THE
UNITED
STATES
ITS HISTORY AND NEIGHBORS

 Harcourt Brace Jovanovich, Inc.

Holt, Rinehart and Winston, Inc.

Orlando · Austin · San Diego · Chicago · Dallas · Toronto

SENIOR EDITORIAL ADVISER

Dr. Phillip Bacon is a professor Emeritus of Geography and Anthropology at the University of Houston. Dr. Bacon has also served on the faculties of Columbia University and the University of Washington. Formerly Dean of the Graduate School of Peabody College for Teachers at Vanderbilt University, Dr. Bacon began his career in education as a teacher of elementary and secondary social studies. He is the author or editor of more than 36 books, including the *Life Pictorial Atlas of the World*. For 18 years, Dr. Bacon served as a member of the Editorial Advisory Board of the *World Book Encyclopedia*.

Among his numerous honors and awards, Dr. Bacon holds the distinguished titles of Fellow of the Explorers Club and Fellow of the Royal Geographic Society of Great Britain. He is a three-time recipient of the Teaching Excellence Award at the University of Houston. His biography appears in *Who's Who in America* and *American Men and Women in Science*.

ACKNOWLEDGMENTS

For permission to reprint copyrighted material, grateful acknowledgment is made to the following sources:

The British Library: From a letter by William Hammond to Sir Simonds D'Ewes, September 26, 1633.

Joan Daves: From "I Have a Dream" speech by Martin Luther King, Jr. Copyright © 1963 by Martin Luther King, Jr.

E. P. Dutton, a division of Penguin Books USA Inc.: From p. 306 in *Life in Mexico* by Mme. Calderon de la Barca. Published by E. P. Dutton & Co., Inc., 1931.

Harcourt Brace Jovanovich, Inc.: From "#45" in *The People, Yes* by Carl Sandburg. Copyright 1936 by Harcourt Brace Jovanovich, Inc., renewed 1964 by Carl Sandburg.

Houghton Mifflin Company: From "It Is a Strange Thing To Be an American" in *The Human Season* by Archibald MacLeish. Copyright © 1972 by Archibald MacLeish.

Macmillan Publishing Company: Abridged from pp. 162–167 in *Charlie Pippin* by Candy Dawson Boyd. Copyright © 1987 by Candy Dawson Boyd. "The Wilderness Is Tamed" from *Away Goes Sally* by Elizabeth Coatsworth. Copyright 1934 by Macmillan Publishing Company, renewed 1962 by Elizabeth Coatsworth Beston.

National Council for the Social Studies: "This Land Is Ours" by Nona Keen Duffy from *The American Citizens Handbook*, Revised Edition, edited by Joy Elmer Morgan. Originally published in *The Instructor*, March 1941.

G. P. Putnam's Sons: From pp. 17–20 in *The Double Life of Pocahontas* by Jean Fritz. Text copyright © 1983 by Jean Fritz.

Leslie Marmon Silko: From "Prayer to the Pacific" by Leslie Marmon Silko in *Literature of the American Indians*, edited by Abraham Chapman.

Peter Smith Publisher, Gloucester, MA: From *The Journal of Madam Knight* by Madam Knight.

Printed in the United States of America
ISBN 0-15-372624-5

CONTENTS

UNIT ONE
THE GEOGRAPHY OF THE UNITED STATES
◆ 10

CHAPTER ONE

CHAPTER TWO

CHAPTER SIX

Northern Exploration and Settlement ◇ **164**

UNIT REVIEW

◆ **191**

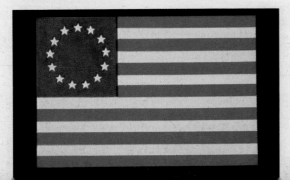

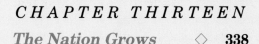

CHAPTER THIRTEEN

The Nation Grows ◇ **338**

CHAPTER FOURTEEN

A Nation on the Move ◇ **362**

UNIT REVIEW

393

UNIT SEVEN

THE NATION DIVIDED

396

UNIT REVIEW

UNIT NINE

THE TWENTIETH CENTURY

502

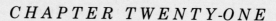

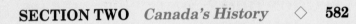

FOR YOUR REFERENCE

R1

PEOPLE MAKE HISTORY

IN FOCUS

CONNECTIONS

SKILLS IN ACTION

READINGS

MAPS AND GLOBES

CHARTS, GRAPHS, DIAGRAMS, AND TIMELINES

Introduction
AMERICAN CITIZENS, PAST AND PRESENT

THIS LAND IS OURS

This land is ours; its golden grains,
Its mountain peaks, and fruited
    plains.
This land is ours to have and hold;
Its wells of oil, its veins of gold.
Its sturdy schools, its churches fine;
Its forest plots of spruce and pine.
Its waterfalls, its caps of snow;
Its ferns and moss where brooklets
    flow!
Its surfaced roads on which we ride
Stretch miles across the country-
    side.
This land is ours; its sun and shade,
Where democratic laws are made.
This land is ours; its fields of corn
Where gentle people of strength are
    born.
This land is ours to love and
    cherish,
To guard, that freedom does not
    perish!

Nona Keen Duffy

This book is about our land and our **heritage.** Our heritage includes ways of thinking, believing, and doing things. You will also read about the many people who have contributed to our nation's heritage in the past. The study of the past is called **history.** History is the means by which we learn of our heritage as citizens and as a nation.

History is seeing the connections between important **events.** Events are things that happen, or occur. One way we show connections in history is to put events in their proper place in time. The picture at the left shows these connections as places along a road. This is a picture history. It shows changes taking place. The picture shows that the past is connected to the present. That is why we study history.

Scholars who study the past are **historians.** To understand life in earlier times, historians use many sources of information. They study diaries written by people long ago. They read descriptions of past events. They look at old pictures, newspapers, and photographs. Using a variety of sources, historians piece together what life was like in the past. In this book you will be reading about some of what they have learned.

To learn about America's past, you need to have a basic knowledge of its **geography.** Geography is the study of the surface of Earth and the ways people use the Earth. In this book you will learn about the geography of the United States.

This book will also describe the **government** of the United States. Government is a group of people who make and carry out the laws by which we live. In the United States, our government is a **democracy.** In a democracy the laws are written and put into practice by the citizens. This year you will study how American democracy came about. You will read about historical events that shaped our government. You will learn what citizens value and respect. You will see what it means to be a citizen of the United States.

USING YOUR TEXTBOOK

Your textbook is divided into several parts. Knowing about these parts will help you use this book to learn about our country.

The Contents

In the Table of Contents you can see that this textbook is divided into 10 units and 23 chapters. Within each chapter are several sections.

Each unit except Unit 1 focuses on a certain period in our country's history. Find Unit 1 in the Contents. What is it called? This unit describes the geography of the United States and tells where its regions, rivers, and resources are located. Knowing these things will help you better understand the history that you will begin learning in Unit 2. Unit 1 has two chapters. What are the names of these chapters? On what page does Chapter 1 begin? What is the name of the first section in Chapter 1?

Sections

Every section begins with **Reading for a Purpose.** It will prepare you to read the section.

Reading for a Purpose begins with a list of key words, people, and places. You will see these words and names again as you read the section. They are printed in dark, or **boldfaced,** letters. Sometimes a boldfaced word is followed by a different spelling. You will see it in parentheses ( ). This spelling tells you how to say the word. For example, the word *bauxite* is followed by (BAWK•syt). In this spelling, the sylla-

ble in capital letters is the syllable that should be accented, or stressed.

Following the word list is a set of questions. From them you will know what kind of information to look for as you read. When you have learned the important words and answered the questions, you should understand the ideas discussed in the section. You can check your understanding by answering the questions in the **Reading Check** at the end of the section.

Features

Each chapter contains three special features. These are called **People Make History, In Focus,** and **Skills in Action.** People Make History focuses on the lives of people who have made a difference in the history of our country. For example, the People Make History feature for Chapter 10, on the American Revolution, is about Paul Revere. Each In Focus explores a topic of high interest. The In Focus for Chapter 16, on the Civil War, is about the Gettysburg Address. Each Skills in Action will help you develop effective language, reading, writing, geography, citizenship, time, critical thinking, or study skills.

Two additional kinds of features are found in every unit. One is called **Connections**. History Connections help you link ideas from the past to the present. Geography Connections help you link ideas from one place to another.

The second feature in each unit is labeled **Reading**. A Reading ends each unit and emphasizes important social studies themes. Some Readings are about special people, events, or other topics related to the unit. Other Readings are stories of a particular time or place within the unit.

The Glossary

Important new words are defined within the sections where they first appear. These words are also defined in the **Glossary** at the end of the book. Like a dictionary, the Glossary lists words alphabetically. It gives the pronunciation of each word and a definition. It also tells you on what page of your book the word is used.

The Index

Perhaps there will be a subject you would like to review. Or you may need to find the answer to a question at the end of a chapter or unit. How can you locate the subject in your book? The quickest way is to find the subject listed in the **Index.**

Important topics, words, people, and places are listed alphabetically in the Index. Each listing shows the page numbers where you can find information on that subject in the reading or in the pictures.

The Atlas, Gazetteer, and Almanac

Because this book takes you all around our country, knowing the locations of places and basic facts about them is very important. The **Atlas, Gazetteer,** and **Almanac** will help you.

The atlas shows maps of our country and our world.

For an overall view of the United States, there is an Atlas at the end of the book. The Atlas is a collection of maps that show the borders of every country in the world and every state in our nation. The Gazetteer also will help you learn about location. It lists the places shown on maps in this textbook. For each place, it gives the location, a brief description, and the number of the page on which the place can be found on a map.

The Almanac is a reference table that presents important facts and figures for each state in our country. It also lists all the Presidents and some facts about them.

Questions to Answer

1. How are units in this book divided?
2. What does the Reading for a Purpose section contain? Why?
3. Name two ways to find the definition of a new word in your book.
4. How is an Atlas useful?

GEOGRAPHY: REVIEW AND PRACTICE

A distant view from space shows the round shape of the Earth. The Earth is a **sphere.** A sphere is anything shaped like a ball.

You probably have something in your classroom that is also a sphere and shows the shape of the Earth. It is a **globe.** A globe is a model of the Earth.

The drawing on the right shows a globe. On the drawing find the **North Pole.** The North Pole is the northernmost point on Earth. At the opposite end of Earth is the **South Pole.** The South Pole is the southernmost point on Earth.

Halfway between the North Pole and the South Pole is the **equator.** The equator is an imaginary line that circles the Earth. It is an equal distance from both the North Pole and the

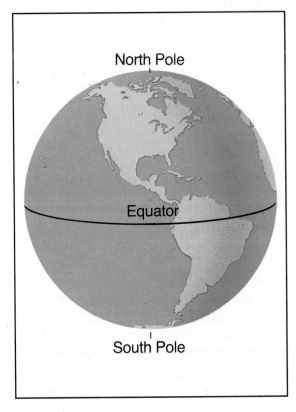

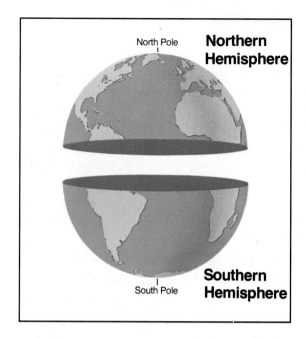

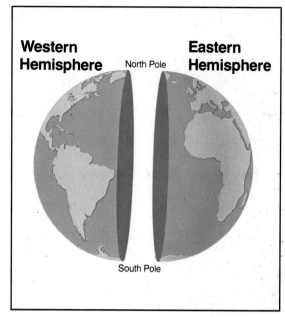

South Pole. To describe locations on Earth, we use the equator to divide the Earth into two equal parts, or halves. Half a sphere is a **hemisphere.** The equator divides the Earth into a **Northern Hemisphere** and a **Southern Hemisphere.**

Another way to divide the Earth is with an imaginary line that circles the Earth through the North Pole and the South Pole. We divide the Earth in this way into an **Eastern Hemisphere** and a **Western Hemisphere.**

Land and Water

A **map** is a drawing of the Earth. The map on page 6 shows the seven **continents,** or great masses of land, in the world. The continents are North America, South America, Europe, Asia, Africa, Australia, and Antarctica. Asia is the largest continent. From the map you can see that Asia is part of an even larger area of land that it shares with the continent of Europe.

Because it includes both Europe and Asia, this entire area is sometimes called Eurasia.

Our country is located on the North American continent. Locate North America on the map on page 6 and on the drawings of the globes on this page. Is North America located in the Northern Hemisphere or the Southern Hemisphere? Is it in the Eastern Hemisphere or the Western Hemisphere?

Most of the Earth's surface is covered by water. In fact, **bodies of water** cover more than 70 percent of the Earth. Bodies of water include rivers, lakes, seas, and oceans.

On the map on page 6, find the four bodies of water called oceans. If you look at the map carefully, you can see that all the oceans are connected. The continents divide the one huge ocean into parts that have separate names. The largest ocean is the Pacific Ocean. The continents of North America and South America separate the Pacific Ocean from the Atlantic Ocean. What are the names of the other two oceans? What two oceans does the continent of Africa separate?

Most of the Earth's water is in these oceans. Oceans, seas, and some lakes contain salt water. This water is too salty for humans to drink or for people to use in farming and manufacturing.

Only about three percent of the Earth's water is fresh, or not salty. Fresh water is found in rivers and most lakes. Therefore, people must depend on the Earth's rivers and lakes for most of their water.

Landforms

The shapes of the Earth's surface are called **landforms.** There are four major kinds of landforms. They are mountains, hills, plateaus, and plains. All four of the major landforms, plus many more kinds of landforms found in the United States, are shown in the Geographic Dictionary on page R41.

Mountains are large, high parts of the land. They rise sharply from the surrounding land. Some mountains have steep slopes and sharp, jagged peaks. **Hills** are not as high as mountains. Unlike mountains, hills are generally rounded at the top. However, hills can also have steep slopes.

Between mountains or hills are valleys. Streams and rivers usually run through valleys. During floods, they deposit **silt,** a mud composed of fine bits of rock and soil. Silt creates fertile soil in the valleys. Valleys can be important farming areas. Valleys are

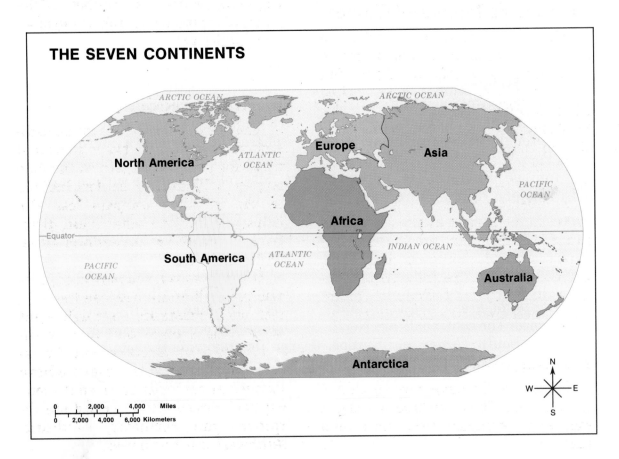

THE SEVEN CONTINENTS

ARCTIC OCEAN

ARCTIC OCEAN

Europe

Asia

North America

ATLANTIC OCEAN

PACIFIC OCEAN

Africa

Equator

INDIAN OCEAN

PACIFIC OCEAN

South America

ATLANTIC OCEAN

Australia

Antarctica

0   2,000   4,000   Miles
0   2,000   4,000   6,000   Kilometers

N
W   E
S

also important as main transportation routes. Because it is easier to travel through a valley than up and down mountains and hills, roads and railroads often follow valleys.

Plateaus are another major landform. Plateaus are high, flat land with steep slopes on at least one side. Some plateaus rise sharply on all sides and have level tops. Such plateaus are then called **tablelands** or **mesas.**

Plains are regions of flat or gently rolling land. They do not have steep hills or deep valleys. Plains generally have fertile land and are important farming areas. Plains bordered by large bodies of water are called **coastal plains.**

Comparing Maps and Globes

Maps have many uses, and there are many different kinds of maps. Some maps give special information about a place. These maps, called **special purpose maps,** may give information about such things as precipitation, temperature, or population.

No matter how useful a map is, it can never be as accurate as a globe. Remember, the Earth is a sphere. It is round in the same way that a globe is round. Globes, then, are the most accurate way to represent the Earth. Globes, however, are not used as often as maps. They are bulky and cannot show small areas in much detail.

Reading Maps

Maps usually have several things in common. These include a title, a map key, a compass rose, and a map scale.

The **title** of a map tells you the subject of the map. What is the title of the map on page 8? Many of the maps in this book show our country as it was in the past. Maps showing the past often have dates next to the title. When you look at a map be sure to pay attention to all of the information given in the title.

Maps may also have a **key.** A map key explains the meaning of each **symbol** used on the map. A symbol is something that stands for something else. A symbol on a map often represents something that is real on the Earth. Symbols may be colors, lines, or other special marks such as circles, triangles, or squares. Look at the map key for the map of the United States on page 8. How does the symbol for the national capital differ from the symbol for a large city?

Finding Directions

The **compass rose** is a guide to directions on a map. It always points out north for you. Look again at the map on page 8. What state borders Indiana on the north? A compass rose also helps you find the other main directions, or **cardinal directions**—east, south, and west.

Often, however, you may need to locate places that are between these directions. For instance, you might want to describe a place that is between south and west. Another word for *between* is intermediate. **Intermediate directions** are those between the four cardinal directions. Intermediate directions are northeast, southeast, southwest, and northwest.

Look at the compass rose on the map below. What intermediate direction best describes the location of Florida? What state borders Colorado on the northeast? What direction is Atlanta from Jacksonville?

Measuring Distances

A **map scale** compares a distance on a map to a distance in the real world. A map scale is useful in finding the real distance between two places. Each map in this book has a scale that shows both miles and kilometers. Find the scale on the map below. Above the line is the scale in miles. Below the line is the scale in kilometers. About how many miles is Boston from New York City? How many kilometers?

On the map of the United States, there are two smaller maps, one of Hawaii and one of Alaska. A small map within a larger map is called an **inset.** An inset may have its own scale. Map scales vary depending on how much area is shown. The use of insets makes it possible to show far-apart places next to each other. How do the map scales differ on these two inset maps? What do they tell you about the comparative sizes of Alaska and Hawaii?

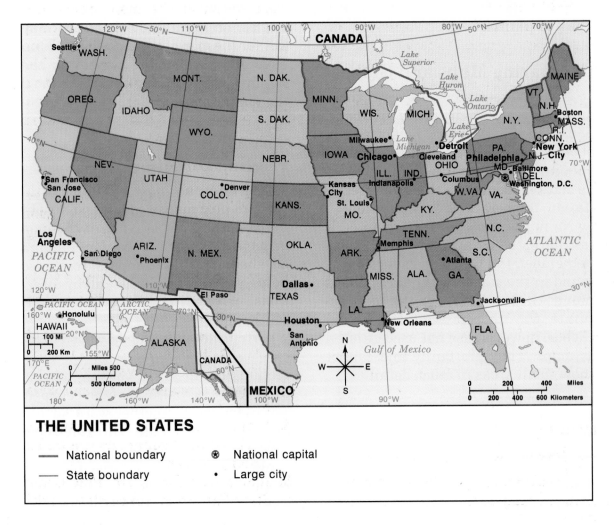

THE UNITED STATES

— National boundary   ⊛ National capital

— State boundary   • Large city

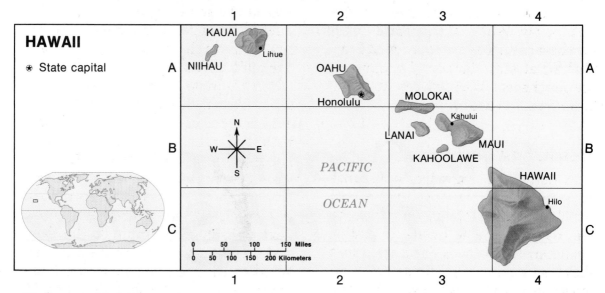

HAWAII

⊛ State capital

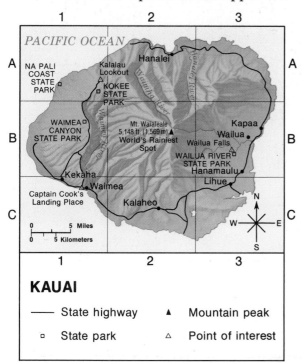

KAUAI

— State highway   ▲ Mountain peak

▫ State park   △ Point of interest

Using a Grid

Mapmakers often put a system of lines on their maps to help people locate places more easily. These north-south and east-west lines cross to form a **grid,** or a pattern of squares. Look at the grid on the map of the state of Hawaii. Find the square in the upper left-hand corner of the map. Above the square is the number *1*. To the side of the same square is the letter *A*. This combination of letter and number identifies this square as *A-1*. What two islands do you find in square *A-1*? Now find square *C-4*. What city is located on the island in *C-4*?

Questions to Answer

Review your map skills by using the map of the Hawaiian island of Kauai (ka•WYE•ee) to answer the following questions.

1. Is the distance from Waimea (C-1) to Kalaheo (C-2) closer to 10 miles or 20 miles?
2. Find Kalalau Lookout in A-1. What does the symbol for Kalalau Lookout tell you about this place?
3. In what direction is Hanalei from Kapaa?
4. What is the symbol for a mountain peak? In what square do you find a mountain peak?
5. About how far is Na Pali Coast State Park from Kokee State Park?

UNIT
1
The Geography of the United States

Some Geographical Facts About the United States

- **Largest States** (by population)

California	Pennsylvania	New Jersey
New York	Illinois	North Carolina
Texas	Ohio	
Florida	Michigan	

- **Largest Cities** (by population)

New York	Philadelphia	San Antonio
Los Angeles	Detroit	Phoenix
Chicago	San Diego	
Houston	Dallas	

The geography of the United States can be seen in towering mountains and vast plains and deserts. It is visible in forested hills and valleys, rocky shores, and sandy beaches. It is found in broad rivers and quiet lakes and streams. This variation in our country's geography allows us to raise many different crops, to mine coal and oil, and to produce other important goods.

In this unit you will study the geography of the United States. You will read about the different ways in which Americans use the land. You will also read about how the resources and the different climates of the United States affect the lives of our citizens.

Think Beyond   How do you think the wide variety of climate and geography in the United States has affected the growth of the country?

• **Tallest Mountains**	• **Longest Rivers**		• **Major Deserts**	• **Largest Lakes**	
McKinley	Mississippi	Red	Chihuahuan	Lake Superior	Lake Erie
Rainier	Missouri	Snake	Great Basin	Lake Huron	Lake Ontario
Pikes Peak	Yukon	Ohio	Mojave	Lake Michigan	Great Salt Lake
Grand Teton	Rio Grande	Brazos	Painted Desert		
	Arkansas	Colorado	Sonoran		

CHAPTER 1

The United States: Its Land and Water

"St. Lawrence marks our northern line as fast her waters flow; And the Rio Grande our southern bound, 'Way down to Mexico; From the great Atlantic Ocean Where the sun begins to dawn, Leap across the Rocky Mountains Far away to Oregon.
Oh, come away! Come away! Come away, I say! Oh, come away! Come away! Come right away!

Oh, come to this country and have no fear of harm, Our Uncle Sam is rich enough To give us all a farm."

—from a song titled "Uncle Sam's Farm," 1850

Look for these important words:

Key Words
- natural regions
- wetlands
- foothills
- piedmont
- volcanoes
- active volcano

Places
- Coastal Plain
- Long Island
- Appalachian Mountains
- Interior Plains
- Central Plains
- Great Plains
- Rocky Mountains
- Intermountain Region

- Great Basin
- Columbia Plateau
- Colorado Plateau
- Pacific Coast Region
- Sierra Nevada
- Cascade Range
- Alaska Range
- Central Valley
- Coast Ranges

Look for answers to these questions:
1. What are natural regions?
2. Which parts of the United States are plains?
3. What are the three major mountain areas of the United States?
4. How are the lands in the eastern United States different from the lands in the western United States?

1   *The American Landscape*

The United States is one of three major countries on the continent of North America. To the north of the United States is Canada. To the south of the United States is Mexico.

Water forms a natural boundary for a large part of the United States. On the east is the Atlantic Ocean. On the west is the Pacific Ocean. Much of the southeastern United States borders on the Gulf of Mexico.

Our American landscape can be divided into **natural regions.** Natural regions are large areas that have something natural in common. For example, regions often share the same kinds of landforms and other natural features such as forests or deserts.

The natural regions of the United States generally run north and south across our nation. Because our nation borders Canada and Mexico, some of these natural regions extend into our neighboring countries as well. Therefore, in addition to sharing the North American continent, the United States also shares many landforms and natural features with Mexico and Canada.

The Coastal Plain

Easternmost in the United States is a natural region called the **Coastal Plain.** It is one of the flattest areas on the North American continent. The Coastal Plain borders the Atlantic Ocean, getting wider as it extends southward. It then extends westward and continues along the Gulf of Mexico into Mexico.

13

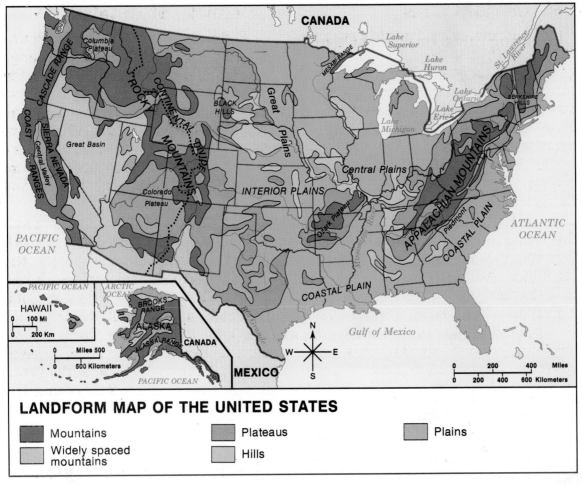

LANDFORM MAP OF THE UNITED STATES

- ■ Mountains
- □ Widely spaced mountains
- ■ Plateaus
- ■ Hills
- ■ Plains

Coastal areas along the Atlantic Ocean and the Gulf of Mexico have many bays and **wetlands.** Wetlands contain large amounts of water and include swamps and marshes. Offshore are islands. The coastal islands are nearly all long, narrow, low sand ridges. With the exception of **Long Island,** New York, the islands off our east coast are generally small and thinly populated.

The Appalachian Mountains

West of the Coastal Plain are the **Appalachian Mountains.** The Appalachian Mountains extend from Alabama to the Gulf of St. Lawrence in Canada. The highest peaks in this large chain of mountains are less than 7,000 feet (2,133 m). Most peaks are less than half that height. However, many of the mountain slopes are steep and heavily forested.

This broad highland region includes the Appalachian Mountains and their surrounding plateaus and hills. There is often an area of gently rolling hills at the base of mountains. These gentle hills are called **foothills,** or the **piedmont.** *Piedmont* means "foot of the mountain." The Appalachian Piedmont is a large area of foothills on the eastern side of the Appalachian Mountains. It separates the Appalachians from the Coastal Plain.

The Interior Plains

In the center of our nation are the **Interior Plains,** a large lowland region that widens toward the north. The Interior Plains cover much of the central part of Canada as well. Within the plains there are areas of hills, mountains, and plateaus.

The Interior Plains are sometimes divided into two areas, depending on the amount of rainfall. They are the **Central Plains** and the **Great Plains.** The Central Plains receive more than 20 inches (51 cm) of rainfall a year. On the Central Plains tall grasses grow well. In fact, this area is sometimes called the Tall-Grass Prairie. The Great Plains receive less than 20 inches (51 cm) of rainfall. This area has short grass and few trees.

Ripe grass waves in the wind in this picture taken on the Tall-Grass Prairie.

The Rocky Mountains

To the west of the Interior Plains there is a sudden and dramatic change in the landscape. As you leave the plains, there appear jagged, snow-capped mountains. These are the **Rocky Mountains.** Extending more than 3,000 miles (4,821 km), the Rocky Mountains stretch all the way from New Mexico north into Canada and Alaska.

The Rocky Mountains are popularly called the "backbone" of North America. These mountains are the largest mountain range in the United States. More than 50 peaks in Colorado alone are higher than 14,000 feet (4,267 m). Parts of the Rocky Mountains have their own names. Among these are the Teton Range, the Front Range, the Wasatch Range, and the Brooks Range.

The Intermountain Region

Intermountain means between the mountains. This is a good name for the **Intermountain Region** because it is between the Rocky Mountains on the east and chains of mountains to the west. Extending from the state of Washington south into Mexico, the Intermountain Region is the largest desert area in our country. Here are desert basins such as the **Great Basin.** Here, too, are major plateaus such as the **Columbia Plateau** to the north and the **Colorado Plateau** to the south. The entire region is a dry and sparsely, or thinly, settled land. The Intermountain Region, however, contains some of the most beautiful landscapes in America.

When most people think of volcanoes they instantly picture molten red lava flowing down a mountainside while hot gases and rocks spew into the air. This dangerous eruption, however, can produce long-term benefits for human beings.

After the volcano has quieted down, we are able to use many by-products from the eruption. For example, pumice, which comes from lava, is used for building roads. Sulphur from volcanoes is often used in making chemicals. In addition, ash and lava from volcanoes make soil very fertile. By interacting with the environment, humans are able to benefit from one of nature's most powerful forces—the volcano.

The Pacific Coast Region

To the west of the Intermountain Region is the **Pacific Coast Region.** Bordering the Pacific Ocean, this region streches from Mexico north to Alaska. It is mainly a mountainous land. High and rugged mountains extend the entire length of the region. On the eastern edge these include the **Sierra Nevada** of California, the **Cascade Range** of Washington and Oregon, and the **Alaska Range** far to the north. Several large valleys, such as the **Central Valley** of California, are sandwiched between these mountain ranges and the lower **Coast Ranges.**

The Coast Ranges hug the Pacific Coast. At many points, the mountains of the Coast Ranges drop sharply into the Pacific Ocean. The Pacific Coast, unlike the Atlantic Coast, has few bays and islands.

The mountains near the Pacific Coast are unique in another way. They include many **volcanoes.** A volcano is a mountain formed by hot rocks, ashes, and gases. These materials rise from the interior of the earth to the surface. When this happens, we say a volcano erupts. A volcano that is erupting or likely to erupt is called an **active volcano.**

Reading Check

1. What natural region is found along the Atlantic Ocean and the Gulf of Mexico?
2. What kind of landform covers the central part of the United States?
3. What is the largest mountain range in the United States?

Think Beyond Why do you think the Atlantic and Pacific coastlines are so different from one another?

People

MAKE HISTORY

John C. Frémont
1813–1890

▶▶▶▶▶▶▶▶▶▶▶▶▶▶▶▶▶

In the 1800s wagon trains rolled westward across the Rocky Mountains and into Oregon in the Pacific Coast region. This long journey followed a rough and dangerous trail. In 1842 the government decided that this trail across the wilderness needed to be mapped. The map would help settlers decide which routes to take and where to settle.

Mapping the area would be a tough job. The person chosen to head the expedition would have to be an explorer, a scientist, and an adventurer. Fortunately, there was one person just right for the job: John C. Frémont.

Frémont was a surveyor who knew how to measure and map the land. He also knew how to handle himself in the wild. He was an expert buffalo hunter and an experienced explorer, able to navigate streams and cross uncharted lands.

Frémont also understood the American Indians and their customs. He knew how to avoid trouble with the Indians, and how to protect his party should problems arise.

Frémont and his group charted the trail and the land surrounding it. They explored streams and rivers to see if boats could use them.

After his glorious expedition of the western frontier, Frémont experienced some hard times. In 1864, he ran against Lincoln for President, but was forced to withdraw. He had money problems, and by 1873 he was bankrupt.

Despite these setbacks Frémont earned a place in history as a great explorer. His work mapping the trail westward helped thousands of Americans settle in the West.

Think Beyond   What kind of job do you think Frémont might seek if he were alive today?

Frémont and crew
race down Platte River

SKILLS IN ACTION

USING LATITUDE AND LONGITUDE

To locate points on Earth, we use a system of imaginary lines. Lines that run in an east-west direction are called **lines of latitude.** Lines that run in a north-south direction are called **lines of longitude.**

Understanding Latitude

The equator is a line of latitude. Lines of latitude always remain the same distance from each other. For this reason lines of latitude are also called **parallels** (PAIR•uh•lels). Parallel lines never meet. They are always the same distance from each other.

Lines of latitude are useful for talking about locations. They make globes and maps easier to use. Look at the globe below.

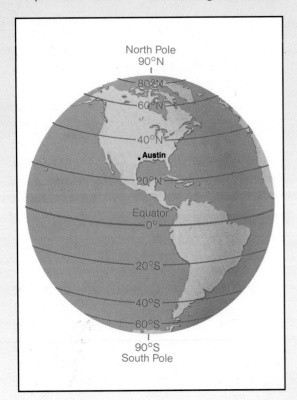

Find the equator on this globe. It is the thick red line around the middle of the globe. Notice that the equator is labeled 0°. This is read as *zero degrees*. (The symbol ° stands for degrees.) A **degree** is a unit of measure used to describe lines of latitude and lines of longitude.

Lines of latitude are also labeled according to direction. Find the red line just above the equator. This parallel is labeled *20°N*—in words, *twenty degrees north*. The N tells you that this parallel is north of the equator. The numeral tells you how far north.

Now find the red line above the one labeled *20°N*. This line is labeled *40°N (forty degrees north)*. The greater the number of a parallel followed by N, the farther north it is. The parallel that is farthest north on this globe is the one labeled *80°N*. The North Pole is the point that is farthest north on Earth. Its latitude is *90°N.*

The parallels to the south of the equator are identified by the letter S, for *south,* following the degree number. Find the red line just below the equator. This line is labeled *20°S (twenty degrees south)*. Which parallel is to the south of this one?

The greater the number of a parallel followed by S, the farther south it is. The parallel that is farthest south on this globe is labeled *60°S*. The South Pole is the point farthest south on Earth. It is labeled *90°S.*

Most globes do not show every parallel. The globe pictured on this page shows every twentieth parallel—20°N, 40°N, and so on. Some globes show only every fifteenth parallel—15°N, 30°N, and so on. Often you need to look between parallels to find a place. Suppose you wanted to find a city with latitude 50°N on a globe showing every twentieth parallel. You would have to look halfway between the parallel labeled *40°N* and the parallel labeled *60°N.*

The degree labels of parallels make it easy to talk about how far north or south something is. For example, if you say that the latitude of Austin, Texas, is 30°N, you are saying how far north the city is from the equator.

Understanding Longitude

When you look at a globe, you will also see lines running north-south. These are lines of longitude, or **meridians.**

Each meridian connects the North Pole and the South Pole. Meridians are numbered much as the parallels are numbered. Look at the globe below.

On this globe the meridians at the equator are 20 degrees apart. Find the line of longitude labeled **Prime Meridian.** It runs north-south near the city of London in Great

Britain. As you can see, this meridian is labeled *0° (zero degrees).*

The meridians to the west of the Prime Meridian are labeled in *degrees west longitude.* Find the meridian just to the west of the Prime Meridian. It is labeled *20°W (twenty degrees west).* The meridian just to the west of this one is labeled *40°W.* As you move west of the Prime Meridian, the numerals, followed by *W,* become greater.

The meridians to the east of the Prime Meridian are labeled in *degrees east longitude.* On this globe the meridian just to the east of the Prime Meridian is labeled *20°E (twenty degrees east).* What meridian on this globe is just to the east of the meridian labeled *20°E?* Again, as you progress farther east of the Prime Meridian, the numerals, followed by *E,* become greater. The meridian on the opposite side of the globe from the Prime Meridian is labeled *180°,* the greatest number of a meridian.

As with parallels, most globes and maps do not show every meridian. This globe shows only every twentieth meridian. If you wanted to find a city at 70°W longitude, you would have to look halfway between the meridians 60°W and 80°W.

The degree labels of meridians are also used in talking about locations. For example, the city of Alexandria, Egypt, is near the meridian labeled *30°E.* Therefore, we say the longitude of Alexandria is 30°E. Manaus, Brazil, is on the meridian labeled *60°W.* The longitude of Manaus is 60°W.

Locating Places on a Map

Together, the lines of latitude and longitude form a **grid.** A grid is a pattern of crossing lines. The grid makes it possible to talk about how far north or south something is and also about how far east or west it is. Neither latitude nor longitude alone is

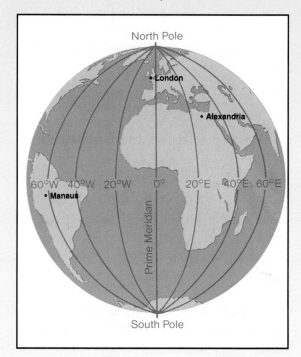

19

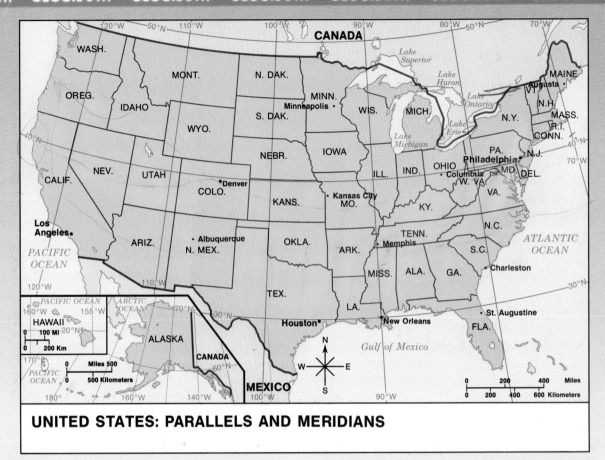

UNITED STATES: PARALLELS AND MERIDIANS

enough to find a place on a globe or map. Both are necessary.

The map on this page shows the mainland United States. It has a grid of parallels and meridians drawn over it.

Every tenth parallel is shown—from 30°N to 50°N. The entire United States lies north of the equator, so all the parallels are written with N, for *north.* Which meridians are shown? The United States lies west of the Prime Meridian, so all the meridians are written with W, for *west.*

Try using both parallels and meridians to find locations. At the side of the map, find the parallel 30°N. At the bottom of the map find the meridian 90°W. Trace these lines to the point at which they meet. The city of New Orleans is not far from this point.

Now try finding the latitude and longitude of a city. Locate Philadelphia,

Pennsylvania, on the map. The parallel that runs through it is labeled *40°N.* The meridian that runs through it is between 70°W and 80°W, or about 75°W. Philadelphia's location is 40°N latitude, 75°W longitude.

CHECKING YOUR SKILLS

Use the map to answer these questions.

1. What is the latitude of Denver, Colorado?

2. What is the longitude of Charleston, South Carolina?

3. What city is located at about 35°N latitude and 90°W longitude?

4. City A is located at 41°N latitude and 74°W longitude. City B is located at 44°N latitude and 100°W longitude. Which city is farther north? Which city is farther east?

Look for these important words:

Key Words
- runoff
- tributaries
- river system
- crest
- drainage basin
- delta
- canyons
- interior drainage

Places
- Continental Divide
- Great Lakes
- St. Lawrence River
- St. Lawrence Seaway
- Mississippi River
- Illinois Waterway

- Fall Line
- Rio Grande
- Grand Canyon
- Great Salt Lake

Look for answers to these questions:

1. Where do rivers east of the Continental Divide drain? rivers west of the Rocky Mountains?
2. What are two of the most important drainage basins in the United States?
3. What is the Fall Line?
4. Why are rivers and waterways important parts of American life?

2 Rivers and Waterways

Rivers are an important part of American life. Big rivers provide transportation routes. Rivers also provide water for farming, for manufacturing, and for everyday use. Rivers are used for recreation as well.

Rain and snow that does not sink into the ground is called **runoff.** Runoff forms streams. These streams flow into other streams and rivers. Streams that flow into other rivers are called **tributaries.** A river and its tributaries is called a **river system.**

River systems drain, or collect, runoff. Look at the map on page 22. An imaginary line running north and south follows the **crest,** or high point, of the Rocky Mountains. This line is

called the **Continental Divide.** East of the Continental Divide, the water in rivers flows to the Atlantic Ocean or to the Gulf of Mexico. West of the Continental Divide, the runoff generally ends up in the Pacific Ocean.

The area drained by a river system is called a **drainage basin.** Two of the largest and most important drainage basins in the United States are the Great Lakes–St. Lawrence River Drainage Basin and the Mississippi River Drainage Basin. Together they drain most of the land located between the Appalachian Mountains and the Rocky Mountains. These two huge drainage basins form the finest natural waterway system in the world.

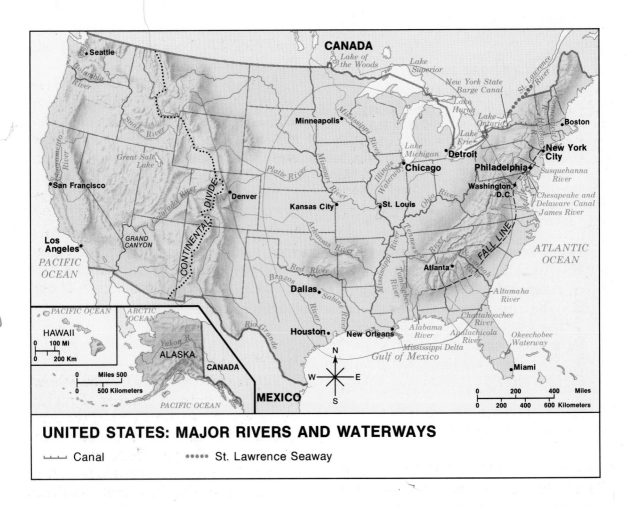

UNITED STATES: MAJOR RIVERS AND WATERWAYS

⊢—⊣ Canal   •••• St. Lawrence Seaway

The Great Lakes—St. Lawrence Drainage Basin

In the northern part of the Interior Plains is the largest body of fresh water in the world, the **Great Lakes.** Five lakes—Lake Superior, Lake Huron, Lake Erie, Lake Ontario, and Lake Michigan—make up the Great Lakes. Canada and the United States share the first four. The fifth, Lake Michigan, is entirely within the boundaries of the United States.

All five of the Great Lakes are connected. Water from the Great Lakes drains northeast into the Atlantic Ocean by way of the **St. Lawrence River.** Together the Great Lakes and the St. Lawrence River drain large areas of the United States and eastern Canada.

The Great Lakes and the St. Lawrence River also provide an important transportation system for both countries. Together the United States and Canada built the **St. Lawrence Seaway.** Completed in 1959, this great project opened the entire Great Lakes—St. Lawrence system to ocean-going vessels. By using the St. Lawrence Seaway, ships are able to sail all the way from the Atlantic Ocean to ports on the Great Lakes.

Shipping vessels can also reach the Great Lakes by traveling through the New York State Barge Canal. This canal connects Lake Erie with the Hudson River. Both the St. Lawrence

Barges are joined into units called *tows* and are pushed or pulled by tugboats.

south for 2,348 miles (3,778 km), all the way to the Gulf of Mexico.

Near its mouth at the Gulf of Mexico, the Mississippi begins to drop silt. The area of fertile land formed by the silt that builds up at the mouth of a river is called a **delta.** A delta has rich soil and makes good farmland.

Through a system of canals, ships are able to travel from the Great Lakes to the Mississippi River. The **Illinois Waterway** connects Lake Michigan with the Mississippi River. In this way the two great drainage basins of our nation are linked together.

Seaway and the New York State Barge Canal allow cities and factories in the interior to gain access to important materials and markets.

The Mississippi Drainage Basin

Most of the central part of the United States and a small part of southern Canada are drained by the mighty **Mississippi River** system with its many tributaries. These tributaries include the Missouri River, the Ohio River, the Arkansas River, and the Red River. Together they create a gigantic drainage basin.

The Mississippi River is the longest river in the United States. From its source in central Minnesota, the Mississippi River flows almost straight

Rivers of the East

The east coast of the United States is well served by a number of major rivers. On the eastern side of the Appalachian Mountains, the rivers run to the Atlantic Ocean. These rivers include the Connecticut, the Hudson, the Susquehanna, the Savannah, and the Altamaha (AWL•tuh•muh•haw).

The rivers first make their way from the mountains through the Piedmont. Where the Piedmont meets the Coastal Plain, there is a hard stone layer. Rivers cannot easily erode, or wear away, this stone layer. Instead, the rivers drop over the stone layer to the plains below, forming a series of waterfalls and rapids.

The place where these waterfalls occur is called the **Fall Line.** In the past, the Fall Line was as far upstream as oceangoing ships could travel. Later it became a good location for the development of water power, which led to manufacturing. For this reason, many of the large cities in the eastern United States are located along the Fall Line.

Rivers of the Southeast

There are many large rivers in the Southeast. The major rivers of this region begin at the southern end of the Appalachian Mountains. From there they flow into the Gulf of Mexico. Important rivers of the Southeast include the Chattahoochee, the Apalachicola (ap•uh•lach•uh•KOH•luh), the Tombigbee, and the Alabama.

Rivers of the Southwest

One major river of the Southwest is the **Rio Grande.** The Rio Grande flows from its source in Colorado to the Gulf of Mexico. For much of its length, the river serves as the border between the United States and Mexico.

Another important river of the Southwest is the Colorado River. Its basin extends from the Rocky Mountains to the Sierra Nevada. The

Over many years, erosion caused by the Colorado River carved out the Grand Canyon.

Colorado has cut its way through layers and layers of earth and rock to reach the Gulf of California. The places where rivers cut deep through the land are called **canyons.** The **Grand Canyon** of the Colorado is one of the world's natural wonders. It extends 217 miles (349 km) through Arizona. It is 4 to 13 miles (6.4 to 20.9 km) wide and about a mile (1.6 km) deep.

Rivers of the West

In the western United States major rivers include the Sacramento, the San Joaquin (SAN wah•KEEN), the Columbia, and the Yukon. Most of the rivers in the western United States flow toward the Pacific Ocean. A few, however, end in shallow or dry lakes in the deserts of Nevada, Utah, and California. This is a region of **interior drainage,** an area where rivers do not flow into an ocean or gulf. Most of the rivers of this region do not even have water in them much of the year. When they do have water, after heavy rainfall or when mountain snows are melting, they flow into desert lakes. Utah's **Great Salt Lake** is the largest of the lakes of this region of interior drainage.

Reading Check

1. What is the Continental Divide? Where is it located?
2. What drainage basin drains most of the central part of the United States?
3. Why do waterfalls occur along the Fall Line?

Think Beyond How do you think America's early settlers made use of the country's rivers and lakes?

Look for these important words:

Key Words
- natural resources
- bauxite
- manganese
- wood pulp
- irrigation
- reservoir
- industries

- economy
- economic resources
- raw materials
- renewable resources
- nonrenewable resources
- conservation

Look for answers to these questions:
1. What are natural resources? What are economic resources?
2. What purposes do reservoirs serve?
3. What is the single most important activity in the economy of the United States?
4. What is conservation?

3 Using Resources

Few nations in the world have as many **natural resources** as the United States. Natural resources are those things found in nature that people use. Trees, water, soil, coal, oil, iron ore, and natural gas are some of the many natural resources found in the United States.

The United States leads the world in the amount of minerals produced. We have vast deposits of coal and are finding new sources of oil both on land and offshore. Our mineral wealth is the most varied in the world. The only minerals that we actually lack in large amounts are tin, **bauxite** (BAWK•syt), and **manganese** (MANG•guh•neez). Bauxite is the ore from which aluminum is made. Manganese is used to make steel. We are able to buy these minerals from other nations.

Our forests and grasslands meet our timber and grazing needs. Forests cover nearly one-third of the United States. Among our many forest products are lumber and **wood pulp.** Wood pulp is used to make paper. Almost one-fourth of the land in the United States is used for pastures and grazing. Beef cattle are our most valuable farm product.

The United States also leads the world in crop production. Our rich soil produces enormous crops. Each farmer in the United States can produce enough food for almost 80 people.

Using the Land

In our country's past, most people lived only where there was enough rain to grow crops. Today, however,

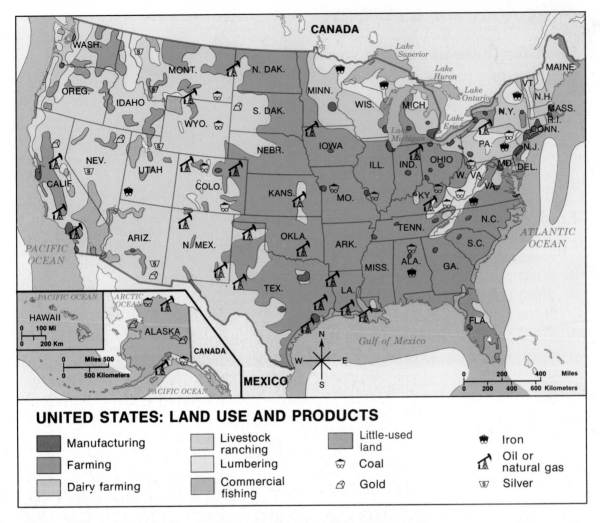

UNITED STATES: LAND USE AND PRODUCTS

- Manufacturing
- Farming
- Dairy farming
- Livestock ranching
- Lumbering
- Commercial fishing
- Little-used land
- Coal
- Gold
- Iron
- Oil or natural gas
- Silver

many dry regions are farming areas because of **irrigation.** *Irrigation* means bringing water to farmland. Water for irrigation comes from rivers, underground wells, or lakes.

In recent years many new lakes have been added to the map of the United States. These lakes have been formed by building dams across rivers. A lake that stores water held back by a dam is called a **reservoir** (REZ•uhr•vwahr).

Reservoirs can serve several purposes. Water rushing through the dams turns machinery to make electricity. Water stored in the reservoirs can be directed through pipes and canals to irrigate farmland. Reservoirs supply water for people living in cities and towns and for factories. Reservoirs are used to help control flooding and for recreational purposes, too.

The use of dams, reservoirs, and irrigation has made it possible to increase the amount of food grown in dry areas. It has also made possible the growth of large cities and **industries** in dry areas. Industries are kinds of manufacturing or businesses.

Look at the map. It shows the main products and uses of land in the United States today. Notice that most of our country is used to produce food, minerals, or manufactured goods.

This coal-processing plant in West Virginia cleans, sorts, and crushes coal to prepare it for use.

Manufacturing

The United States is the world's leading manufacturing nation. Manufacturing is the single most important activity in the **economy** of the United States. An economy is the way people use resources to produce and sell goods and services. The resources used to produce goods and services are called **economic resources.** Economic resources include anything used in the production of goods and services. These include the natural resources that come from the land and water, the people who work to produce the goods and services, and the buildings and machinery they use.

About one-fifth of all workers are employed in manufacturing. Factories in the United States produce huge amounts of goods. These include machinery, electronics, chemicals, and food products.

Many manufacturing centers first developed near areas where **raw materials** were plentiful. Raw materials are natural resources that can be made into useful products. More recently, manufacturing centers have been developing in other parts of the country as well. Improved transportation and communication systems have allowed manufacturing centers to grow in new areas. Raw materials and other economic resources can now be shipped to the factories more easily. Manufactured goods can then be sold to faraway markets by using telephones and computer networks.

27

Conserving Resources

The good life enjoyed by Americans is due in part to our wealth of natural and economic resources. We all use resources. Resources supply the energy we use to run our modern nation. Resources are used to build homes, schools, and other buildings. Factories use resources to manufacture the things we need and want. Resources are used to fertilize farmlands so that better crops can be grown. Other resources are used to make the clothes we wear.

Although the United States is rich in resources, many of our resources are limited. This means that only a certain amount of those resources exists. Some resources have been wasted. Others have been polluted by wastes from cities and factories. Each year the population of the world increases. An increase in people means that more resources will be used.

Some of our resources are more plentiful than others. For example, water is a plentiful resource in many parts of the United States. Yet the United States uses almost 400 billion gallons (1,500 billion liters) of water each day. Most of this is used in manufacturing or in irrigating cropland. In addition, we all use water daily in our personal lives. As the population of the United States increases and cities grow, so too will the demand for water.

Water, soil, and other resources are renewable. **Renewable resources** are the resources that can be reused or remade by humans or nature. Forests are considered a renewable resource because they can be replanted. However, some resources such as coal, nat-

Seedlings such as these are used to replant our nation's forests.

ural gas, and oil are **nonrenewable resources.** This means that neither we nor nature can make more of them.

The **conservation** of all resources is important. *Conservation* means using a resource so as to keep it from being wasted or destroyed. Because almost every part of life depends in some way on the Earth's natural and economic resources, it is important that all our resources be conserved.

Reading Check

1. What three minerals does the United States lack in large amounts?
2. How have the use of irrigation and reservoirs changed dry areas of the United States?
3. Why is manufacturing important to American workers?

Think Beyond   Do you think air is a renewable resource? Why or why not?

IN FOCUS

CARTOGRAPHERS

Almost everyone uses maps. Maps help us plan trips. They help us understand the news. We see them almost every day on television, in newspapers, and in magazines. They help us understand the world around us. In fact, you will be using many maps as you study the pages of this book.

People who draw maps are called **cartographers** (kahr•TAHG•ruh•fuhrs). Cartographers have been at work ever since people first moved about the Earth exploring new lands, trading with others, or looking for new places to settle. Like John Frémont, cartographers in those early days were often explorers. As explorers and pioneers moved westward, they made newer and better maps.

In 1879 the United States Geological Survey was organized. Its job was to draw accurate and detailed maps of the United States. By 1910, road maps for automobile travel came into use. Still later, air travel made new kinds of maps and charts necessary for pilots. Cartographers are still working on ways to show information about the Earth as accurately as possible.

Today, cartographers have ways of drawing maps that would startle the cartographers of the past. They no longer have to go out into the field to survey the land before drawing their maps. Photographs taken from the air provide cartographers with more accurate information than they could gain from photographs taken on the ground.

Satellites orbiting the Earth gather information about places that would be almost impossible to visit. Computers sort the information and even draw the maps for the cartographers. The computer can plot the map on film, on paper, or on a television screen. Cartographers then arrange the information to suit the special purpose of the map.

Life without the work of cartographers would be very confusing. The accurate information that they provide makes understanding locations of places in the world easier.

Think Beyond How do you think the work of cartographers affected the growth of our country?

Cartographers use computers to make maps more accurate.

Look for these important words:

Key Words
- vegetation
- Tropic of Cancer
- Arctic Circle
- Tropic of Capricorn

- Antarctic Circle
- tropics
- northers
- natural vegetation

Look for answers to these questions:
1. How does distance from the equator affect climate?
2. What other factors affect the climate of the United States?
3. How do mountains affect the climate of the western United States?
4. What are the three main groups of natural vegetation in the United States?

4 Climate and Vegetation

Few nations have as many different kinds of climate as the United States. Nearly every kind of climate on Earth is found somewhere in our nation.

Climate and **vegetation**, or plant life, are closely related. The various climates found in the United States influence the kinds of vegetation found in different parts of our country. This variety of climates also makes the United States well suited for growing many different crops. American farmers can produce just about every kind of food grown anywhere in the world.

Latitude and Climate

Lines of latitude measure distances north or south of the equator in degrees. Some lines of latitude have names. The Northern Hemisphere has two named lines of latitude. They are the **Tropic of Cancer** and the **Arctic**

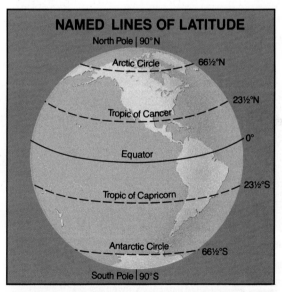

NAMED LINES OF LATITUDE

North Pole | 90°N
Arctic Circle — 66½°N
Tropic of Cancer — 23½°N
Equator — 0°
Tropic of Capricorn — 23½°S
Antarctic Circle — 66½°S
South Pole | 90°S

Circle. The Tropic of Cancer is 23½°N. The Arctic Circle is 66½°N. The Southern Hemisphere also has two named lines of latitude. They are the **Tropic of Capricorn** and the **Antarctic Circle**. The Tropic of Capricorn is 23½°S. The Antarctic Circle is 66½°S.

Because it is nearer to the equator, the area between the Tropic of Cancer and the Tropic of Capricorn receives more direct sunlight than other parts of the Earth. This area, which is called the **tropics,** is generally warm all year. The areas north of the Arctic Circle and south of the Antarctic Circle are generally cold all year. They receive less direct sunlight.

Differences in Climate

The equator is located halfway between the North and South poles. At the poles the weather is extremely cold. Along the equator, the rays of the sun produce high temperatures.

The Earth rotates on its axis, causing day and night. The Earth also revolves around the sun. As the Earth revolves around the sun, seasons change. Because the Earth tilts on its axis, places receive different amounts of sunlight as the Earth revolves.

At different times during the year, places at a distance from the equator receive different amounts of heat from the sun. A place may get more sunlight in summer than in winter. As a result, temperatures are warmer there in summer than in winter.

Most of the United States lies between the Tropic of Cancer and the Arctic Circle. This means that for most places in the United States, there are great differences between the temperatures in the winter and in the summer. Summers for most of the country are long and hot. Winters are usually much colder and often drier than summers. Places nearer the equator, such as Hawaii, Louisiana, Texas, and Florida, are warm much of the year, even in winter. Places farther from the equator, like Alaska and the states bordering Canada, have short, cool summers and long, cold winters.

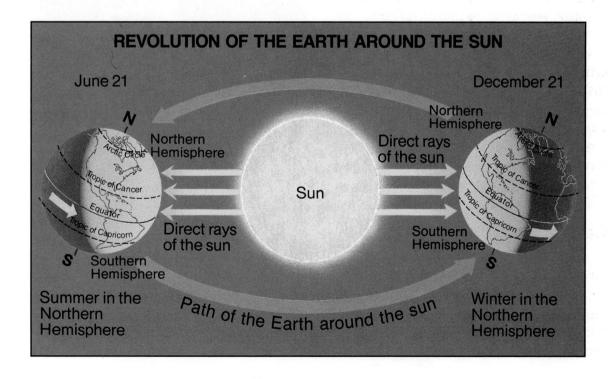

REVOLUTION OF THE EARTH AROUND THE SUN

June 21

December 21

Northern Hemisphere

Direct rays of the sun

N

Sun

Northern Hemisphere

Arctic Circle

Tropic of Cancer

Equator

Tropic of Capricorn

Cold Circle

N

Tropic of Cancer

Equator

Tropic of Capricorn

S

Southern Hemisphere

Direct rays of the sun

Southern Hemisphere

S

Summer in the Northern Hemisphere

Path of the Earth around the sun

Winter in the Northern Hemisphere

Bodies of Water

Distance from oceans and other large bodies of water also affects climate. Water heats and cools more slowly than land. Near the ocean, it is usually not as hot in summer and not as cold in winter. Differences in winter and summer temperatures may be as little as 10 degrees. The ocean helps warm the land in winter and cool the land in summer.

Places far from oceans often experience great differences between winter and summer temperatures. For example, on the plains in the central part of the United States, differences between winter and summer temperatures may be as much as 60 degrees. Temperatures can be very cold in winter and very hot in summer.

Distance from water also affects precipitation, or rain and snow. Land closer to large bodies of water usually receives more precipitation.

Mountains

Mountains also influence climate. Western mountain ranges such as the Sierra Nevada and the Rocky Mountains act like huge walls. They stand in the way of air that flows across the country from west to east. When the air meets the mountains, it is forced to rise. As air rises, it cools. Cool air cannot contain as much moisture as warm air. As a result, rain or snow falls on the western slopes. For example, the average precipitation along the coast of Oregon and Washington is more than 60 inches (152 cm) a year. In some places it equals 150 inches (381 cm).

As the cool air starts to slide down the eastern side of a mountain or

Navajo herders take their sheep to water in a desert at Monument Valley, Utah.

This picture shows a thick rain forest in Olympic National Park, Washington.

32

mountain range, however, it begins to warm. Warm air can hold much more moisture than cool air. As a result, the eastern sides of the mountain ranges are often quite dry. Most of America's deserts are in such locations. Deserts receive an average of less than 10 inches (25 cm) of precipitation a year.

A lack of mountains can affect an area's climate almost as much as having mountains, but in quite a different way. Because there is no mountain range in the central part of the country to block the flow of air, bitterly cold masses of winter air called **northers** can move rapidly out of Canada across the plains. Northers can bring freezing temperatures to places as far south as Texas and Florida. In the summer, the reverse takes place. Warm, moist air from the Gulf of Mexico sometimes brings high temperatures and heavy rains to the entire eastern half of the country. Most of the eastern United States has an annual precipitation that averages between 20 and 60 inches (51 and 152 cm).

All these things—location, large bodies of water, and mountains and plains—create the variety of climates that we find in the United States.

Natural Vegetation

Natural vegetation, or plants growing wild in an area, can be divided into three main groups—forests, grasslands, and scrublands. The vegetation that grows in an area depends on how much precipitation an area receives. Forests require the most precipitation—at least 20 inches (51 cm) a year. Grasslands can develop with far less moisture. Short-grass areas

The Joshua tree is one of the few trees that can survive in the desert.

such as the Great Plains require as little as 10 inches (26 cm) a year. Scrub vegetation such as desert cactus can survive on even less.

Scrublands always develop in dry areas. American scrublands include the cactus deserts of the Southwest, the low, brushy hillsides and valleys of Southern California, and some areas of West Texas.

Reading Check

1. What is the most important reason for differences in climate?
2. What are northers?
3. How does precipitation affect natural vegetation?

Think Beyond Why do you suppose cactuses can grow where the land is too dry for grasses?

SKILLS IN ACTION

USING CLIMATE MAPS

Climate is a word used to talk about the usual weather of a place over a long period of time. Temperatures and the amount of moisture for all seasons are part of climate. Climate maps give information about temperatures and moisture.

A **precipitation map** is one kind of climate map. A precipitation map shows how much moisture falls as rain or snow. The colors on the map tell how much precipitation each area gets. The map key shows that areas tinted dark blue get more than 60 inches (150 cm) of precipitation a year.

A **growing season map** is another kind of climate map. It shows the number of days between the last frost of spring and the first frost of fall. The number of frost-free days is the length of time crops can be grown.

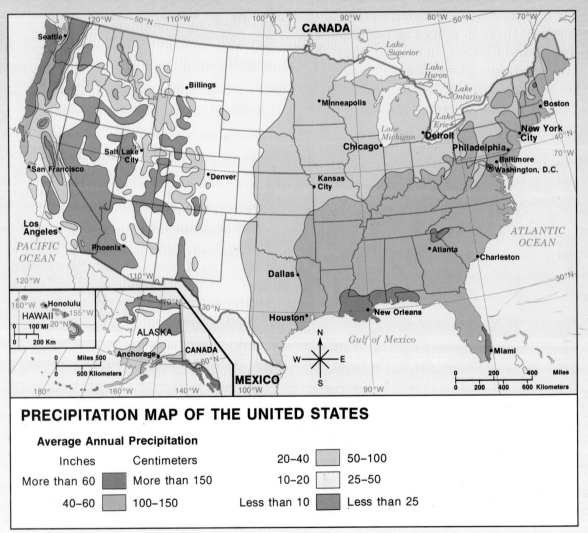

PRECIPITATION MAP OF THE UNITED STATES

Average Annual Precipitation

Inches	Centimeters		
More than 60	More than 150	20–40	50–100
40–60	100–150	10–20	25–50
		Less than 10	Less than 25

Working with Two Climate Maps

You can use a growing season map and a precipitation map together. This is one way to learn about growing conditions in certain places. Find Phoenix, Arizona, on the growing season map. Nearby areas are colored yellow or purple. You can see from the map key that the area near Phoenix has growing seasons that last from five months to seven months or seven months to nine months.

Now look at the precipitation map on page 34. How much precipitation does the Phoenix area have? The area around Phoenix may be too dry for crops to grow naturally. A farmer there may have to irrigate the crops to make them grow.

CHECKING YOUR SKILLS

Use the precipitation map and the growing season map to answer these questions.

1. Cotton needs a growing season at least 6 months long. Would you be more likely to find cotton growing near Denver, Colorado, or near Atlanta, Georgia?

2. Sugarcane grows in a warm, wet climate. Would you find sugarcane near Salt Lake City, Utah, or near Miami, Florida?

3. In general, are growing seasons longer in northern states or in southern states?

4. In general, is there more rainfall in eastern states or in western states?

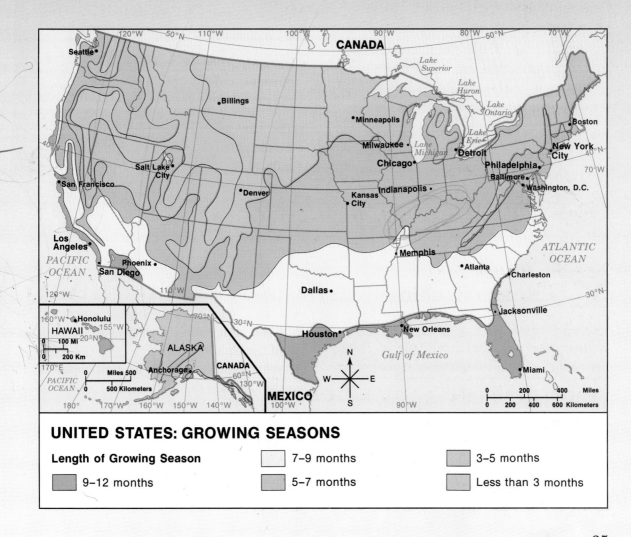

UNITED STATES: GROWING SEASONS

Length of Growing Season

9–12 months	
7–9 months	
5–7 months	
3–5 months	
Less than 3 months	

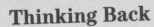

Thinking Back

- Large plains areas are found along the Atlantic Ocean, along the Gulf of Mexico, and in the center of the nation.

- Major mountain areas are the Appalachian Mountains, the Rocky Mountains, and the mountains in the Pacific Coast Region. The largest area of deserts and plateaus is the Intermountain Region.

- Rivers provide transportation routes and water for farming, manufacturing, and everyday use.

- Rivers east of the Continental Divide drain into either the Atlantic Ocean or the Gulf of Mexico. Rivers in the West generally drain into the Pacific Ocean.

- The Great Lakes–St. Lawrence River system and the Mississippi River drain most of the land between the Appalachian and Rocky mountains.

- The United States leads the world in crop and mineral production.

- Dams, reservoirs, and irrigation have increased the amount of food grown and have allowed the growth of large cities and industries in new areas.

- The United States is the world's leading manufacturing nation. Manufacturing is the single most important economic activity in our country.

- Many of the resources of the United States are limited. Conservation of all resources is important.

- Distance from the equator, large bodies of water, and mountains and plains affect the climate of a place.

- The amount of precipitation an area receives generally determines the kind of natural vegetation that will grow in that area.

Check for Understanding

Using Words

Write the meaning of each term below. Then use each term in a complete sentence.

1. conservation
2. delta
3. drainage basin
4. economy
5. irrigation
6. natural resources
7. reservoir
8. river system
9. tributaries
10. vegetation

Reviewing Facts

1. Describe the landscape of the Coastal Plains. Where are these plains located?
2. What mountains are in the eastern part of the United States?
3. What natural region is located between the Appalachian Mountains and the Rocky Mountains?
4. Where is the Intermountain Region?
5. What is the Continental Divide?
6. Name the two largest drainage basins in the United States.
7. What is the Fall Line?

8. Why is it necessary to conserve our resources?
9. List three things that affect climate and describe how each affects the climate of the United States.
10. What effect does climate have on natural vegetation?

Thinking Critically

1. How does the natural region you live in affect the way you live and what you do? Do you think natural regions affect your life more than they did the lives of early settlers? Why or why not?
2. The United States may have the finest natural inland waterway system in the world. How has this affected the growth of the United States?
3. How have natural and economic resources helped the United States become a great nation?
4. How does climate affect how you live and what you do?

Writing About It

Write two paragraphs describing the climate in your region of the country. In your paragraphs include what you like about the climate and what you would like to change.

Practicing Skills: Geography

1. **Latitude and Longitude**
   Use the map on page 20 to answer these questions.
   a. What city is at 30°N latitude, 90°W longitude?
   b. Name three states that have northern borders at 35°N latitude.
   c. What line of latitude forms the northern borders for the states of New York and Vermont?

2. **Climate Maps**
   Use the maps on pages 34 and 35 to answer these questions.
   a. The tastiest apples are grown in climates that have growing seasons of 3 to 6 months. Would apples grow well near Atlanta? near Boston?
   b. Oranges need mild temperatures and a growing season of 9 to 12 months. Would oranges grow well near Los Angeles? Near Seattle?
   c. What is the average precipitation of Billings? Of Houston?

On Your Own

Social Studies at Home

1. Make a list of things in your room at home that were made from renewable resources. Add to the list anything in your room that may be made from nonrenewable resources.
2. Draw or trace a map of the United States. On your map, label the Appalachian Mountains, the Rocky Mountains, the St. Lawrence River, the Mississippi River, and the Rio Grande.

Read More About It

Mountains by Clive Catchpole. Pictures by Brian McIntyre. Dial Books. This book offers brief descriptions about mountain creatures and how they are able to live in rugged environments.

The Only Earth We Have by Laurence P. Pringle. Macmillan. This book stresses the importance of living with nature and how pollution affects us all.

Rivers and Lakes by Martin Bramwell. Franklin Watts. This book offers a short introduction to water sources.

CHAPTER 2

Regions of the United States

"First are the capes, then are the shorelands, now
The blue Appalachians faint at the day rise;
The willows shudder with light on the long Ohio:
The lakes scatter the low sun: the prairies
Slide out of the dark: in the eddy of clean air
The smoke goes up from the high plains of Wyoming:
The steep Sierras arise: the struck foam
Flames at the wind's heel on the far Pacific. "
—from the poem "It Is a Strange Thing to Be an American"
by Archibald MacLeish

Reading for a Purpose

Look for these important words:

Key Words
- interdependence
- cape
- glaciers
- megalopolis

Places
- New England
- Cape Cod
- White Mountains
- Green Mountains
- Adirondack Mountains
- Allegheny Mountains
- Massachusetts Bay
- Delaware Bay
- Chesapeake Bay

Look for answers to these questions:
1. What are the major landforms of the Northeast?
2. How did glaciers affect the landscape of the Northeast?
3. Why are manufacturing and trade important to people in the Northeast?
4. How are agriculture and fishing important to people in the Northeast?

The Northeast

The United States is a huge country. It is the fourth-largest country in the world. Only the Soviet Union, Canada, and China are larger in land area.

To help us study and compare areas of our vast country, we can divide it into seven regions. Four of the regions are named after an important body of water or landform. They are the Great Lakes, Plains, Mountain, and Pacific regions. The others—the Northeast, Southeast, and Southwest regions—are named for their locations.

The states in a particular region are alike in some way. For instance, Arizona, New Mexico, Texas, and Oklahoma have many things in common. They share many of the same resources, and their climates are similar. All are located in the southwestern part of the United States. Because of their location, the states also share a similar history.

Sometimes we want to speak of all these states together. Calling this region the Southwest is easier than naming all the states one by one. Look at the map on page 40. This map shows you the locations of the seven regions of the United States.

Each region of the United States is special in some way. All of the regions, however, depend on each other's resources and products. For example, industries in one region of the United States often depend on the raw materials and economic resources of another region. A car driven in California may have been built in Michigan with steel made in Pennsylvania.

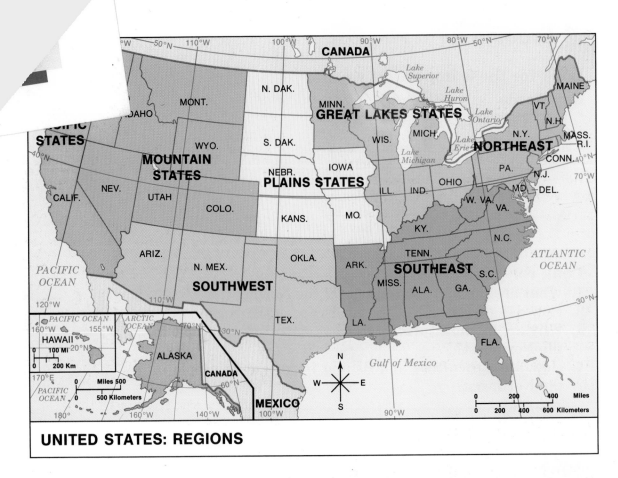

UNITED STATES: REGIONS

Oil from Texas may have been used to fuel the factory in Michigan, and coal from Kentucky may have been used to heat steel furnaces in Pennsylvania. This sharing of resources and products is called **interdependence.** *Interdependence* means depending on one another for the things we want and need.

The Northeastern States

The Northeast is a land of great cities, tiny villages, rocky shores, and sandy beaches. It is also a land rich in history. The Northeast has long influenced the history of our nation. Of the 13 original states, 9 are found in the Northeast.

Extending from Maine to Maryland, 11 states make up the region.

These 11 states are shown on the map on page 42. Settlers in Connecticut, Massachusetts, Maine, New Hampshire, Vermont, and Rhode Island called the land **New England.** Today, these six states of the Northeast are still commonly called New England.

The Land

The Atlantic Ocean borders the Northeast on the east. The coastline is full of bays, inlets, and points of land that extend into the ocean. A point of land that extends into the ocean is called a **cape.** The largest cape in the Northeast is **Cape Cod.**

North of Cape Cod the coastline is rugged and rocky. South of Cape Cod the landscape changes. Miles of sandy beaches stretch along the shores of the

40

Atlantic Ocean. This is the Atlantic Coastal Plain. The land here is generally flat or gently rolling.

Inland from the coast, much of the Northeast is a rugged land of hills. In fact, three-fourths of the Northeast is made up of highlands. The Appalachian Mountains run through the center of this region. In the Northeast, parts of the Appalachians have their own names. They are the **White Mountains** of New Hampshire, the **Green Mountains** of Vermont, the **Adirondack Mountains** of New York, and the **Allegheny Mountains** of Pennsylvania. The Appalachians separate the Atlantic Coastal Plain from the lowlands along the shores of the Great Lakes.

An Icy Landscape

The rugged land of the Northeast is the result of giant sheets of ice called **glaciers.** Thousands of years before the Americas were discovered, the Earth was much colder than it is now. Great quantities of snow fell on northern Canada. It was so cold that the snow did not melt. Instead, the snow was packed down by more snow. Slowly, the packed snow turned to ice. The ice continued to grow. In places it was almost two miles (3.2 km) high.

As the ice piled higher and higher, it began to spread out. Slowly the glaciers inched forward. Much of the Northeast was buried beneath tons of ice. The ice scraped over the land. It carried away soil. It wore down hills and rounded off mountains.

In time the climate warmed and the glaciers melted. However, much of the landscape of the Northeast had

Waters off the Maine coast are also used for recreation.

Storms, water, and ice have worn down the peaks of Vermont's Green Mountains.

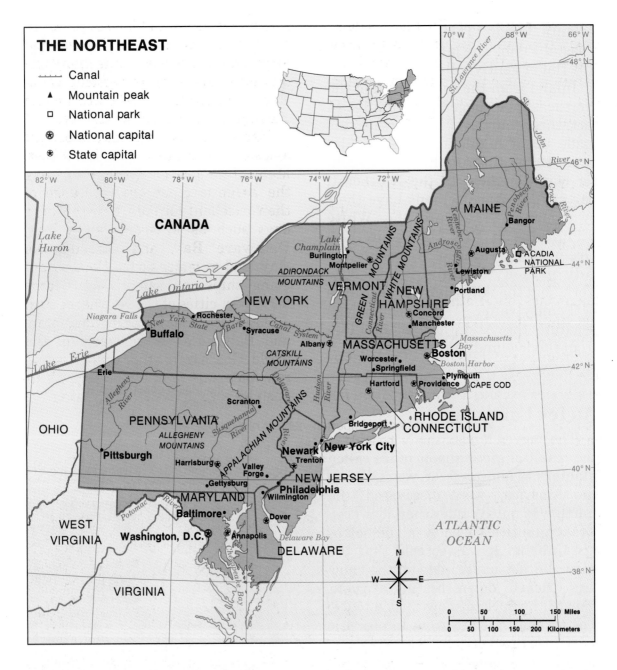

THE NORTHEAST

- ▬▬▬ Canal
- ▲ Mountain peak
- □ National park
- ⊛ National capital
- ✳ State capital

changed. Some places, particularly those in higher areas, were left with poor, rocky soil. In other places hills and valleys were formed.

Land of Cities

The Northeast is densely, or thickly, populated. In area the Northeast is the smallest of our seven regions. However, the Northeast is one of our most populated regions. In fact, more people live in this region than in any other region except the Southeast. Many of these northeasterners live in cities.

Years ago there were large areas of empty land between the cities of the Northeast. Today, these cities almost run into one another. They form a long, broad string of cities stretching all the way from southern Maine to northern Virginia. Some people call this string of cities a **megalopolis** (meg•uh•LAHP•uh•luhs), which in Greek means "giant city."

Economy of the Northeast

The Northeast is an important manufacturing region of the United States. The factories of the region produce a variety of goods ranging from steel and heavy machinery to books, magazines, and clothing. Manufacturing employs more people in the Northeast than any other kind of work.

Trade has always been important to the Northeast, too. The Northeast generally has excellent transportation for carrying goods from place to place. In addition to railroads, highways, and airports, the Northeast has many important rivers. The Connecticut, Delaware, and Hudson rivers are among the region's important waterways.

Each year tons of goods are bought and sold in the cities of the Northeast. Many of the large cities located along the Atlantic coast grew because of their excellent harbors. Several large bays such as **Massachusetts Bay, Delaware Bay,** and **Chesapeake Bay** lead to major ports. Here ocean-going ships can safely dock. Goods leave port cities of the Northeast such as Boston, New York City, Philadelphia, and Baltimore for all parts of the world. Goods from other countries and raw materials used in the region's industries also arrive at these ports.

New York City is one of the world's most important centers of industry, trade, and finance. It is also one of the world's largest seaports.

Workers in the nation's capital perform many service jobs in government.

Serving Other People

Many businesses in the Northeast provide services. New York City, our country's largest city, is sometimes called the financial capital of the world. Billions of dollars change hands in its banks every working day. Many insurance companies have their headquarters in Connecticut and New York. In our nation's capital, Washington, D.C., half of the workers have service jobs with the government. Altogether, more than one out of every five workers in the Northeast is employed in service industries.

Earning a Living on Land and Water

Most of the Northeast has cold, snowy winters. Buffalo, New York, for example, may receive more than 100 inches (254 cm) of snow each year. Summers are warm and humid. In New England, summers and growing seasons are generally shorter than in the rest of the Northeast.

Despite the poor, rocky soil left behind by the glaciers, there are some areas with good soil. Farming is important to the region's economy. Fruits and vegetables grow well in New York, Pennsylvania, Maryland, Delaware, and New Jersey. The Connecticut River valley produces tobacco, apples, and vegetables. Maine is famous for its potatoes and blueberries. Cranberries are harvested on Cape Cod, and New York produces fine grapes.

Dairy products come from all the states in the Northeast. However, dairy and poultry farms are especially well suited to the soil and climate found in the northern areas of the region. The rocky soil and the short growing season in much of New England make it difficult to grow many crops. Instead, farmers raise dairy cattle and poultry. These require little land, and the animals can be fed on grain that is shipped from other regions of the country.

Tomatoes grown on a New Jersey farm are harvested for shipment to market.

Fishing boats and lobster traps are found along the coast of Maine. Maine's lobster catch is the largest of any state.

Fishing is also important to the economy of the Northeast. Fishers from this region bring in about one-third of the total fish catch of our entire country. Chesapeake Bay and the waters off Cape Cod are especially productive.

Other people earn their living from the region's forests. Trees from the Appalachian Mountains provide both lumber and pulp for the region's many paper mills. Maple syrup is one of Vermont's main products.

Depending on the Northeast

The Northeast's excellent transportation system and its fine harbors and ports have made the region an important area for trade. Northeastern industries manufacture many different goods. These products are then transported to other regions to be used by people all over our country.

Although farming is important to the region's economy, the Northeast depends on other regions of the United States for much of its food needs. Large areas of land in the Northeast hold the region's cities, leaving less land available for farming. Therefore, the Northeast is not able to raise enough food for its large population. The Northeast is a good example of interdependence among the regions of our country.

Reading Check

1. Why does much of the Northeast have rocky soil?
2. What kind of work employs the most people in the Northeast?
3. Why is dairy and poultry farming well suited to the northern areas of the Northeast?

Think Beyond How do you think the economy of the Northeast has influenced its growth?

45

SKILLS IN ACTION

USING PHYSICAL MAPS

Reading a Relief Map

Maps show the shapes of countries and continents. Often they also show what the surface of the land is like. Look at the drawing below.

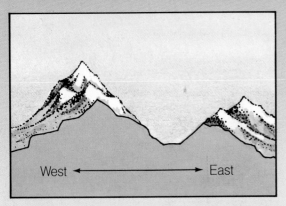

West ←——————→ East

The drawing shows a cross section. A cross section shows what the land would look like if it were sliced. Imagine slicing a pear from top to bottom. The exposed part of the pear would be the cross section.

In the cross section the mountain range to the west is quite high. The mountain range to the east is lower. Between the mountain ranges is a valley.

These landforms are also shown on the sample map. The top of the high mountain range is the heavily shaded area. The lightly shaded area near the eastern edge of the map is the lower mountain range. The valley, the lowest area, is not shaded.

This type of map is called a **relief map.** A relief map uses shading to show the shape of landforms. The relief map below shows part of the northeastern United States.

Find the darkly shaded area in the western part of the map. The shading tells you that this is a mountainous area. Which mountains are to the south of the Adirondack Mountains?

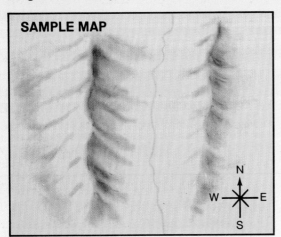

SAMPLE MAP

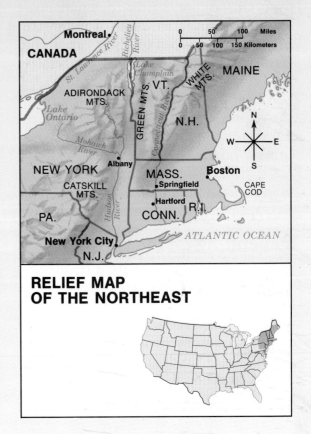

RELIEF MAP OF THE NORTHEAST

46

Find the Mohawk River on the map. It runs from west to east between the two mountain ranges. The land near this river is not shaded. This tells you that the land is lower than the mountainous lands to the north and south.

Find the Connecticut River on the map. Between what mountains does it flow?

Which states seem to have no mountains? According to this map, would you find mountains along the Maine seacoast? Why or why not?

Reading an Elevation Map

The relief map shows mountains. However, the map does not tell you *how high* the mountains are. For this information you must look at an **elevation map.** An elevation map shows the heights of land areas. The word *elevation* means height.

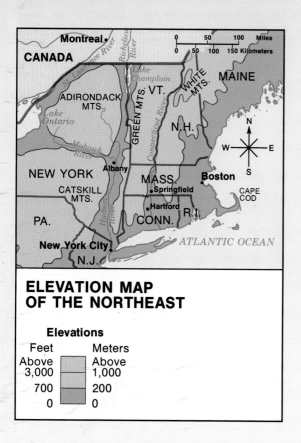

ELEVATION MAP OF THE NORTHEAST

Elevations

Feet		Meters
Above 3,000		Above 1,000
700		200
0		0

Most elevation maps use color to show elevations above sea level. Look at the elevation map below. The map key tells you which colors are used to show different elevations.

For example, dark green is used for land that is between sea level and 700 feet (200 m) high. You can see that the eastern part of Massachusetts is dark green. This tells you that the land is between 0 (sea level) and 700 feet (200 m) in elevation. Most of the Adirondack mountain region is colored light green. How high is this land? Is there any place on the map above 3,000 feet (1,000 m)? Where is it?

Finding Out Which Way Rivers Flow

You can use an elevation map to find out which way a river flows. Water flows in a downhill direction, from high ground to low ground. The colors showing elevation will tell you which part of the river is on high ground, which on low ground.

Look at the Connecticut River on the elevation map. Its source is in New Hampshire near the Canadian border. According to the map, what is the elevation of the river in upper New Hampshire? In Massachusetts the Connecticut River drops in elevation. What is its elevation as it flows through Massachusetts and Connecticut? You can see that the Connecticut River flows southward. It flows from a higher elevation through lower elevations until it reaches the Atlantic Ocean.

Sometimes we describe places in relation to a river as **downstream** or **upstream.** Suppose you are in Springfield, Massachusetts, and you follow the direction in which the Connecticut River flows. You come to Hartford, Connecticut. Hartford is downstream from Springfield. A place reached by going against the river flow is upstream. Springfield is upstream from Hartford.

Physical Maps

Maps that show both relief and elevation are usually called **physical maps.** These maps use shading *and* color to show the shape and height of the land surface.

The combination of shading and color can help you understand the true shape of the land. Find the Catskill Mountains on the map below. The light green color shows that the Catskills have an elevation of between 700 and 3,000 feet (200 and 1,000 m). The shading shows where the Catskills are the steepest.

Uses of a Physical Map

It is much easier to travel on a level trail than on a steep, rough one. Walking up and down mountains is hard work, and it makes for slow traveling. A physical map can show the best travel routes because it shows which areas are flat and which are mountainous.

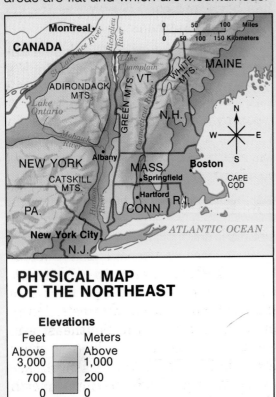

PHYSICAL MAP OF THE NORTHEAST

Elevations

Feet	Meters
Above 3,000	Above 1,000
700	200
0	0

By showing elevation, a physical map can also make clear which way rivers flow.

Imagine that you are hiking from the St. Lawrence River near Montreal to New York City. With your finger, trace the easiest route on the map. You probably would follow the Richelieu (RISH•uh•loo) River to Lake Champlain. Then you would go south until you came to the Hudson River. You would follow the Hudson all the way to New York City. This route would be much faster and easier than a route straight through the Adirondack Mountains.

CHECKING YOUR SKILLS

Answer the following questions. Use the information in this lesson to help you.

1. To find the elevation of the Green Mountains, should you use a relief map or an elevation map?

2. Will a relief map tell you if southern Connecticut is generally flat or hilly? Will a relief map tell you the elevation of southern Connecticut?

3. Does the Hudson River flow from north to south or from south to north? How do you know? Explain your answer.

4. Is the land in northern New Hampshire hilly or flat? How high are the highest areas in northern New Hampshire?

5. Which are higher, the Adirondack Mountains or the White Mountains?

6. What is the elevation of Boston?

7. Is Albany upstream or downstream from New York City?

8. Imagine that you want to travel between Hartford and Springfield by canoe. Would it be easier to begin your trip in Hartford or in Springfield? Why?

Look for these important words:

Key Words
- textiles
- petrochemical
- refineries
- phosphate
- Sun Belt

Places
- Lake Okeechobee
- Okefenokee Swamp
- Everglades
- Blue Ridge Mountains
- Great Smoky Mountains

Look for answers to these questions:
1. What major landforms make up the Southeast?
2. What are some of the Southeast's important crops? major industries?
3. What are some of the Southeast's major ports?
4. What is the Sun Belt?

2 The Southeast

The Southeast is a changing region. Cities are growing rapidly, and people from all over the United States are moving to this land of sunshine. Yet the Southeast is also a land of history and tradition. Like the Northeast, the Southeast has influenced our nation's history from its beginnings. The states that make up this large region are shown on the map on page 51.

The Coastal Landscape

The Southeast borders both the Atlantic Ocean and the Gulf of Mexico. Offshore are many low, sandy islands. The coastline itself is deeply indented with bays.

Water is a plentiful resource in the Southeast. Many broad rivers flow across the region. Also, lakes such as **Lake Okeechobee** in Florida are an important part of the landscape. Lake Okeechobee is one of our country's largest lakes. Water transportation has been and continues to be important in the Southeast.

The Coastal Plain covers much of the Southeast. Most parts of the Coastal Plain have large areas of rich soil. Other parts, however, are wet and swampy. The **Okefenokee Swamp** in Georgia and the **Everglades** in Florida are two of the most famous swamps in the world.

The Piedmont and the Appalachians

Just west of the Atlantic Coastal Plain, the land rises to the Piedmont. Rich in minerals, the Piedmont also has good farmland and forests. Many of the factories in the Southeast and some of the Southeast's largest cities are found in the Piedmont as well. Atlanta, Georgia, and Charlotte, North Carolina, are two of these cities.

Thoroughbred horses are raised in the Bluegrass region of Kentucky.

The Appalachian Mountains are an important part of the Southeast, too. In this region the forested highland area has two special names. The highlands that stretch from Maryland to Georgia are called the **Blue Ridge Mountains.** Southwest of the Blue Ridge Mountains are the **Great Smoky Mountains** of North Carolina and Tennessee. Just west of the Appalachians, more lowland stretches across much of western Kentucky and Tennessee.

Chicken production is important to the economy of the Southeast.

The Economy of the Southeast

The climate of the Southeast is generally warm and sunny. Summers are usually hot, long, and humid. Winters are short and often mild. However, snowfalls and freezing temperatures are common during winter in northern areas of the region.

All of the states in the Southeast receive more than 40 inches (102 cm) of precipitation each year. The rain and long growing seasons help farmers here grow many different crops.

Farming has always been important to the Southeast's economy. North Carolina, Kentucky, Tennessee, and South Carolina are the nation's leading tobacco-producing states. Florida produces large crops of sugarcane, oranges, grapefruits, and tangerines. Georgia is our nation's leading peanut grower. Arkansas leads the country in the production of rice. Louisiana ranks third in rice production. Soybeans and cotton are important crops in several Southeastern states.

Farmers in the Southeast also raise beef cattle, dairy cows, hogs, and poultry. Florida, for example, is an important ranching area and a leading state for beef cattle. Kentucky, Virginia, and Florida are known for their horse farms.

The Southeast is an important source of chickens for meat. Three out of every four broiler chickens in the United States are raised in the Southeast. North Carolina is our country's leading turkey-producing state. The states of Georgia and Arkansas rank fourth and sixth in the production of eggs.

THE SOUTHEAST

□ National park

⊛ State capital

Shipping and Fishing

The waters of the Southeast play an important part in the region's economy. Many of the Southeast's largest cities are ports. They are located along the Atlantic and Gulf coasts as well as on the Mississippi River. Norfolk, Virginia, is one of the largest ports on the Atlantic. Tampa, Florida, and Mobile, Alabama, are large ports on the Gulf of Mexico.

Ports such as New Orleans, Louisiana, serve the thousands of ships and barges that move up and down the Mississippi River. Located about 100 miles (160 km) inland, New Orleans is one of the largest seaports in the

About 5,000 ships from 60 nations dock each year at New Orleans.

United States. Products from all over the country are transported to New Orleans and other ports in the Southeast before being shipped to markets around the world. Goods from other countries and raw materials used in American factories arrive through these ports as well.

Fishing is another important part of the Southeast's economy. Large catches are taken each year from the warm coastal waters of the region. Virginia, North Carolina, Mississippi, Florida, and Louisiana are all important fishing states.

Industry in the Southeast

The first factories in the Southeast were built along the Fall Line. Water power ran the machines that turned out **textiles,** or cloth. Today, textile manufacturing is still an important industry in the Southeast. Other factories process the many fruits and vegetables grown in the Southeast.

The forests of the Southeast are an important economic resource for manufacturing. Furniture manufacturing is a leading industry in the region, especially in the Appalachians and the Piedmont. Forests in these areas supply the hardwood needed to make fine furniture. Georgia, Alabama, Louisiana, and Virginia are all important paper-manufacturing states. Wood pulp for paper is produced from the Southeast's many pine forests. More paper comes from the pine forests of the Southeast than from anywhere else in the United States.

Coal and oil are among the Southeast's most important resources. Coal is used most often as a fuel to run the machinery that makes electricity. Oil

Coal miners enter a mine in West Virginia to begin a new workday.

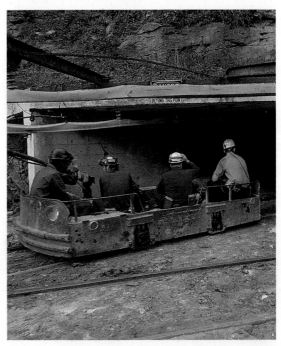

discoveries off the coast of Louisiana have led to the growth of a large **petrochemical** industry. The petrochemical industry produces goods made from oil. These include plastics, paints, fertilizers, and fuels. Factories called **refineries** change the oil into fuels such as gasoline and heating oil.

Mining is a major industry in the Southeast. In addition to coal, large amounts of iron ore and limestone are mined each year. The Appalachian Mountains contain large amounts of these minerals. Florida is the world's largest producer of **phosphate** (FAHS•fayt). Phosphate is used to make fertilizer and glass.

The Sun Belt

The Southeast is part of our nation's **Sun Belt,** an area stretching across the southern part of the United States. It is a land with lots of sunshine, a long growing season, and mild winters.

The Sun Belt is one of the most rapidly growing parts of the United States. People from all over the country are moving to Sun Belt states to work or retire in the pleasant climate. Many businesses are also relocating in the Southeast and the other states of the Sun Belt. New industries are developing. These new factories and growing businesses continue to attract people to the Southeast to fill jobs.

Depending on the Southeast

Farming and fishing in the Southeast affect people all across the United States. The region's fertile land and rich fishing areas contribute much to our food needs. For example, you may drink orange juice made from oranges grown in Florida or eat peanut butter made from peanuts grown in Georgia. These are just two of the many foods that come from the Southeast.

Southeastern industry also contributes much to our country. Petrochemical products, textiles, furniture, paper goods, coal, and oil are just a few of these contributions. These products and resources are used by people in all regions of the United States.

Tourism is important to all the Southeastern states. In fact, tourism is probably more important to the economy of the Southeast than to any other single region of the United States. Many businesses depend on the visitors from all over the world who flock to the Southeast to enjoy the region's sunny climate and many attractions.

Disney World, Epcot Center, and Sea World attract millions of visitors to Orlando, Florida, each year. Other cities offer visitors tours of museums, historical sites, and fine old southern mansions. Nashville, Tennessee, is famous for its Grand Ole Opry. Huntsville, Alabama, is the home of the Alabama Space Rocket Center, which has the largest collection of space-related materials in the world.

Reading Check

1. What two mountain chains are part of the Appalachian Mountains in the Southeast?
2. What does the petrochemical industry produce?
3. Why are people moving to the Sun Belt states?

Think Beyond What challenges might a rapidly growing region face?

APPALACHIAN CRAFTS

Many years ago when a child in the Appalachian Mountains got a birthday present, it was usually something made by hand. It might have been a doll made from cornhusks or a toy horse carved out of wood. Because the Appalachian regions of Kentucky, Tennessee, and Virginia were so isolated from the rest of the world, people had to make whatever they needed out of the materials they had.

Although the region is no longer isolated, people there still take pride in their handmade crafts. Scraps of cloth from worn-out clothing are still used to sew big, thick quilts. Sometimes several women gather for a work session, known as a quilting bee, to create the colorful patterns of the quilt.

The dulcimer, a musical instrument that is kin to a banjo, is another popular item crafted in the Appalachians. Dulcimers are made in different shapes and sizes. They may be intricately carved, or they may be very plain and simple.

No matter how they are shaped or decorated, all mountain dulcimers are played in the same way. The player positions the dulcimer on his or her lap and then picks and strums the strings. Its lilting notes prove that the dulcimer is well named—*dulcimer* means "sweet song."

Toys are also popular crafts. A person with a whittling knife can become a toy factory. One toy, called Ball and Cup, is a wooden cup attached to a long stick. A string with a small wooden ball at its end is tied to the stick. Children hold the stick in one hand and swing the toy so that the ball will drop into the cup.

In the past, only people in Appalachia could enjoy their beautiful handmade crafts. Now, however, handmade quilts, toys, games, and musical instruments from Appalachia can be found in stores and museum shops. Now everyone can enjoy the talents of the Appalachian people.

Think Beyond   How do you think life has changed for the people in Appalachia now that they are no longer isolated?

Handmade mountain dulcimer

Look for these important words:

Key Words
- Heartland of America
- cultivate
- Corn Belt
- Dairyland
- winter wheat
- spring wheat

Places
- Black Hills
- Badlands
- Ozark Highlands
- Ozark Mountains
- Mesabi Range

Look for answers to these questions:

1. What is the most important landform in the Great Lakes and Plains States regions?
2. What are the important resources of the Heartland?
3. Why is the Heartland sometimes called the "breadbasket of the world"?
4. How have waterways contributed to manufacturing in the Heartland?

3 The Great Lakes and Plains States

Giant glaciers pushed south over the middle part of our country thousands of years ago. As in the Northeast, these glaciers flattened hills and filled in valleys. They formed plains and deposited rich soil on the plains. The glaciers also dug out five deep areas in the earth. When the glaciers melted, water filled these areas and formed the Great Lakes. The glaciers formed thousands of smaller lakes as well.

The Great Lakes States region is a land rich in minerals and other resources. It has fertile farmland, large cities, and thousands of factories. The states bordering the Great Lakes are called the Great Lakes states. They are Ohio, Indiana, Illinois, Michigan, Wisconsin, and Minnesota. These states are shown on the map on page 56.

The Plains States region, one of the world's best farming and ranching areas, is to the west of the Great Lakes States region. Six states are part of the Plains States region. They are North Dakota, South Dakota, Nebraska, Iowa, Kansas, and Missouri. These six states are shown on the map on page 56.

Heartland of America

The Great Lakes and Plains States regions are often called the **Heartland of America.** Together they form one of the most important farming and manufacturing regions on Earth. Heartland fields produce food for people throughout the world. The Heartland's factories produce half of the steel and most of the cars in the United

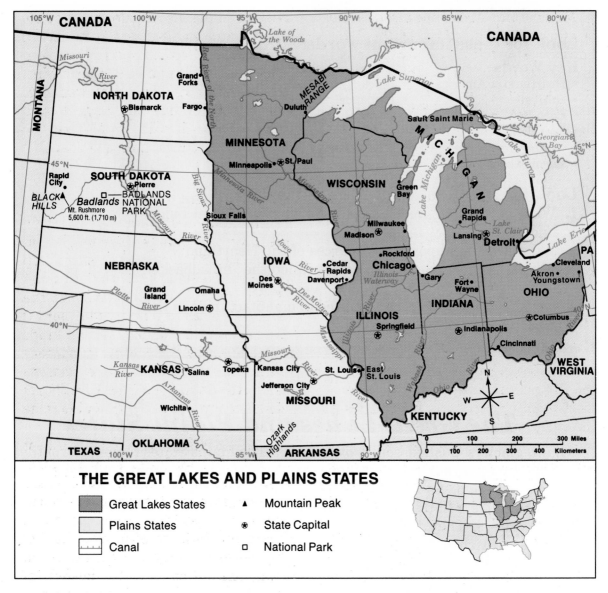

THE GREAT LAKES AND PLAINS STATES

- ▨ Great Lakes States
- ▨ Plains States
- ⊡ Canal
- ▲ Mountain Peak
- ✳ State Capital
- ▢ National Park

States. In its great cities, skyscrapers, steel mills, and flour mills reach up toward the sky.

Beyond the cities, fields of corn and wheat planted on fertile plains and rolling hills thrive in the warm summer sun. Summers are generally sunny and humid. Rainfall is plentiful in the Great Lakes states. The Plains states, however, are drier.

In winter, snows cover these same fields with glistening blankets of white. Winters are generally long,

cold, and snowy. In the southern Plains states, winters are milder.

The Land

Most of the Heartland is a shallow basin lying between higher ground to the east, south, and west. It is a region in which plains are the most important feature of the landscape. Most of the land lies within the Interior Plains of the United States. Fertile soil makes this a valuable farm region.

56

Much of the land of the plains areas is amazingly flat. Part of the land, however, is a rolling landscape. Some hills are found in the northern parts of the Great Lakes states. In a few places, like the **Black Hills** of South Dakota, the land rises to more than 7,000 feet (2,130 m). These pine-covered hills are the highest place in the Plains states. East of the Black Hills is an area of dry land called the **Badlands.** The land is wild and rugged. Few plants grow. In southwestern Missouri are the **Ozark Highlands** and the **Ozark Mountains.** Here the land rises sharply above the plains.

Resources and the Economy

The Great Lakes and the rivers of the Heartland may be the region's most valuable resource. Few places in the entire world have as fine a system of lakes and rivers as the Heartland. The Missouri River joins the Mississippi in the state of Missouri near St. Louis. Together these two rivers are more than 3,700 miles (5,920 km) long.

The waterways of the Heartland contribute to its economy. They provide transportation routes for the region's goods and products. The St. Lawrence Seaway and the Illinois Waterway allow oceangoing ships to carry the Heartland's products to markets around the world.

In addition to waterways, the Heartland has other important natural resources. Large forests cover much of northern Minnesota, Wisconsin, and Michigan. They are part of a great pine forest that spreads across Canada. Wide layers of coal lie beneath the soil in Illinois and Indiana.

North Dakota also has large amounts of coal and oil. Iron ore is mined in Minnesota, Michigan, and Wisconsin. The **Mesabi Range** in northern Minnesota has large mines of iron ore. South Dakota has the largest gold mine in the United States. Many of the states also produce sand and gravel.

Food for the World

The land itself is another valuable resource. Flat plains, rich soil, warm summers, and plenty of moisture help make the Heartland the "breadbasket of the world." The flat land and the large size of farms allow the farmers of this region to use many different kinds of machinery. Modern machinery means that a small number of farmers can **cultivate** large areas. To *cultivate* means to prepare and use land to raise crops.

The Heartland is one of the best areas of the world for growing corn, soybeans, and wheat. Four out of every ten bushels of corn grown in the world are raised by Heartland farmers. Heartland farmers also grow half of the world's supply of soybeans and about one out of every ten bushels of wheat. A large part of these crops is shipped overseas by way of the Mississippi River or the Great Lakes. The harvest helps feed many people around the world.

Corn and Livestock

The warm humid summers of the Central Plains are ideal for corn. In fact, this crop is so important that much of the Central Plains area is called the **Corn Belt.**

Grain is stored in the silos on this grain and hog farm in Iowa.

Milking machines are used on this modern Wisconsin dairy farm.

Corn feeds people, but corn also feeds livestock. Many farmers in the Corn Belt grow corn as food for hogs and beef cattle. Iowa raises more hogs than any other state in the United States. Only four other states raise more beef cattle than Iowa.

Dairyland

Wisconsin has more dairy cows than any other state in the United States. The hay that dairy cows eat can grow in a climate that is too cool for corn. **Dairyland,** then, is north of the Corn Belt.

A modern dairy farm is much like a factory. There are machines to wash the cows before milking as well as machines to milk the cows. The milking is done twice a day, every day of the year, in a building called a milking parlor. The milk goes from the milking machines into a refrigerated tank. In this way the milk has no contact with the air at all. This helps prevent the milk from spoiling.

Few farms require as much work as a dairy farm. Many dairy farmers work 15 hours a day. Barns must be kept spotlessly clean. The cows must have regular examinations to make sure they are healthy. The machinery must be cleaned after each milking. Hay must be cut and stored.

Many Dairyland farms keep as many as 50 cows. That many cows provide about 800 gallons (3,082 l) of milk each day. The money that the farmer makes depends largely on the cost of shipping the milk from the farm to the market. Therefore, many Wisconsin dairy farms are located close to the large cities along the shores of Lake Michigan.

Wheatland

Wheat requires less rainfall than corn and most other crops. North Dakota and Kansas are the two leading wheat-producing states. In Kansas wheat is planted in the fall. By early summer it is ready to be harvested. Wheat that is planted in the fall is called **winter wheat** because it can survive the cold winter weather. Winter wheat is used mainly for making bread.

Farther north in the Dakotas, however, winters are too cold for winter wheat. In North Dakota and South Dakota, wheat is planted in the spring. It is ready to be harvested in the late summer. North and South Dakota, then, are lands of **spring wheat.** Spring wheat makes good macaroni and spaghetti.

Modern combines are used by farmers to cut and thresh wheat crops.

Heartland Factories

The Heartland produces more than one-fourth of all the goods manufactured in the United States. Many of the Heartland's factories are centered in the large cities found along the Great Lakes and the Mississippi River system. Chicago, Illinois, located on the shores of Lake Michigan, is the largest city in the Heartland.

The location of this productive region in the center of our country makes it the crossroads of the North American continent. Many of the major transportation routes in the United States pass through Heartland cities. Many of these cities, like Chicago, grew in part because they were in the center of the transportation system. Today Chicago has our country's second-busiest airport and is one of the country's busiest rail cities.

Factories have developed in the Heartland cities because their locations along major waterways and railroad routes allow raw materials and manufactured products to be shipped easily. For example, iron ore mined in northern Minnesota is shipped on the Great Lakes to Heartland steel mills. Coal used to fire the furnaces in the mills is shipped from nearby areas to Heartland cities.

The Heartland has a variety of industries. Around the southern end of Lake Michigan, from Chicago to Gary, Indiana, is one of the largest steelmaking centers in the world. Cleveland, Ohio; Detroit, Michigan; and Youngstown, Ohio, are also important steel centers. Detroit is the center of the automobile industry. Akron, Ohio, and many other Heartland cities make automobile parts. Farm machinery

Chicago, Illinois, our nation's third-largest city, is an important transportation center for the United States.

comes from Heartland factories, too. Omaha, Nebraska; Kansas City, Kansas; and other Heartland cities have huge meat-packing plants. Minneapolis, Minnesota; St. Louis, Missouri; and Des Moines, Iowa, are all important flour-milling cities.

Depending on the Heartland

The Heartland gives much to the United States. The corn, soybeans, and wheat raised on its fertile plains help feed not only the people of the United States but also people around the world. Its manufactured goods and its many products are used daily by people in every part of our country.

Neighboring regions depend on the Heartland for other things, too. The Great Lakes, the Illinois Waterway, and the Mississippi River system connect large parts of the United States. Many regions of the United States ship goods and raw materials on the Heartland's waterways and on its other transportation systems.

Even though the Great Lakes and Plains states are rich in natural resources, they do not have everything they need. The Heartland, too, depends on other regions of the United States. For example, the industries and the large cities of the area require huge amounts of energy. The Heartland, however, cannot meet all of its energy needs by itself. The Great Lakes and Plains states depend on coal and oil from the Southeast and other regions of our country to help meet that need.

Reading Check

1. What landform covers most of the area in the Great Lakes and Plains States regions?
2. What important resource is mined in the Mesabi Range?
3. What three crops are raised in large amounts in the Heartland?

Think Beyond What are the advantages of Chicago's location?

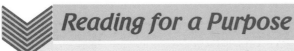
Look for these important words:

Key Words	Places
• uranium	• Guadalupe Mountains
• potash	• Santa Elena Canyon
	• Sonoran Desert
	• Chihuahuan Desert
	• Painted Desert
	• Houston Ship Channel
	• Hoover Dam
	• Lake Mead

Look for answers to these questions:
1. In general, how does the landscape of the Southwest change from east to west?
2. How have the Indians and the Spanish influenced the growth of the Southwest?
3. How have energy resources contributed to the growth of manufacturing in the Southwest?
4. How has the Southwest met its growing demands for water?

4 The Southwest

The Southwest is a land of wide, open spaces. It is a land of cattle ranches and dusty trails. However, the Southwest is also a region of modern cities, eight-lane freeways, and rapidly growing industries.

The Southwest is larger than the Northeast and the Great Lakes States combined. Yet just four states make up the Southwest. They are Texas, Oklahoma, New Mexico, and Arizona. These states are shown on the map of the Southwest on page 62.

The Gulf of Mexico forms part of the region's southeastern border. Mexico borders the region on the south. Along the Texas–Mexico border the Rio Grande flows 1,241 miles (1,997 km)

southeast before emptying into the Gulf of Mexico. The Colorado River forms the region's western border.

The Land

All of the major landforms can be found in the Southwest. The eastern half of Texas and most of Oklahoma are plains regions. Rainfall is plentiful, and several large rivers flow across the plains.

Farther west, hills begin to replace plains in some places. In other places the plains just get higher. This area of high plains is part of the Great Plains. In the Southwest, the Great Plains extend from Texas into eastern New

61

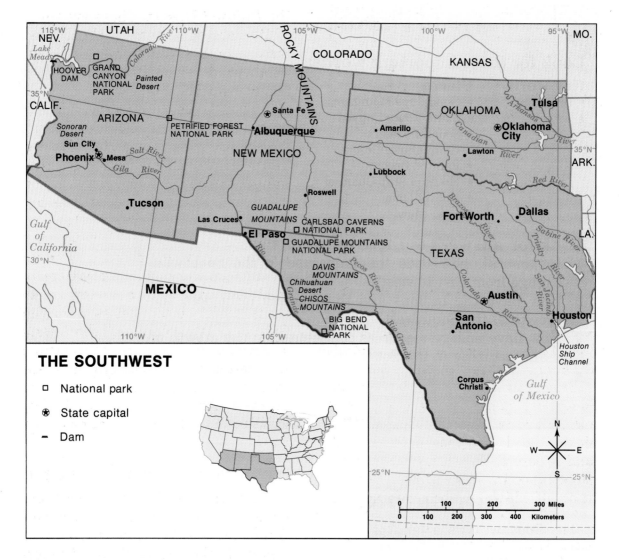

THE SOUTHWEST

- ☐ National park
- ✳ State capital
- − Dam

Mexico. Elevations on the Great Plains range from 2,500 to over 5,000 feet (762 to 1,524 m) above sea level. This land of short grass was once home to millions of buffalo. Today it is a land of cattle ranches.

As you continue west on the plains, mountains begin to appear. The highest are the Rocky Mountains in northern New Mexico. Several other, smaller mountain ranges extend south across New Mexico and into western Texas. Among these are the beautiful **Guadalupe** (gwah•dah•LOOP) **Mountains**. The Rio Grande and its tributary, the Pecos River, are the only major rivers in this dry, mountainous area of the Southwest. The Rio Grande has cut deep canyons through the land. The **Santa Elena Canyon** in Big Bend National Park is one of the most beautiful.

In northern Arizona and New Mexico, the Colorado Plateau covers much of the region. Named for the Colorado River, which runs through it, the Colorado Plateau is a rough land of very little rainfall. This is the land of the Grand Canyon. Farther south are more mountains. Finally, in southern

Yucca plants grow in the desert regions of the southwestern United States.

Arizona and New Mexico, elevations drop. Plains are found along the Salt and Gila (HEE•luh) rivers.

From east to west the land of the Southwest generally becomes drier and drier. In western Texas, New Mexico, and Arizona, much of the land is desert. Here are the **Sonoran** (suh•NOH•ruhn) **Desert,** the **Chihuahuan** (chuh•WAH•wahn) **Desert,** and

Spanish influences in the Southwest can be seen in this Texas community.

the **Painted Desert.** These are three of the largest deserts in the United States. Both the Sonoran and Chihuahuan deserts extend south into neighboring Mexico.

Just as there are variations in the landforms of the Southwest, the climate of this region varies, too. Eastern Texas and Oklahoma have long, hot, humid summers. Summers in the western areas of the region are hot but drier.

Although severe cold spells and snowfalls sometimes occur, winters throughout the region are generally mild. This mild winter climate attracts thousands of winter visitors to the Rio Grande valley of Texas and the deserts of Arizona. However, heavy snowfalls and bitterly cold temperatures are common in winter in the mountains of northern Arizona and New Mexico, particularly at higher elevations.

Indian and Spanish Influence

Vast areas of the Southwest are home to many American Indian tribes. Oklahoma has the largest Indian population in the United States. California ranks second, and Arizona and New Mexico rank third and fourth.

Everywhere in the Southwest are reminders of the days when much of this region was governed by Spain and later Mexico. Spanish place names are often as common as English ones on street signs. Spanish is the native language of many people living in communities in Texas, New Mexico, and Arizona. Many of these people are Mexican Americans. They have contributed much to the Southwest's history and growth.

Members of a drilling crew on a Texas oil rig install additional pipes.

Many factories use the Houston Ship Channel to transport their goods.

Resources and the Economy

Oil, natural gas, coal, and **uranium** are all sources of energy. Uranium is an ore used in making nuclear energy. These important resources are plentiful in the Southwest. The production of energy sources are important to the Southwest's economy.

Texas leads the nation in oil and natural gas production. The state of Texas alone produces more oil than any country in the world with the exception of the Soviet Union, Saudi Arabia, and Iran. Texas also produces about one-sixth of the world's natural gas. Along with Texas, New Mexico also ranks in the top seven oil-producing states.

All four of the Southwestern states also have rich deposits of coal. New Mexico produces about half of our country's uranium. Two other valuable minerals, copper and **potash,** are mined in the desert areas of the Southwest. Potash is used in fertilizers.

Industry in the Southwest

Energy is the basis for much of the industry in the Southwest. Many oil products are manufactured in this region. These products make such cities as Tulsa and Oklahoma City, Oklahoma, and Houston, Texas, important centers for the petrochemical industry.

Houston is the center of our nation's petrochemical industry. Because of its role in the oil industry, Houston is also an important international trade center. Like New Orleans, Houston is an inland port. Connected to the Gulf of Mexico by a wide waterway called the **Houston Ship Channel**, it is our country's third-largest port.

One of the most rapidly growing areas for industry is the triangle formed by three Texas cities—San Antonio, Houston, and Dallas. These are three of the ten largest cities in the United States. They form one of the world's leading centers of electronic and space technology. Austin, the capital of Texas, and Dallas are both important manufacturing centers for computers. Phoenix, Arizona, another of the ten largest cities in the country, is also an important electronics center. Factories in several large southwestern cities build airplanes and rockets.

Manufacturing is the leading economic activity in Phoenix, Arizona.

Some ranchers in the Southwest still use horses to round up cattle for market.

Ranching and Farming

Ranching is important to the Southwest's economy. Even though four of the ten largest cities in the United States are found in the region, the Southwest is still a land of farms and sprawling ranches. More cattle and sheep are raised in Texas than in any other state.

Farming is also important in the Southwest. Cotton is grown in all the Southwestern states. It is the region's largest crop. Wheat grows on farms in Oklahoma, eastern New Mexico, and northern Texas. These areas are at the southern end of the Great Plains. Arizona also grows wheat. Fruits and vegetables thrive in the fertile valleys of the Rio Grande and the Gila and Colorado rivers. Rice grows on the Coastal Plain in eastern Texas.

Crops can grow all year round in some parts of the Southwest. The farming areas have rich, red soil. In many places in the Southwest, however, the farmland needs irrigation.

Growth in the Southwest

The Southwest, like the Southeast, is part of the Sun Belt. The mild climate of the Sun Belt has been like a magnet, attracting industry and workers. This has helped make Phoenix and Tucson, Arizona; Albuquerque, New Mexico; and El Paso, Texas, some of the fastest-growing cities in the United States. In addition, thousands of people have moved to this region to retire. Many service industries have developed to meet the needs of all the people who have moved to new homes in the land of sunshine.

Increases in population and industry have put a high demand on the region's most valued natural resource—water. Having more people and industry means that more water is needed. To help meet this need for more water, wells have been dug and dams have been built. One such dam, the **Hoover Dam,** spans the Colorado River. **Lake Mead,** the reservoir formed by the dam, stores the Colorado River's water. The Hoover Dam provides water and electricity to many

Hoover Dam provides water and electricity for large areas of the Southwest.

parts of the Southwest. In addition, through irrigation, the water from Lake Mead has opened a million acres (404,700 ha) of desert land to farming. The wise use and protection of valuable water resources will insure continued growth in the Southwest.

Depending on the Southwest

Few regions anyplace in the world have the variety of scenery that is found in the Southwest. The Southwest, however, gives much more to the United States than beautiful scenery. The Southwest is a land of energy. This region's oil, natural gas, coal, and uranium provide for much of the energy needs of our country. In fact, the entire nation depends on the energy that this region provides.

In addition to energy, our nation depends on the petrochemical industry of the Southwest. This industry produces such things as cosmetics, detergents, plastics, and fertilizers. The Southwest is also the world's leading center for electronic and space technology. As an important cattle- and sheep-raising area, the region contributes to our nation's food needs as well. This fast-growing region contributes much to our nation and its people.

Reading Check

1. What three large deserts are found in the Southwest?
2. Which state has the largest Indian population?
3. What sources of energy are plentiful in the Southwest?

Think Beyond Why would the Southwest be a good area in which to live?

People
MAKE HISTORY

Ansel Adams
1902–1984

▶▶▶▶▶▶▶▶▶▶▶▶▶▶▶

In 1916, a young piano teacher went hiking in California's Yosemite National Park. Along the way he took some pictures with an inexpensive camera. Those few grainy photos would mark the beginning of a career for Ansel Adams. Within a few years he would become a world famous photographer.

Adams spent years taking black-and-white pictures of towering mountains, peaceful lakes, and swooping valleys. His photographs showed the untouched beauty of the land. They also showed the way light and shadow affect natural objects. His most famous photo, "Moonrise," shows a full moon shining over a dusty New Mexico town.

Ansel Adams proved that a photographer is truly an artist. "You don't take a photograph," he often said, "you *make* it." Making a picture means waiting for the proper lighting, framing the scene, and carefully adjusting the camera to achieve the proper setting and focus. It also means developing the picture in the darkroom. Adams compared photography to music, saying, "The negative is the musical score. The print is the performance."

Ansel Adams was more than a photographer. He was also a conservationist, a teacher, and a writer. As a conservationist, he testified before Congress about the importance of conserving America's woodlands. As a teacher, he held yearly seminars at which hundreds of photographers could learn his techniques.

Through his writing, he explained how to make beautiful photos.

When Ansel Adams died in 1984, he was one of the most popular photographers in the world. His photos, which include portraits and still-lifes as well as his famous landscapes, hang in museums all over the United States and Europe.

Think Beyond How can Adams's photographs help you appreciate the beauty of our country?

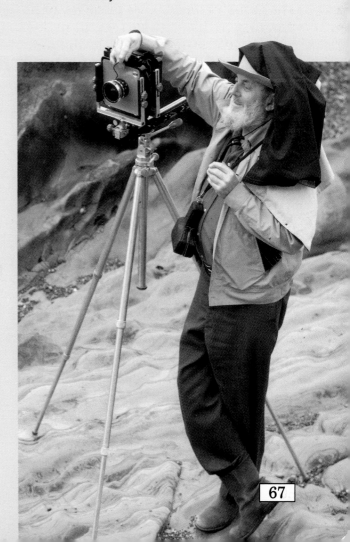

Look for these important words:

Key Words
- Inuits
- Eskimos
- Trans-Alaska Pipeline

Places
- Mount McKinley
- Mount Rainier
- Mount Waialeale
- Death Valley
- Mojave Desert

- Imperial Valley
- Puget Sound

Look for answers to these questions:
1. Which major landforms are found in the Mountain and Pacific states?
2. Which state has the largest population? the smallest population?
3. Which major resources come from the land and sea in the Mountain and Pacific states?
4. Which state leads the nation in manufacturing?

5 *The Mountain and Pacific States*

The Mountain States and the Pacific States regions combine to form a vast region in the western United States. The wettest and the driest places and the warmest and the coldest places in the entire country are found in the Mountain and Pacific States regions. These regions have our highest mountains and our only active volcanoes. There are about 80 active volcanoes in the western United States, including Hawaii.

The longest mountain range in our country, the Rocky Mountains, stretches through all of the Mountain States region. There are six large states in this region. They are Montana, Idaho, Wyoming, Colorado, Utah, and Nevada. These states are shown on the map on page 70.

The Pacific states are bordered by the Pacific Ocean. The five states that make up this region are shown on the map on page 70. They are California, Oregon, Washington, Alaska, and Hawaii. Alaska is our country's northernmost state. Along its eastern boundary, Alaska borders Canada. Hawaii, our country's southernmost state, is the only state that is not on the North American continent.

Mountains and Plains

Rugged mountains can be seen almost everywhere in the Mountain and Pacific states. Much of the land in the Mountain states and parts of Alaska are covered by the Rocky Mountains. The Brooks Range in northern Alaska is part of the Rocky Mountains. South of the Brooks Range is the Alaska Range. Alaska's **Mount McKinley,** the highest point in North America, is in the Alaska Range. Mount McKinley has an elevation of 20,320 feet (6,194 m). The Cascade Range and the Sierra Nevada of Washington, Oregon, and California have jagged peaks that are often covered with snow and ice. West of the Cascades and the Sierra Nevada, along the Pacific Coast, are the Coast Ranges.

Even Hawaii is a land of mountains. In fact, each of the islands that make up our 50th state is really the upper part of a gigantic volcano. These volcanoes, now mostly inactive, reach above the waters of the Pacific from deep on the ocean floor.

The mountains and the Pacific Ocean act together to cause a variety of climates in the huge Pacific States region. Because Alaska is so far north,

Diamond Head, an extinct volcano, towers over Waikiki Beach.

winters in northern Alaska are long and bitterly cold. Yet the Pacific Ocean helps keep winter temperatures along Alaska's coast fairly mild. The ocean brings warmer temperatures and rain to southern Alaska in the summer months.

Winds from the Pacific Ocean bring heavy precipitation to the Coast Ranges and to the western slopes of the Cascades and the Sierra Nevada in Washington, Oregon, and northern California. Where it is very rainy, the trees grow tall. The mountain slopes are covered with Douglas firs and other kinds of pine trees. Redwoods, some of the world's tallest trees, grow here as well. The eastern slopes of the Cascades and the Sierra Nevada have a much drier climate, as does southern California.

Winters in the Coast Ranges are generally mild. In the Cascades and the Sierra Nevada, however, winters are much colder than along the coast. Snowfall is heavy. **Mount Rainier,** in eastern Washington, once recorded a winter snowfall of 1,027 inches (2,609 cm). This is the largest winter snowfall ever recorded in the United States.

Winds from the Pacific Ocean also bring heavy rainfalls to much of Hawaii. **Mount Waialeale** (wy•ahl• ay•AHL•ay) on the island of Kauai is one of the wettest spots in the world. It gets at least 460 inches (1,168 cm) of rain each year.

The eastern area of the Mountain States region is part of the Great Plains. Here the plains slope upward toward the Rocky Mountains. In Colorado, Wyoming, and Montana the plains are nearly a mile (1.6 km) above sea level.

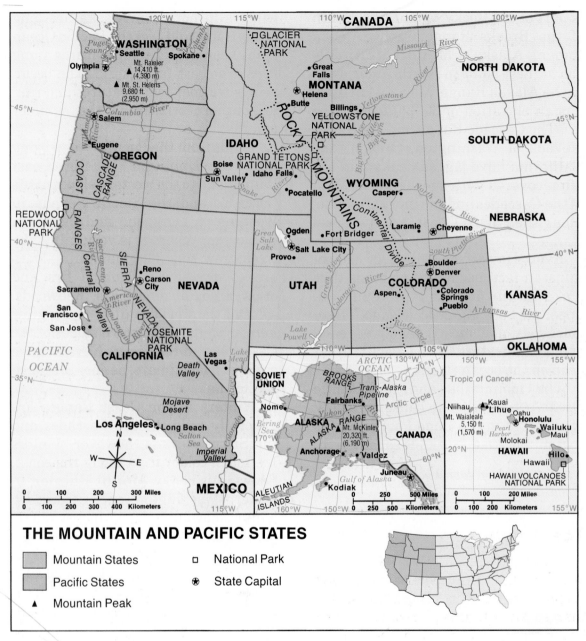

THE MOUNTAIN AND PACIFIC STATES

- Mountain States
- Pacific States
- ▲ Mountain Peak
- ☐ National Park
- ✪ State Capital

Mountains affect the climate of the plains in the Mountain States region. The mountains prevent the moist Pacific winds from reaching this area, making it the driest part of the United States. In the northern states of the region, winters are generally long and cold. Summers are warm and mild. In the southern states summers can be hot. Winters are generally mild.

Plateaus and Basins

Between the Rocky Mountains and the Cascades and Sierra Nevada is the Intermountain Region of the United States, a broad basin consisting of plateaus and smaller mountains. Much of this basin is desert. The Great Basin covers much of Nevada and Utah. The Columbia Plateau, an area of high, dry land, covers parts of Washington, Oregon, and Idaho. This plateau gets only 10 to 20 inches (25–50 cm) of rain a year. The Colorado Plateau, another area of high, dry land, covers the southern parts of Colorado and Utah.

Valleys

The Pacific States region has some important valleys as well. One of the most famous is **Death Valley,** the lowest place in North America. Found in California's **Mojave** (muh•HAHV•ee) **Desert,** Death Valley is 282 feet (86 m) below sea level. Also in California is the great Central Valley. Farmers here use water from the Sacramento River and the San Joaquin River to make the farmland of this valley some of the richest in the United States. Farmers use water from the Colorado River to irrigate the fertile **Imperial Valley.** The Imperial Valley, in southeastern California, is part of the Sonoran Desert.

The People

All the Mountain states are large, but they are thinly populated. Fewer people live in the Mountain states than in any other region of our country. By contrast, most of the Pacific states are heavily populated. However, Alaska, our largest state in land area, has the fewest people. The people of Alaska are not evenly distributed, or spread out, over the state. Nearly half live in the city of Anchorage. Much of Alaska is still unsettled.

In some areas, particularly along the shores of the Arctic Ocean, Native Americans are the only inhabitants.

These Native Americans call themselves **Inuits** (IN•yuh•wuhts). Others call them **Eskimos.**

California has more people than any other state. Nine out of ten Californians live in cities and towns. San Francisco is the largest city in northern California. Los Angeles, farther to the south, is California's largest city.

California has a great mix of people. Mexican Americans have always played an important part in this state. Many people continue to come to California today from Mexico. People from Asia also are arriving on the West Coast in large numbers. In recent years many Asian Americans have settled in the cities of the Pacific states.

No state has a greater mix of people than Hawaii. The beauty of the islands attracts people from many parts of the world.

San Francisco's Chinatown is our nation's largest Chinese community.

Earning a Living from Land and Sea

Forests are important to the economies of both the Mountain states and the Pacific states. They provide much of the lumber used in construction all over the United States. Oregon, California, and Washington are our leading, lumber-producing states.

All of the Pacific states provide large amounts of seafood. Salmon and halibut are especially important. Fish, crab, and oysters are harvested from the waters around the Pacific states and sold in markets all over the world.

Dreams of wealth from gold and silver mines brought many of the first settlers to the Mountain states and to California and Alaska as well. Miners are still busy in all of these states. Almost 200 minerals and fuels are found in the Mountain states alone. Except for Wyoming, the Mountain states have huge amounts of copper. Gold and

An Oregon logger cuts trees for shipment to a nearby lumber mill.

silver are found in all these states. Coal comes from Colorado, Wyoming, Montana, and Utah. Wyoming is also rich in oil and natural gas.

Oil is found in large amounts in northern Alaska, too. The **Trans-Alaska Pipeline** brings oil 800 miles (1,287 km) to Alaska's southern coast. There the oil is transported to refineries around the country.

Farms and Ranches

Ranches can be found in all of the Mountain and Pacific states. Raising beef cattle, sheep, and dairy cows is important to both the regions.

Wheat is the most valuable crop in the Mountain states. Large wheat farms occupy much of the Great Plains in Montana, Wyoming, and Colorado.

Farmers in the Mountain states grow other crops by irrigating the land. Some of these crops are peas, beans, and sugar beets. Idaho is famous for its potatoes.

Farmers in Washington and Oregon grow many crops. Both states are famous for their fruit orchards. More apples are grown in Washington than in any other state. Oregon leads the nation in the production of pears.

Hawaii is famous for its flowers. Orchids grown in Hawaii are delivered to mainland florists by airplanes. Hawaiians also raise sugar cane, pineapples, nuts, and coffee.

California farmers produce over 200 different crops, including nearly 70 kinds of fruits and nuts. Grapes are California's most valuable fruit. California leads the nation in the production of peaches and ranks second in orange production. California also grows a wide variety of vegetables.

Manufacturing

Manufacturing provides many jobs in the Mountain and Pacific states. Colorado is the leading manufacturing state in the Mountain States region. Construction equipment and farm machinery are its leading products. Meat packing is an important industry in Denver. Food-processing plants contribute to the economy of Idaho.

Manufacturing is especially important in the Pacific states. California leads the entire nation in manufacturing. It is best known for its electronic and communications equipment. Washington and Oregon have large paper mills. The city of Seattle, Washington, ships large amounts of lumber through **Puget Sound.** Seattle also has large aircraft factories. Aircraft factories are important in Los Angeles and San Diego, California, as well.

Depending on the Mountain and Pacific States

Food, lumber, oil, minerals, and manufactured goods are just a few of the many things the Mountain and Pacific states give to our country. These regions are also important to our nation's transportation system. Railroads and highways that pass through the Mountain states connect the eastern United States with the West Coast.

The Pacific states have several harbors that make the region important for shipping. Five of the region's largest seaports are Seattle, Washington; San Francisco, Los Angeles, and Long Beach, California; and Honolulu, Hawaii. Goods and raw materials from all over the world arrive through these

Workers in California produce microchips used in computers and electronics.

ports. These ports are especially important for transporting goods and raw materials between the United States and nations in western South America and Asia.

Service industries are important to all 11 states in the Mountain States and Pacific States regions, which attract large numbers of tourists every year. In addition, Denver, San Francisco, Los Angeles, and Honolulu are all important banking and business centers for the western United States.

Reading Check

1. What is the highest point in North America? the lowest point?
2. How does oil from northern Alaska reach refineries located around the country?
3. How is farming possible in the dry lands of the Mountain and Pacific states?

Think Beyond Why do you think so few people live in the Mountain states?

73

Thinking Back

- The United States can be divided into seven regions. These regions share similar locations, landforms, climates, vegetation, resources, and histories.

- Each region is special in several ways. All the regions, however, depend on each other's resources and products. This sharing of resources and products is called *interdependence*.

- In area the Northeast is the smallest region. However, the Northeast is densely populated and is an important manufacturing area. Its excellent transportation system and fine harbors and ports have made the region an important area for trade.

- As part of our nation's Sun Belt, the Southeast is a changing region. Cities are growing rapidly, yet farming remains important to the region's economy. Coal and oil are among the Southeast's most important resources.

- The Great Lakes and Plains States regions are sometimes called the Heartland of America. Together they form one of the most important farming and manufacturing regions on Earth.

- The Southwest is a land of energy. This region's oil, natural gas, coal, and uranium provide for much of our country's energy needs. In addition, the Southwest is the world's leading center for electronic and space technology. It continues to be an important farming and ranching area as well.

- A land of sharp contrasts, the Mountain States and Pacific States regions combine to form a vast region in the western United States. Food, lumber, oil, minerals, and manufactured goods are just a few of the many things the Mountain and Pacific states give to our country.

Check for Understanding

Using Words

Match each term with the correct definition.

1. cape
2. cultivate
3. glaciers
4. interdependence
5. megalopolis
6. phosphate
7. refineries
8. Sun Belt
9. textiles
10. uranium

a. a "giant city"
b. an area with a mild climate stretching across the southern part of the United States
c. a point of land that extends into the ocean
d. cloth
e. a substance used to make fertilizer and glass
f. depending on one another for the things we want and need
g. an ore used in making nuclear energy
h. giant sheets of ice
i. prepare and use land to raise crops
j. factories that change oil into fuels

Reviewing Facts

1. How did glaciers affect the land of the Northeast region?
2. Describe the landscape of the Coastal Plain in the Southeast region.
3. Why are the Great Lakes and Plains States regions sometimes called "the breadbasket of the world"?
4. How have energy resources affected the economy in the Southwest?
5. How are farmers in the dry areas of the Mountain States and Pacific States regions able to raise crops?

Thinking Critically

1. How do landforms and resources affect the ways people make a living in the various regions of the United States?
2. How does the development of one industry in an area lead to the development of other industries in the area?
3. Why do you think a reliable source of water is necessary for continued growth in the Southwest?
4. How has interdependence among the regions of the United States contributed to our country's overall growth?

Writing About It

Write two paragraphs in which you describe what you think it would be like to live near a rain forest, a volcano, or a desert. Describe the sights and sounds you might experience by living near one of these features.

Practicing Skills: Geography

Using Physical Maps

Use the physical map of the Northeast on page 48 to answer these questions.

1. Which major rivers come together just north of Albany?

2. In what direction does the Mohawk River flow? Would it be easier in a canoe to travel east or west on the Mohawk River?
3. If you lived in the White Mountains, could you easily reach Albany by foot or by canoe? Explain.

On Your Own

Social Studies at Home

1. Cut from old magazines and newspapers pictures of food products that may have been grown in the Heartland. Paste the pictures on poster board to display for the class.
2. Talk with friends or members of your family who have lived in other regions of the country. Write a short report telling how that region is different from the one in which you live.

Read More About It

House on Spruce Street by John J. Loeper, Atheneum. This book leads the reader through the history of an imaginary 200-year old house in Philadelphia.

Northeast States by Henry Gilfond. Franklin Watts. By providing information about the history, agriculture, and cities of the region, this book will help provide information about the Northeast.

Pacific States by Don Lawson. Watts. This book contains much information about our westernmost geographical area.

Rocky Mountain States by L.B. Taylor, Jr. Franklin Watts. This book describes America's western mountain region.

Southeast States by Gilda Berger. Franklin Watts. Containing information on the history, geography, and sights of the Southeast, this book gives a flavor of the region.

THE PEOPLE, YES

by Carl Sandburg

In every region of our country there are stories or tall tales about people and nature. In creating these tales, people use their imaginations to entertain themselves and others. In many ways they are also commenting on their environment.

> They have yarns
> Of a skyscraper so tall they had to put hinges
> On the two top stories so to let the moon go by,
> Of one corn crop in Missouri when the roots
> Went so deep and drew off so much water
> The Mississippi riverbed that year was dry,
> Of pancakes so thin they had only one side,

Of "a fog so thick we shingled the barn and six feet out on the fog,"
Of Pecos Pete straddling a cyclone in Texas and riding it to the west
   coast where "it rained out under him,"
Of the man who drove a swarm of bees across the Rocky Mountains and
   the Desert "and didn't lose a bee,"
Of a mountain railroad curve where the engineer in his cab can touch
   the caboose and spit in the conductor's eye,

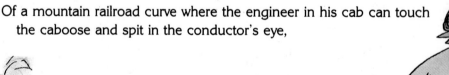

Of the boy who climbed a cornstalk growing so fast he would have
starved to death if they hadn't shot biscuits up to him,
Of the old man's whiskers: "When the wind was with him his whiskers
arrived a day before he did,"
Of the hen laying a square egg and cackling, "Ouch!" and of hens laying
eggs with the dates printed on them,
Of the ship captain's shadow: it froze to the deck one cold winter night,
Of mutineers on that same ship put to chipping rust with rubber
hammers,
Of the sheep counter who was fast and accurate: "I just count their feet
and divide by four,"
Of the man so tall he must climb a ladder to shave himself,
Of the runt so teeny-weeny it takes two men and a boy to see him,
Of mosquitoes: one can kill a dog, two of them a man,
Of a cyclone that sucked cookstoves out of the kitchen, up the chimney
flue, and on to the next town,
Of the same cyclone picking up wagon-tracks in Nebraska and dropping
them over in the Dakotas,
Of the hook-and-eye snake unlocking itself into forty pieces, each piece
two inches long, then in nine seconds flat snapping itself together
again,

Of the watch swallowed by the cow—when they butchered her a year
     later the watch was running and had the correct time,
Of horned snakes, hoop snakes that roll themselves where they want to
     go, and rattlesnakes carrying bells instead of rattles on their tails,
Of the herd of cattle in California getting lost in a giant redwood tree
     that had hollowed out,
Of the man who killed a snake by putting its tail in its mouth so it
     swallowed itself,
Of railroad trains whizzing along so fast they reach the station before
     the whistle,
Of pigs so thin the farmer had to tie knots in their tails to keep them
     from crawling through the cracks in their pens,
Of Paul Bunyan's big blue ox, Babe, measuring between the eyes forty-
     two ax-handles and a plug of Star tobacco exactly,
Of John Henry's hammer and the curve of its swing and his singing of
     it as "a rainbow round my shoulder."

"Do tell!"
"I want to know!"

Unit Review

Words to Remember

Number your paper from 1 to 10. Use the terms below to complete the sentences that follow. Write the correct term next to each number.

conservation	natural vegetation
drainage basin	petrochemical
economy	raw materials
glaciers	reservoir
natural resources	river system

1. A river and its tributaries are called a _____ .

2. The area drained by a river and its tributaries is called a _____ .

3. _____ are those things found in nature that people use.

4. A lake that stores water held back by a dam is called a _____ .

5. The way people use resources to produce and sell goods and services is called the _____ .

6. _____ are natural resources that can be made into useful products.

7. _____ is using a resource so as to keep it from being wasted or destroyed.

8. Plants that grow wild in an area are called _____ .

9. _____ are giant sheets of ice.

10. The _____ industry produces goods made from oil.

Focus on Main Ideas

1. Why do the United States, Canada, and Mexico have many landforms and natural features in common?

2. What is the largest mountain range in the eastern United States? in the western United States?

3. What two large plains areas are found in the United States?

4. What are the two most important drainage basins in the United States?

5. How are ships able to travel from the Atlantic Ocean to the Great Lakes? from the Great Lakes to the Mississippi River?

6. How have dams, reservoirs, and irrigation affected growth in the dry areas of the United States?

7. Name three things that affect climate.

8. How were the landforms of the Northeast, the Great Lakes, and the Plains States regions affected by glaciers?

9. Why is the Sun Belt a rapidly growing area of the United States?

10. What region of the United States has the most people? the fewest people?

Think/Write

Think about why the conservation of our nation's resources is important. Then write a radio commercial urging people to conserve a natural resource important to your region of the United States.

Activities

1. **ART** Make a collage about the geography of the United States. Include pictures

79

showing how the people of the United States use our nation's resources in their work and personal lives.

2. **Research/Art** Find out more about how mountains affect the climate of the western United States. Then draw a poster that illustrates how the mountains affect the climate in that area.

3. **Research/Art** Choose one of the regions of our country and research how people use that region's landforms for recreation. Then illustrate the recreation in a travel brochure. Your pictures should make people want to visit that region.

4. **Writing** Write a poem describing the beauty of the American landscape.

5. **Research/Writing** Choose one of the regions of the United States discussed in Chapter 2. Find out more about the region. Then write a report that describes the climate, the landforms, the resources, and the work that people do in that region.

6. **Reading/Reporting** There are many books about the different regions of our country. Read one and find an unusual fact about one of the regions of the United States. Then share this fact with your class.

Skills Review

1. **Using Latitude and Longitude** Use the political map of the United States in the Atlas to answer these questions.
    a. What line of latitude forms the southern border of Tennessee? the northern border of Wyoming?

    b. What line of longitude forms part of the border between the states of Texas and Oklahoma?
    c. What state capital is located near 40°N and 105°W?
    d. What large city is located near 40°N and 75°W?

2. **Using Climate Maps** Use the maps on pages 34 and 35 to answer these questions.
    a. Is the average yearly precipitation of San Francisco, California, more like that of Chicago, Illinois, or New Orleans, Louisiana?
    b. Is the average yearly precipitation of Anchorage, Alaska, more like that of Denver, Colorado, or Charleston, South Carolina?
    c. What is the growing season of the area near San Francisco? Is it more like that of New Orleans, Louisiana, or Boston, Massachusetts?
    d. Does Kansas City, Missouri, have a growing season of at least eight months? Does Dallas, Texas?

3. **Using Physical Maps** Use the physical map of the United States in the Atlas to answer these questions.
    a. What is the elevation of the land around Houston, Texas? around El Paso, Texas?
    b. Is the elevation of the land in western Wyoming higher or lower than the elevation in eastern Wyoming? Is eastern or western North Carolina higher?
    c. In what general direction does the Colorado River flow? Where is its mouth located?

EXPLORING
YOUR STATE'S GEOGRAPHY

Every state has its own geography. It has its own natural regions. It has its own landforms, rivers and waterways, natural resources, and climate. Although your state may share many of these natural features with neighboring states, each state is unique.

The activities below will help you learn more about the geography of your state. Some of the activities will require you to do research. You will find information about your state in many books in the library. You may want to keep a notebook about your state's geography and add to it as you learn more details.

Learning About Your State's Location and Size

1. Find your state on a map of the United States. What states, countries, or bodies of water form the boundaries of your state?

2. Measure the longest part of your state from north to south. Then measure the widest part of your state. Use the map scale to find out the real distances.

Learning About Your State's Landforms, Natural Regions, and Rivers

3. Draw a large outline map of your state. Show the major rivers of your state on the map. What are their tributaries? In what direction do these rivers flow? Where do they drain?

4. Use books from the library to find out the major natural regions in your state. Which natural regions of the United States are found in your state?

Learning About Your State's Climate

5. What is the climate of your state? What is the average annual precipitation for your state? What is the length of the growing season? Use the maps on pages 34 and 35 as well as books from the library to find out.

Learning About Your State's Resources and Economy

6. What natural resources are plentiful in your state? Choose one of these resources. Then list some of the manufactured goods that are made in your state using this resource.

Learning About Interdependence

7. You have learned that people throughout the United States depend on one another for their wants and needs. Select three resources and products from your state. How might these be used by people in other regions of the United States? Think of three things your family uses that cannot be found in your state. Where do these things come from? How might they have been transported to your state?

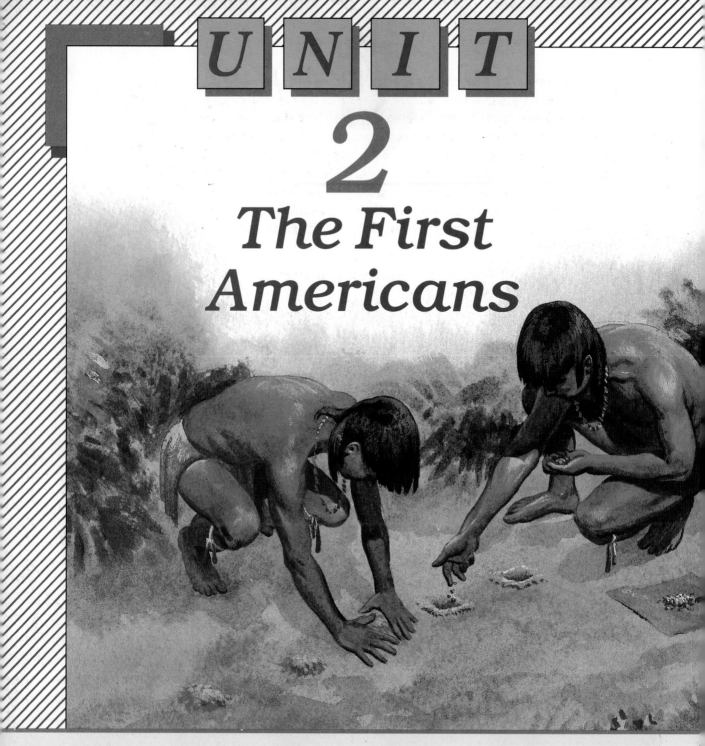

UNIT 2

The First Americans

• 70,000–10,000 years ago	• 40,000–20,000 years ago	• 10,000 years ago	• By 7,000 years ago	• 4,000 years ago	• 300 B.C.–A.D. 900
The last Ice Age	Ancestors of American Indians cross from Asia to North America	Big animals disappear People begin hunting and gathering	People of the Americas were farming	Eskimos come to North America	Height of Maya civilization

*F*or thousands of years before the arrival of the first Europeans, the American Indians lived in North and South America. They hunted for food in the vast forests. They glided up and down the rivers in bark canoes. They learned how to grow vegetables in the rich soil. That heritage still lives today. Many words from the American Indians have been adopted into the English language. Many of the foods first cultivated by the American Indians are still eaten. To understand the culture of the Americas, we must understand the heritage of the American Indians.

Think Beyond   Why do you think learning to farm was important to the American Indians?

• A.D. **600**	• A.D. **1200**	• A.D. **1276**	• A.D. **1438–1532**	• A.D. **1570**
Hohokam build irrigation canals	Height of Mississippian culture	Drought starts in Southwest	Height of Inca civilization	League of Iroquois formed

CHAPTER 3

Passage to a New World

> *Thirty thousand years ago*
> *Indians came riding across the ocean*
> *carried by giant sea-turtles.*
> *Waves were high that day*
> *great sea-turtles waded slowly out*
> *from the grey sundown sea.*
> *Grandfather Turtle rolled in the sand four times*
> *and disappeared*
> *swimming into the sea.*
> —from "Prayer to the Pacific" by Leslie Silko

Look for these important words:

Key Words	land bridge	Places
• Ice Age	• migration	• Bering Strait
• mammoths	• Stone Age	
• strait	• flint	

Look for answers to these questions:
1. Why could people and animals move from Asia to North America during the Ice Age?
2. What kinds of tools did these first Americans use?
3. What happened when the big animals disappeared?

Stone Age People from Asia

Thousands of years ago sheets of ice nearly two miles (3.2 km) thick were creeping over parts of North America. These glaciers covered most of what is now Canada and the northern parts of the present-day United States. This was the time of the last **Ice Age.** It lasted from about 70,000 years ago to about 10,000 years ago.

All sorts of animals roamed North America at the time of the Ice Age. There were huge, hairy elephants called **mammoths.** There were giant bison, similar to the buffalo, with horns 6 feet (1.8 m) across. Ground sloths were as large as cows or even elephants. In the wet meadowlands lived beavers as big as bears. Elsewhere there were bears as big as horses. In the skies flew giant vultures.

The most common animals in North America were camels and horses. Other grass-eating animals were the buffalo, deer, moose, caribou, and elk. Tigers, lions, wolves, coyotes, and cougars hunted these animals.

At the peak of the Ice Age, so much water turned into ice that the level of the oceans dropped. More land was uncovered. Today 55 miles (89 km) of sea separate North America from Asia at the **Bering Strait. A strait** is a narrow passageway between two large bodies of water. During the last Ice Age, however, a **land bridge** a thousand miles (1,609 km) wide connected the two continents. The land bridge was free of ice. Grass grew there. Herds of animals from Asia came to graze. Following the animals across the land bridge were the people. They depended on the animals for their food, clothing, and shelter. Where the animals went, they went also. These people were the ancestors of American Indians.

This movement of people and animals from Asia to North America is called a **migration.** The migration of people and animals took place over a period lasting 20,000 years.

The migrating animals and people crossed the land bridge, then moved

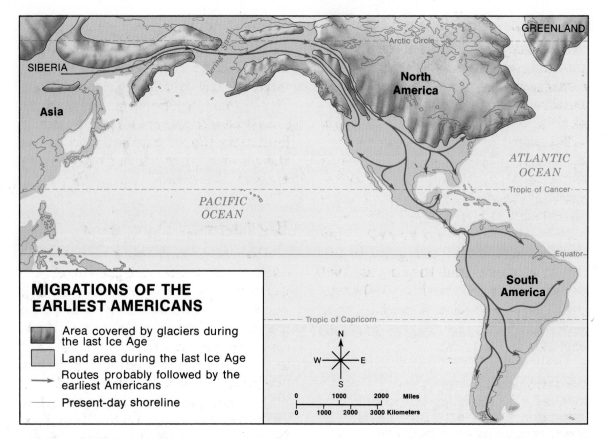

MIGRATIONS OF THE EARLIEST AMERICANS

- Area covered by glaciers during the last Ice Age
- Land area during the last Ice Age
- → Routes probably followed by the earliest Americans
- — Present-day shoreline

south along an ice-free passageway between two glaciers. These first Americans knew how to use fire. Without it, they might not have survived the cold of the Far North. With fire they could keep warm, and they could cook meat.

In time these hunting people traveled throughout North and South America. Some went as far south as the tip of South America. Others moved into the eastern parts of both North and South America.

The first Americans who came all had straight black hair and copper-colored skin. In other ways they were different from one another. They did not all speak the same language. Neither did they all look alike. Some were short and some were tall. Others were of medium height.

These hunting people used stone and bone to make their tools. For this reason we sometimes give the name **Stone Age** to the time in which they lived. During the Stone Age **flint** was the stone most often used for tools. Flint can be as hard as steel, yet it can be chipped easily. The hunters made scrapers, knives, and spear points from it. They also shaped bone into tools. They made spear shafts from splinters of the leg bones of mammoths.

Using spears, these earliest Americans worked together to hunt animals many times larger than themselves. With knives they cut up the animals they had killed. With scrapers of bone or flint, they cleaned animal skins. With bone needles and strips of rawhide, the hunters made clothing and footwear.

Scientists Solving Puzzles

For many years scientists did not agree on how long the Indians had been in America. Then they found proof that the ancestors of American Indians had been in North America for at least 10,000 years. In the early 1900s a cowboy found a pit full of old animal bones near Folsom, New Mexico. In 1926 scientists looking at the pit found a stone spear point buried among some animal rib bones. Scientists knew that the rib bones were those of a giant bison. They also knew that the animal had vanished from the earth 10,000 years ago. They concluded therefore that people must have been in America at least 10,000 years ago.

Early American hunters chipped flint, quartz, and other rocks into spear points. These spear points were found in Arizona buried among the bones of mammoths.

Since 1926 scientists have found many more tools made by early people. Most of them now agree that people were in North America more than 20,000 years ago. Some scientists think people have been here for 40,000 years. Scientists continue to work to fill in the missing pieces of the story of the earliest Americans.

Big Animals Disappear

About 10,000 years ago big animals such as mammoths disappeared. Camels and horses also disappeared from the Western Hemisphere. Scientists do not know why so many animals vanished. Some think that a changing climate was a reason. Some think that the hunters destroyed the animals.

As the big animals disappeared, the early American hunters had to change their way of life. No longer able to depend on big animals for their basic needs, people started hunting smaller animals such as deer and rabbits. They developed new tools such as the bow and arrow for hunting the smaller, swifter animals. They began to gather the roots and seeds of plants. People near the sea began to gather shellfish. For several thousand years people lived by both gathering and hunting.

Reading Check

1. Where was the land bridge connecting North America and Asia?
2. What is a migration?
3. How do we know people were in North America at least 10,000 years ago?

Think Beyond What might have happened if the big animals had not disappeared?

IN FOCUS

THE MAMMOTHS

A favorite game animal of early hunters was the mammoth. It was the largest animal on earth. A mammoth looked much like an elephant, but it was bigger. A male mammoth stood 16 feet (5 m) at the shoulder, or about as tall as a two-story house. That is much bigger than today's largest elephant, which stands about 13 feet (4 m). The mammoth was 7 feet (2 m) wide and walked on legs 18 inches (46 cm) thick. Its long, curved tusks grew to lengths of 8 to 9 feet (2.4 to 2.7 m).

These gigantic animals were peaceable. Their favorite food was the new green leaves of trees. The mammoths were big enough to fight off the fierce saber-toothed tigers. Yet often, hunters working together were able to kill these huge beasts. We know this because stone spear points have been found among mammoth bones.

In the Arctic parts of North America, Asia, and Europe, people hunted another kind of mammoth. This mammoth, which was covered with hair, is called the Wooly Mammoth.

There are places in the Far North where the ground never thaws. For that reason, parts of mammoth bodies, as well as mammoth bones, have been found.

Scientists were thrilled in 1977 when Russian gold miners uncovered a whole baby male mammoth. Scientists named the baby Dima. Forty thousand years ago, Dima had become separated from his mother. With only three baby teeth, he could not survive by eating grass. Starving, he fell into a pit and there died. His body froze and then was covered by landslides.

When a Russian scientist first saw the frozen baby mammoth, he said: "I put my hand on the dark skin and felt the chill of centuries long gone. It was as if I had touched the Stone Age."

Think Beyond Why do you think the discovery of a whole baby mammoth was important to scientists?

Life-size model of a mammoth

88

Reading for a Purpose

Look for these important words:

Key Words
- agriculture
- surplus
- specialize
- civilizations

- Mayas
- Incas
- Aztecs
- Mound Builders
- mounds

- culture
- Hopewell
- obsidian
- mica
- Mississippian

Places
- Cahokia

Look for answers to these questions:
1. How did knowledge of farming change people's lives?
2. What is a civilization? What is a culture?
3. What cultures developed in eastern North America?

2 Farming and Settled Life

Ancestors of the American Indians began to experiment with planting seeds about 7,000 years ago. The Indian farmers started with a small wild grass with only a few seeds on it. By always planting the best-looking seeds, the farmers slowly developed corn. Gradually they learned more and more about **agriculture,** or farming.

Once people learned how to raise food plants, they were able to settle down in one place. They did not always have to search for food to survive. Early farmers found that planting, weeding, watering, and harvesting crops did not take all their time. There was time left over for doing other things. The farming people began to use this time to build homes, to make new tools, and to make pottery.

The development of agriculture also resulted in a **surplus** of food. A surplus is an amount more than what is needed. People with a surplus of grain traded their surplus for other things, such as flint or salt.

Having a surplus also meant that not everyone had to farm. With agriculture, one person could grow the food for several. The result was that people could **specialize.** *To specialize* means to spend most of your time doing one kind of job. If there is extra food, then some people do not have to spend time raising or finding food. They can spend time instead making pots or weaving.

Agriculture made possible the development of **civilizations.** A civilization usually has large cities, complex government, and highly developed arts and sciences. The **Mayas,** Indian peoples of Central America and Mexico, developed a civilization over 1,000 years ago. They had a government and laws. They built huge temples and pyramids. They knew how to make objects of great beauty. They studied the skies and developed a very accurate calendar. They had a system of writing.

Later the **Incas** in Peru and the **Aztecs** in Mexico developed major

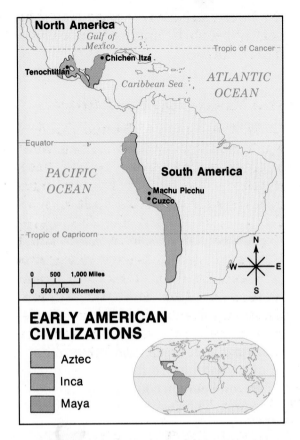

EARLY AMERICAN CIVILIZATIONS

- Aztec
- Inca
- Maya

civilizations. Both were important at the time the first Europeans arrived in the Americas. Both depended on agriculture.

The Mound Builders

Agriculture was also important to the way of life of Indians living in what is now the United States. In the eastern half of our country lived the **Mound Builders.** They made large **mounds,** or heaps of earth. Some mounds were miles long. Some of these mounds were for burials. Others were built as bases for temples and living quarters. Still other mounds had no purpose that we can discover.

The Mound Builders lived in villages and towns. They could do so because a surplus of food made it pos-

sible to specialize. There were those who designed and built mounds. Some farmed or hunted. Others worked at crafts. Still others were warriors or traders. A few were rulers.

The way of life shared by a group of people is called a **culture.** The people in a culture usually speak the same language, follow similar customs, use similar tools, and have similar beliefs.

Scientists have divided the Mound Builders into several cultures. They include the Hopewell culture and the Mississippian culture.

The Hopewell Culture

The people of the **Hopewell** culture farmed in the Illinois and Ohio river valleys about 2,000 years ago. They grew corn, squash, beans, and tobacco.

The Hopewell people were great traders. They traveled long distances to get the objects they valued. Some traders went to the Rocky Mountains to get grizzly-bear teeth and **obsidian** (uhb•SID•ee•un). Obsidian is a glassy, black, volcanic rock that made excellent arrow points and scrapers.

Some Hopewell traders went to the Gulf of Mexico for sea-turtle shells and shark teeth. Others went to the Great Lakes region to get copper nuggets to hammer into ornaments. From Florida the traders brought back alligator teeth.

The Hopewell people made beautiful pipes in the shapes of animals and birds. They wove a cloth using thread made from soft bark. The people wore clothing made of leather, fur, or cloth. They decorated their clothing with freshwater pearls and ornaments made of copper and **mica** (MY•kah). Mica is a clear rock that comes apart in thin sheets.

In their mounds the Hopewell people buried their important dead. They placed with them objects the dead had used in everyday life. Most of what we know about the Hopewell people comes from studying objects found in the burial mounds.

In time the Hopewell created another kind of mound-building culture. These Hopewell mounds were built in the shapes of animals and birds. Some of these animal-and-bird shapes are so large that the only way to see one as a whole is from an airplane!

The Hopewell culture gradually disappeared. We do not know why. Some scientists think it is possible that the Hopewell culture was destroyed by nearby people belonging to more warlike cultures.

The Mississippian Culture

Another group of Mound Builders was the **Mississippian** culture. Most of their mounds had a square base, sloping sides, and a flat top. Such mounds were pyramids built without the familiar pointed top. The Mississippian culture was most active about 700 years ago. Its biggest center was at **Cahokia** (kuh•HOH•kee•uh), near present-day East St. Louis, Illinois. Other important centers of the Mississippian culture were in present-day Oklahoma, Alabama, and Georgia.

Mound Builders constructed this giant serpent at least 1,300 years ago. Located in southern Ohio, the Serpent Mound is about a quarter of a mile long. Do you see the small mound in the snake's open jaws?

From approximately A.D. 1000 to A.D. 1500, Mississippian Indians built villages and mounds, ground corn they had grown, and crafted tools and pots near what is now Memphis, Tennessee. One of these villages, called Chucalissa, has been partially reconstructed. Here visitors may stand in the shadows of mounds and walk along ancient paths once trod by Indians.

At Chucalissa scientists have carefully dug into the earth to discover more about the lives of the ancient Mississippians. Many of these discoveries, such as tools, weapons, and pottery, may be viewed at the Chucalissa museum. The mounds, the discoveries of the scientists, and the museum connect us across time with the ancient culture of the Mississippians.

Scientists think that at one time Cahokia was a city of 30,000 people. The community had about 100 mounds, including the largest earth pyramid in the world. The large pyramid at Cahokia is 100 feet (30.5 m) tall, as high as a ten-story building.

Some of the mounds at Cahokia were used for burials. Others were platforms for religious temples and for houses of important people.

Along Cahokia Creek was a large marketplace for traders and craftsworkers. The traders came in canoes heavy with furs, shells, mica, flint, and copper. The craftsworkers included toolmakers, potters, weavers, jewelers, and leather workers. Some people mined flint nearby and turned it into knives and hoe blades. Others boiled water from a salt spring in order to get salt.

Cahokia was a busy community as late as 500 years ago. Then its people left. We do not know the reasons.

Reading Check

1. What is a surplus?
2. What does it mean to specialize?
3. Name at least one way the Hopewell culture and the Mississippian culture were alike.

Think Beyond What is the major difference between a civilization and a culture?

Look for these important words:

Key Words
- Anasazi
- dwellings
- drought

- Hohokam
- cooperation
- descendants
- archaeologists

- archaeology
- artifacts
- radiocarbon dating

Look for answers to these questions:

1. Where did the Anasazi live?
2. In what ways did the Anasazi use wild plants?
3. Where did the Hohokam live?
4. How do scientists learn about early peoples?

Early People of the Southwest

Among the sandstone cliffs of the Southwest are the deserted towns of another early people. We know these people as the **Anasazi** (ahn•uh•SAH•zee)—*the old ones*. The Anasazi built their communities in what is called the Four Corners. This is where the borders of four states—Utah, Colorado, New Mexico, and Arizona—meet. In this region rivers have carved deep canyons through pinkish-red sandstone. Mesas extend beyond the canyons. The Anasazi built their homes on the mesas, on the canyon floors, and in the canyon walls. Their homes were like apartment houses, with rooms built on top of other rooms. They used mud bricks and wooden beams to build these **dwellings,** or homes.

The Anasazi raised corn, squash, beans, sunflowers, and cotton on the mesas or on the canyon floor. When necessary, they climbed up and down the cliffs by using toeholds cut in the rock. Today some of their dwellings can be reached only by people using rock-climbing equipment. It is hard to imagine people carrying babies and baskets of food up and down such cliffs.

The Anasazi made use of wild plants. The pinyon tree provided nuts. It also gave resin (REZ•uhn) for waterproofing baskets. The yucca plant supplied soft

The yucca plant provided food, soap, and fiber for Indians of the southwest.

fibers for weaving baskets and hard fibers for needles. The fruit of the yucca plant was good to eat. Its root yielded a soap.

In the Anasazi culture the men farmed, hunted, and wove cotton blankets. The women made pottery, prepared food, and repaired the houses.

A **drought,** a long period of little or no rain, started in 1276. The years of drought made growing food impossible. The Anasazi left their homes in the Four Corners in search of water. Many moved across the Continental Divide to settle in the Rio Grande valley of present-day New Mexico. They were probably the ancestors of today's Pueblo Indians.

The Hohokam Culture

Indians in the **Hohokam** (hoh•HOH•kum) culture learned that the secret of living in the desert was irrigation. Using only digging sticks, these people built miles of irrigation canals in the Gila River area of central Arizona more than 1,300 years ago. Digging

Centuries ago, a group of Anasazi Indians built their homes in this large natural cave. The site is now a part of Mesa Verde National Park.

such canals must have taken a great deal of **cooperation**. *Cooperation* means people working together for a common purpose.

The canals provided enough water to irrigate crops. Food was plentiful. The Hohokam had time for other things. Some made beautiful pottery. Others must have spent hours playing ball games. Large ball courts have been found in Hohokam ruins.

The Hohokam lived in the Southwest for more than 1,000 years. Then about 500 years ago their culture disappeared. No one knows exactly why. Their **descendants** may be the Pima and Papago Indians of Arizona. A descendant is the offspring of an ancestor.

Hohokam potters used repeated designs when they made these beautiful pots.

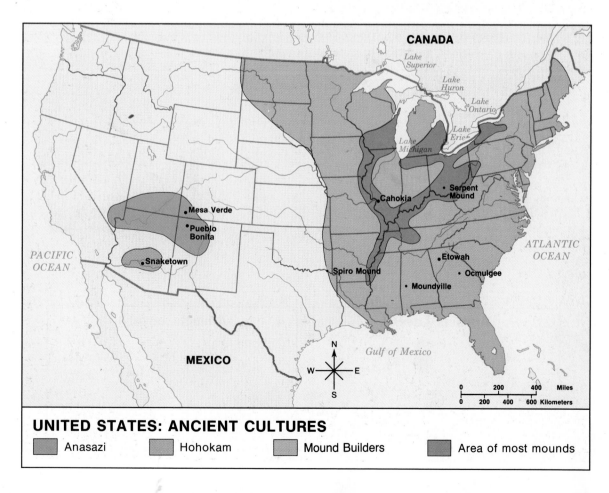

UNITED STATES: ANCIENT CULTURES

◼ Anasazi   ◼ Hohokam   ◼ Mound Builders   ◼ Area of most mounds

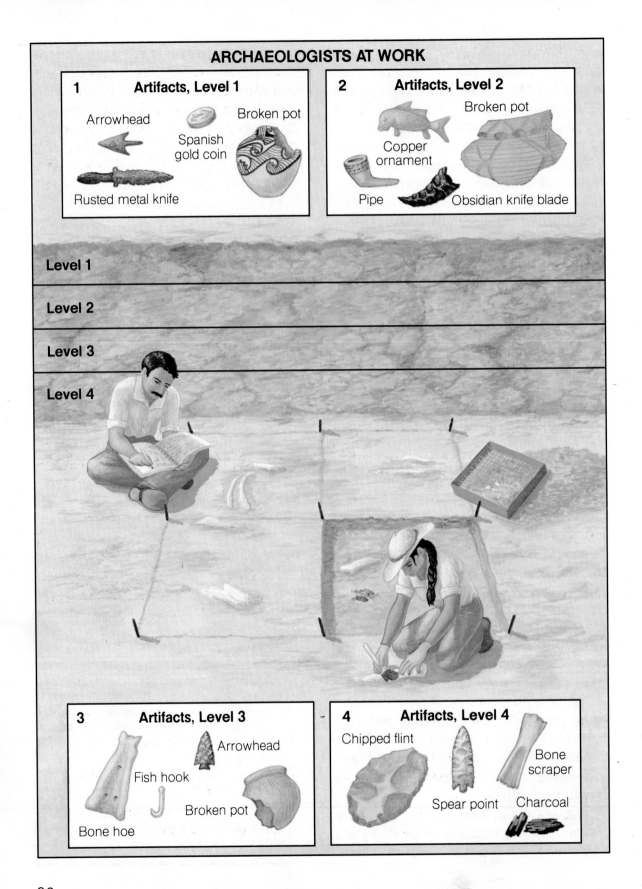

ARCHAEOLOGISTS AT WORK

1 Artifacts, Level 1

Arrowhead

Spanish gold coin

Broken pot

Rusted metal knife

2 Artifacts, Level 2

Copper ornament

Broken pot

Pipe

Obsidian knife blade

Level 1

Level 2

Level 3

Level 4

3 Artifacts, Level 3

Fish hook

Arrowhead

Broken pot

Bone hoe

4 Artifacts, Level 4

Chipped flint

Bone scraper

Spear point

Charcoal

Learning from Remains

Early people left no written records. How then do we know about those who lived long ago? Some did leave spear points and pottery, bits of which survive. Others left their mounds, their irrigation ditches, their cliff houses. From those remains scientists learn about the people who lived in the past.

The scientists who study remains to learn about the past are called **archaeologists** (ahr•kee•AHL•uh•juhsts). Their science is **archaeology** (ahr•kee•AHL•uh•jee).

To study the distant past, archaeologists dig into the earth. They choose to dig in places where people might have lived or camped. They search carefully for bones, weapons, tools, and pieces of pottery that early cultures may have left behind. Objects used by people in the past are called **artifacts.**

When archaeologists find artifacts, they try to figure out how old they are. One way to do this is to figure the age of the layer of earth where each artifact was found. Generally, objects near the surface were made more recently than objects buried farther down. An archaeologist may find a pot 2 feet (61 cm) below the ground and a spear 6 feet (183 cm) below the ground. The archaeologist figures that the person who made the pot lived more recently than the person who used the spear.

What if an arrowhead is found near some pottery? The archaeologist figures that the same people who used the pottery also hunted. Seeds, bones, and shells that are found give clues as to what people ate.

Archaeologists use other methods to find out the exact age of an object. One such method is counting tree rings.

If you look at the cut surface of a sawed-off tree, you will see many rings. Each ring represents one year of that tree's growth. Scientists count and compare the rings on pieces of wood. By working backward from a known year, they have a kind of calendar of tree rings. An archaeologist who finds an ancient piece of wood can figure out from tree rings the year the tree was cut down. Using tree rings to date objects works quite well in the dry climate of the Southwest. There, tree rings have been used to date artifacts 2,000 years old.

Archaeologists also use a technique called **radiocarbon dating.** All plants, animals, and human beings on earth contain radiocarbon. When a living thing dies, the radiocarbon within it begins to disappear very slowly and regularly. By measuring the radiocarbon in an object, scientists can figure out its approximate age. Radiocarbon dating works best for objects between 500 and 50,000 years old.

Archaeologists are the great detectives of science. They work slowly and carefully, putting their clues together to solve each new puzzle. With each archaeological conclusion, we come nearer to understanding the mysteries of the past.

Reading Check

1. What were the natural features of the area where the Anasazi lived?
2. Why could the Hohokam grow food in the desert?
3. Name two methods archaeologists use to date objects.

Think Beyond Why was it so important for the people of the Hohokam culture to work together?

People MAKE HISTORY

Willard Libby
1908–1980

▶▶▶▶▶▶▶▶▶▶▶▶▶▶▶

In 1947 a shepherd boy in the Middle Eastern country of Jordan made a great discovery. In a cave he found scrolls hidden in old earthen jars. When the scrolls were unrolled, they revealed ancient writings.

Scientists were very excited about these manuscripts, known as the Dead Sea Scrolls, and wanted to know how old they were. To find out, they asked Dr. Willard Libby to test them.

Dr. Libby was a chemist who had developed a way to determine the age of ancient materials. Known as radiocarbon dating, Libby's method measures the amount of the element carbon-14 that exists in once-living material. By examining the fibers of the linen in which the scrolls were wrapped, Libby was able to date the scrolls to 33 B.C.

Dr. Libby's development of the radiocarbon dating method was the result of years of study and research. Libby studied chemistry at the University of California at Berkeley. After graduating in 1933 he began teaching at Berkeley. He remained there until 1945, when he left to teach at the Institute of Nuclear Studies at the University of Chicago. In 1950 he became a consultant to the Atomic Energy Commission.

Over the next few years Dr. Libby continued to study carbon-14, and in 1952 he published *Radiocarbon Dating,* a book explaining his method. It was such a breakthrough for scientists that in 1960 Dr. Libby was awarded the Nobel Prize for chemistry.

Willard Libby's dating technique helps scientists discover facts about the age of the Earth and all that has lived on it. Although radiocarbon dating cannot date things exactly, it is a valuable tool in our quest to learn more about the history of our planet and ourselves.

Think Beyond   What things in your classroom do you think could be carbon dated? Explain.

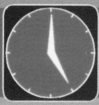

SKILLS IN ACTION

USING TIMELINES TO UNDERSTAND DATES

Why is it important to understand dates? When you talk about your own life, it is easy to say that something happened 5 years ago. When you talk about events in history, it is different. Saying that something happened 183 years ago or 310 years ago is awkward. It is easier to talk about events if you can say that something happened in 1500 or 1860. Understanding dates helps you understand time.

An easy way to think about time is to look at a **timeline.** A timeline is a diagram that shows a certain period of time. It may look something like a ruler. Important events are marked on a timeline at the points when they happened. Look at timeline *A* below.

This timeline shows a **decade,** a period of ten years. The space between each pair of dates is a year. The timeline begins with 1960 and ends with 1970. As you can see, the earliest date is on the left of the timeline. The most recent date is on the right. The decade of 1960–1970 can also be called the 1960s.

Three important events in the history of space travel are shown on timeline *A*. The earliest event shown is the date that the first person was launched into space. This happened in April, 1961. The line for this event is just to the right of the mark that begins the year 1961. The next line shows the date the first spacecraft landed on the moon. This

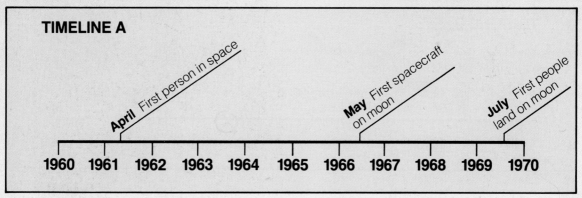

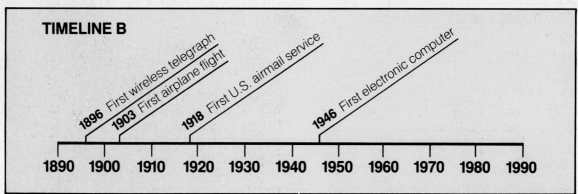

line is to the right of the mark that begins the year 1966. What is the most recent event shown on this timeline?

Timeline *A* shows a period of ten years. Imagine trying to use the same kind of timeline to show a period of 1,000 years. It would have to be 100 times longer than this timeline. How can one make a timeline covering many years without using a piece of paper several feet long?

One kind of timeline can show decades. Look at timeline *B*. It is read from left to right, just as timeline *A* was. On this timeline, only every tenth year is shown. The space between each pair of dates is a decade. Look at the first decade on the left. It begins with the year 1890. A line to the right of the the mark for the year 1890 shows the date of the first wireless telegraph. This line is a little more than halfway between the two marks. This line represents the year 1896. From left to right, read the dates and descriptions of the events shown on the timeline. Which event is the earliest? Which is the most recent?

Another kind of timeline can show centuries. A **century** is a period of 100 years. Now look at timeline *C* below.

The earliest date shown on this timeline is 1500. The space between the first two dates covers a period of 100 years. The earliest event shown on this timeline is Ponce de León's landing in Florida in 1513. What is the next event? Read the timeline from left to right. What two events happened after the Civil War?

When we talk about modern times, we often refer to the time we live in as the *twentieth century*. Timeline *D* below shows how centuries are counted. The years between 1000 and 1100 are known as the *eleventh century*. The years between 1100 and 1200 are the *twelfth century*. What is the name of the century between 1800 and 1900?

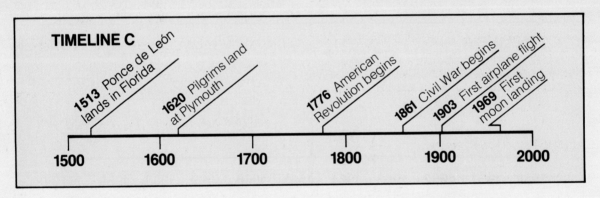

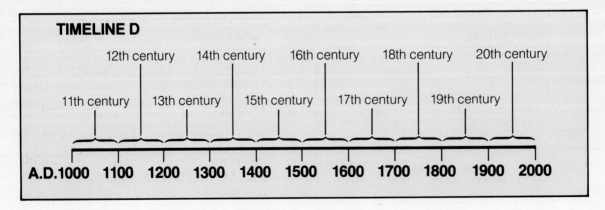

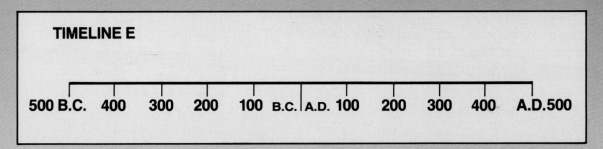

TIMELINE E

500 B.C.   400   300   200   100 B.C. | A.D. 100   200   300   400   A.D. 500

All of the dates you have been reading could be written with the letters A.D. before them. We measure years backward and forward from the birth of Jesus Christ. Years labeled A.D. come *after* the birth of Christ. The letters A.D. stand for *anno Domini,* Latin words meaning "in the year of the Lord."

Events that took place before the birth of Jesus Christ are always labeled B.C. This stands for "before Christ." A date followed by the letters B.C. tells how many years something happened before the birth of Christ. In other words, an event happening in 45 B.C. took place 45 years *before* the birth of Christ. Look at timeline *E* above.

Scientists tell us that the Hopewell culture existed from 200 B.C. to A.D. 500. How many centuries is that? How many years?

How many centuries are there between 300 B.C. and A.D. 200? If an event took place 2,500 years ago, did it happen before or after the birth of Christ?

Not all timelines are horizontal, or go across the page. Some timelines are vertical. Vertical timelines are read from top to bottom, with the earliest date at the top. Look at timeline F. What is the first event on this timeline? What is the most recent event?

CHECKING YOUR SKILLS

Answer the following questions. Use the information in this lesson to help you.

1. What is the definition of each of these words?
   timeline
   decade
   century
   A.D.
   B.C.

2. Find timeline C on page 100. This timeline shows the years from 1500 to 2000. How many years does the space between each pair of dates stand for?

3. In what year did the Pilgrims land at Plymouth?

4. In what century did the Pilgrims land?

5. The first 100 years after the birth of Christ are called the first century A.D. What would the 100 years before the birth of Christ be called?

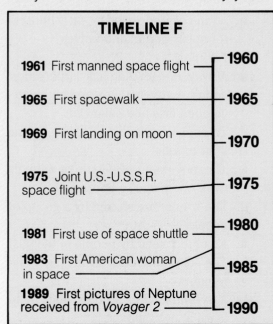

TIMELINE F

1961 First manned space flight — 1960

1965 First spacewalk — 1965

1969 First landing on moon — 1970

1975 Joint U.S.-U.S.S.R. space flight — 1975

1980

1981 First use of space shuttle — 1980

1983 First American woman in space — 1985

1989 First pictures of Neptune received from *Voyager 2* — 1990

101

Thinking Back

- During the last Ice Age, glaciers covered parts of North America. Giant animals roamed the land.

- Herds of animals crossed a land bridge from Asia into North America. Hunters who depended upon these animals followed them. They worked together to kill animals much larger than themselves.

- When the big animals disappeared, new tools were developed to hunt smaller animals. People also began to gather the roots and seeds of plants.

- Ancestors of the American Indians began to experiment with growing seeds.

As they learned to grow plants they no longer had to travel in search of food. They could settle in one place.

- Agriculture made civilization possible. The Mayas, the Incas, and the Aztecs developed major civilizations. Agriculture was also important to the Indians living in what is now the United States.

- Mound Builders, such as the Hopewell and Mississippians, developed cultures in the eastern part of our country.

- The Anasazi and Hohokam lived in the southwestern part of our country.

- Archaeologists learn about the past by studying artifacts. Radiocarbon dating can help determine the age of an object.

Check for Understanding

Using Words

Write down the words below. Next to each word, write the correct definition from the list in the next column.

1. agriculture
2. archaeologist
3. archaeology
4. artifact
5. civilization
6. culture
7. flint
8. migration
9. specialize
10. surplus

a. An amount more than what is needed
b. A kind of stone used by early hunters for spear points and knives
c. Farming
d. A way of life that has large cities, complex government, and highly developed arts and sciences
e. To spend most of one's time at one kind of job
f. The movement of people or animals from one place to another
g. The way of life shared by a group of people
h. An object used by people in the past
i. The scientific study of artifacts and remains
j. A scientist who studies objects to learn about the past

Reviewing Facts

1. Why were people and animals able to migrate from Asia to North America during the Ice Age?
2. What materials did early hunters use to make their tools?
3. How did farming make possible a settled life?
4. How do we know the Hopewell people were great traders?
5. What are the outstanding remains of Mississippian culture?

Thinking Critically

1. Imagine that you are with archaeologists who have just found two obsidian arrows and a carved, decorated clay pot. What do these objects tell you about the people who once used them?
2. Advanced Indian cultures depended on specialization. What kind of specialization is there in your community?
3. All human cultures depend on some kind of cooperation. What examples of this statement can you find in this chapter? How is cooperation important today?

Writing About It

Imagine you are an archaeologist who has just discovered a clue that explains what happened to the Anasazi. Write a journal entry that explains what the clue is and how you feel about finding it.

Practicing Time Skills

Using Timelines to Understand Dates
Answer these questions.

1. Which came more recently, 400 B.C. or A.D. 200?
2. What is the name of the present decade? present century?
3. In what century was the year 1492?
4. In what century was the year 1805?

On Your Own

Social Studies at Home

1. Use clay to make miniature mounds like those built by the Hopewell Indians. You may want to carve shapes of birds or other animals.
2. Show your family the picture of Mesa Verde National Park on page 94. Discuss with them what it was like living among these cliffs. Write a paragraph that summarizes your family's comments about how the Anasazi lived.

Read More About It

The Ancient Maya by Barbara L. Beck. Franklin Watts. This book provides an account of the rise of the Mayans.

Art of the Southwest Indians by Shirley Glubok. Macmillan. This book contains pictures of the arts and crafts of the Southwest groups.

From Map to Museum: Uncovering Mysteries of the Past by Joan Anderson. William Morrow. A curator takes the reader on a dig off the Georgia coast and follows the journey of the artifacts to the museum.

Going on a Dig by Velma Ford Morrison. Dodd, Mead. An overview of archaeological methods is presented. One section deals with the discovery of the Illinois Mound Builders.

The Memory String by Chester G. Osborne. Atheneum. This novel relates the story of 13-year-old Dorath, a prehistoric nomad, who crossed from overpopulated Siberia into North America.

CHAPTER 4

Major Indian Groups

We are part of the earth and it is part of us. The perfumed flowers are our sisters; the deer, the horse, the great eagle, these are our brothers. The rocky crests, the flowers in the meadow, the body heat of the pony, and man—all belong to the same family.

—Chief Seattle of the Suquamish, 1854

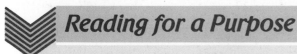

Reading for a Purpose

Look for these important words:

Key Words
- natural environment
- shamans

Look for answers to these questions:
1. What did Indian groups have in common?
2. In what ways did Indians learn from each other?
3. How did life change for the Indians after the Europeans came?

1 Indians of North America

American Indians all had a form of religion. Many thought of the earth as a mother and of the sky as a father. Their religion also included a belief in using their **natural environment** with great care. The land, water, plants, and animals around them were all part of the natural environment.

The Indians used the land and natural features around them. However, they did not believe that anyone could own a part of Mother Earth or of any of her creatures. Many American Indians believed that there were spirits in nature. They believed in living in harmony with these spirits.

The Indian groups had **shamans** (SHAH•muhnz). Shamans were both priests and healers. Shamans could answer questions about disease, about life and death, about right and wrong. Shamans tried to explain to people why things happened the way they did. Shamans knew the stories of how the world came to be. Because there were many different Indian groups, there were many different stories.

The Indians had ceremonies that included dancing and singing to drums. Sometimes dances were held for important religious reasons, such as to pray for rain or good crops. Sometimes they were held before or after a battle.

Learning from Each Other

Traveling long distances by canoe or on foot, Indians were able to trade with each other. As they traded different objects of value, they also exchanged ideas and new ways of doing things. For hundreds of years the American Indians learned from one another. They learned how to grow corn, how to build mounds, how to make pottery, and how to weave cloth.

When the Europeans came, the Indians continued to learn. They quickly learned to use whatever helped them. They welcomed iron tools and eagerly traded for iron knives, kettles, and axes. The sheep, goats, cattle, and horses brought by the Europeans became the basis of new Indian cultures.

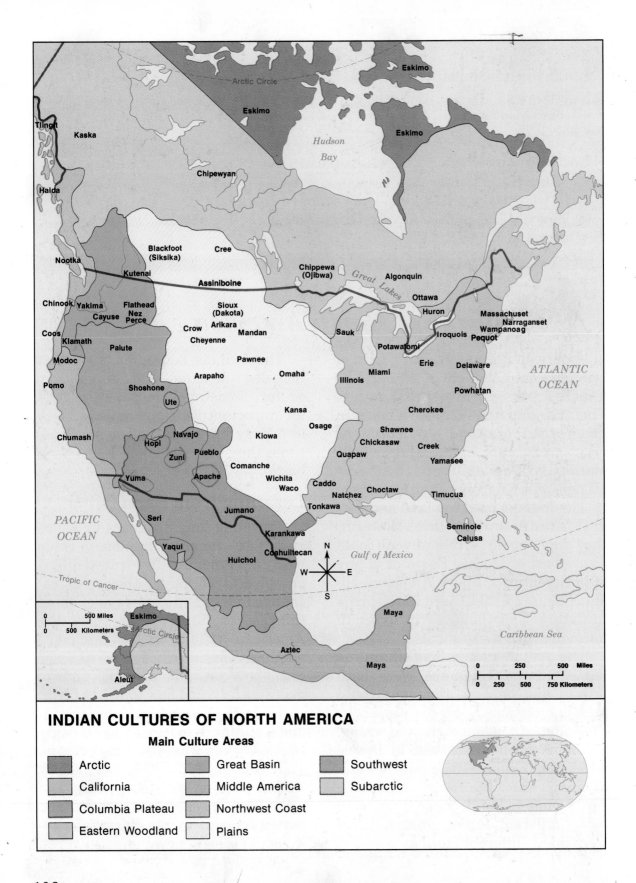

INDIAN CULTURES OF NORTH AMERICA

Main Culture Areas

- Arctic
- California
- Columbia Plateau
- Eastern Woodland
- Great Basin
- Middle America
- Northwest Coast
- Plains
- Southwest
- Subarctic

Religion was important to all Indian cultures. In this model, Iroquois dancers in the False-Face ceremony seek to cure a person's toothache.

Many Indian cultures did not survive the coming of the Europeans. One reason for this was that many Indians were forced to give up the land of their ancestors. This land was productive. Losing the land destroyed the foundation of many cultures. Another reason Indian cultures did not survive was disease. European diseases like measles, flu, and smallpox killed millions in North America.

With more advanced tools, the Europeans changed the land the Indians knew so well. The Indians could no longer live as their ancestors had. The history of American Indians for the last 300 years is a history of a people trying to keep their chosen ways. Many Indian cultures are now gone. Yet countless numbers of places—cities and towns, rivers and mountains—carry the names and memories of these first Americans.

Reading Check

1. What is a natural environment?
2. What is a shaman?
3. Why did many Indian cultures not survive the coming of Europeans?

Think Beyond What could Europeans have learned from the Indians?

SKILLS IN ACTION

USING CULTURAL MAPS

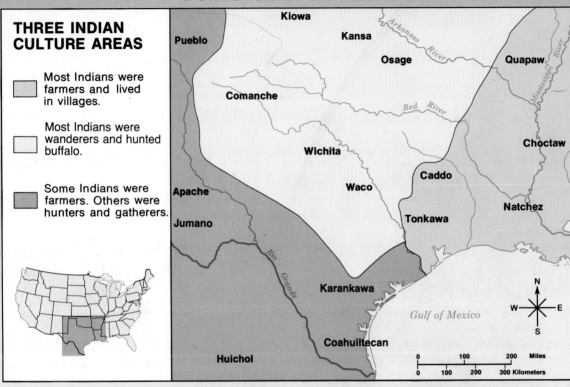

A cultural map shows the location of particular cultures. A culture is a group of people who share a similar way of life. On a cultural map, each culture is identified by a name placed in the center of its territory. Look at the cultural map above.

This map shows parts of Texas, New Mexico, and Oklahoma. On it are the names of the Indian groups who once lived there. Find the homelands of the Wichita group. Did the Kiowas live north or south of the Wichita?

A color key is used to show three regions on the map. Find the lands of the Caddo Indians. As you can see, they are green. The map key gives the meaning of green. It tells you that the Caddo farmed and lived in villages as did other Woodland Indians.

CHECKING YOUR SKILLS

Use the cultural map above to answer these questions:

1. Did the Comanche Indians farm or hunt buffalo?

2. Would you find buffalo hunters among the Choctaws or among the Kiowas?

3. Does the map tell you whether or not the Apaches were farmers?

4. Were the Wichita Indians more like the Natchez or more like the Comanches?

5. How did the Indians living in the areas shown in green get their food? How does this compare with those living in the cultural areas shown in yellow?

108

Look for these important words:

Key Words
- palisade
- slash-and-burn
- extinct
- wigwams

- longhouses
- wampum
- league
- Six Nations
- Five Civilized Tribes

People
- Hiawatha

Look for answers to these questions:
1. How did the Woodland Indians use the forests around them?
2. How did the Woodland Indians clear land for farming?
3. What was life like in an Iroquois village?
4. What was life like among the Creek Indians?

2 Woodland Indians

When the first Europeans came to North America, they found the eastern part of the continent covered with vast forests. The Indians who lived in the forests of the Northeast and Southeast are called Woodland Indians.

The kinds of trees and shrubs varied from north to south, but everywhere they sheltered many kinds of animals. Swift deer, shy elk, and fat bears fed in the woods. In the streams and meadows were sleek beaver and muskrats. There were squirrels, opossums, and many birds, including wild turkeys.

The Woodland Indians made use of the trees for many things. They used trees and tree bark to make canoes and shelters. They used some trees for food. Nuts came from trees like the walnut and hickory. In the Northeast maple sugar was made from the sap of the maple tree.

The Woodland Indians were farmers, gatherers, and hunters. In the Northeast the Indians did more gathering and hunting than farming. In the Southeast the soil and climate were better for agriculture. There the Indians depended on farming for their food. In their fields, the Woodland Indians raised corn, beans, squash, and pumpkins.

Because they farmed, the Woodland Indians lived in villages. The villages of the Woodland Indians often included a community building for meetings and ceremonies. Surrounding each village was a wall made of sharpened tree trunks. Such a wall is a **palisade.** The fields lay outside the wall.

The Indians made clearings in the woods for their fields. They had no tools sharp or powerful enough to cut down trees. They killed a tree by cutting away a circle of bark in the fall. By spring the tree was dead. With the leaves gone, the sun shone through the branches to the ground. Among the dead trees, Indians planted crops.

After a year or two the Indians burned the dead trees. After several more years a field might be completely cleared. This method of agriculture is called **slash-and-burn.**

Some Indians used fish as a fertilizer. Others did not. Without fertilizer a field wore out in about ten years and no longer produced good crops. Then the village moved to a new location and started clearing new fields.

Although the Woodland Indians raised much of their food, they also gathered and hunted. They gathered nuts, berries, wild fruits, greens, and shellfish. They caught fish and hunted bear, beaver, porcupine, deer, and birds.

The most common food bird was the passenger pigeon, which traveled in flocks of hundreds of thousands. Sometimes so many flew overhead that the sky was dark for hours. At night they roosted in trees, weighing down the branches. There they were easy to catch and kill. Early white settlers also killed and ate great numbers of passenger pigeons. Today they are **extinct.** That means there is not one left.

Woodland Indians also hunted to get animal skins for clothing. Furry beaver and bear skins made warm robes, capes, and blankets. Scraped and tanned deerhide made soft buckskin for lighter clothes.

This scene shows daily life in an Algonquian village. At left, a woman prepares to skin a deer. What other activities do you see?

This cut-away model shows a cooking scene in an Iroquois longhouse. Notice the high shelf for storage.

The Northeast Indians

The Woodland Indians of the Northeast included two main language groups, the Algonquian (al•GAHN•kwee•uhn) and the Iroquois (IR•uh•kwoy). The Algonquian lived along the Atlantic coast. In their villages they lived in round, bark-covered shelters called **wigwams.**

The Iroquois lived inland. Their dwellings are called **longhouses.** The Iroquois longhouses were made of poles covered with elm bark. Each longhouse had a hall down its middle with small, open rooms on each side. One family lived in each room. From eight to ten families lived in each longhouse. The families in each longhouse were related to the woman who was head of the longhouse.

Women were important in Iroquois culture. Women controlled the longhouse, the farming tools, and the fields. Women did the farming. They also decided which men would be chiefs.

Families cooked their meals on fires built in the main hall of the longhouse. On high shelves each family kept mats, baskets, buckets made of bark, pots, tobacco pipes, and wooden bowls. There might also be digging sticks for planting corn and snowshoes for getting around in the winter.

The shelves also held **wampum.** Wampum were beads made from porcupine quills or seashells. Wampum was woven into belts or strung into necklaces. The Iroquois used wampum to help them remember important events. They also used wampum as money.

This wampum belt was made in 1683 by Delaware Indians as a gift of peace.

The Iroquois were famous warriors. About 1570 the shaman **Hiawatha** (hy·uh·WAW·thuh) persuaded five of the Iroquois tribes to stop fighting each other and to unite in a **league.** A league is a union of people joined for a common purpose. By the middle of the 1600s the league used armies of 500 to 1,000 men to conquer its Indian neighbors. After a sixth group joined the league, it was called the **Six Nations.** The Iroquois became the most powerful of the Indian groups in the Northeast.

Indians of the Southeast

The Indian peoples of the Southeast also lived in farming villages. Their villages were scattered along the fertile coastal plain, in the foothills of the mountains, and along the rich valley of the Mississippi River.

The villages of the Southeastern Indians often contained as many as 100 dwellings built around a central square. The dwellings were made of a framework of poles and covered with grass or mud plaster. In the Deep South, where the weather was warm, dwellings were often roofed platforms. Wealthy families might have as many as four dwellings, to be used as storehouses, a summer house, and a winter house.

The Creek Indians of the Southeast divided their year into two seasons: winter and summer. The year started with the corn harvest in the month of Much Heat (August). The months that followed were Little Chestnut (September), Big Chestnut (October), Frost (November), Big Winter (December), and Little Winter (January). Their summer started with the month of Wind (February). The months after Wind were Little Spring (March), Big Spring (April), Mulberry (May), Blackberry (June), and Little Heat (July).

After the corn had been harvested in the fall, the Creek men went hunting. These hunting parties lasted as long as five and six months. The men returned in time to work the fields and plant the crops in the spring. Both men and women had to work in the fields. There were fines for those who tried to avoid work. The people worked and planted to songs in the morning. In the afternoons they played ball games. In the evenings they danced.

When summer came, war parties left to attack their enemies. The war parties often brought back captives. The captives became slaves, but children of slaves were born free.

This picture of the Algonquian village of Secoton, North Carolina, was painted about 1585. At the bottom right, Indians are performing a ceremonial dance. The three fields show newly sprouted corn, green corn, and ripe corn.

The Creek Indians in what are now Georgia and Alabama were organized into a league of towns. The towns were divided into red towns and white towns. The red towns supplied war leaders. The white towns were concerned with peaceful activities and supplied the principal chiefs.

After the arrival of white people, the Creeks, Choctaws (CHAHK·taws), Chickasaws, Cherokees, and Seminoles (SEM·uh·nohls) were called the **Five Civilized Tribes.** They quickly accepted parts of the culture of white settlers. Many raised animals, had large farms, and became Christians.

 Reading Check

1. What is slash-and-burn farming?
2. Why was wampum important?
3. What was the Six Nations?

Think Beyond   Do you think women or men were considered more important in the Iroquois culture? Explain.

People MAKE HISTORY

Jacques Le Moyne
?–1588

▶▶▶▶▶▶▶▶▶▶▶▶▶▶▶▶

The Timucuan (tihm•uh•KOO•uhn) Indians of North Florida no longer exist. They died out due to diseases brought by the Europeans. However, when French settlers arrived in Florida in 1564, it was the Timucuans who welcomed them ashore and helped them build Fort Caroline.

Thanks to a settler named Jacques Le Moyne (ZHAHK luh•MOYN) the Timucuan way of life is not lost to us. Le Moyne's job was to make maps of the settlement and to draw pictures of the plants, animals, and people of Florida. He began to attend the Timucuans' festivals and ceremonies, drawing pictures and writing long descriptions of what he saw. From Le Moyne's work, we learn that the Timucuans dressed in deerskin clothing decorated with beads. They grew corn and beans, tilling the soil with hoes made of fish bones and shells. They also had elaborate feasts and held picnics on neighboring islands.

Le Moyne's pictures of the Timucuans were almost lost when the Spanish soldiers attacked Fort Caroline in the summer of 1565. Le Moyne escaped, however, and eventually returned to France. His drawings were published in 1591, three years after his death.

Le Moyne's maps and drawings helped other Europeans decide where to settle in Florida. More important, they provided a permanent record of the Florida countryside and the people who lived there. The Timucuan way of life has disappeared, and some of the plants and animals in the drawings are now extinct. Thanks to Jacques Le Moyne, however, the Timucuans are not forgotten.

Think Beyond   If our way of life became extinct, what would be the most important thing for other people to remember about us?

A Le Moyne watercolor, 1564

114

Reading for a Purpose

Look for these important words:

Key Words
- lodges
- sod
- nomads
- tepee
- travois

Look for answers to these questions:
1. In what ways did Indians of the Central Plains use their environment?
2. How did Indians live on the Great Plains?
3. Why was cooperation particularly important for the Great Plains Indians?

3 Indians of the Plains

West of the great area of the woodlands were the grassy plains. Few trees grew there. In places, one could see for miles.

Among the Indians who lived on the tall-grass prairies of the Central Plains were the Sioux (SOO), the Mandans, the Pawnees, and the Omahas. They were both farmers and hunters. They farmed the rich land in the river valleys. They hunted deer, elk, and buffalo.

In their villages these Indians lived in circular houses called **lodges.** Each lodge was built over a shallow pit. In the northern parts of the prairie, the lodges were covered with **sod.** Sod is the ground cover that includes both grass and grass roots. Such a house was warm and protected in the cold winters. In the southern parts of the prairie, the lodges were covered with grass, animal skins, or mats.

Some of the villages along the Missouri River often were trade centers for Indians from far places. Later they became centers for the trade between white people and Indians. The site of

Pierre, South Dakota, for example, was capital of the Arikara (uh•RIK•uh•ruh) Indian nation for 400 years. It then became a fur-trading center for the French and Indians.

Indians of the Central Plains lived in lodges like the one in this picture. Here, women pound corn, weave, and tend to their children in front of the lodge.

Life for the Plains Indians depended on cooperation in hunting the buffalo. Here, Indians, disguising themselves in wolf skins, creep up on a herd of grazing buffalo.

The Plains Nomads

The people who lived on the Great Plains did not farm or live in villages. Here there were no rich river valleys. The roots of the short grass were very tough. It was impossible to dig the soil using a tool such as a digging stick.

Instead, the Indians on the Great Plains were hunters and **nomads.** Although nomads may have no fixed dwellings, they usually claim certain territory. The Indian nomads followed certain routes within this territory. Their route usually depended on the movement of the buffalo. Sometimes they sought ripening wild plums or berries.

Among the Plains nomads were people of the Kiowa, Comanche, Cheyenne, and Crow tribes. Their dwellings, their clothing, their food, even the fuel for their fires, came from the buffalo. For fuel the Plains nomads used dried buffalo droppings called chips.

The dwelling of the Plains nomads was a **tepee.** It was made by lashing poles together to make a cone. Over the poles were hung skins that had been sewn together. Smoke from the buffalo-chip fire inside the tepee went out a smoke hole at the top. Blankets and robes of buffalo skins helped keep people warm inside the tepee.

Because few trees grew on the Plains, wood was very hard to find. The Indians therefore placed great value on their wooden tepee poles. They transported the poles by turning them into a kind of carrier called a **travois** (truh•VOY). Two poles were fastened to

The buffalo provided food, clothing, and shelter for this Comanche village on the Great Plains. What activities are taking place here?

a harness on a dog. Belongings were hung between the poles. The ends of the poles dragged behind. Later the Indians used horses, which they called "big dogs," to do the same job.

For village dwellers, pottery was a big help for storing, cooking, and eating food. But pots break easily, and they can be heavy. For the nomads, pots were not a help. Instead, the nomadic Indians made containers of buffalo skins. They even cooked in skin pots. Liquid foods were cooked in the containers by dropping in hot stones. The hot stones caused the liquid to boil.

In the nomadic way of life, each person was a part of the group. There was much work to be done, and everyone had to help. No person was born more important than anyone else. A man became chief because he proved himself a good hunter and a good leader of people. He was chief because his people chose him to be chief.

Anyone who did not follow the ways of the group was made to leave it. Sending a person out on the Plains alone was often a death sentence. Survival on the Plains depended on people working together.

A travois

Reading Check

1. Name the two ways the Central Plains Indians got their food.
2. What kind of person did the Plains nomads choose as chief?
3. Compare the Indian dwellings of the Central Plains with those of the Great Plains.

Think Beyond What might cause one Plains tribe to quarrel with another tribe?

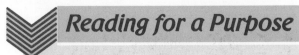
Look for these important words:

Key Words
- staple food
- assembly

Look for answers to these questions:
1. What did the Indians of the Great Basin, the Columbia Plateau, and California have in common?
2. Which of these groups of Indians was the poorest? Why?
3. What foods did different environments provide?

Hunters and Gatherers

The Great Plains stop at the base of the Rocky Mountains. Indians rarely went into these high mountains, so the mountains were like a great fence between Indian groups.

In an area that stretched from the Rocky Mountains to the Pacific Ocean lived the Indians of California, of the Columbia Plateau, and of the Great Basin. They were all similar because their main foods came from gathering and hunting. They did not farm.

Indians of the Great Basin

The Great Basin lies between the Rocky Mountains and the Sierra Nevada. The valleys, mountains, and plateaus of the Great Basin receive little rainfall. This land can be beautiful, but it can also be very harsh. The Indians of the Great Basin were the poorest Indians because the Great Basin is mostly desert. Animals and food plants are harder to find here than in other areas.

The Indians of the Great Basin included the Utes (YOOTS), the Shoshones (shu•SHOW•nees), and the Paiutes (PY•yoots). They lived in small family groups, moving often to look for food. In the summer they moved into the mountain valleys to get fruits and berries. In the fall they gathered nuts from the pine cones of the pinyon trees. They hunted rabbit and occasionally deer and antelope. They wore few clothes but used blankets made of rabbit skins to keep warm in winter. Their dwellings were huts made of brush. The women made fine baskets for gathering, storing, and cooking food.

The people of the Great Basin ate whatever they could catch. Besides rabbits, birds, and antelopes, they ate grasshoppers, prairie dogs, lizards, snakes, and mice.

Indians of the Plateau

The Columbia Plateau is east of the Cascade Mountains. Some areas have

118

forests and rivers. Indians there also lived by gathering, but they had a richer life than those of the Great Basin. Streams and rivers of the region were full of salmon and other fish. Salmon was their **staple food.** A staple food is the food that people depend on most for nourishment.

The Indians of the Plateau included the Nez Perce (nez•PUHRS), the Klamath, the Yakima (YAK•uh•mah), and the Flathead Indians. They lived in villages. Each village had a chief and an **assembly,** a lawmaking body. Any citizen, man or woman, could speak or vote in the assembly. Like the Plains Indians, the Indians of the Columbia Plateau chose leaders whom they respected. Both men and women served as chiefs and shamans.

California Indians

The Indians of California lived on the land between the Pacific Ocean and the Sierra Nevada. This land of broad river valleys and rolling hills was covered with grass and oak trees.

In this gentle land lived a patchwork of people speaking more than 100 different languages. All these people depended on gathering and hunting for their food.

The staple food of the California Indians was acorns, the nuts from oak trees. Oak trees were so plentiful that the Indians did not have to worry about what they would eat. In the fall they had only to gather enough acorns to get them through the year. The acorns were ground and soaked in water to get rid of bitterness. Then the mixture was turned into mush by cooking it in a basket with red-hot stones.

A Karok woman of California cooks acorn mush in a woven basket.

To their acorn diet the California Indians added all kinds of berries, greens, and roots. Those who lived close to the seashore gathered shellfish. In the fall the Indians hunted deer, elk, antelope, ducks, and geese.

Reading Check

1. How did the Indians of California, the Columbia Plateau, and the Great Basin get their food?
2. What kinds of foods did Indians of the Great Basin eat?
3. Why were the California Indians better off than Indians of the Great Basin?

Think Beyond   What might be a disadvantage to having only one staple food?

119

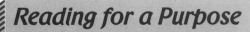
Look for these important words:

Key Words
- springs
- hogans
- totems
- potlatches
- tundra
- kayaks
- igloo

Places
- Arctic Plains

Look for answers to these questions:
1. How did the Indians in the Southwest make use of their natural environment?
2. In what ways did the Northwest Coast Indians use the resources of their environment?
3. What tools did the Eskimos develop to help them survive in the Far North?

5　The Southwest and Northwest

The Southwest is a land of mountains and deserts, of high plateaus and deep canyons. The skies are usually sunny. There is little rainfall. Indian farmers of the Southwest learned long ago to make the desert bloom by using water.

Some used irrigation to get water from the rivers to their crops. Others built their villages near **springs.** Springs are places where underground water breaks through the earth's surface.

Indians of the Southwest who lived in villages and farmed were called Pueblo Indians. Pueblo is the Spanish word for *village*. The staple foods of these Indians were corn, beans, and squash. They raised turkeys for their feathers. They wove the feathers to make warm robes.

The men did the farming and wove cotton cloth. The women made pottery and wove baskets. Like the Iroquois, the women of many Pueblo groups owned the houses.

The Pueblo Indians believed in being peaceful. They fought only to protect themselves. One of the Pueblo groups is the Hopi (HOH•pee). In their language *Hopi* means "the peaceful."

Other Indian groups in the Southwest farmed but did not depend on their crops the way the Pueblo Indians did. These Indians also hunted and gathered. They included the Apaches and the Navajos.

The Navajos did not live in villages like the Pueblo Indians. Instead families lived in scattered dwellings called **hogans.** A hogan is a round or a six-sided dwelling made of logs and dried mud. A family might have several hogans to use during the year.

Sheep, which were brought by the first Europeans, became an important part of Navajo life. Navajos became known as good herders and weavers.

120

Indians of the Northwest

The coastal area between the Pacific Ocean and the Cascade Range was home to many Indian groups. The rainfall is heavy on the ocean coast. Great cedars grow in the forests. These trees grow so tall that they can block sunlight from the forest floor.

Like their neighbors on the Columbia Plateau, the Indians of the Northwest Coast depended on fish as a staple food. Salmon, halibut, cod, and shellfish were all plentiful in the coastal waters. Some groups even went far out in the ocean to hunt whales.

The Northwest Coast Indians had leisure time, too. They developed crafts and arts. They were excellent wood-

Cedar trees tower behind this lodge and totem pole of Northwest Coast Indians.

workers. In addition to making huge canoes of wood, they also made carved bowls and masks.

The Indians of the Northwest Coast believed in animal spirits called **totems.** They asked such totems as the eagle, beaver, raven, bear, and whale for protection. The masks they made for their religious ceremonies were made to look like these totems.

Family groups identified themselves with particular totems. A person could have many totems in his or her family history. To show family history, the Northwest Coast Indians carved totem poles. These were placed in front of their homes or in their burial places.

The Northwest Indians also made blankets of cedar bark and the hair of mountain goats. Their clothing was made of shredded cedar bark. In the winter they used furs and hides as robes.

The chiefs were wealthy people. Wealth was measured by the number of slaves and the number of things a person had. The wealthy people were expected to have great feasts to which many people came. These feasts were called **potlatches.** At a potlatch the host not only fed people but also gave them presents. Sometimes he gave away all his wealth. That made him even more respected.

Eskimos of the Far North

In the Far North lived the Eskimos. Their ancestors probably crossed in boats from Asia about 4,000 years ago. The Eskimo culture ranged across the Far North from Alaska to Greenland. It replaced earlier cultures in the area.

The Eskimos learned to live in a land of ice and snow. A thick fur coat and mittens keep this Eskimo warm as he builds an igloo of snow blocks.

Life is difficult in the Far North. In winter there is no sun for several months. When there is sun, the sun's reflection off the ice can cause blindness. In winter, temperatures can drop as low as −60°F (−51°C).

Much of the land is **tundra.** Tundra is flat, treeless land that stays frozen much of the year. When the land thaws during the summer, it becomes a grassy swamp. There is little soil for flowers or bushes to grow. These parts of the Far North are called the **Arctic Plains.**

The Eskimos developed tools to live in this harsh climate. Those who lived near the ocean fished and hunted seals, walruses, and whales. To do so, they made strong fish hooks and harpoons. Those who lived inland hunted game animals with spears. For their clothing Eskimos used animal skins. Such skins could keep them warm in the coldest weather. Even their canoes, called **kayaks,** were covered with skin.

For their dwellings they used skins, stone, sod, or even chunks of snow. A house made of snow blocks is called an **igloo.**

To journey on the ice and snow, the Eskimos invented a dog-drawn sled. To protect their eyes from the sun, they invented goggles. Their goggles had tiny slits to see through. To get light in the dark winter, they burned fish oil in lamps. Like other early Americans, the Eskimos developed ways to live in their natural environment.

 Reading Check

1. What group of Southwest Indians lived in villages? in hogans?
2. Name at least three ways in which the Northwest Indians used wood.
3. Why did Indians of the Northwest make totem poles?

Think Beyond Why was it so important for the American Indians to treat their environment with care?

IN FOCUS

KACHINA DOLLS

When Pueblo Indian children play with Kachina (kuh•CHEE•nuh) dolls, they are doing more than just playing. They are also learning about the religious beliefs and customs of their people. The *Kachina* dolls represent spirits that watch over the Indians.

According to Pueblo legend, Kachina spirits bring rain, healthy crops, and fertility to all the people of the tribe. The Pueblos believe that the Kachina once lived with them and danced at all their ceremonies. The Kachina, however, were forced to leave, and the Pueblo men were ordered to take their place at the ceremonies. The men dress up in elaborate masks and costumes to resemble the Kachina. The Pueblos believe that the Kachina are brought to life again as the men dance. Young children believe that the dancers are real Kachina who will punish them if they do not behave.

The Pueblo men make all the masks and costumes for the Kachina dances. They also make dolls that look like Kachina to give to all the children of the tribe. The children learn many stories about the Kachina.

Kachina dolls are made from flat pieces of cottonwood or cactus root. They may be only a few inches high or more than four feet tall. Although the dolls are all shaped the same, each is specially decorated to look like a particular Kachina. The color, feathers, leather, and fabric are

used to tell which Kachina it is. For example, Iaqan, the squirrel spirit, has large red ears, a rodentlike face, and a headdress of brown and white feathers.

Kachina dolls are used in many ways. For example, if someone is sick, a doll will be laid on the doorstep to help the person get well. When children are between 6 and 12 years old, they learn that the Kachina dancers are not real Kachina. The boys of the tribe learn how to make Kachina dolls, which they then give to the younger children.

Think Beyond Why do you think the boys of the tribe give Kachina dolls to the younger children?

Kachina dolls

SKILLS IN ACTION

USING THE LIBRARY TO WRITE A REPORT

Suppose you want to find out more about American Indians and write a report on what you learn. Where do you start? A good place is the library.

Libraries have three main sections: those for fiction, nonfiction, and reference books.

Fiction books tell stories. Sometimes the stories are based on real events. Sometimes they are about imaginary people or events. Many people enjoy reading fiction. For information about a subject, however, nonfiction and reference books are best.

Nonfiction books give facts about real people and real things. All nonfiction books are organized on shelves by subject. Each subject has its own call number.

Reference books are collections of facts. A reference book has an *R* (for "reference") and a call number on its spine. Reference books are for use in the library. They may not be taken home.

Using the Card Catalog or Computer

To find a nonfiction book in the library, you have to know its **call number.** Call numbers can be found in the card catalog or in the library computer. There every book in the library is listed by **title,** by **author,** and by **subject.** Each card or entry carries the call number of the book it lists. Look at the title card/computer entry below.

Title Card/Computer Entry

Indians.

j970.1
T

Tunis, Edwin. Written and illustrated by Edwin Tunis. Revised edition. New York: Crowell, 1979.
157 p. illus.

The title card lists the call number in the upper left-hand corner. The first line lists the title. Look at the author card below. How does it differ from the title card?

Author Card/Computer Entry

Tunis, Edwin

j970.1
T

Indians. Written and illustrated by Edwin Tunis. Revised edition. New York: Crowell, 1979.
157 p. illus.

Below is a subject card. Notice that the subject is listed before the author or title.

Subject Card/Computer Entry

INDIANS OF NORTH AMERICA

j970.1
T

Tunis, Edwin
Indians. Written and illustrated by Edwin Tunis. Revised edition. New York: Crowell, 1979.
157 p. illus.

Using Reference Books

To find information about a subject, you may need to use reference books. One of the most commonly used reference books is an **encyclopedia.** An encyclopedia has articles on a great many subjects. The articles in an encyclopedia, also called entries, are arranged alphabetically. Most encyclopedias consist of many books, or volumes.

To find information about American Indians in the encyclopedia, first use the index. The index is usually in the last volume of the encyclopedia.

124

Look at the index below. The main article about American Indians is in the I-J volume. The article begins on page 163. But there are also many other articles about American Indians in the encyclopedia. For example, there is an article about Indian foods beginning on page 337 of the E-F volume. Where in the encyclopedia can you look to find out about Indian masks? Will you find a picture or a map with this article?

India ink I-J:162
Indian, American I-J:163 *with maps and pictures*
> Arizona **A:536**
> Fur Traders **E-F:379** *with picture*
> Rocky Mountain States **Q-R:273**

Culture
> Arrowheads **A:557** *with picture*
> Cliff Dwellers **C:420**
> Foods **E-F:337**
> Languages **L:259** *with map*
> Masks **M:77** *with picture*
> Mound Builders **M:694**

Other useful reference materials are atlases, almanacs, magazines, and dictionaries.

An atlas is a book that contains many maps. There are different kinds of atlases. If you want to find information from a map, ask the librarian to help you find the right kind of atlas.

Almanacs are collections of facts, records, and general information. An almanac is an excellent source of information about the most recent years.

Magazine articles can be useful sources of information. Most libraries have an index listing magazine articles by subject. A librarian can help you find magazine articles or show you how to use the index.

A dictionary contains words listed in alphabetical order. Dictionaries explain the meanings and show the pronunciations of words. A dictionary is a good place to check on the spelling of a word.

Beginning a Report

You know that you can find information in nonfiction books and reference materials. Now think about what you have to do to write a report. First you want to find information on your subject. If your subject is American Indians, start by looking through books on the subject. Look at the pictures. Look at the tables of contents. Read what interests you. You will be learning about the subject while also finding out what information is available.

Now you must limit your subject. You cannot give every bit of available information about American Indians in one short report. One of your choices is to write a report about some part of Indian life. You could write about dwellings, food, clothing, or art. Another choice is to write about just one group of American Indians. You could write about the Anasazi or the Sioux or the Iroquois. If you find you still have too much information, limit your subject even more. Instead of writing about the Iroquois, you might choose to write just about longhouses.

Look through the books or articles to find information on your subject. Use the table of contents and the index to help you quickly find what you need.

As you read, make notes on index cards or pieces of paper. Use a different card or piece of paper for each **source.** A source is the author, the name of the book, and the page. Write your source in the upper right-hand corner of the card or paper.

If you copy down the exact words of your source, be sure to use quotation marks. If you use the quotation in your paper, be sure to tell the source.

Organizing Your Report

After you have found all your information, you will have to organize your report. The easiest way to do this is by putting your notes in order. Make a separate pile of note cards for each topic. Then decide which topic to write about first, which to write about next, and so on.

When you have notes that do not seem to fit, set them aside. You may end up using them, or you may throw them out. You do not have to use all the information you have gathered.

Writing the First Draft

The **first draft** is your first try at writing the report. As you write your first draft, write quickly. Do not worry about perfect spelling or penmanship yet. It is important to get your ideas down on paper before you forget them.

A report usually has three parts: an **introduction,** a **body,** and a **conclusion.** The first part is the introduction, or opening paragraph. This tells the reader what to expect in the report. When you write your introduction, keep it very simple. Write just a few sentences that tell what your report is about.

The body is the main part of the report. It gives the information you have gathered about the subject. The paragraphs in the body should follow the order in which you have organized your notes.

How do you write a paragraph for your report? Pick up your first pile of notes. Make sure they are all about the same topic. Begin each paragraph with a sentence that explains why the topic is important. This sentence is the topic sentence of the paragraph.

Write the rest of your report in the same way. Begin each paragraph with a topic sentence.

The third part of a report is the conclusion, or closing paragraph. It reminds the reader of what you have said in your report. It tells again why the subject you wrote about is important.

After you have finished your first draft, read it aloud to yourself. As you read, circle the words whose spelling you want to check. Underline any sentences that do not make very good sense. Then make your corrections on this first draft.

Next, share the first draft with another person. Ask if any part of the report is not clear. Use that person's suggestions to improve your paper.

Finishing the Report

Now copy the report over carefully, with all of the corrections and changes you have made.

The last thing to add is a **bibliography.** This is a list, in alphabetical order, of the sources of information you have used. List books by the author's last name. List encyclopedias by title and give the name of the article and volume.

CHECKING YOUR SKILLS

Answer the following questions.

1. What are the best kinds of books to use for finding information?

2. How could you find the call number of a book titled *The Art of the Woodland Indians?*

3. Why is it important to limit your subject?

4. What is a way to organize notes before writing a report?

5. What are the three parts of a report?

6. What is a bibliography?

Thinking Back

- All American Indian groups had some form of religion and ceremonies to go with it. All developed ways to live in their environment.

- Indians traded objects and ideas with each other and with the Europeans.

- Many Indian groups were forced to give up their lands to Europeans. Millions died from European diseases.

- The Woodland Indians of the Southeast farmed. The Woodland Indians of the Northeast also farmed but did more hunting and gathering.

- In the Iroquois culture, women were important. They controlled longhouses, tools, and fields. Women decided which men would be the chiefs.

- Hiawatha persuaded the Iroquois to form a league that grew into the Six Nations. The Iroquois became the most powerful group in the Northeast.

- The Five Civilized Tribes quickly accepted parts of the culture of the white settlers.

- The Central Plains Indians farmed the rich river valleys. The Great Plains Indians were nomads who followed the buffalo. Indians of the Great Basin, the Columbia Plateau, and California were hunters and gatherers.

- The Pueblo Indians of the Southwest were farmers. Other Indian groups of the Southwest farmed, but they were also hunters and gatherers.

- Indians of the Northwest Coast depended upon fish for much of their food. The Eskimos developed ways to live in the harsh environment of the Far North.

Check for Understanding

Using Words

Explain the meaning of each term below. Then use each term in a complete sentence.

1. extinct
2. league
3. natural environments
4. nomads
5. palisade
6. shamans
7. sod
8. staple food
9. totems
10. wampum

Reviewing Facts

1. How did the Woodland Indians clear fields for their crops?

2. In what important way were the Iroquois and Algonquian alike? Name two ways in which they were different.

3. Why is Hiawatha remembered as an important person?

4. Who were the "Civilized Tribes"? Why were they called that?

5. Describe the two main groups of Plains Indians.

6. Describe the staple foods of the Indians of the Columbia Plateau and California. What did the Great Basin Indians eat?

7. In what ways were the Navajos and the Hopis different?

8. How did the Northwest Coast Indians use their environment?

9. How did Eskimos meet their needs for clothing, transportation, and housing?

10. Which group of Indians used kayaks? travois? wampum?

Thinking Critically

1. Indian ways were often a response to different natural environments. Choose two Indian groups from different natural environments. Compare and contrast how each group made use of its natural environment.

2. In what way was the life of a nomad different from the life of a person who lived in a village? What were some of the advantages and disadvantages of nomadic life?

3. What are some examples of cooperation among Indian groups? What are examples of cooperation in your life?

Writing About It

Write a report about an Indian group you studied in this chapter. In your report include where the Indians lived, what kind of food they ate, and how they dressed.

Practicing Geography Skills

Using Cultural Maps

Use the map on page 108 to answer the following questions.

1. How did the Kansa Indians get their food?

2. Is it likely the Natchez Indians were farmers? Why or why not?

3. Were the Caddo Indians or Choctaw Indians more likely to see buffalo? Why?

On Your Own

Social Studies at Home

1. Read the description on page 116 of how Plains nomads made tepees. Using that information and the picture of tepees on page 117, make your own miniature tepee from a piece of cloth and several small sticks. Decorate the outside of your tepee with crayons or paint.

2. The Creek Indians had special names, such as "Much Heat" for August and "Wind" for February, which they used for the months of the year. Use your yearly activities and holidays to make a list of how you would name the months of the year.

Read More About It

Hiawatha by Henry Wadsworth Longfellow. Pictures by Susan Jeffers. Dial Books. This classic poem gives a nineteenth-century view of the Woodland Indians.

The Pueblo by Charlotte Yue. Houghton Mifflin. This book brings to life the everyday routines of people living in a pueblo.

The Tipi: A Center of Native American Life by Charlotte Yue. Alfred A. Knopf. The book discusses the movable dwelling of the nomadic tribes of the Great Plains.

Why the Possum's Tail Is Bare and Other North American Indian Nature Tales by James E. Connolly. Illustrated by Andrea Adams. T. Y. Crowell. This collection of 13 legends captures the flavor of the stories of 8 North American Indian groups.

AMERICAN INDIANS TODAY

Indians have made their mark on every part of American life and culture. Many of our 50 states take their names from Indian words. For example, the word *Oregon* comes from the Indian word *wauregan,* which means "beautiful water." Mississippi's name comes from the Chippewa words *mici sibi,* or "big water." Hundreds of cities, rivers, lakes, and mountains carry Indian names, too. *Raccoon, moose, skunk, canoe,* and *moccasin* are just a few of the Indian words that are part of our everyday language. Many of the foods we enjoy were first raised by Indians. Among these are corn, beans, peanuts, peppers, potatoes, squash, and tomatoes. Some of our modern highways even follow paths first used by Indians.

Today, more than one and a half million Indians live in the United States. Many of these Indians live on special Indian lands called **reservations.** Wherever they live in the United States, however, most American Indians find themselves members of two cultures. They have strong ties to their Indian heritage and are trying to preserve that heritage. At the same time they are living and working in modern America.

In the following pages you will meet four modern-day American Indians. All four have a deep sense of the culture, history, and traditions of their ancestors. Each carries the strength of an Indian heritage to an occupation in the modern world.

Dan Namingha—Artist

The Hopi and Tewa Indians of the Southwest have long made some of the world's most beautiful pottery. Dan Namingha's family has been a part of this tradition. His great-

Dan Namingha works on one of his paintings.

great-grandmother, Nampeyo (nam·PAY·yoh), was one of the greatest Hopi potters. His mother and grandmother are also well known for their pottery.

When Dan Namingha was a child, he began to draw the graceful designs he saw on the pots around his home. His second-grade teacher noticed these drawings and knew that he had talent. Every day for five years she gave him art lessons.

These lessons paid off. When Dan Namingha was 16, he earned a scholarship to study art at the University of Kansas. He later studied art in both Santa Fe, New Mexico, and Chicago, Illinois. Today, Dan Namingha is a successful artist. His paintings and sculptures have won many prizes.

Dan Namingha uses strong colors to show his feelings about the Hopi and the Southwest. Sometimes he paints from memories of stories his grandmother used to tell. He also tries to picture certain scenes from his childhood. "A lot of my paintings are of a feeling I had at the moment I saw something," Mr. Namingha says. Working in a studio that he built with his own hands, he draws from the past to communicate to the present.

Hoksina Wayagobi checks the cattle on his ranch.

Hoksina Wayagobi— Rancher

Some years ago Joe Day lost control of his car on an icy Montana road. The car flipped into a snowbank. Badly injured, Joe Day lay for several hours waiting for help. As he lay there, Joe Day thought about his life and how close he was to death. He decided he wanted very much to be alive, to make more out of life. He knew he needed to get closer to his Indian heritage. He was part Sioux and part Assiniboine (uh·SIHN·uh·boyn).

▲ ▲ ▲ ▲ ▲ ▲ ▲ ▲

"If we take care of the earth, the earth will take care of us."

▼ ▼ ▼ ▼ ▼ ▼ ▼ ▼

Joe Day recovered from that terrible accident. Today he prefers to use his Indian name, Hoksina Wayagobi (HAWK·shih·nah wah·YAH·guh·bee). He owns his own cattle ranch, the 5,000-acre (2,023.5-ha) Thunderbird Ranch in eastern Montana. "I came out of that experience a different man," he says. "I guess before, I didn't know the meaning of Indian self-respect, not really."

Now Hoksina Wayagobi is an active supporter of Indian rights in

Montana. He and Emily, his wife, are active in tribal affairs at the Fort Peck Indian Reservation.

Running a cattle ranch is hard work. Hoksina Wayagobi makes the Thunderbird Ranch successful with constant attention to the land. He makes sure that he never has too many cattle grazing. Too many cattle would ruin the grassland. He checks his fences and water systems almost every day. Like his ancestors, Hoksina Wayagobi cares about the land. "If we take care of the earth," he says, "the earth will take care of us."

Adele Little Dog—School Principal

Tucked away on the Standing Rock Sioux Reservation in South Dakota is the small town of Little Eagle. There is an elementary school in Little Eagle. The principal of this school is Adele Little Dog, a Sioux Indian.

A few years ago Adele Little Dog was worried about the education the children of Little Eagle were receiving. She knew that there were problems with Indian education all over America. Only 1 of 100 children had Indian teachers. Indians were dropping out of school twice as often as other youth. Indian children

◀ Adele Little Dog helps a Sioux student with his work.

were not learning how to read and write.

These days Adele Little Dog is much more hopeful about the future. A 1972 law, the Indian Education Act, provides money to train Indians as teachers. It also provides money to help Indian schools pay for field trips, hire tutors, and perform other activities.

When Mrs. Little Dog's son Dana was 10 years old, he had no Indian teachers. By the time Dana entered high school, the situation was quite different. "Now our people are trained as certified teachers," says Mrs. Little Dog. "We have Sioux teachers who understand our children." She hopes that, as a result, the children will do better in school.

Adele Little Dog knows how important education is to the well-being of American Indians. She feels that the millions of dollars being spent on Indian education will also be of great benefit to all Americans. "We are spending money," she says, "on our future, and I can't think of a better way to spend it."

George Horse Capture—Museum Curator

In Cody, Wyoming, the Buffalo Bill Historical Center focuses on Western life and history. One of the museums in the Center tells about the Plains Indians. The curator, or person in charge, of the museum is George P. Horse Capture, a member of the Gros Ventre (GROH VAHN·truh) tribe.

The Plains Indian Museum tells the story of the great buffalo-hunting tribes. Inside you can see war bonnets, shields, painted buffalo skulls, blankets, and necklaces made of grizzly bear claws.

The tepee room has a 50-foot-high ceiling. The beautifully decorated tepees seem to reach up to the heavens. One of the tepees has a special blue and white design. The maker of the tepee was told in a dream that the special design would bring him luck in buffalo hunts.

Mr. Horse Capture and other Indians helped design the museum building. The entrance faces east, toward the rising sun, just as the Indians' lodges faced east. The building is shaped like a circle. "Nature is round," explains George Horse Capture. "The world, the seasons, even the ages of man from childhood to childhood are round."

George Horse Capture has worked to build a place where people can learn about the culture of Plains Indians, past and present. Among those who come are busloads of Indian children. "It is a time of wonderment and appreciation when they come," Mr. Horse Capture says.

George Horse Capture works to further the understanding of Plains Indian Culture.

Unit Review

Words to Remember

Number your paper from 1 to 10. Use the terms below to complete the sentences that follow. Write the correct term next to each number.

agriculture   natural environments
archaeologists   nomads
cultures   shamans
league   specialize
migration   staple food

1. There was a _____ of both animals and people across the land bridge.

2. Experimenting with seeds led to the development of _____ .

3. A surplus of food makes it possible for people to _____ .

4. Scientists who study objects to learn about the past are _____ .

5. The Indians of North America lived in many different _____ .

6. Indian leaders who acted as priests and healers were called _____ .

7. Many Indian _____ did not survive the coming of the Europeans.

8. The Iroquois formed a _____ of Indians called the Six Nations.

9. Plains Indians who depended on the buffalo for food, shelter, and clothing were _____ .

10. Fish was a _____ for Indian groups who lived close to rivers and streams.

Focus on Main Ideas

1. What route did the first Americans follow from Asia to America?

2. Name at least four food plants the American Indians developed.

3. Describe how agriculture makes settled life possible.

4. How do we know about ancient Indian cultures?

5. Describe at least three ways in which the Woodland Indians made use of their environment.

6. What was the difference between the nomads of the Great Plains and the hunting-and-gathering Indians of the Great Basin?

7. Identify the staple foods of
   a. the Indians of the Southwest
   b. the Indians of California
   c. the Indians of the Columbia Plateau
   d. the Indians of the Northwest Coast
   e. the Eskimos

8. Why was the shaman important in Indian cultures?

9. Describe the natural environment of the people who lived in
   a. igloos
   b. skin tepees
   c. longhouses
   d. round lodges
   e. brush huts
   f. pueblos

10. Explain the purpose of each of these items: wampum, palisade, travois.

133

Think/Write

Thousands of buffalo once roamed the American plains. Yet today few remain. The passenger pigeon once traveled in flocks of hundreds of thousands. Today it is extinct. "Man was the most terrible tiger," one scientist has said. What do you think the scientist meant by this statement? Do you think this statement is true today?

Activities

1. **Research/Writing** Choose one North American Indian group that interests you. Go to your school or public library to find information. Write a report telling where the group lived and describing its culture.

2. **Reading** Read legends or stories as told by an American Indian group. Retell one of the stories in your own words.

3. **Acting** Imagine you and several fellow students each belong to a different Indian group. You all meet at a trading village. Exchange information about how each of you lives.

4. **Art** On pages 107 and 111 are pictures of dioramas. A diorama shows a real-life scene by using objects and figures. Choose an Indian group you have studied and make a small diorama showing a scene of life for that group.

Skills Review

1. **Using the Library to Write a Report** Read each statement below. On a piece of paper write whether it is true or false. If it is false, rewrite it to make the statement true.

a. Books that give facts and information are fiction books.

b. An encyclopedia has articles on many subjects.

c. The best place to find the call number of a book is in the card catalog or library computer.

d. You should limit your topic after you have written the first draft.

e. As you read, you should take notes.

f. It is important to write down the author or title of a book you use.

g. You should organize your notes before you begin to write your report.

h. Most reports have two parts: an introduction and a body.

i. You should show your first draft to another person for suggestions to improve it.

2. **Using a Timeline** Look at the timeline below to answer the following questions.

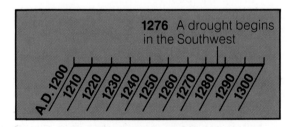

a. What is the number of years between A.D. 1200 and A.D. 1300 called?

b. What is the name for the number of years between 1240 and 1250?

c. What letters are used to show that a date occurred after the birth of Christ?

d. In what decade did a drought begin in the Southwest?

e. What is the name of the century starting in A.D. 1200?

Important events have happened in your state, maybe even in your home town. The Exploring Your State's History activities in each unit review will help you learn about the history of your home state as well as the history of your country. You may want to use a special notebook for the activities of this section. You can find information for these activities in books about your state.

Many American Indian cultures developed in what is now the United States. These cultures differed from each other in their foods. They differed in the materials they used for clothing, tools, and dwellings. They differed in their language and their arts.

The following activities can help you learn about Indian cultures in your state.

Learning About Indian Culture

1. Find out which Indian groups lived in your state before Europeans came to America. Write the names of the groups in your notebook. In the library learn more about one of these groups. In your notebook write about how that group lived.

2. Make an Indian culture map of your state. Show where different cultures lived. Show whether they were primarily nomads, hunters and gatherers, or farmers living in villages.

3. Indians used wild plants and animals for food, clothing, and medicine. Find out how Indians from your state used wild plants and animals. If possible, bring to class some of the wild plants and explain how the Indians used them.

4. Many city and state museums have exhibits about Indian life as it was. Is there such a museum in your area? Where is it? Visit the museum and then report on what you learned.

5. In the picture below a Hopi woman weaves a basket as her ancestors did. What arts and crafts were practiced by Indians in your state? Learn about one of these arts or crafts. Share what you learned with the class.

Learning About Geography

6. Many places in the United States have Indian names. Make a list of the places in your state that have Indian names. Can you find out what any of the names mean?

UNIT
3
Exploration and Settlement

- **About 1,000 years ago**

  Leif Ericson sails to North America

- **1492**

  Christopher Columbus reaches America

- **1519**

  Ferdinand Magellan sails around the world

- **1534**

  Jacques Cartier makes first voyage to Canada

- **1540–1542**

  Coronado explores the American Southwest

*T*he armor of a Spanish soldier shines in the sun. French fur traders paddle a bark canoe. The Dutch build windmills on Manhattan Island. English families build houses in New England. All are signs that European settlement is beginning in North America. The Spanish, the French, the Dutch, and the English were not the first Europeans to come to North America. However, they were the ones who changed the course of its history. In this unit you will learn about the Europeans who explored and settled our country.

Think Beyond   What do you think it would be like to start a new life in a new country?

• **1541**	• **1585**	• **1607**	• **1609**	• **1620**
Hernando de Soto finds the Mississippi River	The English settle at Roanoke	The English settle at Jamestown	Henry Hudson explores the Hudson River	The Pilgrims land at Plymouth

CHAPTER 5

Europeans Come to America

"*La Española* is marvelous, the sierras and the mountains and the plains and the meadows and the lands are so beautiful and rich for planting and sowing, and for livestock of every sort, and for building towns and villages. The harbors of the sea here are such as you could not believe it without seeing them; and so the rivers, many and great, and good streams, the most of which bear gold."

—from a letter written by
Christopher Columbus, 1492

Look for these important words:

Key Words	People	Places
• Vikings	• Bjarni Herjulfsson	• Iceland
• navigators	• Eric the Red	• Greenland
• sagas	• Leif Ericson	• Scandinavia
		• Vinland
		• Newfoundland

Look for answers to these questions:
1. Who were the Vikings?
2. Who was Leif Ericson?
3. Where was Vinland?
4. How do we know about Leif Ericson?

Leif Ericson Sails to Vinland

One summer about a thousand years ago a young man named **Bjarni Herjulfsson** (BYAHR•nee HER•yahlf• suhn) was sailing from **Iceland** to **Greenland.** He was captain of a cargo boat. A terrible Arctic storm arose and blew the boat off course.

When the storm was over, Bjarni could see a low, flat land covered with trees. This was the Atlantic coast of North America. His sailors wanted to stop and explore, but Bjarni had been told that Greenland had glaciers. This land did not have glaciers, so it could not be Greenland. He decided to sail north until he found Greenland.

Greenland had been discovered and settled some years before by **Eric the Red.** Bjarni's story was told during the long winter evenings by settlers in Greenland. Among those who heard Bjarni's story were Eric the Red and his son, **Leif Ericson.** They decided they would try to find the land Bjarni had seen. On the day they were to leave, Eric the Red hurt his leg. Leif alone was left to command the voyage.

The Vikings

For the men who set out on that voyage of discovery, travel was a way of life. They were members of a group of people sometimes called **Vikings** and sometimes called Norsemen. The Vikings first lived in the region of what is now known as **Scandinavia.** Scandinavia includes the countries of Norway, Sweden, and Denmark.

Several hundred years before the time of Leif Ericson, many Vikings left their homeland in boats searching for adventure, riches, and new lands to settle. Some settled in Iceland.

The Vikings were good **navigators.** That means they knew how to find their way on the seas. They were also excellent boatbuilders. They had learned to build a type of cargo boat that was good for ocean travel.

Remains of a Viking settlement have been found at L'Anse Aux Meadows in Newfoundland. There these Viking dwellings have been rebuilt.

It was in such a boat that Leif Ericson and his crew of about 30 men set out to find the land Bjarni had described. Leif hoped to return to Greenland with his boat full of lumber. Few trees grew in Greenland, and the Viking settlers needed wood. They needed wood to build their boats. They needed wooden beams to support the sod roofs of their houses.

Arrival at Vinland

Leif Ericson and his crew found the land Bjarni described. Leif called it **Vinland.** The land had fine grassland and berry vines. The Icelandic word *vin* can mean either "grassland" or "wine." Leif spent the winter in Vinland before returning to Greenland with a cargo of wood.

The stories about the deeds of the Vikings are called **sagas.** We now know the sagas about Leif Ericson are based on truth. Archaeologists have discovered the remains of a Viking settlement in **Newfoundland,** Canada. This is the earliest European settlement in North America that is known to us. We know Vikings lived there about 1,000 years ago.

The Viking discovery of North America was forgotten. Dim memories of Vinland remained only in the sagas. Almost 500 years passed before Europeans again came to North America.

 Reading Check

1. How did Leif Ericson know about another land?
2. What did Leif Ericson hope to find?
3. Why do we now believe the sagas?

Think Beyond Why do you think the Vikings did not settle permanently in North America?

140

SKILLS IN ACTION

USING HISTORICAL MAPS

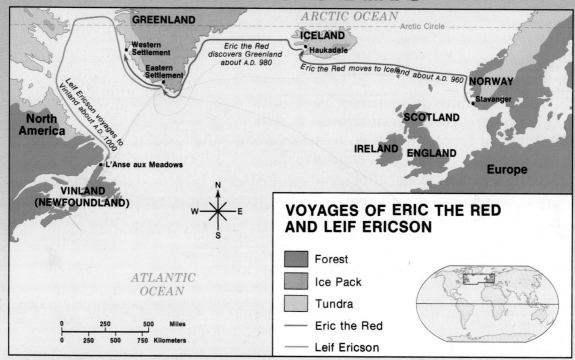

A **historical map** gives information about a past event or time. It can show where past events took place. Historical maps can show cities and nations that existed at a particular time in the past.

The map above shows the routes of Eric the Red and Leif Ericson. Some historical maps give dates in the title. On this map the dates are next to the routes.

Like other maps, historical maps have keys that explain colors or symbols on the map. Look at the key for this map.

Leif Ericson sailed to a place he called Vinland. Vinland is on the map. However, its present name, Newfoundland, appears in parentheses. Historical maps often show past names for places.

Historical maps may show natural features because natural features can be im-

portant to explaining past events. On this map three natural features are shown: forest, ice pack, and tundra. *Tundra* describes the treeless plains of the Far North. The map shows these features to help you understand why finding lumber was so important to the settlers of Greenland.

CHECKING YOUR SKILLS

Use the map to answer these questions.

1. What land did Eric the Red leave in A.D. 960?

2. When did Eric the Red move to Iceland?

3. When did Leif Ericson make his voyage?

4. Would it have been easier for the Greenland Vikings to voyage east rather than west to find lumber? Why or why not?

141

Look for these important words:

Key Words	People	Places
• compass	• Marco Polo	• Middle East
• charts	• Prince Henry	• Arabia
• navigation	• Bartholomeu Dias	• Indies
• expedition	• Vasco da Gama	• West Indies
• journal	• Christopher Columbus	• Caribbean Sea
	• Amerigo Vespucci	• Isthmus of Panama
	• Ferdinand Magellan	• Strait of Magellan
	• Vasco Núñez de Balboa	

Look for answers to these questions:
1. Why were Europeans interested in Asia?
2. Why did Europeans desire to find an ocean route to Asia?
3. What discoveries did Columbus make?
4. Why was the voyage of Magellan important?

2 Early Voyagers

Most Europeans took little note of the Viking discovery. They were looking east toward Asia, not toward the west. They desired gold, silk, perfumes, spices, and jewels. These things came from Asia.

One traveler to Asia was **Marco Polo.** He was about 17 years old in 1271 when he left his home in Venice, Italy. It took him four years to reach China. It was another 24 years before Marco Polo came home, his pockets full of jewels.

Marco Polo wrote a book about his adventures and the amazing things he had seen. He described the wealth to be found in Asia. At the time many people who heard Marco Polo's stories thought he was making them up. Years later, however, his stories excited Europeans. Many Europeans had

begun to wonder what the rest of the world was like.

Trade in the Middle East

Travel to Asia was difficult. Most European traders did not go all the way to China or Japan. Instead they traveled to such cities in the **Middle East** as Damascus and Alexandria. There they met other traders, who came with goods from **Arabia** and Africa. The traders also carried goods from India, China, and the **Indies** (the islands of Southeast Asia).

The Italian merchants of Venice and Genoa (JEN•uh•wuh) tried to keep the Middle East trade for themselves. If they could control the trade, then they could charge high prices. Other Europeans wished there were ways to get goods from the East without depending on the Italians or the Arabs. Could there be another route to Asia besides the long and difficult route through the Middle East?

Prince Henry of Portugal

Henry, a prince of Portugal, hoped to find a water route to Asia. To do so, **Prince Henry** knew he must learn more about the ocean. He encouraged ship captains to record information about winds, ocean currents, and the shapes of coastlines. One of the most important tools that captains used was the **compass,** an instrument for finding directions.

Prince Henry talked to captains returning from voyages. He listened carefully to their stories. Henry and his sailors began to make **charts,** or maps, of the coastlines and the ocean. Prince Henry's efforts led to the science of **navigation.** *Navigation* means figuring out a ship's direction and location and the distance it travels.

During the 1400s the Portuguese explored farther and farther down the African coast. Prince Henry died in

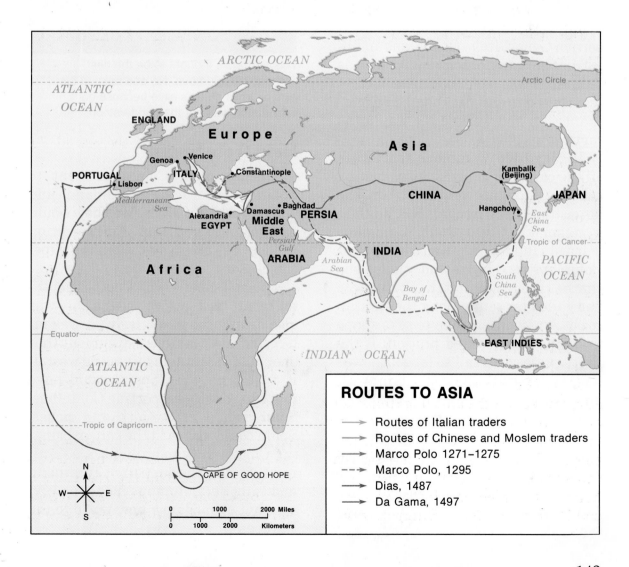

1460 before the Portuguese crossed the equator. Yet he had laid the foundation for later discoveries. **Bartholomeu Dias,** a Portuguese captain, reached the southern tip of Africa in 1487. Ten years later **Vasco da Gama,** also a Portuguese sea captain, sailed around Africa to India. He found the new route to Asia that Prince Henry had dreamed of.

Christopher Columbus

Christopher Columbus is one of the most famous persons in history. His fame comes from his discovery in 1492 of a world unknown to Europeans.

The son of a weaver, Columbus was born in Genoa, Italy. Genoa was an important port, full of activity. As soon as Columbus was old enough, he went to sea. He began as a deckhand on a merchant ship and worked his way up to captain.

In May 1476, Columbus's ship sank off the coast of Portugal. After coming ashore, Columbus went to Lisbon, the largest city in Portugal. His brother, a mapmaker, lived there. Columbus learned mapmaking from his brother. Columbus read books and studied sea charts. He learned that the Portuguese had sailed far south along the African coast. A new idea began to take shape in his head. He asked himself: If the Portuguese could sail so far south, was it possible that he could sail as far west and find Asia?

Columbus took his idea to the king of Portugal, the country most advanced in the science of navigation. The king was interested. However, he turned Columbus down in order to continue the exploration of the African coast.

This portrait is thought to be the best likeness of Columbus. No one painted his picture while he was alive because his importance was not then understood.

Help from Spain

Disappointed, Columbus went to Spain to see King Ferdinand and Queen Isabella. He hoped they would pay for an **expedition.** An expedition is a journey or voyage taken for a special reason.

Queen Isabella was a well-read, intelligent, and active ruler. She was also deeply religious. Isabella was interested in Columbus's argument that one could reach Asia by sailing west. If it were true, then Spain would have much to gain by supporting Columbus. Spain would get wealth and riches. Spain could also lead the way in bringing Christianity to millions of Asians. In 1492, with the support of Ferdinand and Isabella, Columbus made the voyage that opened up a new world to the Europeans.

On Board Ship

On August 3, 1492, three little ships set sail from Palos on the coast of Spain. The ships were the *Nina,* the *Pinta,* and the *Santa Maria.* Columbus sailed in the *Santa Maria,* the largest of the ships.

In his cabin Columbus kept a careful **journal,** or daily record, of the voyage. He recorded the weather, what the sailors saw, the latitude, and his estimates of the distance traveled. These records would help him to repeat the voyage.

More than 30 days passed at sea with no sight of land. The sailors were restless and afraid. They asked themselves: Would they ever reach land? Would they ever see home again?

Finally, on October 11, the sailors saw a carved stick in the water and a piece of cane. From these signs they knew land to be near. Land!

Columbus Finds Land

On October 12 the ships anchored safely off an island Columbus named San Salvador. Columbus believed he had reached Asia and was now in the Indies. For this reason he called the people of the island *Indians.* We use that name to this day to refer to the first people of the Americas. We use

HISTORY CONNECTION

Christopher Columbus carefully drew the last line on his map of Hispaniola—an island he had visited in 1492. As Columbus looked at his map, he must have wondered who might use the map to retrace his route or who might use his navigational information to discover new places in the world.

Today, just as Columbus did in the 1400s, scientists are drawing a special map to help modern-day explorers. This twentieth-century map will not show oceans and continents, however. Instead, it will glitter with stars and planets. It will be a map of the Milky Way galaxy—the star system in which we live. Scientists hope that just as maps of the 1400s were used as navigational tools by later explorers, the map of the galaxy will help future astronauts who venture into the frontier of space. Using maps, whether in outer space or on the seas, connects us to our past.

Columbus's map of Hispaniola.

the name **West Indies** to refer to the islands Columbus visited. The West Indies are located in the **Caribbean** (kar•uh•BEE•uhn) **Sea.**

Columbus had come to find gold. Finding none, he sailed on. He visited the big island of Cuba. Disappointed, he again set sail. Columbus and his sailors next came to an island he named Hispaniola (his•puhn•YOH•luh). Today Hispaniola is divided into the nations of Haiti (HAIT•ee) and the Dominican Republic.

While sailing off the coast of Hispaniola on Christmas Day, the *Santa Maria* was wrecked on a reef. People of Hispaniola helped Columbus's crew to carry the ship's cargo to shore. Columbus's despair about his ship turned to delight when he found that the people had pieces of gold and gold ornaments. He saw enough gold to hope for more.

When Columbus returned to Spain with news of his discoveries, all of Europe was excited. The Portuguese, the English, the French, and the Spanish soon sent out expeditions of discovery. Columbus made three more voyages himself and lived out his life believing that he had sailed west to Asia.

Another ocean traveler, **Amerigo Vespucci** (ahm•uh•REE•goh ve•SPOO•chee), may have been the first to realize a new continent had been found. He called it a "new world." A German mapmaker proposed that the new land be called America in his honor.

First Voyage Around the World

Columbus had dreamed of sailing west to find the Indies. **Ferdinand Magellan** did just that. Magellan grew up in Portugal. When he was 25 years old, he was able to go on a Portuguese ship to India. Magellan became a good sailor and navigator.

After ten years Magellan returned to Portugal with an idea. He too wanted to reach the Indies by sailing west. He started studying all the charts he could find. From these he learned that Columbus did not reach the Indies. He also learned that **Vasco Núñez de Balboa** (VAS•coh NOO•nyez day bahl•BOH•ah) had crossed the **Isthmus of Panama** in 1513 and seen a vast ocean. Balboa called it the South Sea. Magellan later called it the Pacific Ocean. *Pacific* means peaceful.

Magellan thought that he could find a way to the ocean Balboa had

Magellan became interested in navigation at an early age. He learned about the voyages of other explorers while serving as a page in the royal court.

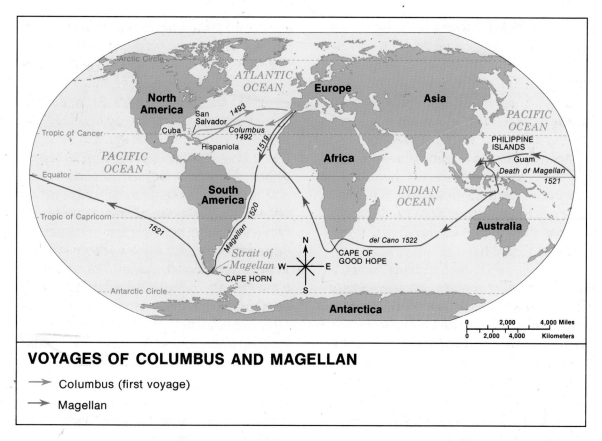

VOYAGES OF COLUMBUS AND MAGELLAN

→ Columbus (first voyage)

→ Magellan

seen. Then he could sail to Asia. When the king of Portugal refused Magellan's request for money, Magellan went to Spain. The king of Spain agreed to pay for the voyage.

Magellan set sail in August 1519. He was in command of five ships. On those ships were 240 men. Magellan, like Columbus, thought the world was smaller than it actually was. He was not prepared for the terrible journey that lay ahead. The voyage around the world was full of hardship—shipwreck, disease, and hunger. Four ships were lost and Magellan himself was killed by natives in the present-day Philippine Islands. Finally, on September 9, 1522, one ship and 18 starving men limped into the Spanish port of Seville.

Despite the terrible losses, Magellan's voyage had proved that one could sail around the world. Near the tip of South America, Magellan had found the waterway to the Pacific Ocean. We now call that waterway the **Strait of Magellan.**

Magellan's voyage showed that there was much more water than land on Earth. It also proved that the lands Columbus found were not part of Asia but a new world.

Reading Check

1. Where did Marco Polo travel?
2. Where did the traders from Venice meet Arab traders?
3. What did Europeans learn from Magellan's voyage?

Think Beyond Why do you think explorers were willing to face hardships and even death in their searches?

IN FOCUS

NAVIGATIONAL INSTRUMENTS

In ancient times, sailors had only the sun, the moon, and the stars to aid them in navigation. By Columbus's time, mariners had begun to rely on special instruments to assist them in their travels.

An important early aid was the *log,* which measured speed. It got its name because the first one actually was a log. It was thrown overboard at the front of the ship, and the sailors counted how long it took the ship to sail past the log. The captain recorded the speed of the ship in a book, which also became known as a log.

Later, the log was replaced by the *log line,* a rope knotted at intervals of 42 feet (12.8 m). It was thrown over the back of the ship, and the sailors counted how many knots passed as a clock ran out.

Austrian
sextant, 1800

This is where we get the expression "knots" to describe a ship's speed.

The most important navigational instrument was the *compass.* Invented more than 1,000 years ago, the first compass was a small bar of magnetized iron floated on a reed in a bowl of water. The magnet in the iron would make the reed point toward the magnetically-charged North Pole, so sailors could tell in which direction they were going.

Later, navigators developed instruments to plot a ship's position on maps and charts. The *cross-staff,* an adjustable T-shaped piece of wood, measured the angle of stars above the horizon. Since the position of stars never changed, the sailors could plot their positions by noting the changes in the angle of the stars as the ship moved.

The cross-staff was developed into the *sextant,* which used a mirror to reflect the sun, moon, or stars onto a glass plate. By comparing the reflection to the horizon line, sailors could map their positions.

Today's mariners use sonar, radar, and other equipment to navigate. However, the captain's record is still called the log, speed is still measured in knots, and many sailors still look to the stars to guide them as they travel.

Think Beyond   Why do you think it was important for early navigators to be able to measure their speed?

Look for these important words:

Key Words	People		Places
• conquistador	• Hernando Cortés	• Juan Cabrillo	• New Spain
• legend	• Montezuma	• Hernando de Soto	• Tenochtitlán
• viceroy	• Ponce de León		• Mexico City
• pueblo	• Francisco Pizarro		• Lima
	• Atahualpa		
	• Cabeza de Vaca		
	• Francisco Coronado		

Look for answers to these questions:
1. How did Cortés conquer Mexico?
2. What people did Pizarro conquer?
3. What was the purpose of Coronado's expedition?
4. What did the Spanish explorers accomplish in North America?

3 Spanish Explorers

The Spanish came to the new world for gold, glory, and God. For the Spanish who conquered the new world, gold meant wealth, power, and fame. Bringing Christianity to the new world was also very important to the Spanish.

Hernando Cortés was one of the most famous of the Spanish explorers. He was a **conquistador** (kawn•KEES•tuh•dawr), the Spanish word for *conqueror*. He dreamed of finding both adventure and gold. His chance came in 1519. In that year he led an expedition to conquer Mexico.

On the east coast of Mexico, Cortés founded the town of Veracruz. He called the land he was exploring **New Spain.** From Veracruz, Cortés then started across the mountains to **Tenochtitlán** (tay•nawch•tee•TLAHN), capital city of the Aztecs.

The Aztec ruler was **Montezuma.** Montezuma ruled over 11 million people. Many of them belonged to Indian groups that the Aztecs had conquered.

Cortés had with him 400 soldiers, 16 horses, 10 cannons, and 13 guns. Cortés also had the help of Indians who were unhappy with Aztec rule. They gave food to the Spanish. They even helped Cortés fight the Aztecs.

Perhaps the greatest help Cortés had was an Aztec **legend.** A legend is a story about the past. It may or may not be true. This legend was about a god named Quetzalcoatl (ket•sahl•KWAHT•uhl). Quetzalcoatl was an Indian god of wind and light. He was also the god of wisdom and knowledge.

About 500 years before Cortés, a famous king also named Quetzalcoatl ruled. He had light skin and a beard.

149

Then this king left, sailing to the east. He promised to return.

Montezuma may have believed Cortés was King Quetzalcoatl. He sent presents of gold to Cortés as Cortés was journeying toward Tenochtitlán. Montezuma asked Cortés not to come to Tenochtitlán. Hoping to encourage Cortés to turn back, Montezuma sent him even more presents. The presents only made Cortés greedy for more gold, and he pushed on toward Tenochtitlán.

Arrival at Tenochtitlán

The Spanish were amazed at the powerful civilization that lay before them. In Tenochtitlán they saw great stone towers. They saw villages built along a network of canals. There were thousands of houses and many more thousands of people. There were beautiful palaces surrounded by gardens, fragrant with flowers and fruit trees.

Montezuma welcomed Cortés and gave him a palace to live in. Four days later Cortés made Montezuma his prisoner. He hoped to rule the Aztecs by capturing their king.

Fighting broke out. Montezuma tried to stop the fighting by speaking to his people. While he was talking, someone threw a stone at Montezuma's head and killed him. The Spanish left Tenochtitlán but only after heavy fighting. Half of them died.

Cortés and his group found safety with the Indians who had helped them earlier. The next year, in 1521, Cortés returned to Tenochtitlán. With the help of 6,000 Indians, the Spanish destroyed the great city. Only by destroying the city did Cortés think he could break the power of the Aztecs.

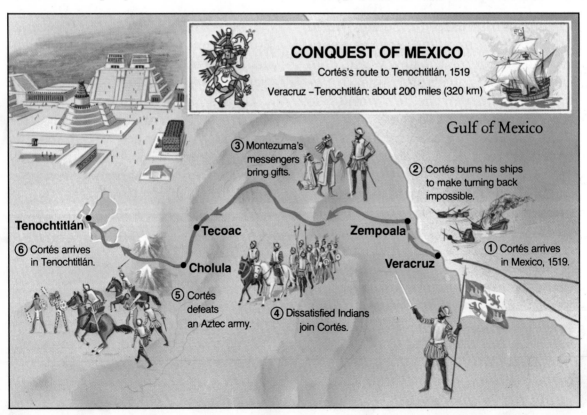

CONQUEST OF MEXICO
—— Cortés's route to Tenochtitlán, 1519
Veracruz – Tenochtitlán: about 200 miles (320 km)

Gulf of Mexico

③ Montezuma's messengers bring gifts.

② Cortés burns his ships to make turning back impossible.

Tenochtitlán

⑥ Cortés arrives in Tenochtitlán.

Tecoac

Zempoala

① Cortés arrives in Mexico, 1519.

Cholula

Veracruz

⑤ Cortés defeats an Aztec army.

④ Dissatisfied Indians join Cortés.

On the ashes of Tenochtitlán the Spanish built present-day **Mexico City.** Mexico City became the capital of New Spain.

The Spanish made the Indians of Mexico their slaves. They were forced to work in mines, to carry heavy loads, and to work the land. Millions died from disease and cruel treatment.

Ponce de León

Excited by the news of Cortés and his golden land, other Spaniards came to explore the Americas. **Juan Ponce de León** had explored the coast of Florida in 1513 and claimed it for Spain. Some people said he was looking for a fountain of youth. Water from this fountain, it was said, would keep a person from growing old. After hearing of Cortés's conquest of Mexico, he returned to Florida in 1521. Fierce Indians, however, drove the Spaniards back into the sea. Ponce de León died of an arrow wound from the battle.

Pizarro in Peru

Francisco Pizarro (puh•ZAHR•oh) heard rumors of a rich empire far south of Mexico. He longed to find out if the rumors were true. With the king of Spain's permission, Pizarro led an expedition to the coast of Peru. There, in 1532, he defeated the powerful Incas.

The Inca kingdom covered 3,000 miles (4,827 km) of the western coast of South America. At least 12 million people lived there. A network of roads connected the towns.

When Pizarro arrived in Peru, the ruler of the Incas was **Atahualpa** (aht•uh•WAHL•puh). Pizarro's men cap-

Pizarro is shown here in the grand armor of a conqueror.

tured Atahualpa. Atahualpa then offered to fill a large room with gold in return for his freedom. Pizarro agreed.

Indians came from all over the country with gifts of gold. After two months Pizarro had received about 13,000 pounds (5,896 kg) of gold and 26,000 pounds (11,791 kg) of silver. He then had Atahualpa killed.

After Atahualpa's death, Pizarro took the Inca capital without a struggle. He founded the new city of **Lima** on the coast. Inca land and wealth were divided among his supporters.

Search for Golden Cities

The gold found in the new world encouraged the Spanish to believe in an old legend. This was the legend of the Seven Golden Cities. It told about seven bishops who had once left Spain.

151

They were said to have crossed the ocean and to have founded seven cities of gold.

Spanish hopes were raised by the story of **Cabeza de Vaca** (kuh•BAY•zuh day VAHK•uh). Cabeza de Vaca was one of four survivors of an expedition to Florida. After being shipwrecked on the east coast of Texas, the survivors had spent eight years living with different groups of Indians. They had wandered through what is now Texas, New Mexico, Arizona, and northern Mexico. At last they had come to the Indian trail leading to Mexico City.

In Mexico City, Cabeza de Vaca gave a report to the **viceroy,** the king's representative in New Spain. He described the mountains and the fertile lands he had crossed. He also said that the Indians had told him of large cities to the north. Could these be the Seven Golden Cities? The Spaniards decided to find out.

The Expedition of Coronado

Francisco Coronado was assigned the job of exploring the area north of Mexico. Coronado first sent out an advance group led by a priest, Friar Marcos. His guide was a slave named Estéban, one of Cabeza de Vaca's fellow survivors.

When Estéban reached the Zuni Indian town of Cibola, the Zunis killed him. After Friar Marcos learned of Estéban's death, he decided not to go to Cibola himself. From a distance he viewed Cibola and then turned toward Mexico "with much more fear than food." When he was again in Mexico, he reported that Cibola was "larger

than the city of Mexico." Those who heard Friar Marcos's report used it to feed their own dreams of riches. With such a rumor, Coronado had no trouble finding people to go on an expedition.

In high spirits, the Coronado expedition started from Compostela in the winter of 1540. The route Coronado followed led north through northern Mexico into the valley of the Rio Grande. The expedition moved slowly. Eager to reach Cibola, Coronado and a small group of followers went ahead.

When Coronado and his followers reached Cibola, what disappointment they felt! It was no grand city. It was a **pueblo**—a small village. After a brief battle, the people of Cibola withdrew, leaving the pueblo to Coronado.

From Cibola, Coronado sent out a scouting party to the west. Led by Garcia López de Cárdenas the party went as far as the Grand Canyon. They were the first Europeans to gaze into the deep canyon. From the rim they could see the Colorado River a mile (1.6 km) below them. They spent three days trying to find a way down the canyon before turning back.

The hope of a rich Cibola had led Coronado to the interior of North America. The hope of reaching a rich city called Quivira (kee•VEER•uh) kept him there for another year. Quivira was in the region we know as Kansas. Coronado wanted to go there because he had been told that it held a wealth of gold. Maybe it was one of the Seven Golden Cities.

On their way to Quivira, the Spaniards traveled through what is now New Mexico, Texas, Oklahoma, and Kansas. These flat plains were a new experience. "There is nowhere a stone,

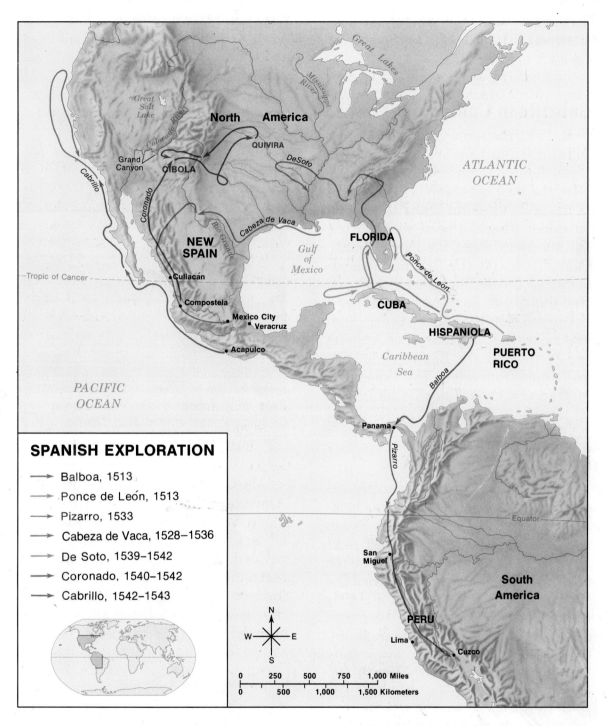

SPANISH EXPLORATION

→ Balboa, 1513

→ Ponce de León, 1513

→ Pizarro, 1533

→ Cabeza de Vaca, 1528–1536

→ De Soto, 1539–1542

→ Coronado, 1540–1542

→ Cabrillo, 1542–1543

a hill, a tree, or a bush. But there are many pastures with fine grass," wrote Pedro de Castañeda, one of the travelers. There were so many buffalo on the plains that Coronado said he never lost sight of them.

What did Coronado find in Quivira? Only a village of grass huts. The Wichita Indian village was located near the middle of present-day Kansas.

Soon after reaching Quivira, Coronado was badly injured in a fall from his horse. Weak, homesick, and very disappointed, Coronado led his followers back to Mexico.

Cabrillo in California

In 1542, the same year that Coronado returned to Mexico City, a Spanish expedition set forth from Mexico to explore the west coast of North America. In charge was **Juan Cabrillo,** a conquistador who had been with Cortés. Sailing north along the Pacific Coast, Cabrillo became the first Spanish explorer of California. Cabrillo discovered San Diego Bay and landed there. His expedition then made other landings near what are today Los Angeles and Santa Barbara. Early in 1543 Cabrillo died from a fall. The expedition continued without Cabrillo, sailing as far north as Oregon.

Hernando de Soto

Meanwhile, another Spanish explorer, **Hernando de Soto,** was looking in the Southeast for the Seven Golden Cities. De Soto landed near Tampa Bay in Florida. He started north, looking for gold. He reached the Savannah River in Georgia. Finding no gold there, he turned west and crossed the lower Appalachian Mountains. His wanderings eventually brought him to the Mississippi River. De Soto and his men were the first Europeans to see the mighty Mississippi.

After spending three fruitless years looking for gold, de Soto died of fever in 1542. He was buried in the Mississippi River. The Spaniards did not want the Indians to find his body and to know they had lost their leader.

Eager for European goods, Indians along California's coast offered Juan Cabrillo fresh fish, water, and firewood.

Most Spanish explorers in North America did not find gold, wealth, or glory. Some explorers lost their lives. Others went home poor and disappointed. The explorers, however, did learn much about the continent. They learned about its geography and about the people who lived there. They claimed new lands for Spain.

Reading Check

1. How did Cortés treat the conquered Indians in Mexico?
2. How did Pizarro conquer the Incas?
3. What did Coronado find in Cibola?

Think Beyond Did the conquistadors feel that their explorations were successful? Explain.

People
MAKE HISTORY

Doña Marina
1502?–1527?

▶▶▶▶▶▶▶▶▶▶▶▶▶▶▶

Hernando Cortés was not alone when he greeted Montezuma at Tenochtitlán. With him were a few of his soldiers and a beautiful Mexican-Indian woman named Doña Marina. She served as Cortés's interpreter and adviser. It was Doña Marina who persuaded Montezuma with "smooth speeches" to surrender to Cortés.

Doña Marina was born into a noble Indian family south of Veracruz. After her father died, her mother remarried and was forced to give her daughter to a band of traders. The traders sold the young Indian woman in the city of Tabasco.

When Cortés defeated the Indians in Tabasco, he was given 20 women as slaves. One of these women spoke both the Mayan and Aztec languages. She was known by the name *La Malinche*. Cortés baptized her and renamed her Doña Marina. With her help, Cortés was able to communicate with the Aztecs.

Doña Marina proved to be a loyal and brave adviser to Cortés. Despite constant danger, she never appeared to be afraid. She warned Cortés of attacks and skillfully argued for him before Indian chiefs. As a result, Cortés gained the support of some Indians as he made his way across Mexico. However, Doña Marina's greatest contribution to the conquest came at Tenochtitlán. It took her only two hours to persuade the powerful Montezuma to surrender to Cortés.

After the conquest at Tenochtitlán, Doña Marina married one of Cortés's captains. She settled in what is now Mexico City. Today, although some Mexicans remember her as a traitor to her people, others think of her as the true conqueror of New Spain.

Think Beyond   Why do you think Montezuma listened to Doña Marina?

Aztec calendar

Look for these important words:

Key Words
- colony
- colonists
- missionaries

- missions
- presidio

People
- Bartolomé de las Casas

Places
- St. Augustine

Look for answers to these questions:
1. What did Bartolomé de las Casas do for the Indians?
2. What kinds of settlements did the Spanish establish in the Southwest and in California?
3. What changes did the Spanish way of life bring to North America?

Spanish Settlement

After the first Spanish explorers had come to the new world, colonies were established. A **colony** is a settlement that is ruled by a faraway country. People who come from a mother country to live in a colony are called **colonists.**

Bartolomé de las Casas (bahr•TAHL•o•may day lahs KAHS•us) settled in Hispaniola in 1502 as a colonist. Like other Spanish settlers, he was given land. He was also given the right to force Indians to work on his land as slaves.

Las Casas first became a successful farmer and then a priest in the Roman Catholic Church. In time he grew concerned about the cruel treatment of the Indians. When he asked the Indians how they were, they always replied, "Hungry, hungry, hungry." Nine of every ten Indians on Hispaniola died from disease or overwork.

Las Casas announced he would no longer keep Indian slaves. He began to work to get better treatment for the Indians. He became known as the Protector of the Indians. Once he described how a captive Indian girl had found a gold nugget weighing 35 pounds (15.9 kg). The Spanish miners she worked

Las Casas, a thoughtful man, saw Indians as human beings with a right to fair treatment and freedom.

156

A SPANISH MISSION

River

Cornfields

Aqueduct

Vineyard

Olive trees

Olive crusher

Vegetable garden

Storerooms

Weaver

Indian village

Wash trough

Fruit orchard

Workshops

Patio

Candle making

Tallow maker

Priests' quarters

Cemetery

Fountain

Church

Majordomo's quarters

Mission cross

Tannery

for celebrated by roasting a pig. "But," Las Casas wrote, "the poor girl who found the nugget did not receive anything—not even a single bite of the pig."

The king of Spain listened to the words of Las Casas. In 1542 the king ruled that Indians could not be made slaves. In 1550 the king ordered that all conquests of Indian peoples be stopped.

Our Spanish Heritage

The Spanish once controlled most of the southern part of what is now the United States. As a result, many Spanish buildings, place names, and words have become part of our American heritage.

Visitors today can tour the fort built by the Spanish in **St. Augustine,** Florida. Founded in 1565, St. Augustine is the oldest city built by Europeans in the United States. Other cities established by the Spanish include San Antonio, Texas; Santa Fe, New Mexico; and San Diego, California.

Americans use Spanish words such as *canyon, key,* and *mesa* to describe landforms. The first cowboys were Spanish. Words like *lasso, corral, ranch,* and *rodeo* all come from the Spanish. Other words taken from Spanish are *alligator, mosquito,* and *tornado.*

Most Spanish settlement in what is now the United States took place in the Southwest and in California. The first to settle in these parts were usually Catholic **missionaries.** They were priests who hoped to convert the Indians to the Christian faith.

Besides their religion, the missionaries brought fruit trees, cattle, sheep, and horses. Their settlements were called **missions.** Missions included a church and the buildings necessary to farming and ranching. The missionaries forced many Indians to work on the mission lands against their will.

Soldiers usually accompanied the missionaries. Once a mission was established, the soldiers built a fort, called a **presidio** (pri•SEED•ee•oh). After the missionaries and soldiers had settled, then colonists came to settle on nearby lands.

The missionaries, soldiers, and colonists established a Spanish way of life where they settled. In Texas and California, cattle were particularly important to that way of life. The hides and animal fat were traded for manufactured goods from Mexico and Spain. In New Mexico, Spanish colonists found that sheep did well in the dry climate.

The animals introduced by the Spanish changed life for many Indians. The horses brought by colonists to New Mexico multiplied and formed into herds of wild mustangs. The Plains Indians quickly learned to tame these horses. They were soon using them for hunting buffalo and for warfare. The Indians of the Southwest started to herd sheep. They began weaving sheep's wool into beautiful garments and blankets for themselves.

Reading Check

1. Who was known as the Protector of the Indians?
2. Name four cities that were founded by the Spanish.
3. What animals did the Spanish introduce to North America?

Think Beyond Did the Spanish treat the Indians fairly? Explain.

SKILLS IN ACTION

USING CHARTS AND TABLES

Reading an Organizational Chart

Some information is easiest to understand when it is shown in a drawing. The drawing below is an **organizational** (or•guh•nuh•ZAY•shun•uhl) **chart.**

This chart shows how the Spanish government ruled Mexico. The person at the top of the chart is the most powerful. In this case the king of Spain ruled Spain and its possessions, including Mexico. He gave orders to the viceroy of Mexico. The viceroy passed the orders along to the governors of the different parts of Mexico. Each governor then passed orders down to the **alcaldes** (al•KAHL•days), the officials ruling in each town.

Power flows only in one direction on this chart, from top to bottom. The viceroy gives orders to the governor of a province. The governor of a province never gives orders to the viceroy. Could a governor give orders to another governor?

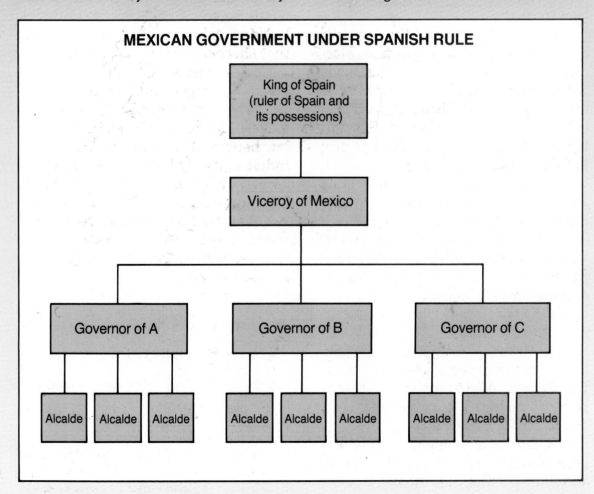

MEXICAN GOVERNMENT UNDER SPANISH RULE

159

Reading a Flow Chart

Another useful chart is a **flow chart.** A flow chart shows the order in which tasks are done or something happens. An arrow on a flow chart points from one task to the next task, from beginning to end. Here is a flow chart that shows how one would organize an expedition.

Look at the top of the chart. The first task is making clear the purpose of the expedition. Follow the arrow to the next job. What is the next step in organizing an expedition? Read the rest of the steps in order. Do you buy supplies before or after you know how many people are coming? What is the last thing you do?

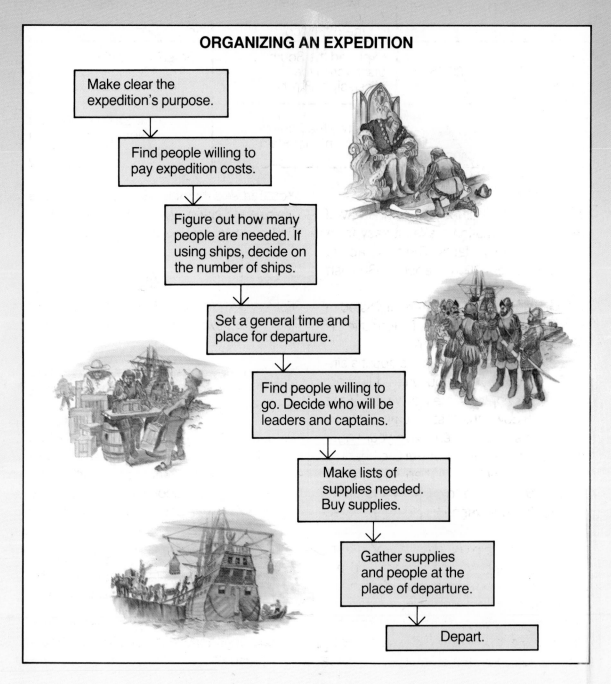

ORGANIZING AN EXPEDITION

Make clear the expedition's purpose.

Find people willing to pay expedition costs.

Figure out how many people are needed. If using ships, decide on the number of ships.

Set a general time and place for departure.

Find people willing to go. Decide who will be leaders and captains.

Make lists of supplies needed. Buy supplies.

Gather supplies and people at the place of departure.

Depart.

SPANISH EXPLORERS OF NORTH AMERICA

Explorer	Dates of Exploration	Achievements	Results
Hernando Cortés	1519-1535	Conquered the Aztecs of Mexico, discovered Lower (Baja) California	Claimed Mexico for Spain and settled it under Spanish rule
Cabeza de Vaca	1528-1536	Wandered through what is now Texas, New Mexico, Arizona, and northern Mexico	Brought back information and stories that interested others in this region
Hernando de Soto	1539-1542	Explored the Southeast; discovered the Mississippi River	Increased Spain's knowledge of North America; claimed land for Spain
Francisco Coronado	1540-1542	Explored the Southwest and the Interior Plains	Increased Spain's knowledge of North America; claimed land for Spain

Reading a Table

A **table** lists bits of information. This way of presenting information makes it easy for a reader to compare facts. The table above presents information about Spanish explorers.

The names of the explorers are listed in the first column. What kind of information is listed in the second column?

Each row across gives facts about a single explorer. Suppose you want to find out when Cortés explored the new world. Move your finger down the first column until you find Cortés's name. Then move your finger across the row until it is under the heading *Dates of Exploration*. When did Cortés explore the new world? Follow the same steps to find out when Coronado explored the Southwest.

A table can help you compare members of a group. Suppose you want to find out which of these explorers came first to the new world. Scan the column headed *Dates of Exploration* until you find the earliest date. It is 1519. Point to it and move your finger to the left until you are pointing to a name.

You can see that the earliest explorer was Hernando Cortés. Follow the same steps to find out who was the latest explorer.

CHECKING YOUR SKILLS

For each question below, decide whether the best answer is an organizational chart, a flow chart, or a table.

1. Suppose you want to explain how to make a kite. How can you best present this information?

2. Suppose you want to present facts about different states, such as when they became states, what their capitals are, and how many people live in each state. What is the best way to show this information?

3. Suppose you want to show the responsibilities of class or school officers. How can you best present this information?

4. What is the best way to present facts comparing the kinds of ships the Spanish used?

Thinking Back

- Leif Ericson, a Viking explorer, established the earliest European settlement in North America. This settlement was in what is now Newfoundland.

- Europeans thought that a water route to Asia would make goods such as spice and perfume less expensive. The water route was found by the Portuguese.

- Christopher Columbus's voyage across the Atlantic Ocean was important because it opened up North and South America to European exploration.

- America was named for Amerigo Vespucci, the first to realize that Columbus had discovered a "new world."

- Ferdinand Magellan's voyage around the world proved that the Earth was larger than previously believed.

- In their search for riches, Spanish conquistadors destroyed the Aztec and Inca civilizations.

- Spanish explorers learned about the new world's geography and its people while claiming additional lands for Spain.

- The first Spanish settlers were usually Catholic missionaries and Spanish soldiers. Later, colonists settled on land near the missions.

- These missionaries and settlers contributed Spanish architecture, place names, and words to our American heritage.

Check for Understanding

Using Words

Explain the meaning of each word listed below. Then use each word in a complete sentence.

1. **colony**
2. **conquistador**
3. **expedition**
4. **legend**
5. **missionaries**

Reviewing Facts

1. What were the Vikings looking for in North America?
2. Why did Europeans want to find a water route to Asia?
3. What new idea did Columbus have?
4. Name three reasons Queen Isabella was interested in helping Columbus.
5. How did America get its name?
6. What knowledge did the voyage of Magellan bring to the world?
7. How did the legend of Quetzalcoatl help Cortés conquer Mexico?
8. What people did Pizarro conquer?
9. What was the purpose of Coronado's expedition?
10. How did Bartolomé de las Casas influence the king of Spain?

Thinking Critically

1. People learn from the experiences of others. What examples of this idea can you find in this chapter?

2. We know that the Vikings visited America 500 years before Columbus. Why do we consider Columbus so important?

3. What skills and abilities do you think the explorers needed? Why were their explorations important?

4. We know that Columbus is credited with discovering America. Why then do you think the country was named after Amerigo Vespucci instead of Columbus?

Writing About It

Pretend that you are Christopher Columbus. Write a journal entry for October 12, 1492. Include in your entry what the weather was like, how the new land looked, and how your crew members reacted. Finally, record your feelings about sighting land at long last.

Practicing Chart Skills

Making a Flow Chart

Write the following sentences on slips of paper. Then arrange them in the order in which they happened. Paste the slips on a sheet of paper and add arrows to make a flow chart. Give a title to this chart.

a. Montezuma welcomes Cortés to his palace.

b. Cortés and his men begin to build Mexico City.

c. Cortés journeys to Tenochtitlán.

d. Cortés escapes to safety. The next year he returns to destroy Tenochtitlán.

e. Cortés takes Montezuma prisoner and fighting breaks out.

f. Cortés founds the town of Veracruz.

g. Montezuma sends gifts to Cortés.

On Your Own

Social Studies at Home

1. Make a historical map using an outline map of the world. Show the discovery voyages of da Gama, Dias, Columbus (the first voyage), and Magellan. Use a color for each voyage. Tell the dates of each.

2. Make a table of Spanish explorers. Start with the information in the table on page 161. Add these names to your table: Juan Ponce de León and Juan Cabrillo. You may want to add illustrations to your table.

Read More About It

Magellan, First Around the World by Ronald Syme. Morrow. This biography relates the story of the man who organized the first trip around the world.

Marco Polo by Gian Paolo Ceserani. G. P. Putnam's. This book contains an illustrated account of Marco Polo's life and travels.

Spanish Pioneers of the Southwest by Joan Anderson. Photographs by George Ancona. E. P. Dutton. This photographic essay shows life in a settlement in the Southwest. It centers on the Spanish pioneers who settled the harsh land and left the legacy of their culture and language.

Vikings by Elizabeth Janeway. Random House. This book, based on Norse sagas, tells of the voyages of Eric the Red and his son, Leif Ericson.

Where Do You Think You're Going, Christopher Columbus? by Jean Fritz. G. P. Putnam's. This biography portrays Columbus as a navigator and characterizes him as an opponent of tradition.

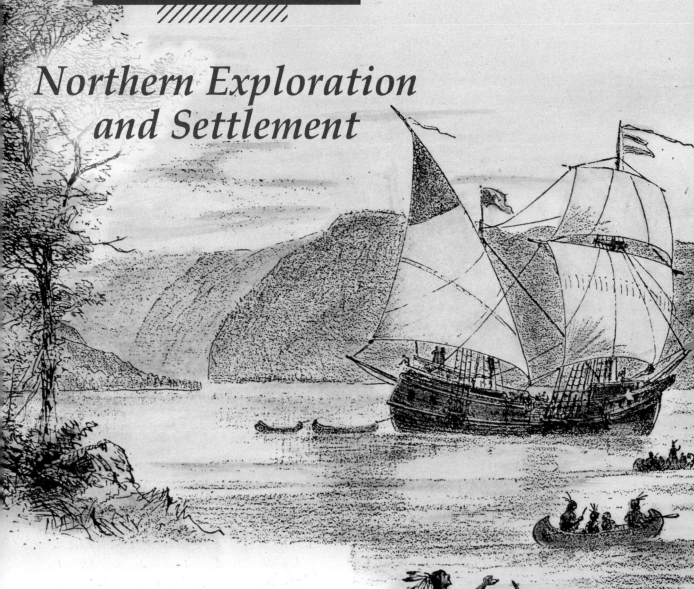

CHAPTER 6

Northern Exploration and Settlement

> Afterwards they (as many as were able) began to plant ther corne, in which servise Squanto stood them in great stead, showing them both the manner how to set it, and after how to dress and tend it. Also he tould them excepte they gott fish and set with it (in these old grounds) it would come to nothing . . .

—Bradford's History of Plymouth Plantation, 1621

Look for these important words:

Key Words
- northwest passage
- sea dogs
- Spanish Armada

People
- John Cabot
- Giovanni Verrazano
- Jacques Cartier
- Francis Drake
- Sir Walter Raleigh
- Henry Hudson
- Samuel de Champlain
- Louis Joliet
- Jacques Marquette
- Robert La Salle

Places
- Grand Banks
- Roanoke Island
- Quebec

Look for answers to these questions:
1. Why were the French interested in finding a new route to Asia?
2. Why could England challenge Spain's power in the new world?
3. Where were the first English settlements in North America? What happened to them?
4. Who encouraged French settlement of North America?

1 England, France, and Holland Claim Land

The first English expedition reached the new world in 1497. It was led by an Italian, Giovanni Caboto (jo•VAHN•ee kah•BOH•toh), who lived in England. The English called him **John Cabot** (CAB•uht). He wanted to sail west like Columbus. The king of England approved his idea. Cabot would claim any lands he found for England.

Cabot's course across the Atlantic Ocean was far north of Columbus's course. He reached a large island he called Newfoundland and claimed it for England. Off the coast of Newfoundland the waters were rich with fish. The English could simply lower baskets into the water and draw them up filled with fish. The name of this rich fishing area is the **Grand Banks.**

Cabot made another voyage in 1498, but he was lost at sea. English fishermen, however, remembered the Grand Banks. In small boats, they set out each spring to cross the stormy North Atlantic to catch codfish.

The Northwest Passage

The route around South America to Asia was long and difficult. Explorers hoped to find a **northwest passage,** a waterway leading to Asia through North America.

The king of France was one of those who wanted to find a northwest passage. In the 1500s Spain was the richest nation in Europe. Spain was growing wealthier from its conquests of Mexico and Peru. Portugal too was becoming powerful and rich from its trade with Africa and India. If France could discover a new route to Asia, perhaps it might also have a chance to gain such wealth.

In 1524 the king of France sent an Italian, **Giovanni Verrazano** (ver•uh•ZAHN•oh), to find a northwest passage. Verrazano first touched land on the coast of present-day North Carolina. Verrazano sailed northward, finding the harbors of present-day New York City and, later, Newport, Rhode Island. He went beyond Cape Cod before returning to France. A northwest passage did not exist, he told the king.

Ten years later **Jacques Cartier** (ZHAHK kahr•tee•AY) tried again to find a northwest passage for France. Between 1534 and 1536 Cartier made the voyages that opened up North America to the French.

In 1534 Cartier explored the northern Atlantic coast of North America. Cartier returned to North America the next year. The Hurons, an Iroquois tribe, told him of a great river that was the "road of Canada." Cartier then sailed up the St. Lawrence River. He had hoped the St. Lawrence River would lead him to China. His hopes disappeared when he came upon great rapids. No boat could travel through

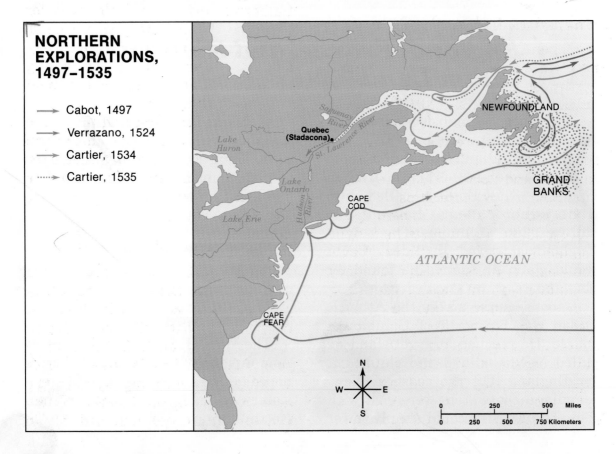

NORTHERN EXPLORATIONS, 1497–1535

→ Cabot, 1497
→ Verrazano, 1524
→ Cartier, 1534
⋯→ Cartier, 1535

the fast, tumbling water of the rapids. The expedition was forced to turn back.

Cartier made a third voyage to Canada, but he was never able to find a northwest passage. Yet French fishermen knew a good thing when they saw it. Like the English, they returned each summer to fish in the Grand Banks and at the mouth of the St. Lawrence River.

Some of the French fishermen found the Indians willing to trade furs. There were many kinds of fur in that region. Deer, bear, beaver, otter, and seal in large numbers lived in North America. The Europeans wanted the furs for their hats and coats. The Indians in turn liked the beads, hatchets, knives, and kettles of the French.

England Challenges Spain

England had found no gold in the new world. Nor had England found a northwest passage to Asia. England did not have Spain's wealth, but it was rich in another way. It had speedy ships and skilled ocean sailors. At first the English sailors went after the fish in the Grand Banks. Then they went after Spanish treasure ships.

England's queen, Elizabeth I, encouraged English sea captains to seize Spanish treasure. English merchants and sea captains used their own money to build ships in hope of capturing Spanish treasure. When they succeeded, they had money to build more ships. The commanders of these English warships were called **sea dogs.** They were really pirates, but Elizabeth protected them because they shared their wealth with England.

Francis Drake was the most famous of the English sea dogs. In 1577 Drake started his most famous voyage. In his ship the *Golden Hind,* Drake sailed through the Strait of Magellan to the Pacific Ocean. Off the coast of South America, Drake captured a Spanish treasure ship. It took four days for Drake's men to transfer the cargo to the *Golden Hind.* They had captured 13 chests of silver coins, 26 tons (23.6 T) of silver bars, and 80 pounds (36.3 kg) of gold. There were also countless boxes of jewels and pearls. The cargo was worth millions of dollars.

Drake did not want to follow the same route home. He was afraid that Spanish warships would find him. He therefore sailed up the Pacific coast. He stopped near San Francisco Bay in California and claimed the land for England. He may even have gone as far north as Vancouver Island, Canada. He returned home by sailing across the Pacific Ocean and around the world to England.

Drake was the first Englishman to sail around the world. Upon his return he was greeted as a hero. Queen Elizabeth gave him a special reward. She made him a knight.

Settling Roanoke Island

The Spanish treasure taken by sea dogs such as Drake increased England's power. With wealth from the treasure, England built a strong navy. A strong navy made England more powerful. Some English people began to think of controlling land in the new world as Spain did. **Sir Walter Raleigh** (RAHL•ee) dreamed of an

At Roanoke in 1590, John White finds chests of rotting books and a mysterious message carved on a tree. "What does this mean?" he asks.

English settlement in North America. Hoping to find a good place for a settlement, Raleigh sent out some ships to explore the Atlantic coast. They visited **Roanoke Island** in 1584. Raleigh claimed the land for England, calling it Virginia.

The next year Raleigh sent a group of colonists to settle and build a fort on Roanoke Island. The settlers, however, did not expect to work. They expected the Indians to feed them. It is not surprising that relations between the English and the Indians soured. Francis Drake stopped by the settlement in 1586. Finding the colonists starving, he took them back to England with him.

In 1587 Raleigh sent a second group of people to colonize Roanoke Island. This group was led by John White.

White's granddaughter, Virginia Dare, was the first English child born in the new world.

We do not know what happened to the second colony. White stayed only one summer before returning to England to get more supplies. Forced then to serve in the navy, he could not return to the new world until 1590. He found the colony deserted. Carved on a log was a single word: "CROATOAN." Croatoan was the name of a nearby island. White wanted to search for the settlers, but a storm was coming. The ship's captain said they must leave immediately. White was never able to answer questions that we still ask. Were the settlers on Roanoke Island killed by the Indians? Did they leave to settle on Croatoan? Did they join the Indians?

Spanish Armada

Spain was not as powerful as the rest of the world thought. The successful attacks of the English sea dogs on Spanish ships showed that. Philip II, the king of Spain, became angry that Elizabeth approved of the sea dogs. He was also angered by the English attempts to colonize Virginia. Philip decided to invade England. The Spanish gathered together a huge fleet of warships, called the **Spanish Armada.** In 1588 the Spanish Armada set out to conquer England. However, the English, with the help of a storm, defeated the Spanish at sea. England's defeat of the Spanish Armada left Spain weak. Spain could no longer claim all the new world for itself.

Henry Hudson

European explorers continued to probe the North American coastline looking for a northwest passage. **Henry Hudson,** an Englishman, was one such explorer. On his first trip to North America in 1609, Hudson sailed as captain of a Dutch ship. He explored Chesapeake Bay and then New York harbor. He sailed up the river he named for himself—the Hudson River. Hudson's voyage gave Holland claim to the Hudson River valley. Soon the Dutch were establishing fur trading posts along the river. Iroquois Indians were willing to trade skins of beaver and otter.

On his second voyage to North America in 1610 Hudson sailed for an English company. The company asked him to explore the northern part of Canada. Hudson explored the bay that also carries his name—Hudson Bay.

Samuel de Champlain

The French meanwhile had renewed their interest in Canada, a land rich in both furs and fish. In 1603 an expedition was sent to explore New France. Its geographer and mapmaker was **Samuel de Champlain** (duh‧sham‧PLAYN). In 1608 he returned to establish the first successful French settlement in the new world at **Quebec** (kwi‧BEK).

Champlain was known as a strong leader of men. He was also known for his fairness and politeness to defeated enemies. His leadership encouraged French exploration and settlement of North America. For that reason he is called the Father of New France.

As the French explored the interior of North America, they set up trading posts. The French missionaries and fur traders got along well with most Indians. There were several reasons for this:

- The French learned the Indian languages.
- Unlike the English, the French traders were not interested in taking land from the Indians.
- The traders and the Indians treated each other like business partners, as equals. The Indians welcomed the iron tools they exchanged for furs. In the business of getting and selling furs, French traders and Indians depended on each other.

Exploring the Mississippi

The French continued to explore the rivers and lakes that led into the interior of North America. In 1673 one French expedition traveled across

The French built trading posts like this one at Fond-du-Lac, Wisconsin.

EXPLORATION OF NORTH AMERICA, 1500-1700

1513 Ponce de León explores Florida

1519 Cortés invades Mexico

1524 Verrazano explores Atlantic coast

1534-35 Cartier explores St. Lawrence River valley

1540-42 Coronado explores the interior

1540-42 De Soto explores the Southeast

1584 Raleigh establishes Virginia

1609-10 Hudson explores Hudson River and Hudson Bay

1673 Joliet and Marquette explore Mississippi River

1682 La Salle reaches Gulf of Mexico

1500
1550
1600
1650
1700

huge Lake Michigan, down the Wisconsin River, and then down the Mississippi River. Traveling in birchbark canoes, the explorers reached as far south as the mouth of the Arkansas River. After four months, the expedition had traveled about 2,500 miles (4,022 km).

This famous expedition was led by **Louis Joliet** (LOO•ee zhol•YAY), a fur trader, and **Jacques Marquette** (ZHAHK mahr•KET), a priest who knew Indian languages.

Another French explorer, **Robert La Salle** (luh•SAL), began his exploration of the Mississippi River in 1679. In Illinois La Salle established Fort Crevecoeur (KREHV•kuhr). All kinds of problems delayed the expedition, but at last, in 1682, La Salle reached the mouth of the Mississippi. He claimed the Mississippi River basin for France.

The city of New Orleans was founded by the French in 1718. By that time the French had established small trading posts and villages throughout the Mississippi River valley. That is why many place names there are French—names such as St. Louis, Des Moines, Detroit, and Louisville.

Reading Check

1. Why was a northwest passage so important?
2. How did England benefit from the activities of sea dogs such as Francis Drake?
3. How did Sir Walter Raleigh help achieve English settlement in North America?

Think Beyond How were the explorers of the new world like today's astronauts?

BEAVERS

The first French explorers in North America had looked for gold and diamonds. Later explorers decided the most precious resource was the furry beaver. Probably 100 million beavers then lived in North America. Before long, trapping beavers and trading their pelts became the biggest business in northern America.

Beavers belong to the rodent family, as do squirrels, mice, and rats. The average beaver is about 3 feet (1 m) long and weighs about 50 pounds (23 kg). Beavers use their sharp teeth to eat the bark and young buds of trees.

Beavers are excellent swimmers. They have large, flat tails that they use to steer themselves through the water. They also slap their tails on the water to signal other beavers that danger is nearby. They live in groups and work together to build dams and shelters.

Trappers were interested in beavers because the skins were valued for making coats and hats. Beaver fur provides excellent protection against cold and moisture.

In the 1600s, trappers combed the eastern part of North America in search of beavers. In those days a trapper could trade 12 beaver pelts for a musket. One pelt could be traded for 4 pounds (1.8 kg) of gunpowder, a new kettle, or 1 pound (0.5 kg) of tobacco.

During the early 1800s fur trading spread west and became an even bigger business. Huge fortunes were made. Trappers who were called "mountain men" moved into the wildest reaches of the Rocky Mountains. Soon, some trappers were catching as many as 100 beavers a week. By the mid-1800s, not many beavers were left. As a result, trapping beavers was no longer profitable.

Today, most states have laws that protect beavers, and beaver populations are higher now than they were a century ago. However, some trapping is still permitted so that the beaver population does not grow too large.

Think Beyond Why do you think there are laws that protect beavers?

Beavers chew trees even when there is no place to build a dam.

Look for these important words:

Key Words
- Virginia Company
- stock
- profit
- indentured servant
- House of Burgesses
- Pilgrims
- *Mayflower*
- compact
- Mayflower Compact

People
- John Smith
- Powhatan
- Pocahontas
- Massasoit
- Squanto
- William Bradford
- Miles Standish

Places
- Jamestown
- New England
- Plymouth

Look for answers to these questions:

1. How was the Jamestown colony able to survive and eventually prosper?
2. How was Virginia governed after 1619?
3. Who were the Pilgrims? Why did they come to the new world?
4. Why did the Plymouth colony survive and prosper?

2

Early Colonists

The English settlements at Roanoke Island failed, but the idea of settling a colony lived on. A group of English merchants decided to try again. To establish a new colony, they needed permission from the king of England. In the English view the king controlled all land claimed by England. With the permission of King James the group of London merchants organized the **Virginia Company.** The aim of these merchants was to start trading posts.

The Virginia Company was owned by many people. They each had given money to organize the company. In return, each had received shares of ownership in the company. These shares were called **stock.** This kind of company was a stock company. The Virginia Company hoped that in the long run it would make a **profit.** A profit is the money left over after expenses have been paid.

Three ships sent by the Virginia Company sailed into Chesapeake Bay early in 1607. They came to a large river, which they called the James River to honor their king. They settled on a shore of the James River in a place that would be easy to defend. They named the settlement **Jamestown.**

The 105 men and boys who arrived to settle Jamestown hoped to find gold. These colonists were not used to working with their hands. They did not know how to farm or to fish. The settlers were simply not prepared to take care

Today, visitors imagine life in early Jamestown as they stroll down its streets. The buildings are copies of the original structures.

of themselves. They depended on the Indians or on ships from England for food. Within a year, half had died of starvation, disease, or Indian attacks.

Jamestown might have disappeared, like the earlier settlement at Roanoke, but for **John Smith.** Smith was a soldier, an explorer, and a writer. Most of all, he was a practical person.

On an expedition to explore the countryside around Jamestown, Smith was captured by Powhatan (pow•uh•TAN) Indians. Their chief, also named **Powhatan,** sentenced him to death. Then, **Pocahontas** (poh•kuh•HAHNT•uhs), the chief's 12-year-old daughter, pleaded for Smith's life. Powhatan agreed to spare Smith.

Friendly relations were then established between the Jamestown settlers and Powhatan's tribe. The Indians began to bring corn and turkeys to the English. Pocahontas herself brought food. Smith wrote that Pocahontas kept the colony from death, starvation, and "utter confusion."

Smith himself did much to keep the colony going. He declared that anyone who did not work would not eat. Every able person was soon busy—sawing wood, building houses, planting gardens, or hunting for food.

The Jamestown colony began to prosper, or do well, when the colonists began to cultivate tobacco. Tobacco was a plant native to the Western Hemisphere. A Jamestown leader, John Rolfe, experimented with various types of tobacco and ways of drying it. By 1613 he had developed a tobacco that the English liked. The Virginians were soon sending tobacco to England. There it sold for very high prices.

A turning point for the Jamestown colony came in about 1616. At that time the Virginia Company began to give land to settlers who had stayed seven years. Until then, there had been no private ownership of land. Everyone was supposed to work on company land. After receiving land of their own, the colonists worked harder. The Virginia colonists worked harder for themselves in one day than they did in a week for the company, Smith said.

The Growth of Virginia

Tobacco encouraged the growth of Virginia. Stories of the money to be made by growing tobacco attracted more settlers. Most of the early settlers had not planned to settle in Virginia for life. They hoped to make a fortune and return to England. To encourage people to settle permanently in Virginia, the Virginia Company sent 90 women to Jamestown in 1619.

The high price of tobacco created a demand for people to work in the fields. A system was developed to provide workers for Virginia. In return for ocean passage, a person agreed to work for a period of time. At the end of that time, generally five to seven years, the person was free. Such a person was called an **indentured servant.**

In 1619 a Dutch trading ship arrived in Jamestown with a group of 20 Africans. For more than 100 years the

Dutch traders sold the first Africans to Jamestown in 1619. For years to come, blacks torn from their homeland would be forced into slavery.

The House of Burgesses was the first colonial assembly in Virginia.

Spanish had brought Africans as slaves to the new world. The African slaves worked in the fields and mines. However, the first Africans in Jamestown were treated not as slaves but as indentured servants. After serving the agreed number of years, they were freed like other indentured servants.

As more field workers were needed, black people were made indentured servants for life. By the middle of the 1600s, all black people coming to America were considered slaves. Slavery was made legal in Virginia in 1661.

By 1619 Virginia had about 1,000 settlers. In that year the Virginia Company said that the English in America would live under English laws. They would have the same rights as those in England. One of those rights was the right to establish and maintain a lawmaking assembly.

In Virginia the colonists elected people to represent them in the law-making assembly. This assembly was called the **House of Burgesses.** The House of Burgesses gave the Virginia colonists valuable experience in self-government.

Relations with Indians

After Chief Powhatan died, the Powhatan Indians stopped being helpful. They did not like losing their fishing and hunting lands to the Virginia settlers. In 1622, to stop the growing colony, the Indians attacked and killed 347 people. Having lost about one-third of their people, the English started an all-out war against the Indians. They finally defeated the Powhatans and took over their lands.

This pattern was repeated many times in American history. Indians and English settlers were generally friendly to each other at first. As more and more settlers pushed into Indian territory, however, friendly relations turned to bloody conflicts.

After the Indian attack of 1622, King James took away the rights of the Virginia Company. He took over direct responsibility for the colony. The king, of course, was on the other side of the Atlantic Ocean. He could not very well look after all the concerns and problems of the colonists. To represent him, the king appointed a governor for the colony. This governor shared ruling power with the House of Burgesses.

The Pilgrims Land at Plymouth

The hope of making a profit from trade was the main reason the Virginia Company founded Jamestown. Religion was the main reason for another English colony.

In 1614 John Smith had explored the Atlantic Coast above the Hudson River. He named this area **New England.** Smith mapped the coastline and described the landscape.

Among those who read Smith's description of New England was a group of English people in Holland. This group had left Scrooby, England, in 1608 because they disapproved of the Church of England. At that time everyone had to belong to the Church of England. To practice religion as they wanted, the Scrooby group fled to Holland. We call them **Pilgrims.** A pilgrim is a person who makes a journey for a religious reason.

In Holland the Pilgrims could practice their religion freely. Still, they worried about their children losing their English ways. Finding a place of their own might solve the problem.

After landing at Plymouth, the Pilgrims huddled around fires for warmth.

The Virginia Company gave the Pilgrims permission to settle near the Hudson River. London merchants agreed to pay for the voyage and provide workers. In turn, the Pilgrims agreed to repay the merchants in furs, fish, and lumber.

The Pilgrims hired a ship, the **Mayflower,** to take them to their new home in the fall of 1620. About one-third of the 102 travelers on the *Mayflower* were Pilgrims. Others were their servants and people hired by the London merchants.

The *Mayflower* had a long and dreadful voyage lasting 66 days. Violent storms drove the Pilgrims off course, and they ended up far north of their destination. When the Pilgrims finally sighted land, they were at Cape Cod in Massachusetts.

The Pilgrims faced an immediate problem. Cape Cod was north of the land governed by the Virginia Company. They were in a place without government. Without government, there were no laws. To meet that problem, the Pilgrim leaders on the *Mayflower* made a **compact,** or agreement. All the men signed the **Mayflower Compact.** They agreed that "just and equal" laws would be made for the general good of the colony. They further agreed that they would obey these laws. In other words, they would govern themselves. We take this idea for granted. But when kings and queens ruled, it was a brave idea.

Another major problem faced the Pilgrims. The windy shores of Cape Cod were not a good place to settle. For four weeks the Pilgrims explored the bay in the raw, cold winds. They finally chose to settle at the place John Smith had named **Plymouth.** It had a harbor, open fields nearby, and fresh water.

The Pilgrims faced a hard winter. They were weak from the stormy voyage. They were hungry from lack of proper food. For a long time they could build no adequate shelter against the cold. Half the group died.

Help from Indians

When spring arrived, the Pilgrims' spirits rose. Those who had been sick started to get better. Best of all, help came. Although the Pilgrims had seen Indians, they had not had any contact with them. Then one day an Indian walked into their midst and said, "Welcome, Englishmen."

In a place without government, the Pilgrims agree to govern themselves. William Bradford leads the signing of the Mayflower Compact.

How surprised the English were! The Indian, named Samoset, had learned some English from contacts with English fishermen. Several days later, **Massasoit** (mas•uh•SAW•it), the chief of the Wampanoag (WAMP•uhn•oh•ahg) Indians, accompanied Samoset on a visit to the Pilgrims.

Among the Indians with Massasoit was an English-speaking Indian named **Squanto.** Squanto had been kidnapped years before to be sold as a slave in Spain. He had escaped and spent several years in England before returning to his native land.

Squanto showed the Pilgrims how to plant corn and catch fish. Because he knew both languages, Squanto also helped keep Pilgrim-Indian relations smooth. Squanto helped the colonists survive.

The Plymouth colony also survived because it had strong leaders. One of them was **William Bradford.** Bradford, an English farmer, had gone with the Pilgrims to Holland and then to Plymouth. He was elected governor of Plymouth in 1621. Most of what we know about Plymouth comes from Bradford's history of the colony. Another leader was **Miles Standish.** Standish was a military man. He was responsible for the colony's defense.

The First Thanksgiving

The Pilgrims harvested their first crops in the fall of 1621. Governor Bradford thought the Pilgrims should have a celebration. He sent men to the forest to shoot turkeys so that the people might "rejoice together" to give thanks to God. Fish, clams, oysters, and lobsters were also gathered.

The Pilgrims invited their Indian neighbors to come. Imagine their surprise when 90 Indians showed up! The Pilgrims did not have food for so many. Massasoit quickly understood the situation. He sent his braves to the woods to get deer. With five deer added to the feast, there was enough for all. This was the first Thanksgiving.

The Pilgrims Prosper

When the Pilgrims first arrived in Plymouth, everyone worked for the community. That meant that there was no private ownership of land. The harvest was divided equally among the families. People began to complain about this because some were working harder than others. In 1623 the land was divided among the settlers. They learned the same lesson the settlers in Jamestown had learned. People work harder on their own land. However, the idea of people sharing with one another remained strong.

The Pilgrims at Plymouth began to prosper with their fishing, farming, and fur trading. When the next wave of settlers arrived, the Pilgrims had a surplus of goods. They then sold milk, meat, and produce to the new settlers.

Reading Check

1. Why was tobacco important to the success of the Jamestown colony?
2. What was the House of Burgesses? Why was it important?
3. How did the Indians help the Pilgrims survive?

Think Beyond Would you rather have been a Jamestown colonist or a Pilgrim at Plymouth? Explain.

Look for these important words:

Key Words	People	Places	
• Puritans	• Peter Stuyvesant	• Massachusetts Bay Colony	• Manhattan
• inflation		• Boston	• New Amsterdam
		• New Netherland	• New Sweden
			• New York

Look for answers to these questions:
1. Who were the Puritans? What were their reasons for coming to America?
2. Where did the Dutch settle? How was their settlement ruled?
3. How did the English gain control of New Amsterdam?

3   *Boston and New Amsterdam*

The Pilgrims were poor people who started their settlement with fewer than 100 colonists. The later settlement of **Massachusetts Bay Colony** at **Boston** was quite different. Here, in 1630, 15 ships arrived carrying more than 1,000 settlers. These settlers, as the Pilgrims did, disapproved of many practices of the Church of England. They did not separate from the church, like the Pilgrims, but wished to make it more "pure." For this reason, these people are called **Puritans.** Like the Pilgrims, the Puritans hoped to establish a community where they could put Christian ideals into practice.

The Puritans had other reasons for coming to New England. In England itself Puritan farmers had found it harder and harder to make a living. Those who owned their land complained of high taxes. Farmers who rented land complained of rising rents. Yet the amount they received for their

John Winthrop, who led the Puritans from England to Boston, governed them for nearly 20 years.

crops stayed the same. Craftspeople also found it difficult to make money. Prices were rising faster than wages. The same amount of money bought fewer goods. England was suffering from **inflation,** or the steady rise of prices.

The Puritan settlement in Boston was successful from the start and continued to grow. Many communities were soon established near Boston.

New Netherland

While the English were settling Virginia and New England, the Dutch started settlements along the Hudson River. They had claimed that area since Henry Hudson had explored the river for Holland. They named the area **New Netherland**.

In 1624 a Dutch company set up a trading post at Fort Orange. Fort Orange is the present-day Albany, capital of New York. In 1626 the company bought the island of **Manhattan** from the Indians and established a trading post called **New Amsterdam.** There they built a wall to keep out wolves and Indians. The street running alongside the wall was known as Wall Street. Wall Street is famous today as a center of banking and finance.

The Dutch company welcomed a variety of settlers. French, Danes, Italians, Spaniards, and Jews all found homes in New Amsterdam.

New Amsterdam prospered after the Dutch company appointed **Peter Stuyvesant** (STY·vuh·sunt) as governor. Stuyvesant had lost his right leg in a Dutch attack on a French fort. Thereafter he walked on a wooden leg called a peg leg. That gave him a nickname of Pegleg Peter.

New Amsterdam was a community of about 1,000 people in 1650. Notice the ships in the harbor and the windmills in the distance.

Peter Stuyvesant strides forward to meet the English who have landed. A harsh and unpleasant leader, Stuyvesant was unable to get the citizens of New Amsterdam to fight the English.

Stuyvesant was a powerful and stubborn governor. He ruled the Dutch colony as he chose. There were often strong disagreements between Stuyvesant and the citizens of New Amsterdam. The citizens wanted more say in government and disliked Stuyvesant's strong-handed rule.

In 1655 Stuyvesant took over the small colony of **New Sweden.** This Swedish colony was centered at Fort Cristina, in what is now Wilmington, Delaware.

Compared to the English colonies, there were few people in the Dutch colony of New Netherland. Knowing this, the king of England declared war on Holland. The king told his brother, the Duke of York, that he could have the Dutch colonies. In 1664 the Duke of York sailed into the harbor of New Amsterdam. Stuyvesant tried to get the citizens of New Amsterdam to fight the English. They refused, and Stuyvesant had to surrender without firing a shot. New Amsterdam was renamed **New York.** The English now controlled most of the Atlantic Coast of North America.

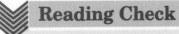

Reading Check

1. Where did the Puritans settle?
2. Why did the Puritans come to New England?
3. Why was England able to take over New Netherland?

Think Beyond Do you think Peter Stuyvesant would be a popular leader today? Explain.

People
MAKE HISTORY

Deborah Moody
?–1658

Officials of Massachusetts Bay Colony said she was "a dangerous woeman." They said she could not live in the colony unless she promised to "leave her opinions behinde her."

Who was this dangerous woman? And what were her opinions? Her name was Deborah Moody. Her opinions were beliefs in religious freedom and in equal rights for men and women.

The widow of an English lord, Lady Moody had come to the American colonies as a protest after the English government tried to tell her where she could and could not live in England. She settled in the Massachusetts Bay Colony in 1639 and joined a local church. A few years later, however, Lady Moody decided that the opinions of her minister did not match her own views.

Lady Moody decided she would have a better chance to live as she chose in the Dutch colony of New Netherland, in what is now New York State. In 1643 the Dutch government granted her a plot of land on Long Island, and Lady Moody established the first English settlement in that area.

The settlement, called Gravesend, was the first settlement in America to be headed by a woman. With the aid of a town council, Lady Moody led town meetings and made rules governing town planning.

In 1657 Lady Moody converted to the Quaker faith, which believed in equality between men and women. Soon, Gravesend was the center of Quaker life on Long Island.

Under Lady Moody, Gravesend became a center of religious tolerance and equal rights. People who came there were able to speak their minds and worship as they chose. As a result, even Lady Moody's enemies began to respect her. When she died in 1658, the governor who had barred her from Massachusetts called her "a wise and anciently religious woman."

Think Beyond Can you think of a famous person today who, due to his or her ideas, is set apart from other people?

Map of Gravesend

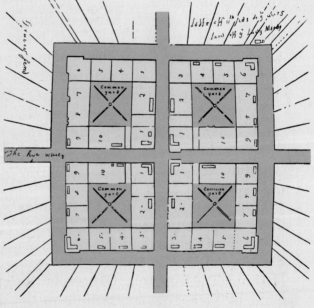

Ye Ancient Plot of ye Towne of s'Gravesende
1645

182

SKILLS IN ACTION

FINDING DIRECTIONS

The explorers and settlers of America faced a long, dangerous voyage. For weeks they were tossed about in small ships. No land was visible. Only the cold, gray waves of the Atlantic could be seen. How did they know the direction in which they were sailing?

Using the Sun

Early sailors used the sun to find directions. They knew, as you do, that the sun rises in the east and sets in the west. If you head toward the sun in the late afternoon, you are moving westward. If the late afternoon sun is at your back, in which direction are you facing?

The farther one lives from the equator, the more the position of the sun varies with the seasons. In northern parts of the world, the sun sets southwest in winter and northwest in summer. If you want to use the sun to find direction, you must learn its position in every hour of every day in every season.

Using the Stars

Early sailors also found their direction using stars. One important star, the North Star, always shines from the direction of the North Pole. It also has the name **Polaris** (puh•LAR•uhs), the pole star.

To find the North Star, you must first be able to locate two star patterns, the **Big Dipper** and the **Little Dipper.** Like the hands of a clock, these star patterns rotate around the North Star. To locate the North Star, first find the two stars forming the "cup" opposite the handle of the Big Dipper. Those stars are always in a straight line with the North Star. Notice that the North Star is in the handle of the Little Dipper.

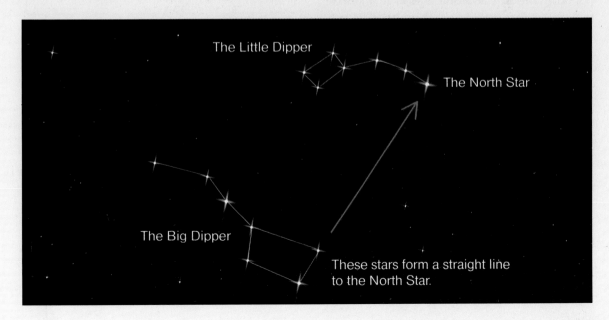

The Little Dipper

The North Star

The Big Dipper

These stars form a straight line to the North Star.

183

Using a Compass

How do you tell directions if you can't see the stars or sun? The invention of the compass solved this problem. With a compass sailors could find their direction in any weather, day or night. The compass is still an important tool.

The most important part of a compass is its magnetic needle. This needle will always line up in a north-south direction, with one end pointing north. Most compasses have the directions printed on them.

When you use a compass, you must make sure it is not near large metal objects. These can make the compass needle point in a false direction. Hold the compass steady until the needle is still. Then slowly turn your body until the needle points to the letter *N* on the compass. You and your compass will be facing north.

Orienting Maps

To use a map to go somewhere, you must first **orient** (OHR•ee•uhnt) the map. *To orient* means to line up in the right direction. One way to orient a map is to figure your direction from the position of the sun. If it is three o'clock in the afternoon, the sun is in the west. Turn your map so that west on the map lines up with the sun.

A better way to orient a map is to use a compass. With a compass you can make sure that north on the map is really pointing toward the North Pole. You can use a compass to do this. First, line up the needle and the *N* on the compass to find out which direction is north. Then turn the map so that *N* on the map is also pointing in the same direction as the compass needle. Now your map is oriented.

Look at the map on this page. Imagine that you are standing where the map shows you are. The street you are on runs east and

west. You know this because *N* on the compass rose points in the same direction as north on the compass you're holding. You see a big street on your left that runs north and south. What street is that? You want to walk to the courthouse. Is it north or south of where you are? Should you turn right or left when you reach Main Street?

CHECKING YOUR SKILLS

Answer the following questions.

1. How can you figure out which way is west in the late afternoon?

2. How can you figure out which way is north at night?

3. You want to use a compass to orient yourself. When you hold it up, the needle is pointing to the letter *W* on the compass face. What should you do?

4. You want to orient your street map with the compass. What should you do?

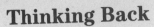
Thinking Back

- England and France hoped to find a northwest passage to Asia through North America. Due to their exploration, both England and France claimed lands in North America.

- Spanish treasures seized by English sea captains made England powerful. Sir Walter Raleigh made two unsuccessful attempts to settle Roanoke Island.

- Samuel de Champlain established a successful French settlement at Quebec. The French explored the interior of North America and maintained friendly relations with the Indians.

- The Virginia Company founded Jamestown, the first permanent English colony. Jamestown prospered when colonists began to cultivate tobacco.

- Indentured servants, including people from Africa, were sent to Virginia to provide labor. Eventually, however, all black people coming to America were considered slaves.

- The Virginia colonists gained valuable experience in self-government when the House of Burgesses was established.

- The Pilgrims came to America to find a place where they could worship freely. Before landing at Plymouth, they signed the Mayflower Compact.

- The Puritans came to America for both religious and economic reasons.

- The Dutch settled lands along the Hudson River but had to surrender them when the English king declared war on Holland. After this, England controlled most of the Atlantic coast.

Check for Understanding

Using Words

Number your paper from 1 to 10. Write the name that best fits each description.

William Bradford   Henry Hudson
John Cabot   Robert La Salle
Jacques Cartier   Walter Raleigh
Samuel   John Smith
   de Champlain   Peter
Francis Drake   Stuyvesant

1. This man was the leader of Jamestown.
2. He explored the St. Lawrence River area looking for a northwest passage.
3. This explorer claimed the Mississippi River basin for France.
4. He discovered the Grand Banks.
5. The Pilgrims elected this man governor of Plymouth in 1621.
6. He was responsible for the first English settlements in North America.
7. This sea dog captured Spanish treasure.
8. New Amsterdam prospered after he was appointed governor.
9. This man explored for both Holland and England.
10. This explorer is also called the Father of New France.

Reviewing Facts

1. How did fast ships and good sailors help England become powerful?
2. Name three reasons why the French and most Indians remained friendly.
3. Why was Jamestown founded? Plymouth? New Amsterdam?
4. What leaders were important in the Jamestown and Plymouth colonies? Why was each important?
5. What was the House of Burgesses?

Thinking Critically

1. The fur trade was an important reason for both French and Dutch settlement in North America. How did trade benefit both the Europeans and the Indians?
2. What does it mean to be "in a place without government"? Why do you think the Pilgrims felt it necessary to write and sign the Mayflower Compact?
3. What changes might have been seen in Jamestown between 1607 and 1619? in Plymouth between 1620 and 1630?

Writing About It

Write a short report describing the ways in which the American Indians helped the early settlers. In your report, include what you think might have happened if the Indians had not provided help.

Practicing Geography Skills

Finding Directions

Answer the following questions:

1. If you turn your back to the sun at three o'clock in the afternoon, what general direction are you facing?
2. If you face a rising sun, what general direction is to your left? to your right?

3. In which direction does the compass needle point?

On Your Own

Social Studies at Home

1. Write a short play about what you think happened to the settlers of the second colony on Roanoke Island. Include Sir Walter Raleigh and John White as characters. Be sure to explain in your play why you think the settlers carved the word *Croatoan* on a tree.
2. Read the description of New Amsterdam on page 180. Then draw pictures of how you think Wall Street might have looked. Next, look through current magazines and newspapers and cut out pictures of modern-day Wall Street. Use both your drawings and the pictures you cut out to make a poster that illustrates how New York City has changed since 1626.

Read More About It

The Carving on the Tree by Elizabeth Campbell. Little, Brown. This story suggests an explanation of the mysterious carving on the tree at Roanoke Island.

The First Thanksgiving Feast by Jean Anderson. Photographs by George Ancona. Clarion Books. This book contains black-and-white photos shot at the re-creation of Plymouth Plantation. The photos are based on original documentation of the first Thanksgiving.

The House on Stink Alley: A Story about the Pilgrims in Holland by F. N. Monjo. Illustrated by Robert Quackenbush. Holt, Rinehart and Winston. Love Brewster recounts Pilgrim life in Leyden, Holland, before the voyage to the new world.

The Double Life of
POCAHONTAS

by Jean Fritz

Pocahontas lived in two worlds, the world of her ancestors and the world of the newcomers to America. For a while she thought that there might be friendship between her people and the English. It seemed so in the beginning when she helped to adopt John Smith into her family.

Pocahontas was present in her father's great longhouse when John Smith arrived, a short, straight-standing man with a furry beard and bright, fearless eyes. He marched past two hundred of Powhatan's bodyguards, all glaring at him, but John Smith showed no fear. Not even before Powhatan himself who sat high on his matted throne—a large, stately figure, every inch a king.

Of course Pocahontas was impressed by this short stranger. Indians always admired courage, and, according to all reports, this man had not only stood up alone to two hundred warriors, he had struck fear into their hearts. Not just by his gun but by himself. By his very boldness. And here he was striding into an enemy stronghold, into her father's court, without the slightest sign that he felt danger. She watched him wash his hands in the water that was brought to him and dry them on feathers as if this was his daily custom. And when Powhatan questioned him, she marveled that he did not flinch and quail as so many prisoners did. No, he spoke out firmly.

Why had the English come? Powhatan wanted to know.

It was all a mistake, John Smith said. They had been fighting their enemy, the Spanish, and had been blown here by a storm.

Why were they staying?

Oh, they were just waiting for Captain Newport to come back. Then they'd go home.

Perhaps Powhatan had already decided what to do with John Smith; perhaps he decided later. In any case, he had guns on his mind. And if he adopted John Smith into the tribe, John would be required to give him gifts. What better gift than guns? A couple of cannon to start off with, maybe. Then, as his mind ran on, Powhatan may have caught the eye of Pocahontas. She looked so interested, eager—well, why not let her be the man's sponsor?

All John Smith knew, however, was that a fire was being lighted. The priests were wailing and calling on their gods as if they were preparing for a sacrifice. Powhatan was conferring with his chiefs. Then he gave an order and John was dragged forward and forced to lay his head on two huge stones. Tall men stood around him with raised clubs, and at any moment John expected to have his brains bashed out.

Suddenly a little girl rushed up to him. She put his head in her arms and begged for his life. Maybe this was prearranged; maybe not. No one can know for sure, but the important thing was: John was saved. The men with the clubs drew back and John was helped to his feet. Of course he was delighted to have his brains intact. And pleased to make the acquaintance of Pocahontas, who had been his savior.

But she was more than that. In her view, she was his sister now. He was her brother, and Powhatan was father to them both. He could live at Werowocomoco, as adopted members of a family often did. He could play games with her, string beads, and make hatchets for her father. They had a special kinship, and if he stayed he would be her countryman.

Did he understand?

Powhatan also wanted to make sure that John Smith understood he'd been adopted into the tribe. To make it seem official, Powhatan and two hundred of his warriors painted themselves black and descended on John Smith one night. Powhatan explained that John Smith was not only Powhatan's adopted son, he was a chief. Like all his chiefs, he would be expected to give Powhatan gifts. What Powhatan wanted right now were two thunder weapons (cannon) and a millstone for grinding corn. Rawhunt

(Powhatan's lieutenant) and twelve guards would go to Jamestown with John Smith to bring back the gifts.

John Smith agreed. Pocahontas would not have let him go without saying goodbye, and John would have made a formal farewell to Powhatan, whom he gladly called "father."

Once at the settlement, John showed Rawhunt the millstone. Rawhunt's body was deformed so that he did not expect to move the millstone himself, but none of the twelve guards could move it either.

Well, there were the cannon, John Smith pointed out. Rawhunt knew how much Powhatan was counting on those cannon, so he urged the guards to try hard, to use every muscle. But it was no use. Each cannon weighed between 3,000 and 4,500 pounds.

It was too bad, John said, that the Indians couldn't take the cannon home. He'd give them other gifts instead. He gathered up some trinkets, bells, baubles of glass and copper.

But Powhatan was expecting thunder.

No thunder, John said.

So the Indians went home, disgruntled, while John Smith, a free man again after six weeks of captivity, walked happily into Jamestown to report to the council on his narrow escape.

You can read more about the fascinating life of Pocahontas in the award winning book, *The Double Life of Pocahontas* by Jean Fritz. (G.P. Putnam's Sons, copyright 1983)

Unit Review

Words to Remember

Read each sentence. Then replace the underlined words in each sentence with the correct word or words from this list. Write the new sentences on your paper.

colonies
compass
conquistadors
expeditions
indentured
  servants
legend
missionaries
navigation
northwest
  passage
profit

1. Prince Henry encouraged a way for sailors to find their way on the seas.

2. An important instrument for sea captains was a tool for finding directions.

3. After Columbus there were many European journeys that explored the Americas.

4. The Aztec and Inca civilizations were destroyed by Spanish conquerors.

5. A story about the past that may or may not be true helped Cortés conquer the Aztecs.

6. After Columbus, Europeans started coming to the Americas to live in settlements ruled by a faraway country.

7. Europeans who came to the new world included people who wanted to bring Christianity to the Indians.

8. Several explorers searched for a waterway leading to Asia through North America.

9. Traders and businesses in the new world hoped to make a sum of money after meeting expenses.

10. People who agreed to work for a period of time in exchange for passage to the new world provided workers for the settlement in Virginia.

Focus on Main Ideas

1. Why were the Vikings important? How do we know about them?

2. Why did Europeans try to find new routes to Asia?

3. Why was the voyage of Christopher Columbus so important?

4. How did Magellan's voyage contribute to knowledge about the world?

5. Make a table comparing the conquests of Cortés and Pizarro. What people did each conquer? When?

6. Give three examples of how the Spanish culture has influenced our American heritage.

7. Why did the English sea-dog attacks on Spanish ships help England become a strong nation?

8. Why did the helpfulness that Indians showed the first English settlers often turn into conflict? Why were the French usually able to get along better with the Indians?

9. Why are the House of Burgesses and the Mayflower Compact important? What were their purposes?

10. How did the main reasons for settling Jamestown, Plymouth, and the Massachusetts Bay Colony differ?

Think/Write

Describing New England, John Smith wrote, "Here every man may be master and owner of his own labor and land." What do you think Smith meant by this statement? What changes helped the Virginia settlers and the Pilgrims reach this goal?

Activities

1. **Research/Art** Find out more about one of the first settlements: Plymouth, New Amsterdam, Fort Orange, or Jamestown. Draw a picture of one.

2. **Research/Art/Writing** Find out more about one of these ships: the *Santa Maria*, the *Golden Hind*, the *Mayflower*. Draw a picture of the ship. Write a short report describing the size of the ship, the kind of ship it is, and its history.

3. **Reading/Reporting** Ask your school librarian to help you find a book about the foods native to our country. Find an interesting fact to report to your class.

4. **Writing** Pretend that you were with one of the explorers or settlers. Write a letter home describing one or two days in your life.

Skills Review

1. **Historical Maps** Use the map on this page to answer these questions.
   a. When did Coronado leave the town of Compostela?
   b. When did Cárdenas reach the Grand Canyon?

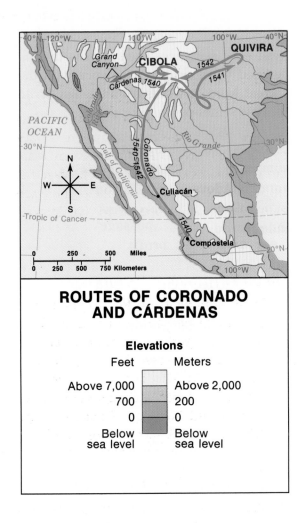

ROUTES OF CORONADO AND CÁRDENAS

Elevations

Feet	Meters
Above 7,000	Above 2,000
700	200
0	0
Below sea level	Below sea level

   c. When did Coronado leave Quivira?
   d. When did Coronado return to Compostela?

2. **Finding Directions** Use the map on this page to answer these questions.
   a. In what direction did Cárdenas travel to reach the Grand Canyon?
   b. How could Cárdenas have used the sun to help him find his way?
   c. When Coronado left Culiacán in 1540, why do you think he traveled northwest rather than traveling due north?

Explorers from many European lands came to the new world. The early explorers did more than just discover places. They brought their languages, cultures, and ways of life to the areas they found. Every state bears the mark of the people who first settled it. These activities may help you learn about the first Europeans to live in your state.

Learning About People

1. Explorers such as Cortés, Coronado, and La Salle helped shape our nation. Find out the name of a famous explorer who discovered or passed through your state. Write a short report on this explorer. Be sure to find out the explorer's native country and language. What hardships did this explorer face in your state?

Learning About Geography

2. Many of the early explorers and settlers dreamed of great riches. They hoped to profit from the gold, beaver fur, and other natural resources they found. Find out which natural resources were discovered by the settlers of your state. Can these resources still be found in your state?

3. Imagine that you are an early explorer of your state. Write a letter to a friend back in Europe and tell about the wild territory you have found. Does it seem like a good place to live? Should your friend come and join you here? Why?

Learning About Culture

4. French and Spanish names are common in our country. French names often begin with the words *Saint, Le, La, De,* or *Des.* Spanish names may begin with *San, Santa, Los, El, La,* or *Del.* Look in an atlas of your state. Are there any French or Spanish names?

5. The picture below shows a copy, or reconstruction, of the *Mayflower.* There are also reconstructions of the early settlements of Plymouth and Jamestown. Can reconstructions of early ships or settlements be found in your state? If so, learn what you can about a reconstruction and what it shows.

UNIT

4
Life in the American Colonies

- **1632**
George Calvert founds colony of Maryland

- **1636**
Roger Williams founds colony of Rhode Island
Thomas Hooker starts settlement in Connecticut

- **1670**
Founding of Charleston, South Carolina

- **1675**
King Philip's War in New England

- **1682**
William Penn founds colony of Pennsylvania

*S*uppose that you could go back in time and visit the American colonies in 1733. The picture below shows the kinds of things you might see. Instead of cars and buses rolling along on paved highways, you would see wagons pulled by horses on dirt roads. Instead of grocery stores you would find pantries filled with food from the family garden. You can nearly feel the hustle and bustle that helped our country grow. In this unit you will discover how people in the colonies built lives in a new and different world.

Think Beyond   Do you think there were any advantages to living during the 1700s? Do you see any advantages in this picture? Explain your answer.

• **1723**

Benjamin Franklin
moves to
Philadelphia

• **1733**

James Oglethorpe
founds Georgia

• **1743**

Eliza Lucas
develops indigo

CHAPTER 7

The New England Colonies

"We dwell in a place which is called marthateutyeis bay. It is a place full of islands that the sea compassed them in, and we have many good harbors for the ships to ride in. First, for the country, it is a very good air, for we have none sick here. We have much champaign ground, many hills which are rocky, much marsh ground with fresh rivers, many great ponds two or three miles about . . . "

—Massachusetts settler
William Hammond, 1633

Look for these important words:

Key Words
- deciduous
- navigable
- naval stores
- common
- village green
- meetinghouse
- authority
- meeting
- town meeting
- offices
- official

Places
- Connecticut River

Look for answers to these questions:
1. What are the natural features of New England?
2. How were New England villages laid out?
3. In what ways was religion important to the Puritans?
4. What kind of town government did the Puritan settlers have?

1 Geography and Towns of New England

Ten thousand years before the Pilgrims landed at Plymouth, glaciers covered much of New England. As the glaciers melted, they left a new landscape behind. There were gentle hills, sharp mountains, and a rocky, jagged coastline with many harbors. The melting glaciers had left behind huge amounts of stones and boulders.

With the disappearance of the glaciers, great forests took root. These included forests of evergreen trees and **deciduous** (di•SIJ•uh•wus) trees. Deciduous trees are hardwood trees that lose their leaves in the fall. Maple, ash, and walnut are deciduous trees that grow in New England.

Clear, fast rivers tumbled down from the mountains to the Atlantic Ocean. Because of the many waterfalls most rivers were not **navigable.** That means they were not wide, deep, or gentle enough for cargo-carrying boats. An exception was the **Connecticut River,** the longest river in New England. Much of this river was navigable, which made the Connecticut valley attractive to early settlers.

Early settlers made good use of New England's natural resources. The fish in the ocean, the forests, the harbors, the rushing streams, and even the rocky fields helped New England to prosper. Because the New Englanders could catch more fish than they needed, they had a surplus. The surplus catch could be sold or traded to the West Indies or Europe. Fishing and trading encouraged shipbuilding.

The forests of New England provided the materials needed for shipbuilding. Logs were floated down rivers to the harbor towns. There the logs were turned into **naval stores.** Naval stores included the planks, masts, pitch, tar, and turpentine used in shipbuilding. Well-built ships encouraged even more trade.

The New Englanders also used the fast streams to turn waterwheels. The waterwheels then turned machinery for grinding grain or sawing wood.

It took hard work to clear the fields of rocks and boulders. The crop that grew best in the rocky soil and short New England summers was corn. The hardworking farmers also grew crops like barley, wheat, rye, and oats. Cows, sheep, and horses grazed in pastures.

The New England Village

Most life in colonial New England centered around the village. Farming was carried on in fields outside the village. Puritan settlers brought this pattern with them from England. They often brought the names of their English villages as well. Boston, Salem, Ipswich, and Groton are some of the New England towns named after English towns.

In the center of the New England village was the **common,** or **village green.** This was a parklike pasture shared by the villagers. At one end was the church, called a **meetinghouse.** Houses lined other sides of the village green. Over the years other buildings were added. Among these were a blacksmith shop, an inn, a school, a village store, and a mill. Beyond the village were the fields and woods.

The Puritans liked the village plan because they thought of themselves as a community. The closeness of village life made it easier for people to help each other. It was easier to get to the meetinghouse.

Village life also made it easier for church ministers to exercise their **authority,** or control. In Puritan New England the minister was the most important person in the village. The Puritans had clear ideas about what was right and what was wrong. The duty of the minister was to help keep people on the right path.

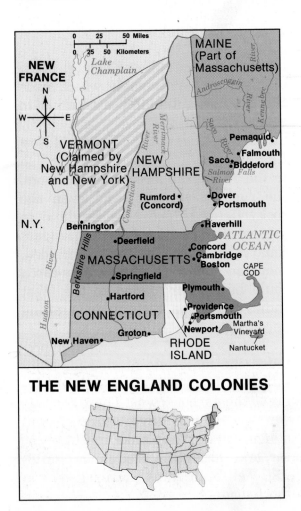

THE NEW ENGLAND COLONIES

The Meetinghouse

Just as the minister was the most important person, so was the meetinghouse the most important building. Everyone had to attend **meeting,** or church, on Sunday. The major part of meeting was the minister's sermon. A sermon often lasted for several hours. The meeting lasted most of the day, with

A NEW ENGLAND VILLAGE

Fields

Mill

Minister's house

Craft shops

Blacksmith

Inn

Meetinghouse

Stocks

Green or common

School

Furniture maker

Well

Cooper

Soapmaking

199

A warming box

a break at noon. At noon villagers gathered in nearby homes for warmth, conversation, and a hot meal.

In the meetinghouse each person had an assigned place to sit. Important people had the best seats. Those who failed to sit in their assigned seats were fined. Sometimes people fell asleep during the long sermons. It was the job of one person to awaken them by tickling their faces with a feather.

There was no heat in the meetinghouse. In winter it could be painfully cold. The women and girls often brought metal boxes full of hot coals to meetings. They rested their feet on the boxes to keep warm. Dogs were welcome in the meetinghouse. A dog curled up at his master's feet helped keep him warm, too. Of course, dogs had to behave. One person had the job of Dog Whipper and put out dogs that barked.

The outside wall of the meetinghouse was a kind of a bulletin board. Notices were nailed to the walls announcing livestock and land sales, intended marriages, and auctions. In the early days, wolves' heads might also decorate the outside of the meetinghouse. People were paid for every wolf they killed.

The Town Meeting

Town business was conducted at a **town meeting.** This meeting, usually held in the meetinghouse, was open to everyone. At first, a man had to be a member of the church to vote. By the end of the 1600s, a man could vote if he owned property. At the town meeting all the town's needs and problems were discussed.

Each year men were elected to a number of **offices.** An office in this sense is a job one does for the good of the community. A person holding an office is an **official** (uh•FISH•uhl). Some of the offices in colonial times were constable, drummer, town crier, digger of graves, sweeper of the meetinghouse, and fence viewer. The constable was in charge of keeping the peace. The town crier called out important announcements. The fence viewer made sure that the pasture fences were kept in repair.

There were other tasks. In Haverhill, Massachusetts, the town meeting appointed a man to keep the measles out of town. How he managed that job, we do not know. The Haverhill meeting also appointed a man to run the ferry. He could not charge what he wanted, however. The town meeting set the charges at 3 pence a horse, 1 penny a person, all ministers free. The town meeting also chose the schoolteacher and decided the teacher's salary.

Reading Check

1. How did colonists make use of New England's natural resources?
2. Why did Puritan settlers like the village plan?
3. What are examples of the importance of religion in New England?

Think Beyond Why was it important to attend the town meeting?

Look for these important words:

Key Words
- Training Day
- militia
- barter

Look for answers to these questions:
1. How did people in New England villages celebrate?
2. What kinds of work did women and girls do?
3. What kinds of work did men and boys do?
4. Why did the Puritans think education important?

2 Everyday Life in New England

The village green was at first used by settlers as grazing land for their livestock. As time passed, however, the green was used less for livestock and more as a place for village gatherings. After their chores were done, children used the green as a community playground. The children enjoyed playing ball or flying kites.

The biggest holiday of the year, **Training Day,** took place on the green. At least once a year all able-bodied men had to report for military drills. A military unit made up of volunteers is called a **militia** (muh•LISH•uh). Men in the militia marched and practiced firing their muskets. After the drill, there were contests and games, and plenty to eat and drink.

Other occasions for celebration included times when people helped one another put up barns or houses. An event in early spring was collecting sap from the maple trees and boiling it down to sugar. Weddings were always a cause for a village celebration.

Home Life

The most important room of a New England house contained the great fireplace. A fire was always kept burning in the fireplace. To let a fire go out

At a house raising, the neighbors would celebrate after the timbers were put up.

In colonial kitchens many activities took place. In the back a woman churns butter. Another spins. One woman cooks while another rolls out dough. A grandfather peels apples. Toddlers play.

caused great trouble because there were no matches. A new fire could be started only by striking flint against metal to make sparks. Most villagers started new fires by borrowing burning coals from a neighbor.

All cooking was done in the fireplace. Baking was done in a small oven in the side of the fireplace. Most food was roasted over the fire or simmered in large iron kettles. Kettles were also used to heat water for cooking and washing.

Women and girls spent long days doing necessary chores. Most of the chores were centered around feeding and clothing the family. Women turned milk into butter and cheese. They dried and preserved fruits such as peaches, pears, and apples. They pickled cabbage and other vegetables from the garden. Pickling vegetables preserved them throughout winter.

The women also made all the clothing for the family. They started with wool from their sheep. They had to spin the wool before weaving it into cloth. From the flax plants in their fields, they spun and wove linen. Pieces of worn-out clothing were used to make patchwork quilts for bedding. Nothing useful was ever wasted.

Farm Work

In New England farmers could raise only enough crops to meet the needs of their families. The men and boys spent long hours working in the fields. They had to remove the rocks, which they used for fences. Once the fields were clear of rocks, the men tilled the soil. To do this, they walked behind oxen pulling a heavy wooden plow. They then planted, weeded, and harvested their crops. Their crops included corn and rye and maybe barley and wheat. Pumpkins and squash grew among the corn.

The men and boys also took care of the cattle, hogs, and sheep. These animals were used as sources of food, leather, and wool. Pig bristles, or hair, were used to make brushes. Animal fat was turned into soap and candles.

Colonial farmers might get barrels from a cooper, or barrelmaker.

Like the women, the men were skilled in a number of crafts. They made their own work tools, such as plows and rakes. During the evenings a colonial farmer might work leather from his animals into shoes, straps, and work pants. He might also make wooden barrels. Barrels were used to store grain, salted meats, and other foods.

Sometimes a farmer specialized in a craft. A man who was a good blacksmith might make nails for a neighbor. In exchange the neighbor would make barrels for the blacksmith. This system of exchanging goods and services without using money is called **barter.** In the early days of colonial life, money was rarely used.

Schools

It was very important to the Puritans that every person be able to read the Bible. Parents were expected to see that their children and servants learned to read. Every town of 50 families or more had a school.

Both men and women were teachers in these schools, which at first were in homes. As time passed, villages began to build their own schools.

School met all year. There was no summer vacation. The Puritans would have called such a vacation a waste of "God's precious time." Working hard, they believed, was a way to please God.

Even though school was open all year round, many children attended only 10 or 12 weeks a year. At other times their parents needed them to do work at home or in the fields. Parents were expected to pay a small amount each week their children attended school. In some places parents paid one

Children in New England often learned reading, writing, and arithmetic at small schools run by women in their homes.

Making this sampler was the way young Patty Goodeshall learned both her stitches and her letters.

price for a student to learn to read. If a student were to be taught arithmetic, it cost more.

Paper was very scarce and expensive in the colonies. Students often learned to write on pieces of birch bark. Girls might learn both their letters and their needlework by stitching samplers.

Boys could go to grammar schools to prepare for college. Harvard College, in Cambridge, Massachusetts, was founded in 1636. It was the first college in the colonies. The Puritans wanted their leaders and ministers to be well educated. Some women received excellent educations at home, but they were not allowed to attend college.

Reading Check

1. What was Training Day?
2. Name three skills women needed.
3. What does *barter* mean?

Think Beyond How was a Puritan school like the school you attend?

People
MAKE HISTORY

John Harvard
1607–1638

▶▶▶▶▶▶▶▶▶▶▶▶▶▶▶▶

In 1636 a group of prominent colonists asked the government of the Massachusetts Bay Colony to set up a college for young men. Many of the colonists had been educated at England's finest universities, and they wanted their sons to have similar educational opportunities.

A few miles away, a young minister was dying of a lung disease. He had come to America only a few months before to start a new life with his bride. A graduate of England's Cambridge University, the minister believed strongly in education. When he learned he was going to die, he wrote a will. In it, he left half of his estate to the new college.

The young minister, John Harvard, had lived a difficult life. Both his parents died when he was small, leaving him in the care of his stepmother. Luckily, his stepmother was kind, and she made sure that John got an education. She sent him to Cambridge, where he received his Master's degree in 1636. She also gave him some money so that he could marry and take his wife, Anne, to America.

The couple sailed on the ship *Hector,* arriving in Massachusetts in 1637. Harvard was soon granted the rights of a freeman, or citizen, of the colony. He used his citizenship to gain 120 acres (48.5 ha) of land, where he built a home. Inside the house was a large library, where John Harvard stored the more than 400 books he owned.

After only 10 months in America, Harvard died. His bequest to the new college totaled almost twice the amount the government had set aside for the school. Harvard also left all his books to the college. Books were so scarce in the colonies that this gift was almost as valuable as the money.

In gratitude for Harvard's generosity, the General Court of Massachusetts decided to name the college in his honor. Today, Harvard University is recognized as one of the finest schools in the United States, thanks in part to a young minister who believed that education was vital to the success of America's youth.

Think Beyond How do you think John Harvard's gift has helped our country?

Look for these important words:

Key Words
- Pequot Indians
- King Philip's War
- frontier
- exports
- imports
- triangle trade route

People
- Roger Williams
- Anne Hutchinson
- Thomas Hooker
- Metacomet
- Olaudah Equiano

Places
- Providence
- Rhode Island
- Portsmouth
- Hartford
- Connecticut
- Vermont
- Maine
- New Hampshire
- Nantucket

Look for answers to these questions:
1. Which members of the Massachusetts Bay Colony founded new settlements? Why?
2. What caused the Indian wars in the Connecticut valley?
3. In what ways did New England colonists become prosperous?
4. How did the slave trade work?

3 New England Grows

The early Puritans of Massachusetts did not welcome people with different ideas. They feared change in their lives. When they disapproved of someone's ideas, that person was punished.

Such a person was **Roger Williams.** He had unpopular ideas about the Puritan Church. He also thought that the Indians, not the king, should have power to grant land to the colonists. Williams's ideas angered the Puritan leaders. They voted to expel Williams from the Massachusetts Bay Colony.

Not allowed to stay in Massachusetts, Roger Williams fled south to Narragansett (nar•uh•GAN•suht) Bay. There he received food and protection from the Narragansett Indians. In 1636 he bought land from the Indians and founded the settlement of **Providence.** It later became part of a new colony called **Rhode Island.** People of all religions were welcome to settle there. In this colony the idea of freedom of religion grew.

A strong and spirited woman named **Anne Hutchinson** was also forced to leave the Massachusetts Bay Colony. This happened after she had begun to question the authority of the Puritan ministers. With her family and many followers, she founded a settlement at **Portsmouth,** Rhode Island, not far from Providence.

Thomas Hooker left Massachusetts too, but for another reason. He had looked with longing at the fertile lands of the Connecticut River valley. Hooker and his followers made the move in 1636. They left the rocky fields of the Massachusetts colony to start

Thomas Hooker led his followers to the fertile valley of the Connecticut River.

a settlement at **Hartford**. Later their settlement joined with others to form the colony of **Connecticut**.

Indian Wars

When settlers first moved into the Connecticut valley, the **Pequot** (PEE-kwaht) **Indians** attacked them. The Connecticut settlers, with help from Massachusetts settlers, struck back and soundly defeated the Pequots.

Meanwhile the English tried to keep peace with other Indians of New England by buying their land. But ownership of land meant different things to the English and the Indians. In the Indian view, no one could own the land. People could only use it. When Indians "sold" land, they thought they were sharing, not giving it up. The English, however, thought the Indians would leave the land after they had sold it.

The ill feelings between the English and the Indians broke out in an all-out war in 1675. This war was called **King Philip's War**. King Philip was the name the English gave to **Metacomet**, the leader of the Wampanoags and the son of Massasoit.

For both Indians and settlers, King Philip's War was bloody and cruel. By this time the Indians had become deadly shots with muskets. Indians attacked and destroyed many New England towns. The Indians were defeated only when the English destroyed their grain crops. Without food, they lost their will to fight. They were either killed or sold into slavery. Their lands were given to soldiers.

The Frontier

King Philip's War cleared New England of Indian resistance. Waves of settlers began pushing up the Connecticut River into the Berkshire Hills. Others moved north into the areas of present-day **Vermont, Maine,** and **New Hampshire.**

The **frontier** was moving westward. A frontier is the area that separates settled land and the wilderness. When the Pilgrims arrived in Plymouth, they were on a frontier. As more and more people carved settlements out of the wilderness, the frontier moved westward.

Settlers who left the coastal areas were looking for good farming land. They settled where they liked the land. They did not necessarily settle in villages. They were independent. With an ax, a knife, and a gun, frontier settlers could take care of most of their needs.

Yet it was usually not long before people organized themselves into communities. Laws and rules were needed to protect the rights of people. Militias were needed to defend the new settlements. Even while these new communities were being formed, other settlers were restlessly pushing the frontier westward.

Towns and Trade

As time passed, life in New England became more comfortable. Fewer people had to struggle to make a living. By 1770 the great-grandchildren of early settlers were living in bigger houses. Many could afford luxuries such as tea and cloth from England.

This prosperity was based on the success of fishers, boatbuilders, and traders. By 1700 many of the 12,000 people in Boston earned their living from the sea.

The town of **Nantucket** on Nantucket Island grew quickly in the 1700s because its sailors began catching great whales. Oil made from whale blubber was in great demand because it burned clear and bright. One lamp of burning whale oil gave as much light as three candles. A large whale might have 500 gallons of such oil.

Whaling ships left their home ports on sea voyages lasting up to five years. Whaling was very dangerous and difficult work. When a whale was killed,

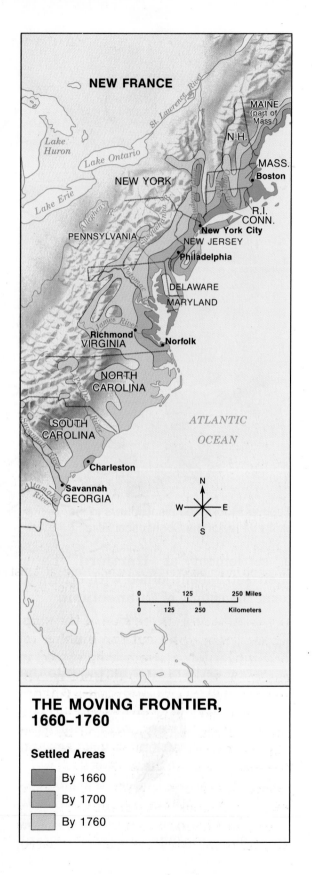

THE MOVING FRONTIER, 1660–1760

Settled Areas

- By 1660
- By 1700
- By 1760

Whaling could be dangerous work. Here, an artist shows an angry sperm whale attacking whalers by smashing their boat.

it was attached to the side of the ship. There the seamen cut the blubber off in chunks, which were then stored in casks. A whaling ship did not return to port until all its casks were filled.

Many New England fortunes were made in trade. Ships owned by New England merchants carried trade goods between the colonies and England. Goods leaving a country are called **exports.** Goods brought into a country are called **imports.** Exports from New England included cargoes of tobacco,

furs, lumber, and dried fish. The English expected their colonies to export raw products only to England or English colonies. The English also expected the colonists to buy all manufactured goods from England.

The independent colonists usually ignored this part of English law. Some started small factories where they made iron products and wove cloth. Others made a regular practice of smuggling items not made in England into the colonies.

Trading for Slaves

Some New England trading ships followed the **triangle trade route.** The triangle trade route was one of the most important English trade routes. It looked like a giant triangle on the Atlantic Ocean.

The triangle trade worked this way. Ships carried molasses from English colonies in the West Indies to ports like Boston, New Haven, and New York. In these ports the molasses was turned into rum. Ships then carried cargoes of rum and iron products to the coast of Africa. There ship captains sold their cargo and bought slaves. They then carried the slaves to the West Indies. In the West Indies they sold the slaves for molasses. In the American colonies they might buy rum again. At each point in the trade shipowners and merchants hoped to make a profit.

The trade in slaves was cruel. In 1764, for example, one Yankee captain in the triangle trade sold rum, candles, guns, and iron chains in Africa. With the money he received, the captain then bought 196 slaves. Before the ship reached the West Indies, 109 of those slaves had died. Some died before the voyage began. Some rebelled during the voyage and were shot. Many

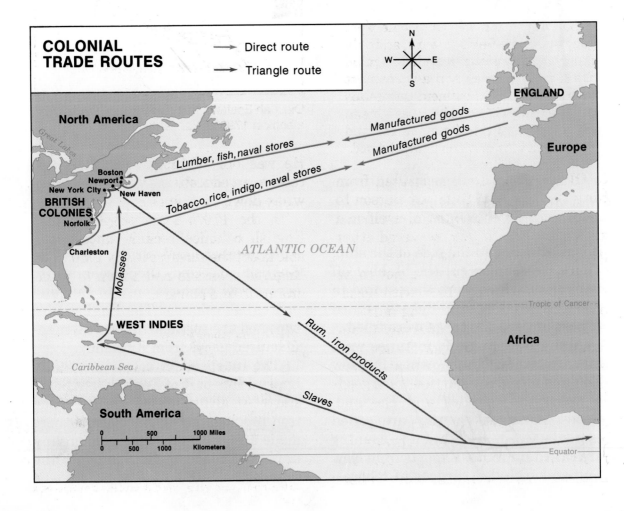

COLONIAL TRADE ROUTES

→ Direct route
→ Triangle route

North America

Great Lakes

Boston
Newport
New York City • • New Haven
BRITISH COLONIES
Norfolk

Charleston

Molasses

ATLANTIC OCEAN

WEST INDIES

Caribbean Sea

South America

Lumber, fish, naval stores

Manufactured goods

Manufactured goods

ENGLAND

Europe

Tobacco, rice, indigo, naval stores

Rum, iron products

Slaves

Tropic of Cancer

Africa

Equator

0   500   1000 Miles
0   500   1000   Kilometers

took their own lives by jumping overboard.

Millions of Africans were sold into slavery. Some had been slaves in Africa. Most had been born free. They had come from many different African cultures. Some were highly skilled as leaders, weavers, sculptors, metalsmiths, and storytellers. Most had been either kidnapped or captured in raids on villages.

Their voyage across the Atlantic in stinking, cramped quarters was part of a vast business. It was the business of providing workers for the new world.

Olaudah Equiano (OL•uh•dah eh•kwee•AH•noh) was 11 years old when he was kidnapped from his village. He described the event:

> One day, when all our people were gone out to the fields to work, and only I and my dear sister were left to mind the house, two men and a woman got over our walls. In a moment they seized us both, and without giving us time to cry out, they stopped our mouths and ran off with us into the nearest wood.

Olaudah was soon separated from his sister and sold from one person to another. In time he found himself on a slave ship. There he discovered other people who spoke his language.

"I asked them if I were not to be eaten by those white men with horrible looks, red faces, and long hair."

As the voyage got underway, Olaudah wished he were dead. He saw two men, chained together, jump overboard. He was whipped when he did not feel like eating. He heard the moans and cries of people suffering from disease, hardship, and homesickness.

At the end of the voyage, Olaudah Equiano was sold in the West Indies.

Olaudah Equiano, taken as a slave, wrote a book in 1793 about his life.

He was one of those rare slaves to receive an education. In later years he wrote down his life story.

In the 1700s some people in the English colonies became uncomfortable about the slave trade. By 1750 New England colonists had begun to form groups to end slavery.

 Reading Check

1. Why did Roger Williams and Anne Hutchinson leave Massachusetts?
2. What were the most important tools of the frontier settler?
3. Explain the triangle trade.

Think Beyond How did the growth of New England affect the Indians?

IN FOCUS

THE YANKEE WHALERS

"Thar she blows! Thar she blows!" cried the lookout perched in the crow's nest high atop the ship. This familiar shout meant that whales had been sighted. At this signal, the hardy sailors lowered a whale boat into the water. The six men aboard quietly rowed "wood to black skin," which meant that the boat was so close that it almost touched the whale.

Then one man with a harpoon, or spear, stood up and took aim. When the harpoon hit the whale, the whalers' job became dangerous. Because the harpoon was connected to the boat by a very long rope, the whales sometimes dragged the boats many miles at high speeds trying to

Whistles, decorative items, and spoons made from whalebone

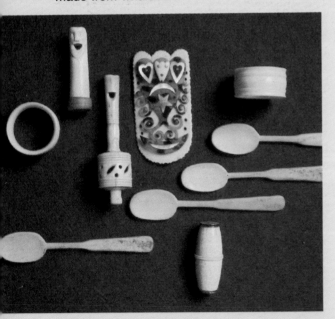

escape. The sailors called this adventure a "Nantucket sleigh ride." At other times, the whales would rise up out of the water and smash the whale boats.

For generations, these huge creatures, which sometimes weigh more than 100,000 pounds (45,351.5 kg) and can span 50 feet (15.2 m), provided a leading industry for New England. Nearly every part of the whale's body was used. Whale oil provided fuel for lamps in homes and on city streets and was used to lubricate machines. Whalebone was used in umbrellas, buggy whips, clothing, and hairbrushes. Whale meat was eaten.

New England whaling reached its peak during the 1800s. By the twentieth century, there was not as much demand for whale products. Petroleum oil replaced whale oil for fuel and lubrication. Electric lights soon made oil lamps unnecessary.

Whaling in New England dropped sharply for another important reason. The whalers had killed too many whales. Each year they had to travel farther and farther to find whales. Their voyages became increasingly difficult and expensive.

We know today that whales are not fish. Whales, like dolphins and porpoises, are highly intelligent mammals. Most nations now do not allow whaling because people do not want whales to become extinct.

Think Beyond What do you think happened to the economy of New England after the whale industry died?

SKILLS IN ACTION

READING BAR GRAPHS

A **graph** makes it easy to compare facts. A **bar graph** compares facts by using solid bars or lines to stand for numbers.

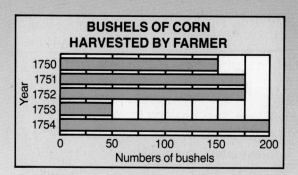

BUSHELS OF CORN HARVESTED BY FARMER

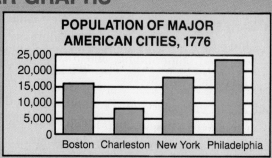

POPULATION OF MAJOR AMERICAN CITIES, 1776

This graph shows how many bushels of corn were harvested by one farmer during a five-year period. Each bar shows the number of bushels harvested in one year. Notice that the lines are labeled 0, 50, 100, and so on. The bar for the year 1753 ends at the line marked 50. This means that 50 bushels of corn were harvested by this farmer in 1753. The bar for 1750 extends to the line marked 150. What does this mean? How many bushels of corn did this farmer harvest in 1752? When did the farmer harvest the most corn?

Sometimes a graph can hint at important events. Find the shortest bar on the graph. This bar tells you that the number of bushels harvested in 1753 was very low. You can guess that something unusual happened that year. Perhaps the crops were ruined by bad weather or fire.

A bar graph is useful because it makes it easy to compare amounts. Yet it often does not give you exact figures. Sometimes you have to estimate actual numbers as you read a bar graph.

Sometimes a bar graph is to be read from bottom to top. The graph above compares the population of four major cities in the American colonies in 1776. The names of the cities are listed at the bottom of the graph. Population figures are listed on the side of the graph. The first line represents 5,000 people. How many people does the second line represent?

Find Boston. Follow the bar above it. The bar passes through the line marked 15,000 but does not reach the line marked 20,000. You can see that the end of the bar is closer to 15,000 than 20,000. From this you can estimate that the population of Boston in 1776 was about 16,000.

CHECKING YOUR SKILLS

Answer these questions.

1. What is a bar graph?

2. Does a bar graph always give exact numbers? Explain your answer.

3. About how many people were there in New York City in 1776?

4. Which city shown on the graph had the smallest population? What was it?

213

Thinking Back

- Early settlers made good use of New England's resources. Fishing and trading encouraged shipbuilding, and forests provided the naval stores.

- Life in colonial New England centered around the village. The minister was the most important person in the village.

- Town business was conducted at a town meeting, which was open to everyone. Each year men were elected to hold offices such as constable, drummer, and town crier.

- Roger Williams and Anne Hutchinson were forced to leave Massachusetts because their ideas differed from those of the Puritans. Both later founded their own towns.

- Thomas Hooker desired better farmland in the fertile Connecticut River Valley. He and his followers settled Hartford.

- Differing views on land ownership caused war between the Indians and settlers. The English won King Philip's War, and many Indians were killed or sold into slavery. The frontier then moved westward.

- Life in New England became more comfortable due to the success of fishers, boatbuilders, and traders.

- Some trading ships followed the important triangle trade route between New England, Africa, and the West Indies. Millions of Africans were sold into slavery and brought to the new world following this route.

Check for Understanding

Using Words

Number your paper from 1 to 10. Use the words below to complete the sentences that follow.

authority	imports
barter	meetinghouse
common	militia
exports	navigable
frontier	officials

1. Most rivers in New England were not _____ .

2. In town meetings New England settlers elected _____ to do necessary community jobs.

3. The center of a New England village was its _____ , or village green.

4. Puritan ministers had much _____ over early settlers.

5. The most important building in a New England village was the _____ .

6. The _____ was a group of volunteers organized to defend a settlement.

7. Most early settlers exchanged goods and services by using a system of _____ .

8. A _____ is an area between settled land and wilderness.

9. Goods that are sent from a country are called _____ .

10. Goods that are brought into a country are called _____ .

Reviewing Facts

1. How did colonists use New England's natural resources to make a living?
2. Give three examples that show the importance and authority of Puritan ministers in Massachusetts.
3. What did Roger Williams, Anne Hutchinson, and Thomas Hooker all have in common?
4. How did the English and the Indians differ about land ownership?
5. Why was the frontier always moving?

Thinking Critically

1. Early settlers had to work very hard just to meet their basic needs for food, shelter, and clothing. What kinds of skills did they need? How do these differ from the skills needed today to meet needs?
2. In what ways did the meetinghouse serve both religious needs and the needs of village government?
3. How was life for Puritan children different from life for modern-day children?

Writing About It

Write a story about the barter system. Characters in your story should include a blacksmith, a farmer, a shoemaker, or any other craftsperson. As you write dialogue for your characters, have them talk about the kinds of items they produce and the way they barter with each other to meet their needs.

Practicing Graph Skills

Reading Bar Graphs

Use the city population graph on page 213 to answer these questions.

1. Which had the greater population in 1776, New York or Boston?

2. Which city had a population of about 18,000?

On Your Own

Social Studies at Home

1. Look at the picture on page 202. Make a list of the items found in this kitchen that are not found in a modern-day kitchen. Then ask your family to help you make a list of things in your kitchen at home that are not shown in this picture. Which kitchen do you think requires more work? Explain.
2. The farmers of New England grew corn, rye, barley, wheat, pumpkins, and squash. They also raised cattle, hogs, and sheep. Using these foods, plan a sample dinner that would feed a large family.

Read More About It

The Courage of Sara Noble by Alice Dalgliesh. Scribner. This classic tale is the story of a girl who accompanies her father into untamed Connecticut territory to build a family homestead.

Fur Trappers and Traders: The Indians, the Pilgrims, and the Beaver by Beatrice Siegel. Walker. The historical impact of the fur trade is discussed in this book.

A New England Village by Eva Deutsch Costabel. Atheneum. This book describes homes and schools in a New England village.

The Sign of the Beaver by Elizabeth George Speare. Houghton Mifflin. This is a stirring tale about a boy left alone to hold his family's claim to land in Maine.

When Daylight Comes by Ellen Howard. Atheneum. This story helps us to better understand the slave trade and the suffering it caused.

CHAPTER 8

The Middle Colonies

"You have also to remove your shoes or you are not allowed to enter the ladies salon, or best decorated room, but it will be opened and you will be allowed to look in from the threshold. However limited their means, the linen must be fine and clean. Therefore the smith's workshops have been banished from Amsterdam, so that the smoke and soot should not begrime their fine roofs and gables."

—English traveler in New Amsterdam describing life in colonial New York

216

Reading for a Purpose

Look for these important words:

Key Words
- proprietor
- delegates

Places
- New York
- New Jersey
- Delaware

- Pennsylvania
- New York City
- Philadelphia

Look for answers to these questions:
1. How was the geography of the Middle colonies different from that of the New England colonies?
2. Why were the Middle colonies also called the breadbasket colonies?
3. How were the Middle colonies ruled?

1 The Breadbasket Colonies

The Middle colonies were **New York, New Jersey, Delaware,** and **Pennsylvania.** These colonies were all alike in an important way. Living in them were people from different countries and of different religions.

Large, navigable rivers flowed through each of these colonies. Near the mouths of these rivers great cities grew. **New York City** grew at the mouth of the Hudson River. The city of **Philadelphia** was founded near the mouth of the Delaware River.

The rivers flowed through plains and gently rolling hills. When the first white settlers arrived, most of the land was covered with deciduous hardwood trees. The land was good for farming. The soil was less rocky and more fertile than that of New England. The climate was better for growing crops. The summers were longer, and the amount of rain, 30 to 50 inches (76.2 to 127 cm) a year, was just right.

One farmer used poetry to describe his feelings about the land:

The fields, most beautiful, yield such crops of wheat,
And other things most excellent to eat. . . .

So much wheat was produced in the Middle colonies that they were called the "breadbasket colonies." Ships docked at the ports of Philadelphia and New York City to pick up cargoes of wheat flour. The wheat flour was carried to other colonies and to people across the sea.

As one followed the rivers west to the Appalachian Mountains, the rivers gradually ceased to become navigable at the waterfalls on the Fall Line. This made it difficult for settlers to get supplies or to ship products to markets. For many years people did not settle beyond the Fall Line because river transportation was not possible.

217

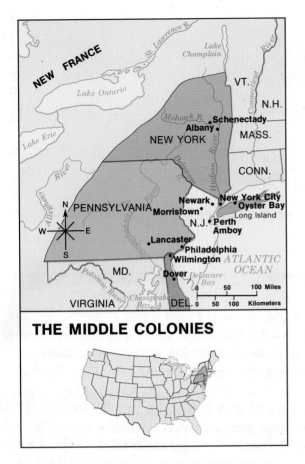

THE MIDDLE COLONIES

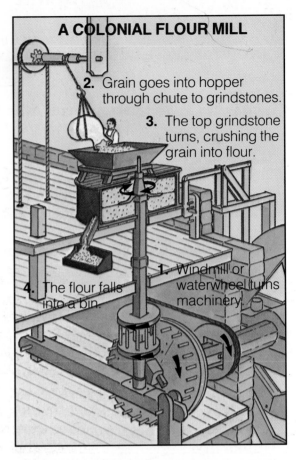

A COLONIAL FLOUR MILL

2. Grain goes into hopper through chute to grindstones.

3. The top grindstone turns, crushing the grain into flour.

1. Windmill or waterwheel turns machinery.

4. The flour falls into a bin.

However, as in New England, frontier settlers began to go into the hills and mountains. There they settled in small clearings, often far from towns.

Rule by Proprietors

Each one of the Middle colonies belonged to an owner who ruled the colony. Such an owner was called a **proprietor** (pruh•PRY•uht•uhr).

At first the proprietor could make all the laws. The proprietor of New York, the Duke of York, ruled as he wished. In 1664 he gave the province of New Jersey to two friends. They in turn became its proprietors. The New Jersey proprietors promised freedom of religion and a lawmaking assembly.

The king, however, had control over each proprietor. In time, King Charles

II of England limited the power of proprietors. The king said that all laws made by proprietors had to be approved by colonial assemblies. These assemblies were made up of **delegates,** people elected by colonists to represent them. In the assemblies the delegates learned valuable lessons in lawmaking and self-government.

Reading Check

1. Describe the geography of the Middle colonies.
2. Why did people usually settle below the Fall Line?
3. How did King Charles II encourage self-government?

Think Beyond How was a town with a town meeting governed differently than a town with a proprietor?

Reading for a Purpose

Look for these important words:

Key Words
- influence
- stoop

People
- Sarah Knight

Look for answers to these questions:
1. What was travel between Boston and New York City like in the early 1700s?
2. What was colonial New York City like?
3. How does our language reflect a Dutch heritage?

2 Colonial New York City

Today it is possible to travel by airplane from Boston to New York City in less than an hour. In colonial times the trip took much longer. By boat the journey from Boston to New York City took from 2 to 14 days, depending on the weather.

A journey by land was also long and often unpleasant. At that time the only way to travel on land was by horseback or on foot. Later, the trails through the forest were widened so that carriages could be used.

In October 1704, Madam **Sarah Knight** made a journey by horseback from Boston to New York City. Madam Knight faced many problems along the way. Of part of her trip she wrote:

The roads all along this way are very bad, with rocks and mountainous passages. After about eight miles riding, in going over a bridge under which the river ran very swift, my horse stumbled, and very narrowly escaped falling over into the water.

Not all rivers had bridges. Near Providence, Rhode Island, Sarah Knight and her guide came to a wide, swift river. She was afraid to ride her horse into it. A boy with a canoe was found to take her across while her horse swam. The canoe was very small and shallow. Sarah Knight held fast to each side, her eyes steady. She dared not even move her tongue for fear the canoe would tip.

There were few inns along the road. Sometimes it was necessary to travel late into the night before reaching an inn. At night the trail became a scary place. Madam Knight sometimes thought she saw an enemy in the dark shadow of a tree or bush.

When Madam Knight reached New York City, she noted that the city of New York was a "pleasant" place. It was located on a river with a "fine harbour for shipping." She found New York City different from Boston in many ways.

The Dutch had been the first European settlers of New York, but a mixture of people had soon settled there. In addition to the English who came, there were also free blacks, French, and

219

Jews. New York differed from Boston in part because of this mixture of peoples.

Sarah Knight noted that most people in New York City belonged to the Church of England. "They are not as strict in keeping the Sabbath as in Boston," she observed.

Dutch Influence

When Sarah Knight visited New York, the Dutch **influence** was still strong. *Influence* means the power of people or things to act on others. Dutch women, she noticed, wore earrings "with jewels of a large size and many in number." Their fingers were "hooped with rings, some with large stones of many colors." Women in Boston did not wear such fancy jewelry.

For winter entertainment the people of New York City rode sleighs to inns about three or four miles (4.8 or 6.5 km) out of town. When Madam Knight was taken on such a ride, she wrote, "I believe we met 50 or 60 sleighs that day—they fly with great swiftness and turn out of the path for none except a loaded cart."

The step-like roofs, the stoops, and the half-doors of these houses all show Dutch influence in colonial New York City.

Some skaters arrive by sleigh, while others warm themselves at a fire in this scene of New York City in about 1700.

Many Dutch houses were built using bricks of different colors. A Dutch house often had a **stoop,** which is a wide, high doorstep. On the stoop were benches where a family could sit on warm evenings. There the family members spent pleasant hours talking with each other and with neighbors passing by.

The door of a Dutch house also made it easy to be friendly to passersby. The door had two parts. The top part could be open while the bottom part stayed closed. A closed bottom door kept dogs and pigs from wandering into the house.

Pigs were common in colonial cities. People threw their garbage into the gutters. The wandering pigs were absolutely necessary to get rid of the garbage.

Today, the skyline of New York City is filled with huge skyscrapers. Even in the 1700s New York had an interesting skyline. Large windmills stood on top of the highest hills. The windmills provided power for grinding grain into flour.

Our language reflects the Dutch heritage of New York. Words that come from the Dutch are *boss, stoop, cookie, Santa Claus, sleigh,* and *waffle*.

Reading Check

1. Describe the roads Sarah Knight traveled from Boston to New York.
2. How did the design of Dutch houses encourage friendliness?
3. What did the people of New York use as a source of power to grind grain?

Think Beyond Sarah Knight believed New York was very different from Boston. Do you think that is true today? Explain.

221

In the "Legend of Sleepy Hollow" the Headless Horseman gallops wildly through a Dutch village in New York. In "Rip Van Winkle" a ne'er-do-well awakens after 20 years in a deep sleep. Both these tales from *The Sketchbook of Geoffrey Crayon, Gent.* are like snapshots that capture life in Dutch New York and hold it still for us to examine. Who was Geoffrey Crayon? You may know him better by another name—Washington Irving.

Irving created Rip Van Winkle and many other characters that have become standards of American folklore. He was the first American to write stories for children. The *Sketchbook* was the first modern collection of short stories.

Irving also wrote biographies of great Americans such as George Washington and history books about famous explorers and their trips. He wrote satires, too—stories that poke fun at people's customs and attitudes.

Irving was successful at a young age. At 19 he was a published author. At 23 he became a lawyer. He was also a businessman, working in his family's knife business.

When he was still in his 20s, Irving went to Europe. He traveled the continent, reading, studying, and attending the great theaters in England, Italy, and France. He also wrote many stories there. Some of the stories were translated into other languages, making him as famous in Europe as he was in America.

Today, many scholars say that American literature began with Washington Irving. His writing made readers curious about America and its people and proved that America was an interesting place in which to live.

Think Beyond Why do you think it was important for America to establish its own special literature?

Rip Van Winkle wakes up.

Look for these important words:

Key Words	• immigrants	**People**
• Quakers	• Conestoga wagon	• William Penn
• refuge	• Scotch-Irish	

Look for answers to these questions:
1. Who was William Penn?
2. What peoples settled in Pennsylvania? What were their reasons for settling there?
3. What things were German settlers known for?
4. How did relations between the Indians and Pennsylvania settlers change?

3 Pennsylvania

William Penn became the proprietor of Pennsylvania in 1681. The next year he planned out the town of Philadelphia. Philadelphia's name comes from Greek words meaning "brotherly love." Penn planned out the town so that it had the look of a checkerboard, with straight streets and squares. Philadelphia's location was excellent for shipping and trading. By 1760 it was the largest city in America.

William Penn belonged to a church group called the **Quakers.** The Quakers believed in simple and plain living. They believed that all people were equal and that all people were basically good. The Quakers refused to bear arms or to fight. They believed in the peaceful solution of problems.

For these ideas the Quakers were made to suffer, both in England and in New England. Any Quakers who came to New England were whipped and forced to leave. Some were hanged.

William Penn offered Pennsylvania as a **refuge,** a place of safety, for the Quakers. He also offered land and freedom of religion to any who settled in Pennsylvania.

The early Quakers in Pennsylvania lived simply. People were expected to dress plainly—no bright colors or satin cloth, no jewelry or silver buckles. Their homes were also plain. There was no silver or gold or fancy furniture.

Even their conversation was plain. Quakers frowned on chatter, gossip, or boasting. Dancing, music, and theater were all thought to be sinful. The Quakers agreed with the Puritans in at least one way. They thought that each moment should be spent in a useful task or in good thoughts.

The Quakers also showed great concern for the poor. Penn wrote that he expected the town meetings "to supply the wants of the poor." Further, they were to care for "widows and orphans and such as are helpless." Quakers very early decided that slavery was evil. They freed their slaves and opposed slavery.

The Pennsylvania Germans became famous for the way they decorated everyday objects with pictures of flowers, birds, and animals.

Pennsylvania Germans

Pennsylvania became a refuge not only for the Quakers but also for other groups. These new settlers were **immigrants.** Immigrants are people who come from one country to live in another country.

Among the immigrants were many German-speaking people seeking religious freedom and a better life. The first Germans in Pennsylvania wrote back enthusiastic letters. "If a workman will only work four or five days in a week, he can live grandly," one wrote.

The Germans who came to Pennsylvania included both farmers and skilled workers. Among the skilled workers were bakers, masons, carpenters, shoemakers, tailors, butchers, coopers, millers, and blacksmiths. They often set up craft shops in towns where they engaged in their crafts.

The Germans were great lovers of music. They often made musical instruments such as organs and pianos. At any German gathering there was likely to be music. There were also likely to be quantities of food. German foods included sauerkraut, sausage, doughnuts, gingerbread, and apple pies.

German gunmakers developed the excellent, long-barrel rifle called the Pennsylvania rifle. In the 1700s it was the most accurate rifle in the world. It was particularly valued on the frontier. Because famous frontiersmen from Kentucky used the rifle, it later became known as the Kentucky rifle.

The excellent and hardworking German farmers built great barns to shelter livestock in winter. These barns, or barns like them, are still found in Pennsylvania.

The German houses were often built over a cellar, or earth basement. In the cellar was a spring or well for water. The earth walls and water helped keep the cellar cool for storing food. Fruit, cheese, milk, and butter could be found there.

The farmers had to figure out how to get their crops and livestock to market. To deal with this problem, the **Conestoga wagon** was invented. This wagon was well suited for carrying heavy freight over bad roads. Pulled by teams of four or six horses, it could carry loads as heavy as 6 tons (5.4 T). The wagon's wheels were wide, which usually kept them from sinking into the mud. A curved floor in the wagon kept the wagon's contents from moving about. A white canvas cover protected the freight from bad weather.

The wagons were painted blue. The horses often wore bows made of bells. Farmers were proud to drive these grand and beautiful wagons.

The Scotch-Irish

Scotch-Irish settlers also came to Pennsylvania. These were people from Scotland who had settled in northern Ireland in the 1600s. Many of them and their descendants had then come to America. Like other immigrants, they were looking for religious freedom and opportunities to make a living. They entered the country through the port of Philadelphia. Then they fanned out into the hilly frontiers of the Appalachians from Pennsylvania to Georgia. The Scotch-Irish were among the first to settle beyond the Fall Line. They

Pennsylvania farmers carried their goods to market in Conestoga wagons. Here, they stop for a rest and a chance to exchange news.

This painting shows William Penn and the Delaware Indians making a peace agreement in 1681. Penn never broke the treaty, but others did.

lived in small clearings, making a living as best they could from farming and hunting.

Relations with Indians

William Penn tried to be very fair in his dealings with the Indians. The Indians respected Penn and looked on him as a friend. "Let them have justice, and you win them," he said.

Despite this early friendship, the pattern of the other colonies repeated itself in Pennsylvania. As the number of settlers increased, the settlers took lands from the Indians. The Scotch-Irish, in particular, were known as "hard neighbors to the Indians." They paid no attention to the agreements the Quakers had made with the Indians.

When the Indians reacted by attacking frontier settlements, the settlers demanded military protection and help. The Quakers, most of whom did not live on the frontier, insisted on peaceful behavior. They refused to provide military help. The settlers on the western frontier then felt great bitterness toward the city Quakers.

Reading Check

1. Why did Philadelphia become an important city?
2. Why was the Conestoga wagon developed?
3. Why did bitterness develop toward the Quakers?

Think Beyond Would you have enjoyed living as a Quaker? Explain.

Reading for a Purpose

Look for these important words:

Key Words • lightning rod   **People**
• apprentice   • Benjamin Franklin

Look for answers to these questions:
1. How did Benjamin Franklin learn to be a printer?
2. Why was Franklin the most important citizen of Philadelphia?
3. What contributions did Franklin make to science?

Benjamin Franklin

Benjamin Franklin was the most important citizen of colonial Philadelphia. Franklin was born in Boston, the fifteenth of 17 children. His father was a candlemaker. One of his earliest teachers was Sarah Knight, the lady who went on horseback from Boston to New York.

Benjamin Franklin was always curious and eager to try out new ideas. One hot day when he was a boy, he was flying a kite from the edge of a pond. He tied the kite down so he could go for a swim. Then he decided to try swimming and flying a kite at the same time.

He lay on his back in the water and held on to the kite string. "I began to cross the pond with my kite, which carried me quite over without the least fatigue, and with the greatest pleasure," he wrote.

Franklin Becomes a Printer

Young Franklin showed great interest in reading and books. Because of this, his father had Benjamin's older brother, a printer, take him as an **apprentice** (uh•PREHNT•uhs). An apprentice worked a certain number of years for a person skilled in a craft. An apprentice lived with the skilled worker's family while he practiced and learned the craft.

The apprentice system was the most common way for boys to learn skills. Girls usually learned skills from their mothers. Sometimes girls worked in households as indentured servants.

Franklin was 12 years old when he became an apprentice. As a printer's apprentice, the young Franklin learned how to set type, or put together the letters for the press. He also learned to work the press, which pressed paper onto the type and printed it. In his spare time Franklin read books and worked at improving his own writing.

Benjamin Franklin did not get along well with his older brother. In 1723, when he was 17 years old, he ran away. He sold his books to buy passage on a boat from Boston to New York. When he arrived in New York, Franklin went to a printer to get work. The printer had no work for him, and he suggested that Franklin go to Philadelphia.

Franklin made his way by boat and on foot to Philadelphia. Hungry, tired, and poor, he finally arrived. The first thing he did was ask at a bakery for 3 pence worth of bread. He was given three large loaves, much more than he expected. He ate one and gave the other two to a woman and her child who had been on the boat with him. Then he found work as a printer.

Citizen and Inventor

Franklin did very well as a printer. Yet he said that he would rather live a useful life than die rich. When he could, he worked as a citizen, a scientist, and an inventor.

As a citizen, Franklin left a strong mark on the growing city of Philadelphia. He organized the first trained fire department. He worked to establish the first public library and the first hospital in Philadelphia. He organized a militia to protect Philadelphia and the frontier settlements.

As a scientist, Franklin is most famous for his experiments in electricity. Using the kite of his childhood, he proved that lightning is electricity. A result of his experiments was his invention of the **lightning rod.** A lightning rod is a rod of metal attached to the top of a house, barn, or boat. It conducts lightning bolts into the ground. Until the invention of the lightning rod, buildings or boats struck by lightning were likely to burst into flames.

Franklin's mind was always looking for a better way to do things. Unhappy with smoky fireplaces, he

In Philadelphia Benjamin Franklin oversees the latest printing to come off his press.

invented an iron stove. This stove, called the Franklin stove, threw heat, but no smoke, into a room. This type of stove is still in use.

Benjamin Franklin would be famous if he had done no more. However, some of his most important work was still to come. As a statesman, he would help his country become an independent and respected nation.

Reading Check

1. What is an apprentice?
2. Why was Franklin important to Philadelphia?
3. Name two of Franklin's inventions.

Think Beyond What did Franklin mean when he said that he would rather live a useful life than die rich?

IN FOCUS

THE FIRST FIRE DEPARTMENT

Colonists who lived in the growing cities were free of many of the dangers and hardships of the frontier. But one kind of danger was still present—fire.

In the cities of colonial America, houses were built very close together. Homes were heated by fires fueled with wood and coal. Homes and city streets were lighted by lamps that burned oil. Because of these conditions, houses and buildings were easily set on fire. When fires did occur, they could spread quickly and were difficult to put out.

Colonists knew that something had to be done. One of those colonists was Benjamin Franklin. As a child, Franklin remembered watching as a huge fire ran wild in Boston. He saw the panic on the faces of his parents and their friends. As an adult, Franklin watched in fear as a great fire nearly destroyed Philadelphia. Franklin set his keen mind on solving the problem of fighting fires.

Franklin used his job as a printer and writer to publish articles about preventing fires in the home. Then, in 1736, Franklin joined with other Philadelphians to organize America's first fully trained volunteer fire department. It was called the Union Fire Company. Its men were trained to respond to fire alarms quickly and to put out fires. The men also learned ways to rescue people who were trapped in burning buildings. Soon other cities copied Franklin's idea and began forming their own fire departments.

Think Beyond   Do you think fire is as big a threat to cities today as it was in colonial times? Why or why not?

A colonial fire brigade (side)
Benjamin Franklin (bottom)

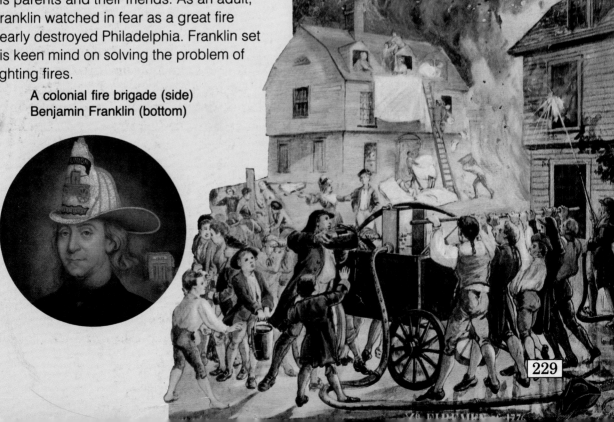

229

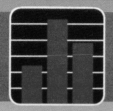

SKILLS IN ACTION

READING PICTURE, CIRCLE, AND LINE GRAPHS

You have learned that graphs are a way of comparing amounts. Many kinds of graphs exist. In addition to bar graphs, there are picture, circle, and line graphs.

Picture graphs use symbols to stand for numbers. The graph below compares the population of the four Middle colonies in 1760. Each symbol stands for 10,000 people. Half of a symbol stands for about 5,000 people. Three complete symbols are shown for Delaware. To find the population represented by these figures, you must multiply 10,000 by 3. The answer is 30,000. How many symbols are shown for New Jersey? What was the population of New Jersey in 1760?

Reading Circle Graphs

A **circle graph** shows parts of a whole. For example, in a flock of 10 chickens, 8 chickens lay eggs and 2 chickens do not. A circle graph shows this fact in this way:

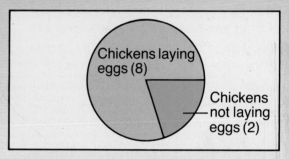

The circle graph below shows how the population of Pennsylvania could be divided up in 1760.

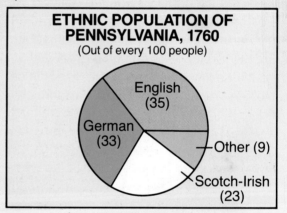

ETHNIC POPULATION OF PENNSYLVANIA, 1760
(Out of every 100 people)

- English (35)
- German (33)
- Other (9)
- Scotch-Irish (23)

The circle represents 100 people in Pennsylvania in 1760. Of every 100 people, 33 were of German origin and 35 were of English origin. The Germans and the English made up the largest part of Pennsylvania's population. Find the next largest section of the circle. What group is that? How many of every 100 people in Pennsylvania were Scotch-Irish?

POPULATION OF THE MIDDLE COLONIES, 1760

New York	𝗫 𝗫 𝗫 𝗫 𝗫 𝗫 𝗫 𝗫 𝗫 𝗫 𝗫
New Jersey	𝗫 𝗫 𝗫 𝗫 𝗫 𝗫 𝗫 𝗫 𝗫 𝗫 𝗫
Delaware	𝗫 𝗫 𝗫
Pennsylvania	𝗫 𝗫 𝗫 𝗫 𝗫 𝗫 𝗫 𝗫 𝗫 𝗫 𝗫 𝗫 𝗫 𝗫 𝗫 𝗫

𝗫 = 10,000 people

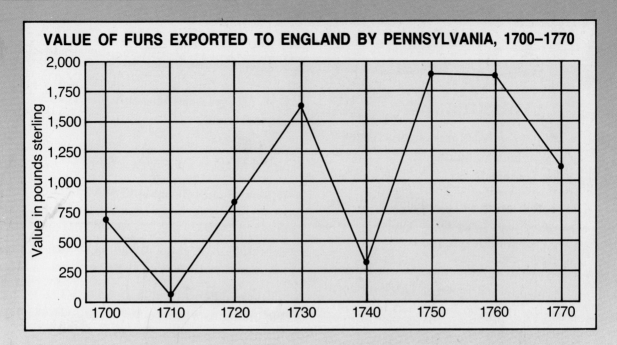

VALUE OF FURS EXPORTED TO ENGLAND BY PENNSYLVANIA, 1700–1770

Reading a Line Graph

A **line graph** shows change. The graph above shows the value of furs exported to England by Pennsylvania from 1700 to 1770. On the left side of the graph are numbers. These numbers represent the value of the furs in English money called pounds sterling.

Across the bottom of the chart are dates. Years shown here are 10 years apart. Find the year 1720. Trace the line up until you reach the dot. Then move your finger across to the number beside it. You can see that in 1720 the value of furs was about 850 pounds sterling. Now find the year 1730. Move your finger up the line until you come to the dot. What was the value of furs in that year?

Find the highest point on the graph. What year is it?

The lines that connect the dots are there to help you see a pattern in the dots. You can see that the dots drop in 1710 and then rise until 1730. In 1730 they begin to fall, before rising again to values higher than before. These up and down patterns are called **trends.**

The overall trend in the value of Pennsylvania exports was an increase. However, between 1700 and 1770, there were bad years for fur exports. A historian would look at these figures and try to find out what they meant. Perhaps the overall increase was due to an increase in the number of people hunting and trading. What might have happened to cause the sudden drops in exports?

CHECKING YOUR SKILLS

Answer the following questions. Use the information in this skill lesson to help you.

1. What kind of graph makes it easy to see parts of a whole?

2. What kind of graph uses symbols to stand for numbers of things?

3. What kind of graph shows change?

4. What kind of graph could you use to show the trend of your grades on spelling tests between September and January?

Thinking Back

- The Middle colonies grew so much wheat that they became known as the "breadbasket colonies."

- Navigable rivers and good harbors led to the growth of large cities such as New York City and Philadelphia.

- Each of the Middle colonies was owned and ruled by a proprietor. Later, all laws made by the proprietors had to be approved by assemblies.

- Travel between the colonies was very difficult. Journeys were often long and unpleasant.

- New York City differed from Boston. All of Boston's settlers were Puritans. New York, however, had a mixture of religions and nationalities.

- Colonial New York was strongly influenced by the early Dutch settlers.

- William Penn offered land and freedom of religion to anyone who settled in Pennsylvania. Many Quakers, Germans, and Scotch-Irish seeking religious freedom and a better life settled there.

- Settlers in Pennsylvania took lands from the Indians, who reacted by attacking frontier settlements. The settlers felt bitter because the Quakers would not provide military aid against the Indians.

- Benjamin Franklin was the most important citizen of Philadelphia. He also helped his country become independent.

Check for Understanding

Using Words

Explain the meaning of each term below. Then use each in a complete sentence.

1. apprentice
2. delegate
3. immigrants
4. influence
5. lightning rod
6. proprietor

Reviewing Facts

1. How did the geography of the Middle colonies encourage the development of agriculture and trading?

2. Why was shipping the most common way to transport people and goods?

3. How did Dutch influence show in the style of building, the recreation, and the language of New York City?

4. Who founded Philadelphia? Why?

5. How did King Charles II put controls on the authority of the proprietor? What was the result?

6. What groups of people made their home in Pennsylvania?

7. Would each of the following more likely be found among the Dutch, Quaker, or Pennsylvania German settlers?
   a. sleigh rides
   b. stoops
   c. windmills

d. plain furniture

e. organs and pianos

f. Conestoga wagon

g. gingerbread

h. waffles

8. What examples can you give that show Benjamin Franklin's willingness to try new ideas?

Thinking Critically

1. The Middle colonies were settled by a mixture of people from different countries. What were some of the contributions those groups made? How do our lives today show our heritage from people of many countries?

2. When people face new challenges, they often come up with new ideas and inventions. What examples of this idea are in this chapter? Can you think of some other examples?

3. Benjamin Franklin was famous for his curiosity and eagerness to try new ideas. How was this shown when he was young? What other qualities does a successful scientist and inventor need?

Writing About It

Write an article for the Philadelphia newspaper that describes Benjamin Franklin's latest invention—the lightning rod. Explain how Franklin came to invent the lightning rod, how it is to be used, and how it will help improve life.

Practicing Graph Skills

Reading Picture and Circle Graphs

1. Picture Graphs Make a picture graph showing the number of ships leaving co-lonial harbors in the 1750s. Use this information: Boston, 600 ships; New York City, 500 ships; Philadelphia, 650 ships; Charleston, 400 ships.

2. Circle Graphs During colonial times hundreds of ships left harbors each year. Draw a circle to represent 100 of those ships. Then make a circle graph showing where the ships went. Use the following numbers: Europe, 25; Caribbean, 25; American colonies, 50.

On Your Own

Social Studies at Home

1. Make a facts booklet that lists ten facts about the Pennsylvania Germans that you learned in this chapter. Illustrate your booklet.

2. Make up a game by writing down riddles taken from facts in this chapter. For instance, you might ask, "My name means 'brotherly love.' What am I?" When you have finished writing your riddles, ask your family to play the game with you.

Read More About It

Night Journeys by Avi. Pantheon Books. A Quaker family's involvement in the escape of indentured servants propels this story, set in eighteenth-century Pennsylvania.

The Tavern at the Ferry by Edwin Tunis. T. Y. Crowell. Through Henry Baker, a Delaware Valley tavern owner, the author gives a social history of the 100 years preceding the Revolutionary War.

What's the Big Idea, Ben Franklin? by Jean Fritz. Coward. This book provides a humorous look at Benjamin Franklin's life.

CHAPTER 9

The Southern Colonies

"All of Maryland that we have seen, is high land, with few or no meadows, but possessing such a rich and fertile soil, as persons living there assured me that they had raised tobacco off the same piece of land for thirty consecutive years. The inhabitants, who are generally English, are most engaged in this production."

—a visitor to Maryland, 1679

Look for these important words:

Key Words
- indigo
- cash crops
- tidewater

People
- George Calvert
- Lord Baltimore
- James Oglethorpe

Places
- Maryland

- Virginia
- North Carolina
- South Carolina
- Georgia
- Charleston
- Albemarle Sound
- Savannah

Look for answers to these questions:
1. How did people in the South use the natural resources of the land?
2. Why was the colony of Maryland settled?
3. Why was Carolina founded? Why did it split into two parts?
4. Why was Georgia founded?

Settlement of the South

In the 1700s the Southern colonies included **Maryland, Virginia, North Carolina, South Carolina,** and **Georgia.** The soil and climate of the Southern colonies were excellent for crops like tobacco, rice, and **indigo** (IN•di•goh). Indigo is a plant that produces a blue dye. Colonial landowners in the South usually grew one of these **cash crops.** Cash crops are crops that people grow in order to sell and make a profit. Cash crops were the most important part of the Southern economy.

Tobacco grew best in the rich soil of the Chesapeake Bay **tidewater.** A tidewater is a low coastal plain full of waterways. These waterways made it easy for boats to get the tobacco to market in England. Tobacco and other cash crops from the Southern colonies sold for very high prices in English markets.

In South Carolina and Georgia many navigable rivers flow through the Coastal Plain. Along these rivers were both fertile land and swamps. Rice grew well in the swamplands.

The Coastal Plain rises gradually until it meets the Piedmont. Here the land was covered with forests of pine and hardwoods. Settlers in the Piedmont raised tobacco, cotton, wheat, and corn.

Founding of Maryland

In 1632 the king of England gave a large piece of Virginia to his friend **George Calvert.** Calvert was a Roman Catholic. Catholics could not worship as they chose in England. Because of this, Calvert intended his colony to be a place where Catholics could settle in safety and freedom.

In this portrait Lord Baltimore hands a map of Maryland to his young son.

After Calvert's death, his dream was carried out by his son, **Lord Baltimore**. He named the new colony Maryland. As proprietor, Lord Baltimore had complete control over the laws in Maryland. In 1649 the Maryland assembly approved his suggestion that Maryland provide religious freedom to all Christians.

The Maryland colony was first centered at St. Mary's City. It was located not far from the mouth of the Potomac River. The colony at St. Mary's City had learned from the experiences of other colonies. The colonists knew no period of starvation and fought no Indian wars. Jamestown was nearby in case the new colony needed supplies or help.

Nature smiled on the settlers at St. Mary's City. One of the first colonists there wrote:

The soil appears particularly fertile, and strawberries, vines, sassafras, hickory nuts, and walnuts, we tread upon every where, in the thickest woods. There is an infinite number of birds of various colors, as eagles, herons, swans, geese, and partridges.

The mild climate, rich soil, and good river system helped the settlers to prosper. Lord Baltimore granted some people large pieces of land. However, most settlers who came to Maryland were indentured servants. Of these, most were men between the ages of 18 and 22.

The indentured servants in Maryland did better than those in other colonies. When their terms were finished, they were helped to start their own farms. Each was given 50 acres (20.2 ha) of land, a suit of clothes, an ax, two hoes, and three barrels of corn.

The Carolinas

By the end of the 1600s Virginia had neighbors to the south. These were the colonies of North Carolina and South Carolina.

North Carolina and South Carolina were each part of an original grant called Carolina. King Charles II of England had given Carolina to eight men. They hoped to gain wealth through the settlement and development of Carolina. Their idea was to raise silkworms, olives, and wine grapes.

The Carolina proprietors sent three ships from England in 1669. Only one of these ships reached the Carolina coast. Its captain sailed along the coast looking for a suitable place for a settlement. He considered Port Royal but decided that it was too close to the Spanish. The Spanish controlled Florida from their port at St. Augustine.

An Indian whom the English met at Port Royal had a suggestion. He described a wonderful place farther north. Excited, the captain, with the Indian on board, sailed to this place.

There he found a good harbor fed by two rivers. It was a good place to settle. Spanish ships would not be able to see the harbor from the sea. It would be easy to protect. On land between the rivers he established the new settlement. It was named Charles Towne in honor of the king.

Today we call Charles Towne **Charleston,** South Carolina. At first the settlement survived by trading with the Indians for furs and deerskins. Deerskin was valued in Europe for gloves. The early settlers also raised livestock and made barrel parts from timber. It was not long before Charleston became an important trading and agricultural center.

Other settlements in Carolina were in the area of **Albemarle Sound.** These settlements were a long way from the settlement at Charleston. Because of this, the proprietors divided Carolina into two parts: South Carolina and North Carolina. Most of North Carolina was hillier than the Chesapeake Bay tidelands and the flatlands of South Carolina. It did not attract large landholders because it was not as fertile. Most of North Carolina became a land of small farms.

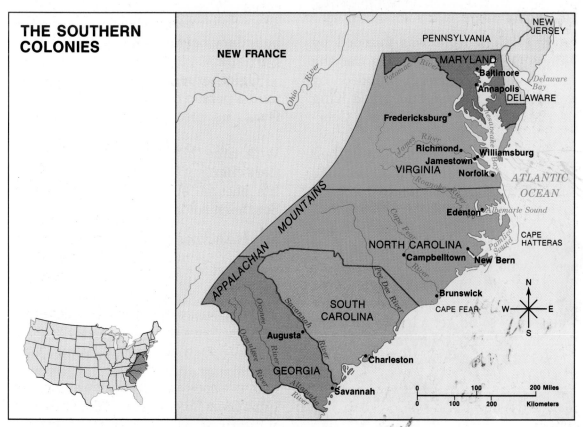

THE SOUTHERN COLONIES

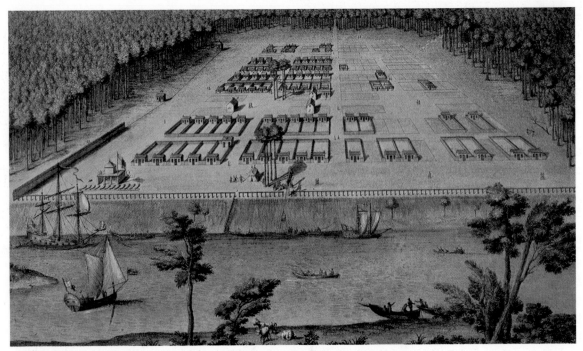

James Oglethorpe laid out a city plan for Savannah, Georgia. The plan called for straight streets and square blocks. The houses were spaced widely apart to guard against the spread of fires.

Georgia

In 1733 Georgia was founded by **James Oglethorpe.** Georgia was the last American colony founded by England. Oglethorpe had urged King George II to approve a colony in Georgia. Oglethorpe hoped an English colony in Georgia would strengthen England's claim to the land. At the time Spain, France, and England all claimed Georgia.

Oglethorpe also hoped to help the poor people of England. In England people who could not pay their debts could be put in prison. Oglethorpe thought that such people needed a place where they could get a fresh start. For that, he looked to Georgia.

In 1733 Oglethorpe and a group of 114 settlers established the new colony at **Savannah,** which was located at the mouth of the Savannah River.

The Savannah River formed the boundary between Georgia and South Carolina.

Oglethorpe limited the amount of land a person could own. To avoid conflicts, he also forbade trading with Indians. Finally, he forbade slavery. With time, however, the Georgia settlers changed these laws. Their way of life became similar to that in other Southern colonies.

 Reading Check

1. What is a cash crop?
2. Why was the site chosen for Charleston a good place to settle?
3. What were Oglethorpe's reasons for starting a colony in Georgia?

Think Beyond Do you think you could start a 50-acre farm with just one ax, two hoes, and three barrels of corn? Why or why not?

Look for these important words:

Key Words
- plantation
- planters
- broker

- public service
- society

People
- William Byrd II

Places
- Annapolis
- Williamsburg
- Richmond
- Baltimore

Look for answers to these questions:
1. What was a plantation?
2. How did the plantation economy work?
3. Why did towns grow slowly in the tidewater region?

2 *The World of the Planter*

In colonial times the English called any farm a plantation. In later times **plantation** came to mean a Southern farm, particularly a large farm. The people who owned these farms were called **planters.**

In the tidewater areas of Virginia and Maryland a plantation was usually located in a clearing along a waterway. The main building was the planter's house, but there were many other buildings as well. Some were cottages for servants or slaves. Others were used for food storage and for cooking. There were sheds for drying and storing tobacco. There were barns for livestock. There was a henhouse. Each plantation had a private landing wharf. This allowed boats to dock right at the plantation and to load tobacco.

Surrounding the buildings of the plantation were a vegetable garden, a corn plot, and an orchard. The tobacco fields were farther away. The planters grew or made what they could. Other things they imported from England.

Money was rarely used in the plantation economy. Tobacco was used instead. Ship peddlers from England would travel up the waterways selling English goods. Imagine the delight of the household when the peddlers showed up. Shoes, pretty lace, colorful thread, iron pans, iron hoes, china dishes—all these tempted the planter's household. The planters bartered tobacco for the things the family chose.

Large planters arranged to sell tobacco through a London **broker.** A broker is a person who gets paid to buy and sell for someone else. Planters sent their tobacco to England with a shopping list of what they wanted for the next year. The list might include carriages, books, and hoes.

The broker in London sold the tobacco, bought what the planter wanted, and sent it back. Sometimes a planter did not make enough money to pay for all the things he wanted. As a result, many planters were often in debt to their English brokers.

Barn

Cattle pen

Slave cabins

Brick making

Blacksmith

Smokehouse

Stable

Storage

Vegetable garden

Carpenter

Spinning and weaving shed

Office

Laundry

Main house

Kitchen

Tobacco field

Tobacco barn

Dock

A SOUTHERN PLANTATION

Towns in the Tidewater

Towns and cities in the tidewater areas grew slowly. Early towns, including **Annapolis,** Maryland, and **Williamsburg,** Virginia, remained small. In New England and the Middle colonies, towns grew where there were good harbors. Towns were a necessary part of trading activities. But in the tidewater areas, goods could be bought and sold from the plantation docks. Towns were not necessary for the planters to buy and sell.

Planters were always having to clear new land to raise tobacco. Tobacco used up the soil in about four years. As land wore out near the coast, planters began to move up the rivers to higher land.

In time important towns grew at the Fall Line. They included **Richmond,** Virginia, and **Baltimore,** Maryland. Farmers who lived above the Fall Line brought their crops to these towns. There the crops were sold and shipped down the river to other markets.

Life on a Plantation

Plantations were often far from each other. Therefore, company was always welcome. When guests came, the men might amuse themselves racing horses. Dancing and card games were favorite pastimes of both men and women.

There were few schools. People lived too far apart. Some plantations had their own small schools for teaching basic reading and writing. Planters often hired teachers from Scotland for their children. When they were about 12 or 13 years old, the young people might attend special town schools. Later students might go to England in order to complete their schooling.

Southern planters were among the best-educated people in the colonies.

Most planters and their families belonged to the Church of England. This was true even in Maryland. To attend church, the family might have to travel an hour by horseback or carriage. Church of England ministers did not have the authority they did in New England. In Southern society planters were more important than ministers. Unlike the Puritans, the members of the Church of England celebrated Christmas. It was the most important holiday in the South.

Plantation Duties

Although slaves did most of the hard work, a planter had important responsibilities. A planter had to see that the crops were planted and harvested. Once the tobacco was harvested, it had to be hung correctly to dry. The planter then had to make arrangements to ship the tobacco to England. He had to keep careful records.

A planter was also responsible for taking care of all those on his plantation. Often the planter or his wife acted as a doctor. Both gave medicines and nursed the sick.

A planter's duties also included **public service.** Public service is doing a job to help the community or **society** as a whole. *Society* means a broad grouping of people who are bound by common laws, traditions, and activities. Public service for a planter could mean serving as a judge or as a representative to the assembly. Some planters served as advisers to the governor, and some did all these things. This tradition of public service may

William Byrd was a Virginia planter who left a diary describing his everyday life.

As part of his public service, William Byrd sat here, in the House of Burgesses.

explain why many planters were leaders in the American colonies.

One of the most famous of early Virginia planters was **William Byrd II.** We know much about him because he kept a diary. Byrd had learned law in England and business methods in Holland. Like many Southern planters, he had a lifelong interest in learning.

Life was often difficult on the plantation. Byrd's diary is full of reports of sickness and death. Sometimes Byrd had servants whipped for lying or for "a hundred faults." Sometimes he heard that the boats carrying his tobacco to London had sunk at sea. His neighbors gave him problems. He wrote:

> In the evening I took a walk about the plantation and found that some of my good neighbors had dug down the bank of my ditch to let their hogs into my pasture, for which I was out of humor.

A planter's wife needed the same skills as other colonial women. She needed to know how to spin and weave, make clothes, and preserve and cook food. Although she did not do all these tasks herself, she had to see that they were done. Her large household—family, servants, and slaves—sometimes numbered in the hundreds. She had to see that all these people had food, clothing, and medical care.

Reading Check

1. What was used for money in the plantation economy?
2. What is a broker?
3. Why did towns at the Fall Line become important?

Think Beyond Why was public service work done by the planters?

CANDLEMAKING

Imagine for a moment that everyone had to make his or her light bulbs. It was almost like that in colonial America, because most people lit their homes with something they made themselves—a candle.

When the first settlers came to America, they used knots of pine wood soaked in resin to light their homes. The pine knots, however, made the rooms too smoky, and people decided that candles would be better. In towns and cities, people could buy candles from a *chandler,* or candlemaker. In rural areas, however, people had to make their own candles.

Candles were made in three steps: braiding the wick, cooking the wax, and dipping or molding the candles.

The strings for the wick were made of cotton or linen and had to be braided in a special way so they would not curl or fall over as they burned. The braided wick was soaked in salt solution and then dried. The salt hardened the wick and made it burn more slowly, so the candle would last longer.

Next, the wax for the candle was made. Candle wax could be made from several ingredients, such as beeswax, bayberries, whale oil, or animal fat called tallow. Most early colonists used tallow, which they cooked in large pots until it was hot and smooth.

The candlemaker tied the wick to a stick, known as a *dipping spindle.* When the tallow was hot enough, the candlemaker dipped the wick into the hot fat. The wick was pulled out, allowed to cool, and dipped over and over again until the candle was the right size. Sometimes, candles were made by pouring the tallow into wooden molds.

Candle-making methods have not changed much since colonial times, except that today's candlemakers use wax made from petroleum instead of tallow. Few people make candles at home anymore, but the candles we buy today are made in the same way the colonists made them 200 years ago.

Think Beyond   Why do you think candles are still popular today even though we have electric lights?

Getting ready to dip the candles

SKILLS IN ACTION

EVALUATING INFORMATION

We get information from many sources. These sources may include television, radio, books, newspapers, and magazines. When we first hear or read information, we must **evaluate** it. To evaluate information means to decide how much of the information is true and whether or not we can trust the information.

The first thing to do when evaluating information is to determine if the statement is a **fact.** A fact is a statement that can be proved true. Dates in history, important events, and numbers are examples of facts. You can look in encyclopedias, almanacs, history books, or other references to see if a fact is true.

Look at the table below. This table lists some of William Byrd's property in 1746. Consider the statement, "William Byrd owned horses, sheep, and goats." Since the table lists 24 mares, 1 colt, 239 sheep, and 15 goats as among Byrd's property, you can prove the statement is true.

William Byrd's Livestock, 1746			
Cattle	**Horses**	**Sheep**	**Goats**
Steers 119 Cows 251 Calves 92	Mares 24 Colts 1	239	15

The following letter is based on an actual letter William Byrd wrote to a friend in England. Byrd had just brought his new wife from England to Virginia for the first time. Look for the facts in the letter. One example of a fact is the date it was written. Another example is that the wind had broken the topmast of the ship.

Virginia, the 5th of July, 1726
My Lord,
Soon after my arrival I wrote to your Lordship that we had happily escaped all the dangers of the sea, and were safely landed at my own house. There was nothing frightful in the whole voyage but a sudden puff of wind that carried away our topmast, which in the falling gave a very loud crack.

The beautiful bloom of spring when we came ashore, gave Mrs. Byrd a good impression of the country. She now begins to be seasoned to the heat, and to think more favorably of our climate.

After your September is over, I shall wish your Lordship a little of our sunshine, to disperse all that fog and smoke with which your atmosphere is loaded. It is miraculous that my lungs can breathe in an air compounded of so many vapors as that of dirty London.

Besides the advantages of a pure air, we abound in all kinds of provisions, without expense (I mean we who have plantations). I have a large family and my doors are open to everybody, yet I have no bills to pay. I have my flocks and my herds, and every sort of trade among my own servants, so that I live a kind of interdependence with every one.

Another thing my Lord, that recommends this country very much, we sit securely under our vines, and our fig trees without any danger to our property. We have no such trades carried on among us as that of house-breakers, highwaymen, or beggars. We can rest securely in our beds, with all our doors and windows open.

I most heartily wish to hear from your Lordship, for I am as much as any man alive, my Lord your humble servant.

William Byrd II

Some of the statements in this letter cannot be proved true. This kind of statement is called an **opinion.** Sometimes an opinion is a guess, or it may be a conclusion drawn on certain facts. An opinion can be sensible or foolish. It often expresses the beliefs, wishes, hopes, or fears of the speaker or writer.

In the first paragraph of the letter, Byrd says: "There was nothing frightful in the whole voyage but a sudden puff of wind that carried away our topmast. . ." This was his opinion. Others on the voyage might have been frightened by the tossing of the ship on the waves or by rumors of pirates. There is no way to prove that nothing else was frightful to any of the other passengers on that voyage. Even if hundreds of people agreed with Byrd's statement, it would still be an opinion.

How can you recognize an opinion? Certain key words or phrases such as *I think, I believe, in my opinion,* and *I doubt* give a hint. They tell you that someone is about to give an opinion.

Words such as *beautiful, wonderful, terrible,* and *terrific* are expressions of opinion. There is no way for everybody to agree on what is wonderful or terrible. A wonderful book to one person may be a terrible book to someone else. Experts may agree that something is wonderful or terrible, but they are still giving opinions.

No one can see into the future, so any statement about it is an opinion. Some people are expert enough to tell what is likely to happen in the future. Yet these statements do not become facts until the events have taken place.

Even though opinions cannot be proved, they still can be valuable. Some opinions are based on factual evidence. These carefully developed, "educated" opinions can help us understand the past and prepare for the future. Historians, for example, use documents such as Byrd's letter to help explain the past. Archaeologists recover buried artifacts such as pottery and tools. This evidence helps them reconstruct the ways our ancestors lived. Although their findings are often opinions, they are valuable because they are based on facts.

Sometimes, however, opinions are influenced far more by the things a person likes or dislikes than by factual evidence. These opinions are based on personal feelings rather than on facts. These opinions are less valuable when gathering information.

It is important that we evaluate information to see if we should believe it and use it. Identifying facts and opinions will help you to evaluate information. Deciding whether an opinion is based on facts or on a person's personal feelings will help you to judge the value of information.

CHECKING YOUR SKILLS

Which of these statements are facts and which are opinions? Explain why.

1. Plantation life in the Southern colonies was always wonderful.

2. William Byrd owned a plantation in Virginia.

3. Mrs. Byrd arrived in Virginia in the spring.

4. I think voyages from England were very exciting.

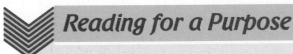

Reading for a Purpose

Look for these important words:

Key Words
- field slaves
- house slaves
- overseer

People
- Benjamin Banneker

Look for answers to these questions:
1. Why did planters depend upon slave labor?
2. What kind of life did slaves lead?
3. How were the rights of free blacks restricted?

Slavery in the South

During the 1600s most plantations in Maryland and Virginia were small. Most used indentured servants from Europe. When tobacco prices were high, everybody did well. When tobacco prices were low, many small planters had trouble. They found it difficult to pay for servants to do farm work.

The big planters could afford to buy slaves to do the work. Slaves cost more than the passage of an indentured servant, but a slave worked for life. An indentured servant worked only for about five years. The more slaves a planter had, the more tobacco he could raise.

By 1700 slaves were becoming an important part of plantation life. Plantations themselves were becoming larger as small planters sold out. The use of slaves changed life in the South. A way of life developed that depended on cheap, plentiful slave labor. Slave labor replaced hired labor wherever tobacco, rice, and indigo were raised.

There were generally two kinds of slaves: **field slaves** and **house slaves.** The person directly responsible for field slaves was the **overseer.** He was hired to see that slaves did the work they were supposed to. Some overseers were free blacks. Some were white. Overseers could be harsh and cruel. Whippings and beatings were common.

House slaves had more contact with the planter and his family. They often were clothed, fed, and housed better than field slaves. Women who were house slaves did the work of washing, spinning, cooking, cleaning, and sewing. Men who were house slaves drove carriages, took care of horses, and practiced skills like carpentry. Children of house slaves were often playmates of the planter's children.

Slaves were treated well or cruelly depending on their owners. Some planters took pride in being fair and kind to their slaves. In turn the slaves gave them loyalty and affection. There was no protection, however, for slaves who had cruel masters. A slave owner was free to beat, whip, or insult any slave. However, by law, a slave owner could not willfully kill a slave.

Slaves As Property

The cruelest part of slavery, however, was not whips. It was that one person could own another. The slaves had no direct control over their own lives. Thousands of white people had come to America looking for freedom and opportunity. At the same time, freedom and opportunity were denied to people of black skin.

Slaves were considered property, like horses or cattle. As with other property, slaves could be bought and sold. That meant that slave families were often separated. Husbands were separated from wives. Parents and children were separated, often never to see each other again.

Slave Children

Separated slave families who lived on nearby plantations were more fortunate than most. When family members lived relatively close together, fathers could visit their families. Slavery made it almost impossible, however, to have a family life.

Slave children under the age of ten lived with their mothers. Starting about age eight, they too began to work. Children of field slaves usually worked in the fields with their mothers. Children of house slaves might learn skills. Boys might learn to make barrels or wheels or do carpentry—all important crafts on a plantation. Young girls might learn the skills of sewing, cooking, or weaving. Some helped take care of the planter's children. Slave children were rarely taught to read or write.

Most slave children beyond the age of ten left their mothers. Some went to stay with relatives. Others were sold.

Millions of people were carried in ships from Africa to the Americas. This picture shows how they were wedged into dark, airless spaces between the ship's decks. Thousands of Africans died of disease, suffocation, or misery during the ocean passage.

The Call of Freedom

Slaves made repeated efforts to escape. Many slaves, separated from their families, ran away to return to their loved ones. Others ran away because they wanted to be free.

Ann Joice had come to Maryland as an indentured servant but had been made a slave. Her grandson, Peter Harbard, said that he often heard his grandmother say that she and all her children "ought to be free." In 1748 Peter Harbard ran away twice. Each time he was recaptured. Finally he was able to buy his freedom.

Some slaves were able to buy their freedom because they had learned useful crafts. They had been allowed to earn money by working as skilled workers. These workers often settled in towns and cities.

In folk stories Brer Rabbit, although smaller, outwits larger animals like greedy Brer Fox.

The total number of slaves who gained freedom, however, was small. Most remained on a plantation, toiling from dawn to dusk six days a week. It was a life of sameness, often boredom. It was a life that did not let grown people be adults. They could not make decisions for themselves or be responsible for their own children.

Few slaves ever wrote about their experiences. Most of what we know about how slaves felt comes from their songs and stories. Music, dance, and stories were all ways they expressed their feelings. Their music included work songs, sad songs, and merry songs. Music and dancing were part of Saturday night gaiety and holidays. One such song went:

Rabbit in the briar patch,
Squirrel in the tree,
Wish I could go hunting
But I ain't free.

Rooster's in the henhouse,
Hen's in the patch.
Love to go shooting,
But I ain't free.

Stories told from one generation to another helped keep alive some memories of family history. Folk stories about Brer Rabbit, Brer Fox, and Brer Bear had their roots in African stories. In these stories Brer Rabbit usually outwits the more powerful animals like Brer Bear. Through music, dance, and stories, blacks held onto their own world of inner feelings.

In time the Christian religion became a source of strength for millions of slaves. At first little effort was made to introduce Christianity to black people. Many of them continued to hold on to African beliefs and traditions. In the late 1700s, however, the Baptists and Methodists began to bring Christianity to the slaves. From then on Christianity became increasingly important in black society.

Free Blacks

At first free blacks had all the rights of citizenship. Free black men could vote. Gradually these rights were taken away in the South. Virginia took away the vote in 1723, and Georgia, in 1761.

Most free blacks, particularly in cities, learned to read and write. To do so was a struggle and sometimes against the law. Both Virginia and Georgia passed laws forbidding education for blacks. Nevertheless, free blacks organized themselves to provide schooling for their children.

Benjamin Banneker was a free black in Maryland. Through education he became an important scientist.

Banneker was the son of a free woman and a slave father. Because his mother was free, Banneker was born free. They lived on a prosperous farm in Maryland. When a Quaker opened a school nearby, Banneker enrolled at the age of 12. A new world opened up to him. He particularly excelled in mathematics. One day he saw a pocket watch for the first time. He was fascinated. He began studying to find out how clocks worked. Banneker then spent his spare time making his own clock. Carved entirely of wood, it was finished in 1753, and was the first clock made in America. It kept perfect time for 48 years.

Later, Banneker gained fame for his almanac. An almanac gives information about natural events. When will the sun rise and set on different days of the year in different places? What will the weather be like? How high will the tide be at a certain place at a certain time? Such information is very helpful to farmers and sailors.

Benjamin Banneker, one of America's first scientists, published an almanac.

Reading Check

1. Name the two main kinds of slaves.
2. What was the responsibility of an overseer?
3. Who was Benjamin Banneker?

Think Beyond If you had been a slave, would you have tried to escape?

People MAKE HISTORY

John Russwurm
1799–1851

▶▶▶▶▶▶▶▶▶▶▶▶▶▶▶

Samuel Cornish
1795–1858

John Russwurm and Samuel Cornish, their hands stained with ink, stared at the page in front of them. It was March 16, 1827, and the two men were looking at the first issue of *Freedom's Journal,* the first newspaper published by blacks in the United States.

In 1827 slavery still existed in the American South. *Freedom's Journal,* with its call for equality for black people, made many white people angry. Communities of black people were attacked, and the homes of those who read the *Journal* were burned.

Violence and threats did not stop Russwurm and Cornish, however. They persuaded black merchants throughout the United States to sell the *Journal.* Black people in Canada and England also began to order the paper.

Russwurm and Cornish had never intended to become newspaper publishers. Russwurm, the second black person to graduate from college, had planned to be a doctor. Cornish, a minister, was a leader in the movement to end slavery.

In 1826 a group of black citizens approached Cornish about starting a newspaper for, by, and about black people. He asked Russwurm to join him in editing the paper.

Many of the leaders in the movement to end slavery were white people. However, Russwurm and Cornish believed that black people had to speak for themselves. In the *Journal*'s first issue, the edi-

tors proclaimed: "Too long have others spoken for us."

In 1829 *Freedom's Journal* stopped publication. By this time, however, two brave men had paved the way for all the newspapers and magazines that are published by African Americans today.

Think Beyond How important do you think *Freedom's Journal* was to black people in 1827? Explain.

Russwurm at right, and Cornish at left

Look for these important words:

People | Places
- Eliza Lucas | • Columbia

Look for answers to these questions:
1. For what reasons did Charleston become a major city?
2. How did geography influence the life and work of the colonists in South Carolina?
3. Why was slavery important on rice plantations?
4. What contribution did Eliza Lucas make to the economy of South Carolina?

The Growth of South Carolina

Large numbers of French people came to South Carolina in 1680. These French people were seeking religious

Charleston, South Carolina, was one of the prettiest and busiest of colonial cities.

freedom. Many of them were skilled in a number of crafts. They also liked town life. As the small colony began to grow, Charleston turned into one of the most beautiful cities of colonial America.

Visitors called Charleston a neat and pretty town. Flocks of buzzards helped it stay that way. Buzzards were protected by law because they cleaned up the garbage.

Because of its excellent harbor, Charleston became one of the most important colonial ports. Only Boston, New York City, and Philadelphia were larger.

Growing Rice

Charleston grew because it became the center of a rice-growing region. Rice needs land that can be flooded while the rice is growing. When the rice is ready for harvest, the land must be drained of water. The low, flat land of South Carolina with its swamps and streams was ideal for growing rice.

The legend of how rice first arrived in the United States goes like this: It was a stormy night in the mid-1600s. A ship from Madagascar, a country in Africa, was being tossed around on rough waves off the coast of South Carolina. As the wind whipped up the waves and the ocean roared, the ship became badly damaged. The captain quickly headed for refuge in a nearby harbor—a harbor named Charleston.

After the storm had blown itself out, the ship's crew repaired their ship and sailed away. However, before they cast off, they did one important thing. As a thank-you to the people of Charleston, they presented the governor of the colony with a bag of seed rice. Ever since that time, rice has been a major economic factor in Charleston.

Although we cannot be sure if this legend is true, it does symbolize how the transportation of goods can affect history and connect us with the rest of the world.

Growing rice was not as easy as growing tobacco. The planter had to construct canals to flood and drain the fields. Sometimes a hurricane or a flooded river ruined the canals and the crops.

Many workers were needed to do the backbreaking work of building canals, planting rice, and harvesting it. To do this work the South Carolina planters depended on slaves. Women usually waded in the black muck of the wet fields to plant the rice. Near harvest time children had the job of scaring the birds away.

The watery fields were full of mosquitoes. Often their bites carried the germs of the disease malaria.

The summers in the lowlands of South Carolina could be very hot and humid. The skies opened with great thunderstorms. Mosquitoes and sand flies swarmed everywhere. To escape such summers, the planters went to Charleston. In Charleston they lived in houses that had wide verandas to catch the ocean breezes. The summer months were merry with parties, dances, and musical gatherings.

Eliza Lucas

One of those who enjoyed the summer gaiety of Charleston was **Eliza Lucas.** At the age of 17, she was in charge of three plantations. Her father, who owned the plantations, lived in an English colony in the West Indies. He was afraid of a war with Spain and sent his family to South Carolina for safety.

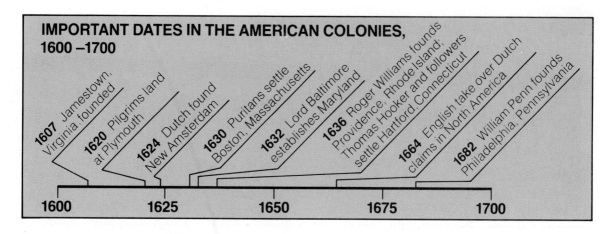

IMPORTANT DATES IN THE AMERICAN COLONIES, 1600–1700

1607 Jamestown, Virginia, founded

1620 Pilgrims land at Plymouth

1624 Dutch found New Amsterdam

1630 Puritans settle Boston, Massachusetts

1632 Lord Baltimore establishes Maryland

1636 Roger Williams founds Providence, Rhode Island; Thomas Hooker and followers settle Hartford, Connecticut

1664 English take over Dutch claims in North America

1682 William Penn founds Philadelphia, Pennsylvania

1600   1625   1650   1675   1700

Eliza Lucas described her busy life in a letter to a friend:

> I have a little library well furnished in which I spend part of my time. My music and the garden, which I am very fond of, take up the rest of my time that is not employed in business.

The business of running three plantations, she wrote, "requires much writing and more business and fatigue of other sorts than you can imagine."

In other letters Eliza described teaching two black girls to read so that they could teach other black children. This was a very advanced idea for that time.

Another of Eliza Lucas's projects was raising indigo plants. People did not learn to make chemical dyes until the 1800s. Until then, indigo was one of the most important dyes. Chemical indigo is widely used today to dye denim for blue jeans.

Using seeds sent by her father, Eliza spent several years growing different types of indigo. In 1743 samples of her dye were judged in London to be of the best quality. Eliza gave indigo seeds to her neighbors and friends. Within a few years South Carolina planters were selling a million pounds (453.6 T) of indigo a year. The South Carolina planters could grow indigo on land where rice did not grow.

Settlers in the Piedmont

While plantations were growing in coastal areas, people were moving into other regions. They spread out beyond the Coastal Plain. There the soil was good, and people began to establish tobacco and cotton plantations.

Many Scots settled beyond the Fall Line. The Scots, used to raising cattle, drove their herds to Charleston for export. The way of life of these frontier cowboys did not depend on slaves.

As in other colonies, important towns developed at the Fall Line. They included **Columbia,** the capital of South Carolina.

Reading Check

1. Give two reasons Charleston became an important city.
2. Why was coastal South Carolina a good place to grow rice?
3. What work did slaves do on rice plantations?

Think Beyond What do you think made Eliza Lucas so independent for a girl of her age in the 1740s?

Thinking Back

- English settlements in the South first centered around the Chesapeake Bay area and the coastal lands of the Southeast. Settlers grew cash crops and used waterways for transportation.

- Maryland was founded so that Catholics could live in safety and freedom. Carolina was founded to earn profits through trade and agriculture.

- Georgia was founded to strengthen England's claims and to provide a place for poor people to make a fresh start.

- Plantations developed along Southern waterways. Tobacco was used to pay for things in the plantation economy.

- Towns grew slowly in the tidewater region because goods could be traded from each plantation's dock. In time, large towns grew along the Fall Line.

- A planter had many duties, including taking care of the people on the plantation and doing public service.

- By the 1700s slaves were becoming an important part of plantation life. Slaves were considered property and had no direct control over their own lives.

- At first free blacks had all the rights of citizenship, but these rights were gradually taken away.

- Charleston became an important city because of its excellent harbor and because it was in the center of the rice-growing region.

- South Carolina was a perfect place to grow rice and indigo. Planters depended on slaves to plant and harvest crops.

Check for Understanding

Using Words

Number your paper from 1 to 9. Use the terms below to complete the paragraph that follows. Use each term once.

broker	planters
cash crop	public service
indigo	society
overseer	tidewater
plantations	

Large farms were called __(1)__ in the South. Persons who owned these farms were called __(2)__. In the __(3)__ areas tobacco was the main __(4)__. In South Carolina, rice and __(5)__ were grown. Farmers often sold their crops through a London __(6)__. Among their duties, landowners helped __(7)__ by giving time to __(8)__ . They often hired an __(9)__, who was in charge of the field slaves.

Reviewing Facts

1. What were the important cash crops of the Southern colonies?
2. Why was Maryland founded?
3. Why was Carolina divided?
4. What were James Oglethorpe's reasons for founding Georgia?
5. Why weren't there any large towns in the tidewater areas?
6. What were a planter's responsibilities?

7. Why did slave labor replace hired labor where cash crops were grown?
8. How did the buying and selling of slaves affect the slaves' family lives?
9. Name three important Southern cities that were established at the Fall Line.
10. Describe the achievements of Benjamin Banneker and Eliza Lucas.

Thinking Critically

1. How were geography, cash crops, and slavery connected? Why was slavery less important where there were smaller farms and fewer cash crops?
2. How was the life of a slave different from the life of a plantation owner? How was it different from that of a small farmer?
3. Four of our first five Presidents were from the planter class of people. From what you have read, can you explain why many of our early leaders came from the South?

Writing About It

Write a short biography of William Byrd using the information given on pages 242 and 244–245. Include in your biography Byrd's place of birth, his educational background, and his family life. Try to make the character of William Byrd come alive.

Practicing Thinking Skills

Evaluating Information

Decide which of the statements below are fact and which are opinion. Then number your paper from 1 to 4 and write *F* if the statement is a fact. Write *O* if it is an opinion.

1. I think Charleston is the most beautiful city in the United States.
2. Georgia was the last American colony founded by England.
3. James Oglethorpe was a wonderful man.
4. Southern planters would have made more money if they had raised more corn and less tobacco.

On Your Own

Social Studies at Home

1. As James Oglethorpe did, you must design a new city. Decide what shape your city will be and how many streets it will have. Will the buildings be close together or far apart? Draw your city, complete with buildings and streets, on a piece of paper. You may want to take suggestions from your family on what to name your city.
2. Make up your own story about how Brer Rabbit outsmarts Brer Bear or Brer Fox. When you are finished with your story, try to make up a melody to go with it or sing it to the tune of a familiar song.

Read More About It

Benjamin Banneker, Astronomer and Scientist by Margaret Goff Clark. Garrard. This biography tells the story of Banneker and his rise from slave to scientist.

Fair Wind to Virginia by Cornelia Meigs. Macmillan. This tale of political opponents exiled by King George reveals much about life in the Virginia colony.

Shaw's Fortune: The Picture Story of a Colonial Plantation by Edwin Tunis. T. Y. Crowell. The reader tours a plantation in the Chesapeake Bay area.

A Williamsburg Household by Joan Anderson. Photos by George Ancona. Ticknor and Fields. This book guides readers through a tour of Williamsburg.

A Visit to Williamsburg

In colonial Virginia, a visit to Williamsburg was an exciting event. It was always something to look forward to. Many planter families went twice a year to Williamsburg. They traveled on horseback or in horse-drawn carriages over narrow dirt roads. They went during the most pleasant times of the year, spring and fall. The blossoming trees of woods and orchards perfumed the spring air. In the fall the air was crisp, and the trees were aflame with colors.

In 1780 the capital of Virginia was moved from Williamsburg to Richmond. Richmond was on the fall line of the James River. By then more and more people had moved inland. It was easier for them to get to Richmond than to Williamsburg. *(continued on page 258)*

On Training Day the militia drilled on the green at Williamsburg. Musicians playing fifes and drums marched in front of the soldiers. Afterwards, sports, races, and other contests were held on the green. At Williamsburg today you can see musicians march as they ◄ once did.

The blacksmith was one of the most important colonial craftsmen. Today at the blacksmith's forge on Prince George Street, the fire turns the iron red-hot and ready for shaping. As in colonial times, this blacksmith makes horseshoes as well as candleholders, farm tools, and wagon wheels.

At Williamsburg today ◄ you can visit the Spinning and Weaving House. At the spinning wheel a woman turns fibers from the flax plant into linen thread. At other times she might turn sheep's wool into yarn. Hanging from the rafters are skeins of wool yarn that have been dyed different colors. Weavers at large looms make fabric using the linen and wool yarns. In colonial times a good weaver could produce about 3 yards (2.7m) of cloth a day.

On a visit to Williamsburg ► ladies would come to the Margaret Hunter Shop, which was run by Margaret Hunter and her sister Jane. Today, the Hunter Shop continues to sell ladies' hats, fans, buttons, shoes, and other fine fashions of the colonial period.

After the capital was moved, the village of Williamsburg lost its importance. Plantation owners and government officials no longer had reason to visit. By 1900 historic Williamsburg showed little of its former sparkle.

Then, in 1926, the project of rebuilding Williamsburg began. First, old maps and drawings were studied. Then the buildings that remained from the 1700s were **restored,** or returned, to their original appearance. Even the colonial gardens were replanted as they had been.

A visit to Williamsburg is like a trip back 250 years in a time machine. Here are all the sights and sounds of colonial life. You hear the hammering of the blacksmith and the clip-clops of horses' hooves. You see the trimmed hedges and the church's high steeple. The sights and sounds of Williamsburg let us experience our colonial heritage.

▲ The Prentis Store today, restored to look as it did in colonial times.

◄ The Prentis Store was a gas station in the 1920s when this photo was taken.

Unit Review

Words to Remember

Number your paper from 1 to 15. Use the words below to complete the sentences that follow. Use each term once.

apprentice
authority
barter
cash crops
delegates
exports
frontier
immigrants
meetinghouse
militias
naval stores
navigable
plantations
proprietor
tidewater

1. There were few _____ rivers in New England.

2. The most important building in a New England town was the _____ .

3. Furs, lumber, and fish were all _____ of the American colonies.

4. In New England the church leaders had a great deal of _____ .

5. Wars between Indians and colonists broke out as settlers continued to push the _____ westward.

6. It was common for American colonists to _____ instead of using money.

7. The forests of New England provided _____ such as pitch, tar, and turpentine that were used in shipbuilding.

8. William Penn became the _____ of Pennsylvania in 1681.

9. The Germans and Scotch-Irish were among the many _____ who settled in Pennsylvania.

10. King Charles II said proprietors had to consult with an assembly of _____ chosen by the colonists.

11. When he was 12 years old Benjamin Franklin became an _____ to his brother, a printer.

12. In the South the first settlements were in the _____ regions of Virginia and Maryland.

13. Farms in the South were called _____ .

14. Tobacco, rice, and indigo were the _____ in the South.

15. Colonists everywhere organized _____ to provide for their defense.

Focus on Main Ideas

1. Why did many colonial cities grow near good harbors? Why did other cities develop at the Fall Line?

2. Compare and contrast agriculture in the New England colonies, the Middle colonies, and the Southern colonies. Discuss the size and fertility of farms, the kinds of crops grown, and the source of farm labor.

3. Religion was an important influence in colonial life. What examples of this statement can you find in the unit?

4. In colonial times fighting was common between the settlers and the Indians. Why? Give two examples of Indian-settler conflict to support your answer.

5. In what ways did the American colonists gain experience in self-government?

6. How did slavery begin in the southern colonies? What conditions allowed slavery to grow?

259

Think/Write

Imagine you are a girl or boy living in one of the colonies. Name the place where you imagine you live. Then write what happens during one day in your life.

Activities

1. **Research/Oral Report** Choose a person in this unit who interested you. Find out more about that person. Share what you learn with the class.

2. **Research/Art** Benjamin Franklin invented a stove, bifocals, and many other things. Find out about one of his inventions. Describe it or draw a picture of it.

3. **Art** Describe an invention or draw a picture of an invention you would like to see. Make sure you explain how it would work.

4. **Research/Art** People in the colonies practiced many different crafts, such as candlemaking, weaving, and making musical instruments. Research one of these crafts and share your findings with the class. If you can, give a simple demonstration of the craft.

5. **Past and Present** Compare and contrast today and colonial times with respect to transportation, food, clothing, shelter, schooling, light, and power. Do this by making a chart. If you wish, include pictures on your chart.

6. **Art** Imagine you are coming to America to start a colony. Build a model showing the kind of location you would look for. Show natural features on your model.

Skills Review

1. **Reading Bar Graphs** This is a graph that shows the number of pelts a fur trapper sold one year. Use the graph to answer the questions that follow.

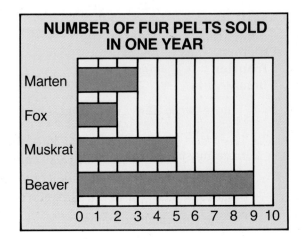

NUMBER OF FUR PELTS SOLD IN ONE YEAR

a. Which animal supplied the most pelts?

b. Which animal supplied the fewest pelts?

c. How many fox pelts were sold?

2. **Evaluating Information** Which of the following are fact and which are opinion?

a. The Connecticut River is the longest river in New England.

b. King Charles II of England was a terrible ruler.

c. In 1760 Philadelphia was the largest city in America.

d. I think Benjamin Franklin's greatest work was as an inventor.

e. Georgia was founded by James Oglethorpe in 1733.

f. The Breadbasket colonies were the best colonies to live in.

American colonists learned to use the different natural resources they found. They learned to use the land, the forests, the rivers, the swamps, and the harbors. Most of the activities below can help you learn about the natural resources or economy of your state.

Learning About Geography

1. The table below shows five important resources. Make a copy of this table in your scrapbook. Find out which of these resources your state has. Next to each resource, give information about this resource in your state.

NATURAL RESOURCES IN OUR STATE	
Navigable rivers	
Fertile soil	
Good ports and harbors	
Forests	
Valuable minerals	

2. Most American colonists lived near rivers. Rivers helped communication and shipping and provided water for agriculture. Many of our first cities also developed along rivers. What cities in your state were built along rivers?

3. Farming was important to all the colonists. The Southern colonies grew tobacco, cotton, and rice. The Middle and New England colonies raised wheat, barley, and corn. Which of these crops are grown in your state?

Learning About Culture

4. Williamsburg, Virginia, is a town that shows life as it was in colonial America. Have any places in your state been restored or rebuilt to show some period in American history? Find out about these places and share your information with the class.

Learning About Economics

5. The English colonies were not the only colonial settlements in what is now the United States. By 1750 there were French settlements in the Mississippi River valley. The Spanish had settled in Texas, New Mexico, and Florida. The Russians had fur-trading posts in Alaska. Were there any European settlements in your state by 1750? If so, describe the economy of these settlements.

UNIT

5

The American Revolution

- **1754–1763**
  French and Indian War

- **1765**
  The Stamp Act taxes paper

- **1767**
  The Townshend Acts tax imports

- **1773**
  Boston Tea Party

- **1774**
  First Continental Congress meets

*I*ndependence Day, July 4, is our most important national holiday. On that day we celebrate the birth of our nation in 1776. Before then, the British king George III ruled the people of the 13 American colonies. The picture below shows angry colonists pulling down a statue of King George. On July 4, 1776, in Philadelphia, Pennsylvania, Americans did much more than pull down a statue. They declared they would no longer obey King George or any king. They would govern themselves from that day forward.

Think Beyond　What advantages do you think there would be to self-government? Do you think there would be any disadvantages? Explain.

- **1775**
  April: Battles of Lexington and Concord

- **1776**
  July: Declaration of Independence

- **1777**
  Victory at Saratoga brings help from France

- **1781**
  Battle of Yorktown

- **1783**
  Britain and the United States sign a peace treaty

CHAPTER 10

Background of the Revolution

❝ . . . Tears stand in my eyes when I think . . . of this once happy . . . land of liberty. All is anarchy and confusion . . . We are all in arms . . . The sound of war echoes from north to south. Every plain is full of armed men . . . May God put a speedy end to this grand and important contest between the mother and her children. The colonies do not wish to be independent; they only deny the right of taxation in Parliament. ❞

—Citizen of Virginia, 1775

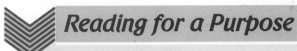
Look for these important words:

Key Words	**People**	**Places**
• revolution	• George Washington	• Ohio River valley
• French and Indian War	• Edward Braddock	• Fort Duquesne
• allies		• Fort Necessity

Look for answers to these questions:
1. What led to the French and Indian War?
2. Why were the French and Indians often able to defeat the British?
3. How did the war end?

The French and Indian War

By 1750 life was good for most Americans. In the growing cities, merchants and traders were doing well. Carpenters, coopers, smiths, printers—all were busy. Farmers in the settled areas were able to sell their animals and crops for a nice profit to help feed people in the growing cities.

Meanwhile, settlers kept pushing the frontier westward. Log cabins and cleared land were gradually replacing the wilderness. Some people began to think of crossing the Appalachian Mountains and settling in the rich valleys on the other side.

The American colonies were still ruled by England, but England was 3,000 miles (about 4,830 km) away. Each colony had become used to governing itself.

Important events would soon lead to the American Revolution. A **revolution** is a large, sudden change in government. The first of these events was the **French and Indian War.** This war started because both France and England claimed the land of the **Ohio River valley.**

France had become worried about the growing American colonies. There were a million and a half people in the British colonies and only 80,000 in New France. If colonists started to spill over the Appalachian Mountains, they could threaten French settlements.

The French decided to protect themselves by building a string of forts in the upper part of the Ohio River valley. One of these was **Fort Duquesne** (doo•KAYN), where Pittsburgh, Pennsylvania, is now. Fort Duquesne was on land claimed by Virginia.

The governor of Virginia sent young **George Washington,** then 21, to warn the French that they were on Virginia territory. The French replied that they would stay.

The governor immediately sent Washington with an army of 150 men to drive out the French. Near Fort Duquesne, Washington and his men

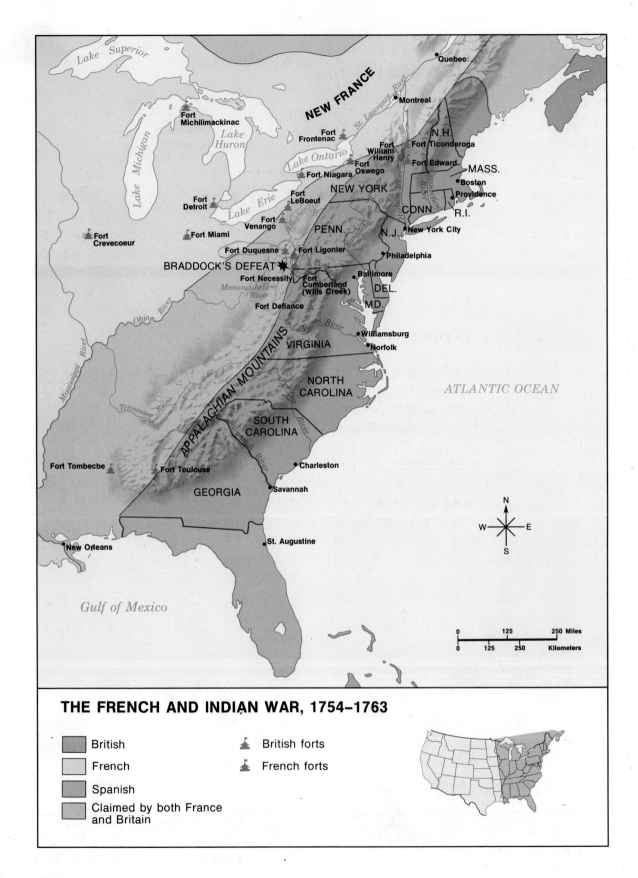

Lake Superior

Lake Huron

Lake Michigan

Lake Ontario

Lake Erie

NEW FRANCE

Quebec

Montreal

St. Lawrence River

Fort Michilimackinac

Fort Frontenac

Fort William Henry

Fort Ticonderoga

Fort Oswego

Fort Edward

N.H.

MASS.

Fort Niagara

Fort Detroit

Fort LeBoeuf

Fort Venango

NEW YORK

Boston

Providence

CONN.

R.I.

Fort Crevecoeur

Fort Miami

Allegheny River

PENN.

Hudson River

Connecticut River

Susquehanna River

N.J.

New York City

Fort Duquesne

Fort Ligonier

Philadelphia

BRADDOCK'S DEFEAT ★

Baltimore

Fort Necessity

Fort Cumberland (Wills Creek)

DEL.

Ohio River

Monongahela River

Fort Defiance

MD.

James River

Williamsburg

Norfolk

VIRGINIA

Mississippi River

Tennessee River

APPALACHIAN MOUNTAINS

NORTH CAROLINA

ATLANTIC OCEAN

SOUTH CAROLINA

Savannah River

Fort Tombecbe

Fort Toulouse

Charleston

GEORGIA

Savannah

New Orleans

St. Augustine

N
W   E
S

Gulf of Mexico

125   250 Miles

0   125   250   Kilometers

THE FRENCH AND INDIAN WAR, 1754–1763

British

French

Spanish

Claimed by both France and Britain

British forts

French forts

hurriedly built a fort which they fittingly called **Fort Necessity.** It lay in a low place. Then the French attacked the fort. Outnumbered, Washington and his men held out until runoff from a heavy rainstorm soaked all their gunpowder. Without dry powder to fire their guns, Washington's small army was forced to surrender.

Washington learned from his experience. He never again built a camp in a low place. Like many Americans, Washington was to learn about war from fighting the French.

Braddock's Defeat

At first it looked as if Britain would lose to France in North America. In 1754 the British general, **Edward Braddock,** led troops through the wilderness to attack Fort Duquesne. His army included British troops in red coats and Virginians in blue coats. George Washington later described the beauty of the red and blue uniforms against the green of the forest. Near Fort Duquesne the French attacked Braddock's troops. His men, numbering 1,459, were badly beaten by about 200 French soldiers and about 600 Indians. The Indians had long been trading partners of the French. Now they were also **allies,** or friends in war, of the French.

Braddock's troops never had fought Indians. The Indians were hard to see in the forest. In contrast, the colorful British made easy targets. Indian war whoops were terrifying to British ears. The British fled in panic. That day almost 1,000 of the British army were wounded or killed. General Braddock was one of those who died.

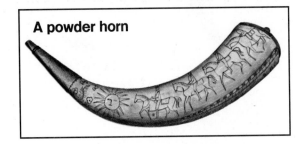

A powder horn

Such British defeats left the frontier without defenses. Even more Indians decided to side with the French. Indian war parties began to attack frontier settlements in Pennsylvania, Maryland, and Virginia. Hundreds of men, women, and children were killed. The colonists blamed the French for these attacks.

In 1757 the war turned in Britain's favor. The British government sent more armies to North America. With fresh generals and thousands more troops, Britain began to win battles against the French and Indians.

In 1763 the French and Indian War ended with victory for Britain. As a result, the French left North America. The British flag now flew over Canada and the Ohio River valley. France gave Spain the rest of its North American territory. Britain now claimed all of North America east of the Mississippi River. Spain claimed all lands west of the Mississippi.

Reading Check

1. Why did the Indians help the French?
2. What caused Braddock's defeat?
3. What parts of North America did Britain win from France?

Think Beyond How do you think the British and the Indians got along after the war?

267

Reading for a Purpose

Look for these important words:

Key Words
- Stamp Act
- trial by jury
- Parliament
- House of Lords
- House of Commons
- petitions
- repeal
- Sons of Liberty
- liberty
- Townshend Acts
- boycott

People
- Sam Adams

Look for answers to these questions:
1. What were the main disagreements between Britain and the colonies?
2. What kinds of taxes did Britain put on the colonists?
3. Why did these taxes make the colonists angry?
4. What methods did they use to protest the taxes?

2 New Laws Anger the Colonists

The French and Indian War led to disagreements between Britain and its American colonies. One of these disagreements was about the frontier and the new lands won from France. Many colonists were eager to move into the Ohio River valley. Britain, however, wanted to keep those lands for the Indians. Britain did not want more wars between its colonists and the Indians. In 1763 Britain passed a law that forbade colonists to settle west of the Appalachian Mountains. This law made many Americans angry.

The next major disagreement between Britain and the colonies was about money. The long war between France and Britain had cost a great deal of money. Britain had borrowed much of the money and now had to pay it back. The British thought the colonists should pay part of the cost. After all, one reason for the war was to defend the colonies.

The Stamp Act

Britain decided to raise money by taxing paper in the colonies. In 1765 paper was very valuable. Every piece of paper had to carry a stamp to show that the tax had been paid. This law was called the **Stamp Act.** A person could not get a license, a diploma, a calendar, or even a newspaper without paying the stamp tax. People who did not obey the new law could be tried in special courts, without **trial by jury.**

Trial by jury had been a right of British people for hundreds of years. A person accused of breaking the law could be tried only by a jury of fellow citizens. The colonists felt this basic right was now threatened.

The Stamp Act took away another important right, Americans said. That was the right to vote their own taxes. The Stamp Act had not been voted for by the colonists' own assemblies.

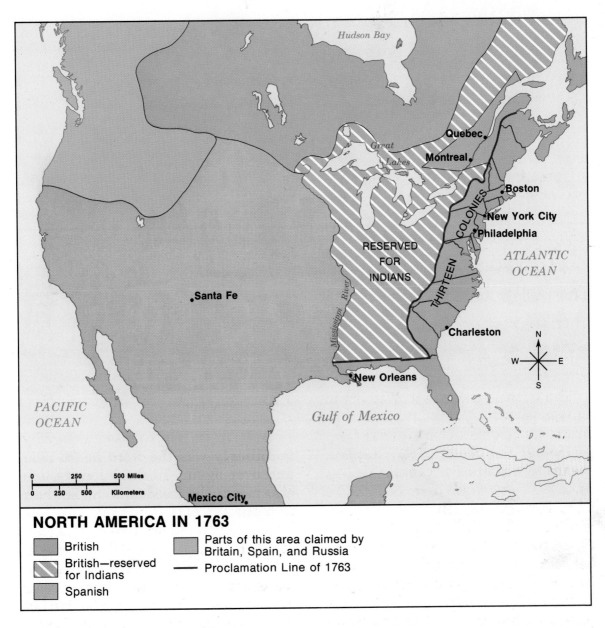

NORTH AMERICA IN 1763

- British
- British—reserved for Indians
- Spanish
- Parts of this area claimed by Britain, Spain, and Russia
- — Proclamation Line of 1763

The British **Parliament** (PAHR•luh•muhnt) had passed the Stamp Act. Parliament was the lawmaking body of Britain. Parliament had two parts, or **houses.** Members of the **House of Lords** held office because of their noble birth. On the other hand, members of the **House of Commons** were elected by the people in Britain. The British felt that Parliament represented British people everywhere.

Not so, said the Americans. Only colonial assemblies had the right to pass taxes in the American colonies. They had not elected people to Parliament. Therefore, they said, Parliament could not tax them.

The Stamp Act made the colonists furious. Colonial leaders made their feelings known to Parliament in the form of **petitions.** Petitions are written requests. They asked Parliament

A protest against the Stamp Act takes place under Boston's Liberty Tree. From the branches swing straw dummies of British tax collectors.

to **repeal** the Stamp Act. *To repeal* means to withdraw or cancel.

Sons of Liberty

At the same time, citizens in every seaport organized themselves into groups called **Sons of Liberty.** The Sons of Liberty burned the stamped paper and attacked British tax officers. A tax officer in New York said he would "cram the Stamp Act down the people's throats." Mobs then attacked his house.

In Boston a lawyer named **Sam Adams** organized protests around an elm tree in Boston Common. The tree became known as the Liberty Tree. Straw dummies dressed as British officials were often hung from the limbs of the Liberty Tree.

Liberty was the word heard over and over again. To the colonists, *liberty* meant the freedom to make their own laws.

The Townshend Acts

The furious and often violent reaction to the Stamp Act forced Parliament to repeal it in 1766. Britain still needed money, however. The next year, Parliament passed the **Townshend Acts.** These laws raised taxes on many imported goods. Lead, paper, paint, glass, and tea now all cost more to buy. Once again the colonists were angry.

The British government had paid little attention to its American colonies in 150 years. It had let them do pretty much as they pleased. Then Parliament changed. It seemed to be

In Boston angry citizens make a bonfire of Stamp Act paper.

Merchants who did not boycott British goods were named on lists like this.

A LIST of the Names of *those*
who AUDACIOUSLY continue to counteract the UNITED SENTIMENTS of the BODY of Merchants thro'out NORTH-AMERICA ; by importing British Goods contrary to the Agreement.

John Bernard,
(In King-Street, almost opposite Vernon's Head.

James McMasters,
(On Treat's Wharf.

Patrick McMasters,
(Opposite the Sign of the Lamb.

John Mein,
(Opposite the White-Horse, and in King-Street.

Nathaniel Rogers,
(Opposite Mr. Henderson Inches Store lower End King-Street.

William Jackson,
At the Brazen Head, Cornhill, near the Town-House.

Theophilus Lillie,
(Near Mr. Pemberton's Meeting-House, North-End.

John Taylor,
(Nearly opposite the Heart and Crown in Cornhill.

Ame & Elizabeth Cummings,
(Opposite the Old Brick Meeting House, all of Boston.

Israel Williams, Esq; & Son,
(Traders in the Town of Hatfield.

And, *Henry Barnes,*
(Trader in the Town of Marlboro'.

treating the colonies like children. Parliament did not accept the idea that the colonies had grown up and were now able to handle their own affairs. "This is the mother country. They are the children. They must obey," said a member of Parliament.

A Boycott Begins

The colonists began to **boycott** British goods. A boycott is a refusal to buy something in order to show disapproval. A boycott of British goods would cause British merchants to lose money. These merchants might in turn pressure Parliament to repeal the taxes. At town meetings people voted to make things for themselves and not to buy imported goods. Some who did not boycott British goods were covered with tar or molasses and dusted with feathers.

The boycott began to work. Imports decreased by half in several colonies. Women were particularly important in making the boycott a success. Many met in groups to spin and weave as their grandmothers had done.

Again the colonists were successful in forcing Parliament to repeal most of the taxes on imports. King George insisted, however, that the tax on tea remain. He wanted the Americans to remember who was boss.

 Reading Check

1. Why was the Stamp Act passed?
2. Why did colonists protest the Stamp Act?
3. Who were the Sons of Liberty?

Think Beyond Is a boycott a useful form of protest? Explain.

Look for these important words:

Key Words
- Redcoats
- massacre
- Boston Massacre
- Committee of Correspondence
- monopoly

- Boston Tea Party
- quartered
- Intolerable Acts
- tyranny
- resist
- First Continental Congress

People
- Crispus Attucks
- Paul Revere
- John Adams
- Patrick Henry

Look for answers to these questions:
1. Why did fighting first break out between the colonists and British soldiers?
2. What were the Committees of Correspondence?
3. What was the Boston Tea Party?
4. How did Britain punish the colonies after the Boston Tea Party?
5. What were some achievements of the First Continental Congress?

3 *Protests in Boston*

Ten thousand British soldiers had been sent to America in 1763 to keep peace on the frontier. If these soldiers had gone to the frontier, Americans would not have minded. Instead, the soldiers stayed in the cities. In Boston the soldiers took over a church for their living quarters. They even rode their horses in the church. That kind of thing greatly angered Americans.

British soldiers were paid so little that they were willing to work at odd jobs for low wages. They took jobs away from American workers. That also angered Americans.

Many colonists made fun of the British soldiers in their red jackets. They called them **Redcoats** and "lobster-backs."

The Boston Massacre

In several cities, Americans got into serious fights with British soldiers. The worst fight happened in Boston. On March 5, 1770, an angry crowd of boys and men began throwing snowballs at a British soldier on duty. More soldiers and their captain arrived on the scene. For half an hour they stood their ground listening to the jeers of the mob: "Come on, you rascals, you bloody backs, you lobster scoundrels! Fire if you dare!"

Suddenly one soldier, hit with a club, fired. Other soldiers followed. When the smoke cleared, five American men were dead or dying. The first to die was a black man, **Crispus Attucks** (AT•uhks).

Many Americans in Boston and elsewhere were angered. Now the hated

272

With this picture of the Boston Massacre, Paul Revere helped create angry feelings against the British.

British soldiers had actually killed people they were supposed to be protecting. At least 10,000 persons turned out for the funeral processions of the dead men. The shops and stores of Boston and neighboring towns were closed. Everywhere church bells tolled.

Paul Revere, a silversmith, made a picture showing the British troops firing on the people of Boston. He titled it *The Bloody Massacre.* A **massacre** (MAS•uh•kuhr) is the killing of large numbers of people who cannot defend themselves. The shooting in Boston was not really a massacre, but to this day we call the event the **Boston Massacre.**

The British captain in charge of the soldiers was tried for murder. **John Adams,** a cousin of Sam Adams, defended him. It took courage for John

Adams to do this because the British were so unpopular. John Adams was a strong believer in justice. He believed that the British soldiers had fired in self-defense. The Boston jury found the British captain not guilty.

Meanwhile Sam Adams had persuaded Boston's Town Meeting to set up a **Committee of Correspondence.** The job of committee members was to write to colonists in other places to keep track of events. By 1774 most colonies had such committees. The committees did much to bind the colonists together against the British.

Boston Tea Party

The three years following the Boston Massacre were quiet. Historians have called it "the calm before the storm." The storm came when Parliament again passed a law that angered Americans.

The new law of May 1773 gave a **monopoly** (muh•NAHP•uh•lee) on tea to the East India Company. A monopoly is complete control over a product or service. According to the law, only the East India Company could import tea into the American colonies. That meant that American merchants and traders could no longer make money in the tea trade.

Tea would cost less under the monopoly, but Americans did not care. They remembered that they were still paying a tax on tea, and they feared monopolies. Merchants worried that Parliament might establish other monopolies and drive them out of business.

During the Boston Tea Party people cheered when the Sons of Liberty, dressed as Indians, threw chests of tea into the harbor.

Three ships carrying East India tea sailed into Boston Harbor in December 1773. The colonists refused to let the tea come ashore. The British governor then said that the tea would be unloaded under the protection of cannons and guns.

Now the Sons of Liberty acted. Disguised as Mohawk Indians, they headed for the Boston docks. As they marched to the docks, the Sons of Liberty sang a song that started:

Rally, Mohawks! bring out your axes,
And tell King George we'll pay no taxes
On his foreign tea. . . .

The "Mohawks" scrambled onto the British ships. They split the chests of tea with their axes. They threw the tea into the water. Newspapers called this the **Boston Tea Party.**

In Britain the king and Parliament passed laws to punish the colonists. In the spring of 1774, an angry Parliament closed the port of Boston to all shipping until the city paid for the destroyed tea. Shipping was the most important business of Boston. Without shipping, the people of Boston had few goods to buy or sell, including food.

To make things worse, Parliament did away with the elected assembly of Massachusetts. A British general, Thomas Gage, was named to govern Massachusetts. Town meetings were forbidden without his approval.

Parliament also said British soldiers could be **quartered,** or housed, in American homes. Americans had to pay for the soldiers' blankets, their food, and their cooking pots. People even had to buy rum for the soldiers.

The colonists called these harsh new laws the **Intolerable Acts.** "Tyr-

anny!" they shouted. **Tyranny** (TIHR•uh•nee) is harsh and unjust rule.

The Colonists Unite

The Intolerable Acts united the colonies as nothing else had. People in all the colonies sent food, clothing, fuel, and money to Boston. In Philadelphia a committee of citizens declared, "We consider our brethren, at Boston, as suffering in the common cause of America."

The Philadelphia committee members invited the colonies to send delegates to Philadelphia. They wanted to discuss how the colonists could **resist,** or act against, British tyranny. In September 1774, 55 men chosen by committees in 12 states met in the **First Continental Congress.**

The men at the First Continental Congress worked hard to develop a statement of rights. They stated these rights in a petition to Parliament. People had a right to life, liberty, and property, they said. People had a right to trial by jury. People had the right to make laws in their own assemblies. People had the right not to have soldiers living in their homes.

The Continental Congress also voted another boycott of British goods. Americans were asked not to import or use British goods. Furthermore, the Congress asked Americans not to sell anything to the British.

In Virginia some members of the House of Burgesses thought that Americans and British would end up fighting each other. They suggested that the militias start preparing for war. Others strongly opposed the suggestion. In response, **Patrick Henry**

George Washington strides out of a session of the First Continental Congress. With him are Patrick Henry and William Henry Lee, both from Virginia. Although Washington had not yet taken command of the army, the artist paints him in uniform to show that in spirit, Washington was ready to fight for his country. The Continental Congress met in Carpenters' Hall, later renamed Independence Hall.

rose. He gave the most famous speech of his career. Americans have long remembered its last words:

> Is life so dear, or peace so sweet, as to be purchased at the price of chains and slavery? Forbid it, Almighty God! I know not what course others may take; but as for me, give me liberty or give me death!

Reading Check

1. What was the Boston Massacre?
2. What was the Boston Tea Party?
3. What important rights were stated in a petition to Parliament?

Think Beyond How do you think residents felt about having British soldiers living in their homes?

IN FOCUS

HISTORICAL PHILADELPHIA

In what city did Betsy Ross sew the first American flag? In what city did the First Continental Congress meet? In what city did Presidents George Washington and John Adams take their oaths of office? The answer to each of these questions is Philadelphia.

Philadelphia calls itself "The Most Historic City in America"—and with good reason. It was the capital of the United States from 1790 to 1800. It is the city that claims dozens of America's firsts, including the first hospital, first library, and first fire department.

Philadelphia first earned its place in history in 1774, when the First Continental Congress met in Carpenters' Hall in the city's center. Over the next 30 years, many of the most important events in American history took place in Philadelphia. The Declaration of Independence and the Constitution were written and signed in Independence Hall. The United States Supreme Court met for the very first time in Old City Hall. The Liberty Bell had its first home in the Pennsylvania State House, located in Philadelphia. And Presidents Madison, Monroe, Jackson, and William Henry Harrison all served as congressional representatives inside the city's Congress Hall.

Many great Americans called Philadelphia their home. George Washington lived there during much of his presidency. Benjamin Franklin built a large house in the center of town. Betsy Ross lived on Arch Street, just a few blocks from Independence Hall.

Each year, history comes alive for millions of Americans as they walk through Philadelphia's old buildings. Many areas of downtown Philadelphia are now part of Independence National Historical Park, a place where the city's historic past is preserved.

Think Beyond   Why do you think it is important to preserve historic cities such as Philadelphia?

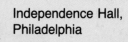

Independence Hall, Philadelphia

Look for these important words:

Key Words	Places
• Minutemen	• Concord
	• Lexington

Look for answers to these questions:

1. Why did the British plan to march to Lexington and Concord?
2. Who warned the countryside that the British were on the way?
3. Why were the battles of Lexington and Concord important to the colonists?

4 Lexington and Concord

Americans now felt they would have to fight to protect their rights and their liberties. In Massachusetts men took time from their work to practice marching and firing guns. Because these volunteer soldiers were to be ready at a moment's notice, they were called **Minutemen.** The Minutemen began collecting military supplies and storing them at **Concord,** a village about 15 miles (24.1 km) west of Boston.

In Boston the British governor became alarmed at the activities of the Minutemen. He decided to make a quick strike to seize the military supplies at Concord. He also hoped to arrest the American leaders, Sam Adams and John Hancock. Both belonged to the Minutemen. They were staying in **Lexington,** a town near Concord.

From Boston, the British could get to Concord in two ways. One was to go the long way around by land. The other was to go across the Charles River before starting their march.

Paul Revere had made arrangements to signal the movements of British troops. If the British were to go by water, two lanterns would shine in Boston's Old North Church. If they were to go by land, one lantern would shine. These arrangements were made in case other plans for warning the countryside failed.

On April 17, 1775, William Dawes was sent by the land route to warn that the British would soon be coming. No one knew yet by what route. On the night of April 18, the Minutemen of Boston realized that the British were leaving by boat. With this knowledge, Paul Revere was to go by the water route and alert the countryside.

Making certain two lanterns were shining in the tower of the Old North Church, Revere set off across the Charles River in a small boat. On the other side, friends met him with a good horse. At a gallop, Revere set off to warn that the British were coming. He raced

278

down the dark roads pounding on doors, shouting his warning. As Paul Revere later said, "I alarmed almost every house till I got to Lexington."

In Lexington, Revere warned Hancock and Adams. Joined there by William Dawes, Revere then set off to alert Concord. On the road, a young doctor joined them. The midnight ride of Dawes and Revere came to an end when they were stopped by a British patrol. The doctor, however, escaped by jumping his horse over a low stone wall and reached Concord.

Meanwhile, the Minutemen gathered on Lexington Green. At dawn the first British troops arrived. There were far more soldiers than the Minutemen were prepared to fight. Seeing this, the captain of the Minutemen ordered his men to return to their homes. At about the same time, the British captain, on his horse, yelled, "Ye villains, ye Rebels, disperse!" As the Minutemen were breaking up, a shot was fired. No one knows who fired first, but each side was soon firing at the other. Within minutes eight Minutemen lay dead or dying.

The smell of gunpowder was still in the air in Lexington Green when the British army marched on to Concord. There they found some wooden carts used to hold cannons. As they burned them, the smoke rose above the town.

Meanwhile, the news of the shots at Lexington had spread. Minutemen from nearby villages began to gather near Concord's North Bridge. The bridge was half a mile (0.8 km) from Concord. When the Minutemen saw the smoke from the gun carts, they thought the British were burning the town. They decided to march to save the town or

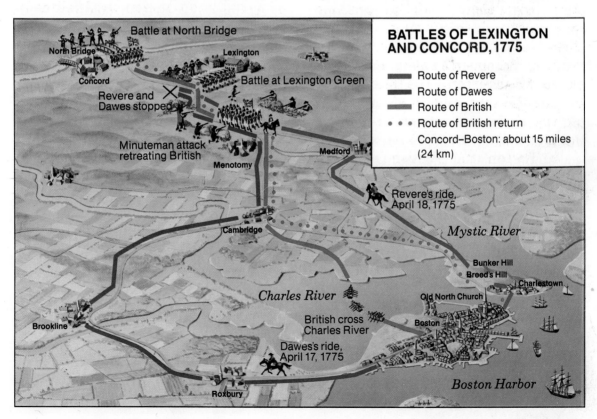

BATTLES OF LEXINGTON AND CONCORD, 1775

▬▬ Route of Revere
▬▬ Route of Dawes
▬▬ Route of British
• • • Route of British return

Concord–Boston: about 15 miles (24 km)

Battle at North Bridge
North Bridge
Concord
Lexington
Battle at Lexington Green
Revere and Dawes stopped
Minuteman attack retreating British
Menotomy
Medford
Revere's ride, April 18, 1775
Mystic River
Cambridge
Bunker Hill
Breed's Hill
Charlestown
Charles River
Old North Church
British cross Charles River
Boston
Brookline
Dawes's ride, April 17, 1775
Boston Harbor
Roxbury

The British Redcoats retreat from Lexington while Minutemen fire on them from behind walls and hedges.

die in the attempt. The Redcoats and Minutemen faced each other and fired in a brief battle at the North Bridge.

After several Redcoats were killed, the British troops fled back into Concord. The Minutemen began to take up positions behind stone walls around Concord. Fearing the numbers of Minutemen they could see gathering, the British started to march back to Boston. Their red coats stood out against the new spring grass, budding trees, and stone fences of the countryside.

Behind the trees and stone fences was hidden an army of Minutemen. These farmers, shopkeepers, craftsmen, and schoolteachers peppered the Redcoats with musket fire. The hail of musket fire created panic in the British troops. "It seemed as if men came down from the clouds," one Redcoat later said. The Redcoats had been trained to fight on a battlefield against an enemy they could see. How could they fight an enemy that hid behind trees and buildings?

It took the British half a day to reach the outskirts of Boston. On the river were British warships with guns ready. At last they were safe.

At least 72 British soldiers were killed that day. Some 49 Americans died. Neither the British governor nor the Americans had looked for battle, but that day it had happened.

The battles of Lexington and Concord on April 19 produced the shots "heard round the world." They announced that Americans meant to fight the British for their rights. They were the shots that started a war.

 Reading Check

1. Why did the British decide to march to Lexington and Concord?
2. What did two lanterns signal?
3. Which men set out to warn the countryside?

Think Beyond Do you think the minutemen had any advantages over the British soldiers? Explain.

Paul Revere
1735–1818

▶▶▶▶▶▶▶▶▶▶▶▶▶▶

People MAKE HISTORY

Listen, my children and you shall hear
Of the midnight ride of Paul Revere.
—Henry Wadsworth Longfellow

These are the first lines of a famous poem about Paul Revere's ride to Lexington. Henry Wadsworth Longfellow wrote the poem in 1863, many years after the ride.

Paul Revere was famous in his own day, but not for his daring ride. He was famous then as a silversmith.

Revere had learned to make silver pitchers and bowls from his father. His father had come to Boston from France to find religious freedom. When young Paul was old enough, he became an apprentice to his father.

Paul Revere learned quickly. He soon became one of New England's finest silversmiths. For his wealthy customers Revere fashioned large silver punch bowls and fancy serving dishes. Paul Revere also made things for everyday use. He made spoons, dog collars, baby rattles, and even false teeth.

In 1765, when the Stamp Act was passed, Paul Revere joined the Sons of Liberty. Some members served their cause by writing or speaking. Revere served as a messenger.

Few people had horses in the city of Boston in those days. Paul Revere kept a horse because he loved to spend free hours galloping through the countryside. Because he had a horse, Revere often carried messages from Boston to committees of correspondence in other towns. His most amazing ride took place in December 1773. He rode to Philadelphia to bring news of the Boston Tea Party. He made the 700-mile (about 1,125-km) round trip in just 11 days.

His most famous ride was to Lexington on April 18, 1775. After that night, Revere could not return to Boston. The British would have jailed him. Instead, he continued to act as a messenger for the Sons of Liberty. Later he served in the Continental Army.

Paul Revere was well known as a silversmith. Today, partly because of Longfellow's poem, he is more famous as a rider for liberty.

Think Beyond What are some different ways in which people might serve our country today?

SKILLS IN ACTION

UNDERSTANDING CAUSE AND EFFECT

Imagine you are waiting for a bus. You discover you have forgotten your homework. You run back home to get it, and you miss your bus.

Something that makes something else happen is a **cause.** What happens is called the **effect.** Forgetting your homework is the cause of your missing the bus. Missing the bus is the effect of forgetting your homework.

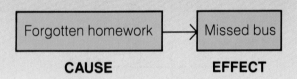

| Forgotten homework | → | Missed bus |

CAUSE   **EFFECT**

Suppose you kick a ball too high. It flies over a fence and breaks a window. What is the effect? What is the cause?

(*Reading hint:* The word *cause* has two meanings. Its main meaning is "something that makes something else happen." Its second meaning is "goal" or "struggle," as in "fighting for the cause of freedom." Only the main meaning is used in this section.)

Life is full of causes and effects. Because history is about life in the past, history too is full of causes and effects. So are history books!

Sometimes causes or effects are labeled. You might see sentences like this in a history book:

The *cause* of the war was an attack on the fort.
The *effect* of the attack was war.
The attack *caused* a war.

All three sentences mean the same thing. There was an attack. It was the cause of something else. There was a war. The war was an effect of something, the attack.

Often, word clues can help you find causes or effects. Such word clues include *because, as a result of,* and *therefore.* Here are some examples:

a. The French and Indian War started *because* the French and the English both wanted to control the Ohio River valley.

b. *As a result of* General Braddock's defeat, Indians began attacking the frontier settlements.

c. As the British and Minutemen faced each other at Lexington, someone fired a shot. *Therefore,* both sides started shooting.

In sentence <u>a</u> the word *because* signals the cause: The French and the English both wanted the Ohio River valley. The effect is that the French and Indian War started. What is the cause in sentence <u>b</u>? What is the cause in sentence <u>c</u>? What is the effect?

Sometimes, however, there are no word clues. Writers cannot always use word clues, and the reader does not always need them. Let's look at some sentences you have already read.

Imagine you are waiting for a bus. You discover you have forgotten your homework. You run back home to get it, and you miss the bus.

In these sentences, word clues are not needed. You, the reader, put them in. You know that forgetting your homework comes before missing your bus. You figure that what comes first probably *caused* or had an *effect* on what came later.

Events often have more than one cause. Suppose that you are hurrying to school. It is raining, and the sidewalks are slippery. You are wearing shoes with slick soles. There are wet leaves on the sidewalk. Your feet slip on the leaves and you fall.

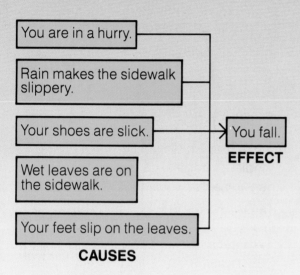

CAUSES

The chart below shows the cause of the Stamp Act. What is it? It shows two effects of the Stamp Act. What are they? Notice the way in which an effect can become a cause of the next event.

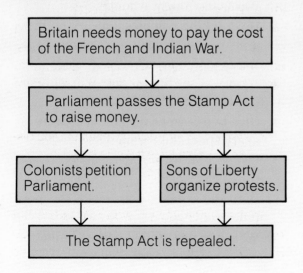

CHECKING YOUR SKILLS

Look at this chart and answer the questions that follow.

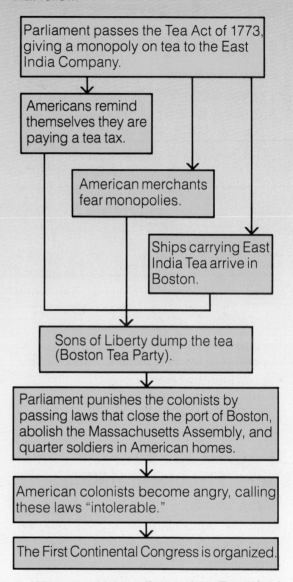

1. What were three effects of the Tea Act of 1773?

2. What was the effect of the Boston Tea Party?

3. What was the cause of Massachusetts losing its assembly?

4. Why did the American colonists become angry? What was an effect of this anger?

283

Thinking Back

- The French and Indian War started because both France and England claimed the land of the Ohio River valley. The Indians became allies of the French.

- Britain won the war and gained control of all lands in North America east of the Mississippi River, including Canada.

- The war caused disagreements between Britain and its colonies. Colonists wanted to settle the new lands, but Britain wanted to keep them for the Indians. The British Parliament decided to tax the colonies to pay for the war.

- The colonists felt these taxes were unfair. Protests forced Parliament to repeal most of the taxes.

- British soldiers in American cities further angered the colonists. In several cities, fights broke out. The worst of these fights resulted in the Boston Massacre.

- The Committees of Correspondence helped keep colonists informed of happenings in other colonies.

- To protest the tea monopoly, a shipment of tea was dumped into Boston Harbor. Parliament then passed the Intolerable Acts to punish the colonists.

- The First Continental Congress met to discuss ways to resist British tyranny.

- When British soldiers decided to seize the Minutemen's supplies and arrest their leaders, fighting broke out. The battles of Lexington and Concord proved that Americans were willing to fight the British for their rights.

Check for Understanding

Using Words

Write the numbers from 1 to 10 on your paper. Explain the meaning of each of the words below.

1. allies
2. boycott
3. liberty
4. massacre
5. monopoly
6. petition
7. quartered
8. repeal
9. resist
10. tyranny

Reviewing Facts

1. What started the French and Indian War? Who fought whom?

2. How did the colonies and Britain disagree over settlement west of the Appalachian Mountains?

3. What was the Stamp Act? Why did Parliament pass it?

4. Give two reasons the colonists were so angry about the Stamp Act.

5. List several ways Americans protested the Stamp Act.

6. How did women help make the boycotts a success?

7. What was the purpose of the Committee of Correspondence?

8. Why did American merchants fear monopolies?

9. What were the Intolerable Acts? Why did they so anger the colonists?

10. What was the effect of the battles of Lexington and Concord?

Thinking Critically

1. Why did it take courage for John Adams to defend the British captain? Can you think of other examples of courage in this chapter? Do you think some things take more courage than others? Why?

2. Do you think it was fair for Parliament to ask the colonies to help pay for the French and Indian War? Explain.

Writing About It

It is the spring of 1774. Imagine that you are a member of the Committee of Correspondence in Boston. Write a letter to a fellow member in Philadelphia describing events taking place in Boston.

Practicing Thinking Skills

Using Cause and Effect

Study the chart below. Answer the questions that follow.

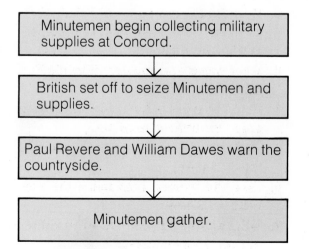

Minutemen begin collecting military supplies at Concord.

↓

British set off to seize Minutemen and supplies.

↓

Paul Revere and William Dawes warn the countryside.

↓

Minutemen gather.

1. Why did the British set off for Concord?
2. Why did Paul Revere and William Dawes warn the countryside?
3. What was the effect of this warning?

On Your Own

Social Studies at Home

1. Imagine that you are a silversmith like Paul Revere. Using modeling clay, craft a pitcher, tray, or some other item. Be sure to sign your work.

2. Discuss with your family the idea of a boycott. Then have them help you look through newspapers and magazines to find examples of modern-day boycotts. Cut out the examples and paste them onto posterboard for display in class.

Read More About It

The American Revolutionaries: A History in Their Own Words 1750–1800 edited by Milton Meltzer. T. Y. Crowell. This collection of diaries and newspaper articles captures the spirit of the American Revolution.

Johnny Tremain by Esther Forbes. Houghton Mifflin. This story offers an "eye-witness" account of revolutionary turmoil in Boston in the 1770s.

Paul Revere's Ride by Henry Wadsworth Longfellow. Illustrated by Nancy Winslow Parker. Greenwillow. This picture book includes the famous poem's full text along with explanatory notes.

Why Don't You Get a Horse, Sam Adams? by Jean Fritz. Illustrated by Trina Schart Hyman. Coward, McCann, & Geoghegan. This book provides a humorous look at an American patriot's historical contributions and his refusal to ride a horse.

CHAPTER 11

The Revolutionary War

"I lay here two nights and one day and had not a morsel of anything to eat all the time, save half of a small pumpkin, which I cooked by placing it upon a rock, the skin uppermost, and making a fire upon it. By the time it was heat through I devoured it with as keen an appetite as I should a pie made of it at some other time."

—Valley Forge soldier, 1777

Look for these important words:

Key Words

- Second Continental Congress
- Patriots
- Loyalists
- declaration
- Continental Army
- earthworks

- Battle of Bunker Hill
- independence
- Olive Branch Petition
- mercenaries

- Declaration of Independence
- Independence Day

People
- Thomas Paine
- Thomas Jefferson

Places
- Mount Vernon

Look for answers to these questions:

1. How did the colonists prepare to fight the British?
2. Why did most Americans want to avoid war with Britain?
3. Why did Americans finally declare independence from Britain?

1 On the Road to Independence

After the battles of Lexington and Concord, the Continental Congress met again in Philadelphia. This was the **Second Continental Congress.** Some of the wisest men in America attended. From Massachusetts came Sam Adams, John Adams, and John Hancock. From Pennsylvania came Benjamin Franklin, and from Virginia, Patrick Henry and George Washington.

These men were called **Patriots.** Patriots believed that the American colonists were right to stand up for their liberties. About one-third of the American colonists were Patriots. About one-third of the colonists sided with Britain. They were called **Loyalists,** or Tories. Another third of the colonists did not choose either side.

Few members of the Second Continental Congress wanted a complete break with Britain. In a **declaration,** or statement, the Second Continental

Congress said, "We fight not for glory or for conquest." Colonists had started fighting, they said, because they felt they had no choice.

Even though it hoped for peace, the Continental Congress created an army and navy to fight the British. It appointed George Washington to be commander in chief of the new **Continental Army.** John Adams had suggested Washington for the job. Washington's skill, great talents, and excellent character would command the respect of all Americans, Adams said. He proved to be right.

Washington would rather have returned to his Virginia plantation, **Mount Vernon.** Instead, he accepted the position of commander in chief. He felt it was his duty to do so. He wrote Martha Washington, his wife, that he hoped his going would "answer some good purpose."

Battle of Bunker Hill

After the battles at Lexington and Concord, the angry citizens of Massachusetts started to build **earthworks,** or walls of dirt and stone, near Boston. Earthworks would protect Patriot soldiers if there were another battle. The Patriots had taken over control of the countryside. A British soldier was not safe if he tried to leave Boston. The British troops were hemmed in, able to enter and leave Boston only by sea.

The Patriots began to build new earthworks on a small hill near Charlestown on June 16, 1775. At this, the British commander decided the time had come for action. He called out his troops. On June 17, lines of Redcoats started marching up the hill to the roll of drums. Behind the earthworks the Patriots waited, muskets ready. "Don't fire until you see the whites of their eyes," they were told. When the British drew close to the earthworks, the Patriots let loose a deadly hail of shot.

The British were forced back several times. Finally, the Patriots ran out of ammunition and retreated. The British took the hill, but at great cost. On that day about half of the British army were killed or wounded. The Patriot losses were much fewer. The Americans were proud of how well they had done. They felt the victory was really theirs. From this battle, the **Battle of Bunker Hill,** the British learned that it would be no easy job fighting the Americans.

Hopes for Peace

Most Americans still did not want war. They considered themselves loyal

At the Battle of Bunker Hill, Patriot soldiers prepare to defend themselves against lines of British Redcoats.

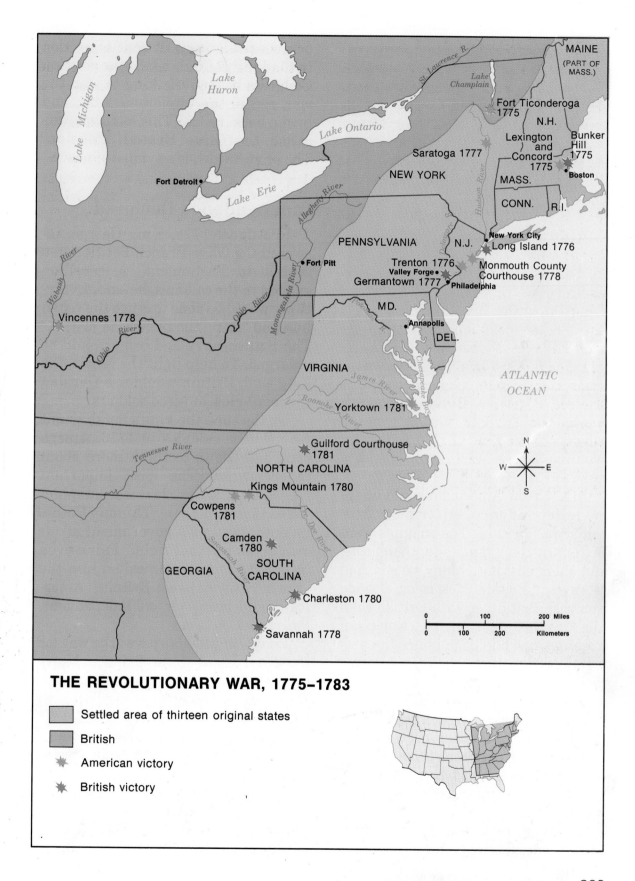

Lake Huron

Lake Michigan

Lake Ontario

St. Lawrence R.

Lake Champlain

MAINE
(PART OF MASS.)

Fort Ticonderoga 1775

N.H.

Saratoga 1777

Lexington and Concord 1775

Bunker Hill 1775

NEW YORK

Boston

Fort Detroit

Lake Erie

MASS.

CONN.

R.I.

Allegheny River

Hudson River

PENNSYLVANIA

New York City
Long Island 1776

N.J.

Fort Pitt

Trenton 1776
Valley Forge
Germantown 1777

Monmouth County Courthouse 1778

Philadelphia

Wabash River

Ohio River

Monongahela River

MD.

Vincennes 1778

Ohio River

Annapolis

DEL.

VIRGINIA

ATLANTIC OCEAN

James River

Chesapeake Bay

Tennessee River

Roanoke River

Yorktown 1781

Guilford Courthouse 1781

NORTH CAROLINA

Kings Mountain 1780

Cowpens 1781

Pee Dee River

Camden 1780

N
W E
S

GEORGIA

SOUTH CAROLINA

Savannah River

Charleston 1780

Savannah 1778

0   100   200 Miles
0 100 200 Kilometers

THE REVOLUTIONARY WAR, 1775–1783

Settled area of thirteen original states

British

★ American victory

★ British victory

In his right hand King George III holds the scepter, symbol of his right to rule.

peace with Britain. It sent a petition to the king of England. In the petition Congress begged the king to stop the war, repeal the Intolerable Acts, and bring back peace. This petition was called the **Olive Branch Petition.** The olive branch is a symbol of peace.

Independence Declared

In August 1775, King George answered the Olive Branch Petition in a speech to Parliament. A rebellion existed in the colonies, he said. Everything would be done to crush the rebellion and "bring the traitors to justice." The British navy and army would be enlarged. To help fight the rebels, the king said, Britain would use German **mercenaries,** or hired soldiers.

By the time the king's harsh words reached the colonies in 1776, Americans had begun to think more about independence. The most important reason for this change was a pamphlet called *Common Sense.* **Thomas Paine,** its author, said, "A government of our own is our natural right." Paine even attacked the king. He called him the "Royal Brute of Great Britain." America would be better off independent, Paine said.

Paine's arguments paved the way for the final break from Britain. Many colonists began to urge independence. That was the only way, they said, to ensure liberty. "By every post [mail] and every day, independence rolls in on us like a torrent," John Adams wrote from the Congress.

In June of 1776, the Congress asked a committee to write a declaration of independence. **Thomas Jefferson,** a Virginia planter and scholar, was a

subjects of the king of England. Each evening George Washington drank a toast to King George.

In 1775 few Americans could imagine **independence,** or complete freedom, from Britain. The colonies were British in their language, their laws, and their customs. Many people had relatives in Britain. Most colonial trade was with Britain or with British colonies in the West Indies. American trading ships had been under the protection of the British navy wherever they sailed. The British navy was the most powerful in the world.

If the colonies did fight a war against Britain, how could they hope to win? If the colonies cut themselves off from the king, how would they be ruled? They could not imagine a government without a king.

In July 1775, the Continental Congress made another effort to achieve

Thomas Jefferson presents the Declaration of Independence.
On his left is Benjamin Franklin. On his far right is John Adams.

member of this committee. Using a goose quill pen, Jefferson wrote every evening for 17 days. The committee suggested some changes. At last the document was ready.

On July 4, 1776, the members of the Continental Congress voted for the **Declaration of Independence.** Writing to his wife, Abigail, John Adams said that **Independence Day** should be remembered with shows, games, sports, guns, bells, bonfires, and fireworks "from this time forward forever more."

The Declaration of Independence announced to the world why the American colonies had to cut their ties with Britain. Now the colonies were the United States of America. After the declaration was read out loud in Philadelphia, the Liberty Bell rang out.

Yet saying the 13 colonies were the United States of America did not make it so. The United States had to prove their strength and push the British troops off their soil.

 Reading Check

1. Why did the Second Continental Congress appoint George Washington commander in chief?
2. Why could few Americans imagine independence in 1775?
3. Why was *Common Sense* written?

Think Beyond If the Declaration of Independence did not make the colonies free, why was it so important?

SKILLS IN ACTION

READING A DOCUMENT:
THE DECLARATION OF INDEPENDENCE

Wars are fought with words as well as with guns. Thomas Jefferson, the main writer of the Declaration of Independence, firmly believed it was right to be fighting against British rule. He wrote the Declaration of Independence to win support for the American Revolution. Jefferson wanted his words to help the new nation win its battle for freedom.

In order to do this, Jefferson had to plan and write carefully. He had to state facts to convince people independence was necessary. He also had to speak to people's hearts. He had to make people *feel* that the Americans were right and the British were wrong.

Jefferson organized the Declaration of Independence into several main parts. In the first part, or introduction, he said why the Declaration was necessary. In the second part, Jefferson explained the colonists' basic beliefs about rights and government.

You can view the original Declaration of Independence in the National Archives.

In the third part, he listed the wrongs done by the king. In the fourth part, or conclusion, Jefferson said that the colonies were now free and independent.

Introduction: When In the Course of Human Events

Jefferson began the Declaration with words that mean this:

> Sometimes a group of people must cut themselves off from the country they once belonged to. They find they have no choice but to form a new nation with the same powers of other independent countries. When people do this, they should explain their reasons. In that way, they show respect for the opinions of others.

The modern paragraph above gives the basic meaning of Jefferson's words. The words Jefferson actually used were these:

> *When, in the course of human events, it becomes necessary for one people to dissolve the political bands which have connected them with another, and to assume, among the powers of the earth, the separate and equal station to which the laws of nature and of nature's God entitle them, a decent respect to the opinions of mankind requires that they should declare the causes which impel them to the separation.*

Notice that Jefferson's words form one long sentence. It is a serious, dignified sentence. It moves slowly and surely, like a great river, toward the last word and key idea: *separation.*

This very special sentence may be hard for you to understand. However the declaration was easily understood by the people of 1776. In fact, it was written much more simply and honestly than many other important writings of that time. The people who read the Declaration of Independence found it effective and stirring.

Beliefs: All Men Are Created Equal

In the second part of the Declaration, Jefferson stated the Patriots' main ideas about government. He began with a sentence that means this:

> We believe in certain ideas. Anyone can see how true these ideas are. God has given all people some rights that are a natural part of them. These rights include the right to live, the right to be free, and the right to try to be happy. People cannot give up or take away these rights. In these ways, all people are born equal.

Below are the words Jefferson actually used. They say what Patriots believed in 1776 and what Americans believe today:

> *We hold these truths to be self-evident: that all men are created equal; that they are endowed by their Creator with certain inalienable rights; that among these are life, liberty, and the pursuit of happiness.*

These words are as clear and powerful today as when they were first written. They are among the most famous in history. Since they were written, they have stirred people in many nations to fight against cruel and unfair governments.

Jefferson believed that a government must protect the basic rights of its people.

For him, this was the purpose of government. If a nation's government does not protect these rights, he said, people have the right to change or get rid of the government. Jefferson warned, though, that action against a government is a very serious thing. It should not be done except when a government has treated its people very badly for a long time.

Wrongs: The King Has Wronged Us

In the third and longest part of the Declaration, Jefferson tells how badly the king of England had governed America. Jefferson listed more than 25 ways in which the king had wronged the American colonists. Here are three examples in modern language:

- The king has not let the colonies pass laws of their choice.
- The king has not given any power to representatives from the colonies.
- The king has sent soldiers to live among the colonists. He has not punished these soldiers when they have broken laws.

In this part Jefferson used strong language to make people very angry at the king of England. In his words:

> *He has plundered our seas, ravaged our coasts, burnt our towns, and destroyed the lives of our people.*

Plunder means to take by force. *Ravage* means to destroy. If you had been a colonist, how would you feel about a king who did such things?

Jefferson did not stop there. He pointed out that the king was now doing something even worse. The king was sending German mercenaries, to do even more damage.

293

He is, at this time, transporting large armies of foreign mercenaries to complete the works of death, desolation, and tyranny already begun.

Perhaps, after reading a long list of wrongs, someone might still ask, "But did you try to settle these problems peacefully?" So Jefferson explained that the colonists had often asked the king to correct these wrongs. They had sent many petitions to the king, but he had ignored them. Such a king, Jefferson said, was "unfit to be the ruler of a free people."

Conclusion: We Are Free and Independent

In the last part of the Declaration, Jefferson announced independence in words that mean this:

We, the representatives of the United States of America, say this: the colonies are now free and independent. They no longer have any connection with the British king or government. As an independent country, we now have the right to make peace or war, and to trade with other nations. We now have all the other rights that other nations have.

Jefferson knew that *saying* such things would not be enough. American patriots now had to fight and win a war with Britain. Only then would the United States be a free and independent country.

Jefferson added one last sentence to the Declaration. He wanted to make clear that he and the other Patriots meant every word.

And, for the support of this declaration, with a firm reliance on the protection of Divine Providence [God], we mutually pledge to each other our lives, our fortunes, and our sacred honor.

Jefferson and other Patriots then signed their names to the Declaration. They were telling the world that they were willing to die for the cause of independence. They wanted to set an example for all Americans who would join them. They made a promise to give their property, even their lives, to the struggle. They promised to do this upon their sacred honor, the most serious and deep promise they could make.

By writing the Declaration of Independence in clear and powerful words, Jefferson helped the Patriot cause. His words also laid the foundation for a new kind of government, one dedicated to protecting the rights of its people.

CHECKING YOUR SKILLS

Copy the sentences below. Use the information in this skill lesson to find the words that best complete each sentence. When the sentences are complete, you will have a list of the main ideas of the Declaration of Independence.

1. The colonists say they are breaking off from _____. They promise to explain their reasons for doing this.

2. The colonists explain their belief that all people have some basic rights. These rights are _____, _____, and _____.

3. They list the _____ the king had done to them. They explain how they tried to settle these problems _____.

4. They declare their _____, and they declare that they want the rights of nations.

5. The signers pledge their _____, their _____, and their _____ to the cause of freedom.

Look for these important words:

People
- Marquis de Lafayette
- Friedrich von Steuben

Places
- Trenton
- Saratoga
- Valley Forge

Look for answers to these questions:
1. What difficulties did the Continental Army face?
2. How was George Washington able to hold an army together?
3. How did women help in the Revolutionary War?
4. How did Europeans help the Patriots?

2 Americans Fight for Liberty

In the summer of 1775, George Washington arrived in Massachusetts to take command of the 15,000 soldiers gathered there. Washington's problems were great and would remain so throughout the war.

Washington's major problem was feeding and supplying the Continental Army. Most soldiers in the war never did have uniforms. They fought in the clothes they had. Thousands marched and fought without shoes. Thousands never had blankets or tents. The historian Samuel Eliot Morison has written:

> Altogether, the private soldier of the War of Independence was so badly fed, clothed, and cared for...that one is surprised and grateful that any continued to fight.

Another problem Washington faced was the lack of discipline. The soldiers knew little of drills or marching in lines. The men who came to fight were not used to taking orders. They were independent people—backwoodsmen, fishermen, farmers, and craftsmen. Washington's job was to turn these soldiers into a well-trained army able to take on the British forces.

Another problem was keeping men in the army. Washington's army at times had more than 15,000 men. At other times it shrank to as few as 2,000. Most men served in the army less than a year. Many would go home when it was time to plant or harvest crops. Others joined the army only when the fighting was nearby. They were like the farmer Reuben Stebbins. He had paid little attention to the war until he heard the sounds of a battle near his farm in New York state. Then he saddled his horse and rode off to fight the British. "We'll see who's going to own this farm," he shouted.

Washington was able to hold his army together only because people respected him so much. Soldiers were

These ragged Continental soldiers proudly march forward in this painting by Howard Pyle. In the front line is the drummer, one of the most important persons in the army. Drum beats directed soldiers to advance, to retreat, or to halt.

willing to follow Washington when they were hungry, cold, or even barefoot. Washington's simple presence brought respect, as a boy soldier later remembered.

Israel Trask, at the age of 10, was a cook and messenger boy in Washington's army. He was with the army in Massachusetts when a group of soldiers from Virginia arrived. The Virginia soldiers wore white, fringed shirts that came to their knees.

The New Englanders, who dressed differently, began to make fun of the Virginians. At first the Virginians were patient and took the teasing, but then they scooped up the snow at their feet and started throwing snowballs. Soon the snowball fight turned into a free-for-all with 1,000 soldiers kicking, biting, and hitting each other.

Young Israel watched. Then, Israel Trask remembered, George Washington appeared. "With the spring of a deer, he leaped from his saddle, threw the reins of his bridle into the hands of his servant, and rushed into the thickest of the fight."

Washington was a strong man, 6 feet 3 inches (190.5 cm) tall. With an iron grip he "seized two tall, brawny, athletic, savage-looking riflemen by the throat, keeping them at arm's length, alternately shaking and talking to them." As soon as the other soldiers saw the general, they ran away as fast as they could. Only Washington and the two soldiers in his grip remained on the field.

Women in the Revolution

The story of the War of Independence may seem to be the story of men. Men made the important battle decisions. Men did most of the fighting. Men did most of the dying. Yet women were as important in winning the war. When the men went off to fight, the women took over the businesses, shops, and farms.

Many women formed groups to raise money for the war. Others worked hard to sew shirts and knit socks for the soldiers.

Women were spies and messengers. Some, left alone in their homes, resisted the British either by wit or by guns. When women at Groton, Connecticut, heard that the British were approaching, they dressed in men's clothes. Armed with pitchforks, sling shots, and guns, they successfully turned back the Redcoats.

Lead for bullets was in short supply during the war. Because lead was an important part of pewter, women gave up their pewter pots and plates, their pewter spoons and forks. Many family treasures were melted down for bullets.

Hundreds of women shared the uncomfortable army life. These women, often with children, followed their husbands. In army camps they cooked food and washed clothes. Some, like Martha Washington, nursed the sick and wounded. On the battlefield women brought water and sometimes loaded cannons. A few dressed and fought as men.

The British knew how important the women were. One officer wrote that even if the British destroyed all the men in America, "we should have enough to do to conquer the women."

Victory at Trenton

By the fall of 1776, Washington and his ragged army moved south from

Molly Pitcher grabs a rammer to load cannon even though an officer tries to order her off the field. "Molly Pitcher" was the nickname of Mary Ludwig Hayes. She earned the nickname by bringing water to troops suffering through a long, hot battle at Monmouth, New Jersey.

This famous painting shows George Washington crossing the icy Delaware River on Christmas Day before the attack on Trenton.

Massachusetts. They went first to New York and then to New Jersey. The British had defeated the army several times and were chasing what remained of it. The Americans were in despair.

Then came new hope. On Christmas Day, 1776, Washington and his army of 2,400 men crossed the Delaware River in boats. By night in freezing weather, the shivering soldiers silently marched toward **Trenton,** New Jersey. There the German mercenaries were celebrating Christmas.

At daybreak the Americans made a surprise attack. Over 900 Germans surrendered. Only four Americans were wounded. Two others froze to death. The Continental Army found many weapons and supplies at Trenton. Patriots everywhere were overjoyed at the news. Perhaps there was hope after all!

Help from Europe

The year 1777 brought help to the Patriots. From Europe came men eager to fight for the idea of liberty. The most important of these was the **Marquis de Lafayette** (mahr·KEE duh lahf·ee·ET), then only 20 years old. A rich Frenchman, he hired French soldiers to come with him to America. Washington liked the young Lafayette and immediately gave him important duties.

Another who came was Johann de Kalb, a German-born professional soldier. From Poland came Casimir Pulaski (KAZ·ih·mihr puh·LAS·kee) and Thaddeus Kosciuszko (THAD·ee·uhs kahs·ih·UHS·koh). Later Kosciuszko returned to Poland to lead a revolution for Polish liberty.

The best news of October 1777 was an American victory at **Saratoga,** New

It is a snowy, cold day at Valley Forge in 1777 as George Washington and the Marquis de Lafayette observe the hungry and weary troops.

York. There the Americans soundly defeated a large British army. This victory brought America an ally—France.

Benjamin Franklin had gone to France to try to win help for the Americans. At news of the American victory at Saratoga, the French decided to help the struggling nation. In this way the French hoped to get back at Britain, their old enemy.

Later in 1777, Washington's army faced another hard winter. After losing Philadelphia to the British, Washington established his winter camp at **Valley Forge,** about 20 miles (32 km) away. While the British were warm and comfortable in Philadelphia, the Americans were hungry, cold, and sick at Valley Forge. Things looked bad indeed for the Continental Army.

In these hard times a German soldier showed up to help. **Friedrich von Steuben** (FREE•drihk vahn STYOO•buhn) took on the job of organizing and drilling the army so that it could move quickly on command. He taught the soldiers how to use bayonets. Bayonets were standard equipment for European soldiers but were unknown in America. By spring the troops were marching smartly.

 Reading Check

1. How did women contribute to the Revolution?
2. Name at least three Europeans who helped the Patriots.
3. Why did France decide to help the American Patriots?

Think Beyond How did Washington's personality affect his army?

YANKEE DOODLE

Almost every American knows the song "Yankee Doodle": "Yankee Doodle went to town / Riding on a pony, / Stuck a feather in his cap / And called it macaroni!" It has become one of our most popular patriotic songs, and it can be heard at Fourth of July celebrations and at other occasions honoring the United States. "Yankee Doodle" was written, however, not to honor Americans but to make fun of them.

During the French and Indian War, the British enlisted American colonists to help them fight the French. Although the Americans were good soldiers, some of them looked rough and ragged. Most of them lived on farms or in remote regions. They were not as well-dressed or as polished as the British Redcoats.

According to legend, a British doctor named Richard Schuckburg went to Albany, New York, to tend wounded British soldiers. While there, he saw a group of colonial soldiers assembling in the city square. Their ragged clothing and unruly behavior amused Dr. Schuckburg, and he wrote a song to make fun of them:

"Father and I went down to camp / Along with Captain Goodwin, / And there we saw the men and boys / As thick as hasty puddin'. / Yankee Doodle, keep it up, / Yankee Doodle dandy. / Mind the music and the step / And with the girls be handy."

No one is sure if Dr. Schuckburg really wrote the song, but by 1767 it was being sung in all of the colonies. During the American Revolution, too, British troops used the song to make fun of the American troops. When the British left Boston to march on Lexington and Concord in 1775, they marched to the tune of "Yankee Doodle." One story says that after the British were defeated at Concord, the colonists sang "Yankee Doodle" as they chased the Redcoats back to Boston. Ever since, "Yankee Doodle" has been sung by Americans to celebrate being Americans.

Think Beyond Why do you think the colonial soldiers did not have uniforms like the British?

Rough and ragged colonial soldiers

Look for these important words:

Key Words	People	Places
• treaty	• Nathanael Greene	• Yorktown
	• John Paul Jones	
	• George Rogers Clark	
	• Francis Marion	
	• Charles Cornwallis	

Look for answers to these questions:
1. What leaders helped win the war? What did each accomplish?
2. What happened at the Battle of Yorktown?
3. Why was the United States able to defeat Britain?

3 The Push to Victory

Starting in 1778, most of the fighting shifted to the South, particularly South Carolina. The Americans suffered some terrible defeats, but under the leadership of General **Nathanael** (nuh•THAN•yuhl) **Greene,** they began to hold their own. Victories at Kings Mountain, Cowpens, and Guilford Courthouse gave new heart to the Southern forces.

The British were able to take many important cities in America. But they could not win the war, for no one city was the heart of America. America's heart was in the farms and villages of its 13 states. As the British tried to stamp out the fire of independence in one place, they found that it only sprang up in another place. "We fight, get beat, rise, and fight again," Nathanael Greene wrote.

During the war Americans were cheered by news of many brave people. **John Paul Jones,** a navy commander, battled British ships in their own waters. In one famous battle the British demanded his surrender. He replied, "I have not yet begun to fight."

In the Ohio River valley, **George Rogers Clark** helped safeguard the frontier by attacking the British and their Indian allies. Clark became known as the "Washington of the West."

From bases in the swamps of South Carolina, **Francis Marion** led daring raids against the British. They called Marion the "Swamp Fox" because they could never catch him and his men.

Thousands of blacks, both slave and free, fought on both sides of the Revolution. The British offered freedom and land in Canada to slaves who would join the Loyalists. The blacks who fought for the Patriots did so with courage and skill. Black soldiers from Rhode Island were "the best under arms," a French officer wrote.

In the Revolution's most famous naval battle, John Paul Jones's ship *Bonhomme Richard,* left, fought all night against the British *Serapis.*

Francis Marion and his followers cross the Pee Dee River in the swamps of South Carolina. The British never could catch him.

French troops march toward the battle line in the siege of Yorktown, 1781. In the distance is Yorktown itself. Behind earthworks, French and American gunners fire their cannons into the British positions.

Victory at Yorktown

In October 1781, the last major battle of the war was fought at **Yorktown,** Virginia. Yorktown was a small town on Chesapeake Bay, not far from Williamsburg. The British general **Charles Cornwallis** had set up headquarters at Yorktown because it was easy for British ships to bring supplies.

The French and Americans made a plan to defeat Cornwallis. First, the French troops in Rhode Island marched south to join Washington's army. Along the way, Americans turned out to stare at the trim and colorful uniforms of the French. The French soldiers looked so fancy compared to the poorly clothed Continental soldiers. Everywhere the French went they carried war chests full of silver and gold coins. With the coins they could buy all the supplies and food they needed.

The French army joined George Washington's army near New York City. Together, the two armies continued marching toward Virginia. Meanwhile, the French navy gained control of Chesapeake Bay, as planned. Hearing the news, Washington whooped with joy and swung his hat in the air. Now, even the British navy could not help Cornwallis, trapped at Yorktown.

The French and American armies began to surround and bombard the British at Yorktown. To do this, they started on September 28 to dig trenches, or large ditches. The trenches protected the soldiers from most bullets and cannonballs. For two weeks they dug trenches closer and closer to the British. Day and night the two sides fired cannonballs at each other. At night the cannonballs looked like shooting stars.

During the battle Sarah Osborn was taking food to her husband and others in the trenches. Each day she brought beef, bread, and a gallon pot of coffee. On one of her trips she met George Washington. "Are you not afraid of the cannonballs?" he asked. "No," she said. "It would not do for the men to starve as well as fight."

Cornwallis, knowing he could not win, decided to surrender. A drummer boy in a red coat appeared on top of a British earthwork. He beat his drums until French and American gunners saw him. One by one they stopped their fire. A British officer then appeared with a white flag, a sign of surrender.

Two days later British and German soldiers marched out of Yorktown to lay down their arms in a field. Their bands played sad music. One of the songs was named "The World Turned Upside Down." Americans were joyful. When news of the victory reached Philadelphia, the Liberty Bell rang out loud and clear.

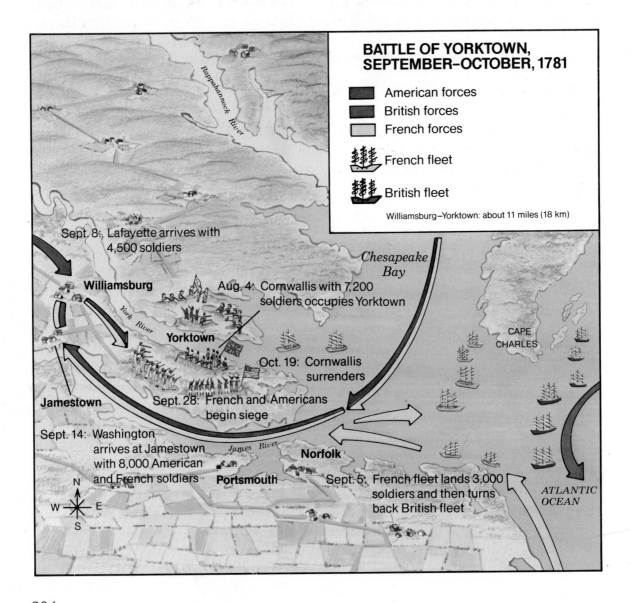

BATTLE OF YORKTOWN, SEPTEMBER–OCTOBER, 1781

- American forces
- British forces
- French forces
- French fleet
- British fleet

Williamsburg–Yorktown: about 11 miles (18 km)

Rappahannock River

Sept. 8: Lafayette arrives with 4,500 soldiers

Williamsburg

Chesapeake Bay

Aug. 4: Cornwallis with 7,200 soldiers occupies Yorktown

York River

Yorktown

CAPE CHARLES

Oct. 19: Cornwallis surrenders

Jamestown

Sept. 28: French and Americans begin siege

Sept. 14: Washington arrives at Jamestown with 8,000 American and French soldiers

James River

Norfolk

Portsmouth

Sept. 5: French fleet lands 3,000 soldiers and then turns back British fleet

ATLANTIC OCEAN

N W E S

The War Is Over

The Battle of Yorktown was the last major battle of the war. Yet a peace **treaty,** or formal agreement, did not become final until 1783. By that time George Washington and his officers had made their headquarters in New York City.

In early December 1783, George Washington and his officers met at the Fraunces (FRAWN•sehs) Tavern for a farewell dinner. Famous for its food, the tavern was in a fine, old New York mansion. Samuel Fraunces, the owner, was a black man from the West Indies. Before the war, his tavern had been a favorite meeting place for the Sons of Liberty.

Near the end of the dinner, Washington stood up. "With a heart full of love and gratitude, I now take my leave of you," he said to the men before him.

One by one, each man at the dinner came up to say good-bye to the commander in chief. Tears streaming down his cheeks, Washington hugged each one. "Such a scene of sorrow and weeping I have never before seen," wrote one of the officers. They were sad because they thought they would never again see George Washington. He was the man who had led them through the long and bloody war. He was the man who had led his country to glory and independence.

After saying his farewells, Washington started home to Mount Vernon. On the way he stopped in Annapolis, Maryland, where the Continental Congress was meeting. He told the Congress that, with peace, his work was done. "I retire from the great theater of action," Washington said. He was leaving public life forever, he thought. Saying his good-byes, Washington mounted his favorite horse, Nelson. By riding hard, he reached Mount Vernon on Christmas Eve.

Great as their joy was in victory, American officers were sad to say good-bye to each other. In Fraunces Tavern in New York City, George Washington bids each of his officers a final, tearful farewell.

In 1853 Ann Pamela Cunningham learned about a run-down farm in Virginia. This farm had once been George Washington's beautiful estate. When she heard about Mount Vernon's condition she tried to imagine how it must have looked when George Washington lived there.

During the 1700s, Mount Vernon had been a beautiful mansion surrounded by a sweeping green lawn. On the lawn were fragrant flower gardens planted alongside fruit and shade trees. After Washington's death, however, the house and its grounds were neglected.

Thus, when Cunningham heard about the mansion in 1853, she knew something had to be done to help. She and others formed the Mount Vernon Ladies' Association. As a result of their work, money was raised to restore the house and grounds. Thanks to the Mount Vernon Ladies' Association, today we can connect to our history by visiting the home of our first President.

Why the Americans Won

The Americans had beaten the powerful British army. How was this possible? All during the war the British army had problems. First of all, it was far from Britain and had to depend on supplies delivered by ship. The army could not set up and hold bases far from the sea. Generals of the British army often did not work together.

On the other hand, the Americans were fighting on their own soil. If they lost the war, many Patriots knew they would be hanged for treason. Americans were also fighting for liberty, an idea dear to their hearts. For these reasons they fought harder, and they would not give up. The Americans also had important help, particularly from the French. Finally, the Americans won because they had fine leaders. Soldiers respected these leaders and followed them even when times were hard. The finest of these leaders was George Washington.

 Reading Check

1. Why could the British capture important cities but not win the war?
2. When was a peace treaty finally signed between Britain and the United States?
3. What problems did the British face during the war? What advantages did the Americans have?

Think Beyond How important was cooperation between American and French leaders in determining the outcome of the war?

Thinking Back

- The Second Continental Congress created an army and a navy. It appointed George Washington to lead the Continental Army.

- Most Americans still considered themselves loyal subjects of the king. Congress made another effort to achieve peace with Britain.

- King George refused to stop the war. On July 4, 1776, Congress approved the Declaration of Independence.

- The Continental Army faced serious shortages, and its soldiers generally lacked discipline. Washington was able to hold his army together only because people respected him so much.

- American women played an important part in winning the war. Europeans eager to fight for the idea of liberty came to help.

- After the American victory at Saratoga, France became an ally of the United States.

- The British captured many important American cities, but they could not win the war. When the British tried to stamp out the fire of independence in one place, it flared up in another.

- The last major battle of the war was fought at Yorktown, where General Cornwallis surrendered his British forces. However, a formal peace treaty did not become final until 1783.

Check for Understanding

Using Words

Explain the meaning of the words below. Then use each word in a complete sentence.

1. declaration
2. independence
3. Patriots
4. mercenaries
5. treaty

Reviewing Facts

1. Why did the Patriots consider the Battle of Bunker Hill a victory?
2. How did the Second Continental Congress try to achieve peace with Britain?
3. What personal strengths did George Washington have?
4. How did Thomas Paine's *Common Sense* influence the Revolution?
5. What did the Declaration of Independence announce to the world?
6. Why was Washington's victory at Trenton important?
7. Why was the Battle of Saratoga a turning point in the war?
8. Name at least four Patriot military leaders in addition to George Washington. Why is each famous?
9. How was French help important at the Battle of Yorktown?
10. Put these events in order: Battle of Yorktown, Battle of Bunker Hill,

Declaration of Independence, *Common Sense*, Battle of Saratoga.

Thinking Critically

1. You may know the saying "The pen is mightier than the sword." This means that words can be more powerful than weapons. Do you think the saying is true? Explain your answer by using examples.

2. George Washington faced many problems as leader of the army. Yet he led the army to victory. What other leaders can you think of? What qualities should a good leader have?

3. You have read about the Battle of Yorktown from the point of view of the Americans. Imagine what a British account of the battle might say. How might it be different from the American account?

4. Most leaders of the Revolution were fairly rich. They were people of education and property. Why do you think they risked everything they had for the American Revolution?

Writing About It

Imagine that you are George Washington's wife, Martha. Describe how you feel about General Washington finally returning home to stay. Include your reaction when your husband finally reached Mount Vernon on Christmas Eve.

Practicing Reading Skills

Reading a Document

Use pages 292–294 to answer the following questions about the Declaration of Independence.

1. What methods of persuasion did Thomas Jefferson use in writing the Declaration of Independence?

2. What are the four main parts of the Declaration of Independence?

3. According to Jefferson, what three rights do all people have?

4. What did the Declaration of Independence achieve?

5. What is the main idea in the last sentence of the Declaration of Independence?

On Your Own

Social Studies at Home

1. George Rogers Clark was known as the "Washington of the West." Francis Marion was called the "Swamp Fox." Write down your own nicknames for King George III, the Marquis de Lafayette, John Paul Jones, and Charles Cornwallis. Explain how you decided on the nicknames.

2. Read the History Connection on page 306 to your family. Then draw pictures of how you think Mount Vernon looked both before and after it was restored. Have family members help you make sure your pictures show at least five things that are different.

Read More About It

Black Heroes of the American Revolution by Burke Davis. Harcourt Brace Jovanovich. By showing us some of the 5,000 black soldiers who fought in the Revolutionary War, this book reminds us that we owe our independence to patriots of all races and backgrounds.

My Brother Sam Is Dead by James Lincoln Collier. Four Winds Press. A younger brother narrates as Sam defies their Loyalist father and joins the Continental Army.

AMERICANS FOR FREEDOM

Without great leaders, the American Revolution would have failed. It would also have failed without the courage and skill of many other Americans. In the next pages, you will read about six of these people.

Mercy Otis Warren

In the 1760s few Americans thought seriously about independence from Britain. One who did was Mercy Otis Warren of Plymouth, Massachusetts.

Mercy Otis Warren was the sister of James Otis, a lawyer and Patriot. James and Mercy were educated together until it was time for James to go to college. In the 1700s women did not go to college. Mercy kept up her studies at home, however, and often wrote to James.

James Otis was one of the very first to write and speak against British rule. He was the first to use the phrase "no taxation without representation." Otis was a fiery speaker. His motto was "Where liberty is, there is my country!" Mercy Otis Warren shared her brother's views.

Mercy and her husband, James Warren, opened their house to many of the early Revolutionary leaders. These included Sam Adams, John Hancock, and John and Abigail Adams.

Mercy Warren was also a friend of Thomas Jefferson and Martha Washington. In her letters, Mercy Warren kept these Virginians informed of events in New England.

In 1769 James Otis was seriously injured. He could no longer write and speak for the Patriot cause. Mercy Warren

Mercy Otis Warren often met with other Patriots to discuss the Revolution.

Peter Salem fights bravely at the Battle of Bunker Hill.

continued her brother's work. She was a fine writer. She could have written as her brother did, with reason and fiery words. Instead, she chose another way of attacking the British and the Loyalists. She chose to make fun of them in her poems and plays. She made the British look like "blockheads" who were too stupid, greedy, or silly to rule a free country.

In 1775 Mercy Warren was almost 50. The American Revolution had begun, and Mercy Warren had helped start it. She began to write a three-volume history of the Revolution. She finished it 30 years later, at the age of 77. It is still read by historians today.

Peter Salem

Of the Minutemen who faced the British soldiers at Concord Green on April 19, 1775, at least five were black. Several were slaves, but all were volunteers. One of them was Peter Salem.

Peter Salem heard Major John Pitcairn (PIHT·kairn), the British commander, shout, "Disperse, ye rebels!" When the death and confusion started, Peter Salem held his ground. He fired again and again.

A few weeks later, Peter Salem was in the Battle of Bunker Hill. He was one of about 20 blacks. The Americans waited as more than 2,000 British soldiers marched toward them. Closer and closer the British came. Three times the British marched up the hill, and three times they were stopped by American musket fire.

Running out of gunpowder, the Americans began to retreat. When a British officer saw the retreat, he ran forward, shouting to his men, "Follow me, the day is ours!" Peter Salem raised his musket and shot him dead. The British officer was Major John Pitcairn.

After the Battle of Bunker Hill, George Washington asked to meet Peter Salem. Two years later, Salem fought at the important Battle of Saratoga. In 1779 he took part in a surprise bayonet attack on a British camp at Stony Point, New York. In 1816 Peter Salem died in his home town, Framingham, Massachusetts.

John Honeyman

John Honeyman was a weaver from Ireland who lived near Trenton, New Jersey. As a young man, Honeyman had been taken from his home and forced to serve in the British army. Honeyman hated the British and their king. With all his heart, John Honeyman was a Patriot.

George Washington asked Honeyman to pretend that he was a Loyalist. He asked Honeyman to make fun of the Patriots and to cheer when they lost a battle. He asked him to praise the king of England. George Washington needed a spy in the Trenton area.

Honeyman played his part. His Patriot neighbors came to hate him and even threatened him with death. Their friends scorned his wife and children. Almost no one knew that Honeyman was a secret Patriot. Several times American soldiers tried to kill him.

In the winter of 1776, Washington's army was on the run. It had lost battle after battle. The Patriots were discouraged. Washington needed a victory to keep the war going. John Honeyman made such a victory possible.

Honeyman told Washington that hired German soldiers were planning to celebrate Christmas in Trenton. He made detailed drawings of where all the soldiers and guns were. Honeyman was almost killed by Patriots while trying to get to Washington's camp with this information. Washington asked him to go back to Trenton. Once again, fearful for his life, Honeyman crept through the line of Patriot soldiers.

Finally Honeyman reached Trenton. There he was questioned by the German commander. Was it true that Washington's army was tired, starving, freezing? Yes, said Honeyman. Honeyman convinced the commander that Washington was a fool and was ready to give up. Hearing the news, the Germans went ahead with their Christmas party. They did not even bother to post guards.

George Washington captured Trenton on December 26, 1776. The German soldiers were still asleep after their party.

George Washington thanks John Honeyman for his services.

The victory enabled the Americans to get food, clothing, and arms. With these supplies, the army could go on and fight again.

John Honeyman told no one that he had helped win the Battle of Trenton. For the rest of the war, his neighbors disliked him. After the war, the state of New Jersey brought him to trial as a traitor. Honeyman was a simple man. He could not bring himself to say that he had worked for the great George Washington. Perhaps he thought no one would believe him. Honeyman was almost hanged as a traitor. In the nick of time, an American officer got to the trial and saved Honeyman's life. Honeyman's neighbors were still suspicious. They still thought he had worked for the British. They refused to trust or like him.

Then one day in 1784, Honeyman's neighbors were astonished to see George Washington himself ride up to Honeyman's house. In a voice that all the neighbors could hear, Washington said to Honeyman: "Thank you, sir, for your service to me and to your country. I am grateful, and your country, sir, is grateful."

Lydia Darragh

Washington's army was camped near Philadelphia in early December 1777. But for one woman, Washington and his army might have been destroyed. Lydia Darragh (DAR·ah) showed great bravery by warning the army of its danger.

Lydia Darragh's family were Quakers. Quakers did not believe in war. They thought it wrong to kill another human being for any reason.

As a Quaker, Lydia Darragh's oldest son also hated violence. But he also believed in the Patriot cause. Finally, he decided he must fight. He joined Washington's army. Early in December 1777, he was with Washington at Whitemarsh, about 8 miles (12.8 km) from Philadelphia.

The British had captured Philadelphia. The British asked to have a meeting in the Darragh house. They told Lydia Darragh to put her family to bed early. She did what she was told. Later that night, however, she listened at the keyhole as

Lydia Darragh overhears the British plan an attack on Washington's army.

the officers talked. They were planning a surprise attack on Washington's army. Lydia Darragh heard the whole plan.

Early next morning, Lydia Darragh left her house carrying a flour sack. The British soldiers believed she was only on her way to get flour. She walked five miles (8 km) to the miller's and left her sack to be filled. Then she walked on toward the Continental Army. She finally met a Continental officer on the road and told him of the planned attack.

Lydia Darragh then returned to the miller's. She paid for her flour and quietly returned home. She did not tell her husband what she had done. That day Lydia Darragh had made a choice. In doing so she had bravely supported the Patriots and independence.

James Armistead

The Battle of Yorktown was over. Charles Cornwallis, the defeated British commander, paid a visit to the headquarters of the Marquis de Lafayette. Cornwallis was astonished to see the young French nobleman chatting and laughing with a black man, James Armistead. Armistead had been Cornwallis's servant. Cornwallis had used Armistead as a spy against the Americans. Why hadn't the Americans shot this spy?

Like John Honeyman, James Armistead was what we call a double agent. He had pretended to spy for the British. He had passed false information to them. In reality, Armistead had been working for Lafayette. While he served dinner to Cornwallis and other officers, he listened to their plans. Then he passed these plans on to Lafayette and George Washington. Information from Armistead helped make possible the plan that led to defeat of the British at Yorktown.

Like Washington himself, Armistead admired the dashing young Lafayette. After the war, Armistead changed his name to James Armistead Lafayette. In 1786 the General Assembly of Virginia held a vote. The lawmakers voted to buy the freedom of the slave James Armistead Lafayette. They did so with these words: "At the peril of his life, he found means to visit the British camp, and there perfectly did many jobs."

Charles Cornwallis is surprised to see James Armistead with the Marquis de Lafayette.

Mary Katherine Goddard checks a page coming off her printing press.

Mary Katherine Goddard

Two years after the Battle of Yorktown, many Americans were still not sure they had won the war. There were still many British soldiers in frontier forts. To the north, Canada was still British. Would the British try to take back their former colonies?

On February 19, 1783, readers of the *Maryland Journal and Baltimore Advertiser* knew for sure. They learned that Britain had agreed to recognize the new nation. The British would withdraw their soldiers. The *Journal* was a newspaper that went to many readers in many states. It had "scooped" the story. It had got the story to its readers before any other newspaper.

The *Journal* was run by Mary Katherine Goddard (GAHD·uhrd). She gathered the news and decided what stories to print. Then she printed copies of her newspaper one at a time on a big printing press.

During the American Revolution, Mary Goddard kept her readers informed of everything that happened. She was the first to publish reports of the battles at Lexington and Concord. She was the first to print a signed copy of the Declaration of Independence.

Mary Goddard was a Patriot and made no bones about it. She was also a newspaperwoman. She printed whatever she thought would interest her readers. Once during the war, she printed an unsigned letter that poked fun at the Second Continental Congress. Baltimore Patriots thought the letter gave support to the British. They demanded to know the name of the letter writer so they could arrest and punish him.

No, said Mary Goddard. If that happened, people would be afraid to tell newspapers anything. Then the only place to get news would be the government. The government would become too powerful. That, said Goddard, is not the way to have freedom.

Some Patriots threatened to wreck her newspaper. Mary Goddard still refused to name the letter writer. Finally the case went to the Maryland lawmakers. They decided that Mary Goddard was right. It was important to protect the freedom of the press.

Unit Review

Words to Remember

Number your paper from 1 to 10. Complete the sentences below with the words or names in the list. Write the correct answers on your paper.

allies   Patriots
boycott   repeal
independence   revolution
Loyalists   treaty
monopoly   tyranny

     In 1763 the British and Americans won a war against the French and their Indian __(1)__. When the British passed the Stamp Act in 1765, Americans accused them of __(2)__. Americans asked the British to __(3)__ the Stamp Act. To make their feelings clear, Americans started a __(4)__ of British goods. When Britain gave a __(5)__ to the East India Company to import tea, angry Americans threw the tea into Boston Harbor. In July 1776, the Continental Congress voted to declare __(6)__. People who supported the fight against Britain were called __(7)__. People who supported the British were called __(8)__. The struggle of American Patriots to overthrow British rule was a __(9)__. In 1783 a peace __(10)__ recognized America's independence from Britain.

Focus on Main Ideas

1. How did the French and Indian War lead to the Stamp Act?

2. What events led to disagreements between Britain and the 13 colonies?

3. What rights did the colonists consider important?

4. What caused the American colonists and the British to start shooting at each other?

5. What was the Olive Branch Petition? What was the king's response?

6. What was the purpose of the Declaration of Independence?

7. Why is the Liberty Bell a symbol of American freedom and independence?

8. How was each of the following battles important?
   a. Lexington and Concord
   b. Bunker Hill
   c. Trenton
   d. Saratoga
   e. Yorktown

9. Why did the Americans win the war?

10. How did each of these people contribute to the American Revolution?
   a. Sam Adams
   b. John Adams
   c. Paul Revere
   d. Thomas Paine
   e. Thomas Jefferson
   f. George Washington
   g. Marquis de Lafayette
   h. Patrick Henry
   i. Friedrich von Steuben
   j. Nathanael Greene
   k. Crispus Attucks
   l. George Rogers Clark
   m. John Paul Jones
   n. Francis Marion

Think/Write

The Patriots who signed the Declaration of Independence and many other courageous people were willing to die for the cause of American independence. What do you think makes a person courageous? What characteristics do courageous people possess?

Activities

1. **Research/Writing** You have read about many people who had the courage to fight for their beliefs. Find out more about the person who interests you most. Write a report about that person.

2. **Research/Report** The three main parts of an army in the 1700s were the artillery, the cavalry, and the infantry. Find out what each of these words means. Describe what a soldier did in the artillery, in the cavalry, and in the infantry.

Skills Review

1. **Understanding Cause and Effect** Read the following paragraph. Then answer the questions.

Benjamin Franklin went to Paris in 1775 to persuade the French government to help the Americans. In Paris, Franklin was well liked. The French liked Franklin because he dressed plainly. They also admired his experiments with electricity. Finally, the French enjoyed Franklin's witty sayings. When news of the Battle of Saratoga came in 1777, Benjamin Franklin urged the French to send help to the United States. This time the French leaders agreed.

a. Why did Franklin go to Paris?
b. What were the reasons for Franklin's popularity in Paris?
c. What effect did the American victory at Saratoga have in France?

2. **Reading a Document** You have read about *Common Sense* by Thomas Paine. In *Common Sense*, Paine tried to persuade people that America should be independent. As did Thomas Jefferson, Paine used reason to convince people he was right. He also used words and ideas that appealed to people's feelings.

Here is a part of *Common Sense* rewritten in modern language. Read it and answer the questions that follow.

Some people say that America has grown rich and strong under the control of Britain. They say that America will continue to grow if it stays under Britain's control. I answer this way: America would have grown rich and strong even without Britain.

Some people say that Britain is the parent country. If that is true, then the more shame on Britain. Even animals do not make war against their families. People have come here to get away from Britain because it was cruel to them. I believe, too, that Europe, and not Britain, is the parent of America. America is a home for lovers of liberty from *every part* of Europe.

a. Name at least one reason Thomas Paine believed America should break away from Britain.
b. What ideas or words of Paine made people feel good about America? Which of Paine's ideas or words made people dislike Britain?
c. How does Paine use "parent" as an idea in his argument?

The American Revolution took place mainly in the 13 original states. Is your state one of these? Is it near one of the original states?

During the American Revolution, other things were happening in the places that later became states. West of the Appalachians, people were exploring and settling. Spanish-speaking people were settling an area that stretched from the Mississippi River to California. They were building towns, trading, and exploring. They were naming the mountains, rivers, plains, and deserts of half a continent.

Whaling ships were stopping at Hawaii to get fresh vegetables, fruit, and water. In Alaska, Russian fur traders were setting up trading posts.

To know what else was happening in other places is to have a "sense of history." You can begin to develop this sense by learning more about your own state's history. Here are some things you can do.

Learning About Geography

1. Your state probably looked very different during the Revolution than it does today. What was your state like? Were there towns and cities? What kinds of people lived in your state? What did they do? Try to find a map of your state or region during the time of the Revolution. Use what you have learned about your state to make your own map for the years 1763–1781.

2. Because the American Revolution was so important, many places are named after Patriots. In the United States today, cities, rivers, streets, schools, and even mountains carry the names of Washington, Jefferson, and Adams. Towns carry the names of de Kalb, Lafayette and Pulaski. Are there streets or schools in your town named after any of the Patriots?

Find your state in an atlas. What places in your state are named after Patriots of the Revolution?

Learning About People

3. You may know about some courageous people who lived in your state during the time of the Revolution. They may have been war heroes, traders, explorers, or settlers. Learn more about one of these people. Write a short report on the person you choose. Share your report with the class.

Making a Timeline

4. Important events may have happened in your state during the Revolution. Make a timeline showing these events. Then add to it some key events of the American Revolution. Start with the French and Indian War. Add the Boston Tea Party and the Battle of Yorktown.

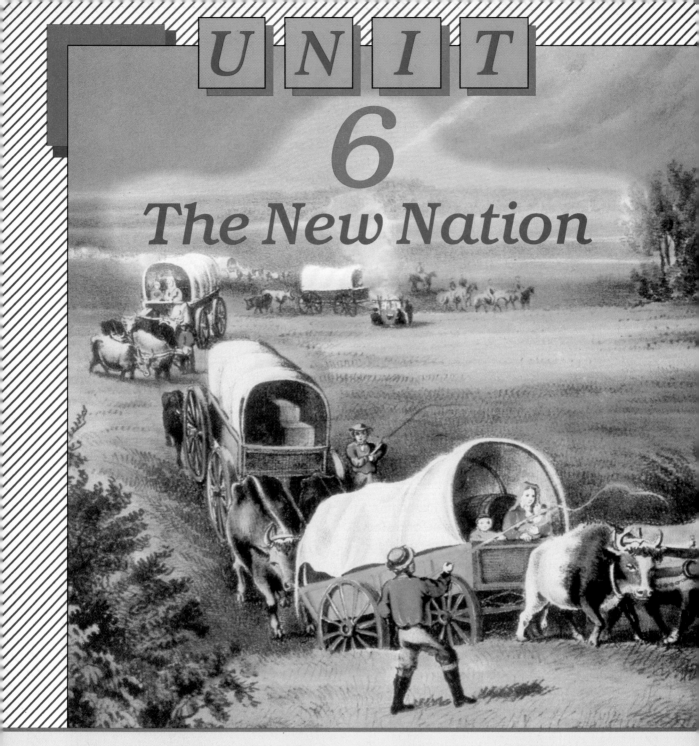

UNIT
6
The New Nation

- **1769**
Daniel Boone
explores Kentucky

- **1787**
Constitutional
Convention meets in
Philadelphia

- **1789**
The Constitution
becomes the law of
the land

- **1803**
The United States
buys the territory
of Louisiana

- **1804–1806**
Lewis and Clark
explore the
Louisiana
Purchase

After winning its independence, the United States formed a new government that combined strong power with great freedom. While many people in the Northeast were busy establishing this new government, other people were looking toward the western frontier. Wagon trains rolled across the mountains and prairies and into California. The United States now stretched from shore to shore—all the way from the Atlantic Ocean to the Pacific Ocean.

This pioneer spirit left a strong mark on our country's history. Americans have become known for finding new ways of doing things and inventing whatever they need.

Think Beyond   How do you think the pioneer spirit is shown in America today?

• 1812–1814	• 1830	• 1836	• 1846–1848	• 1848
The War of 1812	First U.S. railroads use steam locomotives	Texas declares independence	The Mexican War	Gold discovered in California

CHAPTER 12

The U.S. Constitution

"Peace made, my dear friend, a new scene opens. The object will be to make our independence a blessing. To do this we must secure our Union on solid foundations—a herculean task—and to effect which mountains of prejudice must be levelled! It requires all the virtue and all the abilities of our country."

—Alexander Hamilton, 1782

Look for these important words:

Key Words
- Constitution
- Articles of Confederation
- republic
- creditors
- debtors
- territory
- survey
- townships
- Northwest Ordinance
- compromise
- federal
- Preamble

People
- James Madison

Places
- Northwest Territory

Look for answers to these questions:
1. What problems did the United States face after the American Revolution?
2. Who is called the Father of the Constitution?
3. What form of government did the Constitution establish?
4. What did the writers of the Constitution hope to achieve?

1 The American Republic

The Constitution did not become law until 1789. Before then, the United States was governed under rules of the **Articles of Confederation** (kuhn•fed•uh•RAY•shuhn). The Articles of Confederation gave most powers of government to the states. The states sent representatives to a congress. It was this congress that conducted the Revolutionary War.

By the end of the war George Washington had become the symbol of the new country. He was treated as a hero wherever he went. One general said this of Washington: "First in war, first in peace, and first in the hearts of his countrymen."

Some thought that Washington, not Congress, should run the country. Instead, Washington retired to his beloved Mount Vernon. For this, the American people admired him even more. By retiring to private life, Washington showed that he believed in a **republic.** A republic is a form of government in which people elect representatives. These representatives, sitting in an assembly, make the laws and decisions.

The Nation Faces Problems

Washington had high hopes for the new nation. Soon, however, the government under the Articles of Confederation began to fall apart. War against Britain no longer held the states together. They began to quarrel and bicker with each other. They quarreled over boundary lines. They passed taxes on goods imported from neighboring states. New York had a tax on all farm produce from New Jersey. Connecticut taxed goods coming from Massachusetts. Such taxes discouraged trade between the states. Business owners and merchants disliked the taxes, but Congress had no power to lift them.

Under the Articles of Confederation, Congress had no means of solving the nation's money problems. Congress could not pass taxes. Congress could only ask each state to pay its share toward running the government. Congress could not force the states to pay.

Congress could print paper money, but it printed too much paper money. The result was terrible inflation. A $20 paper bill in 1779 was worth only 2¢ in 1782.

Congress had borrowed a great sum of money to pay for the war. It owed money to the suppliers of food, clothing, and military equipment. It owed money to the soldiers. For three years Congress could not even pay the salaries of its own members.

These money problems greatly upset all kinds of people. **Creditors,** the people who had loaned money, wanted to be paid back in gold or silver, not with worthless paper money. **Debtors,** the people who owed money, could not pay in gold or silver. They wanted to use paper money. Debtors were often jailed for not paying in gold or silver. Some groups of debtors attacked courthouses and local governments.

The young country faced other problems. Britain did not allow American trading ships in its ports. Spain was threatening to close the Mississippi River and the port of New Orleans to American traders.

American statesmen tried to make trade agreements with England and Spain. But these powerful nations had no respect for young America. In England John Adams was asked, "Do you represent one nation or thirteen?"

Governing the Ohio Valley

In this time of troubles, Congress made several decisions of lasting importance. Congress decided how to divide and how to govern America's western lands.

Britain had refused to allow settlement west of the Appalachian Mountains. With independence, the frontier was opened. Settlers poured into the Ohio valley. The land north of the Ohio River and east of the Mississippi River was called the **Northwest Territory.** A **territory** is an area of land belonging to a government.

In 1785 Congress established a system to **survey** (suhr•VEY) the western lands. *To survey* means to make land measurements. The land was to be marked off in squares called **townships.** Each side of the township measured 6 miles (9.7 km). Each township, in turn, was divided into 36 squares, or sections. This survey system of townships and sections continues to be used in parts of the United States.

In 1787 Congress passed the **Northwest Ordinance** (ORD•uhn•uhns). This law outlined the steps by which new states would be formed. It forbade slavery in the Northwest Territory. It also declared that one section of each township was to be used to support public schools.

The Northwest Ordinance was an excellent plan for America's growth. It was fair and forward-looking. Still, few people took Congress seriously.

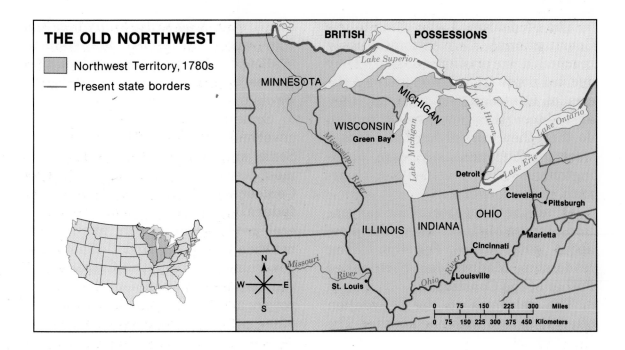

THE OLD NORTHWEST

Northwest Territory, 1780s

Present state borders

BRITISH POSSESSIONS

Lake Superior

MINNESOTA

MICHIGAN

WISCONSIN

Green Bay

Lake Michigan

Lake Huron

Lake Ontario

Lake Erie

Detroit

Cleveland

Pittsburgh

Mississippi River

ILLINOIS

INDIANA

OHIO

Marietta

Cincinnati

Missouri River

Ohio River

Louisville

St. Louis

N
W — E
S

| 0 | 75 | 150 | 225 | 300 | Miles |
| 0 | 75 | 150 | 225 | 300 | 375 | 450 | Kilometers |

A Rope of Sand

James Madison was a member of Congress under the Articles of Confederation. In 1779 Madison had been elected to Congress from Virginia. Then 29 years old, he was its youngest member. He was to spend the rest of his life in public service. Madison became a student of government. He read everything he could find about ancient and modern governments.

Madison was disturbed by the weakness of the Articles of Confederation. Under the Articles of Confederation each state was almost a nation by itself. Congress had little power over the states. Madison said he feared Congress had become a "rope of sand."

Such leaders as George Washington, John Adams, and Thomas Jefferson agreed with Madison. Madison began to argue for a stronger national government. Only a strong national government could keep the country from breaking apart, Madison said.

Others, including Patrick Henry, preferred the Articles of Confederation. They were afraid of a strong government. A rope of sand, they said, was better than a rod of iron.

A New Constitution

In 1787 Congress invited the states to a convention in Philadelphia to consider changing the Articles of Confederation. The delegates began to gather in Philadelphia in May 1787. Early to arrive was George Washington. By attending the convention, Washington was again letting Americans know that he supported the republican form of government.

In 1787 Washington was 55 years old. He arrived in Philadelphia in a great black coach pulled by six high-stepping horses. He promptly called on Benjamin Franklin, then 81 years old. At that time Franklin was governor of Pennsylvania.

The 55 delegates who came to the Constitutional Convention quickly reached a surprising decision. They decided not to try to patch up the Articles of Confederation. Instead, they agreed to write a new constitution. To do this, they worked hard six days a week for four months. George Washington served as president, or chairman, of the convention.

Of all the delegates to the convention, James Madison knew the most about government. For his strong leadership, Madison has been called Father of the Constitution.

The delegates to the convention often disagreed with one another. The constitution was written only because they were willing to **compromise** (KAHM·pruh·myz). *To compromise* means to give up some of what one wants in order to reach agreement.

Some delegates wanted the national government to have most of the power. Some wanted the states to have the most power, as under the Articles of Confederation. The compromise was a **federal** form of government. In a federal government powers are shared between the states and the national government. Under the Constitution the national government has some powers and the state governments have other powers. Still other powers are

In this famous painting, George Washington directs the signing of the Constitution. Benjamin Franklin is seated, lower left. James Madison is seated at the table to Franklin's left. Alexander Hamilton is at his right.

Is 13 an unlucky number? Charles Thomson did not think so when he designed the front of the Great Seal of the United States in 1782. The eagle carries a 13-leaf olive branch in one talon and 13 arrows in the other. Above the eagle's head are 13 stars, and on its chest are 13 stripes. Why did Thomson use 13 so many times? That number symbolizes our original 13 colonies. The Great Seal on official documents and on the one dollar bill helps remind us of the original 13 colonies.

shared by the national and state governments.

The convention delegates thought about the problems the country faced under the Articles of Confederation. They agreed to give the national government the powers it needed to meet these problems. The national government was given strong powers to collect taxes and to regulate trade between states. It was also given the powers to raise an army and to deal with foreign nations.

The Constitution's Purpose

The first part of the Constitution is the **Preamble** (PREE-am-buhl), or introduction. The Preamble tells the purpose of the Constitution.

We the people of the United States, in order to form a more perfect union, establish justice, insure domestic tranquility, provide for the common defense, promote the general welfare, and secure the blessings of liberty to ourselves and our posterity, do ordain and establish this Constitution for the United States of America.

The Preamble is short and dignified, but it may be hard for you to understand. What it means is this:

We the people of the United States have made the Constitution for the following reasons. We wish to bind together our people, our places, and our states in a better way. We wish to set up courts in which people can get fair treatment. We wish to make certain that there will be peace and order within the country. We wish to set up an army and navy so we can defend our country. We wish to be able to do what is necessary to make the lives of our people better. And finally, we wish to make certain that we and those who live after us remain a free people.

Reading Check

1. What problems did America face under the Articles of Confederation?
2. Why is Madison called the Father of the Constitution?
3. According to the Preamble, what is the purpose of the Constitution?

Think Beyond Why do you think people have been willing to die to defend the Constitution?

Look for these important words:

Key Words
- legislative
- executive
- judicial
- House of Representatives
- Senate
- President
- Supreme Court
- constitutional
- checks and balances
- veto
- amendments
- democracy
- majority

Look for answers to these questions:
1. How is our government set up?
2. What does it mean to have checks and balances in the Constitution?
3. Why is the Constitution a remarkable document?
4. What do we mean by *democracy*?

2 The Structure of the Government

The new Constitution called for three branches of government. These were the **legislative** (LEJ•uh•slay•tiv), the **executive** (ek•ZEK•yuh•tiv), and the **judicial** (joo•DISH•uhl) branches. The legislative, or lawmaking, branch was the Congress. It was divided into two houses—the **House of Representatives** and the **Senate.** The legislative branch was given the power to pass taxes and make laws.

A **President** would head the executive, or management, branch. The President's main duties were to carry out the laws and head the armed forces.

The judicial branch would be the system of courts, headed by the **Supreme Court.** The President would appoint justices, or judges, to the Supreme Court. The Supreme Court would have power to decide whether laws were **constitutional** (kahn•stuh•TOO•shuhn•ul). *Constitutional* means lawful according to our Constitution.

The framers of the Constitution were afraid to give to any part of government too much power. Therefore, they established a system of **checks and balances.** Each branch of the government would have controls on the power of the other branches.

For example, only Congress can make laws. After Congress has voted for a law, the President shows his approval by signing the law. If the President disapproves of the proposed law, he can **veto,** or refuse, it. The Supreme Court can decide if laws are constitutional or not. If not, then the law ceases to exist.

The States Compromise

A major disagreement at the convention was between small and large states. Small states like Delaware and New Jersey wanted to have an equal voice with the large states. They were afraid that large states like Pennsylvania and New York would have more power because they had more people.

The large states and small states then compromised. Each state would have two senators, so all states would have equal representation in the Senate. In contrast, the number of members in the House of Representatives would depend on the population of each state.

The delegates also disagreed on how people would be elected to Congress. All the delegates believed in a republican form of government. Even so, some were suspicious of letting the people have too much direct influence. They remembered the mobs of angry debtors who had attacked the courts. Others had more faith in the people.

Again a compromise was reached. Members of the House of Representatives would be elected directly by the people. The senators would be elected by state legislative bodies. That part of the Constitution has since been changed. Senators today are elected directly by the people.

A Living Document

Not everyone was satisfied with the new Constitution. Some of the delegates refused to sign it. Most followed the lead of Benjamin Franklin. "I consent . . . to this Constitution because I expect no better, and because I am not sure that it is not the best," he said.

The Constitution as hammered together by the convention in 1787 is

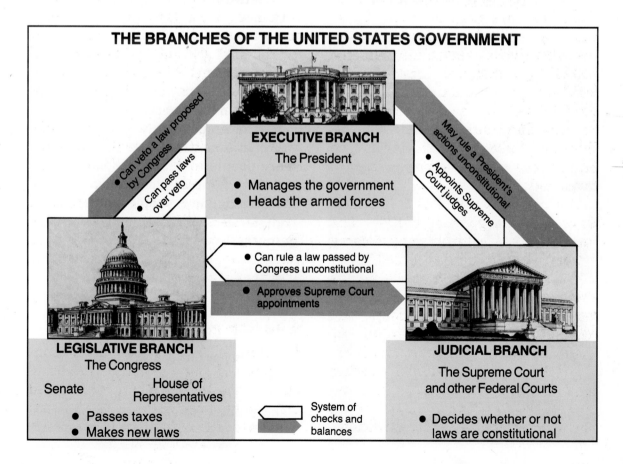

THE BRANCHES OF THE UNITED STATES GOVERNMENT

Can veto a law proposed by Congress

Can pass laws over veto

May rule a President's actions unconstitutional

Appoints Supreme Court judges

EXECUTIVE BRANCH

The President

- Manages the government
- Heads the armed forces

- Can rule a law passed by Congress unconstitutional

- Approves Supreme Court appointments

LEGISLATIVE BRANCH

The Congress

Senate   House of Representatives

- Passes taxes
- Makes new laws

System of checks and balances

JUDICIAL BRANCH

The Supreme Court and other Federal Courts

- Decides whether or not laws are constitutional

remarkable. It has been the framework of our government for 200 years. It has been a model for the constitutions of other nations. As the law of the land, it has served the nation well. Over the years there have been **amendments,** or changes, to the Constitution. These have reflected the will of new generations of Americans.

Under the Constitution the 13 United States have become 50 United States. The population has grown from 4 million to 234 million. Americans have gone from horse-and-buggy days to the space age. The Constitution has given us a strong form of government and yet allowed change. For that reason we call it a living document.

The Constitution was the foundation of our government when there were but 13 states. It remains so today.

The Meaning of Democracy

Our form of government under the Constitution remains a republic. We continue to elect representatives to make laws and decisions. The United States is also a **democracy.** *Democracy* is an ancient Greek word meaning "rule by the people." People in a democratic nation like ours can make many choices about their lives. They have many rights and freedoms.

Democracy depends on respecting the wishes of the **majority,** or greatest number. Democracy can be found working all over the United States. In class meetings, in school government, in town meetings, you can find democracy. Whenever and wherever people decide something by voting, democracy is working.

Since the Constitution was written, our country has become more democratic. In 1789 only white men who owned property could vote. Women and poor white men could not vote. Millions of slaves had no rights or representation in government. The Indians were not considered citizens. With time more people were represented in government because they could vote. As more and more people achieved the right to vote, the nation became more democratic.

Reading Check

1. What does it mean to veto a law?
2. Why is the Constitution called a living document?
3. How has our country become more democratic?

Think Beyond Why do you think our country needs a President as well as the Congress and the federal courts?

IN FOCUS

THE NATIONAL ARCHIVES

Inside a building in Washington, D.C., is a huge room filled with boxes. Those boxes are filled with American history.

The room is located in the *National Archives and Records Service,* and the boxes contain records of the United States government. Peace treaties, Presidential proclamations, Acts of Congress, and millions of other historical documents are all carefully stored at the National Archives' headquarters.

America's historical records once were scattered all over the country, in universities, museums, and private collections. However, in 1934, Congress decided that all these documents should be stored in a single place, known as the National Archives.

Three of our country's most important documents, the Declaration of Independence, the United States Constitution, and the Bill of Rights may be viewed at the National Archives. These documents are sealed in bronze-and-glass cases. In case of fire or other emergency, the documents can be lowered immediately into a large fireproof safe.

The National Archives also stores many other types of documents. Some are paper documents, such as transcripts of Senate hearings. Others are recordings, photographs, films, videotapes, and books. Anything that relates to the government may be included.

Anyone can look at the records in the National Archives. Each year, thousands of reporters, historians, and private citizens examine records in special "search rooms" located in the National Archives building. Although no one but government officials may take records from the National Archives building, people may make photocopies of the records they want to keep.

The National Archives preserves America's past. Its records remind us of the growth and triumph the United States has experienced in 200 years as a nation.

Think Beyond   What kinds of items might a historian or reporter be searching for at the National Archives?

Americans view the Declaration of Independence

Look for these important words:

Key Words
- Bill of Rights
- Cabinet
- Federalists
- Republicans

People
- John Adams
- Thomas Jefferson
- Alexander Hamilton

Places
- District of Columbia
- Washington

Look for answers to these questions:
1. What is the Bill of Rights? Why did Americans think it necessary?
2. Who were the first men to serve in the government? What were their jobs?
3. In what ways did some of these men disagree about what was best for the nation?

3 *A New Government Begins*

The new Constitution could not become law until two-thirds of the states had approved it. After reading it, many people were upset that the Constitution said nothing about individual rights. Many Americans remembered all too clearly how they had fought for liberty and for their rights. They wanted to make certain that tyranny could not raise its head in America. Never again, they vowed, could the government take away their liberties.

Those who wanted the Constitution promised to add a bill of rights that protected the individual. When the Constitution was approved, Madison wrote the **Bill of Rights,** the first ten amendments to the Constitution.

In 1789 George Washington was elected President, and **John Adams,** vice president. Leaving Mount Vernon in his shining coach, Washington traveled to New York, the temporary capital. There the most popular man in America took the oath of office as President. As his advisers, he chose **Thomas Jefferson** and **Alexander Hamilton.** Jefferson would be secretary of state and Hamilton would be secretary of the treasury. Such advisers later became known as the **Cabinet.**

Congress faced the task of passing laws to make the government work. "We are in a wilderness without a single footstep to guide us," said James Madison.

Hamilton and Jefferson

Alexander Hamilton and Thomas Jefferson often argued about what each thought was best for the United States. Washington respected and listened to both men. Hamilton thought that the country should encourage manufacturing and the growth of cities. Jefferson thought that the country should continue to depend on agriculture. Like

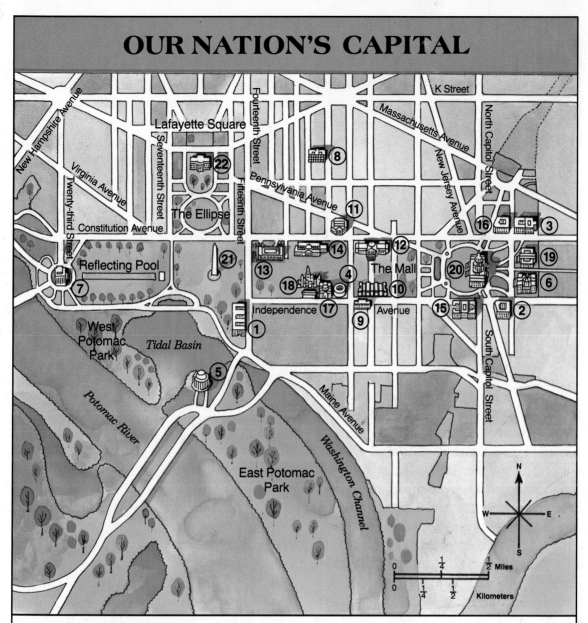

OUR NATION'S CAPITAL

WASHINGTON, D.C.

Index to Buildings and Monuments

1. Bureau of Engraving and Printing
2. Cannon House Office Building
3. Dirksen and Hart Senate Office Buildings
4. Hirshhorn Museum and Sculpture Garden
5. Jefferson Memorial
6. Library of Congress
7. Lincoln Memorial
8. Martin Luther King Memorial Library
9. National Aeronautics and Space Administration
10. National Air and Space Museum
11. National Archives

12. National Gallery of Art
13. National Museum of American History
14. National Museum of Natural History
15. Rayburn House Office Building
16. Russell Senate Office Building
17. Smithsonian Arts and Industries Building
18. Smithsonian Institution building (offices) (Smithsonian museums: 4, 10, 12, 13, 14, 17)
19. Supreme Court Building
20. United States Capitol
21. Washington Monument
22. White House

Thomas Jefferson was an important leader during Washington's Presidency.

Adams Becomes President

George Washington served as President for two terms, each term four years long. Many people wanted him to remain President for a third term. Washington refused, saying two terms were enough. In refusing, Washington set an example for future American Presidents.

Washington retired to Mount Vernon for a well-deserved rest. When he left, the nation was on its feet. The government established by the Constitution was working.

John Adams followed Washington as the next President. The government then moved to Washington, D.C. John and Abigail Adams were the first to live in the newly built White House.

At that time the White House was called the President's Palace. When the Adamses moved in, the now-lovely East Room was unfinished. There Mrs. Adams hung the family wash to dry. She complained that she had trouble getting enough firewood. Thirteen fireplaces, all going at the same time, were necessary to keep out the damp cold of the Washington winter. Despite the problems, Mrs. Adams was hopeful. "This House is built for ages to come," she wrote. The same could be said of the Constitution.

many of his day, Jefferson felt that farmers were a better sort than city dwellers. Hamilton wanted a strong national government. Jefferson favored as little government as possible.

From the disagreements of Hamilton and Jefferson were born political parties. The supporters of Hamilton's ideas called themselves **Federalists.** The supporters of Jefferson's ideas called themselves **Republicans.** Political parties are not part of the Constitution. They have, however, become important to the way our government works.

Sometimes Hamilton and Jefferson had to compromise so that laws could get passed. In one compromise, it was agreed that the national capital would be built in the South. It would not be part of any state. Created from land given by Virginia and Maryland, the site would be called the **District of Columbia.** George Washington himself chose the site for the capital city. It would carry his name, **Washington.**

Reading Check

1. Why did people want a bill of rights added to the Constitution?
2. What is the Cabinet?
3. What led to the beginning of the first political parties in America?

Think Beyond Why do you think government leaders decided to build a new national capital?

People MAKE HISTORY

Abigail Adams
1744–1818

▶▶▶▶▶▶▶▶▶▶▶▶▶▶▶▶

Only one woman in American history has been the wife of one President and the mother of another President. That was Abigail Adams. Her husband, John, was the second President of the United States. Her son, John Quincy Adams, became our sixth President. Abigail herself was an important person.

We know a great deal about Abigail's life because she wrote and received thousands of letters. Many of these letters still exist. Like most young girls of her day, Abigail did not attend school. She learned reading and writing from her family at home.

In 1764, one month before her twentieth birthday, Abigail married John Adams, then a young lawyer. Because of John's political career, they were separated frequently. During such times Abigail managed the family farm, raised the children, and ran the household. Abigail and John wrote frequently to each other during these separations.

In 1776 John Adams was elected to the Continental Congress. Abigail wrote him a long letter expressing her ideas on liberty. "In the new Code of Laws which I suppose it will be necessary for you to make," she wrote, "I desire you would Remember the Ladies, and be more generous and favorable to them than your ancestors. Do not put such unlimited power into the hands of the Husbands." Why could women not have a voice in the making of laws? she asked. This was a revolutionary idea at that time.

Abigail Adams taught all her children to think for themselves. She taught them to fight for what they believed. Early in his political career, young John Quincy Adams decided to leave his father's party, the Federalists. His father was upset, but Abigail defended her son for following his conscience. "I pride myself more in being the Mother of such a son," she wrote, "than in all the honors and titles which a Monarch could bestow."

John Quincy Adams could have been equally proud of his mother. Abigail Adams was not only a capable woman, but also an independent thinker.

Think Beyond   Do you think expressing your opinions can help to persuade others? Explain.

Abigail Adams in her later years

SKILLS IN ACTION

UNDERSTANDING THE BILL OF RIGHTS

In 1791 ten amendments were added to the United States Constitution. These first ten amendments are known as the Bill of Rights. They protect the rights of United States citizens.

Americans had fought long and hard to break free from the unfair laws of the king of England. They wanted to make their hard-won rights part of the new Constitution.

This list tells you what rights each amendment protects.

- **Amendment I** promises freedom of religion, freedom of speech, and the freedom to hold meetings. It also says that Americans have the right to ask the government to correct wrongs.
- **Amendment II** says that the people's right to own weapons cannot be taken away. This is because weapons are needed to maintain militias.
- **Amendment III** says that no one can be forced to give room and board to soldiers.
- **Amendment IV** says that people and their property cannot be searched without good reason.
- **Amendment V** says that no one can be brought to trial twice for the same crime. No one can be forced to be a witness against himself or herself. No one can be punished without a fair trial. The government cannot take a person's property without paying for it.
- **Amendment VI** says that everyone has the right to a fair trial within a short time. A person has the right to defend himself or herself against charges.

- **Amendment VII** says that the right to a jury trial cannot be taken away.
- **Amendment VIII** says that no one should have to pay unreasonable bail or fines. No one should be given cruel and unfair punishment for any crime.
- **Amendment IX** says that the people will have all basic rights. They will have these rights even if they are not mentioned in the Constitution.
- **Amendment X** says that the states will keep all those powers not given to the federal government by the Constitution.

The Important First Amendment

The First Amendment guarantees some of our most important freedoms. Read it as it is written in the Constitution:

Congress shall make no law respecting an establishment of religion, or prohibiting the free exercise thereof; or abridging the freedom of speech, or of the press; or the right of the people peaceably to assemble, and to petition the government for a redress of grievances.

Look at the first part of this amendment: "Congress shall make no law respecting an establishment of religion, or prohibiting the free exercise thereof." What does this mean? It means that Congress cannot pass a law saying that one religion is the nation's only religion. Congress cannot say that any religion is against the law.

In England there had been fights over religion for centuries. At times people were fined for not attending services of the Church of England. At other times certain churches were forbidden to meet. Americans did not want this to happen in their new nation. The First Amendment guarantees religious freedom. Americans have the right to believe or not to believe whatever they want.

Next, the First Amendment says Congress cannot **abridge** the freedom of speech or of the press. *To abridge* something is to cut it off. In England in the time before the American Revolution, people could not always talk freely. They could be thrown in jail if they complained about the king or the government. Without free speech people cannot talk about ways to change the government.

In a country that allows free speech, some people may express ideas unpopular at first. As people discuss these ideas, they may decide that some of them are wise after all. At one time, for example, it was unpopular to say that women should be able to vote. It was unpopular to say that factories must be safe places to work. After talking about these situations, though, people began to change their minds. They called for laws allowing women to vote and for making factories safer. Acceptance of these once

The right to read what we choose is one of our most precious freedoms.

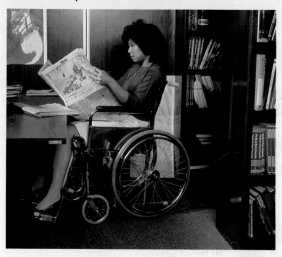

unpopular opinions has made the United States a better place to live.

The last part of the First Amendment says that people have the right to meet peacefully. It says they also can ask the government for help if they think they have been wronged.

CHECKING YOUR SKILLS

Imagine a completely different United States. Imagine that after the Revolution no one had written the Constitution or the Bill of Rights. Imagine that rulers passed only the laws they liked. Read what could happen. Then answer the questions.

1. You want to have a birthday party, but the law says you can have only four people. Why would rulers want to limit the number of people who gather together? What part of the First Amendment keeps this from happening in our country?

2. The rulers of the country have set up the Church of North America. They say you cannot go to public schools unless you belong to this church. You cannot hold a public office unless you belong to this church. What part of the First Amendment keeps this from happening?

3. Imagine that a ruler wants only good things said about him. You draw a cartoon that makes fun of the ruler. A newspaper prints your cartoon. For this you are thrown in jail and the newspaper is shut down. What part of the First Amendment protects you from this sort of thing?

4. You are riding a public bus and you say to someone next to you, "The government has too much power." Someone reports you, and you have to pay a $100 fine for complaining. What keeps this from happening in our country?

335

Thinking Back

- After gaining independence, the United States was governed by the rules of the Articles of Confederation, which caused the government serious problems. The states began to quarrel among themselves, and Congress had no means of solving the nation's money problems.

- Delegates to the Constitutional Convention agreed to write a new plan of government. The plan was a compromise that established a federal form of government in which the states and the national government shared powers.

- The Constitution established three branches of government and created a system of checks and balances to prevent any part of the government from becoming too powerful.

- The Constitution has given us a lasting form of government, yet it also has allowed for change. Since the Constitution was written, our country has become more democratic.

- The Bill of Rights was added to the Constitution to protect the personal rights and liberties of Americans.

- Early leaders argued about what was best for the future of the United States. These disagreements led to the formation of political parties in our country.

Check for Understanding

Using Words

Read these sentences. Then replace the underlined words in each with the correct word or phrase from the list. Write the new sentences on your paper.

Bill of Rights	executive
checks and balances	judicial
compromise	legislative
Constitution	republic
democracy	Senate

The form of the United States government is a (1) government in which people elect representatives to make laws and decisions. The United States is also a (2) government by the people. Our nation's laws are still based on the (3) framework of government approved in 1789. The organization of our government is based on (4) people giving up some of what they want. The government is divided into three parts: the (5) lawmaking branch, the (6) courts branch, and the (7) management branch. The lawmaking branch is divided into two houses: the House of Representatives and the (8) house in which each state has two votes. Important to our system of government are (9) ways each part has controls on other parts. Individual liberties are protected in the (10) first ten amendments.

Reviewing Facts

1. What decisions did Congress make about the Northwest Territory?

2. Name at least four powers the Constitution gives to the national government.

3. According to the Preamble, what is the purpose of the Constitution?

4. Describe the main purpose of each of the three branches of government.

5. How did Thomas Jefferson's and Alexander Hamilton's ideas differ about what was best for the country?

Thinking Critically

1. Why did James Madison call the Articles of Confederation "a rope of sand"? Why did others say they preferred a rope of sand to a rod of iron?

2. How did the Constitution make the government stronger than it had been under the Articles of Confederation?

3. In what ways is the Constitution a document of compromises? Have you ever compromised on the playground or at home?

Writing About It

Imagine that you are a newspaper reporter covering the Constitutional Convention in 1787. Interview James Madison as he arrives at the convention. Ask him why the convention is being held and what he hopes it will accomplish. Then write your article based on what you think Madison would have said.

Practicing Citizenship Skills

Understanding the Bill of Rights
Answer these questions.

1. What is the purpose of the Bill of Rights?

2. What amendment says that people cannot be searched without good reason?

3. What amendment guarantees freedom of speech?

4. What amendment says that a person has the right to trial by jury?

On Your Own

Social Studies at Home

1. Study the map of Washington, D.C., on page 331. Then imagine that you are a tour guide, and give your family a tour of our national capital. For example, you may want to show them how to get from the White House to the Washington Monument and from the Washington Monument to the Capitol building.

2. The Great Seal of the United States displays symbols important to our country's history. Design a "great seal" for your class with symbols of important class events or items. Draw your seal and compare it with those of your classmates.

Read More About It

George Washington and the Birth of Our Nation by Milton Meltzer. Franklin Watts. This book is a collection of primary sources and photos about Washington as an adult.

Sarah Bishop by Scott O'Dell. Houghton Mifflin. Following the Revolutionary War, orphaned Sarah flees into the wilds of southern New York State.

1787 by Joan Anderson. Illustrated by Alexander Farquharson. Harcourt Brace Jovanovich. In a blend of fact and fiction, an aide to James Madison remembers the summer spent writing the Constitution.

We the People: The Constitution of the United States of America by Peter Spier. Doubleday. This appealing book illustrates the phrases of the Preamble and gives a historical overview of the entire document.

CHAPTER 13

The Nation Grows

"The ax has cut the forest down,
The laboring ox has smoothed all clear,
Apples now grow where pine trees stood,
And slow cows graze instead of deer.

Where Indian fires once raised their smoke
The chimneys of a farmhouse stand,
And cocks crow barnyard challenges
To dawns that once saw savage land.

The ax, the plow, the binding wall,
By these the wilderness is tamed,
By these the white man's will is wrought,
The rivers bridged, the new towns named. "

—"The Wilderness Is Tamed"
by Elizabeth Coatsworth

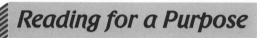
Look for these important words:

Key Words	People	Places
• pioneers	• Daniel Boone	• Kentucky
		• Cumberland Gap
		• Wilderness Trail
		• Boonesborough

Look for answers to these questions:
1. What happened to the frontier after the Revolution?
2. Who was Daniel Boone?
3. Why did the Shawnee and Cherokee Indians resist settlers in Kentucky?
4. How was Kentucky finally settled?

1 Explorations Westward

The United States grew rapidly in the 50 years after the Revolution. In those 50 years the frontier moved from the Appalachian Mountains to the Mississippi River. Pushing the frontier ever west were the **pioneers.** Pioneers are the first people to settle or enter a new territory.

Daniel Boone was one of the most famous American pioneers. Born in Pennsylvania, Boone was 16 years old when his family moved to the Yadkin valley of North Carolina. Boone had always loved roaming the woods. In North Carolina he spent months at a time living and hunting in the woods. He was as comfortable in the woods as in a farmhouse, maybe more so.

After marrying, Boone supported his growing family with some farming and much hunting. Deer were so plentiful that venison was a staple food of frontier life. In the winter Boone trapped beaver and otter for their skins. With the money he received for the skins, he bought guns, gunpowder, and lead for bullets.

Daniel Boone drove a wagon for General Braddock's army during the French and Indian War. While serving in the army, Boone met John Finley, a fur trader. Finley told stories about visiting a wonderful land the Iroquois called *Kentake* (kuhn•TUK•ee). *Kentake* is the Iroquois word for "meadowland."

After the war Boone tried to find this land, **Kentucky,** but he could not find a way over the mountains. He looked in vain for the Warrior's Path, an Indian trail that crossed the mountains. Discouraged, he returned home.

Soon after, a wandering peddler came to the door of the Boone house. He was none other than Boone's old friend, John Finley! With Finley to help him, Boone again made plans to find Kentucky. In 1769 a small party of six men started out. This time they found the Warrior's Path. Following the trail, they crossed the Appalachian Mountains at **Cumberland Gap.** On the other side they found the rolling pastures of the Kentucky River valley thick with buffalo. The woods were full of deer. In the many streams swam great numbers of beaver.

Both Cherokee and Shawnee Indians claimed parts of Kentucky as their hunting grounds. Several times the Shawnees captured Boone. Each time they let him go, but with a warning. "Don't come here anymore, for this is the Indians' hunting ground, and all the animals, skins, and furs are ours," said their chief. He told Boone that if he returned, the wasps and yellow jackets would sting him severely.

Daniel Boone may have looked like this frontiersman. Rifle in hand, he wears buckskins and a coonskin cap.

Boone did not listen. He returned again and again to Kentucky to explore and to hunt. His adventures became legends.

Boone tried to lead several families to Kentucky in 1773. The Cherokees attacked them at Cumberland Gap, however, and Boone's oldest son was killed. The party turned back.

Kentucky Is Settled

Meanwhile, word spread of Kentucky's rich land. People wanted to settle there, but the Indians refused to give up the land. Finally, in 1775, the Virginia militia defeated the Indians in battle. They were forced to give up their claims to Kentucky.

As soon as the treaty had been signed, Daniel Boone was hired by a land developer to clear a road to Kentucky. In March 1775, Boone led a group headed for the Warrior's Path. Slashing trees and bushes to make way for wagons, they carved a road out of the wilderness. This road became known as the **Wilderness Trail.**

When the road was finished, Boone returned to North Carolina. He gathered his relatives and neighbors into a party to move to the new land. It was a slow, difficult trip over the mountains. Getting a cow to walk 300 miles (482 km) was not easy. Sometimes wild animals scared the packhorses so that they scattered in all directions. Indians made surprise attacks. Despite these difficulties, the pioneers were soon busy building the Kentucky settlement of **Boonesborough.**

Soon thousands of pioneers passed over the Wilderness Trail on their way to the valleys beyond. They went west

Settlers west of the Appalachians shipped their goods by flatboat to New Orleans. Boatmen then returned north on horseback or by foot.

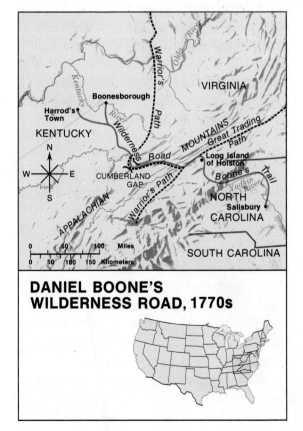

DANIEL BOONE'S WILDERNESS ROAD, 1770s

hoping to find cheap, good land. Land meant new opportunity.

By 1800 Americans were settling as far west as the Mississippi River. Kentucky and Tennessee had become states. Ohio would soon be a state. Farmers in these states shipped their crops and livestock on flatboats down the Mississippi River to New Orleans. From New Orleans the goods went by ship to markets around the country.

Reading Check

1. What is a pioneer?
2. What land did Daniel Boone explore and later settle?
3. Why did pioneers push west?

Think Beyond How would the story of the settlement of Kentucky be different told from the point of view of a Cherokee Indian?

341

IN FOCUS

LOG CABINS

Imagine that it is the late 1700s. You and your family have just moved to Kentucky. What do you do first? Chances are that you build a shelter.

Most early settlers knew how to build houses like those in their homelands. Those houses were built of bricks, stones, or planks of sawed wood. Special tools and a lot of time were required to build homes of those materials. However, new settlers facing the coming of winter were often short of time. Tools were often scarce, too.

Many settlers froze to death in poorly built shelters. What was needed were quickly built houses that would last until finer ones could be built.

In 1638, colonists from Sweden and Finland started building a type of structure that was common in their homeland. It was the log cabin. The only tool needed to build a log cabin was an ax. The only materials needed were plenty of tall, straight trees. Add to that a great deal of hard work, and the result was a sturdy, warm, and safe home.

The typical log cabin was built in six stages. First, the builder selected a number of straight, smooth trees that had about the same width. Then, steel ax flashing, he felled the trees and trimmed them to the right length. The logs were pulled by horses or dragged by hand to the building site. They were notched at the ends so they would fit together. Next, the logs were lifted into place. Finally, the cracks were "chinked." They were filled with mud, clay, or moss. In this manner two people could complete a cabin in a couple of weeks.

Log cabins quickly became popular in Pennsylvania, Ohio, Kentucky, and Tennessee. In these areas where deep forests stretched farther than the eye could see, logs were readily available. It is no wonder, then, that one visitor to a Kentucky village in the 1700s exclaimed, "Almost every house in the settlement was built of logs."

By building log cabins, settlers could make safe, warm homes for themselves in the wilderness of America.

Think Beyond Why do you think log cabins are popular today?

Log cabin homes

Look for these important words:

Key Words
- Louisiana Purchase

- William Clark
- Sacajawea

- Montana
- Snake River
- Columbia River
- Arkansas River
- Red River
- Colorado
- New Mexico

People
- Napoleon Bonaparte
- Meriwether Lewis

Places
- Louisiana
- Missouri River
- North Dakota

Look for answers to these questions:
1. What was the Louisiana Purchase?
2. What did Meriwether Lewis and William Clark achieve?
3. Who explored the Arkansas and Red river valleys for the United States?

2 *The Louisiana Purchase*

Thomas Jefferson, his red hair now gray, became the country's third President in 1801. The country soon faced a major difficulty. Spain closed the port of New Orleans to the farmers of the American West. By closing New Orleans, Spain hoped to stop the westward movement of the U.S. frontier.

After France lost the French and Indian War, it gave Spain its claims to land west of the Mississippi. This land was called **Louisiana.** Then, in 1802, Jefferson learned that Spain had secretly given Louisiana back to France. The French leader, **Napoleon Bonaparte** (nuh•POHL•yuhn BOH•nuh•pahrt), dreamed of again establishing French power in North America.

Jefferson sent representatives to Paris to ask Napoleon to sell New Orleans to the Americans. Jefferson offered $10 million. Napoleon at first refused. Then events in Europe changed his mind. Britain declared war on France.

Needing money to fight the war, Napoleon offered to sell all of Louisiana to the United States. The price was $15 million. The agreement was made in 1803.

This was the greatest real estate bargain the United States ever made. It gained a vast territory ranging west from the Mississippi River to the Rocky Mountains and north to Canada. This territory was known as the **Louisiana Purchase.**

Nobody in the United States knew exactly what lay in the Louisiana Purchase. It was unexplored, an unknown. President Jefferson asked his secretary, **Meriwether Lewis,** to lead an expedition to gather all kinds of information about the new land.

Lewis had had much experience in the wilderness as an army officer in the Northwest Territory. He chose **William Clark,** a good friend, to share the leadership of the expedition. Clark had valuable wilderness experience. He was particularly good at making maps.

Lewis and Clark Head West

The Lewis and Clark expedition left St. Louis, Missouri, in the spring of 1804. It proceeded by canoe up the **Missouri River.** Near the Mandan villages in present-day **North Dakota,** they built a fort in which to spend the winter. While there, they hired a French fur trader to translate some Indian languages for them. The Frenchman was married to a Shoshone named **Sacajawea** (sa•kuh•juh• WEE•uh). Sacajawea had been kidnapped from her people years before. Lewis and Clark hoped that Sacajawea would translate for them when they reached the land of the Shoshones.

In the spring of 1805 the small party of about 40 set out on their historic trip. They had six small canoes and two large ones. "This little fleet, although not quite so respectable as that of Columbus or Captain Cook, was still viewed by us with as much pleasure," wrote Lewis in his journal.

At last the expedition reached the streams that were the source of the Missouri River. The snow-capped peaks of the Rocky Mountains were in sight. The expedition had reached the land we call **Montana.** To cross the high mountains, they would need horses. They put their hopes on the Shoshones. "If we do not find them or some other nation who have horses, I fear the successful issue of our voyage will be very doubtful," Lewis wrote.

Lewis and Clark were so eager to find the Shoshones that they walked

Here, Lewis and Clark have reached the Three Forks of the Missouri. With them is Sacajawea, a Shoshone Indian. The Shoshones loaned horses to the expedition and showed Lewis and Clark a route to the Pacific Ocean.

on land ahead of the slow-moving canoes. They were rewarded only with severe blisters. Their leather moccasins were no match for the sharp rocks and cactuses that were everywhere.

At last the travelers made contact with the Shoshones. Imagine their surprise to learn that the Shoshone chief was Sacajawea's brother! The party was now able to get horses and continue its journey over the mountains.

Once over the Rockies, the explorers built more canoes. They then canoed down the **Snake River** to the **Columbia River.** From there they continued on to the Pacific Ocean. Near the mouth of the Columbia River, they built a small fort. There they spent the winter of 1805–1806. They had hoped to find an American trading ship anchored offshore. Not finding one, they had to return overland as they had come.

The expedition returned to St. Louis in 1806. Under the expert leadership of Lewis and Clark, the expedition had collected a mass of information. Lewis

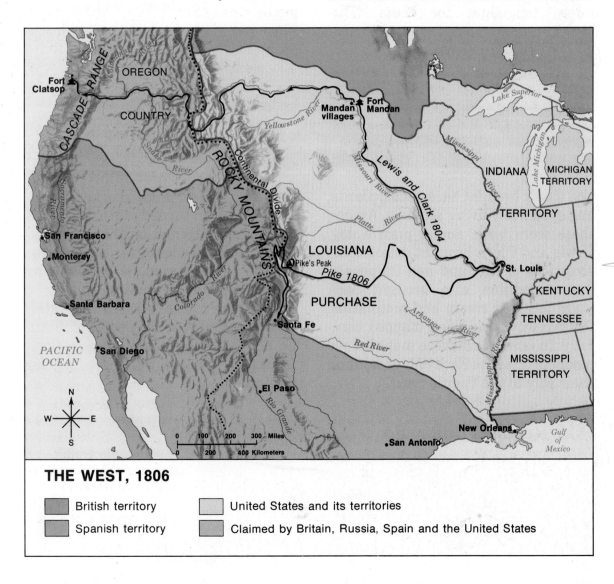

THE WEST, 1806

British territory

Spanish territory

United States and its territories

Claimed by Britain, Russia, Spain and the United States

Zebulon Pike led a government expedition to explore the Arkansas and Red river valleys. In Colorado he tried unsuccessfully to climb the peak that now carries his name. In New Mexico the Spanish captured him for trespassing. They released him a year later.

and Clark brought back seeds, plants, and even a few living animals. Among these were birds and a prairie dog. Lewis and Clark brought detailed descriptions of the land and its people. The expedition also brought back maps locating rivers and mountains. Passageways had been mapped carefully. In later years these maps helped pioneers cross the Rocky Mountains on their way to the Pacific coast.

Pike Reaches Colorado

At the same time as Lewis and Clark were on their expedition, Zebulon Pike was also leading an expedition. He intended to explore the **Arkansas** and **Red** rivers, which flowed through the middle part of the Loui-

siana Purchase. Pike reached **Colorado** and then turned south. He hoped to get more information about Spanish territory. He went too far south, however. In **New Mexico,** he was jailed by the Spanish for trespassing.

After his release about a year later, Pike reported that the people of Santa Fe needed manufactured goods. Soon American traders were heading for Santa Fe.

Reading Check

1. Who owned Louisiana in 1802?
2. Who were Lewis and Clark?
3. What area did Pike explore?

Think Beyond Do you think luck was important in Lewis and Clark's success? Explain.

Reading for a Purpose

Look for these important words:

Key Words	People	Places
• neutral	• Henry Clay	• Fort McHenry
• impressment	• Francis Scott Key	
• War Hawks	• Andrew Jackson	
• *Constitution*		
• *Guerrière*		

Look for answers to these questions:
1. What were some causes of the War of 1812?
2. What American cities did the British attack in the War of 1812? What happened in each case?
3. Who became a national hero after the War of 1812?

3 War of 1812

After the War of Independence, American relations with both France and Britain were troubled. France and Britain were often at war with each other. Neither country recognized the right of a country to be **neutral,** not to take sides. The British seized American ships to stop trade with the French. The French seized American ships to halt trade with the British. Congress decided to do something. It passed laws forbidding Americans to trade with either power until each stopped seizing American ships.

Americans were also furious with Britain for taking sailors off American ships. The British seized the sailors to put them to work on British ships. This was called **impressment.** Americans felt that they and their nation were not getting the respect they deserved.

In 1810 Napoleon Bonaparte announced that France would respect American ships. By then James Madison was President. He announced that the United States would favor France over Britain. This made Madison popular in the West and South.

In the early 1800s the British seized U.S. sailors for work on British ships.

347

People in the West and South favored war with Britain. Those who wanted war were called **War Hawks.** The War Hawks blamed the British in Canada for encouraging Indian attacks on the frontier. The War Hawks were eager for more land. They hoped to take Canada from Britain and Florida from Spain. Senator **Henry Clay** of Kentucky was the most famous of the War Hawks. He urged that the United States "take the whole continent."

Meanwhile, Britain agreed that it, too, would no longer seize American ships or sailors. But it was too late. The desire for war with Britain was too strong. At the urging of the War Hawks, the United States declared war on Britain in 1812.

Britain had the strongest navy in the world. Yet the small United States navy won several important victories. Some of these battles took place on the Great Lakes, some on the high seas.

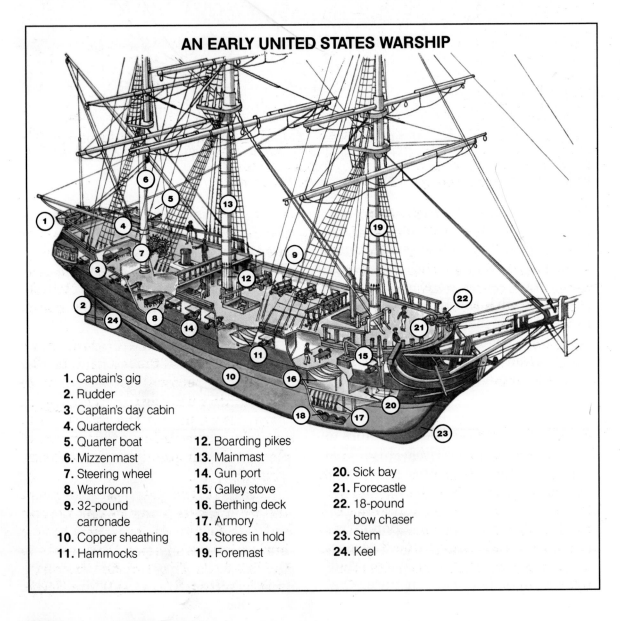

AN EARLY UNITED STATES WARSHIP

1. Captain's gig
2. Rudder
3. Captain's day cabin
4. Quarterdeck
5. Quarter boat
6. Mizzenmast
7. Steering wheel
8. Wardroom
9. 32-pound carronade
10. Copper sheathing
11. Hammocks
12. Boarding pikes
13. Mainmast
14. Gun port
15. Galley stove
16. Berthing deck
17. Armory
18. Stores in hold
19. Foremast
20. Sick bay
21. Forecastle
22. 18-pound bow chaser
23. Stem
24. Keel

Dolley Madison, a quick-witted and patriotic First Lady, rescues George Washington's portrait even as the British march into the Capital.

The U.S. frigate **Constitution,** commanded by Isaac Hull, defeated the British ship **Guerrière** (ge•ri•YAIR) in a hard battle. The British cannonballs could not break through the hard oak sides of the American ship. According to legend, a crew member on the *Constitution* yelled, "Her sides are made of iron." After that the *Constitution* carried the nickname Old Ironsides.

Raid on Washington, D.C.

During the war the American armies made only half-hearted attempts to invade Canada. The British did not invade the United States, but they did conduct hit-and-run raids along the coast. In one raid the British advanced on Washington, D.C., then a city of only 8,000 people.

When President Madison heard that the British were near, he headed for the battlefield 7 miles (11.3 km) away. There, on August 24, 1814, the American army failed to stop the British. The British continued their march toward Washington.

Dolley Madison stayed behind in the White House until the last minute. She had loaded personal goods and state papers into a waiting cart. The British were closing in. Yet she took time to take down the full-length portrait of George Washington in the East Room. Then she fled.

The first British troops to arrive at the White House found the dining room set, with food ready for 40 people. The hungry soldiers helped themselves to the fine foods. They finished their banquet by setting fire to the White House.

The next day Washington was still burning when a great hurricane struck the city. "Roofs of houses were torn off and carried up into the air like sheets of paper," a British soldier wrote. The British lost 30 men buried beneath the ruins. After the storm they quickly retreated to their ships.

Battle at Baltimore

When the British left Washington, they sailed up Chesapeake Bay. The British commander said that he intended to spend the winter in Baltimore. But Baltimore, unlike Washington, was defended by a fort. This was **Fort McHenry.**

The commander at Fort McHenry had earlier requested an American flag. He asked that it be "so large that the British will have no difficulty in seeing it at a distance." Mary Pickersgill and her 13-year-old daughter made an enormous flag for the fort. It measured 42 by 30 feet (12.8 by 9.1 m).

All night on September 13, the British threw a hail of rockets and bombs on Fort McHenry. At dawn **Francis Scott Key,** an American prisoner on a British ship, looked through the reddened sky at the fort. He was overjoyed at what he saw. The Stars and Stripes was still flying! He quickly set down the words to *The Star-Spangled Banner,* our national anthem.

The British bombarded Fort McHenry in Baltimore all night. At dawn the American flag still flew, and the British abandoned their attack.

In New Orleans, Andrew Jackson defeated the British with an army of crack-shot frontiersmen, French-speaking planters, and free blacks.

Battle of New Orleans

Unable to defeat the Americans at Baltimore, the British sailed away to New Orleans. There American soldiers commanded by **Andrew Jackson** were waiting for them.

Earlier that year Andrew Jackson had soundly defeated the Creek Indians at the Battle of Horseshoe Bend in Alabama. The Creeks had sided with the British. By doing so, they hoped to keep Americans off their land.

When word came to Jackson that the British might attack New Orleans, his troops hurried to defend the city. There they withstood an assault of over 5,000 British soldiers. For ten days the British attacked in vain, finally retreating to their ships. For his victories against the Creeks and the British, Jackson became a national hero.

Americans were later to learn that the Battle of New Orleans had not been necessary. Two weeks before the battle, the British and Americans had signed a peace treaty in Europe. However, word that the war was over had not reached New Orleans in time.

 Reading Check

1. What troubles did America have with Britain and France after the War of Independence?
2. Who were the War Hawks?
3. Who was Andrew Jackson?

Think Beyond How do you think the soldiers at New Orleans felt when they found out their battle had been unnecessary?

People

MAKE HISTORY

John J. Audubon
1785–1851

▶▶▶▶▶▶▶▶▶▶▶▶▶▶▶▶▶

In the early 1800s thousands of young Americans moved into the wild new lands of the West to seek their fortunes. Among them was John J. Audubon from France. Audubon ended up making a fortune, but not at all in the way he expected.

Young Audubon tried his hardest to be successful in business. He just did not have the right abilities. He tried his luck as a clerk, a salesperson, and a store manager. None of these efforts was successful. In 1819, at age 34, he was jailed for having too many debts.

John Audubon's real loves were art and exploration. He was fascinated by the millions of multicolored birds and other wild creatures in the backwoods. Soon he began to devote all his time to watching and drawing wildlife.

Audubon had married Lucy Bakewell. To help support their family, she had become a teacher. Her earnings made it possible for Audubon to pursue his love of art.

Audubon traveled throughout America on foot, horseback, flatboat, stagecoach, and river steamer. His goal was to paint every kind of bird in America.

Audubon faced many hardships. Rats ate 200 of his drawings. Spilled gunpowder stained months' worth of painting. Still, Audubon never gave up his dream. He hoped to offer his country "a monument to the varied splendor of American nature."

Finally, in 1838, Audubon completed his greatest work, a book of his paintings called *The Birds of America.* People were amazed by Audubon's colorful drawings of nearly every kind of native bird. The birds seemed ready to fly off the page at any moment. *The Birds of America* brought him both fame and money.

Audubon died in 1851. Within a few years many of the birds he had drawn were extinct. Only from his drawings do we know what such birds as the Carolina parakeet and the great auk looked like. Today, Audubon's name has become a symbol for preserving what is wild, beautiful, and unspoiled.

Think Beyond How do you think Audubon's drawings can help people become more aware of the need to protect endangered animals?

Louisiana heron as painted by Audubon

Reading for a Purpose

Look for these important words:

Key Words
- Trail of Tears

People
- Davy Crockett
- Sequoyah

Places
- Oklahoma
- New Echota

Look for answers to these questions:
1. How did the United States grow in territory in its first 50 years?
2. In what ways did democracy grow?
3. What qualities did Andrew Jackson have?
4. What happened to the Indians of the Southeast?

4 Growth of the Country

On July 4, 1826, the United States celebrated its fiftieth birthday. Everywhere Americans rejoiced with parades, speeches, fireworks, and celebrations. Many hoped that those two old Patriots, John Adams and Thomas Jefferson, would live to see the celebration. Both men did live to greet that Fourth of July, but both died before sunset. In Philadelphia the Liberty Bell tolled at their passing.

In the 50 years since the signing of the Declaration of Independence, the Union had increased by 11 states. In New England, Vermont and Maine had become states. Ohio, Illinois, and Indiana were carved from the Northwest Territory. Kentucky and Tennessee also had become states. Louisiana and Missouri had been formed from the Louisiana Purchase. Alabama became a state after the Creek Indians were forced to give up much of their land. Mississippi and the territory of Florida had been created from land once claimed by Spain.

Democracy Grows

The promises of the frontier continued to lure Americans westward. They went seeking land, adventure, and opportunity. On the frontier, people faced the hardships of the wilderness as equals. Settlers had to rely on themselves and yet help their neighbors. Democratic ideas grew on the frontier.

In early America, voting was usually a privilege that came with owning property. In most of the new frontier states, this changed. There the vote was given to all white men, not just to those who owned property. Many of the older states began to follow the example of the frontier states.

Today it does not seem democratic that only white men could vote. In the 1820s, women and most blacks could not vote. Indians were not considered citizens. Yet giving the right to vote to all white men was an important step in the growth of democracy. No other country in the world was so advanced at that time.

When all white men could vote, there was a change in the kind of man elected. Elected officials were no longer always men of education and property. **Davy Crockett** is an example of the new kind of leader. When Davy Crockett first ran for office, he admitted he knew nothing about the government. "I had never read even a newspaper in my life," he said. When he gave election speeches, he told "laughable stories." His "laughable stories" got him elected.

Davy Crockett was like many on the frontier. By being part of the government, he learned about government. He learned much by listening to others make election speeches. Davy Crockett later became a member of Congress.

Election of Andrew Jackson

Andrew Jackson was elected President in 1828. Until the election of Jackson, Presidents had come from either Massachusetts or Virginia. Now, for the first time, a person from the frontier was elected President. It was also the first election in which most American men could vote. They elected Jackson, the hero of the Battle of New Orleans.

Voters liked Jackson because he was a self-made man of the frontier. Jackson had been born in a log cabin. He had taught himself enough law to become a wealthy lawyer and judge in Tennessee. The new voters felt that Jackson was one of them, one of the common men.

Crowds gather to greet Andrew Jackson on his way to Washington, D. C. The popular frontier hero was elected President in 1828.

Jackson first fought the British in the hills of South Carolina during the Revolutionary War. He was only 13 years old at the time. One day Jackson and his brother were captured while trying to find food in a farmhouse. The British officer in charge ordered young Andy Jackson to shine his boots. When Jackson refused, the officer swung his sword toward Jackson's head. Ducking, Jackson put his arm up for protection. He was cut severely on his hand and forehead. The scars were with him all his life.

As the British officer learned, Andrew Jackson was stubborn. Even as a boy he was known for his toughness. One of his friends later remembered him this way: "I could throw him

At 13, Andrew Jackson had to dodge the sword of a British officer angered by Jackson's refusal to shine his boots.

three times out of four, but he would never stay throwed." Such toughness earned Jackson the nickname of Old Hickory. Hickory was the toughest tree growing in the forests of Tennessee.

When Jackson was elected in 1828, his followers were overjoyed. Thousands streamed into Washington for the inauguration. They showed up at the White House for the reception. Rough frontiersmen with muddy boots stood on the satin-covered chairs to get a glimpse of their hero. To keep from being crushed, Jackson had to escape by a back door.

As President, Jackson continued to be both tough and stubborn. He vetoed a bank law that would favor the rich. Government should not help the rich get richer, he said. Government instead should "shower its favors alike on the high and the low, the rich and the poor."

Indian Removal

Jackson's toughness also resulted in harsh and unfair treatment of the Indians east of the Mississippi. He insisted they be removed to land west of the Mississippi. Explorers had reported that the plains west of the Mississippi were useless to white people. At that time people believed that the soil was good only where trees grew. It became a popular idea that all Indians should move west. Jackson made this idea come about.

Congress passed the Indian Removal Act in 1830. Under the terms of the Indian Removal Act, all Indians east of the Mississippi were forced to leave their land and move west. They were to live in a new Indian territory, present-day **Oklahoma.**

Jerome Tiger, a modern artist, caught the feelings of cold, hunger, and despair of his ancestors' Trail of Tears to Oklahoma.

Not all Americans agreed with Jackson's Indian policy. Senator Henry Clay of Kentucky was one who did not. He pleaded with his fellow senators to honor the Indian treaties. His speech brought tears to the eyes of other senators, but they did nothing to stop the removal.

Many Indians resisted the Indian removal policy. In Illinois the government fought the Black Hawk War. This was to force the Sauk and Fox Indians to move. In the Southeast the removal policy was particularly hard on the Five Civilized Tribes. They were the Choc-taws, the Chickasaws, the Cherokees, the Creeks, and the Seminoles. The Seminoles refused to move. The result was the Seminole War. Thousands of Seminoles lost their lives.

The 15,000 Cherokees in Georgia had 22,000 cattle, 1,300 slaves, and 2,000 spinning wheels. They had 18 schools. One Cherokee, **Sequoyah** (si•KWOI•uh), had invented an alphabet for the Cherokee language. When a Cherokee-language newspaper was printed, the Cherokees quickly learned to read and write their language. They established a republic with the capital at **New Echota** (i•KOHT•uh).

The United States had guaranteed the independence of the Cherokee nation by a treaty in 1791. When gold was discovered on Cherokee lands in 1828, Georgia began to take those lands. The Cherokees appealed for help to the national government, but their pleas went unheard.

Instead of supporting the treaty with the Cherokees, Jackson used the army against them. They too were forced to move. They started westward in the winter of 1838. Almost one-fourth of their number died on the trail from disease, hunger, and cold. This journey, like others taken by Indians forced to move west, has been called the **Trail of Tears.**

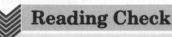

Reading Check

1. Why was Davy Crockett elected?
2. What did frontier voters like about Andrew Jackson?
3. What happened on the Trail of Tears?

Think Beyond What problems do you think were ahead for resettled Indians in an unfamiliar land?

SKILLS IN ACTION

READING POLITICAL CARTOONS

Talking animals, Presidents who look like vegetables, superheroes leaping over buildings—how are they alike? They can all be found in cartoons!

Cartoons can make you laugh. They can tell a story. They can also poke gentle fun or contain deeper meanings behind their humor. They can express opinions about something. Cartoons that express opinions about politics or government are called **political cartoons.** Political cartoons are most often found in newspapers or newsmagazines.

The First American Political Cartoons

Benjamin Franklin drew what is thought to be the first American political cartoon. This famous cartoon appeared in *The Pennsylvania Gazette* in 1754.

In 1754 Benjamin Franklin was representing Pennsylvania at the Albany Congress in New York. At this congress he suggested a "Plan of the Union" for the colonies. He wanted the colonies to unite to defend America's freedom. He used his cartoon to urge union. Each piece of the snake represents one of the colonies. The *Join or Die*

saying was based on a superstition about snakes. The belief was that a snake cut to pieces would come to life again if put back together before sunset. Benjamin Franklin wanted the pieces of the snake (the American colonies) to join together and thus be strong.

Below is another early American political cartoon. It was drawn for a similar reason as Franklin's cartoon: the hope for a united America. This cartoon celebrates New York's approval of the Constitution in 1788. It expressed the hope that North Carolina and Rhode Island would also approve the Constitution.

Symbols in Political Cartoons

Benjamin Franklin's cartoon used a snake to represent the colonies. The second cartoon used pillars of a building to show the states. The snake and the pillars used in these cartoons are **symbols.**

Political cartoons often use symbols. It would be hard to show a picture of colonial unity. How could you show a picture of peace? or war? Symbols are a good way to show these ideas. The use of symbols can make a message easier to understand.

You are probably familiar with some symbols. Many of them are used in political cartoons. Before you read on, try to think of a few symbols you know.

Uncle Sam is probably the best-known symbol of America. The first known cartoon of Uncle Sam was drawn in 1832.

No one knows who first drew Uncle Sam. Yet over the years he developed into the figure we all know. He is the man wearing a blue top hat with stars and red-and-white striped pants. The initials of Uncle Sam are the same as for the United States. In political cartoons Uncle Sam stands for the United States as a whole.

Another symbol often used in American political cartoons was the crown and dress of royalty. America had fought a war to end rule by royalty. Americans wanted to make sure that their leaders did not act like kings. By showing a leader dressed as a king, cartoonists were saying *beware*. This leader's behavior threatened democratic rule. Look at the cartoon below. What do you think this cartoon is saying about Andrew Jackson as President?

GETTIN' BACK AT THE CARTOONISTS.

JIM BERRY NEA

REDEDICATION

CANADA

Animals are often used as symbols in political cartoons. The eagle is used to represent the United States. The dove is used as a symbol of peace. The snail, as in the cartoon on page 358, is used as a symbol of slowness.

Two of our most famous political symbols are also animals. The donkey represents the Democratic party, and the elephant represents the Republican party. The donkey was probably first used to represent Andrew Jackson. Later, the donkey became a symbol for the entire Democratic party. Cartoonist Thomas Nast introduced the elephant as a symbol of the Republican party in 1874. We are still using these symbols today. Political cartoons may combine many symbols at once. The cartoon at the upper right was published in 1938 to honor friendship between the United States and Canada. The dove as a symbol of peace carries an olive branch in its beak. The olive branch is also a symbol of peace. What other symbol do you recognize in this cartoon?

Political cartoons can make important points. It is up to you, however, to decide whether you agree with them.

CHECKING YOUR SKILLS

Answer the following questions. Use the material in this lesson to help you.

1. How is a political cartoon different from other types of cartoons?

2. Where can you find political cartoons?

3. According to the cartoon on page 357, which states had not yet approved the Constitution?

4. Uncle Sam, a symbol himself, carries several other symbols in his clothing. What are they?

5. Name at least four symbols you might find in political cartoons.

6. What do the donkey and elephant stand for?

359

Thinking Back

- After the Revolution the frontier moved westward from the Appalachian Mountains to the Mississippi River. Several new states were added.

- Defeated in battles, many Indians were forced to give up their land and to retreat farther west.

- Meriwether Lewis and William Clark explored the vast new land called the Louisiana Purchase. Zebulon Pike explored the valleys of the Arkansas and Red rivers.

- Americans were furious with Britain for seizing American ships and sailors. The United States declared war on Britain in 1812.

- During the War of 1812, British troops attacked American cities. They captured Washington, D.C., and burned the White House. American troops defended New Orleans, and their leader, Andrew Jackson, became a national hero.

- Democracy grew as states began allowing all white men to vote, whether they owned property or not. A frontiersman, Andrew Jackson, was elected President.

- Congress passed the Indian Removal Act, which required all Indians still living east of the Mississippi River to move to western lands.

Check for Understanding

Using Words

Number your paper from 1 to 10. Use the words below to complete the sentences that follow.

Daniel Boone	Francis Scott Key
William Clark	Meriwether Lewis
Columbia River	Missouri River
Andrew Jackson	neutral
Kentucky	Sacajawea

　__(1)__ led pioneers on a trail through the Cumberland Gap into __(2)__. President Thomas Jefferson sent __(3)__ and __(4)__ to explore the Louisiana Purchase. They first proceeded by canoe up the __(5)__. In North Dakota a Shoshone woman, __(6)__, joined the expedition. The expedition journeyed down the Snake River and the __(7)__ to the Pacific Ocean.

When war broke out between France and Britain, the United States tried to remain __(8)__. When that became impossible, the United States went to war with Britain. While the British bombarded Fort McHenry at Baltimore, __(9)__ wrote "The Star-Spangled Banner." A hero of that war, __(10)__, became President in 1828.

Reviewing Facts

1. Why did Napoleon decide to sell the territory of Louisiana?

2. What was the purpose of the Lewis and Clark expedition?

3. Compare and contrast the British attack on Washington, D.C., with the British attack on Baltimore, Maryland.

4. How did voting requirements change in the early 1800s?

5. In what ways was Andrew Jackson a man of the frontier?

Thinking Critically

1. Compare two events: the expedition of Lewis and Clark, and the Trail of Tears. Why were relations between whites and Indians so different in these situations?

2. How did the experiences of the frontier encourage the growth of democracy?

Writing About It

Write a story that describes how you think Sacajawea felt when she saw her brother again after so many years. Be sure to include dialogue between Sacajawea, her brother, and Lewis and Clark.

Practicing Reading Skills

Reading Political Cartoons

Below is a political cartoon of President Bush. What is the cartoonist's opinion of Bush's stand on the environment? Explain your answer.

Dana Summers/Orlando Sentinel © 1989. Washington Post Writers' Group

I AM THE ENVIRONMENTAL PRESIDENT!

On Your Own

Social Studies at Home

1. Look at the picture of the Trail of Tears on page 356. Discuss this picture with your family and write a short report that tells how the picture makes you feel.

2. Draw a picture of how you think Daniel Boone's Wilderness Trail looked. In your picture include wagons, cows, and pack-horses. Share your picture with the class.

Read More About It

Bold Journey: West with Lewis and Clark by Charles Bohner. Houghton Mifflin. The story of the Lewis and Clark expedition is told from the viewpoint of a young expedition member, Hugh McNeal.

1812: The War Nobody Won by Albert Marrin. Atheneum. This lively history describes the leaders and battles of the War of 1812. It also emphasizes the black soldiers and sailors who participated in the war.

The Story of Daniel Boone by William Cunningham. Scholastic. This story contrasts the life and the legend of a hero.

The Story of the Louisiana Purchase by Mary Kay Phelan. T. Y. Crowell. This book summarizes America's greatest land deal.

Streams to the River, River to the Sea by Scott O'Dell. Houghton Mifflin. This book retells the story of Lewis and Clark's journey from the viewpoint of Sacajawea.

The Young United States, 1783–1830: A Time of Change and Growth, A Time of Learning Democracy, A New Time of New Ways of Living, Thinking, and Doing by Edwin Tunis. T. Y. Crowell. The text and illustrations in this book capture daily life as our country grew.

CHAPTER 14

A Nation on the Move

"*Yesterday was a proud day for the state of New York. The GRAND CANAL [Erie Canal], commenced on the anniversary of American independence, 1817, is completed, and at 10 o'clock yesterday morning, the first boat borne by the waters of Lake Erie, descended into the canal.*"

—New York Gazette and General Advertiser,
October 27, 1825

Look for these important words:

Key Words
- engineers
- Yankee know-how
- locks
- flatboats
- steam engine

People
- De Witt Clinton
- Robert Fulton
- Henry Miller Shreve
- Peter Cooper

Places
- Erie Canal

Look for answers to these questions:
1. Why was the Erie Canal important? How was it built?
2. What effects did the invention of the steamboat have?
3. How did the railroad change life in the United States?

Canals, Steamboats, and Railroads

The early nineteenth century saw an explosion of energy and confidence in the United States. Nothing seemed too difficult. Americans conquered one problem after another. Where there was a will there was a way, they told themselves.

A grand example of this spirit was the building of the **Erie Canal.** New York's governor, **De Witt Clinton,** had urged the building of a canal. The purpose would be to transport both people and goods between the Hudson River and the Great Lakes.

Settlers in western New York and the Great Lakes region had trouble getting their goods to East Coast markets. Roads crossed the Appalachian Mountains in very few places. Those roads more often than not were designed for pack animals, not loaded wagons.

The proposed Erie Canal would be 363 miles (584.1 km) long, the longest in the world. It would connect Troy on the Hudson River with Buffalo on Lake Erie. It was foolish, said critics of the canal, to try to build something so huge. The longest canal in America at the time was just 27 miles (43.4 km) long. But most New York citizens wanted the canal. In 1816 the New York lawmakers voted to build it.

Two lawyers from New York City were named chief **engineers.** As engineers they would be responsible for designing the canal and seeing that it was built. They had some experience surveying, but they knew nothing about building canals. People assumed that the two men could figure out how to build a canal as they went. Americans called this ability to solve practical problems **Yankee know-how.**

The engineers planned the canal to be 40 feet (12.2 m) wide carrying 4 feet (1.2 m) of water. The towpath would be on one side of the canal. Horses pulling the canalboats would walk along the towpath.

Lake Erie is 568 feet (173.1 m) higher than the Hudson River. The

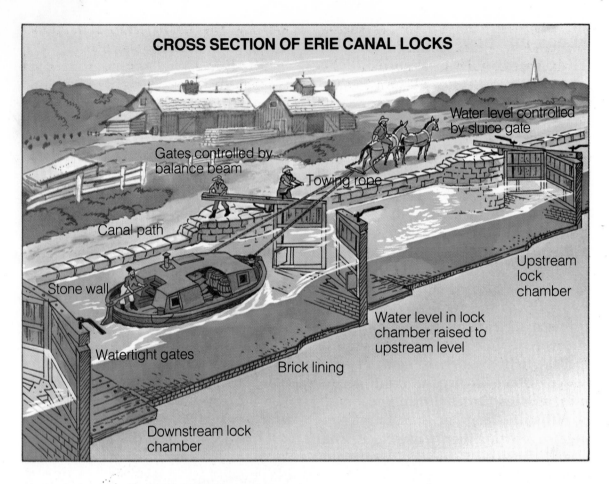

CROSS SECTION OF ERIE CANAL LOCKS

Water level controlled by sluice gate

Gates controlled by balance beam

Towing rope

Canal path

Upstream lock chamber

Stone wall

Water level in lock chamber raised to upstream level

Watertight gates

Brick lining

Downstream lock chamber

main problem they faced was how to get the canal to go uphill. The solution to the problem would be **locks.** The engineers designed 82 locks. A lock is like an elevator of water. In a lock a boat can go to a higher or lower level on the canal.

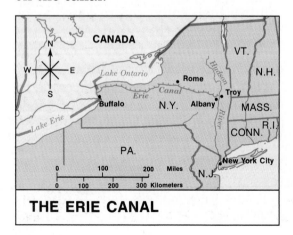

THE ERIE CANAL

The builders of the canal invented new machines to deal with their problems. Cutting down each tree in their path took too much time. So they invented a machine that pulled a tree down from its top. The builders also invented a machine that took great roots out of the ground.

Most of the canal was dug by men using shovels, pick axes, and wheelbarrows. Some 3,000 Irish immigrants made up the labor force. Boatloads of Irish immigrants came to New York City. Their hope was to get jobs working on the "Big Ditch." They would be paid 80¢ a day plus meals and lodging. The Irish could hardly believe their luck. Such wages were three times what they could earn at home. The high wages became a magnet that attracted thousands to a new life in America.

The Erie Canal was finished in 1825. Hundreds of canalboats began to haul both passengers and freight. They moved at the grand speed of 4 miles (6.4 km) an hour. People could now travel more easily between the Atlantic Coast and the Midwest. A steady stream of westward moving settlers began to use the Erie Canal.

Freight charges dropped. In 1817 it had taken 20 days to send a ton (907 kg) of wheat from Buffalo to New York City. The cost was $100. By the 1850s it cost $8 and took 8 days. Freight boats hauled grain from Buffalo to the growing cities of the East. On their return journey, the boats carried manufactured goods made in the cities.

The Erie Canal was opening up a transportation route to the heartland of the country. The opening of this route helped make New York City the leading city in the United States.

Steamboats

While the Erie Canal was being dug, Americans were working on another important problem. This was the problem of moving up mighty rivers. It was easy for farmers to float goods down the Ohio and Mississippi rivers. Farmers used great rafts called **flatboats.** But once the flatboats were downriver,

Horses patiently pulled heavily loaded towboats along the Erie Canal. The boats carried people, grain, and goods.

that was it. They could not return against the river current. The flatboats were sold for lumber in New Orleans. The boatmen had to walk or ride home on horseback. Usually they followed the road called the Natchez Trace.

In 1807 **Robert Fulton** amazed onlookers by chugging up the Hudson River in a steamboat. The **steam engine** had been invented in Britain in the 1700s. A steam engine works by heating water to make steam. The hot steam then drives the machinery. The first steam engines were used to pump water out of mines. Robert Fulton was the first who successfully put a steam engine on a boat. The steam engine turned a paddle wheel, which then pushed the boat through water.

Several years later came the first steamboat trip down the Mississippi. The steamboat *New Orleans* made this first voyage, from Pittsburgh to New Orleans, in 1811. It was probably one of the most difficult trips ever made. Just as the steamboat entered the Mississippi from the Ohio River, it was tossed and thrown about by great waves. The greatest earthquake ever to hit the United States had just struck. The river changed course. Trees toppled pell-mell into the water.

The engine on the *New Orleans* was not powerful enough to drive the boat back up the Mississippi. Yet its voyage showed the possibilities of the steamboat. The man who realized these possibilities was **Henry Miller Shreve.** Shreve designed a more efficient and powerful engine. He installed the engine on a two-deck boat with the paddle wheel in back. Shreve's steamboat could travel up the mighty Mississippi.

By the 1820s great paddle-wheel boats were operating on the Mississippi. They could also be seen on the other large rivers and lakes of the United States. It had taken four months for a flatboat to travel from Pittsburgh to New Orleans. A steamboat could make the trip in a few days.

Coming of the Railroads

Both canals and steamboats were soon challenged by the railroad. Rails had been used for some time to move carts into steep mines. On a Pennsylvania canal, canalboats rode rails to get over hills too steep for locks. Horses and even sails had been used to move rail cars. But it was the steam engine that really made the railroad possible.

The Baltimore and Ohio Railroad was the first American railroad to use a steam locomotive. In 1830 the railroad switched from horses to steam

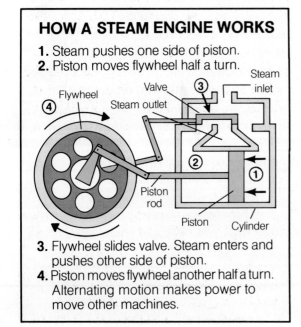

HOW A STEAM ENGINE WORKS

1. Steam pushes one side of piston.
2. Piston moves flywheel half a turn.

Flywheel
Steam outlet
Valve
Steam inlet
Piston rod
Piston
Cylinder

3. Flywheel slides valve. Steam enters and pushes other side of piston.
4. Piston moves flywheel another half a turn. Alternating motion makes power to move other machines.

The *Tom Thumb,* Peter Cooper's locomotive, puffs black smoke in its race with a horse. The *Tom Thumb* lost, but a new age had begun.

locomotives after a locomotive raced a horse. This locomotive was the *Tom Thumb.* It nearly won the race but broke down before the finish line. Even so, it was clear that the steam locomotive could have superior pulling power. The *Tom Thumb* was designed by **Peter Cooper,** a self-taught mechanic. He made the locomotive using an English steam engine and scrap iron.

Also in 1830 the locomotive *Best Friend of Charleston* ran successfully in South Carolina. Doctors had warned that fast speeds would cause human blood to boil. In spite of its speed—up to 30 miles (48.3 km) an hour—the train was a success. After six months the *Best Friend of Charleston* blew up. The train fireman, disliking the hissing of the engine, had sat on the safety-valve.

The coming of the railroad brought many changes. The railroad was the first industry to make heavy use of iron. People, in fact, called the railroad locomotive the Iron Horse. With the railroad, people depended less on rivers for transportation. The railroad opened up new parts of the country. It became easier to move raw materials and manufactured goods. Railroads multiplied rapidly. The country was on the move.

Reading Check

1. Why was the Erie Canal built?
2. What was its effect?
3. What were the advantages of river steamboats?

Think Beyond   Can you think of any harmful effects the steamboat or locomotive might have had? Explain.

IN FOCUS

THE NATIONAL ROAD

One of the worst problems that early settlers faced was the lack of roads. Most towns had no paved roads at all. This made it very difficult for settlers in remote areas to get to town to trade.

By 1801, settlers in Pennsylvania and Ohio were demanding better roads. They especially wanted a road that led from the heavily populated East Coast to the western states. Even more they wanted the federal government to build and pay for this road.

President Thomas Jefferson was upset. He did not think that the federal government should be involved in building roads that would be used only by people in a certain area. But when Ohio became a state in 1803, Congress voted to build a road from the Atlantic Coast to Ohio, to help settlers travel to the new state. This route became known as the *National Road.*

Construction of the National Road began on November 20, 1811. Because the road started in Cumberland, Maryland, it also was known as the Cumberland Road.

The road was built using the best techniques of the day. It was wide and level, and it was paved with stones and tar. It was also long. It stretched from Maryland to Pennsylvania and then on to what would later become West Virginia. From there, it passed through Ohio and Indiana, and finally ended in Vandalia, Illinois.

Builders took years to finish the National Road. It reached West Virginia in 1818, but it was not completed to Vandalia until the mid 1800s. Of course, these efforts were also costly. By the time it was completed, the National Road had cost the taxpayers $3.6 million. The money was well spent, however. The National Road became the main route for settlers traveling to the American West. It proved to the federal government that regional roads could help the entire country.

Think Beyond   Today we can travel by air and rail, as well as on roads. Do you think that good roads are still important? Explain.

Settlers traveled the National Road

Look for these important words:

Key Words
- technology
- mass production
- interchangeable parts

People
- Samuel Slater
- Francis Cabot Lowell
- Eli Whitney

Look for answers to these questions:
1. What were the first factories in the United States?
2. How did textile manufacturing develop?
3. What changes did the cotton gin bring about?
4. How did Eli Whitney change American manufacturing?

2 Growth of Manufacturing

New methods of transportation made it easier for different parts of the country to specialize. People in the West supplied food crops and raw materials. People in the Northeast began to specialize in manufactured goods.

The textile mills of New England were the first important factories in the United States. These mills turned cotton and wool into thread and the thread into cloth. They were built in New England where swift-running streams turned waterwheels to power machinery.

Getting the right machinery for factories had taken great effort. In the 1700s new inventions in Britain made large textile mills possible. These mills turned out great quantities of thread, yarn, and cloth. The new inventions were secret, however. Britain would allow no one to leave the country with factory designs. It wanted no one else in the world copying its success.

Such laws, however, did not discourage **Samuel Slater,** a young man who worked in the British mills. Hoping to go to America, Slater completely memorized the workings of the machines. His memory was the beginning of the New England textile business. He arrived in America in 1789. From memory he designed a spinning mill for a manufacturer named Moses Brown. In less than two years Brown's mill near Pawtucket, Rhode Island, was in operation. The first workers in this factory were six boys and three girls, all between 7 and 12 years of age.

Later, **Francis Cabot Lowell** of New England developed a new system of organizing factories. Lowell spent two years, from 1810 to 1812, observing British textile mills and factories. Like Samuel Slater, he memorized the workings of the machinery. He also memorized the organization of the spinning, dyeing, and weaving mills.

When Lowell returned to America, he started his own factory. He put the spinning, dyeing, and weaving together under one roof. This was different from the usual practice of having a different factory for each process. In Lowell's mill raw cotton went in one end of the mill and came out as cloth at the other end. Nothing like that had ever been done in Britain or America.

To get workers for the mills, Lowell urged young country women to come work. The women lived in boarding houses and worked 12-hour days. Lowell tried to create healthy and happy living conditions for the women. He was unusual in this, too.

Other manufacturers began to follow Lowell's lead in the way they built factories. They did not, however, show his same concern for people. As the number of factory workers grew, working conditions grew worse.

Eli Whitney's Inventions

American manufacturing was given another important boost by the inventions of **Eli Whitney.** Whitney's inventions led to new **technology.** Technology is using tools and knowledge to achieve practical aims.

A New Englander, Eli Whitney went in 1793 to visit a plantation near Savannah, Georgia. There he heard cotton planters tell how hard it was to prepare cotton for market. The cotton fibers had to be separated from the seeds by hand. It was a slow, tiring process. At that time it took a person all day to clean 1 pound (about 0.5 kg) of cotton. It was like picking burrs from socks and sweaters. As a result, cotton was expensive.

Women and children worked in New England's first textile factories. Here, women are making the looms ready for weaving.

The cotton gin made it easy to separate seed from cotton fiber. It meant profits for the planters as well as a demand for more slaves.

Within ten days Whitney invented the cotton gin. The cotton gin did the work 50 times faster and cleaned the cotton better. Whitney's cotton gin made growing cotton profitable for Southern planters. Soon cotton was "king" of Southern crops. The textile mills of New England wanted all the clean cotton the South could produce.

One effect of Whitney's invention was that slavery became more important than ever. Slavery was dying in other parts of the country. In the South, too, people questioned slavery. But the cotton gin changed all that. The demand for field workers increased.

Another effect of the cotton gin was that cotton cloth became common. People have used and valued cotton for several thousand years. Cotton cloth is soft to the touch and cool to wear. It had always been expensive. After the invention of the cotton gin, cotton cloth was no longer a luxury. It became the commonly used cloth.

Mass Production Started

The cotton gin was only a beginning for the inventive Eli Whitney. Another idea of his would change American manufacturing forever. This

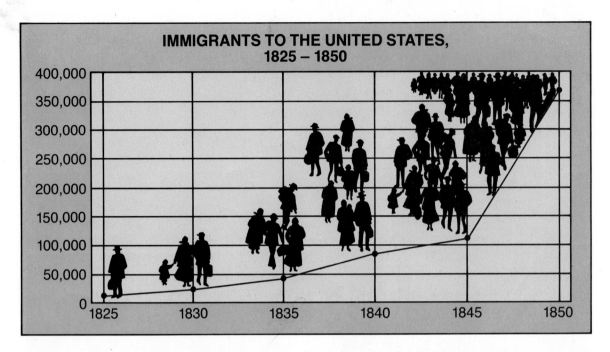

IMMIGRANTS TO THE UNITED STATES, 1825 – 1850

was a new way of manufacturing that could produce huge amounts of goods. We call it **mass production.**

In the old way, a craftsworker made one thing at a time from start to finish. Muskets, for instance, were each made by hand, one at a time. No musket was exactly like any other musket.

Why not make all the musket parts the same and then assemble them? Whitney asked. He presented his idea to the United States government, which then ordered 10,000 muskets. First, Whitney had to make the machines to make the musket parts. When he had 10 muskets, he took them to Washington, D.C. There President John Adams and his Cabinet were amazed at what Whitney showed them. He took the 10 muskets apart, mixed up the parts, then put them back together. These were **interchangeable parts.** Similar parts were identical. Interchangeable parts are the basis of all mass production.

Mass production made it possible to use unskilled workers in factories. No longer was it necessary for a gunsmith to make a musket, or a clockmaker, a clock. Workers could assemble machine-made parts. Using the principle of interchangeable parts, workers could manufacture many more goods than could individual craftsworkers.

By the 1840s thousands of immigrants were taking jobs in the new factories. The populations of cities like New York, Boston, and Baltimore mushroomed. Almost half these immigrants were Irish. Others came from Germany, Poland, and other parts of northern Europe.

 Reading Check

1. Where were the first factories in America?
2. Who introduced the idea of interchangeable parts?
3. Name two effects of the invention of the cotton gin.

Think Beyond How do you think mass production affected the craftspeople?

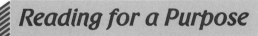
Look for these important words:

Key Words	People	Places
• Battle of Gonzales	• Stephen Austin	• Texas
• Texas Revolution	• Santa Anna	• San Antonio
• Republic of Texas	• William Travis	• Alamo
	• Sam Houston	• San Jacinto River

Look for answers to these questions:

1. Why did Americans first go to Texas?
2. How did relations between the Mexican government and American settlers change?
3. Why is the Alamo famous?
4. How did Texas finally win its independence from Mexico?

3   *The Settling of Texas*

Full of energy and always on the move, people in the early 1800s began to push beyond the country's borders. Land-hungry Americans looked longingly at the Spanish colony of **Texas.** Spain had built missions and forts throughout Texas, yet there were few settlers living on the wide-open land. In 1820 Moses Austin, a banker from Missouri, asked Spanish officials for permission to establish a colony of Americans in Texas. The Spanish gave their approval. However, Austin died before he could carry out his plan.

Stephen Austin continued his father's plan for a colony in Texas. Austin chose land between the Brazos and Colorado rivers for his colony, and the first settlers arrived in 1821. That same year Mexico won its freedom from Spain. Mexico was now an independent country. American settlers would now have to deal with the new government in Mexico.

Encouraged by the work of Austin, the Mexican government decided to allow more settlements. With its rich coastal plains, rolling hills, prairies, and forests, Texas was a good place to raise cotton, corn, and cattle. More Americans were coming to settle in Texas each year. Soon there were more Americans than Mexicans living in Texas.

Mexico Tightens Control

At first the Mexican government generally left the people in Texas alone. In time, however, Mexico became concerned about the growing number of Americans in Texas. Fearful it might lose control of Texas to the United States, Mexico decided to tighten its control over Texas. In 1830 a law was passed that said no more settlers from the United States could come to Texas. Furthermore, the settlers who were already in Texas were told they must obey all Mexican laws and pay more taxes.

Texans were angered by the new laws. Many Texans had family members still living in the United States, and these families could not move to Texas. Then, in 1834, General **Santa Anna** took over the government of Mexico and made himself president for life. When Santa Anna sent more soldiers to collect the taxes and to enforce the Mexican laws, the Texans revolted and fighting broke out.

The Texas Revolution

The **Battle of Gonzales** on October 2, 1835, was the beginning of the **Texas Revolution.** Mexico demanded that a cannon given to the people of Gonzales be returned. When the people of Gonzales refused, Mexican soldiers were sent to take the cannon by force. After a brief battle, the Mexican soldiers fled back to **San Antonio** without the cannon.

Determined to drive Santa Anna's army out of Texas, the Texans attacked the Mexican soldiers at San Antonio in early December 1835. After four days of furious fighting, the Mexicans raised a white flag—the flag of surrender. Mexican forces loyal to Santa Anna departed for Mexico.

The Alamo

A small group of Texans remained in San Antonio at the **Alamo,** an old Spanish mission. Among the people at the Alamo were Americans who had just arrived from the United States. Others, like Juan Sequin, had been born in Texas. These men, along with

some of their wives and children, were using the mission as a fort. Their commander was **William Travis.** Besides Travis, there was Davy Crockett from Tennessee. Jim Bowie, a famous frontiersman, was there too, but lay sick in bed. All were there to fight for the cause of freedom in Texas.

While the men and women at the Alamo were preparing for the fight, Santa Anna was on the move. Alarmed by the earlier defeats of his soldiers, Santa Anna ordered a large army of more than 4,000 soldiers to Texas. Santa Anna himself led the force.

Santa Anna was a handsome man who sat proudly on his gold-stamped saddle. He was also a man of strong will. The Texans, he had decided, would not get away with their revolt. The Mexicans flew a red flag. It meant that no mercy would be shown to their enemies.

Davy Crockett, famous frontiersman, met death at the Battle of the Alamo.

Fighting for independence, Texans fought to the death when Mexican soldiers attacked them at the Alamo. In this picture of the attack, considered to be quite accurate, the Texas flag still flies.

The Mexican army attacked the Alamo on February 23, 1836. For 12 days fewer than 200 Texans successfully fought off the Mexican attack. Additional fighters had slipped into the Alamo after the battle began. Gregorio Esparza, his wife, and their three children joined the defenders. Thirty-two men from Gonzales also joined the defenders inside the Alamo.

Travis knew the fort was doomed. Surrounded by the Mexican army, the Texans were running out of powder and cannonballs. By March 5 the defenders of the Alamo could not return Mexican fire because ammunition was so low. Yet Travis promised never to surrender. The brave fighters in the Alamo would fight to the end.

On March 6, the thirteenth day of the siege, 2,500 Mexican soldiers began the final assault. They used ladders to climb the Alamo's walls. Fighting became hand to hand. One after another, the Texans were killed. Jim Bowie defended himself from his sickbed, but he, too, was killed. Within two hours it was all over. The force of 183 Texans had been killed. More than 600 Mexicans had been killed or wounded.

Santa Anna spared the lives of the women, children, and the two slaves in the Alamo. Suzanna Dickenson, the wife of one of the defenders, was sent by Santa Anna to tell the rest of Texas that the Alamo had fallen. She arrived in Gonzales with the sad news on March 13.

Texas Becomes Independent

During the time of the fighting at the Alamo, Texas leaders met. On March 2, 1836, they formally declared independence from Mexico. The meeting set up a government for the new **Republic of Texas.**

The first job of the new government was to fight Santa Anna's army. The Texans chose **Sam Houston** as commander of their army. Sam Houston had come to Texas from Tennessee. There he was a close friend of the Cherokees and had been adopted into their tribe. He had fought in the War of 1812 under Andrew Jackson.

The war was not going well for the Texans. At Goliad about 300 Texans led by James Fannin were captured and later killed by Santa Anna's army. Thousands of Texans left their homes and started back to the United States.

Sam Houston was not ready to surrender Texas to Santa Anna. Houston had a small army at Gonzales. However, Houston knew that his troops needed better training if they were to defeat the powerful Mexican army. He needed time to train his army. To gain the needed time, Houston decided to pull his army back toward eastern Texas. Along the way Houston trained his troops.

Finally, six weeks after the fall of the Alamo, the Texans struck back. Sam Houston led Texan troops on a surprise attack against Santa Anna's forces near the **San Jacinto** (juh-SINT•oh) **River.** As they bore down on the Mexican army, the Texans yelled their battle cries: "Remember the Alamo." "Remember Goliad." The Texans defeated the Mexicans in a battle that lasted only about 20 minutes. Half the

Sam Houston became leader of the Texans in their fight for independence from Mexico.

Mexicans were killed. The other half were taken prisoner. Among the prisoners was Santa Anna.

Houston offered to spare Santa Anna's life in exchange for Texas' independence. Santa Anna quickly agreed and his army retreated to Mexico. Texas remained an independent republic until it became a state in 1845. Sam Houston later served as president and then governor of Texas.

Reading Check

1. Who was Stephen Austin?
2. In what ways did Mexico try to tighten its control over Texas?
3. What happened when Texans refused to obey Mexican laws?

Think Beyond What do you think it was like inside the Alamo?

People
MAKE HISTORY

Lorenzo de Zavala
?–1836

▶▶▶▶▶▶▶▶▶▶▶▶▶▶▶

In 1836 Mexican armies led by General Antonio Lopez Santa Anna invaded the Republic of Texas. When the Mexican troops reached the Texas capital, Santa Anna gave an order: "Find Lorenzo de Zavala!"

Lorenzo de Zavala was the vice president of Texas. He was also a Mexican. He had served in the Mexican government and was once an aide to Santa Anna. In 1835, however, Zavala went to Texas to help Sam Austin and other Texans fight for independence from Mexico.

Zavala had been Mexico's treasury minister and its minister to France. He had even helped write the Mexican Constitution of 1824. While he was still a Mexican official, he met Sam Austin, and they became friends. At Austin's request Zavala helped change the Mexican constitution so that Anglos could move to Texas.

Zavala even tried to persuade Santa Anna to grant the Texans some limited self-rule. After Santa Anna refused, Zavala decided to help the Texans win their freedom.

Zavala's government service experience helped the Texans greatly. His knowledge of Mexico's constitution aided the Texans in writing their own constitution. The new constitution included many things that Zavala originally had written into the Mexican Constitution. For example, the President served only three years and could not run for a second term.

Also, members of the clergy were not permitted to hold public office.

Zavala died only a few months after he became vice president of Texas. His many contributions to Texas live on, however. He designed the Republic's first flag, and his signature appears on the Texas Declaration of Independence.

Think Beyond How did Zavala's efforts affect the history of our country? Explain.

The Texas flag designed by Zavala

Look for these important words:

Key Words
- Mormons
- forty-niners

- James K. Polk
- Johann Sutter
- James Marshall

- Independence
- South Pass
- St. Louis
- Great Salt Lake
- Utah Territory
- Rio Grande
- Sacramento River valley

People
- Marcus and Narcissa Whitman
- Brigham Young

Places
- Oregon Country
- Cape Horn
- Oregon Trail

Look for answers to these questions:
1. How was Oregon Country settled?
2. Who were the Mormons? Where did they settle?
3. What territory did the U.S. acquire from Mexico? By what means?
4. Why did people rush to settle in California?

4 Oregon, Utah, and California

After Lewis and Clark, the first Americans to go by land to **Oregon Country** were fur traders. Oregon Country included present-day Oregon, Washington, and British Columbia. It was claimed by both Britain and the United States.

The surest way to get to the Pacific coast was to sail around **Cape Horn.** This long and difficult voyage around the tip of South America took six to eight months. Yet Yankee traders regularly sailed this route.

The overland route taken by Lewis and Clark was long and hard. In 1812 an American fur trader found an easier route. The new trail, called the **Oregon Trail,** led northwest from **Independence,** Missouri, to the Platte River. It followed the Platte River to what is now called Wyoming. There, at **South Pass,** it crossed the Continental Divide. On the western side of the Rocky Mountains, the trail followed first the Snake River, then the Columbia River. The end of the trail was the Willamette (wuh•LAM•uht) valley of Oregon.

Among the first pioneers in Oregon Country were **Marcus and Narcissa Whitman.** They were missionaries who made the difficult journey west in 1836. They established a mission in the Walla Walla valley. Travelers on the Oregon Trail often stopped at the mission.

The first settlers in Oregon Country reported lush valleys, wooded hills, and fertile soil. Here was land Easterners could dream of farming. It was not like the treeless Great Plains. In 1843 the first large group of pioneers headed for Oregon. In the next few years thousands more followed.

News of timberlands, rich soil, and sparkling streams in Oregon lured pioneers like these across the vast spaces of the continent.

On the Oregon Trail

Travelers to the West usually gathered in **St. Louis,** Missouri, called the Gateway to the West. From St. Louis they traveled up the Missouri River by steamboat to Independence. In Independence they organized themselves in wagon trains to cross the "prairie ocean." The wagons were similar to Conestoga wagons, but smaller. Because the pioneers thought of the grasslands as a kind of ocean, the covered wagons were nicknamed "Prairie Schooners." A schooner is a kind of sailing ship.

With the coming of spring, the wagon trains headed west across the flower-dotted plains. These plains were "too wide for the eye to measure," wrote one traveler, Francis Parkman. "One day we rode on for hours, without seeing a tree or bush." He saw only an "unbroken carpet of fresh green grass."

The trip took at least three months and often as long as six months. What a hard trip this was! The sun was like a fireball. Fresh water was scarce. Sudden storms drenched the travelers. Wagons broke down. Rivers had to be crossed. Valuable farm animals stumbled into prairie-dog holes and broke their legs. These pioneers put up with great hardship for the hope of good farmland and a fresh start.

The Mormons Settle Utah

In 1846 the **Mormons,** a religious group, joined the migration across America. Under the leadership of Joseph Smith, they had earlier settled in Nauvoo, Illinois. Their religious beliefs caused problems with neighboring settlers. In 1844 a mob killed Joseph Smith. His successor, **Brigham Young,** decided that the Mormons should move to a place where no one would bother them. In 1846 the first group of Mormons started on the overland route to the **Great Salt Lake.**

Under the stern, strong leadership of Brigham Young, the Mormons quickly organized the **Utah Territory.**

One of the first things the Mormons did was build irrigation canals. The canals brought plentiful water from the mountains to the desert plains surrounding Great Salt Lake. The Mormons made the Salt Lake desert bloom with produce, grain, and grass. Soon they were selling supplies to other pioneers headed west.

The Mexican War

When the Mormons settled near Salt Lake, that land belonged to Mexico. In 1848, only two years later, it would become part of the United States.

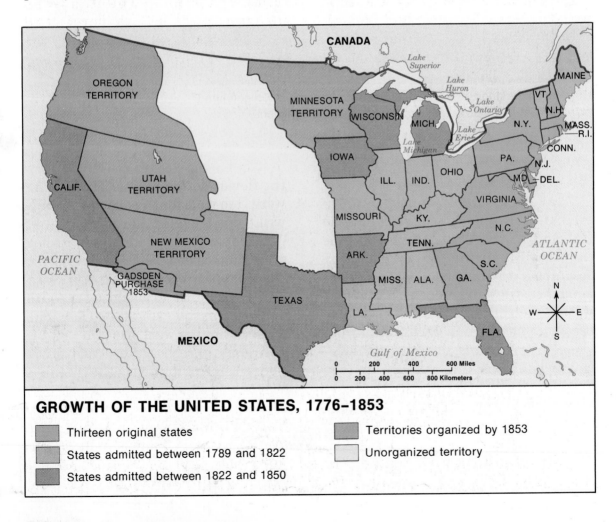

GROWTH OF THE UNITED STATES, 1776–1853

- Thirteen original states
- States admitted between 1789 and 1822
- States admitted between 1822 and 1850
- Territories organized by 1853
- Unorganized territory

James K. Polk had been elected President in 1844. His supporters wanted to see the United States expand to the Pacific Ocean. They thought that Texas, Oregon, and California should all be part of the United States. Indeed, Texas became a state soon after Polk's election. Polk and his followers particularly wanted California.

In January 1846, President Polk sent American troops south into Mexico. They crossed the **Rio Grande,** the Texas-Mexico border. When the Mexican troops ordered the Americans back across the Rio Grande, shooting started. President Polk then asked Congress to declare war on Mexico.

The United States Army won this war with Mexico by invading Mexico in 1847. The army marched from Veracruz to Mexico City. In 1848 Mexico signed a peace treaty ending the war. In the treaty the United States acquired far more than California. It also got land that is now Arizona, Utah, New Mexico, Nevada, and parts of Colorado and Wyoming. The United States purchased additional land from Mexico in 1853.

California Gold Rush

In California many people lived on sprawling ranches. Towns like Monterey, Los Angeles, and San Francisco were still small and sleepy. All this changed with the discovery of gold.

One of those who had settled in California was **Johann Sutter,** a Swiss immigrant. In 1839 Sutter had settled in the **Sacramento River valley.** By 1848 his property included wheat

San Francisco boomed as goldminers poured into California. Along the waterfront, abandoned ships became stores, hotels, and businesses.

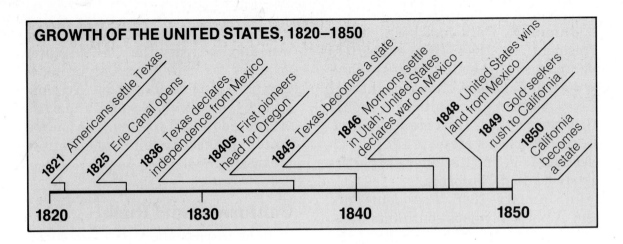

GROWTH OF THE UNITED STATES, 1820–1850

1821 Americans settle Texas

1825 Erie Canal opens

1836 Texas declares independence from Mexico

1840s First pioneers head for Oregon

1845 Texas becomes a state

1846 Mormons settle in Utah; United States declares war on Mexico

1848 United States wins land from Mexico

1849 Gold seekers rush to California

1850 California becomes a state

1820   1830   1840   1850

fields, a cattle ranch, and a tannery. In addition to this, he wanted a water-powered sawmill and hired people to build it.

In January 1848, **James Marshall** was at work building Sutter's water-powered sawmill near Sacramento. Something glittered in the water. He picked it up. It was a piece of gold half the size of a pea. Then he saw another and another.

The news flashed like wildfire to the East. Gold! As in times past, this simple word drew all who dreamed of quick riches.

Sutter's employees themselves caught the fever. They stopped working and started looking for gold. The sawmill was never finished. "Everybody left me from the clerk to the cook," Sutter complained. From his point of view, worse was to come. Soon thousands of people swarmed over his land. They shot and ate his cattle. They claimed his land. They made him a poor man.

Ninety thousand gold seekers came to California in 1849. These were the **forty-niners.** Most traveled the overland trail and then branched south across the Nevada desert to California.

The longer but easier way was to come by water around Cape Horn.

The California gold rush stimulated the building of the clipper ships. These were the fastest and most beautiful ships to sail the seas. Clipper ships were designed to bring fresh tea from China as quickly as possible. Time was just as important in the gold rush. Gold seekers were impatient to reach California and would pay to get there faster. Clipper ships reduced the journey around Cape Horn from eight months to three months.

California filled with new people. By 1850, just one year after the gold rush, California had become a new state.

Reading Check

1. Why did Marcus and Narcissa Whitman travel west?
2. By what means did the United States acquire California, Nevada, Utah, and New Mexico?
3. Why did thousands travel to California in 1849?

Think Beyond What qualities do you think a good pioneer had to have? Explain.

SKILLS IN ACTION

FIGURING OUT TIME AND DISTANCE

The map on this page shows the wagon routes to the West. The map scale can help you figure out how long these routes were. Notice that the map scale shows distance in both miles and kilometers. In this skill exercise you will use only miles to measure distance.

Measure the map scale with your ruler. On this map 1¼ inches equal 400 miles.

One way to measure a curving route is to use a string. Take a piece of string and hold the string on the map. Make a mark with a pencil or pen on the string at the starting place. Then use the string to follow the

WAGON TRAILS WEST

— California Trail   — Oregon Trail

— Mormon Trail   — Santa Fe Trail

— Old Spanish Trail

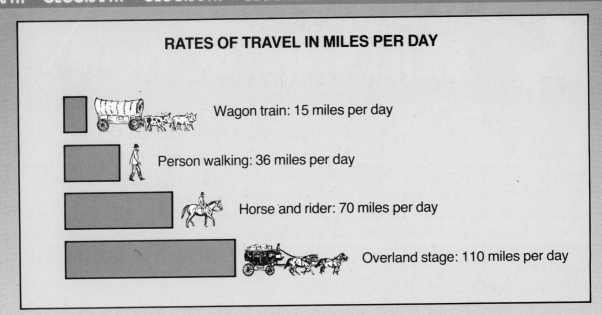

RATES OF TRAVEL IN MILES PER DAY

Wagon train: 15 miles per day

Person walking: 36 miles per day

Horse and rider: 70 miles per day

Overland stage: 110 miles per day

route. Make another mark on the string at the ending place. Place the string against the map scale. You can measure off the distance by making a mark for every 400 miles.

Use a string to measure the distance between Independence and Fort Vancouver along the Oregon Trail. Then mark off the string into 400-mile marks. You should have four 400-mile marks. How many miles does that stand for? The last part of your string measure is less than 1¼ inches. Hold it to the map scale and guess the number of miles it stands for. To figure out the distance between Independence and Fort Vancouver, add the miles represented by each part marked on the string.

The chart above shows travel rates for different forms of transportation.

The first pioneers traveled in covered wagons. They went about 15 miles per day. How many days did it take to get from Independence to Fort Vancouver by wagon? To find out, divide the total number of miles by the rate of travel. Let us assume your mileage figure is 1700 miles. If you divide that number by 15, you get 113. It took pioneers about 113 days to get from Independence, Missouri, to Fort Vancouver by wagon.

Use a string to measure the route between Santa Fe and Los Angeles. How long would it take to make this journey by stagecoach?

CHECKING YOUR SKILLS

Use the map and chart to answer these questions.

1. About how long did it take a covered wagon to travel 600 miles?

2. About how many miles was Salt Lake City from Sacramento, California?

3. About how many days would it take a horse and rider to go from Independence to Fort Laramie?

4. About how far was Santa Fe from Fort Atkinson?

5. About how many miles long was the California Trail? About how many days would it take to walk the California Trail?

Thinking Back

- New means of transportation including canals, steamboats, and railroads were developed in the 1800s.

- The Erie Canal made westward travel easier, cut shipping costs, and helped New York City grow.

- Steamboats allowed travel upriver and made river transportation faster.

- Railroads opened up new parts of the country to settlement and encouraged the growth of cities and industry.

- New methods of transportation made it easier for different parts of the country to specialize. Textile mills were our first important factories.

- The cotton gin made cotton-growing profitable, cotton cloth cheaper, and slavery more important.

- Mass production allowed unskilled workers to assemble interchangeable parts. More goods could be manufactured for less money.

- Settlers in Texas fought a war with Mexico. Texas won its independence and became a republic.

- Americans followed the Oregon Trail to settle in Oregon Country and California. Mormons organized the Utah Territory.

- As a result of winning the war with Mexico, the United States acquired vast new territories.

- In 1849 gold attracted thousands of people to California. One year later California became a state.

Check for Understanding

Using Words

Explain the meaning of each of the terms below. Then use each term in a complete sentence.

1. **canal locks**
2. **interchangeable parts**
3. **mass production**
4. **technology**

Reviewing Facts

1. Describe three effects of the Erie Canal.
2. How did Robert Fulton and Henry Miller Shreve each contribute to the development of the steamboat?
3. What was the importance of the race between the *Tom Thumb* and a horse?
4. Which two men helped establish textile mills in New England?
5. How did the invention of the cotton gin encourage the growth of the textile mills in New England?
6. How did Eli Whitney's idea of interchangeable parts bring about a new way of manufacturing?
7. What happened when Mexican troops attacked the Alamo?
8. Why did people head west on the Oregon Trail?
9. What territory did the United States gain as a result of the Mexican War?

10. How did the gold rush encourage the development of clipper ships?

Thinking Critically

1. How did the Erie Canal encourage the growth of New York City?

2. Why did the railroad mark the beginning of a new age? How did the railroad change people's lives? In what ways does new technology change our lives today?

3. What was it like to cross the country in a wagon train? What problems did travelers face? Why did people cross the country?

4. How did new inventions help bring about growth of the nation, of cities, of manufacturing, and of slavery?

Writing About It

Imagine that you traveled on the Oregon Trail to present-day Washington. Write about the sights, smells, and sounds you encountered.

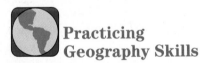

Practicing Geography Skills

Figuring Out Time and Distance

Use the map on page 383 and the Rates of Travel chart on page 384 to answer the following questions.

1. About how many days would it take a wagon train to travel from Fort Bridger to the Whitman mission?

2. About how long would it take to cover the same distance on horseback?

3. Did it generally take a covered wagon more than or less than 35 days to travel from Salt Lake City to Fort Vancouver?

4. About how many days would it take to go on horseback from Independence to Los Angeles?

On Your Own

Social Studies at Home

1. The Irish workers who helped build the Erie Canal were paid 80¢ a day plus meals and lodging. Figure out how much these workers earned each week. Then, with your family, figure out how much more you would need to be able to live today.

2. Write a travel brochure that tells about a trip on a paddle wheeler. Include information on where the trip will go, how much it will cost, and why someone would want to make the trip. Be sure to illustrate your brochure.

Read More About It

Death of the Iron Horse by Paul Goble. Bradbury Press. The Cheyenne triumph over the iron rails of the soldiers in this story based on a true event.

Frontier Living by Edwin Tunis. T. Y. Crowell. This book describes every aspect of the pioneer lifestyle.

The Oregon Trail by Francis Parkman. Penguin. This eyewitness account of the "highway" west provides a taste of the journey taken by Oregon pioneers.

The Railroads by Leonard Everett Fisher. Holiday House. This book provides coverage of the early development of America's railroad system.

Whistles Round the Bend: Travels on America's Waterways by Phil Ault. Dodd, Mead. This book describes water travel from the canoe to the hovercraft. It emphasizes canal traffic of the nineteenth century.

The Wolf's Tooth by G. Clifton Wisler. Lodestar Books. This book is a gripping portrayal of life in frontier Texas.

Lucy Applegate on the Oregon Trail

by Michael DiLeo

The life of a pioneer family is difficult to imagine. Hardship, adventure, surprise, sadness, wonderment—all these are the experiences of Lucy Applegate as she and her family set out on the hazardous journey along the Oregon Trail to make their new home in the West.

Lucy Applegate knew something was up. The minute the Missouri teenager walked into the house, she sensed something special was happening. Her father, Lindsay Applegate, was in the kitchen with Uncle Charles and Uncle Jesse. They all seemed very excited. They were talking about leaving Missouri for the new land of Oregon!

Uncle Jesse, a lanky six-footer, did a lot of the talking. He was going on about how difficult farming had become in Missouri. Bacon prices had dropped. Wheat was down to 15 cents a bushel. You could not give the corn away. Uncle Charles said he had heard the grass grew as high as your eye in Oregon. Lucy heard her dad complain about how Missouri had changed since the slave owners had come. Her family would have nothing to do with slavery.

The decision was made quickly. The families of Jesse, Charles, and Lindsay Applegate were going west on the Oregon Trail! Lucy was thrilled. So were her brothers and her many cousins.

The Applegate families all sold their farms to raise money for the trip. Some of the money was used to buy a few hundred head of cattle. The rest of the money was used to make covered wagons.

The brothers built the wooden boxes for the wagons themselves. They used only well-seasoned hardwoods. Each box measured about 10 feet (3.1 m) long, 4 feet (1.2 m) wide, and 2 feet (0.6 m) deep. The brothers then built arched frames on top of the wagon boxes to support canvas covers. A blacksmith and wheelmaker put together the wagons' moving parts, including the wheels and axles.

Lucy's father placed an advertisement in a local newspaper. The ad invited other families in the area to join the move to Oregon. The idea was to leave from the little town of Elm Grove, Missouri, on May 22, 1843.

On the evening of May 21, the wagons started pouring into Elm Grove. Lucy was astonished to see the huge crowd that had gathered to go west. Uncle Jesse guessed that 1,000 people were going—400 adults and about 600 children. Charles pointed out one of the men to Lucy. His name was Baptiste Charbonneau (SHAR·bon·noh). He was the son of Sacajawea, the Indian guide. Baptiste had been born on the trail during the Lewis and Clark expedition.

A sea of animals accompanied the wagons. There were horses, mules, oxen, beef cattle, and milk cows, not to mention all the dogs.

Lucy went for an evening walk among the wagons. Their canvas covers looked beautiful in the light of the full moon. Lucy peeked inside one of the wagons her father had built. The sides were packed high with supplies and personal belongings. A narrow walkway remained down the middle of the wagon. The frame was just tall enough for a grown-up to stand in the walkway. Lucy's mother had sewn pockets in the canvas cover to hold ammunition, hairbrushes, medicines, and other things.

The next morning the wagons set out. Uncle Jesse rode on horseback and kept the cattle moving. After a few miles of bouncing around in the slow-moving wagon, Lucy decided to walk. It seemed as if most people in the wagon train agreed with her choice.

In the afternoon Lucy took all the Applegate youngsters on a romp to pick wildflowers. They had no trouble catching up again with the poky wagons.

After a few days the wagons reached the Kansas River. There, where Topeka, Kansas, now stands, the train decided to elect a leader. Lucy watched, fascinated. The men who wanted to be leader started out walking across the prairie. People then followed the person of their choice. The person with the longest-line of followers was elected leader. The winner was Peter Burnett. He later became governor of California. Uncle Jesse was chosen to lead the families who had brought large numbers of cattle.

During a normal day on the trail, the wagons plodded on until just before sunset. The leaders then led the drivers to a marked place. The drivers put the wagons in a circle and chained them all together. This circle was not made to defend against Indian attacks, as many people think. Actually, the circle of wagons created an overnight corral for all the livestock.

When all the animals were safely inside the circle, the women started making dinner. Lucy and her friends went to collect fuel for the fire. In the great prairie there was very little firewood. The most common fuel was dried pieces of buffalo dung. These pieces were called buffalo chips.

Lucy was surprised by the bright, clean, odorless flame the buffalo chips made. The biggest problem with the chips was the fights that started during the collections. Sometimes children would steal from each other's piles. That would bring about great fights and shouting matches. Pretty soon the chips would be flying all over the place.

Somehow dinner was cooked every night. Lucy's mother liked to serve potatoes, squash, or rice with buffalo, beef, or deer meat. Occasionally the men would catch trout or catfish. The Applegates always had plenty of dairy products. The jostling wagons turned the milk cows' daily offerings into rich, golden butter.

Sometimes for a special treat, Lucy's mother baked a pie using dried fruit brought from Missouri. The men all loved to drink coffee with their pie. It seemed as if Uncle Jesse could drink gallons of coffee.

As the evening sky darkened, the sounds of music drifted through the camp. Fiddles, harmonicas, and flutes played "O Susanna" and "She'll Be Comin' Round the Mountain." Lucy and the other young people danced in the twinkling starlight.

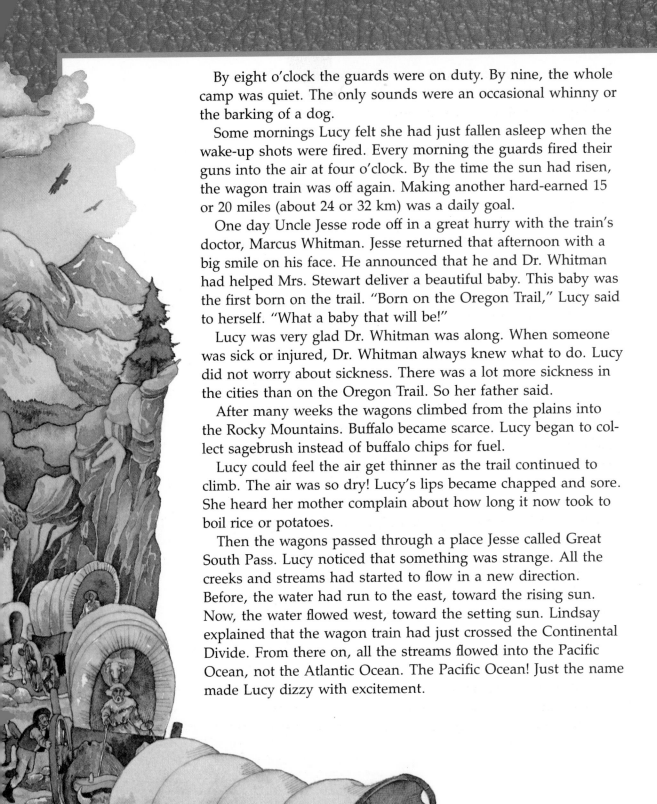

By eight o'clock the guards were on duty. By nine, the whole camp was quiet. The only sounds were an occasional whinny or the barking of a dog.

Some mornings Lucy felt she had just fallen asleep when the wake-up shots were fired. Every morning the guards fired their guns into the air at four o'clock. By the time the sun had risen, the wagon train was off again. Making another hard-earned 15 or 20 miles (about 24 or 32 km) was a daily goal.

One day Uncle Jesse rode off in a great hurry with the train's doctor, Marcus Whitman. Jesse returned that afternoon with a big smile on his face. He announced that he and Dr. Whitman had helped Mrs. Stewart deliver a beautiful baby. This baby was the first born on the trail. "Born on the Oregon Trail," Lucy said to herself. "What a baby that will be!"

Lucy was very glad Dr. Whitman was along. When someone was sick or injured, Dr. Whitman always knew what to do. Lucy did not worry about sickness. There was a lot more sickness in the cities than on the Oregon Trail. So her father said.

After many weeks the wagons climbed from the plains into the Rocky Mountains. Buffalo became scarce. Lucy began to collect sagebrush instead of buffalo chips for fuel.

Lucy could feel the air get thinner as the trail continued to climb. The air was so dry! Lucy's lips became chapped and sore. She heard her mother complain about how long it now took to boil rice or potatoes.

Then the wagons passed through a place Jesse called Great South Pass. Lucy noticed that something was strange. All the creeks and streams had started to flow in a new direction. Before, the water had run to the east, toward the rising sun. Now, the water flowed west, toward the setting sun. Lindsay explained that the wagon train had just crossed the Continental Divide. From there on, all the streams flowed into the Pacific Ocean, not the Atlantic Ocean. The Pacific Ocean! Just the name made Lucy dizzy with excitement.

After leaving South Pass, the Applegates found the journey even more difficult. The wagons had to struggle over giant boulders, wind through steep canyons, and cross swift rivers. Sometimes Lucy thought they would not make it. Somehow Lindsay, Uncle Jesse, and the others always kept the train moving.

A man named Mr. Eyres drowned while the wagons crossed the mighty Snake River. Lucy felt so sorry for his wife and children. What would she ever do without her father and uncles?

The roughest stretch for the Applegate train was the cruel trek through the Blue Mountains. The forests were thick and scary. The hills seemed impossibly steep. It took 40 men five full days to cut a path. Finally the wagons reached the top. There Stickus, Dr. Whitman's Indian guide, raised his arms thankfully to the heavens. Uncle Jesse pointed excitedly to Mt. Hood and other snowy peaks on the horizon. They had made it to Oregon!

Amazingly, this huge wagon train had stayed together nearly all the way across the country. Then, when the pioneers reached the great Columbia River, the wagon train began to split up.

At Fort Walla Walla the Applegates decided to sell their cattle to a trading post. The brothers then built boats to ride down the river. To do so, they sawed boards from huge driftwood logs.

The river trip started well, but soon disaster struck the Applegate family. Just before reaching a dangerous waterfall, the first boat crashed into a rock and splintered. Lucy's younger brother and her ten-year-old cousin were both drowned.

Lucy was heartbroken. She cried until she could not cry anymore. She told her father she did not like Oregon. She wanted to go home. Still, the family had to go on. Jesse and Lindsay led their brave little band downriver. They aimed for the fertile Willamette Valley, a place they would eventually call home.

They reached the place where the Columbia and the Willamette rivers meet. Lucy was lost in thought, remembering the deaths of her brother and cousin. She thought about how tired she felt, how weary her mother and father looked. She thought about this strange new land. She thought about her friends back in Missouri.

Lucy was also able to realize the joys of her great journey. She remembered the feathery grass of Grand Ronde Valley and the buffalo stampede near Fort Laramie. She remembered the boys trying to plug a hot-springs geyser with their hats. She recalled the wildflowers and the spectacular showers of falling stars. She wanted to laugh and to cry at the same time.

Lucy's boat passed an ocean-going schooner of the Hudson's Bay Company. One of the English sailors saw the sad-looking young lady with tears in her eyes. He called out to her, saying she was beautiful. Then he tossed her a red, shiny apple.

Lucy smiled back at the sailor. The darkness of her brother's death left her heart. She wiped away her tears of sorrow and set about starting a new life.

Unit Review

Words to Remember

Number your paper from 1 to 10. For each term below select the correct definition from the list that follows.

1. compromise
2. democracy
3. executive
4. federal
5. legislative
6. mass production
7. neutral
8. republic
9. survey
10. technology

a. not taking sides
b. give up some of what one wants in order to reach agreement
c. a form of government in which power is shared between states and the national government
d. a word meaning "rule by the people"
e. make land measurements
f. a kind of manufacturing in which unskilled factory workers assemble interchangeable parts
g. a new way of doing things as a result of a new invention
h. a form of government in which elected representatives rule
i. the lawmaking part of a government
j. the part of the government headed by the President

Focus on Main Ideas

1. What compromises did delegates to the Constitutional Convention make when they wrote the Constitution?

2. What are the main responsibilities of each of the three branches of America's government?

3. How does the Constitution give strong powers to the national government and yet protect the liberties of the people?

4. Pioneers did not all share the same goals. Tell where each of the following people settled and why.
   a. Daniel Boone
   b. Stephen Austin
   c. Marcus and Narcissa Whitman
   d. Brigham Young
   e. Johann Sutter

5. The United States had troubled relations with both Britain and Mexico. What was the cause of troubles with Britain? with Mexico? What wars were fought? What was the outcome?

6. Explain how each of these people contributed to the growth of the United States: Samuel Slater, Henry Miller Shreve, DeWitt Clinton, Eli Whitney, and Robert Fulton.

7. Why was the steam engine so important in the nineteenth century?

8. In what ways did the United States become more democratic by 1850? How was the nation not democratic?

9. How did manufacturing, the growth of cities, and the frontier all create a need for better transportation?

10. How did new methods of transportation help tie parts of the country together?

Think/Write

Rebecca Boone was Daniel Boone's wife. Imagine what her life was like during Daniel Boone's long absences. What skills and strengths would she have needed? Write about her life as you imagine it.

Activities

1. **Research/Art** Learn more about steam engines and how they were used. Draw or show pictures of what you learn.

2. **Research/Writing** Learn more about transportation in the early nineteenth century. You might choose to read about canals, flatboats, steamboats, or railroads. Write a report on what you learn.

3. **Mapmaking/Art** Make a picture map of the western United States. On your map, show the Alamo, the Whitman mission, prairie schooners on the Oregon Trail, forty-niners, the Mormon settlement, and steamboats on the Missouri River.

4. **Reading/Acting** Many stories have been written about pioneers such as Daniel Boone and Davy Crockett. With other students, read more about a pioneer of your choice. Then act out a scene from that person's life.

5. **Research** Find out more about the naval battles of the War of 1812. Then do one of these activities:
   a. Draw or paint a picture of a battle.
   b. Give a report on a naval battle.

6. **Timeline** Make a timeline showing *one* of the following:
   a. Major Inventions in the United States, 1790–1850

   b. Major Steps in the Growth of Transportation Systems, 1790–1850
   c. The Growth of the United States: New States and Territories, 1776–1850

7. **Reading/Acting** With several classmates, act out a scene from "Lucy Applegate on the Oregon Trail."

Skills Review

Figuring Out Time and Distance Use the map to answer the questions that follow.

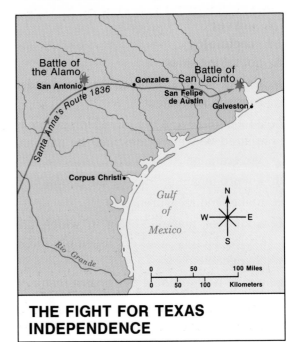

THE FIGHT FOR TEXAS INDEPENDENCE

1. How far did Santa Anna travel between the Rio Grande and San Antonio? At 75 miles a day, how long did it take him?

2. From San Antonio, was it farther to Corpus Christi or to San Felipe de Austin?

3. How many miles did Santa Anna travel between San Antonio and the battle site of San Jacinto?

EXPLORING
YOUR STATE'S HISTORY

After the American Revolution the young American nation grew by leaps and bounds. The population of the United States jumped from about 4 million in 1790 to about 23 million in 1850. The amount of land claimed by the United States more than tripled.

In the East, cities grew as trade and manufacturing increased. In 1790 New York and Philadelphia were the nation's only large cities. By 1840, 13 cities had populations of more than 20,000. Thousands of these people were recent immigrants.

In the West, settlers advanced into the areas first explored by Lewis and Clark. The discovery of gold in California speeded up the settling of the West. The following activities will help you learn about the history of your state during this exciting time.

Learning About Technology

1. In the early nineteenth century our country experienced a transportation revolution. New roads were built for travel by stagecoach. Canals, such as the Erie Canal, helped connect the states by water. Steamboats journeyed up and down on great rivers. Railroads provided a new kind of fast, powerful transportation. Trains carried both raw materials and manufactured products. Learn about your state's first transportation systems and industries. Were there towns that became important as stops for wagon trains, canals, steamboats, or railroads? Were there towns that grew because of increased trade or manufacturing?

Learning About People

2. Was your state settled between 1789 and 1850? Where did people first settle and what did they do? Write a report about the pioneer settlers of your state.

3. If people settled in your state between 1789 and 1850, where did they come from? Why did they choose your state?

Learning About Culture

4. The early years of the westward movement are the source of many wonderful stories. Some of them are real stories. Some of them are tall tales like those told about Pecos Bill or Paul Bunyan. Are there stories about your state in its early days? Draw pictures to go with one of these stories.

Learning About Geography

5. Between 1789 and 1850 many states sent farm products and raw materials to manufacturing states. During these years was your state a manufacturing state or an agricultural state? What were its principal products? How important is agriculture to your state today? manufacturing?

6. In colonial times the trade centers were ocean ports. In the nineteenth century, cities developed inland. What were the important towns or cities in your state before 1850? Why were they important? Are they still important? Why or why not?

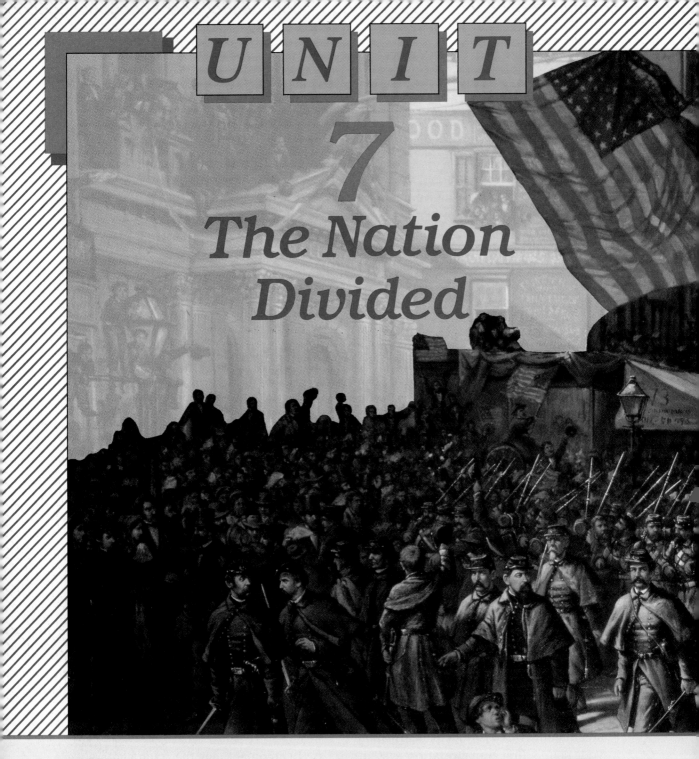

- **1820**
Missouri Compromise limits slavery to the South

- **1850**
Compromise of 1850 tries to keep peace

- **1854**
Kansas-Nebraska Act

- **1860**
Abraham Lincoln elected President

- **April 1861**
War starts at Fort Sumter, South Carolina

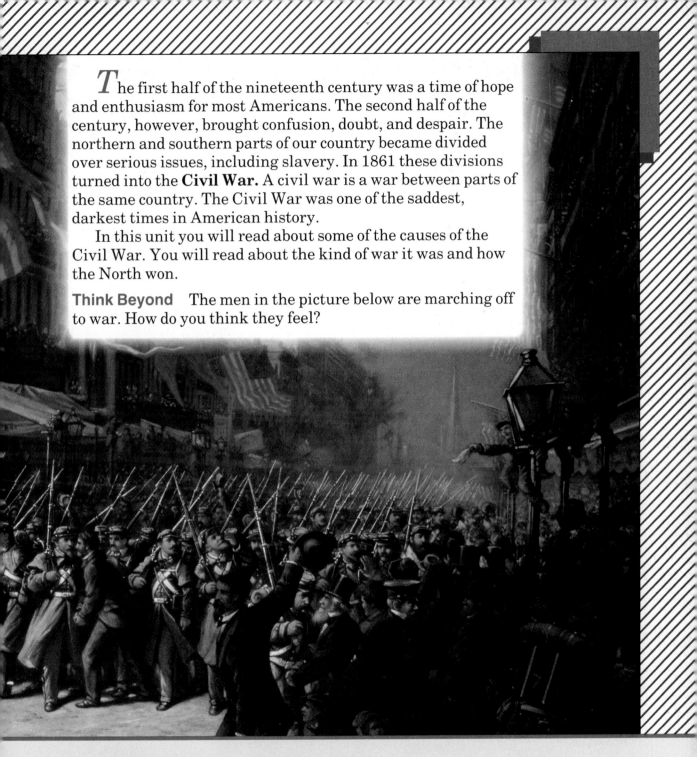

*T*he first half of the nineteenth century was a time of hope and enthusiasm for most Americans. The second half of the century, however, brought confusion, doubt, and despair. The northern and southern parts of our country became divided over serious issues, including slavery. In 1861 these divisions turned into the **Civil War.** A civil war is a war between parts of the same country. The Civil War was one of the saddest, darkest times in American history.

In this unit you will read about some of the causes of the Civil War. You will read about the kind of war it was and how the North won.

Think Beyond　　The men in the picture below are marching off to war. How do you think they feel?

• January 1, 1863	• July 1863	• November 1863	• 1864	• April 9, 1865	• April 15, 1865
Slaves are freed by Lincoln	Battle of Gettysburg	The Gettysburg Address	Union troops march through South	Robert E. Lee surrenders to Ulysses S. Grant	President Lincoln dies

CHAPTER 15

Background to the Conflict

*"*WASHINGTON, March 4.—The day is cool and quiet. Thousands throng the streets. The Inaugural of President Lincoln is brief. It was not completed until 10 A. M. this morning. Acres of human beings have assembled at the East wing of the Capitol.

The indications are that there will be no disturbance, although the troops are under arms. *"*

—Charleston *Daily Courier,* 1861

Reading for a Purpose

Look for these important words:

Key Words
- tariff
- free states
- abolish
- abolitionists
- fugitives
- Underground Railroad
- stations

People
- Nat Turner
- Frederick Douglass
- Harriet Tubman

Look for answers to these questions:
1. What general concerns divided North and South?
2. How did feelings differ about slavery?
3. What was the Underground Railroad?
4. How did Frederick Douglass and Harriet Tubman each work against slavery?

Divisions Between North and South

While the nation was expanding, strong differences were developing between the North and the South. The textile mills and new factories were making the North a center of manufacturing, banking, and trade. Hundreds of thousands of immigrants were arriving from Europe. These immigrants worked in the factories and lived in the cities.

As in colonial days, Southern life continued to center around agriculture. The invention of the cotton gin in 1793 made cotton a profitable crop. Southern planters began growing tens of thousands of acres of cotton. They kept looking for new land on which to raise cotton. By 1830 cotton had become the most important crop in the South. The raw cotton went to textile mills in both Britain and New England.

In Congress, the South favored laws that would help its interests, including agriculture. The North favored laws that would help manufacturing and trade. For instance, the North wanted a high **tariff,** or tax on imported goods. Imported goods would then cost more than goods made in the United States. People would then buy goods made in the United States, and American manufacturing would grow.

The South had little manufacturing of its own. Southerners bought manufactured goods made in Britain or in the northern United States. Southerners wanted to pay the lowest possible price for manufactured goods. Southerners, therefore, did not like tariffs on imported goods.

Division over Slavery

Most planters used slaves to do the hard work. This included planting, hoeing, harvesting, and cleaning cotton. The increasing importance of cotton led to the growth of slavery. In 1820 there were about 1.5 million slaves in the South. By 1860 the number had

RESOURCES OF THE NORTHERN AND SOUTHERN STATES BEFORE 1860

▨ Northern states and territories	⬟ Iron ore
▨ Southern states and territories	✿ Rice
⚓ Port	⚘ Sugar cane
┼┼┼ Railroad	⬗ Textile manufacturing
⛏ Coal	⬧ Tobacco
❦ Cotton	❧ Wheat
⬙ Iron and steel works	

increased to nearly 4 million slaves. In 1820 the price of a good field hand was several hundred dollars. By 1860 the price had risen to a thousand dollars. Slaves were extremely valuable. Free blacks everywhere were in danger of being kidnapped and sold into slavery.

Only one of four families in the South owned slaves. Many owned just a few to help in the house and fields. The planter families who owned many slaves, however, were the leaders. Their way of life and their ideas were accepted by most people in the South.

Until the 1820s most Southern people thought slavery was wrong but necessary. Many, like Thomas Jefferson, hoped that it would end. In 1832 the Virginia House of Burgesses argued about stopping slavery in the state of Virginia.

The argument started because many people had been scared by a slave revolt the year before. The revolt had been led by **Nat Turner.** Turner had been known as a peaceful, God-fearing slave. One August night in 1831, however, he and a band of fellow slaves attacked white families. The slaves, carrying axes and guns, went from house to house, surprising people in their sleep. They killed about 55 people, most of them women and children. Turner was caught, tried, and hanged.

In the end the House of Burgesses voted—73 to 58—not to end slavery. Instead, Virginia joined with other slave states in passing laws that put more controls on slaves. Slaves could not meet in groups after dark. Speaking against slavery became a crime.

Many Southerners began to say that slavery was good. Without slaves, they said, their way of life would be destroyed.

Slavery had gradually disappeared from Northern states. Many of these states had passed laws making slavery against the law. States that did not allow slavery were called **free states.**

GEOGRAPHY CONNECTION

In the picture you see slaves in the Old South plucking cotton bolls from cotton plants. Being picked from the plant, however, was only the first step in a long journey for these cotton bolls.

Next, the cotton bolls were cleaned and baled. Then they were loaded onto a sailing ship bound for a textile mill in Rhode Island, or perhaps New York. There the cotton was spun into thread, which was dyed and woven into cloth. As cloth, the cotton was again loaded onto a ship and returned to the South. There, in a Charleston dry-goods shop, a woman might buy the cloth and make it into a shirt or a dress. In fact, the cloth might even be made into a piece of clothing for the slave who first picked the cotton boll.

Some people thought that slavery should be ended everywhere, including the South. Slavery had been stopped in other parts of the world. Mexico had ended slavery in 1829. Britain had ended slavery in 1833. People wishing to **abolish,** or end, slavery were called **abolitionists** (ab•uh•LISH•uh•nuhsts).

Frederick Douglass

One of the most famous abolitionists was **Frederick Douglass.** Frederick Douglass had been born a slave on a Maryland plantation. As a young boy he often asked himself, "Why am I a slave?" Some of his fellow slaves told of being brought from Africa. Others told how their fathers and mothers had been stolen from Africa. When he was seven or eight years old, he learned an exciting fact. There were states in the North where there was no slavery.

As a child Douglass lived with a family in Baltimore. He wanted to learn to read and write. The wife of his owner began teaching Douglass. She had to stop when her husband reminded her that it was against the law. If slaves could read and write, he said, they might get ideas of freedom. Douglass then taught himself to read and write. He did so by asking questions of neighborhood boys who went to school.

When Douglass was a young man, he escaped by riding a train from Baltimore to New York City. In the North, Douglass became friends with William Lloyd Garrison, a well-known abolitionist. Garrison encouraged Douglass to speak out on slavery. Douglass began to give lectures. Later he started a newspaper.

Douglass described his experiences as a slave. He described the masters he had known, both the kind and the cruel. He described the whippings that men and women received for little or no reason. He described the heartbreak of being sold, the separation of families—husbands, wives, and children. He spoke against the evil of slavery.

Underground Railroad

For most slaves, escape to the North meant a difficult and dangerous journey. People who were seeking to escape from slavery were called **fugitives** (FYOO•juh•tivs).

Fugitives from slavery had to hide by day and travel by night. They kept their direction by following the North Star. They had to avoid patrols looking for escaped slaves. Sometimes they had to go for days without food. Other times they lived on wild plants in the woods. Most fugitives tried to get to Canada. Fugitive slaves caught in the Northern states could still be returned to their owners. Only in Canada was a fugitive slave completely safe.

Often the fugitives had help from other people. This help was called the **Underground Railroad.** It was a network of safe places stretching from points in the South to Canada. The safe places were called **stations.** They were the homes and farms of people who wanted to help the fugitives.

The "conductors" on the Underground Railroad guided the fugitives to freedom. They included fearless men and women of both races. One was John Fairfield, a young white man raised in the South. He helped many slaves reach

Weary from the night's travels, fugitives on their way to Canada seek refuge
at dawn at a station on the Underground Railroad.

freedom. One of them said, "I never saw such a man as Fairfield. He told us he would take us out of slavery or die in the attempt." Fairfield did not return from one trip to the South. Some think he was killed helping the slaves.

Another famous conductor on the Underground Railroad was **Harriet Tubman.** She had escaped from slavery in Maryland. After that she returned time and time again to the South. She guided 300 people to freedom during daring nighttime journeys.

Harriet Tubman was known as Moses. Some nights slaves could hear the song "Go Down Moses" being quietly sung. This was a sign that Harriet Tubman had arrived. Part of that song ran:

> We need not always weep and moan
> Let my people go
> And wear these slavery chains forlorn,
> Let my people go.

 Reading Check

1. What were people called who wished to end slavery everywhere?
2. How did Frederick Douglass fight against slavery once he was free?
3. Who was Harriet Tubman?

Think Beyond Why do you think many people in the South came to believe that slavery was good?

People MAKE HISTORY

Sojourner Truth
1820–1892

▶▶▶▶▶▶▶▶▶▶▶▶▶▶

On June 1, 1843, a black woman named Isabella stood looking at the East River in New York City. She was thinking about her future. She had decided to start a new life, but first she wanted a new name.

Isabella had been born a slave in New York State. She was given her freedom after New York abolished slavery in 1827. For some years Isabella had worked as a household servant. Then she had become a religious missionary on the streets of New York City.

Now Isabella had felt a call from God to "travel up and down the land." So she named herself *Sojourner,* which means "traveler." Sojourner wanted to preach, to bring truth to the world. She chose *Truth* as a last name, calling herself *Sojourner Truth.*

After crossing the East River that day in 1843, Sojourner Truth followed her calling. She set out to talk, preach, and sing to the American people. Before the year was over, she was also preaching freedom for all slaves. Across her chest she wore a banner. On this banner were the same Bible words as are on the Liberty Bell: *Proclaim liberty throughout all the land unto all the inhabitants thereof.*

By 1850 women were organizing to get equality under the law. In simple and strong language Sojourner began to speak out for women's rights. Once she heard a man say that women were naturally weak and unequal to men. Sojourner Truth stood up, bared her right arm, and showed her muscles. "Ain't I a woman? Look at me. Look at my arm. I have ploughed, and planted, and gathered into barns." Her strong words gave spirit to the women's rights movement.

For 40 years Sojourner Truth traveled throughout America speaking out for freedom and equality. Once a man tried to tell Sojourner that her speeches were useless. "Why, I don't care any more for your talk," he boasted, "than I do for the bite of a flea." Sojourner smiled at the man. "Perhaps not," she answered, "but just like the flea, I'll keep you scratching."

Think Beyond   Do you know of anyone who stands up for what he or she believes as Sojourner Truth did? Explain.

Look for these important words:

Key Words
- extension of slavery
- Missouri Compromise
- Compromise of 1850
- *Uncle Tom's Cabin*
- Kansas-Nebraska Act

- secession
- debates

People
- Henry Clay
- Harriet Beecher Stowe

- Stephen Douglas
- Abraham Lincoln
- Dred Scott

Look for answers to these questions:
1. How did North and South disagree about slavery in new territories?
2. How did they work out their differences?
3. What led to fighting in Kansas?
4. What brought national attention to Abraham Lincoln?

2 The Extension of Slavery

Most Northerners were not abolitionists. They were content to let slavery remain in the South. Northerners were generally opposed, however, to the **extension of slavery.** That means they opposed slavery in the new territories of the West. They wanted new states to be free states.

People in slave states felt they had the same rights as other Americans. These included the right to move to new territory. Slaves were their property, they said. Why couldn't they take their property with them?

Important Compromises

In 1820 the North and South reached a compromise. **Henry Clay,** a senator from Kentucky, worked hard on this agreement. It was called the **Missouri Compromise.** The Missouri Compromise said that the new state of Missouri would be a slave state. The new state of Maine would be a free state. The number of free and slave states would remain equal.

The Missouri Compromise set an imaginary line running through the Louisiana Territory. It said that new states north of this line would be free states. New states south of this line would be slave states.

The Missouri Compromise worked to keep peace for almost 30 years. In 1849 there were 15 slave states and 15 free states.

Then, after the Mexican War, the question came up again. How would the new territories be organized? California wanted to be admitted to the Union as a free state. The South did not like that. It would mean 16 free states to 15 slave states. It would give the free states more power in Congress. They could then pass laws that favored the North. The Missouri Compromise no longer worked.

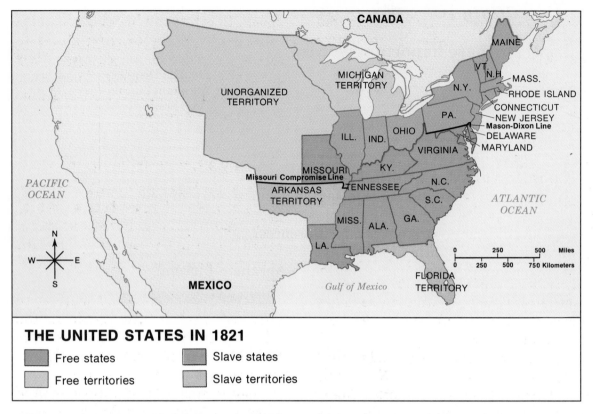

THE UNITED STATES IN 1821

■ Free states
■ Slave states
□ Free territories
■ Slave territories

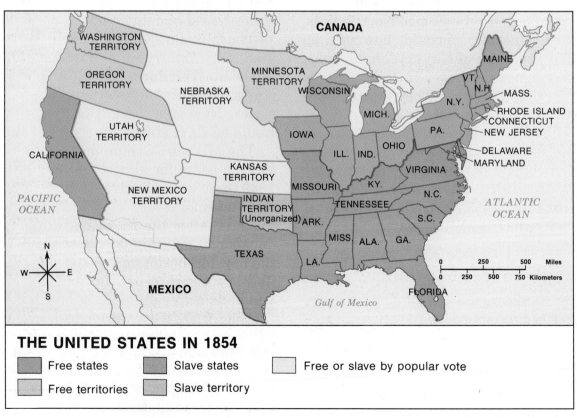

THE UNITED STATES IN 1854

■ Free states
■ Slave states
□ Free or slave by popular vote
■ Free territories
■ Slave territory

In 1850 Congress again hammered out a compromise. The **Compromise of 1850** included several parts:

- California would be a free state.
- The people in the territories of Utah and New Mexico could decide themselves to be free or slave states.
- Any slaves escaping to the North would have to be returned.
- Anybody helping slaves to escape would be punished.

This last part of the compromise was particularly important to the South. Slaves were worth a great deal of money. Southerners were getting quite angry about the help Northerners were giving runaway slaves.

The Compromise of 1850 did not last long. Feelings in both the North and South grew stronger and hotter. Many Northern leaders urged people to disobey the new law by helping runaway

Uncle Tom's Cabin convinced millions of Northerners that slavery was evil.

135,000 SETS, 270,000 VOLUMES SOLD.

UNCLE TOM'S CABIN

SUPERB ILLUSTRATED EDITION, IN 1 Vol., WITH 153 ENGRAVINGS.

FOR SALE HERE.

AN EDITION FOR THE MILLION, COMPLETE IN 1 Vol., PRICE 37 1-2 CENTS.
" " IN GERMAN, IN 1 Vol., PRICE 50 CENTS.
" " IN 2 Vols., CLOTH, 6 PLATES, PRICE $1.50.
SUPERB ILLUSTRATED EDITION, IN 1 Vol., WITH 153 ENGRAVINGS.
PRICES FROM $2.50 TO $5.00.

slaves. Southerners believed that abolitionists were encouraging slaves to revolt as well as to escape. They remembered Nat Turner. They were afraid of the bloodshed that could be part of a slave revolt.

Feelings Grow Stronger

In 1852 **Harriet Beecher Stowe** wrote a novel, **Uncle Tom's Cabin.** She wrote the book based on stories heard from fugitive slaves. It brought tears to the eyes of millions of Northern readers.

Uncle Tom's Cabin did more than anything else to turn people in the North against slavery. Northerners who had paid no attention to the abolitionists now saw slavery as an evil.

Southern people said the stories of slavery in *Uncle Tom's Cabin* were not true. Southern writers also said that slaves were generally better off than most Northern factory workers. Wage earners, they said, had to work longer hours under worse conditions.

Bloodshed in Kansas

Feelings in both North and South were inflamed even more by a new law, the **Kansas-Nebraska Act** of 1854. The Kansas-Nebraska Act said there would no longer be a line to separate slave states and free states. Instead, in each new state the people themselves would decide.

The Kansas-Nebraska Act was written by **Stephen Douglas,** a senator from Illinois. A short man, Douglas was known as the Little Giant. He was a popular man and well known in both North and South.

The people against slavery were furious with the Kansas-Nebraska Act. They agreed with an Illinois lawyer, **Abraham Lincoln.** Lincoln said, "Slavery must be kept out of Kansas." Lincoln did not believe in ending slavery where it existed, but he did not want slavery to expand.

Kansas was one of the places where people would vote to decide whether it was to be a free state or a slave state. Therefore, people both for and against slavery rushed into Kansas. As these two groups fought for control of Kansas, that territory became known as Bleeding Kansas. More than 200 settlers were killed in the first year. After elections were held, Kansas was finally admitted as a free state in 1861.

The bloodshed in Kansas was a sign of things to come. People on both sides of the slavery issue no longer saw compromise as possible. Some in the South began to speak of **secession.** By *secession,* they meant withdrawing from the United States.

Dred Scott Decision

The clouds over North and South became even stormier in 1857. In that year the Supreme Court handed down its decision in the **Dred Scott** case. Dred Scott, a slave, had asked for his freedom because his master had taken him to a free territory.

The Supreme Court ruled that Congress could not keep slavery out of the territories. The Court also said that the Declaration of Independence did not really mean "all men are created equal." Black people were not meant to be included, the Court said. Black people had no rights under the Constitution. Therefore, the Supreme Court said, Dred Scott must remain a slave.

In Illinois, Abraham Lincoln disagreed. Congress did have the power to

A cannonball rips through a pioneer home in eastern Kansas as people for and against slavery fight each other. Kansas would be free or slave depending on how the majority of its people voted. In the end, they voted for Kansas to be a free state.

Thousands came to hear Abraham Lincoln, standing, and Stephen Douglas, at his right, debate about the extension of slavery. Their debates received national attention.

keep slavery out of the territories, he argued. And, he said, when the writers of the Declaration of Independence said "All men are created equal," they meant it. There could be no exceptions.

Lincoln-Douglas Debates

In 1858 Lincoln ran against Stephen Douglas for the office of United States senator from Illinois. Lincoln and Douglas each expressed their ideas in a series of **debates,** or arguments. They debated each other in towns throughout Illinois. Crowds of 15,000 often came to hear them. Newspapers printed what each man said. Their arguments were eagerly read by thousands more.

Douglas argued, "Let each state mind its own business and let its neighbors alone." He said, "This republic can exist forever divided into free and slave states."

Lincoln responded that Douglas's arguments were thin. They were like soup "made by boiling the shadow of a pigeon that starved to death." Lincoln said: "I believe this government cannot endure, permanently half slave and half free. . . . It will become all one thing or all the other."

Douglas won the election, but Lincoln won national fame. People began to talk of the tall man from Illinois.

Reading Check

1. What was the main disagreement between North and South over the extension of slavery?
2. What book turned many in the North against slavery?
3. How did Abraham Lincoln win national fame?

Think Beyond Why were so many people willing to risk their lives to make Kansas a free state?

409

SKILLS IN ACTION

USING POPULATION MAPS

One special kind of map is a population map. A population map shows where people live. Sometimes population maps are called maps of **population density.** *Density* means the amount of crowding. A population density map shows how many people live in different areas. The map at the top of page 411 shows population density of much of the United States in 1860.

To read this map, look first at the key. There you see that different colors have been given to different population densities. Yellow is a symbol for fewer than 2 people per square mile (2.6 sq km). People who lived in parts of the country with this density might have been quite far from their neighbors. It would take 20 minutes to walk to a neighbor's house 1 mile (1.6 km) away. Many lived much farther apart than that.

What does the dark orange color stand for? This population density shows much more crowding. It is an area of smaller farms and many towns. In such an area there is usually a large city.

The map key also shows a dot (·) for cities of over 50,000 people. An even larger dot stands for cities of over 100,000 people. The largest dot is for cities of over 500,000 people.

Special Population Maps

Some population maps show density for only a particular part of the population. The map at the bottom of page 411 shows where slaves lived in 1860.

The key helps you read this map. It tells you that the green area had no slaves or

was unsettled. The remaining color symbols tell you how many slaves there were for every 100 people. The word to describe this way of looking at numbers is *percent*. For instance, find the color that stands for 10 to 30 percent. Ten to 30 percent means that of every 100 people, 10 to 30 were slaves.

CHECKING YOUR SKILLS

Use the maps and keys to answer these questions.

1. What does *density* mean?

2. Was the population density greater or less as one moved west?

3. Where was the greatest number of cities located?

4. Locate South Carolina on the maps. Describe its population density in 1860.

5. How many cities in the United States had more than 500,000 people?

6. Was the density of slaves greater in the northern or the southern states?

7. Locate Texas on the maps. Were there more slaves in eastern or western Texas?

8. Describe the slave population density of South Carolina in 1860.

9. Were slaves more likely to live in areas of greatest population density? Explain your answer.

10. Were areas of low population density always areas of low slave density? Explain.

410

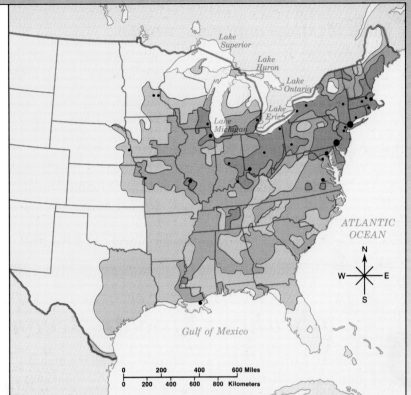

POPULATION DENSITY, 1860

People per square mile	People per square kilometer
More than 45	More than 18
18–45	8–18
2–18	1–8
Less than 2	Less than 1

● City over 500,000 population

• City over 100,000 population

· City over 50,000 population

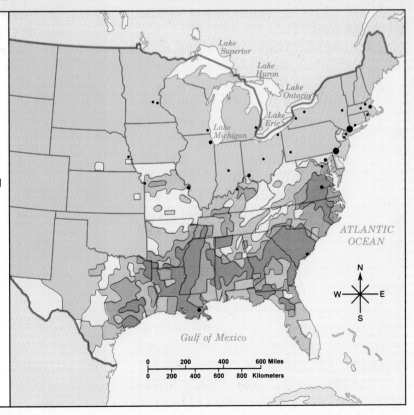

SLAVE POPULATION DENSITY, 1860

Percent of Slaves in Total Population

Over 50 percent
30–50 percent
10–30 percent
Under 10 percent
No slaves or unsettled

● City over 500,000 population

• City over 100,000 population

· City over 50,000 population

411

Reading for a Purpose

Look for these important words:

Key Words
- Union
- secede
- Confederate States of America

- Confederacy
- inauguration

People
- Jefferson Davis

Places
- Fort Sumter

Look for answers to these questions:
1. What personal qualities did Abraham Lincoln have?
2. What views did the Republican party hold?
3. How did the South react to Lincoln's being elected President?
4. Why did a war begin between North and South?

3 Abraham Lincoln Becomes President

Abraham Lincoln had a face one could not forget. "I never saw a more thoughtful face. I never saw a more dignified face. I never saw so sad a face," wrote an observer.

Abraham Lincoln was named after his grandfather, who had been a friend of Daniel Boone's. Grandfather Lincoln had followed Boone into the Kentucky wilderness. His young son Tom was beside him in the fields one day when Indians attacked. Tom saw his father killed. When Tom grew up, he married Nancy Hanks. Their home was a small log cabin with a dirt floor. There, in 1809, Abraham Lincoln was born.

The Lincoln family moved on the edge of the frontier first to Indiana, then to Illinois. In the frontier life there was work aplenty. "I was raised to farm work," Lincoln later wrote. He chopped trees and split them to make rails for fences. He plowed and planted and harvested crops. There was little time

After a long day of farmwork, young Abraham Lincoln read at night by firelight.

Eastman Johnson, American 1824-1906
Boyhood of Lincoln, 1868, oil on canvas, The University of Michigan Museum of Art, bequest of Henry Lewis. © 1983, The Regents of the University of Michigan.

for school. When he could, Lincoln borrowed books to read. He could read only during a lunch break or after finishing his evening chores.

As a young man Lincoln worked taking flatboats loaded with cargo down the Mississippi River. For a time he kept a store. Then he became a surveyor. All the while, he was reading. He taught himself law. In 1836, at age 27, he became a lawyer.

Lincoln became known for his honesty, his fairness, his humor. He was known as the best storyteller around. Once Lincoln was carrying home his two sons, Willie and Tad, both crying. A neighbor asked, "Why, Mr. Lincoln, what's the matter?" Lincoln answered, "Just what's the matter with the whole world. I've got three walnuts and each wants two."

Lincoln had great respect for work. He felt that all people had the right to the rewards of their own labor. No matter how hard slaves worked, they had no hope for a better life. Wage earners might work under conditions as bad, but they had hope that life would improve for themselves and their children. Lincoln supported shoe-factory workers in New England who went on strike for higher wages. Lincoln said, "Thank God that we have a system of labor where there *can* be a strike."

Election of Lincoln

The next year, 1860, the Republican party made Abraham Lincoln its candidate for President. The Republican party had been born in 1854. Its members stood against the extension of slavery and for the preservation of the **Union.** *Union* refers to the union of states that is the United States of America. Republicans did not think that states had the right to **secede,** or withdraw, from the Union. Abraham Lincoln frightened the South. If he were elected, Southerners said, their way of life would come to an end.

Abraham Lincoln was elected in 1860. South Carolina then chose to secede. South Carolina leaders argued that the state had the right to secede. Their reasoning was simple. Because the state had voted to join the Union, it could vote to secede from the Union. Other cotton states quickly followed: Mississippi, Alabama, Georgia, Florida, Louisiana, and Texas. The seceding states formed a new nation, the **Confederate States of America.** It was also called the **Confederacy.**

Jefferson Davis of Mississippi was chosen president of the Confederacy. Davis was a cotton planter. He had fought in the Mexican War and had also been a United States senator. Like Lincoln, he was known for his honesty.

North and South watched to see what Lincoln would do as President. Lincoln's **inauguration** (in•aw•guh•RAY•shuhn), or taking the oath of office, was March 4, 1861. The first thing he did as President was to make a speech, an inaugural (in•AW•gyuh•ruhl) address. In this speech Lincoln took a strong stand. He said that slavery would be left alone in the slave states. Slavery should not, however, be extended to any new places. Lincoln also gave notice that he would do all he could to preserve the Union. He would "hold, occupy, and possess" all property belonging to the United States government. Finally, he pleaded for peace and asked the

The Battle of Fort Sumter in the harbor of Charleston, South Carolina, was the first battle of the Civil War. It resulted in a Confederate victory.

Confederate states to return to the Union. "We are not enemies, but friends," he said. "We must not be enemies."

People in the Confederacy did not trust Lincoln. They had not voted for him. They did not feel Lincoln represented them. Confederate leaders insisted that the states had the right to secede from the Union.

Battle at Fort Sumter

For one month after Lincoln's inauguration, the tension built. People wondered what Lincoln would do about the seceding states. The first test was in South Carolina at **Fort Sumter,** a fort located on an island in Charleston Harbor. When South Carolina seceded, government troops were stationed at the fort. Lincoln had promised to hold all property that be-

longed to the United States. He sent word that ships would bring food to the soldiers at the fort.

On April 12 the Confederate leaders demanded that the fort surrender. The fort's commander refused. Confederate troops then fired their cannon. They bombarded the fort for 30 hours until, at last, Fort Sumter surrendered. War between North and South had begun.

Reading Check

1. Describe three qualities for which Abraham Lincoln was famous.
2. Name three ideas Lincoln expressed in his inaugural address.
3. Where did the Civil War begin?

Think Beyond Do you think the Confederate states had the right to secede? Why or why not?

IN FOCUS

SOUTHERN WOMEN

Southern women of the Civil War period are often pictured in wide-hooped skirts, with dainty parasols and fancy bonnets. However, these Southern belles, as they were called, did not represent most Southern women. Whether they were wives of farmers or of rich planters, white Southern women often worked from before dawn until after nightfall.

The farmers' wives ran their households, fed and clothed their families, and worked in the fields when needed. They spun and wove cotton to make clothes, bedding, and curtains. They nursed sick family members and prepared homemade remedies. They pumped water, carried it to the house, and heated it for baths and laundry. They scrubbed the laundry on washboards and then hung it out to dry.

Confederate wives and mothers also hauled wood for the fireplace. They made the fires and kept them going day and night. The women raised chickens, gathered eggs, and killed and cooked the birds for dinner.

These thrifty women wasted nothing. Feathers from the chickens were stuffed inside cloth to make mattresses. When livestock was killed for food, women saved the hides for leather, bones for soup, and fat for soap.

The Civil War changed the lives of Southern women. When the men went away to war the women had to do the men's work in addition to their own. This included such heavy work as chopping wood, planting and harvesting the crops, and roping and shoeing the horses. Women also traveled to the cities, where they took the place of men in business.

Southern white women may have been born free. Some may have been very rich. However, few spent all their time wearing fancy bonnets and attending parties—unlike those you might see in the movies.

Think Beyond   Why do you think many people have the wrong idea about how Southern women lived?

Southern woman spinning

Thinking Back

- As our country developed, the North became a center of business, while Southern life centered around agriculture. This led to disagreements over such issues as tariffs and slavery.

- Abolitionists spoke against slavery. The Underground Railroad was formed to help slaves escape.

- For many years, compromises helped keep peace between North and South.

- *Uncle Tom's Cabin*, the Dred Scott decision, and the Kansas-Nebraska Act helped inflame feelings about slavery.

- Abraham Lincoln and Stephen Douglas argued their ideas about slavery in a series of debates in Illinois in 1858. These debates brought Lincoln national fame, and two years later he became our sixteenth President.

- After Lincoln's election, several states seceded from the Union and formed a new nation called the Confederate States of America.

- President Lincoln asked the Confederate states to return to the Union, but they refused. Confederate troops then attacked Fort Sumter, and the Civil War began.

Check for Understanding

Using Words

Choose the correct word from the list below to complete the sentences that follow.

abolish   secession
abolitionists   tariff
fugitives

1. Frederick Douglass wanted to _____ slavery.
2. The _____ wanted to end slavery.
3. A tax on imported goods is a _____ .
4. People escaping from slavery were _____ .
5. The act of withdrawing from the Union was called _____ .

Reviewing Facts

1. Explain why the North favored a tariff and the South opposed a tariff.

2. Compare how Frederick Douglass and Harriet Tubman worked against slavery.
3. Compare the opinions of the North and South about the extension of slavery.
4. What were the beliefs of the Republican party when it was formed?
5. What event caused Southern states to secede from the Union?

Thinking Critically

1. How did North and South try to compromise on the extension of slavery? Why did compromise finally fail to work?
2. Compare how Frederick Douglass and Harriet Beecher Stowe fought against slavery. Who do you think had the greater effect? Why?
3. What kinds of problems did fugitive slaves face? Why were people like Harriet Tubman and John Fairfield important to the fugitives?

4. What kind of person was Abraham Lincoln? What were some of his beliefs? How might his early life have had an effect on those beliefs?

5. Imagine two people, one a planter in South Carolina and one a small farmer in Illinois. How might they disagree with each other over these subjects?
   a. the extension of slavery
   b. *Uncle Tom's Cabin*
   c. the election of Abraham Lincoln

6. Why do you think the South attacked Fort Sumter? Do you think war could have been avoided if Fort Sumter had not been attacked?

Writing About It

Imagine you are a soldier inside Fort Sumter on April 12, 1861. Write a diary entry that describes how it feels to be inside the fort. Include in your account the things you see and the sounds you hear.

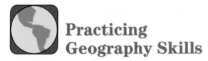
Practicing Geography Skills

Using Population Maps
Answer these questions.

1. What is a population density map?
2. If a map shows a population density of more than 45 people per square mile (2.6 sq km), what kind of place is that likely to be?
3. If a map shows a population density of less than 2 people per square mile (2.6 sq km), what kind of place is that?
4. If a special population map shows that 30 percent of the people were slaves, what does that mean?
5. Name a situation in which a population map might be useful.

On Your Own

Social Studies at Home

1. Harriet Tubman helped slaves escape to freedom in Canada. Create a map showing the route a slave might follow from South Carolina to Canada. Make sure your map shows any rivers or mountains that would have to be crossed.

2. *Uncle Tom's Cabin* made many people in the North think about slavery. Discuss with your family an article, a book or story, or a movie that has made you more aware of an issue or event. Write a short report to share with the class by answering such questions as, Whose point of view was discussed? What differing opinions were there? How did the information make you feel?

Read More About It

Harriet Tubman: Conductor on the Underground Railroad by Ann Petry. T. Y. Crowell. This is a classic biography of the woman who led over 300 slaves to freedom.

Lincoln: A Photobiography by Russell Freedman. Clarion Books. This Newbery Medal winner provides an in-depth look at one of our greatest Presidents. Both photographs and documents are used to describe Lincoln's life.

Nettie's Trip South by Ann Warren Turner. Macmillan. Through pictures and text this book describes a young girl's first exposure to slavery.

Sojourner Truth: A Self-Made Woman by Victoria Ortiz. J. B. Lippincott. This biography provides an in-depth look at the first black woman to crusade openly against slavery.

CHAPTER 16

The Civil War

"*July 1.—I got up early this morning to get my baking done before any fighting would begin. I had just put my bread in the pans when the cannons began to fire, and true enough the battle had begun in earnest, about two miles out on the Chambersburg pike. What to do or where to go, I did not know. People were running here and there, screaming that the town would be shelled. No one knew where to go or what to do.*"

—from the diary of a Gettysburg woman, 1863

Look for these important words:

Key Words	People	Places
• regiments	• Robert E. Lee	• West Virginia
	• Stonewall Jackson	• Bull Run

Look for answers to these questions:
1. What was the mood of Americans at the beginning of the Civil War?
2. What happened at the Battle of Bull Run?
3. What effect did the Battle of Bull Run have?

1 The Fighting Begins

After the battle of Fort Sumter, four more states joined the Confederacy. They were Virginia, North Carolina, Tennessee, and Arkansas. The western counties of Virginia refused to join the Confederate effort. Later they became another state, **West Virginia.** The slave states of Delaware, Maryland, Missouri, and Kentucky stayed with the Union. In these states, which bordered on free states, slavery was not so important a part of the economy.

Both North and South began preparations for war. Men and boys eagerly joined **regiments,** or organized groups of soldiers, made up of their neighbors and friends. In the North the foreign-born organized their own regiments. The Irish, the Italians, the Germans, and the British all had their regiments. Some wore colorful uniforms of red baggy trousers, yellow sashes, and blue coats.

The new soldiers left their homes in a riot of enthusiasm. There were cheers, speeches, and the rousing music of fife-and-drum bands. "On to Washington," cried young soldiers in the South. "On to Richmond," they shouted in the North. Richmond, Virginia, was the Confederate capital.

Those who stayed home formed committees to help with the war effort. They collected funds. Women in both North and South formed societies. They busied themselves making bandages and knitting and sewing for the soldiers. "I do not know when I have seen a woman without knitting in her hand. Socks for the soldiers is the cry," Mary Chesnut, a Southerner, wrote in her diary.

Spirits were high in the South. "Secession is the fashion here," wrote a British newspaper reporter. "Young ladies sing for it. Old ladies pray for it. Young men are dying to fight for it. Old men are ready to demonstrate it."

Spirits were high in the North as well. "We shall crush out this rebellion as an elephant would trample on a mouse," wrote one Northerner. Eager as Northerners were to join the army, they did not always know why. Nathaniel Hawthorne, a writer, was one such man. "Though I approve the war as much as any man, I don't quite understand what we are fighting for," he wrote to his wife.

President Lincoln had hoped that **Robert E. Lee** would command the Union army. Lee had fought bravely in the Mexican War. By the time Lincoln asked Lee to take command, Lee's home state of Virginia had seceded. Lee refused Lincoln's offer. His choice was hard. Lee disliked slavery and had no slaves of his own. He was devoted to the Union. But, Lee wrote, he could not fight "against my relatives, my children, my home."

Robert E. Lee, left, on his horse Traveller, meets with Stonewall Jackson.

First Battle of Bull Run

In the lighthearted days after the battle at Fort Sumter, people thought the war would soon be over. Neither North nor South understood how strongly the other side felt.

The first battle between armies of the North and South was fought in July 1861. The site was near **Bull Run,** a small stream near Manassas Junction, Virginia. Shouting "On to Richmond," the Union army gaily left Washington on July 16. The sun was very hot. Soon clouds of dust covered the bright new uniforms of the marching soldiers. On their backs the soldiers carried their bedding, clothing, muskets, and personal items. As it grew hotter their loads seemed heavier. They began to leave unneccessary items beside the road.

These soldiers showed little discipline. Whenever they felt like it, they wandered off to pick berries or rest. On the day of the battle, July 21, crowds of sightseers came out from Washington in carriages. They brought picnic baskets of food and drink. They carried bright umbrellas to protect themselves from the sun.

Now the two armies found each other. Some soldiers had trouble telling friend from enemy because there were so many different uniforms. In time the Union army would wear blue uniforms. The Confederates would wear gray.

In the fighting at Bull Run that hot July day, the Confederates began to weaken. Then a Confederate general saw a group of Virginians shooting well and standing firm. At their head was Thomas Jackson, a former teacher in a military school. "There is Jackson

At Bull Run, two untrained armies clashed in a confusing, bloody battle. Defeated by the South, Union troops retreated to Washington, D. C.

standing like a stone wall," cried the general. "Rally behind the Virginians!" The Confederates were able to hold their line. Ever after Jackson was known as **Stonewall Jackson.** He became one of the South's best generals.

The Union attack failed. The soldiers began to retreat. The picnickers decided it was time they, too, picked up and went home. The road back to Washington became jammed with carriages, wagons, and running soldiers. Everywhere people were in panic. The fleeing troops left behind 8,000 muskets, many cannons, and quantities of supplies. The Confederates could have followed their victory with a march on Washington. Instead, they chose to celebrate.

The city of Washington was shocked by Bull Run. More than 4,700 men were killed, wounded, or missing. The First Battle of Bull Run, according to a Civil War historian, "ended the rosy time in which men could dream that the war would be short, glorious, and bloodless." The war now became a serious, deadly business. The North would win the war only after four long years of bloody and bitter fighting.

 Reading Check

1. What slave states did not join the Confederacy?
2. Why did Robert E. Lee refuse to command the Union army?
3. Where was the first battle fought?

Think Beyond Do you think the war would have ended differently if the Confederates had attacked Washington right after their victory at Bull Run? Explain.

People MAKE HISTORY

Mathew Brady
1823?–1896

▶▶▶▶▶▶▶▶▶▶▶▶▶▶▶▶▶

Mathew Brady carefully loaded his camera equipment onto a mysterious-looking wagon and set out to follow the Union Army. The soldiers stared at the wagon in wonder and tried to guess what it was. Suddenly, someone shouted, "It's a whatsit!"

The "whatsit" was actually the first news van. Brady and his assistants used it to travel from battle to battle and take photographs of the war. Inside the wagon was everything they needed to develop the photographs that have given us our most vivid impressions of the conflict between North and South.

As a young child, Brady had been interested in art and painting. When Brady was fifteen, William Page, an American historical painter, recognized Brady's special talent. Page offered him the opportunity to study with Samuel F. B. Morse in New York.

At that time Morse was working with daguerreotype (duh•GAIR•uh•typ), an early kind of photography. Brady became very interested in this process and studied with Morse for three years. In 1844 Brady set up his own daguerreotype studio in New York City.

Only two years after opening his business, Brady won the highest prize in the American Institute's contest for best daguerreotype. This launched his career as a photographer. His most famous subject was President Abraham Lincoln. Brady photographed Lincoln throughout the war years.

Thanks to Mathew Brady, we can see Lincoln's worried expression during the war. We can see the tiredness in Lincoln's face at the end of the war. And thanks to Brady and his "whatsit" we have a permanent visual record of one of the most important eras of our country's history— the Civil War.

Think Beyond What can you learn from looking at Brady's pictures of the Civil War?

Brady's "whatsit"

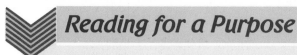
Look for these important words:

Key Words
- strategy
- Anaconda Plan
- blockade

- cavalry

People
- Jeb Stuart

- Ulysses S. Grant
- Mary Ann Bickerdyke
- Sally Tompkins

Look for answers to these questions:
1. What was Lincoln's plan for winning the Civil War?
2. What was the Confederate plan for winning the war?
3. What were the strengths of the South? of the North?
4. How were the sick and wounded treated during the war?

2 *Plans, Strengths of Each Side*

Lincoln's **strategy,** or long-range plan, for winning the war was first to weaken the South, then to invade it. To weaken the South, Lincoln and his advisors adopted a plan the newspapers called the **Anaconda Plan.** An anaconda is a large snake that kills its prey by squeezing. The Union would squeeze the South by not letting it ship its cotton or get necessary supplies. The South was a farming economy. It needed to sell its cash crops and buy manufactured products like cloth, shoes, sugar, and guns. To block the imports was the purpose of the Anaconda Plan. It called for winning control of the Mississippi River and for a naval **blockade** of Confederate seaports. A blockade is the use of warships to prevent other ships from entering or leaving a harbor.

The Confederate strategy rested on the belief that Britain and France would help the South. Both countries depended on Southern cotton to keep their cotton mills going. The South hoped to hold out against the North until European help came. The other hope of the South was that the North would tire of the war. At first, the fighting strategy of the Confederacy was to defend its own territory. Later this strategy was expanded to include brief invasions of the North.

Strengths of the South

Going into the war, the North and South each had different strengths. Southern soldiers had the will and fire that came from fighting on their own soil. They were fighting for a cause clear to them—the independence of the Confederacy. Most Confederate soldiers came from the countryside. They were in better physical shape than the city boys who joined the Union forces. Southern boys learned to ride and shoot at an early age. Soldiers joining the Union army often had to be taught to sit on a horse and how to shoot.

Dashing Jeb Stuart, waving a feathered cap, led the Confederate cavalry. He reported to General Lee on the movements of Union troops.

One of the South's greatest strengths was its generals. These generals had had experience fighting for the United States in the Mexican War. Robert E. Lee became the greatest of the Confederate generals. Lee was a kind and courteous man. He was also a capable and skilled leader. Confederate soldiers cheered wildly when Lee appeared before them riding his huge iron-gray horse, Traveller.

Many of Lee's military successes depended on other fine generals, including Stonewall Jackson, Joseph Johnston, and **Jeb Stuart.** Jeb Stuart was in charge of the **cavalry,** the soldiers on horses. Stuart was a dashing man who wore a large feather in his hat. Stuart and his men acted as the "eyes" of Lee. The cavalry could travel the countryside quickly, leaping walls and fences. It often circled the whole Union army. Stuart then reported the movements of the Union troops.

Strengths of the North

The North went into the war with a greater population. There were 22 million people in the 23 states of the North. The 11 states of the Confederacy had only 5.5 million free people. The North had greater industrial strength. It had at least six times as many factories as the South. It had 22,000 miles (35,398 km) of railroad track to the South's 9,000 miles (14,481 km). The North had most of the nation's coal and iron. Both coal and iron were necessary in the modern age of factories and steam engines.

The North also had the money to build factories, railroads, and ships. It had the money to pay soldiers' wages and purchase war supplies. The gold and silver discovered in California and Colorado were making the Union rich.

Even with all these strengths, the North needed the will to achieve victory. In his speeches Abraham Lincoln gave people this will to fight. Lincoln was a great strength of the Union, perhaps its greatest strength.

When the war started Lincoln had difficulty finding good generals. Toward the end of the war, excellent generals were in command of Union troops. They included **Ulysses S. Grant.** Grant had fought in the Mexican War but had retired. He was a store clerk in Illinois when the war broke out.

Nursing Care in the War

The Civil War claimed more than half a million lives before it ended. Most of those who died were between the ages of 15 and 21. Almost every home, North and South, lost someone in the war.

Thousands upon thousands lost their lives either on the battlefield or from battle wounds. In his diary the poet Walt Whitman described the wounded after a battle on a cold winter day. The

A Catholic nun dies on a Civil War battlefield. Those who braved battlefields to care for the wounded were often innocent victims of stray gunfire.

wounded were lying on the ground, which was frozen hard. The wounded were lucky, Whitman said, if their blankets were spread on layers of pine or hemlock twigs, or even small leaves.

Medical service was poor. Little was then known about germs. Nothing was used to kill germs. Many soldiers died of infections. Painkillers were hard to get. Army doctors sawed off mangled limbs often without giving patients any sort of painkiller.

Thousands of soldiers who survived battle conditions died from disease. The army camps were often dirty and unclean. Water became infected. Disease spread quickly. Twice as many died from disease as from battle.

At that time many people still thought it improper for women to care for sick men. Most nurses were men. But the need for nursing care soon changed people's ideas. In the North and South over 600 trained nurses from Catholic religious orders helped. Several thousand other women also served as volunteer nurses.

One of the most famous of these nurses was **Mary Ann Bickerdyke.** Her church minister asked for a woman to take supplies to the sick and wounded. She volunteered. Arriving at the Union camp at Cairo, Illinois, she was shocked by the conditions. Sick soldiers were lying in dirt and filth.

Mary Ann Bickerdyke announced that no one would get food until he had a bath. On the spot she had barrels sawed in half to make bathtubs. Within hours each sick man was washed, shaved, and dressed in clean clothing. The muck they had been lying on was carted away. Each man was given a mattress filled with clean straw. Only

Mother Bickerdyke, known for her stern tongue and plain dress, scolds an army surgeon for disobeying orders. Thousands of soldiers survived the war thanks to her standards of cleanliness and nursing care.

then did Mary Ann Bickerdyke hand out the fried chicken she had brought.

Mary Ann Bickerdyke came to be called Mother Bickerdyke by the soldiers she cared for. She ended up directing kitchens, rounding up supplies, and starting army laundries. She became the terror of lazy officers and doctors. She was present at a total of 19 battles.

Mother Bickerdyke would do anything to help the sick and wounded under her care. She was with the Union army when it was camped in Tennessee in December 1863. A bitter, cold storm blew in. The sick and wounded were in danger of freezing to death. There was no firewood. The storm was too fierce to send soldiers to chop down trees.

In the camp were walls built of logs. They had been constructed to provide for protection in a recent battle. It was against army orders for anyone to destroy these walls. Mother Bickerdyke did not care. At her command soldiers used mules and chains to tear the logs from the walls. The logs were then used for a great fire that saved many lives.

In the South **Sally Tompkins** gained fame for her private hospital in Richmond, Virginia. There, she took excellent care of both Yankee prisoners and Confederate soldiers. The fine care of her hospital made it different from most. At the end of the war only 73 of 1,333 of her patients had died. In contrast, a visitor described another Richmond hospital. Mary Chesnut wrote in her diary that there were "long rows of them dead, dying. Awful smells, awful sights."

Reading Check

1. What was the Anaconda Plan?
2. Name at least three strengths of the South.
3. Name at least three strengths of the North.

Think Beyond How was the South's position like that of the American colonies during the Revolutionary War?

SKILLS IN ACTION

READING PRIMARY AND SECONDARY SOURCES

Historians use many different sources to gather information about the past. One important source of information used by historians comes from people who lived at the time past events took place and observed the events firsthand. This firsthand information is called a **primary source.** Primary sources then are observations made at the time events take place. Primary sources include photographs, diaries, journals, and letters. Look again at Mary Chesnut's description of a Richmond hospital on page 426. Is this a primary source? What clues tell you that it might be?

Richmond
June 29th, 1862

My dear Mary,
   For the last three days I have been witness of the most stirring events of modern times.
   The fight on Friday was the largest and fiercest of the whole war— some 60,000 or 70, with great preponderance on the side of the enemy. Ground, numbers, armaments, &c all in favor of the enemy. But our men and generals were superior. The higher officers and men behaved with a resolution and dashing heroism that has never been surpassed in any country or in any age.
   Our line, by superior numbers and superior artillery . . . , was three times repulsed when Lee, assembling all the generals to the front, told them that victory depended on carrying the batteries and defeating the army before them, ere night should fall. If night came without victory, all was lost, and that the work must be done by bayonet. Our men then made a rapid and irresistible charge, without powder, and carried everything. The enemy melted before them and ran with the utmost speed. . . .
   The victory of the second day was full and complete. Yesterday there was little or no fighting, but some splendid maneuvering which has placed us completely around them.
   I think the end must be decisive in our favor. We have lost many men and officers. We are fighting again today, will let you know the result as soon as possible. Will be home sometime next week.
   No letter from you yet.
   With devotion, yours,
   James Chesnut, Jr.

Mary Chesnut kept the letter her husband wrote her from the Battle of Richmond.

The letter on page 427 is a primary source. It is part of a letter a Confederate soldier, James Chesnut, Jr., wrote to his wife during a series of battles near Richmond. As you read the letter, notice the language used. The language itself can be another clue that something is a primary source. Because many primary sources were written long ago, the language used might seem unfamiliar to us.

Primary sources can give historians valuable information about past events. Not only do they give important facts about an event, but they can also give interesting descriptions of the people involved. However, primary sources often include people's opinions and personal feelings. Also, the information given in a primary source sometimes may not be accurate or it may be incomplete. For example, people involved in an event may not be able to see everything that is happening. Important information may be left out.

Historians usually describe events long after they have happened. A description of an event after it has happened is called a **secondary source.** Secondary sources include biographies, newspapers, magazines, or anything that describes or shows something from the past. Your textbook is an example of a secondary source. It was written in modern times to tell about past events. The following is a historian's account of the battle near Richmond.

Meanwhile, through most of June [General] McClellan stood before Richmond . . . Estimating Lee's strength at 200,000, he believed he was heavily outnumbered. Although Lee in fact had 85,000 men to pit against his opponents 100,000 or more.

Compare the historian's account of the battle with that of James Chesnut. While Chesnut's letter to his wife was correct in reporting that Lee's troops were outnumbered, he was incorrect in reporting the total number of troops involved in the battles. Historians, therefore, must compare many primary sources of information to get accurate information. They must also separate the facts from the opinions in primary sources.

Secondary sources are a quick and easy reference. Historians have already done the difficult job of researching the information for us.

CHECKING YOUR SKILLS

1. Name three examples of primary sources. Why might these be considered primary sources?

2. What clues might show that something is a primary source?

3. Name three examples of secondary sources. Why are these considered secondary sources?

428

Look for these important words:

Key Words
- casualties
- Emancipation Proclamation
- Pickett's charge
- Gettysburg Address

Places
- Antietam
- Chancellorsville
- Gettysburg

Look for answers to these questions:
1. What were some of the important battles of the first part of the war? Why was each important?
2. What were the effects of Lincoln freeing the slaves?
3. How was the fighting in the Civil War different from that in the Revolutionary War?
4. Why is the Gettysburg Address important?
5. For what goals was the North fighting?

3 The First Part of the War

For more than a year the Union army tried to march on the Confederate capital of Richmond. Each time it failed. Union troops were well armed and well organized, but they seemed no match for the Southern troops. Particularly outstanding were those led by Stonewall Jackson.

In May 1862 Jackson and his troops marched 245 miles (394 km), fought four battles, and won them all. As a result, one-third of the Union army in Virginia was busy chasing Jackson instead of attacking Richmond.

Jackson was a beloved general, who showed great concern for his men. On long marches he made the soldiers lie down and rest ten minutes every hour.

The Northerners had hoped for a short war. They began to be discouraged by the long lists of **casualties.** Casualties are people who have been killed or wounded. Some people began to ask, Why keep fighting?

Union Victory at Antietam

Then, in September 1862, the North won a major victory at **Antietam** (an·TEET·uhm). By then Robert E. Lee was commander of the Southern troops. He had led his army across the Potomac River into Maryland, aiming for Harrisburg, Pennsylvania. There the Confederates planned to cut off railroad communication between the Eastern states and the West. Lee's troops were badly in need of food, shoes, and clothing. They hoped to find these supplies in the North.

Union troops stopped the Confederate army near Sharpsburg, Maryland, at Antietam Creek. The loss of life on that mild September day was great. "Never before or after in all the war were so many men shot on one day," the historian Bruce Catton wrote. Having lost one-fourth of his army, Lee finally retreated back across the Potomac River.

Union and Confederate troops blaze away as each side seeks to control the bridge at Antietam Creek. By dusk, at least 22,500 men had died.

Union victory at Antietam had an important result. The South, besides losing the battle, lost possible help from Britain and France. Both British and French leaders had shown sympathy for the Confederacy. Now it was not certain that the South would win independence. Neither Britain nor France wanted to help a loser.

Slaves Are Freed

By this time Lincoln had decided to free the slaves. He wanted to wait to make the announcement, however, until after a Union victory. After the victory at Antietam, Lincoln issued the **Emancipation Proclamation.** *Emancipation* means freedom. Lincoln announced freedom for the slaves of the Confederacy as of January 1, 1863. The Emancipation Proclamation gave new spirit to the North. It gave Union troops a cause for which to fight. Abolitionists were overjoyed. Their goal had now become the North's goal.

Black Soldiers

When the war started, blacks had not been welcome as soldiers in the army. Runaway slaves who came to Union camps were often returned to their owners. After the Emancipation Proclamation, regiments of black soldiers were organized. Before the end of the war about 180,000 blacks fought in the Union army. Another 30,000 served in the navy.

The black soldiers fought in regiments commanded by white officers. At first black soldiers were paid only half the salary of white soldiers. Some therefore refused to take any pay. By

Proud to be in uniform, this soldier rushed to have his picture taken with a new invention—the camera.

the end of the war, pay for black soldiers and white soldiers was equal. Black soldiers often had to fight with weapons of poor quality. Their hospital care was usually worse than that of whites.

Yet the spirit of black soldiers was high. They were fighting for freedom. Frederick Douglass, the abolitionist, urged free blacks to volunteer for the army. With their help, he said, "four million of our brothers and sisters shall march out into liberty." The secretary of war wrote to Lincoln about the courage of the black soldiers. He said they had "proved themselves among the bravest of the brave."

Lee's Important Victory

Most of the fighting in the East was in northern Virginia. There, for most of the war, Robert E. Lee and his army held back the Union army. General

Lee's most brilliant victory was at **Chancellorsville,** Virginia, in May 1863. Lee's army defeated a Union force twice the size of his. In winning, however, Lee lost his right-hand man. In the confusion of battle, Stonewall Jackson was shot by some of his own soldiers.

The victory at Chancellorsville gave the Confederacy confidence to try again to invade the North. The Confederate goal was to win a clear victory on Northern soil. If they could do so, they hoped the war might end. In June, one month after the victory at Chancellorsville, Lee's troops started north.

The Battle of Gettysburg

The Union army met Lee's army near the town of **Gettysburg,** Pennsylvania. The greatest battle of the war was fought there on the first three days of July 1863. Lee was forced into the battle before he was quite ready. Jeb Stuart and the cavalry had taken off to ride around the Union army. The ride took much longer than they had planned. The "eyes of Lee" had not yet arrived when the battle started. Lee did not have the information he needed about the position of Union troops.

The high point of the fighting came the afternoon of July 3. That morning all had been quiet. The main line of the Union army lay behind a stone wall on a ridge. Across a large field were the Confederates. At one o'clock Confederate guns began firing, all their fire power directed to the ridge. A Union officer on the ridge described the scene: "How the long streams of fire spout from the guns, how the rifled shells hiss, how the smoke deepens and rolls."

The "great ceaseless roar of the guns" lasted two hours. Men and horses lay dead. Gun carriages and wagons were destroyed.

Then "an ocean of armed men" started toward the Union line on the ridge. Marching shoulder to shoulder, 15,000 Confederate troops in a line half a mile (0.8 km) wide moved steadily. This moving wall of Confederate soldiers, led by General George Pickett, is called **Pickett's charge.** "Here they come," shouted the Union soldiers, guns ready.

When the Confederates were within musket range, the Union soldiers fired. "Men were falling all around us, and cannon and muskets were raining death upon us," remembered a Confederate officer. "Still on and up the slope toward the stone fence our men steadily swept." Pickett's men reached the wall but were stopped by the murderous fire of Union guns. Pickett's charge had failed. The Confederate troops retreated, leaving half their number dead and wounded. Lee had to order a retreat.

When Lee's army reached the Potomac, the river was flooding. The troops had to wait for the waters to go down. President Lincoln sent this message to the Union general: "Do not let the enemy escape." While the Union general tried to make plans, the flood waters went down. Lee's army escaped back into Virginia.

HISTORY CONNECTION

T. S. C. Lowe sat nervously hunched in a basket attached to a large gas balloon. Slowly, *The Intrepid* rose into the air and quietly floated above the battle lines. Suddenly, Confederate troops spotted the balloon and began firing at it. Lowe crouched even lower as the shots whizzed by the basket.

The balloon rose higher and higher until it was safe for Lowe to peer out of the basket. After carefully surveying the landscape below, he telegraphed a message that told Union forces where they could safely cross the river.

A new era was born as information was sent from craft hovering overhead to commanders on the ground. Satellites today can send information instantly on everything from the location of foreign military bases to weather conditions.

The battle had cost thousands of lives. Each side lost more than 20,000 men. For Lee, that amounted to one-third of his army.

Battlefield Technology

Casualties were particularly high in the Battle of Gettysburg. The main reason for this was an advance in war technology. There were new kinds of cannons and guns. Most of the cannons could fire a 12-pound (5.4-kg) ball a distance of a mile (1.6 km). The cannons fired not only cannonballs but also special cans filled with nails and shot. When fired, the can would fly into pieces. Nails and shot sprayed murderously in all directions.

In the Revolutionary War bayonets had been a very important part of the fighting. The fighting was often "eyeball to eyeball" because guns were not very accurate and often misfired. There was none of this kind of fighting at Gettysburg. Most of the soldiers on both sides used the rifle musket, a new kind of gun. The new rifle musket had very good aim and firing power. It could kill a person half a mile (0.8 km) away. The gun could also be loaded faster than the old kind. Charging across an open field in the face of such weapons was deadly. Yet some generals continued to order such charges. Pickett's charge failed because it was an old way of fighting a new kind of war.

The Gettysburg Address

In November 1863, President Lincoln went to Gettysburg to honor those who had died there. The speech he gave has become known as the **Gettysburg**

This photograph of Abraham Lincoln shows him tired, but determined.

Address. In his speech Lincoln spoke to the heart of the war-weary North. These thousands had died, Lincoln said, so that "government of the people, by the people, for the people shall not perish from the earth." Lincoln made clear that democracy had become part of the Northern cause. The North was now fighting for three goals. These were preservation of the Union, freedom for the slaves, and defense of democracy.

Reading Check

1. What was an important effect of the Union victory at Antietam?
2. What was the Emancipation Proclamation? When was it issued?
3. Why were the casualties so high at the Battle of Gettysburg?

Think Beyond Why do you think Lincoln's speech renewed the spirits of Northern soldiers? Explain.

IN FOCUS

THE GETTYSBURG ADDRESS

Thursday, November 19, 1863, was a mild day at Gettysburg, Pennsylvania. At least 15,000 people had come to Gettysburg that day for the dedication of a national soldiers' cemetery. There lay buried thousands who had died five months before at the Battle of Gettysburg.

Abraham Lincoln rode to the site on a large chestnut horse. Bands played. When it was Lincoln's turn to speak, he stood up and took two pages of notes from his pocket. In five minutes he delivered the speech known as the Gettysburg Address.

In the Gettysburg Address, Lincoln gave clear and noble expression to the nation's democratic beliefs.

Four score and seven years ago, our fathers brought forth on this continent a new nation, conceived in liberty and dedicated to the proposition that all men are created equal.

Now we are engaged in a great civil war, testing whether that nation—or any nation, so conceived and so dedicated—can long endure.

We are met on a great battlefield of that war. We have come to dedicate a portion of that field as a final resting place for those who here gave their lives that that nation might live.

It is altogether fitting and proper that we should do this.

But, in a larger sense, we cannot dedicate, we cannot consecrate, we cannot hallow, this ground. The brave men, living and dead, who struggled here, have consecrated it, far above our poor power to add or detract.

The world will little note nor long remember what we say here, but it can never forget what they did here.

It is for us, the living, rather, to be dedicated, here, to the unfinished work which they who fought here have thus far so nobly advanced. It is rather for us to be here dedicated to the great task remaining before us—that from these honored dead we take increased devotion to that cause for which they gave the last full measure of devotion; that we here highly resolve that these dead shall not have died in vain; that this nation under God, shall have a new birth of freedom; and that government of the people, by the people, for the people, shall not perish from the earth.

Think Beyond   What do you think Lincoln meant when he said, "that we here highly resolve that these dead shall not have died in vain"?

President Lincoln at Gettysburg

Reading for a Purpose

Look for these important words:

Key Words
- assassination

People
- William Tecumseh Sherman

Places
- Vicksburg
- Chattanooga
- Atlanta
- Appomattox Court House

Look for answers to these questions:
1. Why was the Union victory at Vicksburg important?
2. How did William Tecumseh Sherman wage war against the South?
3. How did the Civil War end?
4. Why did the North win?
5. What event brought grief to the nation?

4 *The Second Part of the War*

In the West, by 1863, the Union forces were in control of New Orleans. Other points along the Mississippi River above **Vicksburg,** Mississippi, were also under their power. But Vicksburg itself belonged to the South. It was on a high bluff overlooking the mighty river. There powerful guns protected that part of the river for the Confederacy. Soldiers, food, and supplies crossed the river from Texas, Louisiana, and Arkansas.

General Ulysses S. Grant started to lay siege to Vicksburg in late May 1863. For 47 days Union guns pounded the city. The people of Vicksburg lived in caves for protection. Finally, on July 3, the Confederate commander at Vicksburg sent up the white flag of surrender. This was about the same time of Pickett's charge at Gettysburg.

Grant's victory at Vicksburg was the worst blow the South had yet received. It cut the South in two. The Union now

Ulysses S. Grant had common sense and a talent for military strategy.

had complete control of the Mississippi River. The Anaconda Plan was working. For his brilliant victory Lincoln would name Grant as his top general.

With the Union now controlling the Mississippi, Grant planned an invasion of the South. In 1864 Union troops started marching from **Chattanooga, Tennessee,** into Georgia. They destroyed everything that the South could use to fight the war. This army, led by General **William Tecumseh Sherman,** attacked and then occupied **Atlanta,** Georgia.

Sherman's March to the Sea

Until 1864 the war was fought between armies. In 1864 the Union army began destroying farms in Virginia. The purpose was to keep food from the Confederate armies. With Grant's permission Sherman marched his army from Atlanta toward the sea to Savannah. His goal was to destroy everything that could help the Southern war effort. Sherman's army burned crops, wrecked bridges, and tore up railroad tracks. Sherman hoped to destroy the spirit and will of the South to keep fighting.

Mrs. Thomas Burge, who lived near Covington, Georgia, was in the path of Sherman's march. She described in her diary what happened.

To my smokehouse, my dairy, pantry, kitchen and cellar, like famished wolves they come, breaking locks and whatever is in their way. The thousand pounds of meat in my smoke-house is gone in a twinkling. My flour, my meat, my lard, butter, eggs, pickles, wine, jars, and jugs are all gone. My eighteen fat turkeys, my hens, chickens, and fowls, my young pigs are shot down in my yard.

Union soldiers under Sherman's command tore up railroad tracks as they marched through Georgia. This was a new kind of warfare.

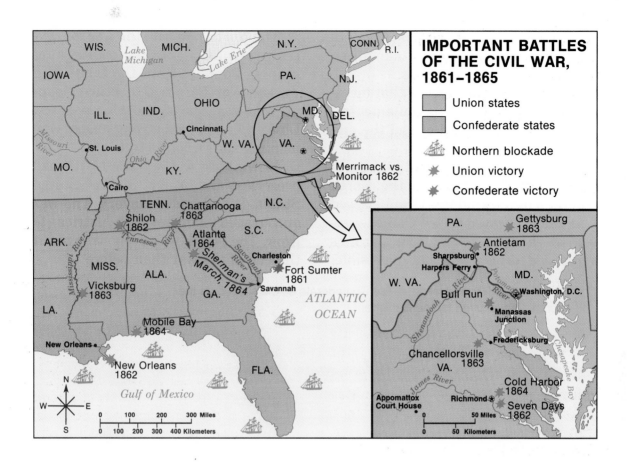

IMPORTANT BATTLES OF THE CIVIL WAR, 1861–1865

- Union states
- Confederate states
- Northern blockade
- Union victory
- Confederate victory

Merrimack vs. Monitor 1862

Shiloh 1862
Chattanooga 1863
Atlanta 1864
Sherman's March, 1864
Charleston
Fort Sumter 1861
Savannah
Vicksburg 1863
Mobile Bay 1864
New Orleans 1862
Cincinnati
St. Louis
Cairo

ATLANTIC OCEAN
Gulf of Mexico

WIS. MICH. N.Y. CONN. R.I.
IOWA PA. N.J.
ILL. IND. OHIO MD. DEL.
MO. KY. W. VA. VA.
ARK. TENN. N.C.
MISS. ALA. GA. S.C.
LA. FLA.

Lake Michigan
Lake Erie
Missouri River
Ohio River
Mississippi River
Tennessee River
Savannah River

N W E S
0 100 200 300 Miles
0 100 200 300 400 Kilometers

Gettysburg 1863
Antietam 1862
Sharpsburg
Harpers Ferry
Bull Run
Manassas Junction
Fredericksburg
Chancellorsville 1863
Cold Harbor 1864
Appomattox Court House
Richmond
Seven Days 1862

PA. W. VA. MD. VA.
Washington, D.C.
Shenandoah River
Potomac River
James River
Chesapeake Bay

0 50 Miles
0 50 Kilometers

Lincoln's Second Term

In March 1865, Lincoln took the oath of office for a second term as President. The end of the war was in sight. Lincoln's words had given will and spirit to the North to carry on the war. Now his words, in the Second Inaugural Address, aimed at healing the nation's wounds. Lincoln said he hoped to see a "just and lasting peace." It would be "with malice toward none, with charity for all."

Surrender at Appomattox

General Grant was now in charge of the Union army fighting in northern Virginia. There Lee's troops were ragged and starving. Grant's soldiers were well armed and well fed. Grant kept pushing the Confederate troops. Lee could no longer protect Richmond. At last Lee was put in a position where he could neither fight nor retreat. He surrendered his army to Grant at the town of **Appomattox Court House** on April 9, 1865.

There in the parlor of a private home, Grant met with Lee. They discussed the terms of the surrender.

Grant told Lee the Confederate soldiers were to lay down their arms. They were also to return to their homes. The men who owned their own horses and mules could keep them, Grant said. They would need the animals to plant crops to get through the next winter. After they had signed the surrender papers, Lee asked Grant for food for his soldiers. Grant told Lee to take all he wanted from Union supplies.

Grant later wrote about that meeting with Lee. He said he could not tell whether Lee was glad or sad the end had come.

Despite Lincoln's Second Inaugural Address, not everyone in the North approved of the kindness Grant showed Lee. Many wanted to see Confederate leaders hanged as traitors. Grant's surrender terms made that impossible.

The North had won the war for several reasons. Lincoln's strategy of keeping supplies from the South had worked. Northern manufacturing supplied the needs of the Union army. Lincoln had been a strong leader who inspired the Union to fight.

In winning the war the North had preserved the union of the United States. It had ended slavery. The war encouraged Northern industries to grow. The North was even stronger at the end of the war than before.

Tired, hungry, and war-saddened, these Confederate soldiers weep as the Confederate flag is furled for the last time.

The Death of Lincoln

Less than a week after the surrender at Appomattox, President Lincoln was attending the theater. There John Wilkes Booth, an actor, shot him. Booth thought he was helping the Confederates. After shooting Lincoln, Booth leaped to the stage. Then he escaped on horseback. He was followed, and 12 days later he was shot while hiding in a barn.

Lincoln was taken to a house across the street. Early the next morning, April 15, his heart stopped. "Now he belongs to the ages," said Lincoln's secretary of war, Edwin Stanton. It was a cold, rainy day. Strong and brave people wept.

The North mourned Lincoln's death. A railroad train carried Lincoln's body from Washington to Illinois. Millions gathered along the route. They grieved for the man who had led the nation through its darkest time.

Secretary of War Stanton blamed Jefferson Davis for the **assassination** (uh•SAS•uhn•ay•shun). An assassination is murder for a political reason. In grief and anger many Northerners wanted to see the South punished. "Hang Jeff Davis," many shouted. Confederate leaders had nothing to do with Lincoln's death, but bad feelings remained. The North forgot Lincoln's words, "with malice toward none, with charity for all." As a result, the nation's wounds were slow to heal.

THE COURSE OF THE CIVIL WAR

Nov. Abraham Lincoln elected President — 1860

Dec. South Carolina secedes

Feb. Confederacy formed — 1861

March Lincoln inaugurated

April Battle at Fort Sumter

July First Battle of Bull Run — 1862

Sept. Battle of Antietam

Jan. Emancipation Proclamation

May Battle of Chancellorville — 1863

July Battle of Gettysburg; Battle of Vicksburg

Nov. Gettysburg Address — 1864

May-December Union troops march through the South

Nov. Lincoln re-elected President — 1865

April 9 Surrender at Appomattox Court House

April 15 President Lincoln dies — 1866

Reading Check

1. Why was the Union victory at Vicksburg a terrible blow to the South?
2. How did General Grant show kindness in the surrender terms?
3. Name three reasons the North won the war.

Think Beyond How do you think the Southern soldiers felt when the war finally ended? Explain.

Thinking Back

- The first battle at Bull Run made people realize that the Civil War would be long and deadly.

- To win the war, the North planned to blockade enemy ports and then to invade the South. The South hoped to get aid from England and France.

- The North and South had different strengths. The South was fighting on its own territory and had experienced generals. The North, however, had greater industrial strength and more resources.

- As a result of the Confederate loss at Antietam, Britain and France decided not to help the South.

- The Emancipation Proclamation gave new spirit to the North. Many black soldiers now joined the Union Army.

- The battle at Gettysburg ended the South's efforts to invade the North.

- The Gettysburg Address gave Northerners a new goal to fight for—the defense of democracy.

- The Union victory at Vicksburg split the Confederacy in two. Union soldiers then marched through the South, destroying much property.

- General Lee surrendered to General Grant at Appomattox Court House on April 9, 1865. Less than a week later, Abraham Lincoln was shot to death.

Check for Understanding

Using Words

For each word below select the correct definition from the list that follows.

1. **assassination**
2. **blockade**
3. **casualties**
4. **regiments**
5. **strategy**
   a. organized groups of soldiers
   b. long-range plan
   c. persons killed or wounded in war
   d. murder for a political reason
   e. using a navy to prevent ships from entering or leaving a harbor

Reviewing Facts

1. Describe the feelings of both North and South before the Battle of Bull Run.
2. Compare and contrast the war strategies of the North and South.
3. How did the strengths of the South give it an early advantage in the war?
4. How did the strengths of the North make an important difference in the long run?
5. In what way did women, in both the North and South, help the soldiers?
6. How did black soldiers help the North? How were they treated?
7. In what ways was the Civil War a different kind of war from the Revolutionary War?
8. What were the three goals of the North? When did Lincoln express each goal?

9. How did the North carry out the Anaconda Plan?

10. What did the North accomplish by winning the war?

Thinking Critically

1. How did technology make a difference in
the war's outcome?

2. How was Abraham Lincoln a strong and
great leader? What are the marks of leadership? Who else discussed in this chapter showed leadership?

3. Which slave states did not join the Confederacy? What reasons might they have
had for staying in the Union?

4. What did Lincoln mean when he said
"with malice toward none, with charity
for all"? Did General Grant carry out that
idea at the war's end?

Writing About It

At the time of the Civil War, the camera was
a new invention. Write a story about members of a family who go to have their picture
taken for the first time. In your story, describe how they felt and what they wore.

Practicing Reading Skills

Reading Primary/Secondary Sources

Identify each of the following as either a
primary or secondary source. Explain your
answers.

1. *Voices of the Civil War*, a Confederate
officer's description of Pickett's charge
at the Battle of Gettysburg

2. *The First Book of the Civil War*, Dorothy
Levenson's history of the Civil War

3. *Mary Chesnut's Civil War*, Mary Chesnut's diary telling about her life during
the Civil War

On Your Own

Social Studies at Home

1. Study the photo of Abraham Lincoln on
page 433. Describe how he looked and
tell what you think he may have been
feeling. Compare your description of Lincoln with those of your classmates.

2. Imagine you are a reporter covering the
Confederate surrender at Appomattox
Court House in 1865. Write a short article
about what you saw and heard as Lee
and Grant left the farmhouse after signing the surrender papers. Read your report to your family.

Read More About It

Anthony Burns by Virginia Hamilton.
Alfred A. Knopf. This book portrays the in-
humanity of slavery by relating the story of
the escape, arrest, and trial of Anthony
Burns.

*The Black Americans: A History in
Their Own Words, 1619–1983* by Milton
Meltzer. T. Y. Crowell. This useful collection
of primary source material covers 350 years
of African-American history.

Charley Skedaddle by Patricia Beatty.
William Morrow. This story of a 12-year-old
soldier's cowardice points out that war is a
deadly serious business.

Clara Barton: Soldier of Mercy by Helen
Dore Boylston. Illustrated by Paula Hutchinson. Random House. This biography documents Clara Barton's efforts to relieve suffering caused by the Civil War.

Which Way Freedom? by Joyce Hansen.
Walker. This novel tells the story of a runaway slave who joins the Union army.

The Civil War at Sea

The *Congress*, a wooden Union warship, was on patrol in the waters near Norfolk, Virginia. An officer on board scanned the horizon with his spyglass. He was looking for Confederate ships. Suddenly he cried out, "That thing! That thing is coming!" It was March 8, 1862.

The other crewmen gathered to see a strange vessel coming toward them. It looked, one of them thought, like a runaway hay barn.

This strange ship was called the *Merrimac*. It was America's first metal warship, then called an *ironclad*. The Confederacy had created it starting with the hull of an old wooden frigate. On the top of the hull a fortress had been built. This fortress had 2-inch (5.1 cm) iron sheets placed on slanted walls of thick pine and oak. The *Merrimac* was slow and very hard to steer, but that did not matter much. The *Merrimac* was almost unsinkable.

The Confederate ironclad Merrimac (right) does battle with the Monitor on March 9, 1862.

So far, no one had invented a shell or cannonball able to pierce iron. The *Merrimac* easily destroyed the *Congress* and another union warship that day. Then it went away for the night. Its intention was to return the next day and finish off the Union vessels.

Confederate sailor
▼

Fortunately for the Union, its navy had an ironclad of its own. Stephen Mallory built the *Merrimac* for the South. At the same time a Swedish immigrant, John Ericsson, designed an iron-covered ship for the North. Ericsson named his creation the *Monitor*.

The *Monitor* had already left New York when President Lincoln heard about the *Merrimac*'s success. He ordered the *Monitor* to rush to Norfolk.

When the *Merrimac* returned on March 9, its crew stared at the strange vessel guarding the harbor. One of the Confederate officers described it as "an immense shingle floating in the water, with a gigantic cheesebox rising from its center."

For four hours the "runaway barn" battled the "floating cheesebox." They fought side by side, each ship landing direct hits on the

" The runaway barn battled the floating cheesebox "

other. Neither ship was seriously damaged, but eventually the *Merrimac* was forced to retreat. A telegram announced the news to President Lincoln. "*Monitor* is uninjured and ready at any moment to repel another attack." Lincoln was overjoyed. The *Monitor* had saved the small Union fleet.

Violent sea battles between Union and Confederacy took place throughout the war. The union won most of these battles. As brave as its sailors were, the South could not match the Union navy.

UNION ADVANTAGES

At the time of the Civil War, the South depended on agriculture. Cotton, tobacco, and rice were the major crops. There was little industry.

Most blockade runners were built in England. They could use either sails or steam engines for power.

The North had the lion's share of factories and ironworks. Most trading ships and merchant seamen were based in the North. Annapolis, the training school for naval officers, was in Maryland, a Union state.

The North's strategy was a blockade of Southern ports. Unable to trade, the South ran short of many necessary items. In fact, the South ran short of almost everything but tobacco, rice, and cotton.

FIGHTING THE BLOCKADE

The South fought against the blockade with all the might and wit at its command. Southern inventors used beer kegs and other metal cases to make exploding underwater bombs. These bombs, called mines or torpedoes, were placed in Southern harbors to sink Union vessels.

Special Confederate ships called **blockade runners** learned to sneak through the blockade. These steamers were painted gray to blend with the coastal fog. Cotton was loaded onto the runners for export to England and other countries. The blockade runners returned carrying food, guns, and luxuries.

BATTLE AT MOBILE BAY

As the war dragged on, the South found itself strangled by the blockade. By 1864 only a few Southern ports remained open. The most important of these ports was Mobile, Alabama.

A Union admiral, David Glasgow Farragut, intended to close the port. In August 1864 he led his fleet to the entrance of Mobile Bay.

Two years earlier Farragut had cleverly slipped his ships past two Confederate forts to capture New Orleans. Two Confederate forts also guarded the entrance to Mobile Bay. This time, however, Farragut would have no chance to slip by.

Farragut chose the morning of August 5 to attack. The tide was coming in. The Union commander hoped that the tide would speed his ships past the two forts. The fleet started out at 6 o'clock. At 7 o'clock the forts began firing. Soon the decks of Farragut's vessel were thick with smoke, blood, and wounded men. But the admiral pressed on.

Farragut climbed high into his ship's rigging to get a better view. An officer tied him to the rigging because the 63-year-old leader had dizzy spells. Farragut hardly noticed he was tied, so intent was he on watching the battle.

The Union ship *Tecumseh* struck a mine, one of many the Confederates had placed. The ship sank

" Damn the torpedoes! Full speed ahead! "

This picture of the Union fleet at the Battle of Vicksburg shows how ships changed during the war. Notice that they are powered by steam engines and have metal decks.
▼

in two minutes. Other Northern ships slowed down, afraid to go on. Farragut knew that if the fleet hesitated, all the ships would be destroyed by gunfire. He guessed that many of the mines, or torpedoes, were too waterlogged to explode. "Damn the torpedoes!" he cried to his captains. "Full speed ahead!"

Except for the *Tecumseh*, the entire fleet made it past the forts. The last obstacle was a mighty ironclad, the *Tennessee*. In a furious struggle all the Union ships turned on the *Tennessee*. Union cannons shot away the heavy

chains that worked *Tennessee's* rudder. The metal monster, 200 feet (60.9 m) long, could not be steered.

Finally, at 10 A.M., the *Tennessee* surrendered. Farragut had taken Mobile Bay. The Union blockade was nearly complete. In April of the next year, General Lee surrendered at Appomattox to end the war.

Civil War naval battles changed the style and technology of fighting at sea forever. Never again would graceful, but frail, wooden sailboats dominate a war. The steam engine had replaced the canvas sail. Metal plates were replacing wooden planks. The use of ironclads, torpedoes, and submarines brought naval warfare into the modern age.

◄ **At the Battle of Mobile Bay in 1864, Union ships successfully broke through Confederate defenses. Admiral Farragut, tied to his ship's rigging, directed the victory.**

446

Unit Review

Words to Remember

Replace the underlined words in the sentences below with the correct word or words from this list. Write the new sentences on your paper.

abolitionists   fugitives
assassination   regiments
a blockade   secession
casualties   strategy
emancipation   tariff

1. North and South had long disagreed over a <u>tax on imported goods.</u>

2. Frederick Douglass and William Lloyd Garrison both were <u>people who wanted slavery ended everywhere.</u>

3. Harriet Tubman helped <u>runaway slaves</u> reach freedom in Canada.

4. After the election of Abraham Lincoln many Southern states voted for <u>withdrawing from the Union.</u>

5. President Lincoln ordered <u>warships to prevent other ships from entering or leaving harbors</u> of Southern ports.

6. Men and boys from both North and South joined with friends and neighbors to form <u>organized groups of soldiers.</u>

7. The Anaconda Plan was the name given to Lincoln's <u>long-range plan</u> for winning the war.

8. The battles of the Civil War resulted in great numbers of <u>people killed or wounded.</u>

9. President Lincoln declared <u>freedom</u> for all slaves in the Confederacy as of January 1, 1863.

10. The North mourned at news of the <u>murder for a political reason</u> of President Lincoln.

Focus on Main Ideas

1. The causes of the Civil War were rooted in the different ways of life in North and South. How did North and South differ?

2. Why was the extension of slavery so important to both North and South?

3. How did North and South use compromise to keep the peace for years?

4. What was the purpose of the Underground Railroad? Who was Harriet Tubman?

5. Why was the fighting in Kansas a sign of the coming Civil War?

6. Describe Abraham Lincoln's ideas on slavery
   a. when he first ran for President.
   b. when he issued the Emancipation Proclamation.

7. When the war started, what were the Confederate states fighting for?

8. Many changes happened during the Civil War. What changes occurred in
   a. the goals of the North?
   b. technology of guns and cannons?
   c. medical care on the battlefield?

9. What were the important ideas of the Gettysburg Address? How did it give the North yet another goal to fight for?

10. What was Lincoln's strategy for winning the Civil War? Did his strategy work? Explain your answer.

Think/Write

Imagine that you are serving in one of the armies in the Civil War as either a soldier or a nurse. Write a letter home telling about your feelings and your experiences.

Activities

1. **Research/Writing** Choose one of the people discussed in this unit. Find out more about that person and write a short report.

2. **Research/Oral Report** With a friend, read more about the Lincoln-Douglas debates. One of you should take Douglas's point of view, and the other should take Lincoln's point of view. Each of you should explain your point of view to the class.

3. **Making a Table** Make a table of the major battles of the Civil War. On the table, list the battles in the order in which they happened. Tell when and where each battle was fought. Tell the importance of the battle.

4. **Reading/Writing** Read a book about Civil War times. It could be a biography of a person or a work of fiction. Write a report telling how the book helped you better understand this time in history.

5. **Timeline** Make a timeline with 1850 as the beginning date and 1865 as the ending date. On your timeline, show the main events leading to the Civil War. Include the major battles and events of the Civil War.

6. **Research/Oral Report** Learn more about one of these subjects and give an oral report on what you learn.
   a. Civil War cavalry
   b. Civil War artillery
   c. Civil War medicine and nursing
   d. Black soldiers in the Civil War

Skills Review

1. **Using Population Maps** Find Florida and Louisiana on the population density maps on page 411. Use the maps to answer these questions.
   a. What was the average population density of northern Florida in 1860? of southern Florida?
   b. Did Florida or Louisiana have a city of over 100,000 people? a city of over 500,000 people?
   c. In 1860 were there probably more slaves in Louisiana or Florida? Explain your answer.

2. **Identifying Primary/Secondary Sources** Which of the following is a primary source and which is a secondary source? Explain your answers.
   a. *Harriet Tubman: Conductor on the Underground Railroad*, Ann Petry's biography of Harriet Tubman
   b. *Year of Lincoln, 1861*, Genevieve Foster's history that describes the Civil War and other world events in 1861
   c. *The Blue and the Gray*, the story of the Civil War as told by those who lived through the war

Most of the fighting in the Civil War took place in the southeastern states. The whole nation, however, felt the effect of this war. The following activities can help you learn about your state during this stormy, difficult time.

Learning About Government

1. Did your state join the Union between 1820 and 1860? If so, did it join the Union as a free state or a slave state? Did people in your state vote whether it would be a free or slave state?

Learning About Economics

2. How did the economy of your state change during the Civil War? Was there an increase in manufacturing? What happened to agriculture? Was your state richer or poorer at the end of the war? Why?

Making a Timeline

3. What important events happened in your state between 1850 and 1865? Make a timeline showing these events. Include on the timeline important Civil War events.

Learning About Geography

4. Were any Civil War battles fought in your state? If so, locate the battle sites on an outline map of your state.

5. Many places in the United States are named after people who were important during the Civil War. What places in your community or state are named after people you have studied in this unit?

6. Find out if you live in a state that had stations on the Underground Railroad.

Learning About People

7. When the Civil War started, Clara Barton began to carry supplies to the wounded. She was called the Angel of the Battlefield. After the war she organized a search for missing persons. Later she founded the American Red Cross. Today the Red Cross is important in every state. Find out what services the Red Cross provides in your state. Find out how volunteers are important to the Red Cross and other service organizations.

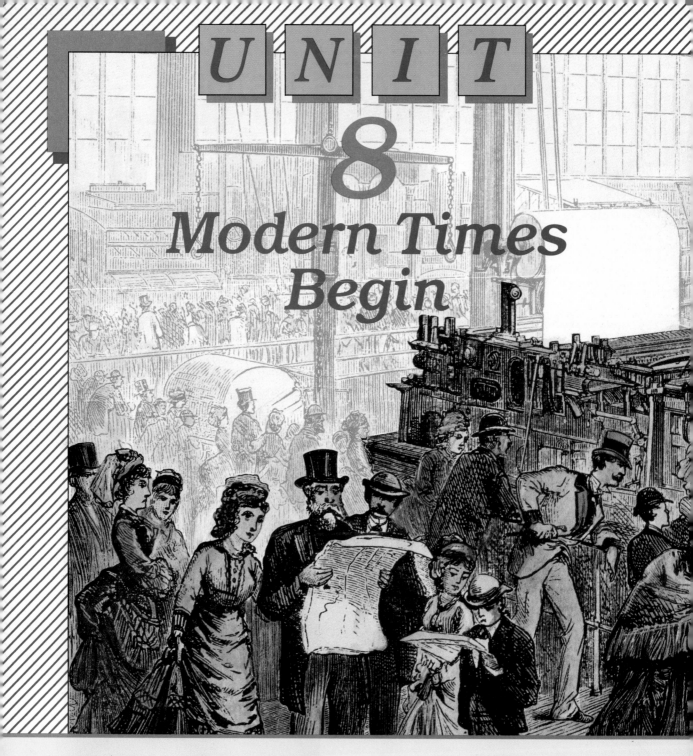

UNIT

8

Modern Times Begin

• **1865**
Civil War ends
Freedmen's Bureau
organized

• **1866**
Fourteenth
Amendment passes
Congress

• **1867**
Military rule in
Southern
states

• **1869**
Transcontinental
railroad completed

• **1872**
Yellowstone becomes
the first national
park

450

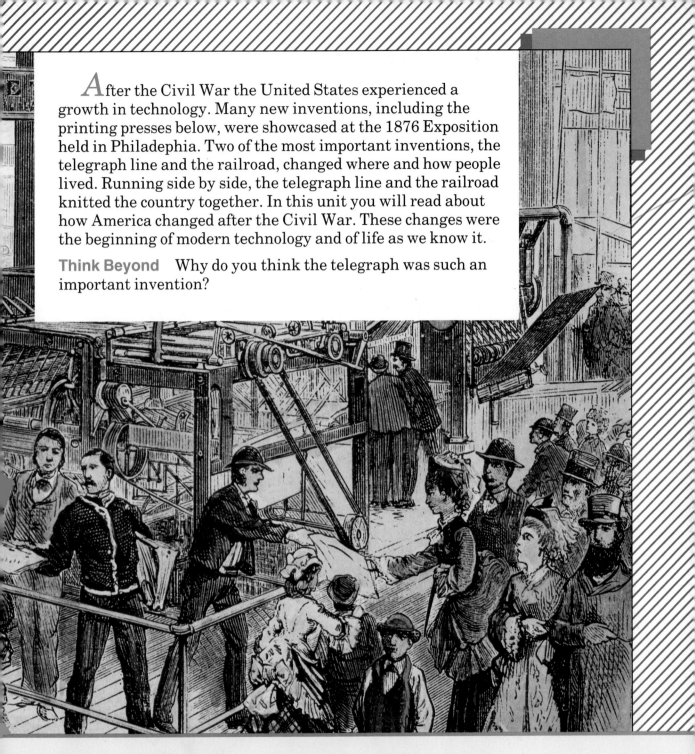

After the Civil War the United States experienced a growth in technology. Many new inventions, including the printing presses below, were showcased at the 1876 Exposition held in Philadephia. Two of the most important inventions, the telegraph line and the railroad, changed where and how people lived. Running side by side, the telegraph line and the railroad knitted the country together. In this unit you will read about how America changed after the Civil War. These changes were the beginning of modern technology and of life as we know it.

Think Beyond   Why do you think the telegraph was such an important invention?

• **1876**	• **1877**	• **1886**	• **1890s**
Battle of the Little Bighorn	Reconstruction ends Chief Joseph surrenders	American Federation of Labor founded	Populist movement

CHAPTER 17

Changes in North and South

❝The roads, long neglected, are in disorder, and having in many places become impassable, new tracks have been made through the woods and fields without much respect to boundaries. Borne down by debts, losses, and accumulating taxes, many who were once the richest among their fellows have disappeared from the scene, and few have risen to take their places. ❞

—English traveler in Tennessee, 1865

Look for these important words:

Key Words
- Reconstruction
- Freedmen's Bureau
- sharecroppers
- tenant farmers
- legislatures
- Black Codes
- second-class citizens
- Fourteenth Amendment
- ratify
- carpetbaggers
- scalawags
- Fifteenth Amendment
- secret ballot
- segregation
- Jim Crow laws
- poll tax

Look for answers to these questions:
1. What problems did freed slaves face after the Civil War?
2. What was the Freedmen's Bureau?
3. Why was military rule established in the South?
4. How did Southern states discourage black people from voting?

1 Reconstruction in the South

The end of the Civil War in 1865 brought the nation three main problems.

- The war had freed millions of slaves. The freed slaves were overjoyed to be free, but what would they do for housing, clothing, and food? How would they earn a living?
- The South was in economic ruin. There was no money. Banks were closed. Stores had little to sell. Railroads, bridges, plantations, and crops had been destroyed. How would the South be rebuilt?
- With the defeat of the Confederacy, the South no longer had any government. How would the Southern states be brought back into the government of the United States?

The government plan for dealing with these problems was called

Reconstruction. The word *reconstruction* means rebuilding. Reconstruction had two distinct parts. The first part was Lincoln's Reconstruction plan. The second part was Congress's Reconstruction plan.

President Lincoln's Reconstruction plan called for a **Freedmen's Bureau.** The Freedmen's Bureau would provide help and education to the former slaves. After Lincoln's death, Andrew Johnson, the new President, started to carry out Lincoln's Reconstruction plan.

The Freedmen's Bureau provided food, clothing, and fuel to both black and white people. It set up law courts. It established schools, perhaps its most important work. The Freedmen's Bureau built more than 4,000 schools and hired teachers for them.

The newly freed blacks were eager for education. "The tiniest children are

453

Freed blacks were eager to learn. Children and grandparents sit side by side in this Freedmen's Bureau school in Vicksburg, Mississippi.

delighted to get a book in their hands," one teacher wrote. Another observer said that they would "starve themselves, and go without clothes, in order to send their children to school." Learning, they knew, was a key to another kind of freedom.

Freed blacks had hoped that they would be given 40 acres (16.2 ha) and a mule. That did not happen, so most worked for their former masters as **sharecroppers** or **tenant farmers.**

Sharecropping worked like this. A landowner gave a sharecropper mules, plows, farming tools, and food. In return, the sharecropper gave the landowner one-third to one-half his crop. Unlike a sharecropper, a tenant farmer owned his animals and tools. He paid rent to the landowner in either crops or money. As sharecroppers or

tenant farmers, millions of freed blacks were now able to earn a living. Southern farms began again to produce crops.

As part of Lincoln's Reconstruction plan, elections were held in the South and state governments were soon back in operation. However, the new state **legislatures,** or lawmaking bodies, soon began to pass laws called **Black Codes.** These laws made newly freed blacks into **second-class citizens.** This meant that blacks did not have the full rights of citizenship. In some states they could by law do only household or field work. Blacks could not vote.

Many members of Congress were upset about what the South was doing. They did not think that blacks should be second-class citizens. Congress replaced Lincoln's Reconstruction plan with one of its own.

Congress's Plan

As part of its plan, Congress proposed the **Fourteenth Amendment** to the Constitution. The Fourteenth Amendment declared that all people born in the United States were citizens. All were to be given equal protection under the law.

Southern states refused to **ratify,** or approve, the Fourteenth Amendment. In response, Congress ordered military rule in the South, beginning in 1867. The South would be governed by the army until each state ratified the Fourteenth Amendment. In a region already torn apart by war, Southern political life was turned upside down.

New people, blacks as well as whites, became leaders in the South. Some were Northerners who had come south to teach school or start factories. Southern whites called these Northerners **carpetbaggers.** A carpetbag was a kind of cheap suitcase made of carpet scraps. It was said the carpetbaggers came south carrying everything they owned in a carpetbag. White Southerners who worked with the Northerners in the Reconstruction governments were called **scalawags.**

Blacks held important positions in the state governments set up under military rule. Many were elected to seats both in state legislatures and in Congress.

The Reconstruction legislatures approved the Fourteenth Amendment, which became law in 1868. They also ratified the **Fifteenth Amendment.** The Fifteenth Amendment says that no citizen shall be denied the right to vote because of color or race.

The Reconstruction legislatures made some important and lasting contributions. They set up schools. They repaired damage to bridges and roads. They had railroads rebuilt. They repealed the Black Codes. They set up new state constitutions that gave the vote to all men. No longer did a person have to own property to vote. Under the state constitutions, a person could no longer be put in prison for debt. This helped the poor.

The End of Reconstruction

The Reconstruction legislatures passed heavy taxes on land. The taxes were used for schools, road repairs, and railroads. The taxes hurt landowners who were trying to get their farms and plantations going again. Many farms had to be sold for unpaid taxes. Planters believed the heavy taxes were strangling them.

Southern landowners began to organize to get back power. One way to achieve such power was to control the way people voted.

At that time there was no **secret ballot.** A secret ballot is a way to vote without anyone knowing how one has voted. Before the secret ballot was used, the names of voters and how they voted were published in newspapers.

Secret societies were formed to keep blacks from voting or to make certain they voted only in certain ways. Those who joined the secret societies included white people who resented the equality of black people.

Members of one secret society, the Ku Klux Klan, wore white hoods and robes. Dressed like this, they delivered

Here a black man casts his first vote.
Later, new laws took away this right.

nighttime warnings to blacks who voted. Klan members also threatened white people with whom they disagreed. They sometimes burned schools and churches. At election time Klan members whipped and even killed black leaders. It was a time of terror for blacks throughout the South. Appeals to Congress fell on deaf ears.

Reconstruction was over by 1877. By then military rule had ended in the South. State governments were controlled by white landowners. Congress no longer showed an interest in protecting the rights of black people.

Blacks in the New South

In the 1870s many Southern blacks were kept from voting or forced to vote in certain ways. In some places, however, they continued to be elected and serve in city, state, and national offices.

In the 1880s practices were established that again made black people second-class citizens. One of these practices was **segregation,** or separation, of the races. Segregation came about gradually. The laws and customs that brought about segregation became known as **Jim Crow laws.** Jim Crow laws established segregation by race in all public places. Schools, theaters, trains, buses, even drinking fountains were segregated. This pattern of segregation lasted for more than 70 years.

At the same time, Southern states began to pass laws that in effect took away the right of black people to vote. One law was that a **poll tax** be paid in order to vote. In Mississippi each adult male had to pay two dollars in order to vote. A poor person might have to work four days to earn two dollars. The poll tax discouraged poor people, both black and white, from voting.

Another law in Southern states said that a person had to prove he could read or understand the state constitution. Officials who gave the tests rarely passed a black person. White people could vote whether or not they could read or understand the constitution. Unable to vote, blacks had little power to bring about changes they wanted. By 1899 there were few black officeholders.

 Reading Check

1. What was Reconstruction?
2. Why did Congress propose the Fourteenth Amendment?
3. What were Jim Crow laws?

Think Beyond How do you think Southern blacks felt about their future in the late 1860s?

Look for these important words:

Key Words
- Industrial Revolution
- Bessemer process
- smelt
- coke
- slag
- industrial
- telegraph
- Morse code
- invested
- reaper

- guarantee
- petroleum
- monopoly

People
- Samuel F. B. Morse
- Andrew Carnegie
- Cyrus McCormick
- John D. Rockefeller
- Alexander Graham Bell

Places
- Pittsburgh
- Lake Superior
- Chicago
- Gary
- Cleveland
- Detroit
- Birmingham

Look for answers to these questions:

1. What happened during the Industrial Revolution?
2. Why did places like Chicago become large cities?
3. What inventions and improvements depended on iron and steel?
4. Why did petroleum become an important resource in the nineteenth century?

2 New Technology, New Inventions

The great growth of technology and business in the nineteenth century changed American life forever. Taken together, these changes are called the **Industrial Revolution.** During the Industrial Revolution, machines replaced hand tools. Factories replaced craft shops. Coal replaced wood as a fuel. Iron became the basis of new technologies.

In 1779 the British built the first all-iron bridge. Soon iron was being used for buildings and railroad tracks as well. The development of railroads depended on iron tracks. As locomotives got bigger and heavier, not even iron tracks were strong enough. Many lasted only about three years.

Steel tracks were harder and lasted longer, but steel was very expensive to make. Steel is made from iron with a small amount of carbon added. Other metals like nickel may also be added. Because of the expense, steel was used only for such objects as knives and swords.

By 1856 inventors in both England and the United States discovered a new way to make steel. It was both cheaper and easier than the old way. Named after the English inventor Henry Bessemer, this new method was called the **Bessemer process.** By 1865 factories in the United States were turning out steel railroad tracks. They were expected to last at least 20 years.

457

Making steel requires a fuel that burns hot enough to **smelt** the iron ore. *To smelt* means to melt ore to separate out the metal. The best fuel, steelmakers discovered, was **coke.** Coke is made from coal and burns much hotter than coal itself.

Steelmaking also requires the use of limestone. Mixed with the molten iron ore, limestone helps remove the **slag.** Slag is the part of the ore that is not iron. After the smelting process, slag is left over as a waste product.

New Cities

New cities were started as the United States became an **industrial** nation. *Industrial* means having many factories. Before this time, important cities were located on good harbors near the ocean. The new industrial cities were built inland. They developed close to resources needed for iron and steel manufacturing.

The Appalachian Plateau, an area west of the Appalachian Mountains, had many such resources. It was rich in iron, coal, and limestone. Because of this, the first iron and steel industry developed in western Pennsylvania. **Pittsburgh** became a great steelmaking center. It remains so today.

The nation's greatest iron ore deposits were found in the 1850s near **Lake Superior** in Michigan. The ore was transported by barge across Lake Superior to Chicago and other Great Lakes cities. To the same cities, trains brought coal from the Appalachian region. **Chicago,** Illinois; **Gary,** Indiana; **Cleveland,** Ohio; and **Detroit,** Michigan, all became centers of iron and steel manufacturing. Other manufacturers who used iron and steel to make their products built their factories nearby.

In the South, **Birmingham,** Alabama, also became a large city. It too was close to iron and coal deposits. It was not on the water, like the older cities of Charleston and New Orleans.

Manufacturers were able to build factories near resources because of the railroads. Railroads could be built almost anywhere. Manufacturers could use them to bring necessary raw materials to their factories. Manufactured goods could be transported by railroad to distant markets. Cities such as Chicago, Illinois; Pittsburgh, Pennsylvania; St. Louis, Missouri; and Atlanta, Georgia, became railroad centers.

In the hot glare of the blast furnaces, workers made steel for the nation.

The Telegraph

The inventions and improvements of the nineteenth century depended on iron and steel. The **telegraph** was one of the most important of these inventions. Both Europeans and Americans had experimented with ways to send messages over long distances. An American inventor, **Samuel F. B. Morse,** experimented with sending electricity along iron wires. To send messages along the wires, Morse invented a code. The code was a system of dots and dashes standing for letters of the alphabet. This system became known as the **Morse code.**

With money from Congress, Morse built the first telegraph line between Washington, D.C., and Baltimore, Maryland. On May 24, 1844, Morse tested the telegraph line. He sat in the Capitol and sent a series of electrical dots and dashes along the iron wire to Baltimore. There his assistant translated the dots and dashes to read, "What hath God wrought!"

The country quickly recognized the importance of the telegraph. Telegraph lines were strung along railroad tracks. With the telegraph, railroads could keep track of train schedules. With the telegraph, news could flash quickly from one part of the country to the next.

By 1861 telegraph poles reached across the continent to California. In

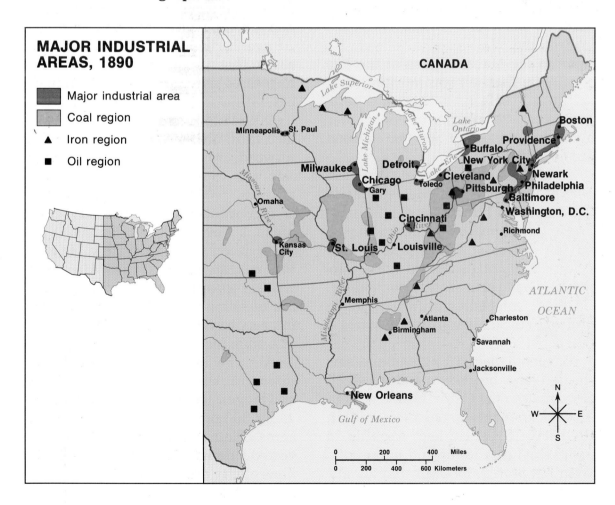

MAJOR INDUSTRIAL AREAS, 1890

- Major industrial area
- Coal region
- ▲ Iron region
- ■ Oil region

1866 a telegraph cable was successfully laid under the Atlantic Ocean. Within hours people on either side of the Atlantic could communicate with one another. Time had speeded up.

After the Civil War most of America's energy was directed to inventing, manufacturing, and selling. In this, inventors were important, but it was businessmen who made fortunes. Huge fortunes were made in new industries, including steel, oil, flour milling, railroads, and lumber. The richest and most important businessmen were called captains of industry.

Andrew Carnegie

The captain of the steel industry was **Andrew Carnegie.** Carnegie was born in Scotland, the son of a weaver. He came to the United States at the age of 12. His first job was working in a textile mill. He then became a telegraph operator on a railroad line. Later he worked as secretary to the railroad president.

As a young man, Carnegie **invested** part of his wages. *To invest* means to use money with the hope of making a profit. Carnegie invested his money by buying shares of stock in new businesses. By buying shares of stock, Carnegie owned parts of these companies. As these companies grew and made profits, stockholders like Carnegie prospered.

Carnegie visited England and saw the Bessemer process for making steel. Returning to the United States, he and several partners started a steel mill in the early 1870s. He kept working to make steel at a lower and lower cost. With his profits, he built and bought more steel mills. Carnegie became one of the richest men in America.

Cyrus McCormick

Cyrus McCormick, both an inventor and businessman, changed life on the farm. For centuries there had been only one method of harvesting grains. This was to use a hand-held scythe (SYTH). It was hard, backbreaking work. A better way to harvest the grain was needed. Many tried to develop a good **reaper,** or harvester, but Cyrus McCormick succeeded.

Cyrus McCormick grew up on a Virginia farm. As a boy he liked to spend time in his father's tool shop. His father had tried to invent a reaper but had given up. McCormick kept trying. At age 22, in 1831, he finally made a reaper that worked. Within hours it had harvested as much grain as could be cut with a scythe in several days.

In 1848 McCormick started a reaper factory in Chicago. There he was close to wood, iron, and steel supplies. He was also close to the grain-growing prairies.

McCormick's selling methods helped make a revolution in business. He advertised his reaper widely. He gave demonstrations to farmers. He gave a written **guarantee,** or promise, that the machine would work. He even let farmers buy reapers by paying a little at a time instead of all at once.

All the while, McCormick was improving the reaper, making it better and bigger. By the 1880s farmers were using 30-horse teams to pull reapers across their fields. Tons of wheat harvested this way were sold to feed millions of city dwellers.

Chicago Historical Society, "The Testing of the First Reaping Machine Near Steele's Tavern, VA. 1831" by the Milwaukee Lithography & Engraving Co, ca1883.

Near Steele's Tavern, Virginia, a crowd gathers to see an invention that will change their lives: Cyrus McCormick's reaping machine. With this invention, farmers could cut as much wheat in one day as they had been able to cut in two weeks using a hand-held scythe.

New Uses for Oil

For years people had been aware of the black oil, or **petroleum,** that gathered on ponds in western Pennsylvania. In the early 1800s the oil was collected and sold in bottles as "American oil." Drinking it was supposed to cure everything from cough to toothache. Yet there seemed to be more oil than Americans could ever take as medicine.

What else could one do with the oil? Scientists were asked to study it. They reported that the oil burned well and was a good grease. Soon more and more uses for petroleum were discovered. Greater efforts were made to collect it from the tops of ponds.

Then in 1859 Edwin Drake started to drill for oil as one drills for water. This was in Titusville, Pennsylvania. People thought he was crazy. But when his well filled up with oil, an oil rush started. Oil towns sprang up all over western Pennsylvania. About 250 refineries in Pittsburgh and Cleveland began processing the oil for grease and kerosene.

John D. Rockefeller

John D. Rockefeller became a captain of the oil industry. Rockefeller lived in Cleveland. He was 23 years old in 1863 when he invested in an oil refinery. He steadily expanded his investment and ended up buying other refineries.

Rockefeller was known as a shrewd businessman who looked after pennies as well as dollars. "To drive a good bargain was the joy of his life," said a writer of the time.

Rockefeller hated to let anyone make a profit off his business. Therefore, his company bought forests to get its own lumber. It bought a barrel factory to make its own barrels. It bought ships and railroad cars to carry its products. Rockefeller set out to get a **monopoly,** or complete control, of the oil business. He succeeded, but he made many enemies. He put out of business many companies that were unable or unwilling to follow his business practices. Many began to question the fairness of these practices.

461

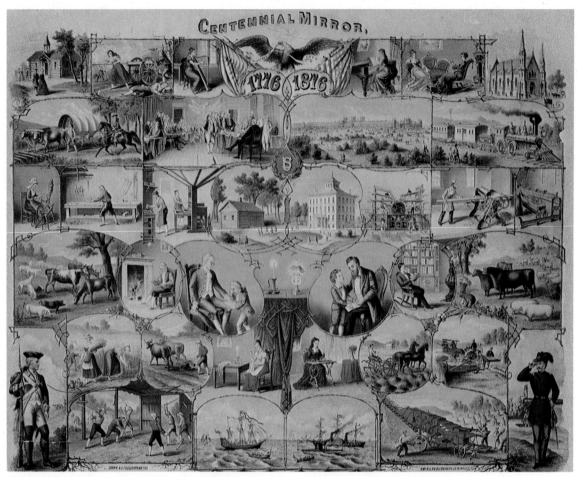

This picture was made in 1876 to show the changes in American life since 1776. Look at it carefully. How many things do you see compared?

The 1876 Exposition

The United States celebrated its one-hundredth birthday in 1876 with a world's fair in Philadelphia. At this fair, the 1876 Exposition, countries from all over the world exhibited their products. The United States did the same. American exhibits included sewing machines, iron cookstoves, locomotives, a knitting machine, and canned food. The center of American pride was a giant steam engine.

Getting less attention at the fair was one new machine. Yet this machine would change communication as much as the telegraph had. **Alexander Graham Bell,** a teacher of the deaf, demonstrated his invention of the first telephone. A professor in Scotland who heard of the invention declared, "It is all humbug, for such a discovery is physically impossible."

 Reading Check

1. Name three resources needed by steelmakers.
2. Who invented the telegraph?
3. Why was the reaper important?

Think Beyond If you have played the board game *Monopoly,* explain how it works. How is winning it like having a monopoly in business?

CARNEGIE HALL

A well-known joke tells of a man who gets lost in New York City. The man stops a cab driver to ask him for directions. "How do you get to Carnegie Hall?" the man asks. "Practice, practice," responds the cab driver.

As the joke points out, only the best performing artists are asked to appear in Carnegie Hall, New York City's most famous concert hall. Many people consider a performance at Carnegie Hall to be the highest accomplishment.

Carnegie Hall was built in 1891 as a home for the New York Philharmonic Orchestra. It was first named the New York Music Hall. In 1898 it was renamed to honor Andrew Carnegie, the steel-making millionaire who gave most of the money to build the hall.

Located at the corner of 57th Street and Seventh Avenue, Carnegie Hall was considered one of the most beautiful music halls of its time. Its main hall had seats for 3,000 people. There was also a smaller stage area, called Carnegie Chamber Music Hall, which could hold 300 people. The people of New York were so excited about the new hall that they held a huge music festival to celebrate its opening. The great Russian composer Tchaikovsky (chy•KAWF•skee) came to New York to conduct the symphony at the opening ceremonies.

In 1959, the great music hall was in danger of being torn down after the New York Philharmonic moved its home to the Lincoln Center. However, a group of citizens, headed by violinist Isaac Stern, wanted to preserve Carnegie Hall. The citizens' group bought the building from New York City for $5 million. Even more was spent to restore and redecorate it. After the restoration, Carnegie Hall was even more beautiful than when it opened in 1891.

Many of the world's most honored performers have played at Carnegie Hall. Today the hall holds all kinds of concerts—even rock, country, and jazz.

Think Beyond   What does his donation of money for the construction of Carnegie Hall tell you about Andrew Carnegie?

Front of Carnegie Hall

Look for these important words:

Key Words
- tenements
- piecework
- sweatshops
- reformers

- Hull House
- labor union
- federation
- American Federation of Labor

- queue
- prejudice

People
- Jane Addams
- Samuel Gompers

Look for answers to these questions:
1. How did thousands of immigrants live in the cities?
2. How was life made better for immigrants and workers?
3. Who was Samuel Gompers? What did he achieve?
4. Why did Asians come to the United States?

3 The Workers of the Nation

The new age of steam and iron created thousands of jobs. People were needed to mine coal, build railroads, cut timber, and keep the smelters going. To fill these jobs came millions of immigrants from Europe. Between 1865 and 1900, 12 million people came from overseas. They came from such countries as Britain, Ireland, Germany, Sweden, Italy, Russia, and Hungary. The immigrants came to get away from poverty, war, or tyranny.

Millions of these immigrants lived in the cities and worked in factories, mines, and mills. Life was hard for them. They lived crowded together in run-down apartment houses called **tenements.** Salaries were so low that everyone in a family had to work. Children had to work from an early age to keep the family fed.

Many children worked at home helping their parents do **piecework.** *Piecework* is work done and paid for by the piece. Piecework was usually sewing of some kind. A family doing piecework might do nothing but sew seams.

To help feed his family, this New York boy carried heavy loads of piecework.

They got paid a few pennies for each piece they sewed.

Children had always helped their parents when they lived on farms. Children who worked on farms got plenty of exercise and fresh air. They learned how to do many things. Children who worked 12 hours a day in stuffy, poorly lit rooms were not healthy. They did not learn new skills.

Long Days in Sweatshops

Often piecework was done in small factories called **sweatshops.** Sweatshops had terrible working conditions. Workers were pushed to work faster and harder and longer. Twelve-hour days were common. So were accidents. "Sometimes in my haste I get my finger caught and the needle goes right through it." This was said by Sadie Frowne, a worker in a sweatshop. "We all have accidents like that," she said. "Sometimes a finger has to come off."

If workers complained about conditions or went on strike, as many did, they were fired. Employers found it easy to hire new immigrants to work at the lowest possible wages.

Help for the City Poor

Many Americans became concerned about the growing problems of the city poor. In Chicago, for example, a group of women forced changes that resulted in better treatment in Chicago's jail and mental hospitals. These women were **reformers,** people who wish to bring about change for the better.

Jane Addams was a reformer who started **Hull House** in 1889. Hull

Jane Addams worked to help immigrants.

House was a community center where immigrants received education and training.

Reformers also worked to improve conditions in tenements. They demanded an eight-hour working day for women. They worked to outlaw child labor and to improve health and safety conditions in factories.

Samuel Gompers

As business grew more powerful, working conditions seemed to grow worse. Workers organized to fight against the power of what was now called "big business." Leading that fight was **Samuel Gompers.**

Samuel Gompers was 13 years old when his family left the tenements of London for America. America sounded good to Samuel's father, a cigar maker. It was hard to make a living in London. Samuel had quit school at the age of 10 to help his father make cigars.

In New York City the Gompers family found life similar to life in London. The whole family worked hard making cigars at home. When he was 16 years old, Samuel Gompers started to work in a cigar maker's shop. There the cigar makers worked from dawn to sunset.

Gompers had joined a cigar maker's **labor union.** A labor union is an organization of workers who seek to protect their interests. Soon Gompers was union leader of the workers in his shop. Then he organized one big union of all the cigar makers. They went on strike for a ten-hour day and better wages, but the strike failed. Tobacco buyers owned many of the tenements where the workers lived. They forced the cigar makers to move. Some ended up begging on the streets.

From this experience Gompers decided that cigar makers should get other workers to join them. All skilled workers in trades like carpentry, plumbing, and bricklaying should get together. They should form one large **federation,** Gompers said. A federa-tion is an organization formed of many member groups. Gompers felt that only skilled workers should be in this federation. If they went on strike, it would be hard to replace them. The strike would have a better chance of success.

Gompers's dream came true in 1886. Representatives of skilled workers formed the **American Federation of Labor,** or AFL. Gompers was elected president of the AFL every year but one until his death in 1924.

Under the wise and strong leadership of Gompers, the AFL grew. Government and business leaders began to listen to its demands. The demands included higher wages and an eight-hour day. The AFL also wanted better working conditions, an end to child labor, and accident insurance. The insurance would pay the salary and medical bills for workers injured on the job. Whenever people asked what the unions wanted, Gompers answered, "More."

Immigrants from Asia

The Chinese first came to America in great numbers after the California gold rush. Like others who flocked to California, they hoped to strike it rich.

About 25,000 Chinese had arrived in San Francisco by 1852. To get there, they had suffered terrible conditions on board ship. Most, however, felt they had no choice. China was a poor country, yet taxes were high. To survive, parents sometimes sold one or more of their children into slavery.

Most of the Chinese immigrants were men. They left their families behind in China and sent back money to them.

Chinese immigrants arrive in "Gold Mountain," their name for California.

To American miners in the goldfields, these Chinese immigrants seemed very strange. They looked different. They wore their hair in one braid called a **queue** (KYOO). Wearing a queue was an important part of Chinese culture. A man without a queue was in disgrace. The Chinese language and religion were also completely unfamiliar to Westerners.

The American miners tried to force the Chinese out of the goldfields. Many Chinese were beaten and even killed.

But the Chinese felt they had no choice but to persist. To go home would mean starvation for their families. Some Chinese began to specialize in meeting two important needs. They began to supply good food and clean clothes. They opened restaurants and laundries all over California. Other Chinese continued mining. In 1870 one-third of the miners in California were Chinese.

As the goldfields gave out, the Chinese did other work. They worked building railroads, draining swamps, and growing crops. They were known as hard workers.

Numbers of Chinese immigrants continued to come to this country looking for opportunity. But by the 1870s many white people wanted to keep out the Chinese. Workers were particularly upset that the Chinese were willing to work for low wages. In 1882 Congress passed a law that stopped the immigration of Chinese workers.

For Chinese in this country, life could be difficult. They continued to

Chinese immigrants, eager for opportunity and willing to work for low pay, laid down the tracks of the Central Pacific Railroad.

Japanese people, like immigrants before them, found opportunity in the United States. Many, like this family, were farmers.

face **prejudice** on the part of white Americans. Prejudice means making negative judgments about people because of their race or religion.

In western states, mobs sometimes attacked the Chinese, even killing them. Sometimes bullies amused themselves by cutting off queues. The police usually looked the other way.

Meanwhile numbers of Japanese had also come to the United States as agricultural workers. Many of these Japanese were able to save enough money to buy small farms. In California they became known as excellent farmers. In time they, too, experienced prejudice as did the Chinese.

The first Asian immigrants faced hard times. However, Asian Americans today have distinguished themselves in all walks of life. One of these people is Hiram L. Fong, a former United States senator. Fong's parents left China to work on sugarcane plan-tations in Hawaii. Life in the tenements of Honolulu was hard. The Fong family was very poor.

To earn money, young Hiram Fong started shining shoes and selling fish and newspapers. He worked hard to earn money to attend school. In time he graduated from law school. Fong became rich by practicing law and investing in business. He also gave time to public service and was elected to Hawaii's legislature. Later he served four terms in the United States Senate.

Reading Check

1. What were conditions like in a sweatshop?
2. What was the purpose of Hull House?
3. Why did Samuel Gompers urge trade unions to join together?

Think Beyond   How might you feel if you were the target of prejudice?

People MAKE HISTORY

Lue Gim Gong
1860–1925

▶▶▶▶▶▶▶▶▶▶▶▶▶▶▶▶▶

When Spanish explorers came to Florida in the 1500s, they brought with them exotic plants. Some of these plants, such as palm trees, grew well in Florida's tropical heat. Others, such as orange trees, were not as strong and healthy as they had been in their native land.

Lue Gim Gong changed the fate of the orange tree in America. Because of the work of this self-taught botanist, citrus fruits have become a major crop in states like Florida, Texas, and California.

As a young man in Massachusetts, Lue worked as a gardener for Fanny Burlingame, the cousin of the U.S. Ambassador to China. When his employer gave him some property in DeLand, Florida, he set up a laboratory there and conducted experiments with fruit. Using methods of cross-pollination that he had learned on his family's farm in China, he combined Florida's sickly oranges with a stronger type of orange. The result was a large, juicy orange that could grow in America.

Lue's orange was so important to American farmers that in 1911, the U.S. Department of Agriculture awarded him the Wilder Medal for his work. The Wilder Medal is the Agriculture Department's highest honor.

Lue experimented with cherries, tomatoes, and even roses, but he will always be remembered for his oranges. Because of Lue Gim Gong's work, many Americans enjoy a glass of orange juice each day, and many people in America have jobs growing oranges.

Think Beyond How do you think Lue's work has affected the economies of Florida, California, and Texas?

Picking Florida oranges

469

SKILLS IN ACTION

USING TIME ZONES

People used to figure time based only on the sun's position. Noon was the hour when the sun reached its **zenith,** or highest point, in the sky. Yet the sun is not at its zenith in all places at the same time. When it is noon in Kansas City, Missouri, it is still morning in San Francisco, California. It is afternoon in Baltimore, Maryland.

Telling time from the sun was not a problem until the railroads began to cross the United States. Railroad managers could not set up train schedules because of the time differences from place to place.

Sandford Fleming of Canada and Charles F. Dowd of the United States had an idea. They proposed that the world be divided into 24 time zones. The time zones would be laid out along every fifteenth meridian from the Prime Meridian at Greenwich, England. Each time zone would be one hour different from neighboring time zones. Each time zone to the west would always be one hour earlier than the time zone to the east. All towns in a time zone would use the same time. In the 1880s railway managers began to adopt this plan. Most countries in the world today follow this plan for figuring time.

On the next page is a time zone map of the mainland United States. Most of the United States is divided into four time zones. Alaska and Hawaii are in other time zones. Notice that the lines between time zones are not as straight as meridians. That is because time zone boundaries may follow state borders or geographic areas.

How can you figure out what time it is in cities in different time zones? First, figure out what time zone each city is in. Find New York City on the map. It is in the eastern time zone. Now find Kansas City in the central time zone, the next time zone to the west. To find the time in Kansas City, subtract one hour from the time in New York. If it is noon in New York, it is 11:00 A.M. in Kansas City. Find Denver on the map. It is in the mountain time zone. It is one hour earlier in Denver than it is in Kansas City. It is two hours earlier in Denver than in New York City.

Move west to Los Angeles. What time zone is Los Angeles in? It is one hour earlier in this zone than it is in Denver. It is two hours earlier than in Kansas City. It is three hours earlier than in New York. When it is noon in New York City, what time is it in Los

THE SUN OVER THE UNITED STATES

Kansas City

San Francisco

Baltimore

Direction of Earth's Rotation ⟶

In San Francisco it is 10:00 A.M.

In Kansas City the sun is at its zenith. It is noon.

In Baltimore it is 1:00 P.M.

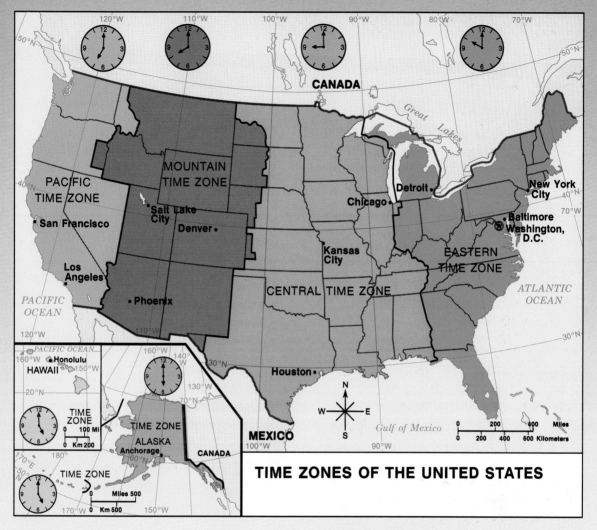

TIME ZONES OF THE UNITED STATES

Angeles? When it is noon in Los Angeles, what time is it in Chicago?

The time in each zone is often abbreviated. *EST* stands for Eastern Standard Time. *CST* stands for Central Standard Time. *MST* stands for Mountain Standard Time. *PST* stands for Pacific Standard Time. When a newspaper announces that the President will speak at 7:00 P.M. (EST), people in other parts of the country have to figure the time for their zone.

From the end of April to the end of October, most places operate on daylight time. This means that the clocks are set ahead an hour. Daylight time lets people have more hours of light at the end of the day. During daylight time the abbreviations in each time zone are *EDT, CDT, MDT,* and *PDT.*

CHECKING YOUR SKILLS

Use the map to answer these questions.

1. In what time zone is Salt Lake City?

2. What time is it in Salt Lake City when it is 4:00 P.M. in New York City?

3. What time is it in Salt Lake City when it is 6:00 A.M. in San Francisco?

4. In what time zone is Houston?

5. When it is 2:00 P.M. in Houston, what time is it on the West Coast?

471

Thinking Back

- After the Civil War the nation faced three major problems: taking care of freed slaves; rebuilding the South; and restoring the South to the U.S. government.

- Lincoln's Reconstruction plan established the Freedmen's Bureau.

- After the Southern states held elections, the new state legislatures passed laws that made the newly freed blacks second-class citizens.

- Congress ordered military rule in the South. State governments set up under military rule ratified both the Fourteenth and Fifteenth amendments.

- After Reconstruction ended, blacks were once again made second-class citizens.

- The Industrial Revolution changed American life forever. Iron and steel became the basis for new technologies and new inventions.

- New industrial cities developed close to resources that were used for iron and steel manufacturing.

- Immigrants came to the United States to fill newly-created jobs and to escape war, tyranny, or poverty.

- The new workers faced many hardships on their jobs. Reformers, such as Jane Addams, worked to improve conditions for the city poor through education and training.

- The American Federation of Labor, founded by Samuel Gompers, demanded better working conditions.

- Chinese and Japanese immigrants came to the United States looking for better living conditions and opportunity.

Check for Understanding

Using Words

Write the words below on a piece of paper. Next to each word, write its definition.

1. federation
2. industrial
3. invest
4. legislatures
5. monopoly
6. prejudice
7. Reconstruction
8. segregation
9. sweatshops
10. tenements

Reviewing Facts

1. What problems did the nation face after the Civil War?

2. What was the purpose of military rule in the South during Reconstruction?

3. What were some achievements of the Reconstruction legislatures?

4. Describe the position of Southern blacks in 1900.

5. What changes were part of the Industrial Revolution?

6. Why did inland cities such as Gary, Pittsburgh, Cleveland, Detroit, and Birmingham become centers of iron and steel manufacturing?

7. Why was the telegraph such an important invention?

8. Why did so many immigrants from Europe come to our country during the last half of the nineteenth century?
9. What problems were Jane Addams and Samuel Gompers concerned about? What did they do about these problems?
10. Why did Chinese immigrants stay in the United States, even though they were often badly treated?

Thinking Critically

1. How did the people discussed in this chapter contribute to American society? Which ones do you think were most important? Explain your answer.
2. Imagine that you live in the 1870s and work 12 hours a day in a sweatshop. Describe your working conditions. How might this way of life affect your future?
3. How is learning a key to freedom? What examples can you think of to support your answer?

Writing About It

Imagine that it is the 1800s and you are an immigrant coming to this country in search of a better life. Write a diary entry that describes your feelings when you first see the Statue of Liberty. Include a paragraph about your dreams for a new life in America.

Practicing Time Skills

Using Time Zones

Use the time zone map on page 471 to answer these questions.

1. Suppose you live in California and want to call your grandmother in New Jersey at 8:00 P.M. her time. At what time would you have to telephone from California?

2. The Olympics are going to be on television at 10:00 A.M. (PDT). What time will the program start in these cities?
   a. Kansas City
   b. New York City
   c. Denver
3. When it is 3:00 P.M. in Los Angeles, what time is it in Honolulu?

On Your Own

Social Studies at Home

1. Samuel Morse invented a code to send messages along telegraph lines. Make up your own code, and practice sending messages with a classmate.
2. Trace the map on page 459. On your map, label the cities that became major centers of iron production. Then trace the route the iron would take going from Lake Superior to Chicago.

Read More About It

The Golden Door: The United States from 1865 to 1918 by Isaac Asimov. Houghton Mifflin. This history of America in the late nineteenth century emphasizes the Industrial Revolution and immigration.

Great Discoveries and Inventions by David Lambert. Facts on File. This book covers major inventions of the nineteenth and twentieth centuries.

Immigrant Girl: Becky of Eldridge Street by Brett Harvey. Holiday. This picture book illustrates how European immigrants lived in the early 20th century.

Trouble at the Mines by Doreen Rappaport. Illustrated by Joan Sandin. Harper/Crowell. This book tells the story of union organizers at a Pennsylvania coal mine.

CHAPTER 18

A Nation Settled and Strong

"Four miles after leaving Omaha, the first stoppage is made. The journey is now fairly begun and every one is on the lookout for new scenery and strange adventures. As mile after mile is left behind, the remark is very generally made that the surrounding country, instead of being wild and desolate, is rich and filled with settlers."

—English train traveler in the American west, 1871

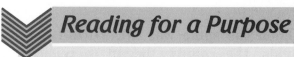

Reading for a Purpose

Look for these important words:

Key Words
- Pony Express
- transcontinental railroad
- stockyards
- stampede
- Homestead Act
- homesteaders

Places
- Kansas City
- St. Louis
- Omaha
- St. Joseph
- Sacramento
- Promontory
- Nueces River valley

- Abilene
- Dodge City
- Ogallala
- Cheyenne
- Chisholm Trail

Look for answers to these questions:

1. How did the railroad bring about new ways of life on the Great Plains?
2. Why did cattlemen in Texas drive their herds north?
3. What inventions were necessary to settlers of the Great Plains? What problems did these pioneers face?

1 Settling the Great Plains

In the 1850s freight wagons and stagecoaches were making regular trips between California and such cities as **Kansas City, St. Louis,** and **Omaha.** In 1860 a private company started the **Pony Express.** Its purpose was to carry letters between **St. Joseph,** Missouri, and **Sacramento,** California.

The Pony Express rider rode as fast as he could. He stopped only when he reached one of the 190 relay stations. There he might get a fresh horse to continue the journey. If not that, he would hand the mail sack to another rider ready to go. In this manner the Pony Express was able to deliver letters quickly. A letter could travel the 1,900 miles (about 3,057 km) from Missouri to California in just ten days.

Galloping across the West was difficult and dangerous work for the Pony Express riders. In a San Francisco newspaper, the Pony Express advertised for riders this way:

> Young skinny wiry fellows, not over eighteen. Must be expert riders, willing to risk death daily. Orphans preferred.

The Pony Express lasted only 18 months. In October 1861, a telegraph line across the country was completed. It put the Pony Express out of business.

Transcontinental Railroad

When Abraham Lincoln ran for President in 1860, the Republican party promised a **transcontinental railroad.** This was to be a railroad that linked the East with the Pacific Coast. When Lincoln was elected, the Republicans kept their promise. In 1862 Congress granted two railroad companies the right to build this railroad. The government gave them land and loaned them money. The Union Pacific would build west from Omaha, Nebraska. The Central Pacific would build east from Sacramento, California.

Each railroad raced to see which could lay the most track before they met. The ribbons of steel were laid at the rate of one or two miles (1.6 or 3.2 km) a day. The Union Pacific used Irish immigrants as laborers. The Central Pacific used Chinese immigrants.

On May 10, 1869, the two railroads met at **Promontory,** Utah. Only the distance of two pieces of track separated them. The last steel spike to be driven in was attached to a telegraph wire. When the spike was hit, an electric charge would announce that the rail line was complete. All over the country, people waited for the news.

Then the spike was hit. Within seconds, the country began to rejoice. Chicago held a parade seven miles (11.3 km) long. Church bells pealed across the nation.

The Union Pacific–Central Pacific did not long remain the only railroad across the West. By the 1890s four more railroads had been built from Midwestern cities to the Pacific.

The telegraph had carried messages across the Great Plains. But it was the steam-belching locomotive on steel tracks that changed the Plains. In the East the railroad had followed settlement. In the West settlement would follow the railroad.

The railroad made possible great cattle ranches. The railroad opened up the Plains to farmers. By the 1890s these farmers were turning the Great Plains into seas of wheat.

Westward-bound settlers, many of them from Europe, travel by railroad to new homesteads on the Plains.

A cowboy gallops to head off a stampeding herd of cattle. This was one of the cowboy's most dangerous jobs.

Railroads and Cowboys

The cowboy is one of the most popular figures of the American past. In his pointed-toe boots, wide-brimmed hat, and leather chaps the cowboy has become legend. Yet cowboy life lasted a rather short time—about 25 years. The railroads helped make the cowboy an important figure. The railroads also brought the settlement that ended the cowboy way of life.

For years Texans had raised longhorn cattle in the **Nueces** (nyoo•AY•suhs) **River valley** south of San Antonio. They had learned from the Mexicans the techniques of rounding up, roping, and branding cattle. The cattle were longhorns—a breed that had been raised for years in northern Mexico. Longhorns were wild, tough beasts that did well on the prairie. Only men on horseback—the cowboys—could control them.

Thousands of cattle grazed in Texas while people in northern cities were hungry for beef. Prices for cattle were low in Texas. Cattlemen could get nearly 20 times as much money for their cattle if they could get them to the cities. The question was *how*.

Railroad lines moving into Kansas provided the answer. Joseph McCoy, a cattle trader, built large cattle pens called **stockyards** near the railroad tracks in **Abilene,** Kansas. Then he sent word to Texas that he would buy herds of cattle. In 1867 Texas cattlemen started driving huge herds of cattle north to Abilene. Later **Dodge City,** Kansas; **Ogallala,** Nebraska; and **Cheyenne,** Wyoming, became important cow towns.

The most famous of the cattle trails was the **Chisholm** (CHIZ•uhm) **Trail.** On the long cattle drives, cowboys rode with the herd. They had a hard job. A constant danger was that the cattle would **stampede,** or run away out of control. Other dangers included prairie fires, flash floods, or attacks by bandits.

In the cow towns the cattle were loaded onto freight cars and shipped to Chicago. There the cattle were butchered. The meat was then sent in refrigerated freight cars to all parts of the East.

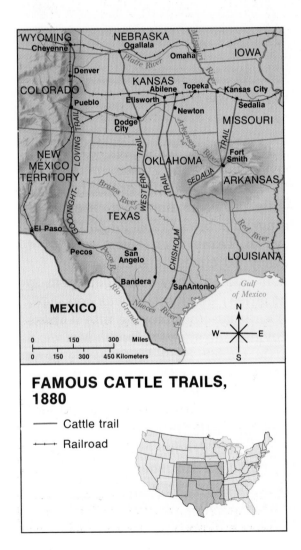

FAMOUS CATTLE TRAILS, 1880

—— Cattle trail
+—+ Railroad

Cattlemen soon started grazing cattle on the ranges of the Great Plains. By this time most of the buffalo had been killed off by sharp-shooting buffalo hunters. The grasslands did not belong to the cattle ranchers, but they used millions of acres for their herds.

Railroads and Homesteaders

The railroads wanted more settlement on the Plains because it would mean more business. They advertised for people to come settle the Plains.

In 1862 Congress had passed the **Homestead Act.** This law gave 160 acres (64.8 ha) of land to anyone willing to live on it for five years. The people who settled the land in this way were called **homesteaders.** Many settlers also bought land from the railroads or the government.

Even with the railroad, settlement of the Plains would have been impossible without three inventions. These important inventions were the steel plow, the windmill, and barbed wire.

In the 1830s a steel plow had been designed that could turn over the tough sod. The invention of the windmill let settlers pump necessary water from hundreds of feet below the surface. The windmill was first used by the railroads. Windmills provided water for the steam lomotives. Soon, windmills marked each new town on the Plains. By the 1890s homesteaders had their own windmills.

The use of barbed wire brought the open range to an end. Barbed wire was invented in 1873. Before then farmers had no way to keep cattle out of their fields. When farmers started enclosing their land with barbed wire,

This pioneer Nebraska family poses outside its sod "dug-out" house. Why do you suppose the wagon and team of horses are in the picture?

ranchers often cut the wire. Some bitter fighting took place between the cattle ranchers and the farmers.

In the end, however, ranchers found barbed wire to be as useful as farmers did. With barbed wire they could make pastures to enclose their cattle. The windmill provided water for the cattle. Pastured cattle meant that fewer cowboys were necessary. Cowboys now needed to be as skilled at digging fence-post holes as roping calves.

With the steel plow, barbed wire, and hard work, pioneer homesteaders conquered the Great Plains. For fuel they used buffalo chips. For houses they used sod. Sod houses were cool in summer and warm in winter, but housekeeping was a problem. Dirt often fell from the sod ceiling. Sometimes snakes did too!

These pioneers faced other hardships. In the years of drought nothing grew. When crops did grow, farmers worried about prairie fires, hail-storms, hot winds, or grasshoppers.

Grasshoppers attacked in force for the first time in 1874. They came in clouds by the millions, eating every green thing. One pioneer woman, Adelheit Viets, was wearing a white dress with a green stripe the day the grasshoppers came. "The grasshoppers settled on me and ate up every bit of green stripe in that dress before anything could be done about it," she remembered.

As hard as life could be on the Great Plains, the settlers had fun, too. Picnics, dances, horseback riding, and fairs were common events.

 ## Reading Check

1. How did the government help build the transcontinental railroad?
2. What work did cowboys do?
3. Why were windmills important?

Think Beyond Imagine that you are a Plains settler. Relate one good and one bad incident of the past year.

SKILLS IN ACTION

USING TRANSPORTATION AND RESOURCE MAPS

Transportation Maps

A **transportation map** shows transportation routes. It may show railways or the regular routes of ships and airlines. It may also show major highways. The map below is a historical transportation map. It shows how people and goods traveled to western states during the 1870s.

Look at the map key. What types of transportation routes are shown on this map? Can you find four rivers on which people journeyed by boat? Notice that many trails on

ROUTES TO THE WEST IN THE 1870s

— Major mail or wagon route   — River route

+++ Railroad

480

the map follow along rivers. They followed trails near rivers because they were level and easy to travel.

The railroads went west much later than the wagons and stagecoaches. Trace the routes of the railroad from east to west. Notice that in places the railroads followed the wagon routes.

The railroads were an improvement over wagons and ships. They speeded up the development of the West. Railroads were faster than wagons and stagecoaches. They could carry more people in greater comfort and safety. They could carry goods at a lower cost. They could also carry the products of the West back to eastern markets. This encouraged people to go west to make a living.

Resource Maps

How could people make a living in the West? A **resource map** shows the location of natural resources and regions. It also may show the manufactured goods of an area. Often resource maps show which crops and livestock do well in certain areas. The map on this page is a historical map that shows some of the natural resources and products of the state of Colorado. It also shows the railroad routes that existed in 1881.

Look at the map key. What mineral regions are shown? What other resources and products are shown on this map? Both sheep and cattle were raised in Colorado. Where was one likely to find the most cattle? Where were sheep generally found?

Study the railroad routes shown on the map. The tracks that run to the edges of the state continue to cities elsewhere. Compare these railroad routes to the ones shown in the map at left. Notice that more routes are shown on the 1881 map. Why might there be more railroads in 1881 than in 1870?

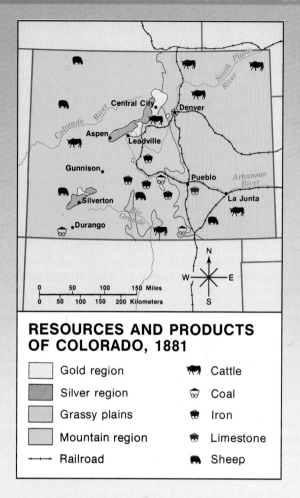

RESOURCES AND PRODUCTS OF COLORADO, 1881

☐	Gold region	🐄	Cattle
▨	Silver region	⬚	Coal
☐	Grassy plains	🐃	Iron
☐	Mountain region	🐃	Limestone
┼────	Railroad	🐑	Sheep

CHECKING YOUR SKILLS

Use the two maps and their keys to answer these questions.

1. Which methods of transportation could someone use to travel from Denver to San Francisco in 1870?

2. Coal, limestone, and iron are needed to make steel. Which town in Colorado was best located for steel mills?

3. Ranchers drove their cattle each year to a town where the cattle could be shipped east by train. Which town in Colorado was likely a cattle center?

4. Could a traveler get to Denver from Kansas City by a water route?

481

Look for these important words:

Key Words
- Sioux
- Battle of the Little Bighorn
- Nez Perce
- Apaches

People
- Chief Red Cloud
- George Custer
- Crazy Horse
- Chief Joseph
- Geronimo

Places
- Black Hills
- South Dakota
- Little Bighorn River
- Sierra Madre

Look for answers to these questions:
1. What did settlement of the Great Plains mean for the Indians who lived there?
2. Why did Indians attack wagon trains, homesteads, and army forts?
3. Who were some of the outstanding Indian leaders of this time?

2 Indian Wars in the West

From the time the Spanish had introduced the horse to the Plains, the Plains Indians had become superb riders. The Indians used the horse to carry themselves and their belongings. Riding fleet horses, the Indians hunted buffalo. As in the past, they depended on buffalo to satisfy most of their needs. With settlement of the Plains, Plains Indian culture came to a rather quick and violent end.

The familiar pattern of conflict between settlers and Indians was repeated in the Great Plains. There, Indians were distressed to see their hunting grounds invaded. Unable to hunt, the Indians lost their economic base. Their whole way of life had depended on hunting. Westward-moving settlers forced one Indian group after another to leave their homes and hunting grounds. Angry about the loss of their hunting grounds, the Indians began to fight back. They attacked wagon trains and homesteads.

In 1865 the **Sioux** (SOO) attacked wagon trains on the Bozeman Trail. This trail led from the Platte Valley Overland Trail to Montana. It also cut through some of the best Sioux hunting grounds. For three years the Sioux, led by **Chief Red Cloud,** fought army troops. The Sioux even forced the army to abandon forts along the trail.

Then, in 1868, Red Cloud signed a peace treaty. The treaty recognized the right of the Sioux to the **Black Hills** of **South Dakota.** The Sioux triumph was short-lived. In 1874 General **George Custer,** ignoring the treaty, led government troops into the Black Hills. Custer was looking for gold, and he found it. With the discovery of gold, the government could not keep miners out of the Black Hills. It was easier to force the Sioux to leave.

In the 1870s the Sioux fought to hold their land in the Black Hills. This picture shows George Custer demanding that the Sioux settle on a reservation.

Crazy Horse was now, in 1876, leader of the Sioux. Groups of Sioux and Cheyennes were camped together on the **Little Bighorn River** in Montana. Custer, at the head of a scouting party, learned about the encampment. He attacked and found his party surrounded by at least 2,500 Indians. In the battle that followed, Custer and all his men were killed. The **Battle of the Little Bighorn** was the last Sioux victory. The army hounded the Sioux until hunger forced the Sioux to give up. Crazy Horse surrendered in 1877. He was killed while in prison.

The Nez Perce and Apaches

The **Nez Perce** (NES PUHRS) lived on the Columbia Plateau in Oregon. They had lived in peace with white people since the coming of Lewis and Clark. Their valley was beautiful. Then settlers began to stream onto their land by the wagonload. The Nez Perce were told to leave.

Some of the young men wanted to fight, but **Joseph,** their chief, said no. He said that there were not enough warriors—only 100. "We were like deer," he said later. The white settlers "were like grizzly bears." Joseph's hopes to lead his people away peacefully were ruined. A settler killed one of Chief Joseph's people. The son of the murdered man in turn led an attack, killing some settlers. The army came in pursuit.

During the summer of 1877 Chief Joseph led his people away. They traveled over 1,700 miles (about 2,735 km) through the states of Idaho, Montana, and Wyoming. Time after time the Nez Perce defeated army troops. Deciding they would never be left in peace, the Nez Perce headed for Canada. Forty miles (64.4 km) south of the border, they were stopped by soldiers. Chief Joseph was forced to surrender. These words he spoke:

> I am tired of fighting. Our chiefs are killed. . . . The old men are killed. It is the young men who say yes or no. He who led the young men is dead. It is cold and we have no blankets. Our little children are freezing to death. I want time to look for my children and see how many of them I may find. Maybe I shall find them among the dead. Hear me, my chiefs, I am tired. My heart is sick and sad. From where the sun now stands, I will fight no more forever.

Chief Joseph and his people failed to find the peace they longed for.

For his bravery, the people of Bismarck, North Dakota, honored Chief Joseph with a dinner. Many Americans, particularly Easterners, began to demand that Congress provide better treatment for the Indians.

Between 1869 and 1874 there were more than 200 major battles. In the end, starvation made the difference. It became government policy to kill as many buffalo as possible. This was to destroy the Indian way of life. Starved and defeated, most Indians had no choice but to move onto government reservations.

In the Southwest a small band of **Apaches** (uh•PACH•ees) held out longer than other Indian groups. These Apaches, led by **Geronimo,** rebelled against conditions on the hot, dry San Carlos Reservation. There it was hard to grow or find food. Government food given to the reservation was often wormy. Geronimo and his followers fled to the **Sierra Madre** of Mexico. From bases in these mountains they made attacks on Arizona settlers. For ten years they escaped capture by United States soldiers. At last, an Apache scout working for the soldiers led them to Geronimo's hiding place. In 1886 Geronimo was forced to surrender.

Reading Check

1. Why did the Indians feel they had to fight?
2. Why did General George Custer break the treaty with the Sioux Indians?
3. Who led the Nez Perce on their long march?

Think Beyond How would you describe the government's policy toward American Indians in the 1800s?

IN FOCUS

HORSES

Christopher Columbus carried some very important passengers during his second voyage to the New World. These passengers would forever change the landscape of North, South, and Central America. Who were Columbus's special passengers? Horses!

About 10,000 years ago, horses roamed all over the Western Hemisphere.

These horses, however, mysteriously disappeared. Thus, when Columbus brought his horses to the Caribbean island of Hispaniola in 1494, it was like a homecoming.

Over the next few years, Spaniards brought more horses to America. By 1500, the Spanish were bringing their horses to Cuba and Central America. Finally, in 1519, horses arrived in North America when explorer Hernando Cortés brought 16 horses to Mexico from Cuba.

Cortés later wrote that the horses were "worth their weight in gold" in conquering Mexico's Indians, because the Indians were awestruck by the giant, trained beasts. Soon, however, the Indians obtained lost, traded, or stolen horses.

Horses changed the Indians' lives forever. The Indians began hunting on horseback, greatly increasing their food supply. They started using horses as draft animals for farming and traveling, saving countless hours.

Horses also changed the American landscape. Lost horses gathered on the North American plains and formed wild herds. Today, descendants of the wild herds still roam America's western plains. The horses are a legacy of Christopher Columbus and a memorial to the Spaniards' and Indians' love of horses.

Think Beyond Why do you think Columbus first brought horses to the Americas?

Modern-day wild horses

485

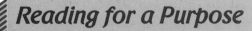
Look for these important words:

Key Words	People	Places
• reforms	• John Muir	• Yellowstone
• Populist	• Gifford Pinchot	• Yosemite
	• Thomas Edison	• Sequoia
	• Guglielmo Marconi	

Look for answers to these questions:
1. Why did Americans become interested in protecting some of America's wilderness?
2. What kinds of changes did farmers ask for?
3. How did women's lives change?
4. What sports did people enjoy in the 1890s?

3 Changes in American Life

The 1890 census reported there was no longer a frontier. The United States was now settled. New states had been organized. These included Colorado, Wyoming, Montana, Idaho, Washington, North Dakota, and South Dakota. Oklahoma had been set aside for American Indians, but it was opened to settlement in 1886. Utah would become a state in 1898, Oklahoma in 1907, Arizona and New Mexico in 1912.

As long as there was a frontier, there was always a place to go. The frontier had been a place for people in trouble, people looking for opportunity, people starting a new life. These kinds of people had often gone to the frontier during the settlement of the continent.

With the frontier gone, Americans began to see their country in a new way. They wanted to protect some of the wild beauty of America. One such place was **Yellowstone.** This part of Wyoming had been visited in 1807 by the Lewis and Clark expedition. Shortly afterward fur trappers and traders began to visit Yellowstone. They told stories of boiling mud pots and steaming geysers, but few believed them. Then in 1870 General Henry Washburn, a government surveyor, led an expedition to Yellowstone. The trappers' stories, he learned, were true. Soon afterward, in 1872, Yellowstone became our first national park.

In California the naturalist **John Muir** wrote about the beauty of **Yosemite** (yoh•SEM•uh•tee) and **Sequoia** (si•KWOI•uh). These places too became national parks in 1890. As with Yellowstone, they were to be preserved for the enjoyment of future generations.

For most of their history, Americans had acted as if the forests would always be there. People had cut trees freely wherever they grew. As early as the 1870s some people began to warn of the danger of using up the forests.

Four-fifths of the nation's forests had already been chopped down. In 1891 Congress responded to the concern by creating national forests. The forests would be managed by foresters. As trees were cut for lumber, new trees would be planted.

Gifford Pinchot (PIHN•shoh) became the nation's chief forester. He had studied how Europeans had used and maintained their forests for hundreds of years. He favored the planned conservation of America's forests, too. Pinchot was the first person to use the word *conservation*.

Here a cedar with a 17-foot diameter dwarfs the lumberjacks about to fell it. Concerned that America's trees would all be used up, Congress established in 1891 a system of national forests.

Reforms from the West

The railroads had opened up the West, but farmers came to hate them. Railroads charged as much as they could, and farmers had to pay. There was no other way to get their crops and livestock to market. In California the Central Pacific was called "the octopus." When farmers complained, neither Congress nor state legislatures listened.

People began to organize to bring about **reforms,** or changes. They wanted to get rid of the wrongs. This movement was called the **Populist,** or People's, movement. Most Populists were farmers who wanted more control over the large corporations. For instance, they wanted railroad rates controlled so that they were fair.

The Populists also wanted government to do more for the farmers. They demanded free mail delivery to rural areas and a parcel post service. The Populists were the first to demand direct election of senators and the secret ballot. They also wanted ways to remove officials who acted improperly. In time many of their demands became laws.

Changes in Women's Lives

One result of the Industrial Revolution was that women had machines to help with housework. Sewing machines reduced the time needed to make clothes. Washing machines reduced the toil of washday. Women no longer had to spend hours growing or storing food. Grocery stores offered canned food and fresh fruits and vegetables. These fresh fruits and vegetables were brought by railroad from California and Florida.

You may not know it, but riding your bicycle connects you with many parts of the world. In 1790 the bicycle was invented in France. This first bicycle was a two-wheeler made of wood. It had no pedals or handlebars but was propelled in much the same way as a skateboard. In Germany in 1816 this idea was improved upon when an inventor added a steering bar to the front wheel.

However, there was still no good way to make the vehicle move. That was taken care of in 1839 when a Scottish inventor added a foot pedal to the front wheel.

Finally, in 1897, the idea traveled to England and at last became commercially successful. The bicycle of 1897 looked very much like the one you ride today.

Ice was now available year round. The iceman delivering ice was a common sight all over America. The icebox made it easier to keep milk and meat cool. The availability of ice helped make ice cream a favorite American treat.

At the end of the nineteenth century, growing numbers of women went to college. Many of these educated women became teachers. Others, like Jane Addams, worked for reform and change.

Still other women entered industry and business. In business offices women at typewriters replaced male clerks. In the growing number of department stores, women were used to run the new cash registers. Women by the thousands began to operate the switchboards of the expanding telephone industry.

Sports

As people spent more of their time working indoors, outdoor sports became popular. One of the most popular pastimes was playing baseball on city streets or vacant lots. Baseball had developed from a children's game. The Knickerbocker Baseball Club of New York was organized in 1845. It wrote down the rules of the game. During the Civil War, New Yorkers taught baseball to other Union soldiers. The game soon grew in popularity.

The invention of the bicycle gave city dwellers a new freedom. Bicycling to the country on holidays became a favorite pastime.

Sports that first became popular in the 1890s were golf and tennis. Basketball was invented in 1891 as a winter sport that could be played in gymnasiums.

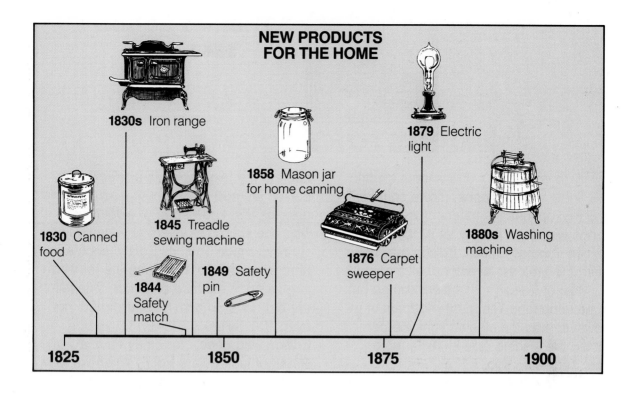

NEW PRODUCTS FOR THE HOME

1830s Iron range

1830 Canned food

1845 Treadle sewing machine

1844 Safety match

1849 Safety pin

1858 Mason jar for home canning

1876 Carpet sweeper

1879 Electric light

1880s Washing machine

1825   1850   1875   1900

New Inventions

New inventions of the 1890s were about to cause even greater changes in American life. The kind of gasoline engine used today had been invented in 1876 by a German engineer. Soon people were putting the engines on horse carriages. In 1895 the first important race between "horseless carriages" was held. It took place on a road between Chicago and Evanston, Illinois. It took these first automobiles almost eight hours to go 54 miles (86.9 km). By 1898, however, there were 50 automobile manufacturers in the United States.

The invention of the telephone by Alexander Graham Bell in 1876 had started a revolution in communications. **Thomas Edison** carried this revolution even further with his invention in 1877 of the phonograph. Edison's first phonograph looked very different from today's stereo systems, but it worked. In the first recording, Edison recited "Mary had a little lamb."

In September 1899 **Guglielmo Marconi** (goo•LYEL•moh mahr•KOH•nee) tried out a new invention to report from sea on a sailing race. Marconi was an Italian inventor. His reports of the race from sea were the first use of radio in America.

The gasoline engine, the automobile, and the radio all were important inventions. They would bring as many changes as the steam engine, the railroad, and the telegraph had.

 Reading Check

1. Why were national parks created?
2. Name three Populist demands.
3. Why did sports become popular?

Think Beyond Why do we need to preserve things in nature?

People MAKE HISTORY

Thomas Edison
1847–1931

▶▶▶▶▶▶▶▶▶▶▶▶▶▶▶▶▶▶

Try to imagine a world without electric lights, phonographs, movie cameras, and microphones. All these marvelous things were invented by an American named Thomas Edison. Edison may have been the greatest inventor of all time.

Most of Edison's inventions turned out to be important. The most important of all, however, was the electric light. He perfected the electric light in 1879, more than 100 years ago.

Inventors had known since 1808 that electricity could provide light. Many people had tried to make a small, practical electric light, but all had failed. After many embarrassing failures and more than a few explosions, Edison finally perfected his electric lamp. The first public demonstration of the miracle invention was given on New Year's Eve, 1879. Three thousand people flocked to Edison's New Jersey laboratory. Edison flipped a switch, and dozens of lamps lit up the darkness. A reporter called the light bulb "a little globe of sunshine." Edison formed a company to sell his invention and quickly became one of the richest people in America.

Edison started young as an inventor. At the age of 10, he set up a laboratory in the basement of his family's home. To get money to buy supplies for his experiments, he sold newspapers on a train. At the age of 12, he set up a laboratory in the train's baggage car. Working on the railroad, young Edison learned how to operate the telegraph. As a telegrapher, Edison learned much about electricity. He drew on that knowledge of electricity when he started to invent an electric light.

What made Thomas Edison such a superb inventor? For one thing, he refused to give up in the face of failure. One failure did not stop him. Neither did 20, nor even 100, failures. "I'll never give up," Edison said once, "for I may have a streak of luck before I die." When we turn on lights, see a movie, or play a record, we can be glad Edison just kept trying.

Think Beyond How do you think someone like Edison goes about inventing something?

Edison with the "Ediphone"—a dictating machine

Thinking Back

- The Pony Express was a mail service that carried letters quickly between Missouri and California.

- A transcontinental railroad opened up the Plains to farmers and cattle ranchers.

- Railroads allowed ranchers to get their cattle to cities, where they received higher prices.

- To encourage settlement of the Plains, Congress passed the Homestead Act. Three inventions that made the settlement of the Plains possible were the steel plow, the windmill, and barbed wire.

- Settlement of the Plains ended the Indians' traditional way of life. Chief Red Cloud, Crazy Horse, Chief Joseph, and Geronimo were important Indian leaders in the West.

- National Parks were established to protect some of the wilderness areas of America.

- People began to organize to bring about reforms. The Populist movement wanted more government control over large corporations, more services for farmers, and political reform.

- Machines to help with housework gave women more time for other things—some went to college, and others entered industry and business.

- Outdoor sports became more popular. Inventions of the 1890s were the automobile with a gasoline engine, the phonograph, and the radio.

Check for Understanding

Using Words

Write the meaning of each word below. Then use each word in a complete sentence.

1. **homesteaders**
2. **reforms**
3. **stampede**
4. **stockyards**
5. **transcontinental railroad**

Reviewing Facts

1. How did the transcontinental railroad change the West?
2. How did the railroad both create and destroy the cowboy's way of life?
3. What were some of the problems homesteaders faced?
4. How did the invention of the steel plow, the windmill, and barbed wire help people live on the Great Plains?
5. Why did the Plains Indians attack wagon trains and settlers' homes?
6. Compare and contrast the experiences of the Sioux led by Chief Crazy Horse with those of the Nez Perce led by Chief Joseph.
7. What finally forced the Indians to move onto reservations?
8. Why did Americans become interested in conservation in the 1890s?
9. How did new inventions change women's lives?

10. What inventions of the late nineteenth century would cause major changes in the twentieth century?

Thinking Critically

1. How did the Indians, cowboys, and homesteaders differ from one another in their use of the resources of the Great Plains? How would each feel about the buffalo, the railroad, and the steel plow? Which way of life on the Great Plains would you choose if you could? Why?
2. The 1890 census reported that there was no longer an American frontier. Do you agree? Are there any frontiers today?
3. The railroad in the West could be viewed as both good and bad. Why?
4. Imagine city life in the 1890s. What things might you use in the house? What recreation would be important?

Writing About It

Imagine that it is 1862 and your job is to write advertisements for the railroad. Write an advertisement that would persuade people to come and live on the Plains. Describe how the Plains look and the advantages of living there.

Practicing Geography Skills

Transportation and Resource Maps

Use the two maps on page 480 and 481 to answer the following questions.

1. In 1870 how would a traveler get from Santa Fe to Los Angeles?
2. If you were building a meat processing plant in Colorado, near what city would you locate it?
3. A traveler from Omaha, Nebraska, wants to go into the Montana territory. What method of transportation would he or she use to begin this trip?
4. If you wanted to work on a sheep ranch in Colorado, would you go to eastern or western Colorado?

On Your Own

Social Studies at Home

1. Draw a picture of what you think a settlement on the Plains looked like. Be sure to include the three important inventions that made life there possible. When you are finished, show your picture to your family and explain why these inventions were so important.
2. Write a short story that describes how a person from the nineteenth century might feel if he or she could visit your home for a few days. In your story, include the person's reactions to at least three modern conveniences that he or she had never dreamed of. Share your story with your family and classmates.

Read More About It

Justin and the Best Biscuits in the World by Mildred Pitts Walter. Lothrop, Lee & Shepard. In a chat with his grandfather, Justin learns how both women and blacks contributed to settling the Great Plains.

The Pony Express by Samuel Hopkins Adams. Illustrated by Lee J. Ames. Random House. This story details one of the greatest adventures in American history.

My Prairie Year: Based on the Diary of Eleanor Plaised by Brett Harvey. Holiday. This diary relates details from a nine-year-old girl's first months of homesteading on the prairie.

HOW BUSINESS WORKS

FRESH CUT
FLOWERS
ROSES **BOUQUETS** CARNATIONS

▲
Small businesses as well as large businesses are an important part of our economy.

Did you ever think about how many things you use in a single day? Where do all these things come from? Many of the things we use are made by people who work in factories. Most of these things they make are sold in shops and stores. Factories

and offices, shops and stores are all part of business. Business provides people with all the things they want or need.

In the United States, businesses can offer for sale many kinds of goods and services. This freedom is called **free enterprise.** In a free enterprise system, people can buy almost anything they might need or want.

In our free enterprise system, the government does not tell businesses what to produce or how much to produce. Instead, people decide what will be produced through the choices they make and the prices they are willing to pay for the goods and services they want and need. These wants and needs are called **demand.** The goods and services offered by businesses are called **supply.** The supply of a good or service generally rises when demand is great. This means businesses will produce more of a product if they believe **consumers,** or buyers, are willing to buy more. If the demand for a product falls, however, businesses will produce less of that product.

Both supply and demand are affected by price. Businesses will not provide goods or services to meet consumers' demands unless businesses can make a profit. Consumers, however, will not buy a product they demand if the price is too high. For example, if you could buy a CD player for $1.00, you would probably rush to buy one. However, a business could not make a profit selling the CD player for that price. Therefore, the business would not be willing to produce the CD player.

On the other hand, if the CD player sold for $10,000, businesses might be eager to sell large numbers for great profit. Consumers, though, would not be willing to purchase the

These shoppers decide how successful a product is by the choices they make.

CD player at such a high price. Without sales, the businesses would make no profit. The price at which businesses can make a profit and at which consumers will buy a product is called the **fair market price.** The fair market price is also called the **market clearing price.** This is the price that satisfies both consumers and businesses.

Today there are millions of businesses in our country meeting consumers' demands for goods and services. Many small businesses are owned by one person. Very large businesses are usually owned by many people. These large businesses, called **corporations,** are owned by **stockholders.** Stockholders are people who have invested money in the company. The stockholders share whatever profit the corporation makes.

How does a business work? To answer this question, let's meet some businesspeople. They are in the business of making and selling something you might use every day— bicycles.

◀ Edna Jones's bicycle shop features a variety of bicycles for her customers to choose from.

A Bicycle Shop

Edna Jones owns a small bicycle shop called Wheels and Deals. Her shop is filled with many different kinds of bicycles, everything from tricycles to ten-speeds. "I'm very proud of my business," she says. "I have one of the most successful bike shops in the city."

Edna Jones explains that her shop did not always have so many bicycles on display. "To start my shop, I needed money," she says. "I needed money to buy a cash register and to get my shop ready for business. I also needed money to buy my first shipment of bicycles from the factory." The money used to start a business and all the equipment needed to run a business are called **capital.**

"At first I had only a few bicycles. Now I have more than 100," she says quite proudly.

How does Edna Jones run her business?

"First of all, it costs money to run a shop like this. I have three people who work for me, and I pay them wages. I pay money each month to rent this building. Even the electricity for the lights and heat costs money."

The amount of money it takes to run a business is called **overhead.** Overhead can be costly.

If it costs so much to run a shop, how does Edna Jones make money?

"I sell bicycles for more than they cost to buy from the factory," Edna Jones explains. "That means that I make some money on each bicycle I sell. With that money I pay my overhead. If business is good, there is a profit left over after I have paid my overhead."

Edna Jones shows an advertisement for her bicycle shop that appeared in the local newspaper. "I use advertisements like this to bring in new customers," she explains. "You see, there are other bicycle shops in the city. We are all trying to offer the best price or the best service. That way we will find new customers." Trying to get new customers is called **competition.** One shop competes with another for business.

Just then a customer comes into the shop. He has come because he saw the advertisement in the newspaper.

"You see, my advertisement is working!" Edna Jones says happily. "And now, please excuse me. In a business like mine, the customer is always the most important person."

◀ **A customer responds to an advertisement.**

A Bicycle Manufacturer

We have seen how bicycles are sold. Now let's look at one business that makes bicycles, the Putnam Bicycle Company. Walter Putnam started the company, but he only owns part of it. The company is a corporation. Mr. Putnam is president of the company, but he must make reports to the stockholders.

Mr. Putnam is happy to show people how bicycles are produced. "More than 100 people work in my company," Walter Putnam says. The people who work in a business are called **employees.** The work they do is called **labor.** "In a company like mine, labor is very important," Mr. Putnam says. "I try to make sure my employees are happy and safe at work."

Walter Putnam points out some of the machines. One large machine shapes the metal bicycle frames. Another machine makes the metal handlebars. Some employees tighten the spokes of the bicycle wheels.

All businesses use **land.** In business, land includes the economic resources that are used to make products. "To make a bicycle," Mr. Putnam says, "we use several different kinds of metals, including aluminum and steel. We use rubber for the brakes and for the tires. To make the bicycle seats, we use plastic or leather. The costs of economic resources run into millions of dollars."

"We are always trying to improve our bikes," he explains. "We sell our product to bicycle shops. They are our customers, just as you might be a customer in a bicycle shop. We want to sell as many bikes as we can. To do that, we try to make the kinds of bicycles our customers will want.

The more customers we have, the more profit we will make." The company's profit may be invested in new machinery or divided among the stockholders.

The job of finding and keeping customers is called **marketing.** "To market a bicycle, you have to talk to the owners of bicycle shops. Then you

People make bicycle parts in a ▶ factory.

A factory employee checks that each bicycle is put together correctly.
▼

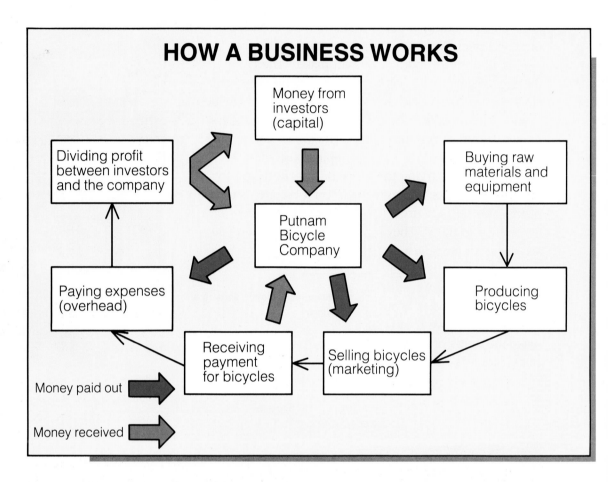

HOW A BUSINESS WORKS

Money from investors (capital)

Dividing profit between investors and the company

Buying raw materials and equipment

Putnam Bicycle Company

Paying expenses (overhead)

Producing bicycles

Receiving payment for bicycles

Selling bicycles (marketing)

Money paid out

Money received

have to make sure that your customers are happy. That's what running a business is all about," Mr. Putnam says.

A bicycle might seem like a simple thing at first. However, producing and selling a bicycle requires capital, land, and labor. It takes people in many different businesses. Edna Jones, Walter Putnam, and their employees are only some of the people. The workers in a steel mill must produce the steel for the bicycle frames. Workers in a rubber company make the rubber for the bicycle tires. A trucking company delivers these resources to Walter Putnam's factory and then delivers the bicycles to stores.

Can you see why business is one of the most important activities in our country? Just think about the number of businesses involved in making one thing, a bicycle! Then remember how many different things you use in a single day. Each one is made by people who are in business.

Unit Review

Words to Remember

Number your paper from 1 to 10. Use the words below to replace the underlined words in the sentences that follow.

federation
homesteaders
invested
prejudice
ratify

reaper
Reconstruction
segregation
sharecroppers
stampede

1. A plan for the <u>rebuilding</u> of the South provided help for freed slaves, for repairing war damage, and for restoring state governments.

2. Most freed blacks could not own land, so they became <u>farmers on rented land.</u>

3. Cyrus McCormick invented a <u>harvester</u> that made it possible to harvest much more grain than was possible by hand.

4. Andrew Carnegie <u>used some of his money to buy shares</u> in companies that were growing.

5. Samuel Gompers organized unions of skilled workers into a <u>single organization representing them all.</u>

6. By 1900 <u>separation</u> of the races was common throughout the South.

7. Chinese and Japanese immigrants faced problems caused by <u>people's negative judgments based on race.</u>

8. Many settlers on the Great Plains were <u>people who were given 160 acres (64.8 ha) of land by the government.</u>

9. When Southern states refused to <u>approve</u> the Fourteenth Amendment, Congress ordered military rule.

10. A danger faced by cowboys on the cattle drives was that the cattle might <u>rush off wildly.</u>

Focus on Main Ideas

1. How did the Freedmen's Bureau and Reconstruction legislatures try to rebuild the South?

2. As businesses grew larger, what reforms did Jane Addams, Samuel Gompers, and Western farmers work for?

3. How did inventions change transportation and communication in the nineteenth century? What are examples in which one invention led to another?

4. Compare and contrast the treatment of the blacks, the Indians, and the Chinese during the late nineteenth century.

5. How did the Industrial Revolution change the way work was done? How are people's lives continuing to change?

Think/Write

As settlers pushed west, Indians were often forced to leave their homes and hunting grounds. Imagine that you are one of these Indians. Write a paragraph describing how you feel about being forced to leave your home and familiar surroundings.

499

Activities

1. **Art** Draw a picture of the Great Plains as they might have been before the railroad. Draw another picture showing how it changed after the railroad.

2. **Research/Oral Report** With a partner, research the Battle of the Little Bighorn. Prepare a class presentation. One partner should describe the battle from the point of view of General Custer. The other should describe the battle from the point of view of Chief Crazy Horse.

3. **Timeline** Make a timeline of important inventions. Use 1830 as the first date and 1900 as the last date.

4. **Field Trip/Report** With your teacher or a family member, visit a business in your community. Find out what kinds of goods the business sells. Who are the customers of this business? Does the business advertise? Make an oral or written report on what you learn.

5. **Research/Writing** Find out more about a person, an invention, or a problem discussed in this unit. Write a report about what you learn.

Skills Review

Transportation and Resource Maps

Look at the map at the bottom of the page to answer these questions.

1. If you were driving cattle north through Oklahoma to Kansas, what river would you have to cross?

2. If you wanted to look for oil, would it be wiser to look in the eastern part or the western part of Kansas?

3. If you wanted to raise pigs, which eat a lot of corn, would Garden City or Topeka be a better place to settle?

4. What towns likely had stockyards near the railroad station? Explain.

5. What products could be found in western Kansas in 1880?

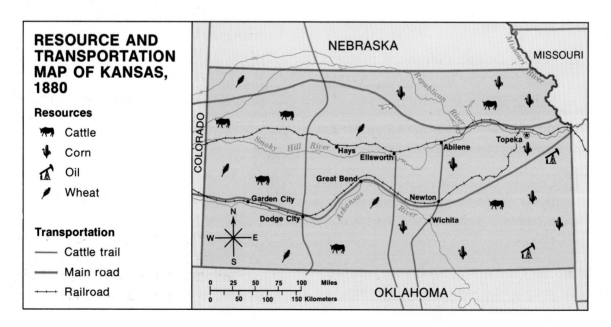

RESOURCE AND TRANSPORTATION MAP OF KANSAS, 1880

Resources
- Cattle
- Corn
- Oil
- Wheat

Transportation
- Cattle trail
- Main road
- Railroad

EXPLORING
YOUR STATE'S HISTORY

Before the Civil War the United States was mainly a land of small towns and farmland. In the years between 1860 and 1900, our nation changed a great deal. Across America great factories sprang up. Little towns sprouted into large cities. Railroads reached out across the land. Great inventions changed the way of life for all Americans.

Each state faced a different challenge during this period. The Eastern states tried to handle the problems of rapid industrial growth. The Southern states tried to recover from the Civil War. On the Great Plains, farmers worked to tame the endless stretches of rolling grassland. In the West people were discovering and developing new resources. The following activities will help you learn about your state as it entered the modern industrial age.

Learning About Geography

1. By the year 1900 most states had one or more large cities. What is the largest city in your state? In what year was this city founded? If you can, find out its population in 1860 and in 1900. How many people live there today?

2. In many states the largest city is also the state capital. In other states, however, the capital is not the largest city. Write a short report on your state's capital city. How did it get its name? How far is it from your hometown? Why was it chosen as the capital?

3. Make a resource and transportation map of your state. Draw the major railroads, highways, and airports. Draw the major rivers. Use picture symbols to show the important mineral, manufacturing, and agricultural resources.

Learning About Economics

4. With the Industrial Revolution, mineral resources such as iron, coal, oil, and copper became very important. Make a table of your state's mineral resources. Tell where they are found. Give examples of manufactured products that use these minerals.

MINERAL RESOURCES IN OUR STATE				
Coal	Oil and Gas	Iron	Gold and Silver	Copper

5. What are the major industries in your state today? Why is your state a good location for these industries?

Learning About Technology

6. Draw a scene in your town as it might have been in 1850. Show the same scene as it might have been in 1900. The two pictures should show some changes that result from progress in technology.

UNIT 9

The Twentieth Century

• **1901**
Theodore Roosevelt
becomes President

• **1903**
First successful
air flight

• **1917**
The United States
enters World War I

• **1920**
Women get the right
to vote

• **1930s**
The Great Depression

502

*T*hroughout their country's history Americans have challenged themselves to explore new horizons, to acquire more knowledge, and to develop the skills needed to meet the future. As in the past, new frontiers are still being explored.

The Wright brothers' flight at Kitty Hawk marked the beginning of a new era. The dream of soaring through the air was achieved. Within 70 years that dream was transformed into a landing on the moon. In this unit you will read about that landing and other major events of the twentieth century.

Think Beyond How do you think space travel has affected the way Americans live?

• **December 7, 1941**	• **1941–1945**	• **1945**	• **1963–1973**	• **July 20, 1969**	• **1988**
Japan bombs Pearl Harbor	World War II	United Nations organized	Vietnam War	Astronauts land on the moon	George Bush elected President

CHAPTER 19

Our Century Begins

" The old pioneer days are gone, with their roughness and their hardship, their incredible toil and their wild half-savage romance. But the need for the pioneer virtues remains the same as ever. The peculiar frontier conditions have vanished; but the manliness and stalwart hardihood of the frontiersmen can be given freer scope under the conditions surrounding the complex industrialism of the present day. "

—President Theodore Roosevelt, 1903

Look for these important words:

Key Words
- Spanish-American War
- Rough Riders
- Battle of San Juan Hill
- armistice
- Polynesians

People
- Theodore Roosevelt
- King Kamehameha I
- Queen Liliuokalani

Places
- Cuba

- Philippine Islands
- Manila Bay
- Guam
- Puerto Rico
- Far East
- Klondike

Look for answers to these questions:
1. Why did the United States go to war with Spain?
2. What territories did the United States acquire from Spain?
3. How did the United States acquire Hawaii? Alaska?

1 Becoming a World Power

By 1900 American settlement and influence extended far beyond America's shores. One reason for this was the **Spanish-American War.**

The Spanish-American War was fought in part because Americans took the side of **Cuba** against Spain.

Cuba was Spain's largest colony in the Western Hemisphere at the time. In 1898 Cubans rebelled against Spain. American newspapers were full of stories about the harsh Spanish rule in nearby Cuba. After Americans read such stories, they wanted to help the Cubans win independence.

Spain was close to granting Cuba independence. Then, in February 1898, an American battleship, the *Maine,* exploded in the harbor at Havana. More than 200 sailors were killed. It was not clear why the ship blew up. The United States, however, blamed Spain and declared war.

"Remember the *Maine*" became a very popular slogan. Americans saw themselves as defenders of Cuba against Old World tyranny. Soon after war was declared, the American navy steamed to the **Philippine Islands.** There the navy destroyed the Spanish fleet and captured **Manila Bay.** George Dewey was the American naval commander. Overnight he became a hero.

In the United States thousands joined up to fight in the war. One of these was **Theodore Roosevelt.** Roosevelt collected a fighting company made up mostly of Western cowboys and sheriffs. They called themselves the **Rough Riders.** Roosevelt hoped to find both action and glory in the war.

At the **Battle of San Juan Hill** in Cuba, Roosevelt found the action and glory he was seeking. The Spanish commanded the top of a hill that lay

505

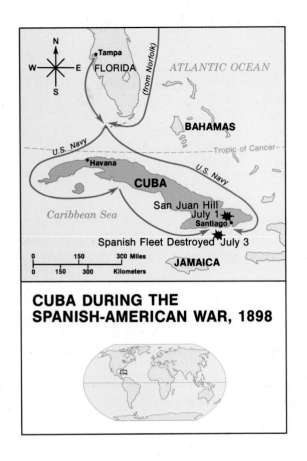

CUBA DURING THE SPANISH-AMERICAN WAR, 1898

between the Americans and the city of Santiago. With bullets ripping the grass around him, Roosevelt yelled "Charge!" and started up the hill. But only five men followed. Mad as could be, Roosevelt retreated. The Rough Riders, it turned out, had not heard his battle cry. Up the hill Roosevelt charged again. This time the Rough Riders followed. Regiments of professional soldiers also charged. After heavy fighting, Santiago at last surrendered.

The Spanish-American War lasted less than four months. In August 1898, Spain signed an **armistice.** An armistice is an agreement to stop fighting.

A peace treaty followed the armistice. The treaty gave the United States control of Cuba, **Guam, Puerto Rico,** and the Philippine Islands. By giving up Cuba and Puerto Rico, Spain gave up the last of its territory in the Western Hemisphere.

This is an artist's idea of Teddy Roosevelt's charge into a rain of Spanish bullets at the Battle of San Juan Hill. In truth, Roosevelt made the charge on foot.

The United States was now a world power. Control of the Philippines meant that Americans became important in the **Far East,** or eastern and southeastern Asia. In the Caribbean, the United States was now the most powerful nation. Europeans showed new respect for the United States.

The United States gave Cuba its independence in 1902. In 1946 the Philippines became an independent country. Puerto Rico and Guam remained territories of the United States.

The Hawaiian Islands

The Hawaiian Islands also came under American control in 1898. These islands are 2,400 miles (3,862 km) west of our Pacific coast. The original inhabitants of Hawaii were **Polynesians** (pahl•uh•NEE•zhuhnz). In the eighth century they had migrated from other Pacific islands to the Hawaiian Islands. Expert navigators, they sailed in ships able to carry as many as 100 people. They carried with them banana and coconut trees.

The Hawaiian Islands were explored in 1778 by Captain James Cook from England. Whaling and trading ships started making regular stops. American missionaries arrived about 1820. Soon after, cattle ranches and sugar plantations were started.

Other people came to live and work in the islands. They included Mexicans, Asians, Filipinos, Portuguese, and Americans.

The Hawaiian Islands had been united under **King Kamehameha I** (kuh•may•uh•MAY•hah) in the early nineteenth century. The sugar planters and missionaries gained much

Queen Liliuokalani failed in her effort to restore royal authority in Hawaii.

influence in the government. In 1893 the Hawaiian ruler, **Queen Liliuokalani** (li•lee•uh•woh•kuh•LAHN•ee), tried to change things. She wanted to restore the ruler's traditional power.

The sugar planters did not want Queen Liliuokalani to regain power. The planters took over the government and set up a republic. They asked to be part of the United States.

Alaska

In 1867 the United States had bought Alaska from Russia. Most native Alaskans were Aleuts and Eskimos. Their way of life depended on hunting and fishing. Many Americans thought the purchase extremely foolish. Why should the United States buy a piece of land so far north? "Polar Bear Garden," some called it.

507

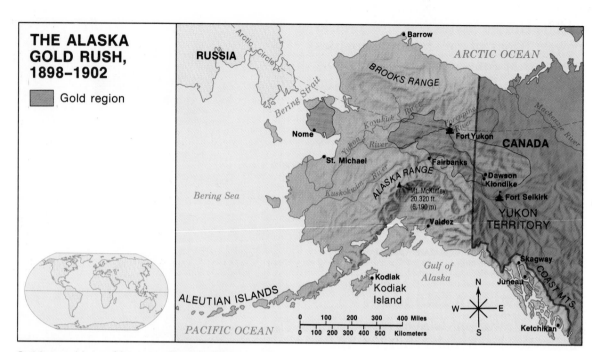

THE ALASKA GOLD RUSH, 1898–1902

Gold region

RUSSIA

ARCTIC OCEAN

Arctic Circle

Barrow

BROOKS RANGE

Bering Strait

Koyukuk River

Porcupine River

Fort Yukon

CANADA

Nome

Yukon River

St. Michael

Fairbanks

Dawson Klondike

Bering Sea

Kuskokwim River

ALASKA RANGE

Mt. McKinley 20,320 ft. (6,190 m)

Fort Selkirk

YUKON TERRITORY

Valdez

Gulf of Alaska

Skagway

ALEUTIAN ISLANDS

Kodiak
Kodiak Island

N
W   E
S

Juneau

COAST MTS.

PACIFIC OCEAN

0   100   200   300   400 Miles
0   100 200 300 400 500   Kilometers

Ketchikan

Gold—and lots of it—was the message of the Klondike News in 1898.

Alaska was almost forgotten. Then, in 1896, gold was discovered in the **Klondike** region. The Klondike was in Yukon Territory, near the Canadian-Alaskan border. The discovery of gold opened up Alaska for settlement. About 100,000 people left by boat from Seattle to head into this newfound land of riches. It was a harsh frontier. Thousands died from sickness, starvation, and the extreme cold of winter.

The Alaska purchase turned out to be a very good bargain. The land is full of valuable mineral resources, including silver, copper, lead, and petroleum.

Reading Check

1. Why did America side with Cuba?
2. How did the Hawaiian Islands become part of the United States?
3. What caused people to become interested in settling Alaska?

Think Beyond What advantages did gaining Alaska and Hawaii give the United States?

Look for these important words:

Key Words
- isthmus
- Progressives
- regulate
- tuberculosis

Places
- Panama Canal
- Colombia

Look for answers to these questions:
1. What were some of Theodore Roosevelt's qualities?
2. Why did Roosevelt urge the building of the Panama Canal?
3. What kinds of reforms did Roosevelt work for?

2 Theodore Roosevelt and His Time

Theodore Roosevelt returned from Cuba a well-known and popular man. He was immediately elected governor of New York. Two years later Roosevelt was chosen to be President William McKinley's Vice President.

Roosevelt had been rather skinny and sickly as a child. When he found he could not defend himself against some bullies, he took boxing lessons. For the rest of his life, Roosevelt was a man of action. He loved outdoor activity—hiking, riding, hunting.

On September 6, 1901, President McKinley was shot in Buffalo, New York. Eight days later McKinley died. Roosevelt was now President.

As President, Theodore Roosevelt was the most popular man in America. Americans liked the athletic, outspoken "Teddy" Roosevelt. They chuckled over stories about his six children romping through the White House. They approved when they heard that the President and his children had pillow fights. On one of his hunting trips, Roosevelt refused to shoot a bear cub. Overnight a new toy came into being—the teddy bear.

This lovable, stuffed toy was Theodore Roosevelt's own teddy bear.

Roosevelt believed that the United States should use its power and influence in the world. He believed that what happened in the rest of the world affected the United States.

When Russia and Japan fought a war in 1904–1905, President Roosevelt offered to help the two nations work out peace terms. For his peace work Roosevelt became the first American to receive the Nobel Peace Prize. First awarded in 1901, the Nobel Peace Prize is given to a person or organization helping to bring peace to the world.

The Panama Canal

The way to get things done, Roosevelt once said, was "to speak softly and carry a big stick." He meant that the nation should try to achieve its aims quietly and properly. If that did not work, however, the nation should be prepared to be forceful. It should be prepared to use a strong navy and army.

Roosevelt used a big stick to get the **Panama Canal.**

For years people had talked about building this canal. It would cut across the **isthmus,** or neck of land, joining South and North America. Such a canal would save ships the hard and lengthy travel time around South America. It would greatly speed up the journey between the Atlantic coast and the Pacific coast. In the 1880s a French company had tried to build such a canal. The jungle and disease had defeated its efforts.

From the White House, Roosevelt urged the building of a canal. The canal could serve both merchant ships and the growing United States Navy.

Congress voted to build the canal. It did so, although the Isthmus of Panama belonged to **Colombia.** The United States offered $10 million to Colombia for the right to build a canal. But Colombia delayed making a decision.

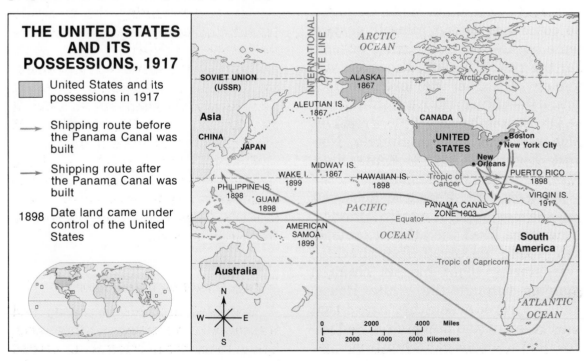

THE UNITED STATES AND ITS POSSESSIONS, 1917

United States and its possessions in 1917

Shipping route before the Panama Canal was built

Shipping route after the Panama Canal was built

1898 Date land came under control of the United States

Railroads hauled away the dirt while the Panama Canal was being built as a link between two oceans.

Roosevelt then made it known that he would welcome a revolution in Panama against Colombia. Roosevelt sent the navy to protect the isthmus. If revolution broke out, the navy was to keep Colombian troops from landing. Within three months such a revolution came about. Roosevelt immediately recognized the new nation of Panama. Panama then gave the United States the right to build the canal. The United States would control a zone on either side of the canal 5 miles (8 km) wide.

Work on the canal began at once. Great earth-moving machines began to tame the jungle. Engineers designed canal locks.

Unlike the Frenchmen, American workers were able to stay healthy. Doctors had learned that mosquitos carried diseases called malaria and yellow fever. Controlling the mosquito helped the Americans succeed where the French had failed.

Building the canal was a tremendous feat. It took ten years. Roosevelt went to visit the canal site in 1908. It was the first time a President had left the United States while in office.

The first ships steamed through the canal on August 15, 1914. Today, the canal continues to be of great importance. It helps world trade as well as American defense.

Progressives and Reform

Roosevelt used his popularity and the power of his office in other ways. One of them was to bring about needed

Glacier National Park in Montana has more than 50 glaciers. It became a national park at the urging of Theodore Roosevelt.

reform at home. Roosevelt and his supporters were called **Progressives.** The Progressives wanted government to **regulate,** or set rules for, business, transportation, and banking.

One business that needed reform was the meat-packing industry, according to a government report. Shredded rope had been found mixed with canned meat. Many of the workers in packing plants had the lung disease **tuberculosis** (too•buhr•kyuh•LOH•suhs). Tuberculosis could spread through the food the sick workers handled. The packing plants were dirty. Roosevelt supported new laws that let the government set standards for purity. Government officials could inspect packing plants to make sure these standards were followed.

New National Parks

When Roosevelt became President, he made conservation popular with Americans. Roosevelt added 194 million acres (78.5 million ha) to the national forests. He successfully pushed for five new national parks. Among them were the Grand Canyon, Mesa Verde, and Glacier national parks.

 Reading Check

1. Why did the United States want to build the Panama Canal?
2. What did Progressives want?
3. Why were reforms needed in the meat-packing business?

Think Beyond How has the Panama Canal affected relations between countries of the Western Hemisphere?

People MAKE HISTORY

William Gorgas
1854–1920

▶▶▶▶▶▶▶▶▶▶▶▶▶▶▶▶

In 1904 the Panama Canal Zone was filthy. Sewage from the many people working on the canal filled the streets, and insects swarmed everywhere. In the area's hospitals, thousands of people lay dying of tropical diseases.

William Gorgas (GAWR•guhs) was a doctor in the United States Army. He was an expert on sanitation methods and on yellow fever. It was his job to clean up the Panama Canal Zone and eliminate yellow fever so that the canal could be built.

Gorgas and his troops first built proper sewage systems and cleaned up the streets. That solved the sanitation problem. Getting rid of yellow fever and malaria, however, would be tougher.

Both diseases were carried by mosquitoes, and mosquitoes were everywhere in Panama. Any standing water—even in rain barrels—served as a breeding ground. Gorgas knew that to get rid of the diseases, he had to get rid of the mosquitoes.

Gorgas ordered his troops to put screens on all the windows of all the buildings. He topped rain barrels with a layer of oil to keep the insects from breeding. He had all buildings sprayed with an insecticide. Thanks to these methods, yellow fever and malaria were wiped out in the Panama Canal Zone within 18 months.

William Gorgas's life seemed to revolve around yellow fever. His mother met his father when she left her hometown to avoid a yellow fever outbreak. Gorgas met his own wife when he treated her for yellow fever. He even contracted the disease himself, but recovered. This made him immune to the fever, so he was able to treat victims without becoming sick.

Gorgas proved that yellow fever could be stopped if mosquitoes were controlled. Today people can be vaccinated against yellow fever, but Gorgas's methods are still used to stop mosquitoes from breeding in tropical areas.

Think Beyond Why is it important both to find ways to prevent diseases and to find cures for them? Explain.

President Roosevelt visits the Panama Canal

Inset: yellow fever mosquito

513

Look for these important words:

Key Words
- glider
- assembly line
- installment buying
- installment
- suburbs
- suffrage
- Nineteenth Amendment

People
- Orville and Wilbur Wright
- Henry Ford
- Lucretia Mott
- Elizabeth Cady Stanton

- Lucy Stone
- Susan B. Anthony
- Abigail Duniway

Places
- Kitty Hawk

Look for answers to these questions:
1. What processes did Orville and Wilbur Wright go through before achieving powered flight?
2. What were some important effects of the automobile?
3. Who were the leaders for women's rights?
4. What does the Nineteenth Amendment say?

3 Steps in Technology and Democracy

The twentieth century has been a time of major achievements in technology. For one, people began to travel through the air in flying machines. **Orville and Wilbur Wright** were the first to achieve the long-held dream of powered flight.

The Wright brothers were bicycle makers in Dayton, Ohio. Like many others of the time, they became fascinated with the possibility of flying. They started out by reading everything already known about flight. They even spent hours studying flying birds.

Then the Wright brothers constructed a **glider,** an aircraft that has no engine. On a windy stretch of beach at **Kitty Hawk,** North Carolina, the Wright brothers experimented with the glider. They developed ways to control and turn the glider in the air. Next they designed a gasoline engine and propellors to power the plane.

Orville and Wilbur Wright took the parts of this new aircraft to Kitty Hawk in September 1903. For the next several months they worked feverishly to get the new aircraft ready for flight. Propellors broke and had to be remade. The brothers raced against time. Winter was near, and they feared others might succeed before them.

At last, on December 17, the Wright brothers were ready. Orville was at the controls. He started the engine and headed into the high winds. The plane flew 120 feet (30.5 m). Orville and Wilbur made three more flights that day. After the last flight they were taking the plane back to its shed. Just then a gust of wind tossed it about, and the plane was smashed. However, history had been made that day.

The Wright brothers continued to make improvements, testing them in a cow pasture near Dayton. When

Theodore Roosevelt became President, powered flight was still a dream. Before his presidency was over, the army had ordered an airplane from the Wright brothers. A new age had begun.

The Automobile

In Detroit, Michigan, another revolution in transportation was in the making. Until 1908 only the rich could afford automobiles. **Henry Ford** wanted to make a cheaper car. Before 1908, cars had been made one at a time. Workers assembled, or fitted together, the many parts. Ford changed this system. His workers stayed in one place, each worker with a specific task to do. The automobile being assembled moved on a conveyor belt from one work station to another. This system was called an **assembly line.**

The first Model Ts came off Ford's assembly line in 1908. Within five years Ford was able to sell a Model T for about $450. Still, many Americans could not afford to buy one. To help people buy automobiles, **installment buying** became common for the first time. This means that rather than paying for something all at once, a buyer at first pays only a small part of the selling price. Then each month, the buyer makes a regular **installment,** or payment, until the debt is paid.

The automobile gave Americans a new freedom of movement. People were no longer dependent on city streetcars. They could use the automobile for getting to work. People began to move to the **suburbs,** or communities near a city.

The automobile created a need for new business and industry. The need for tires led to the growth of the rubber industry. The oil refining business expanded in order to supply gasoline. Gas stations began to replace blacksmith shops. People began to demand that the government build good roads.

Henry Ford, a self-taught engineer, believed that every American could own a car. His Model Ts, or "Tin Lizzies," rolled off the assembly lines by the thousands.

By 1910, 1 of every 200 persons owned a car. By 1930, 1 of every 53 persons owned a car. Today 7 out of 10 people own a car, van, or truck. Now it is difficult to imagine life without automobiles.

The Rights of Women

Another major achievement of the twentieth century has been the continuing growth of democracy. In 1920 women got the right to vote.

The right of women to vote had first been proposed in 1848 at a women's rights meeting. This meeting, which was held in Seneca Falls, New York, was organized by **Lucretia Mott** and **Elizabeth Cady Stanton.** They had met each other while working for the abolition of slavery. At the meeting Elizabeth Cady Stanton read a Declaration of Sentiments. It was modeled on the Declaration of Independence. "We hold these truths to be self-evident: that all men and women are created equal," she said. The declaration demanded that women be given full rights of citizenship, including the right to vote.

From then on, a small group of outstanding women worked for the right to vote. In addition to Stanton and Mott, they included **Lucy Stone** and **Susan B. Anthony.**

Lucy Stone, like Stanton and Mott, was both an abolitionist and a defender of women's rights. As a young woman, she traveled the country giving speeches. "She was the first who really stirred the nation's heart on the subject of women's wrongs," according to Stanton.

Susan B. Anthony became a close friend of Elizabeth Cady Stanton.

Anthony and Stanton started a national organization to promote women's rights.

In 1872 the Supreme Court had supported Illinois in its refusal to let women practice law. Women, said the Court, were naturally timid and delicate. Therefore they were unfit for many occupations. This was a popular idea among people of the time. The facts, however, did not support it.

Settling America would have been impossible without numbers of strong and brave women. The American Revolution would not have been won without the active help of women. Women worked to end slavery and bring about reforms. At telephone switchboards, at typewriters, at cash registers, women were helping American business to grow. Other women became teachers, scientists, writers, and doctors.

Yet in 1900 one-fourth of the states would not let a wife own property. One-third of the states said a woman had no right to her own earnings. They belonged to her husband.

Working for the Vote

In Oregon **Abigail Duniway** felt this system was most unfair. Why, she asked her husband, was the law so one-sided? "Because," he said, "men made the laws."

In 1871 Abigail Duniway started a newspaper to promote **suffrage** for women. Suffrage means the right to vote. If women could vote, then they could change unfair laws. Susan B. Anthony journeyed to Oregon to help her. For years Abigail Duniway wrote and spoke about women's right to vote.

By 1910 the suffrage movement had gained the support of most American

Thousands of women marched in New York City to demand the right to vote. In the Nineteenth Amendment that right was finally recognized.

women. Women started wearing yellow, the color of the cause. Women started holding rallies and parades. Their demands became bolder and stronger. In 1912, 15,000 women marched up Fifth Avenue in New York in a demand for women's suffrage.

A woman who marched in a parade talked about it several years later:

> I didn't walk in New York's first suffrage parade because my mother wouldn't let me. Next year, in 1913, I wanted to march, but my husband asked me not to. This fall I decided that it was up to me to suffer for democracy.

The **Nineteenth Amendment** to the Constitution became law in 1920. For the first time adult women could vote nationwide for President. Another step toward a fuller democracy had been taken.

 Reading Check

1. Why are the Wright brothers still remembered today?
2. What is an assembly line?
3. Why was the 1848 Seneca Falls meeting important?

Think Beyond How do you think the women's suffrage movement affected how our leaders are chosen today?

IN FOCUS

FORD'S MODEL T

What if every other car on the highway looked exactly like yours, with the same design, even the same color? That's how it was for motorists who drove Model Ts in 1913.

Model Ts were made in only one style and in only one color—black. However, the people who drove Model Ts were just glad that there was a car that they could afford to buy. Before the Model T, only a few, wealthy people owned cars. Everyone else used horses or mules for transportation.

The Model T was designed by Henry Ford. Ford worked as an engineer for Thomas Edison's electric company. In his spare time, Ford built cars in his garage. In 1903 he started the Ford Motor Company. His goal was to produce cars the average family could afford. The first Model Ts, in 1908, cost $850. Over the next few years, the price fell to $450.

Model Ts became affordable because they were the first cars made on an assembly line. In this system, each worker had only one job to do. For example, a worker might be in charge of attaching the headlights to the front of the car. The car traveled on a conveyor belt around the factory and stopped in front of each worker, moving on when each task was completed. This method was fast, allowing Ford to produce hundreds of thousands of cars each year. In 19 years, the company made and sold 15 million Model Ts.

By 1927, the era of the Model T was over. People wanted cars that looked different from their neighbors' cars. Ford then began making the Model A. It came in four different colors and 17 different models.

The Model A was successful, but it was never as popular as the Model T had been. In fact, no other car would ever be as popular as the Model T was. And no other car would ever be as important. Ford's Model Ts transformed America into a nation of automobile drivers.

Think Beyond Why do you think Model Ts came in only one style and color?

Family outing in a Model T

SKILLS IN ACTION

LEARNING FROM A NEWSPAPER

Some newspapers have hundreds of pages, and others have just a few. Even so, almost all newspapers are divided into the same parts.

The News Section

The first part of most newspapers is the **news section.** This section begins on the front page. Here you will find the most important international, national, and local stories.

If a story was written someplace besides the newspaper's hometown, it carries a **dateline.** A dateline gives the name of the place where the story was written. At the top or bottom of such a story, you may see the words *Associated Press* or *United Press International.* These are the names of large news agencies that send reporters all over the world. Sometimes only the initials are used—*AP* or *UPI.* The stories written by news agency reporters are sold to many newspapers.

A **by-line** gives the name of the person who wrote the story. Not all newspaper stories have by-lines.

The Editorial Page

Most papers have a special page or section for **columns** and **editorials.** A column is an article that gives the views of a particular writer. An editorial is an article that gives the opinion of the **editor.** The editor directs the newspaper.

Columns and editorials are very different from news stories. News stories present facts and tell what happened. Editorials and columns present opinions. An editorial usually judges something that happened and argues whether it was right or wrong. An editorial may also give advice to leaders or citizens.

The editorial section also presents letters that are written by the paper's readers. In these letters the readers give their opinions about recent events. Political cartoons in the editorial section express opinions about news events.

Other Sections

You will find both news stories and columns in other sections of a newspaper. These include sports, entertainment, and business sections.

You can locate parts of the paper by looking in the paper's table of contents. The table of contents is usually printed on the bottom half of the front page.

Almost all newspapers have a section of small advertisements. These ads are **classified,** or grouped, by what they are offering. Some ads list jobs that are available. Others list cars or boats for sale. Still others list houses for rent or for sale.

Scanning a Newspaper

Very few people have time to read every word in a newspaper. Most people just read articles about things they think are important or interesting. They **scan,** or quickly look through, the newspaper to find articles to read. They do this by looking at **headlines.** The headline is in big type and tells the main

519

PEARY REACHES THE POLE

April 7, 1909

BATTLE HARBOR, Labrador—Commander Robert E. Peary of the United States Navy has reached the North Pole. Peary wired this message yesterday—"I have the pole, April sixth."

For 23 years Peary has explored the Arctic regions. Since 1898 Peary has searched for routes to the North Pole. Now his ambition has been realized.

The ship *Roosevelt* landed the Peary expedition in September near Cape Columbia on Ellesmere Island. In March Peary's expedition left Cape Columbia for the North Pole.

"I decided that I should strain every nerve to make five marches of fifteen miles each," Peary said in his wire. At the end of the fifth march, on April 6, there was a break in the clouds at noon. Peary made his observation. He was at 90°N—the North Pole.

Ready for the Pole, Commander Robert E. Peary posed with his huskies last fall on board the steamer *Roosevelt.*

Peary quoted his original entry for that day:

"The pole at last! The prize of three centuries, my dream and goal for twenty years, mine at last!"

---

idea of a story. After you read the headline, you may then decide to read the story.

News stories are usually written according to one rule: the first paragraph should give all the basic facts. It should answer the questions *Who?, What?, When?,* and *Where?.* Depending on the story, the answers to *How?* or *Why?* may also be included. The paragraphs of a news story are arranged in order of importance. The basic facts are always in the first paragraph or two. Each paragraph that follows gives more details. The least important details are at the end.

Read the news story above. It is based on a 1909 newspaper account.

The first sentence tells *who* did *what* and *where.* Robert Peary discovered the North Pole. The second sentence tells *when*—on April 6.

The paragraphs that follow each give additional information about the facts in the first paragraph. The second paragraph tells that Peary had tried for several years to reach the pole. The third paragraph quotes Peary about the march to the pole. The last paragraph expresses how Peary felt when arriving at the pole.

With each paragraph a reader gets more information. Yet the reader could stop after the first paragraph and have the most important facts. This way of organizing facts lets the reader scan. It lets the reader decide how much of the story to read.

CHECKING YOUR SKILLS

Write the answers to these questions.

1. Where will you find major news stories in a newspaper?

2. What is an editorial?

3. Why is a news story different from an editorial?

4. What should the headline of a news article do?

5. What questions should the first paragraph of a news story answer?

Reading for a Purpose

Look for these important words:

Key Words
- Allied Powers
- Allies
- Central Powers
- no-man's-land
- League of Nations

People
- Woodrow Wilson

Look for answers to these questions:
1. Why did the United States fight in World War I?
2. Where was most of World War I fought?
3. What kinds of jobs did women do during the war?
4. How did the United States make a difference to the outcome of the war?

4 World War I

In 1914 war broke out in Europe. On one side were Russia, France, Britain, and Italy. These were known as the **Allied Powers,** or **Allies.** On the other side were the **Central Powers** —Germany, Austria, and Turkey. Of these, Germany was the strongest nation.

The United States as a country tried to stay neutral in the war. But the feelings of Americans were not in the least neutral. Most Americans favored Britain. The Americans and the British shared the same language and many of the same traditions. Americans were comforted by British control of the seas. On the other hand, people with roots in Germany or Austria favored those nations.

The strategy of Britain was to win the war with a blockade of German ports. German strategy, on the other hand, was to end the blockade and destroy the British navy by using submarines. In 1915 German submarines sank the British passenger ship *Lusitania* with great loss of life. Americans were outraged. Such an attack was against the rules of the sea.

The U.S. Enters the War

Woodrow Wilson was President of the United States at this time. He had hoped to keep America out of the war, but this proved impossible.

In the spring of 1917, Germany announced that its submarines would go after any ships in British waters. The German submarines then sank three ships. American passengers aboard these ships were killed. President Wilson asked Congress to declare war on Germany. It was necessary to fight, he said, for the peace of the world. "The world must be made safe for democracy," he said.

After the United States declared war, a wave of anti-German feeling ran through the country. Schools and colleges stopped teaching the German language. German music was no longer played. Sauerkraut was called "liberty

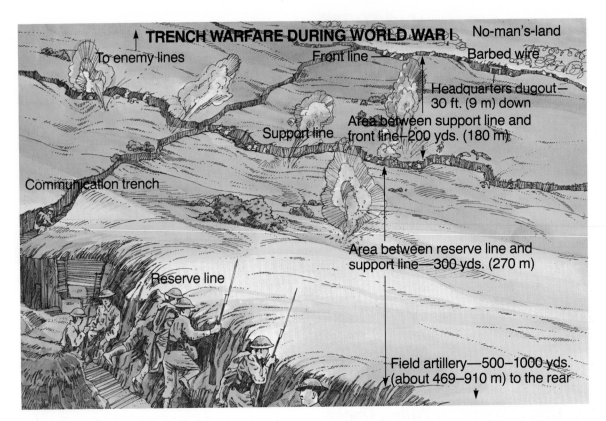

TRENCH WARFARE DURING WORLD WAR I

To enemy lines

Front line

No-man's-land

Barbed wire

Headquarters dugout—30 ft. (9 m) down

Area between support line and front line—200 yds. (180 m)

Support line

Communication trench

Area between reserve line and support line—300 yds. (270 m)

Reserve line

Field artillery—500–1000 yds. (about 469–910 m) to the rear

cabbage." Even German measles were renamed "liberty measles."

Trench Warfare

In Europe the war had bogged down into deadly trench warfare. Most of this warfare was in northern France. The soldiers who lived and died in these trenches were separated by a **no-man's-land.** No-man's-land was the land separating opposing armies. It was laced with barbed wire and mines. The Germans used poison gas for the first time to kill enemy troops.

The English developed a new secret weapon they called a tank. By the end of the war, tanks could cross the no-man's-land, crushing barbed wire. Bullets could not pierce tanks.

Overhead, observation balloons were used to spy on the enemy. During the war each side developed an infant air force. Flying "aces" gained glory for their skill and bravery. They included Germany's "Red Baron," Manfred von Richthofen (RIK•toh•vuhn), and America's Eddie Rickenbacker.

Women in the War

American women went to Europe to serve as nurses and ambulance drivers. Katherine Stinson of San Antonio, Texas, wanted to become a combat pilot in the war. The army refused her. Instead she flew across the United States raising money for the Red Cross. Then she went to Europe as an ambulance driver. Katherine's sister Marjorie taught many Canadian and American men to fly.

Thousands of women joined the navy and army as clerks and telegraph

During World War I women stepped forward to do all kinds of work formerly done by men. Here these women take on the job of delivering blocks of ice—an important job before most people had refrigerators.

operators. Thousands more took over jobs left vacant by men going to war. They worked in fields and factories. They became auto mechanics. As police officers they directed traffic and patrolled the streets.

The War Comes to an End

In Europe the Americans made a difference to the outcome of the war. Enthusiastic American soldiers gave important military help. Shiploads of American wheat, hay, canned goods, and guns poured into France. Working together, the Allies, which now included the United States, began to push back the German army.

On November 11, 1918, an armistice was declared. The war was over, and American troops started coming home. Meanwhile world leaders gathered together to make peace terms. Wilson urged these leaders to accept his idea for a **League of Nations.** The League of Nations would be a world-wide organization to which all nations could belong. The league would work to find peaceful solutions to problems among nations.

The League of Nations was established, but the United States refused to join. The United States Senate must vote approval of all treaties. It voted not to approve the League of Nations treaty. Many senators believed that America should not get involved any more in world affairs.

 Reading Check

1. Who was President in 1917?
2. How did the United States help its allies in World War I?
3. What was the League of Nations?

Think Beyond How might war have been avoided for the United States in 1917?

Thinking Back

- During the early twentieth century, the United States became a major world power.

- As a result of the Spanish-American War, the United States gained Cuba, Puerto Rico, Guam, and the Philippine Islands.

- The Hawaiian Islands came under American control when sugar planters set up a republic and asked to become part of the United States. The United States purchased Alaska from Russia.

- President Theodore Roosevelt believed that the United States should use its power and influence in the world.

- The building of the Panama Canal helped make the United States stronger and allowed ships to travel faster between the Atlantic and the Pacific coasts.

- President Roosevelt and the Progressives favored reforms in business, transportation, and banking.

- In the first decade of the 1900s powered flight was achieved, the automobile became more affordable, and the growth of democracy continued. The suffrage movement resulted in the Nineteenth Amendment.

- The United States entered World War I. With economic and military help from the United States, the Allies won the war.

- At President Wilson's urging, the League of Nations was established. The United States, however, refused to join.

Check for Understanding

Using Words

Match each term with the correct definition on the right.

1. armistice
2. assembly line
3. glider
4. installment
5. isthmus
6. no-man's-land
7. regulate
8. suburbs
9. suffrage
10. tuberculosis

a. a narrow piece of land connecting two larger areas

b. a lung disease

c. the right to vote

d. communities near a city

e. an aircraft with no engine

f. a payment made each month until a debt is paid off

g. the land that separated opposing armies during World War I

h. an agreement to stop fighting

i. set rules for

j. system by which a product being manufactured moves from one work station to another

Reviewing Facts

1. What caused the Spanish-American War?

2. How did the United States defeat Spain in the Spanish-American War?

3. How did the United States gain control of Hawaii? of Alaska?

4. Name three major achievements of President Theodore Roosevelt.

5. Why was the Panama Canal important?

6. What was an example of government regulation of business?

7. How did new technology in transportation bring changes to American life?

8. How did American women show their support of the suffrage movement?

9. Why did the United States join Britain's side in World War I?

10. How was the Spanish-American War similar to World War I? In what ways was it different?

Thinking Critically

1. What beliefs delayed women's suffrage? Can you think of other examples of how beliefs might have interfered with the rights of others?

2. How does the United States use its power to influence world affairs today?

3. If you could choose to live a part of the history you have read about in this chapter, which part would it be? Why?

Writing About It

Imagine that it is 1896 and that you have gone to Alaska to try to find gold. Write a letter to your family back home that describes the climate, the land, and what you do every day.

Practicing Reading Skills

Reading a Newspaper

Look in a newspaper and bring to class an example of these:

- a news article with a by-line
- a column
- an editorial
- a letter to the editor
- a political cartoon
- a sports column

On Your Own

Social Studies at Home

1. With your family's help, write a "how-to" manual on how to care for our national parks. Be sure to list things that you need not do in a national park as well as things that you need to do to help keep the park beautiful.

2. Draw pictures that show events in a day of the life of Theodore Roosevelt. For example, you might make a drawing of Roosevelt having a pillow fight with his children, or you might show him riding his horse. Exchange your pictures with your classmates.

Read More About It

Susan B. Anthony: Pioneer in Woman's Rights by Helen Stone Peterson. Garrard. This book offers much background information about Anthony's work for both women and African Americans.

When I Grew up Long Ago by Alvin Schwartz. J. B. Lippincott. This book is a collection of quotes from people who grew up in the early 1900s.

CHAPTER 20

The Jazz Age, the New Deal, and World War II

"Talkies, squeakies, moanies, songies, squawkies . . . But whatever you call them, I'm absolutely serious in what I have to say about them. Just give them ten years to develop and you're going to see the greatest artistic medium the world has known. Just think: you can get all the movement, the swing, the rhythm and the drive of the best of the old silent movies into them."

—D. W. Griffith, film director, 1929

Look for these important words:

Key Words
- Jazz Age
- Roaring Twenties
- jazz
- spirituals
- stock market
- Great Crash

People
- Charles Lindbergh
- Charlie Chaplin
- Will Rogers
- Herbert Hoover

Look for answers to these questions:
1. What was life like for many Americans in the 1920s?
2. Why did Charles Lindbergh become an American hero?
3. What forms of entertainment were popular in the 1920s?
4. What was the Great Crash?

1 The Jazz Age

The **Jazz Age** and the **Roaring Twenties** are both names given to the 1920s. After the serious days of World War I, Americans were ready for good times. Many had more money than ever before. They spent their money on many of the new products becoming available. Such products included cars, washing machines, phonographs, and radios.

A Pennsylvania radio station was the first to make regular broadcasts in 1920. People who wanted to listen to the station had to make their own radios. Soon companies began to sell manufactured radios. By 1922 more than 500 stations were broadcasting. By 1925, 5 million families had radios.

Radio made possible an audience of millions of people. Listening to the radio, Americans shared in the exciting events of the decade. One of these, in 1926, was a fight for the heavyweight boxing title. Millions listened as Gene Tunney beat Jack Dempsey in a ten-round boxing match. Baseball games were also popular. Yankee fans cheered when Babe Ruth hit his sixtieth home run during the 1927 season.

This listener strains his ears to catch the faint, scratchy sounds of early radio.

Charles Lindbergh

In 1927 Americans listened eagerly when **Charles Lindbergh** flew across the Atlantic Ocean toward Paris. Lindbergh wanted to win a $25,000 prize. The prize was offered to the first person to fly nonstop from New York to Paris. Lindbergh had designed his own small plane, the *Spirit of St. Louis.* On May 20, 1927, Lindbergh climbed into his plane with five sandwiches and a canteen of water. Alone, battling fatigue, he tried to keep his course over the wide ocean. Lindbergh wrote in his journal: "My back is stiff; my shoulders ache; my eyes smart. It seems impossible to go on longer."

Go on he did. Thirty-three and one-half hours after leaving New York, he landed in Paris. The French greeted him as a hero. In that hour Lindbergh became the most popular person in America.

Jazz and the Movies

Over their radios Americans could also hear a new sound of music. It was **jazz.** Jazz grew out of the heritage of the American blacks. That heritage included West African music brought by their ancestors. In America blacks were introduced to the hymns of the Christian missionaries. They gradually changed the hymns. These new versions of hymns became known as **spirituals.** From this tradition of African music and spirituals, jazz was born.

Americans everywhere began to go to the movies. The invention of the

After flying nonstop from New York to Paris, Charles Lindbergh became a national hero. A navy ship brought him and his plane home from France.

Louis Armstrong, born in New Orleans, moved to Chicago in the 1920s. Playing his trumpet or the piano, he was one of the great performers of American jazz.

Looking cold and forlorn, Charlie Chaplin huddles against a door in "A Dog's Life."

movie camera was the basis of the new industry. Based in Hollywood, California, the movie business first turned out silent films. By 1927 Edison had come up with another invention, the talking picture. Soon movies with sound replaced silent films.

Charlie Chaplin was one of the most popular movie stars of the silent films. One of his most famous roles was the "little tramp."

Will Rogers became one of the most popular stars of the "talkies." Will Rogers kept America laughing. Rogers was a cowboy, a stage entertainer, a radio and movie star, and a newspaper writer. He was part Cherokee and had been born in the Indian Territory of Oklahoma. "My ancestors didn't come on the *Mayflower,* but they met the boat," he quipped.

The Good Times End

In 1928 **Herbert Hoover** was elected President. Hoover had gained fame for the excellent way he organized relief after World War I. The poor, the hungry, and the displaced of Europe were helped because of Hoover's efforts.

The good life of the 1920s, many thought, would go on forever. Hoover shared those hopes. "We in America today are nearer to the final triumph over poverty than ever before in the history of any land," he said.

Thousands pinned their hopes on a rich future by investing in the **stock market.** The stock market is a place where people can buy and sell stocks. Stocks are shares of ownership in business corporations. If more people want to buy than sell, the price of shares goes up. The reverse is also true. If more people want to sell than buy, the price of shares goes down. During the 1920s the prices on the New York Stock Exchange kept going higher. People began to borrow money to buy stocks. "How can you lose?" they asked.

On October 29, 1929, nearly everyone lost. Prices on the stock market crashed down like a house of cards. This was called the **Great Crash.** It marked the end of the good times of the Twenties. It was the beginning of hard times ahead.

Reading Check

1. Why did radio become very important in the 1920s?
2. Who was Charles Lindbergh?
3. How did jazz music develop?

Think Beyond How did the collapse of the stock market affect even those who had not bought stock?

IN FOCUS

WOMEN IN THE SKIES

Only seven years after the airplane was invented, a handful of hardy women were already flying. They soared across America in the open, rickety contraptions that were the first airplanes.

In 1912 Harriet Quimby was the first woman to fly across the English Channel. Just before she took off, a friend showed her how to read a compass. Following the compass, she flew safely across the Channel. This brave flier died several months later when her airplane crashed near Boston.

Ruth Law was also a flier. On the day of her first plane ride, she saw Harriet Quimby plunge to her death. Nevertheless, Ruth Law was determined to fly.

Amelia Earhart talks to students.

Within six months she was doing stunt flying, making graceful loops in the air. In 1916 Ruth Law took off from Chicago for New York City. She flew until her sputtering engines told her she was out of gas. She landed in Hormel, New York, setting a long-distance air record of 590 miles (946.3 km). Why did Ruth Law risk danger and death? "My flight was done just purely for the love of accomplishment," she told people.

The most famous of the early women fliers was Amelia Earhart. She was a military nurse in Canada in 1918 when she first saw an airplane. Thrilled at the sight, she started taking flying lessons. In 1932 she was the first woman to fly alone across the Atlantic Ocean. Near the end of the flight, she faced grave problems. Her instruments were out of order, and her engine was failing. Gasoline was leaking into the cockpit. Then just as she feared that she would crash into the ocean, the coast of Ireland appeared. Her plane sputtered to a landing in a cow pasture near Londonderry. To an amazed farmer working nearby, she said, "I've come from America." Her flight of 15 hours, 18 minutes was then the fastest crossing on record.

On an around-the-world flight in 1937, Amelia Earhart disappeared in the South Pacific. At the news, America grieved for this spirited and courageous flier.

Think Beyond What special quality do you think Law, Quimby, and Earhart all shared?

Look for these important words:

Key Words
- Great Depression
- depression
- New Deal
- bureaucracy
- unemployment
- Dust Bowl

- hydroelectric dams
- Tennessee Valley Authority
- Social Security

People
- Franklin Delano Roosevelt

- Eleanor Roosevelt

Places
- Hoover Dam
- Grand Coulee Dam
- Bonneville Dam

Look for answers to these questions:
1. What was life like for many Americans in the 1930s?
2. What qualities did Franklin D. Roosevelt have?
3. What was the New Deal?
4. What was the effect of the government's building huge dams?

2 Depression and New Deal

The hard times of the 1930s were called the **Great Depression.** During a **depression** there is little money and no economic growth.

Most people who had invested in the stock market lost their money. Banks that had lent too much money had to close. When the banks closed, great numbers of people lost their savings.

Because people had little money, they bought few goods. Manufacturers could not sell what they had made. Workers then lost their jobs. Millions of these people had borrowed money to buy cars, radios, and washing machines. When they lost their jobs, they could not pay their debts. This caused even more banks and businesses to fail.

"We saw bank failures everywhere," an Arkansas man remembered. "The most valuable thing we lost

A rich man in the 1920s, Fred Bell sold apples in the 1930s.

was hope. A man can endure a lot if he still has hope."

The farmers had not shared in the boom times of the 1920s. Crop and livestock prices had dropped so low that farmers could make no profit. When they could not pay off loans to the banks, they lost their farms.

Poverty and hardship settled on the face of the land.

There had been hard times in the past. Always the country had come out of them. These hard times too would pass, President Hoover said. The government gave loans to businesses and some aid to the poor. But it was not enough.

Times got even worse. By 1932 one-fourth of American workers were without jobs. Farmers could not afford to ship their goods to market. In the cities, people were starving. Soup kitchens and breadlines gave some relief. There poor people could get free soup and bread.

Studs Terkel is a writer who interviewed people about their memories of the 1930s. One woman he talked to remembered:

> There were many beggars who would come to your back door, and they would say they were hungry. I wouldn't give them money because I didn't have it. But I did take them in and put them in my kitchen and give them something to eat.

Another person told Studs Terkel that her mother used to feed hungry men at the back door. This made the neighbors angry at her mother. "They said it would bring others, and then what would she do? She said, 'I'll feed them till the food runs out.'"

Roosevelt Elected President

In 1932 the American people rejected Hoover as President and elected **Franklin Delano Roosevelt.** Roosevelt was a hearty, likable person. He was married to **Eleanor Roosevelt,** a niece of Theodore Roosevelt.

Eleven years before his election as President, Roosevelt had come down with polio. The disease left him disabled, unable to walk without braces. Roosevelt, however, made a decision not to feel sorry for himself. Though disabled, he would do something worthwhile with his life. Before getting sick, Roosevelt had gained some experience in public service. He reentered politics and was elected governor of New York. Then, in 1932, the Democratic party chose Roosevelt as its Presidential candidate. "I pledge myself to a new deal for the American people,"

Franklin Roosevelt, with Eleanor at his side, gave new hope to many people.

Roosevelt told the Democrats. The words stuck. Roosevelt's program was called the **New Deal.**

Ending the depression, Roosevelt decided, needed bold, new actions from government. On inauguration day Americans listened on the radio to Roosevelt's rich, confident voice. "The only thing we have to fear is fear itself," he said. In those dark days Roosevelt gave people new hope. Things would be all right. The government would do something.

Growth of Government

The new Congress quickly began to pass Roosevelt's proposals. The programs of the New Deal greatly expanded the power of the federal government. These programs were to bring help to the American people. A large **bureaucracy,** or body of government officials, developed along with the government programs.

Help for the Jobless

The New Deal aimed at getting people back to work. The government hired thousands of young men. Their jobs were to build bridges, plant trees, and do other worthwhile things.

Another New Deal program trained unemployed people in new skills. The government hired others to use the skills they had. Librarians, artists, and writers were given jobs. Even with these programs, **unemployment,** the number of people without jobs, remained high. At least unemployment did not increase.

Drought, dust storms, and depression led farmers to abandon their homes, load up their Model Ts, and head to California to look for work.

Help for Farmers

The New Deal gave loans to farmers so they would not lose their farms. Another program limited production. If farmers produced less, then prices would rise. The government began to pay farmers not to plant crops.

On the Great Plains farmers faced another problem. A drought came to the area early in the 1930s. The dry, plowed land blew away in the strong winds. Wind-blown dirt covered fences and roads. The arrival of a dirt storm could turn daylight into the black of night. The western Great Plains became known as the **Dust Bowl.**

To deal with this problem, the New Deal started a conservation program. The aim was to stop the dust storms and preserve the land. An important part of the program was planting trees to serve as windbreaks. In time, better plowing methods, more rainfall, and the new windbreaks ended the Dust Bowl.

Government-built Dams

Until the New Deal, the development of energy was generally left to private business. But Senator George Norris of Nebraska had a different idea. He wanted the government to build **hydroelectric dams,** dams that produce electricity. The government would then sell the electricity at low rates to users. This idea became another part of the New Deal.

In 1933 Congress created the TVA, or **Tennessee Valley Authority.** The purpose of the TVA was to tame the Tennessee River. The plan called for the construction of hydroelectric dams, for locks to help navigation, and for

fertilizer factories. The TVA has made the Tennessee valley a productive and prosperous place.

Other large dams were built by the government during the New Deal. The **Hoover Dam** on the Colorado River was one. Others included the **Grand Coulee** and **Bonneville** dams on the Columbia River. The electricity generated by the Hoover Dam helped southern California and Arizona to grow. The dams on the Columbia River encouraged the agricultural development of eastern Washington and Oregon.

Support for Labor

The New Deal brought new support for the American labor movement. There had often been bitter strikes and conflicts over the right of workers to organize into unions. Roosevelt gave his support to labor unions. New laws gave workers the right to form unions and the right to a minimum wage.

Workers were further helped by **Social Security.** It was one of the most important reforms of the New Deal. Social Security is a kind of insurance program for retired workers. Workers and employers each contribute to Social Security. In turn workers can count on an income when they retire.

Reading Check

1. What was the New Deal?
2. What was the purpose of the Tennessee Valley Authority?
3. How did the New Deal help workers?

Think Beyond What does it mean to say that the most valuable thing lost in the depression was hope?

People MAKE HISTORY

Mary McLeod Bethune
1875–1955

▶▶▶▶▶▶▶▶▶▶▶▶▶▶▶

When a student at her school for girls in Florida became ill, Mary McLeod Bethune immediately took the child to a local hospital. "We can't treat this girl here," the doctor told her. "You'll have to take her to the Negro hospital, 50 miles from here."

Although she encountered prejudice daily, Mrs. Bethune bore no resentment to anyone. When a cab driver refused to give her a ride because she was black, she gently explained why such prejudice was wrong. The man promised never again to discriminate.

Born to emancipated slaves in South Carolina, Mary Bethune was the founder and president of Bethune-Cookman College, which became a model for African American schools. She gave advice on education and racial affairs to Presidents Coolidge, Hoover, Franklin Roosevelt, and Truman. She organized schools, hospitals, athletic clubs, and social groups for the African American community. She helped to integrate the Red Cross and other groups.

Mary Bethune was the first person in her family to go to school, and when she graduated from college she dedicated her life to educating others. Her work for equality and justice earned the respect of some of the most influential people in the country. Oil tycoon John D. Rockefeller gave money to her school. Eleanor Roosevelt was a personal friend, and worked to aid Mrs. Bethune's causes.

Mary Bethune did so much for African Americans that she became known as "Mother Bethune." Her determination and hard work helped African Americans achieve equal rights.

Think Beyond How do you think it would feel to be ill and not be able to receive medical attention because of your color?

Look for these important words:

Key Words
- Nazi party
- storm troopers
- dictator
- World War II
- military draft
- Axis Powers
- Allies
- rationing
- relocation camps
- civilians
- carriers
- D day
- Holocaust

People
- Adolf Hitler
- Benito Mussolini
- Dwight D. Eisenhower
- Harry S. Truman

Places
- Japan
- Austria
- Czechoslovakia
- Poland
- Pearl Harbor
- English Channel
- Normandy
- Berlin
- Hiroshima
- Nagasaki

Look for answers to these questions:
1. What events led to World War II?
2. Why did the United States enter World War II?
3. What was Allied strategy in World War II?
4. What was the Holocaust?
5. What forced Japan to surrender?

3 World War II

Roosevelt was reelected in 1936. Problems at home seemed to be getting better, but world news was bad. Great changes were taking place in Europe. Americans who listened to the radio or read the newspaper were aware of these. In 1936 the news often reported on **Adolf Hitler** in Germany.

After World War I Germany was expected to pay back the costs of the war. Germany did not have the money to pay this huge debt. Its economy suffered. Inflation in Germany was terrible.

Hitler played on German feelings that Germany had not been treated fairly after World War I. In addition, Hitler said that Germans were superior to other peoples of the world.

Hitler joined a political party, the National Socialists, or **Nazi party.** Soon he became a leader of the party. The Nazis promised to make Germany a powerful nation once again. They blamed many of Germany's problems on Jews. The Nazis set up a private army called **storm troopers.** The storm troopers burned books they did not like and attacked Jewish people.

In 1933 the Nazis took over, and representative government in Germany came to an end. Only Hitler ruled. Hitler began to prepare Germany for another war. He had plans for Germany to rule the world.

In Italy **Benito Mussolini** (buh‑NEET‑oh moo‑suh‑LEE‑nee) had come to power. Like Hitler, Mussolini was all-powerful. We call such a ruler a **dictator.** A dictator has no respect for individual rights. A dictator has no respect for democracy or representative government.

On the other side of the world, military officers had started to rule **Japan.** Japan did not have all the resources necessary to become an industrial country. The military leaders said Japan could get oil, rubber, iron, and tin only by conquest. The United States, which controlled the Philippines, stood in the way of Japanese expansion.

War Begins in Europe

In 1938 Germany invaded **Austria** and **Czechoslovakia.** The next year Germany invaded **Poland.** Britain and France declared war on Germany but were almost powerless against the German armies. German armies quickly took over most of Europe. German bombers attacked Britain, but Britain fought on. In 1941 Germany invaded the Soviet Union. **World War II** had begun.

In the United States many people felt that the country should stay out of European conflicts. Few citizens wanted to see the United States fight another war. Yet, as Roosevelt said, war was a disease that could spread. The United States, said Roosevelt, should prepare itself in case war came. The United States started making war equipment such as tanks and bombers. It began to send equipment and supplies to Britain. To build up an army of trained soldiers, Congress started a **military draft.** A military draft is a way of bringing people into the army.

In 1940 German troops marched into Paris passing through the Arc de Triomphe.

America Enters the War

On Sunday, December 7, 1941, World War II came to the United States. At 7:55 A.M. Japanese warplanes swooped through the clouds above **Pearl Harbor.** Pearl Harbor is the American naval base in the Hawaiian Islands. A deadly load of bombs was dropped on the American ships and airfield. It was a day, Roosevelt said, that would "live in infamy." *Infamy* (IHN•fuh•mee) means remembered for being evil.

The United States had been attacked. That meant war. Japan was an ally of Germany and Italy. These countries were known as the **Axis Powers.** The United States joined Britain and the Soviet Union. They were called the **Allies.**

In the now peaceful waters of the Pacific Ocean off the coast of Oahu lies the USS *Arizona* National Memorial. The white steel-and-concrete structure is a tribute to the battleship *Arizona,* which was sunk during the attack on Pearl Harbor in 1941. One thousand and two men were aboard when the ship went down.

Dedicated as a national memorial on May 30, 1962, the structure stands on the site of the attack. In fact, you can still see a section of the battleship sticking out of the water. And after fifty years oil from the giant battleship is still seeping to the surface. The USS *Arizona* National Memorial connects us to our history and helps us remember the men who gave their lives for our country.

The United States immediately speeded up production of airplanes, ships, submarines, jeeps, and tanks. Now, instead of there not being enough jobs, there were not enough workers. As in World War I, women took over many jobs in factories, fields, and offices. Other women joined the army and navy to do nonfighting jobs.

The demands of fighting a world war led to further growth in government. Never had Americans experienced so much control over their lives. Controls were established over prices, wages, and rents. This became necessary in order to produce war supplies and feed thousands of troops. Government rules called for **rationing,** or limiting, what people could buy. Each citizen had a coupon book. It was impossible to buy most goods without coupons. Coupons were needed for such items as shoes, sugar, and gasoline.

The Japanese Americans

When the United States went to war with Japan, prejudice against the Japanese grew. This was particularly true in California.

Military officials believed that the Japanese Americans could not be trusted. They believed they would help Japan invade the United States.

The United States government therefore decided to put Japanese Americans in **relocation camps.** These camps were like prisons. Barbed wire fenced in the camps. Soldiers with guns guarded the camps to keep people from leaving. About 120,000 Japanese Americans spent the war years in these camps.

For them it meant heartache, bitterness, and loss of property. They were forced to leave their land, their businesses, and their homes.

Arrival at the camps themselves was a fearful time, as one woman remembered: "Can you imagine the despair and utter desolation of all of us? Everybody was weeping, youngsters hanging onto parents, fear and terror all around."

While their parents were in the camps, Japanese American soldiers served bravely and well. The Japanese American regiment was, for its size, the most decorated unit in World War II.

Not all Americans agreed with the way Japanese Americans were treated. One who did not was Eleanor Roosevelt. Free societies do not do such things, she said.

Fighting the War

World War II was a different kind of war. Armies did not spend years in trenches as in World War I. Instead, armies moved quickly by tank, ship, and airplane. Radio helped them stay in touch with each other and make quick decisions.

Both sides bombed cities, killing hundreds of thousands of **civilians.** A civilian is a person who is not a soldier.

Bombs dropping from the air destroyed factories, hospitals, apartment houses. They often destroyed old and beautiful buildings, great churches, and museums. Whole cities were destroyed.

The strategy of the Allies called for the following:

· Getting control of the Mediterranean Sea. The Allies would fight the Germans and Italians in North Africa and then invade Italy.
· Landing armies on the coast of France to start pushing back the Germans. At the same time the Russians would push the German armies from the east.
· Forcing the Japanese back from the Pacific lands and islands they had conquered.

Much of London was destroyed by bombs dropped during German air raids.

539

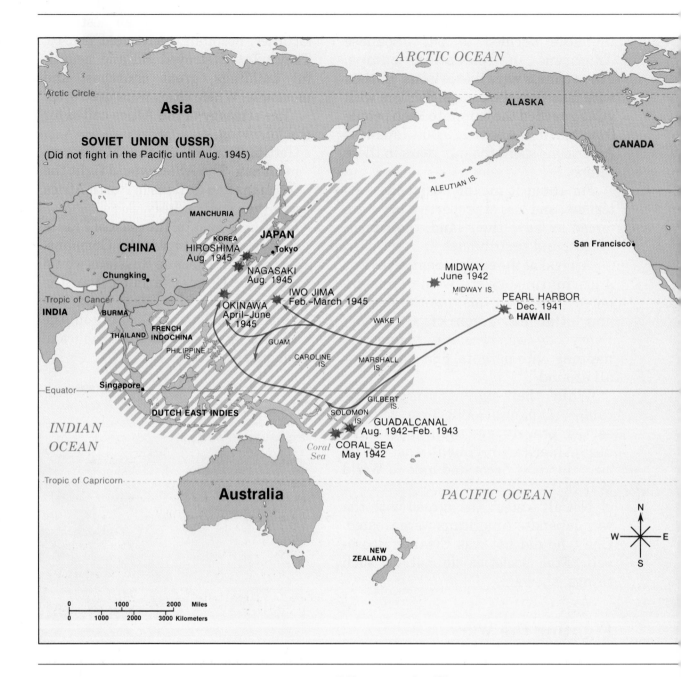

In the Pacific important air battles were fought by planes based on aircraft **carriers.** Carriers are huge ships that serve as bases for fighter planes. American victories at sea began to force the Japanese back. Fighting was fierce as the United States began pushing the Japanese from the Pacific islands.

Victory in Europe

The Allies invaded North Africa in 1942. They started pushing north through Italy in 1943.

On June 6, 1944, the Allies worked together in the greatest seaborne invasion in history. We call it **D day.** General **Dwight D. Eisenhower** led

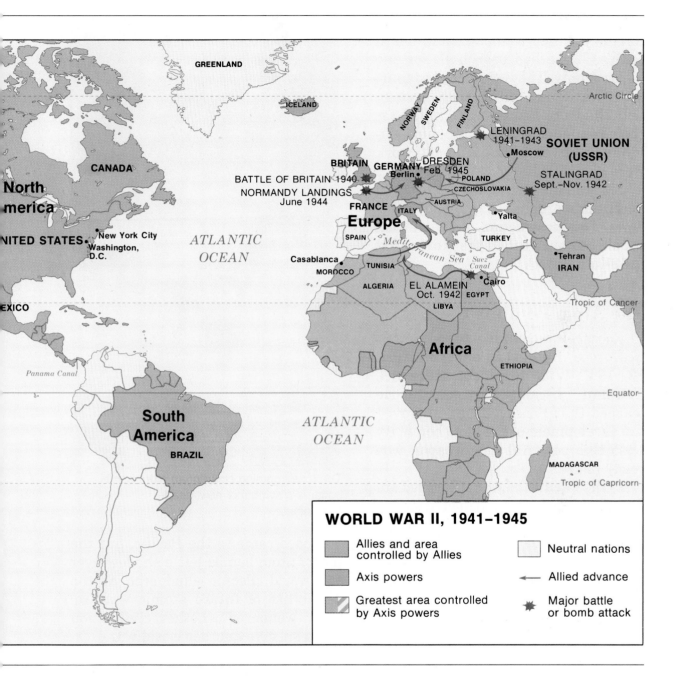

WORLD WAR II, 1941–1945

- Allies and area controlled by Allies
- Axis powers
- Greatest area controlled by Axis powers
- Neutral nations
- ← Allied advance
- ✦ Major battle or bomb attack

the invasion. Allied forces crossed the **English Channel** to land on the beaches of **Normandy** in France. They were met by murderous gunfire from German soldiers, but the invasion was successful. Technology made the difference. The Americans had 6,000 aircraft. The Germans had 900.

The Allies started pushing back the Germans. In May 1945 Allied troops met near **Berlin,** the German capital. There they found out that Hitler had killed himself. The Allied victory in Europe was complete.

Only then did people understand fully the evil nature of Hitler and the

Nazis. Throughout former German territory Allied soldiers found death camps. These had been built for one purpose only. They were used to murder more than 12 million men, women, and children. People were killed for their religious or political beliefs. Civilian captives who could not work were also killed.

Six million people were murdered on Hitler's orders because they were Jews. This destruction of the Jewish people has been called the **Holocaust** (HOH•luh•kawst).

The Atom Bomb Is Used

Roosevelt did not live to see victory in Europe. He died in office on April 12, 1945. Vice President **Harry S. Truman** became President. He learned that Roosevelt had approved the development of the atom bomb. By 1945 this powerful new weapon was ready to use.

In the Pacific the war still raged on. President Truman made the decision to drop the atom bomb on Japan. He wanted to end the war quickly and save American lives. On August 6, 1945, an American bomber, the *Enola Gay,* took off and flew over the industrial city of **Hiroshima** (hihr•uh•SHEE•muh). A single bomb was dropped. There was a flash like an exploding sun. Then a great mushroom cloud rose from the destruction. On that day or soon after, nearly 140,000 people died.

As terrible as the bomb was, Japan did not surrender immediately. On August 9 another atom bomb was dropped, this time on **Nagasaki** (nahg•uh•SAHK•ee). Only then did Japan make plans to surrender.

The mushrooming cloud of an atom bomb became a symbol of new, deadly technology.

Peace came to the Pacific, but the use of atom bombs left a shadow over the world. People shuddered at the possibility of future atomic warfare. They wondered whether civilization could survive another world war.

Reading Check

1. What was a cause of World War II in Europe?
2. Why did the Japanese attack the United States at Pearl Harbor?
3. What happened on D day?

Think Beyond Why do you think Truman decided to use the atom bomb?

SKILLS IN ACTION

CONDUCTING AN INTERVIEW

Interviewing means questioning people about what they have done or what they think. You can learn about events in recent history by interviewing people who took part in them.

Interviewing takes careful planning. You must first decide what event or period you want to learn about. For instance, you might want to learn what it was like to live during the depression. Perhaps you have a relative or a neighbor who lived at that time. If so, ask the person for an interview. Explain why. You might say, "We are studying the depression in school. I would like to find out what it was like to live then."

If the person agrees to an interview, set up an exact time for the meeting. You should also ask for permission if you want to use a tape recorder. Some people do not like to have their words recorded on tape.

Several days before the interview, think about the main questions you want to ask. Try to ask questions that start with *How, What kind of, Where, When,* or *Why.* Write your questions on a sheet of paper. Questions about the Great Depression might include:

- *Where did you live during the depression?*
- *Were you then in school?*
- *How did your family live?*
- *Did you hear Franklin Roosevelt speak?*
- *What kind of entertainment did you have?*
- *Did you have a job? What was it?*

On the day of the interview, be ready well ahead of time. Get out your notebook and have several pens or pencils ready. Dress neatly.

Be on time for the interview. You may spend a few minutes chatting just to relax.

Start by asking the first questions on your list. Remember that a good interviewer listens rather than talks. Do not argue with the person or interrupt.

It is not important that you ask your questions in order. Often your questions will be answered without your asking them. Sometimes, however, the conversation will stop. You can start it up again asking certain kinds of questions. "What happened then?" and "How did you feel when you saw that?" are good for this purpose.

After the interview go over the notes you have taken. Add to them if necessary.

To turn your notes into a report, first look for three or four topics. Use these topics to organize your report. When you are finished, you may want to send a copy of your report to the person you interviewed. You can ask if the information is correct. If there are any corrections, make them in your report. Finally, send a thank-you note to the person you interviewed.

CHECKING YOUR SKILLS

Use the information in this lesson to answer these questions.

1. What are some of the things you should explain in making an appointment for an interview?

2. What kinds of questions should you ask?

3. What should you bring with you to the interview?

4. What should you do after the interview is over?

Thinking Back

- Life was generally good for Americans during the 1920s.

- Radio allowed Americans to share in events and to receive news quickly.

- Charles Lindbergh became a hero by flying nonstop from New York to Paris.

- New forms of entertainment developed in the Roaring Twenties, including radio, phonographs, movies, and jazz music.

- During the Great Crash, prices on the stock market dropped suddenly and many people lost money.

- In the 1930s life was very hard in America because of the Great Depression.

- President Roosevelt's program for ending the Great Depression was called the New Deal.

- World War II was caused by Adolf Hitler's plans for Germany to rule the world, Mussolini's rise to power in Italy, and the Japanese leaders' decision to conquer foreign territories.

- The United States entered the war on the side of the Allies after Japan bombed Pearl Harbor. As a result of the attack, Japanese Americans were placed in relocation camps because military officials feared they would help Japan invade the United States.

- In Germany, Nazis killed more than 12 million people because of their religious or political beliefs. Six million of these people were Jews.

- The Allies first defeated the Axis Powers in Europe. In 1945 the United States used the atomic bomb to force Japan to surrender.

Check for Understanding

Using Words

Number your paper from 1 to 10. Use the terms below to complete the sentences that follow.

bureaucracy	Holocaust
civilians	military draft
depression	rationing
dictator	stock market
jazz	unemployment

1. A music called _____ grew out of the heritage of African Americans.

2. The _____ is where people can buy and sell shares of ownership in large business corporations.

3. In a _____ there is little money and no economic growth.

4. During the Great Depression, there was much _____, or many people were without jobs.

5. A body of government officials is called a _____ .

6. Adolf Hitler was a _____, an all-powerful ruler, of Nazi Germany.

7. When war began in Europe, Congress started a _____, a way to bring people into the army.

8. To provide supplies during the war, government regulations called for _____ to limit what people could buy.

9. Many _____ were killed during the bombing of cities in World War II.

10. The name given to the Nazi murder of millions of people in death camps is the _____ .

Reviewing Facts

1. What forms of entertainment were the result of new technology?

2. How did Roosevelt's New Deal get some people back to work?

3. Describe at least three ways in which government took on new responsibilities under the New Deal.

4. What were three parts of the Allied strategy in World War II?

5. Why did Japan surrender to the United States?

Thinking Critically

1. Compare the 1920s with the 1930s. Use the pictures in this chapter to help you.

2. How was World War I a different kind of war from World War II?

3. Would you agree with the statement "A man can endure a lot if he has hope"? Why or why not?

4. What might life be like under a dictator?

Writing About It

Imagine that you are a newspaper reporter covering the story of Charles Lindbergh flying across the Atlantic Ocean. Write a newspaper article that describes how you think Lindbergh looked when he got off the plane, what you think he said, and how you think the crowd reacted.

Practicing Study Skills

Conducting an Interview

If you were to interview someone, in what order would you do each of the following? Write the phrases in the correct order.

- Ask for an interview.
- Write a report on the interview.
- Tape or take notes of the interview.
- Decide whom you want to interview.
- Send a thank-you letter to the person you interviewed.

On Your Own

Social Studies at Home

1. Use modeling clay to build a replica of the Hoover Dam. You may want to use the picture on page 66 as a guide. Take your model to class to share with other students.

2. Have your family help you look at the stock market report in the newspaper. Choose one stock and follow it for a week. Every day record the stock's closing price. Decide whether you would have lost or made money on the stock if you had invested in it that week. Compare your profits or losses to those of your classmates.

Read More About It

Album of the Great Depression by William Loren Katz. Franklin Watts. This book uses primary sources and illustrations to tell the story of the Great Crash.

Jar of Dreams by Yoshiko Uchida. Atheneum. This book describes the problems of Japanese Americans dealing with prejudice during World War II.

CHAPTER 21

Meeting New Challenges

"I tell you the New Frontier is here, whether we seek it or not. Beyond that frontier are uncharted areas of science and space, unsolved problems of peace and war, unconquered pockets of ignorance and prejudice, and unanswered questions of poverty and surplus. I believe the times demand invention, innovation, imagination, decision. I am asking you to be new pioneers on that New Frontier.

—President John F. Kennedy accepting the Democratic nomination, 1960

Look for these important words:

Key Words
- United Nations
- human rights
- communism
- Cold War
- ideals
- Peace Corps
- Great Society
- Vietnam War
- inflation
- Viet Cong
- Vietnam Veterans Memorial

People
- Dwight D. Eisenhower
- John F. Kennedy
- Fidel Castro
- Lyndon B. Johnson
- Richard M. Nixon

Places
- Soviet Union
- North Korea
- South Korea
- North Vietnam
- South Vietnam

Look for answers to these questions:
1. What problems did the United States face after World War II?
2. What was life like for many Americans in the 1950s?
3. What goals did President Kennedy set forth?
4. How did our country get involved in the Vietnam War?

Leadership in a Changed World

At the end of World War II the people of the world turned again to the idea of an organization of nations. In 1945 delegates from 50 countries met in San Francisco to form the **United Nations.**

The purpose of the United Nations was to keep world peace, promote justice, and establish **human rights.** Human rights are the basic rights and freedoms of all people. Another goal of the United Nations was to work to provide better health care, education, and food supplies for all the people of the world.

The United States came out of World War II as the strongest nation

in the world. The Americans used their strength to help the nations of the world rebuild. Yet even as the war was ending and the plans for peace were being made, the United States found itself facing another foe. This was the **Soviet Union.**

The United States and the Soviet Union had been allies during World War II. After the war, however, the situation changed. The Soviet Union worked to establish **communism** in the eastern European countries it had invaded during the war. Communism is a social and economic system in which all land and industries are owned by the government.

547

Under a strict communist system the government, not the individual, decides what and how much will be produced. There is little personal freedom. The only people with power are members of the Communist party.

The United States saw the spread of communism as a threat to freedom. America began to help countries resist communism by giving them military and economic aid. The United States and its allies against communism are known as the free world.

Hostility, or unfriendliness, developed between the free world and the communist nations. This hostility became known as the **Cold War.** A cold war is generally fought with words, ideas, and money rather than with soldiers or armies.

Helicopters were first used to carry troops into combat in the Korean War.

The Korean War

Sometimes the Cold War became hot. This happened in 1950 when communist **North Korea** invaded **South Korea.** This was the Korean War. North Korea was aided by China, which had become a communist nation in 1949.

The United Nations voted to send troops to support South Korea. Soldiers from 15 countries fought to stop the invasion. Many of these were Americans. Once again, American soldiers found themselves fighting in a far corner of the world.

Dwight D. Eisenhower, the famous World War II general, was elected President in 1952. Raised in Abilene, Kansas, Eisenhower had been a professional soldier. With his broad grin and fatherly manner, he was one of the most popular Americans during the 1950s.

President Eisenhower promised to end the Korean War. In 1953 an armistice was signed. North Korean troops had been pushed back into North Korea. South Korea remained an independent country.

Kennedy Elected President

In 1960 **John F. Kennedy** was elected to succeed Eisenhower as President. Kennedy came from a wealthy Massachusetts family. During World War II Kennedy had fought in the Pacific. As a newspaper reporter, Kennedy reported the founding of the United Nations in San Francisco. In 1946 he began his career in politics by running for a seat in Congress.

At age 43, Kennedy was the youngest person ever elected President. He

President Kennedy is shown here with his wife Jacqueline, their son John, and daughter Caroline.

was particularly popular among young people. Kennedy brought humor and energy to the job of President.

In his inaugural address Kennedy asked that people join the struggle against the common enemies of humankind. These were "tyranny, poverty, disease, and war itself." To Americans he said, "Ask not what your country can do for you—ask what you can do for your country."

Americans responded to the **ideals** set forth by Kennedy. An ideal is a worthwhile goal. One such ideal was helping people in the rest of the world. To do this, Congress founded the **Peace Corps** (KAWR). Thousands of Americans joined the Peace Corps. They carried know-how, help, and concern to far parts of the world.

In October 1962, President Kennedy learned that the Soviet Union planned to install launch sites for missiles in Cuba, just 90 miles (145 km) from American soil. Three years before, **Fidel Castro** had taken control of Cuba. Castro was a communist. Thousands of Cubans had fled to freedom in the United States.

Fearful that the Soviet Union could use the missiles to attack American cities, Kennedy ordered a blockade of the island nation. The Soviet Union stopped the shipment of missiles to Cuba and agreed to remove all existing missiles.

On November 22, 1963, the President and his wife, Jacqueline, visited Dallas, Texas. They were waving to crowds as their car moved through the streets. Suddenly shots rang out. President Kennedy had been assassinated. Hours later, Vice President **Lyndon B. Johnson** took the oath of office of President.

Johnson as President

Lyndon Johnson was a tall, energetic Texan. He had years of experience in Congress, where he was known for his ability to get laws passed.

Johnson was particularly concerned with helping America's poor. As President, he used his skill with Congress to bring about new government programs. These programs were part of Johnson's dream of the **Great Society.** The Great Society programs included medical aid to the elderly and help to the poor with education, housing, and jobs.

At the same time, the United States was fighting the **Vietnam War.** President Johnson said that the nation could pay for both guns and butter. He meant that the nation could afford both a war and prosperity at home. As it turned out, Johnson was wrong. To pay for both the Great Society programs and the Vietnam War, the government had to borrow a great deal of money. This led to **inflation.** Where there is inflation, people can buy less with the money they earn.

The Vietnam War

Like Korea, Vietnam was divided into two countries. **North Vietnam** was communist. **South Vietnam** had an elected government. In the late 1950s the communists, or **Viet Cong,** within South Vietnam tried to take over the government. They were aided by North Vietnam.

To help South Vietnam against the Viet Cong, the United States first sent money and military equipment. Next, soldiers were sent to advise the South Vietnamese army. Later the soldiers were directly fighting the Viet Cong.

When troops failed to defeat the Viet Cong, the President ordered American planes to bomb North Vietnam. He hoped this would stop the flow of supplies from North Vietnam to the Viet Cong. The United States moved to a direct war with North Vietnam. By 1968 there were about 500,000 Americans in Vietnam.

Lyndon Johnson became President after John Kennedy was assassinated.

A Vietnam veteran reaches out to touch the name of a friend who died in the war.

The Vietnam War divided American opinion. As American casualties climbed into the thousands, many people began to consider the war unnecessary and wrong.

Because of the problems caused by the war, President Johnson decided not to run again for President. In 1968 the American people elected a new President, **Richard M. Nixon.** Nixon tried to end the war by bombing the North Vietnamese even harder than before. The protests against the war grew.

In 1973 the United States finally reached a cease-fire agreement with North Vietnam. As part of the agreement, all American troops left Vietnam. In 1975, under President Gerald Ford, the war officially came to an end.

North and South Vietnam became united in one communist country.

In 1982 the **Vietnam Veterans Memorial** was unveiled in Washington, D.C. It is a wall of polished black granite that lists the names of the American men and women who lost their lives in Vietnam.

Reading Check

1. How did the United States help countries resist communism following World War II?
2. What is the ideal behind the Peace Corps?
3. What was the result of President Johnson's borrowing money to pay for the Great Society?

Think Beyond Why did so many people protest the Vietnam War?

Look for these important words:

Key Words
- segregation
- civil rights
- integration
- Civil Rights Act of 1964
- National Organization for Women

People
- Rosa Parks
- Martin Luther King, Jr.
- César Chavez
- Sandra Day O'Connor
- Geraldine Ferraro

Places
- Montgomery
- Birmingham

Look for answers to these questions:
1. What did Martin Luther King, Jr., feel was the best way to bring about change?
2. What steps were taken to bring about equal treatment of the races?
3. What other groups of Americans organized to work for equality?

2 The Struggle for Civil Rights

On December 1, 1955, **Rosa Parks** sank wearily to her seat on the bus in **Montgomery,** Alabama. She was sitting in the middle of the bus. By law African Americans were supposed to sit in the back. They could sit in the middle section only if the seats were not needed for white people.

As the bus filled up, Rosa Parks was asked to give up her seat. She refused. The bus driver called the police, and she was taken to jail.

By her action Rosa Parks had challenged the practice of **segregation,** separation of the races. In the South there were laws that supported segregation. In other parts of the nation, segregation existed by custom and practice. The result was that African Americans often were denied their **civil rights.** Civil rights are the rights of citizens to equal treatment both by law and in practice.

Martin Luther King, Jr.

Martin Luther King, Jr., was a young minister in Montgomery when Rosa Parks was arrested. He was angry when he heard what happened. He called a meeting in his church. Furious also, the people at the meeting decided to let the bus company know how they felt. Its owners depended on the money spent by African Americans. "Don't take the bus on Monday" was the word passed from person to person. In their churches African-American ministers gave the same message. A bus boycott began.

Martin Luther King, Jr., led this protest. For 381 days African Americans in Montgomery boycotted the buses. Often they did so with great hardship to themselves. At last the bus company agreed that African Americans could sit where they wanted. African Americans had learned that by working together they could bring about change peacefully.

Change in a peaceful, or nonviolent, way was important, Martin Luther King, Jr., said. Nonviolence, he said, would change people's minds and hearts. Violence would only make matters worse.

Thousands of white people of all ages began to join the civil rights movement. Together, people of both races worked to break down segregation. Their targets were public places—lunch counters, bus stations, schools, and other public buildings.

Voting is one important way in which people bring about peaceful change. Knowing this, civil rights workers helped to register African-American voters. If more African Americans voted, they could bring about further change.

Support for Civil Rights

In 1954 the United States Supreme Court had declared that separate schools for African-American children were illegal. Such schools did not provide equality of education, according to the Court.

Despite the 1954 Supreme Court decision, most schools in the South remained segregated. In April 1963, King led a march in **Birmingham, Alabama.** The marchers demanded an end to all segregation. In its place they wanted **integration,** or full equality of

the races. For eight days there were marches and police arrests of the marchers. President Kennedy demanded that Congress pass a civil rights law to end segregation in all public places.

To let Congress know how they felt, 200,000 civil rights supporters held a huge march. This was in Washington, D.C., in August 1963. As the marchers gathered before the Lincoln Memorial, Martin Luther King, Jr., spoke to them of his hopes:

I have a dream that one day, on the red hills of Georgia, sons of former slaves and the sons of former slave owners will be able to sit down together at the table of brotherhood. . . .

I have a dream that my four little children will one day live in a nation where they will not be judged by the color of their skin but by the content of their character.

Thousands of people march on Washington, D.C., to show their support for civil rights.

Civil Rights Law Is Passed

President Kennedy had pledged his support to a civil rights law. President Johnson carried out that promise. He pushed Congress until it passed the **Civil Rights Act of 1964.** The new law made segregation in public places illegal. It also said that people should have equal job opportunities.

In 1964 Martin Luther King, Jr., received the Nobel Peace Prize. King had been effective in using nonviolent means to bring about change. However, King himself died from violence. He was killed in April 1968 by an assassin's bullet. In his honor, most states now observe King's birthday as a national holiday.

In the South the walls of segregation tumbled down. At the same time Americans became aware that segregation also existed outside the South. During the 1970s the courts ordered busing of students in many places in an attempt to bring about nationwide integration of schools.

Others Seek Rights

Following the lead of the civil rights movement, other groups of Americans began to organize. They, too, wanted to achieve more rights in American society. American Indians organized to achieve the rights they had been granted in earlier treaties. They began

Martin Luther King, Jr., received the Nobel Peace Prize for his nonviolent efforts to gain civil rights for African Americans.

to take more control over their lands, their mineral resources, and their education.

In California, farm workers, many of them Mexican Americans, had never been able to form a union. Thanks to **César Chavez,** the United Farm Workers Union was organized. Like Martin Luther King, Jr., Chavez emphasized nonviolence as a way to bring about change. By organizing strikes, Chavez was able to reach agreements with the growers and help farm workers gain more rights.

Movement for Women's Rights

In 1966 writer Betty Freidan and others founded the **National Organization for Women** (NOW). NOW gave women a united voice in urging reforms. At this time many jobs were not open to women. When women and men did have the same kind of job, women were often paid less than men.

By the 1970s new laws were passed saying that employers must treat men and women equally. No job could be limited to men only or women only. Women began to do all kinds of work.

Women have done much to achieve equal rights. Many women have entered professions and started businesses. Some have become astronauts. Others have been elected to important positions. Some are mayors of cities. Others serve as members of the United States Congress. In 1981 **Sandra Day O'Connor** became the first woman appointed to the Supreme Court. In 1984 **Geraldine Ferraro** became the first woman nominated by a major political party for Vice President.

Sandra Day O'Connor served as a judge in Arizona before her appointment to the Supreme Court.

 Reading Check

1. How did Rosa Parks challenge the segregation laws?
2. What was the purpose of the Montgomery bus boycott?
3. What did César Chavez work to achieve?

Think Beyond Why do you think it is important for everyone to be treated equally?

Rachel Carson
1907–1964

▶▶▶▶▶▶▶▶▶▶▶▶▶▶▶▶

In 1962 a New York Times headline read, "SILENT SPRING IS NOW NOISY SUMMER." The headline referred to the debate surrounding Rachel Carson's book *Silent Spring,* which showed that pesticides and other chemicals were upsetting the balance of nature and endangering human life.

Carson showed that some pesticides killed birds, fish, and small mammals in addition to the insects they were designed to fight. She reasoned that if other mammals could be endangered by these chemicals, so could humans.

All over the country citizens began to wonder if their health was at risk. As a result, President John F. Kennedy had the U.S. Department of Agriculture investigate Carson's claims.

Chemical companies, afraid that Carson's claims would hurt their business, tried to disprove her facts. Rachel Carson, however, was qualified to make her claims. A biologist educated at Johns Hopkins University, she had worked for many years at the U.S. Fish and Wildlife Service. An expert in marine life, she had won praise for her many articles and books about the oceans and their creatures.

Carson's love for nature grew from her childhood on a Pennsylvania farm. She often wandered through the woods and studied the animals and plants that lived there. Her respect for the land was learned from her parents, who had once refused to allow a coal-mining company to dig through their farmland.

Silent Spring changed the way Americans viewed nature. It made more people aware of environmental concerns and spurred the government to create the Environmental Protection Agency. Thanks to Rachel Carson, Americans are working hard to protect the Earth and its air and water.

Think Beyond What do you think is the relationship between a healthful environment and a healthy person?

Look for these important words:

Key Words	People	Places
• scandal	• Gerald Ford	• Middle East
• Watergate	• Jimmy Carter	• Israel
• hostages	• Ronald Reagan	• Egypt
• terrorism	• Mikhail Gorbachev	• Iran
• *glasnost*		• Teheran
• budget		• Berlin
• Berlin Wall		
• budget deficit		

Look for answers to these questions:

1. Why did Nixon go to China and the Soviet Union?
2. What happened in Iran during Carter's Presidency?
3. What changes has Gorbachev made in the Soviet Union?
4. What problems do Americans and their government face today?

3 *The Challenges of Recent Decades*

In 1968, the year Richard Nixon was elected President, the nation was under stress. People were demonstrating against the Vietnam War. Martin Luther King, Jr., was assassinated. Thousands of young people were rejecting the ways of American society. One historian has called 1968 "the year everything went wrong."

Nixon's Achievements

Nixon's finest achievements as President were in relations with other countries. Although he could not end the Vietnam War as he had hoped, he reduced the tensions of the Cold War. Nixon became the first President to visit both China and the Soviet Union.

The United States had had nothing to do with China since 1949 when China had become a communist nation. There was no trade, no exchange of diplomats or students, no travel back and forth.

In 1972 President Nixon accepted an invitation to go to China. As a result, the two nations agreed to trade. They also agreed to begin an exchange of scientific and cultural groups.

President Nixon also tried to reduce tensions with the Soviet Union. Several months after he visited China, Nixon traveled to the Soviet Union. As a result, the United States and the Soviet Union signed a number of agreements involving a limit on weapons, cooperation on scientific and cultural projects, and an increase in trade.

Nixon Resigns

In 1972 Nixon was reelected President. In his second term, however, the **Watergate scandal** ended his Presidency. A scandal is any action that brings disgrace. The basis of the Watergate scandal was that Nixon knew about improper and illegal activities of people working for his reelection. These activities included breaking into a Democratic Party office in a building named Watergate. Because of the scandal, Nixon was forced to resign as President in August 1974.

Vice President **Gerald Ford** became President when Nixon resigned. Under President Ford American soldiers were withdrawn from Vietnam, and that unpopular war was finally over.

Carter's Presidency

In 1976 American voters had a choice between Gerald Ford and Jimmy Carter as President. They selected **Jimmy Carter.** Carter earned worldwide praise for arranging a peace agreement between two old enemies in the **Middle East, Israel** and **Egypt.** However, a new storm was brewing in **Iran,** another Middle Eastern country.

In 1979 a revolution took place in Iran. Leaders of the revolution were angry at Americans because the United States had been friendly with Iran's previous government. To show their anger, the Iranian revolutionaries attacked the United States Embassy in **Teheran** in November, 1979. They held 53 Americans as **hostages,** or prisoners. More than a year later, on Carter's last day in office, Iran finally released the American hostages.

The American hostages were welcomed home with parades and big yellow ribbons.

The Middle East has continued to be one of the world's trouble spots. People there are divided by religious, cultural, and political differences. Instead of seeking to achieve their goals in peaceful ways, some Middle Eastern groups have turned to **terrorism.** Terrorism is the use of violence to achieve publicity for a cause. Sometimes terrorism is a scream for recognition. At other times its purpose is to force a change in government policy. In the past, forms of terrorism have included kidnapping, murdering, and bombing.

The Reagan Years

In 1980 Americans voted to put **Ronald Reagan** in the White House. Reagan had first been a movie actor and then governor of California.

When Reagan took office, the future looked dim to many Americans. In the 1970s rapidly increasing prices had hurt the buying power of Americans. Many people had lost confidence in the government as a result of the Vietnam War, the Watergate scandal, the Iranian situation, and inflation.

President Reagan helped to change that. He made people feel better about their country. Reagan brought back hopefulness in several ways. First of all, he himself was hopeful and upbeat about the world. He saw no problem that could not be overcome.

Reagan brought back confidence in government by ending inflation. With the end of inflation, it was easier for people to plan for the future because costs of things were more stable.

The Cold War Thaws

Relations between the Soviet Union and the United States warmed up during the Reagan years. This was primarily because in 1985 a new leader came to power in the Soviet Union. This leader was **Mikhail Gorbachev** (mee•khah•EEL gawr•buh•CHAWF).

Gorbachev has changed many of the old Soviet policies and practices. For instance, he has called for **glasnost** (GLAHS•nohst), a Russian word that means "openness." In using the term *glasnost,* Gorbachev meant he wanted more freedom in the Soviet society. One example of the new freedom is that in 1989 the Soviet people had free elections for the first time.

People in other communist countries were also allowed new freedoms. In 1989 people in East Germany were allowed to visit friends and relatives in West Germany. The **Berlin Wall,** which divided the city of **Berlin,** was opened. Changes also were made in other countries, including Poland, Czechoslovakia, and Hungary.

The meeting between Reagan and Gorbachev symbolized the thaw in the Cold War.

George Bush Becomes President

In the presidential election of 1988 Americans chose George Bush. Bush had been Vice President under Ronald Reagan for eight years and had wide experience in government.

Bush asked Americans to rededicate themselves to moral values and to reach out to the less fortunate. He called on Americans "to make kinder the face of the nation and gentler the face of the world."

Unsolved Problems

When Bush entered office, unemployment had dropped and the average income was up. Yet the nation faced some serious economic problems.

One of these concerned the national **budget.** A budget is a plan for spending money. For several years, the government had been spending more than it earned. For this reason the government now had to borrow money to meet its expenses. The amount of money borrowed is called the **budget deficit.**

During Reagan's presidency, the government's debt doubled. In order to maintain a healthy economy, the government now had to either increase its income by raising taxes or reduce its spending.

The prosperity of the Reagan years did not reach everybody. Congress reduced the money spent on social and health programs. This affected the poor, the sick, the disabled, and the unemployed. As a result, thousands of people have become homeless. Local governments and churches have done the most so far to help the homeless.

President George Bush and First Lady Barbara Bush walk down Pennsylvania Avenue after the inauguration.

Americans also took aim at another social problem—the use of drugs. The use of illegal drugs harms, and even kills, the drugtaker. The buying and selling of drugs has led to robberies and murders in city neighborhoods.

The government tries to prevent illegal drugs from entering the United States, but that solves only one part of the problem. The demand for drugs still exists. To stop the demand for drugs, people must be made aware of the damage drugs cause.

Reading Check

1. How did Nixon improve relationships with China and the Soviet Union?
2. What is terrorism?
3. What is a budget deficit?

Think Beyond Why do you think Gorbachev encouraged *glasnost?*

 # SKILLS IN ACTION

SAVING ENERGY

The United States has always been rich in natural resources. Natural resources include oil, coal, natural gas, water, and timber. As our country has grown, we have used increasing amounts of resources to support our technology. Now we face a challenge. How can we keep the world's natural resources from being used up? How can we save resources for the use of future generations? The answer is, save energy.

How can you save energy? One way is to cut down energy use in your home.

Most home energy is used for heating in winter and cooling in summer. You can save energy by using the heater less during cold months. When you feel cold, put on a sweater instead of turning up the heat. Turn the heat down or off when you go to bed at night. After sunset, close the curtains. This will keep the warm air inside from cooling off as it hits the cold windows. Open and close outside doors quickly so that cold air does not sweep inside. Keep windows tightly shut.

In hot months, try not to use the air conditioner unless the temperature is over 90°F (32°C). Close the curtains in the daytime to keep the sun out.

There are many ways to save on electricity use at home. Turn lights off as you leave a room. Check to be sure outdoor lights are not left on all night. Turn off radios, stereos, and television sets if no one is using them.

Washing and drying clothes uses up a lot of energy. Always wash enough laundry at one time to make a full load. You can save energy by drying clothes on a clothesline instead of in a dryer.

A refrigerator also uses up a lot of energy. This is especially so when warm air gets inside and has to be cooled. Holding the refrigerator door open for several minutes lets a lot of warm air in. Open and close the door quickly and not often.

You can help cut down on energy use outside your home, too. Many people waste gas by making unnecessary car trips. Walk or ride your bicycle whenever you can. Take public transportation for longer trips.

The best way to save energy is not to waste anything. When a product is manufactured, energy and raw materials are used. When you no longer have use for things, give them to organizations that take such things. Then they can be used again.

Recycling also saves energy. Using recycled materials to make new products usually takes less energy than using raw materials. Recycling also saves such resources as iron, aluminum, and timber.

CHECKING YOUR SKILLS

Write the answers to these questions.

1. What is an important reason for saving energy?

2. What are some ways you can save energy during the cold months?

3. What are some ways you can cut down on electricity use in your home?

4. What are some ways you can save energy in transportation?

5. How can you save the energy used to manufacture things?

561

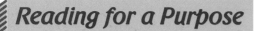

4 *The Space Age*

In October 1957 the Soviet Union stunned the United States by launching *Sputnik* (SPUT•nihk). *Sputnik* was a **satellite.** A satellite is a body, either natural or manufactured, that revolves around a planet. The moon, for example, is a natural satellite of Earth.

As a result of *Sputnik,* the United States speeded up its own space efforts. In 1958 Congress formed the National Aeronautics and Space Administration, also known as **NASA.** Its purpose was to develop and oversee the United States' efforts in the new frontier of space.

Under the guidance of NASA, the United States launched a series of satellites. Today orbiting satellites have become an important part of the way we send and receive information. They provide information about weather on Earth and relay radio, television, and telephone signals.

Reaching the Moon

In 1961 President Kennedy set a goal for the United States. This was to put a person on the moon by the end of the decade. So much was unknown. There were the problems of getting a spacecraft out into space and then back again safely. A spacecraft must break away from Earth's gravity. To do this, it has to reach an enormous speed, almost 25,000 miles (40,225 km) an hour. Away from Earth, a spacecraft experiences both deadly heat and freezing cold. How could a spacecraft be designed to withstand such extreme temperatures? How could people travel safely in an environment where there was no air to breathe?

The men and women working for NASA tackled these and other problems during the 1960s. By 1963 humans had orbited Earth in American spacecraft. The people going into space

562

were called **astronauts.** Then a series of explorations called **Apollo** prepared for a moon landing. In 1968 *Apollo 8* first circled the moon.

By the next year NASA was ready to try a moon landing. On July 16, 1969, *Apollo 11* blasted off from **Cape Canaveral,** Florida. On board were astronauts **Neil Armstrong, Edwin Aldrin, Jr.,** and **Michael Collins.** As they orbited the moon, Armstrong and Aldrin left the spacecraft in a small landing unit. This unit, called a **lunar module,** looked like a big spider. The lunar module landed gently on the moon's surface on July 20.

Millions watched in awe by television as Neil Armstrong climbed from the module onto the moon. "One small step for a man," he said, "one giant leap for mankind."

New Efforts in Space

After a total of six moon landings, NASA began a new series of explorations. Unmanned spaceships were launched far into the solar system. As a result of these efforts, scientists are now learning much more about the other planets in our solar system.

Columbia, America's first **space shuttle,** was launched in 1981. A shuttle is something that goes back and forth. The space shuttle was designed to be reused. Launched like a rocket, it orbits the Earth. When it returns to Earth, it lands like a plane.

Encouraged by the success of *Columbia,* the United States built additional space shuttles. The space shuttle program was a tremendous success. Space shuttles launched satellites as well as spacecraft to probe the solar

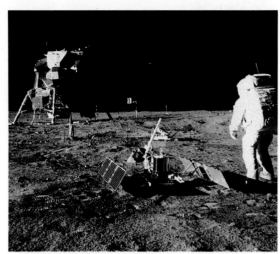

In 1969 American astronauts became the first humans to walk on the moon.

system. Plans were made to build more shuttles, and the number of flights was increased.

Then, in January 1986, tragedy struck. Seconds after lift-off, the space shuttle *Challenger* exploded, killing the crew of five men and two women. One of the women was Christa McAuliffe, a social studies teacher from New Hampshire. To a shocked nation President Reagan promised, "We'll continue our quest in space. . . . Our hopes and our journeys continue."

In 1988 NASA resumed shuttle flights. The nation's space program was back on course.

 Reading Check

1. Why has NASA been important?
2. When did the first astronauts land on the moon?
3. Why are the new spacecraft called space shuttles?

Think Beyond Do you think space exploration has affected your everyday life? Explain.

IN FOCUS

COMPUTERS

Computers are some of the hardest workers in America. They do many tasks that were once done by hand, such as checking out groceries, keeping track of airplane reservations, and welding together auto parts. Until the 1960s, most people had never even heard of computers.

Computers were invented in the 1940s. Early computers stored information and could add, subtract, multiply, and divide at very high speeds. They were so big that they took up entire rooms. In the 1950s and 1960s, companies began using computers to process paychecks and to print bills. Because computers were so large and expensive, many companies shared the same computer. In this system, called *time-sharing,* several companies were linked to one computer by telephone lines.

In the 1970s, scientists invented the *microchip.* Microchips are made of silicon, an element found in the Earth's crust. Because mircrochips are only about one fourth the size of a dime, computers smaller than a suitcase could be made. The microchip also brought lower computer prices.

In the 1980s, the microchip was used to develop the personal computer, or *PC.* The PC is made up of a keyboard, a screen (also called a monitor), and a CPU, or central processing unit. The CPU is the "brain" of the computer. It receives information, either from the keyboard or through program disks, and then stores and processes the information.

PCs have thousands of uses. Architects use them to help draw designs for buildings. Weather forecasters use them to study weather patterns. Businesses use them to store customer information. Teachers use them to teach lessons. Some families use them at home to write letters, to keep track of household expenses, and even to play games.

Think Beyond Why do you think computers have become such an important part of modern life?

Many schools now teach students to use computers.

Thinking Back

- After World War II the United States became a leader of the free world in the struggle against communism.

- The Vietnam War, fought against communist North Vietnam, divided the American people. Unable to defeat the communists, the United States withdrew from Vietnam.

- In the late 1950s Martin Luther King, Jr., became a leader of the civil rights movement. This movement ended segregation and brought about a new civil rights law.

- The civil rights movement encouraged all Americans to be proud of their particular heritage. Native Americans, Hispanics, and women also organized to achieve their civil rights.

- President Richard Nixon worked to improve relations with China and the Soviet Union. In his second term the Watergate scandal forced him to resign.

- President Jimmy Carter arranged a peace agreement between Israel and Egypt. During Carter's presidency 53 Americans were taken hostage in Iran.

- Some Middle Eastern groups have used terrorism to achieve publicity for a cause.

- In the 1980s President Ronald Reagan restored confidence and economic stability to the United States.

- Soviet leader Gorbachev helped people in communist countries gain more rights.

- Space exploration has been one of the major technological achievements of the United States.

Check for Understanding

Using Words

Explain the meaning of each term below. Then use the term in a complete sentence.

1. astronaut
2. budget
3. civil rights
4. communism
5. ideals
6. integration
7. terrorism
8. satellite
9. segregation
10. glasnost

Reviewing Facts

1. What is the purpose of the United Nations? When was it formed?
2. How did relations between the United States and the Soviet Union change after World War II?
3. How did the United States force the Soviet Union to remove nuclear missiles from Cuba?
4. What were some of the Great Society programs?
5. What did Martin Luther King, Jr., feel was the best way to bring about change?
6. What is the importance of the Civil Rights Act of 1964?

7. What rights did women gain in the 1970s?
8. How did the Watergate scandal affect the feelings of Americans?
9. What caused the Cold War to thaw during the late 1980s?
10. Name three current problems that Americans are working to solve.

Thinking Critically

1. How might inflation affect you and your family?
2. Both Martin Luther King, Jr., and César Chavez believed that nonviolence is the best way to achieve goals. What does nonviolence mean? Do you agree with King and Chavez? Why or why not?
3. What do you think could be done to help fight the war against drugs? What can you do to help?
4. What special qualities do you think a person must have to be an astronaut?
5. What changes have occurred in American life since the 1950s? Which do you think are the most important? How have they affected your life?

Writing About It

Imagine that it is December 1, 1955, and that you are Rosa Parks. Write a diary entry for that day that explains what happened, how you were treated, and how you felt. Include in your entry what you hoped to achieve by your actions on that day.

Practicing Thinking Skills

Saving Energy

Use the lesson on page 561 to answer the following questions.

1. Why is it important to conserve energy?
2. How can you help save energy during winter months? during summer months?
3. What are some ways in which you can conserve electricity throughout the year?
4. What is the best way to conserve energy?

On Your Own

Social Studies at Home

1. Make a list of the Presidents of the United States starting with President Eisenhower and ending with President Bush. Beside each name write as many events as you can think of that are associated with that President. Ask older family members to help by thinking of events they remember.
2. Draw pictures about the space program. You may wish to draw the Apollo astronauts landing on the moon or the space shuttle taking off or landing. Be prepared to show your pictures to your class.

Read More About It

Always to Remember: The Story of the Vietnam Veterans Memorial by Brent Ashabranner. Dodd, Mead/Putnam. The history of the Vietnam War and the building of the memorial are briefly described.

César Chavez and La Causa by Maurice Roberts. Childrens Press. This book provides a short biography of Chavez and tells of his struggle for rights for farm workers.

Martin Luther King, Jr., Free at Last by David A. Adler. Illustrated by Robert Casilla. Holiday. This biography brings to life the central figure in a movement that helped change modern American society.

Charlie Pippin

by Candy Dawson Boyd

While doing a social studies report, Charlie learns a lot about the war in Vietnam. However, her father, who is a Vietnam veteran, will not discuss the medal he received for trying to save two of his friends. Charlie comes to understand her father's feelings better after visiting the Vietnam Memorial with her aunt and uncle.

The pathway meandered through a parklike setting. Stark, bare trees lined both sides. There was light snowfall on the ground that crunched beneath her boots. Charlie had expected to see the wall immediately, but instead, the path led down a gradual incline. To her left, in the distance, she saw the grand spire of the Washington Monument.

At last they reached one end of the wall. Charlie remembered that the Vietnam Memorial wall was made of polished black granite. It was V-shaped, with one arm pointed toward the Washington Monument and the other arm aimed at the Lincoln Memorial. She was at the end of the wall that pointed toward the Washington Monument, which explained why she could see the tall spire. The long wall was divided into one hundred and fifty panels, each forty inches wide. On each panel were carved the names of the dead and missing in action. Charlie had to squat down to read the names on the panels at the end. That was because the panels decreased in height from the center of the wall, where they were almost eleven feet high, to the ends of the wall, where they were only eight inches high.

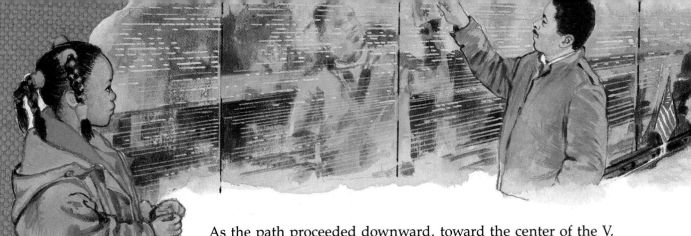

As the path proceeded downward, toward the center of the V, the panels got taller, until they towered above Charlie. She had to stare up to see the names at the top. The wall was like a huge wide V built into the earth, opening its arms in welcome, beckoning her to enter. The black granite panels were so highly polished that she could see her face in them.

Walking along the path, she saw small American flags stuck into the ground below. And taped to a panel was one red, shriveled rose.

The Vietnam Memorial was real. Real. Scary. Beautiful. Each time Charlie looked at a panel she saw her face, Uncle Ben, the naked trees and sky.

Uncle Ben stopped, his eyes sweeping the panel numbers and letters. "Rows and row of names," Charlie heard him mutter, shaking his head. "Rows and rows." From her report, she knew how many names were cut into the stone that had been quarried not far from Bangalore, India—58,007 names.

While Uncle Ben's hand searched, Charlie watched. Then, as if a cold wind had swept over him, she saw his body begin to tremble. His fingers touched the letters of a name. Afraid, Charlie stood there, wishing that her aunt were closer. But Aunt Jessie was talking to the couple with the little girl.

His hand moved again, this time down and to the left. It stopped, and this time he froze. Charlie couldn't see her uncle's face. There were other people around them. He stood there a long time. Finally, she touched his arm. Clearly she saw the two of them and the snow on the ground and the dull, cold sky and the faded red rose. And she saw tears streaming down her uncle's face.

He reached out and held her close, his eyes never leaving the panel. Charlie looked up at him. And she knew that he didn't see her. For a second she thought she was standing there with her father, holding him while he cried.

"Were they your best friends, too, Uncle Ben?" she whispered, thinking of Gerald Moer and Fred Hansen. She had to repeat the question twice before he heard her.

"They were my men," he said. He wiped at his face with his free hand, sniffing. From the way he held his body, Charlie realized that he wanted to stay, so she gently disengaged herself. She had work to do.

A few panels down she discovered the names she sought: Gerald Moer and Fred Hansen. One name was too high for her to touch, but she could see it. Charlie faced her panel.

"Hi, I'm Charlie, Oscar Pippin's daughter," she whispered. "I came to see you. My daddy is fine. I know he still misses you." She took a deep breath and squeezed back the tears. This was not the time to cry. Then she saw the person she needed, the park ranger.

"Mister," Charlie asked, "please make a rubbing of two names for me."

The white-haired man ambled over and took a pencil and two strips of white paper out of his coat pocket. Charlie pointed to the names and repeated them while he laid a piece of white paper over each name. Next, he rubbed the pencil over the raised letters underneath the paper. He handed her the first strip, then started on the second. Charlie stared at the elegant, engraved letters. She thanked the ranger when he handed her the second strip. He moved on to help someone else.

With care, Charlie took the origami flower out of her pocket and wedged the stem into the slight break in the panel midway between the two names. "For you two to remember me and Daddy," she whispered. "And for us to remember you, Fred Hansen and Gerald Moer." Then Charlie bent her head and said a prayer, letting the tears fall. Moments later, she composed herself and took several photographs, making sure to get their names.

"Charlie, you ready? It's getting cold out here," her aunt called. Charlie looked around for her uncle. He was still where she'd left him. Holding the strips carefully in one hand, she reached into her pocket.

"Here, Uncle Ben," she said, going up to him and handing him the origami crane she'd made that morning and the tape she'd grabbed from Aunt Jessie's desk before they left. "I made this."

"The crane is a symbol of peace," she added. "You can tape it to the wall. Like the rose down there."

Smiling a little, he took the golden crane while Charlie tore off a piece of Scotch tape. Then he taped the paper bird to the wall and stepped back.

"Our niece made that crane, Jessie." There was pride in his voice. "Will they throw it away?" he asked.

"Oh, no, Uncle Ben. I read an article that said the rangers collect the things people leave at the Vietnam Memorial and keep them in a special storage room. They even wear gloves when they pick them up," Charlie said.

By now they were walking up an incline, past the other arm of the V that formed the wall, toward the second Vietnam Memorial, a statue of three infantrymen. Charlie looked back to photograph the panels once more. She wondered why the Vietnam Memorial had been called such horrible names. She recalled reading that some said it was "ugly," "a black wound," and "a shameful grave." Charlie thought there was something right about a memorial that honored, name by name, every American who had died or was missing in action. She liked the idea of placing the panels in the earth, but visible to the living eye and open to the air and the sky.

Charlie thought Maya Lin had done a great job. She was the young Chinese-American student whose design was selected for the memorial. Charlie had read that she got a *B* from her teacher on this project. *That* showed that grades weren't everything. She should have gotten an *A*!

You can find out much more about the Vietnam War and Charlie's interest in world peace by reading the fiction book *Charlie Pippin* by Candy Dawson Boyd. (Macmillan Publishing Company, copyright 1987)

Unit Review

Words to Remember

Read each sentence. Then replace the underlined words in each sentence with the correct word from the list. Write the new sentences on your paper.

armistice   inflation
astronauts   integration
bureaucracy   human rights
dictators   glasnost
ideals   unemployment

1. In 1918 the fighting in World War I stopped when the warring nations signed an <u>agreement to stop fighting.</u>

2. During the Great Depression there was a large amount of <u>people out of work.</u>

3. A result of the growth of government since the 1930s has been a large <u>group of government officials.</u>

4. Adolf Hitler and Benito Mussolini were both <u>all-powerful rulers.</u>

5. Martin Luther King, Jr., headed protests to bring about <u>full equality of races in public places.</u>

6. A problem that started under President Johnson was <u>the reduced value of money.</u>

7. Neil Armstrong, one of America's <u>travelers in space,</u> landed on the moon in 1969.

8. One purpose of the United Nations was to establish <u>the basic rights and freedoms of all people.</u>

9. Gorbachev called for <u>more freedom and openness</u> in the Soviet society.

10. Democracy and equality of opportunity are two <u>worthwhile goals</u> held by people in America.

Focus on Main Ideas

1. How did the United States use its power and influence in the Caribbean in the late nineteenth and early twentieth centuries? What were the results?

2. What major progress has been made in the twentieth century toward justice and equality for all Americans?

3. How did the United States use its power and influence

    a. in World War II?
    b. to fight the spread of communism after World War II?
    c. to work for peace among nations?

4. What are some of the great technological achievements of this century? How have they affected American life?

5. What problems does the United States face today? Do you think these problems may be solved by technology? Or, do you think solutions depend on the values of people? Explain.

Think/Write

President John F. Kennedy said, "Ask not what your country can do for you—ask what you can do for your country." What do you think President Kennedy meant by this statement? What kinds of things can you do for your country?

571

Activities

1. **Research/Writing** What will go into history books of the future? Look through newspapers and magazines to collect information you think future historians might use. Choose one major event and write it up as it might appear in a history book.

2. **Timeline** Make a timeline beginning with the year 1900 and ending with the current date. Put at least 20 events on your timeline. If you wish, illustrate your timeline.

3. **Research/Art** Do research on the new freedoms experienced by people in Berlin, Germany in 1989. Cut out pictures that show the Berlin Wall being taken down. Make your pictures into a collage.

4. **Research/Writing** Research the equipment that was used to put humans on the moon. Choose one piece of equipment, such as the lunar module, a space suit, or the control center and write a report about the item you chose. In your report explain why that piece of equipment was important to the moon landing.

5. **Research/Writing** Who do you think is the most interesting or important person of the twentieth century? Write a report on this person.

6. **Making a Table** Make a table listing all the Presidents from 1928 to 1953. On your table, tell the years each President served. Describe one or more of each President's accomplishments.

7. **Newspaper Reading** Read newspapers to find articles that tell about the most recent flight of the space shuttle or the latest satellite launched into space. For each article you find, write several sentences in your own words telling what it is about.

8. **Research/Oral Report** Find out about Sally Ride, the first American female astronaut. What was her training and education? Find out about other female astronauts who have since traveled into space. Report to the class on what you learn.

9. **Research/Art** Find out more about how Americans are using technology to develop new sources of energy. Then draw a poster to illustrate how one new source of energy works. Label your drawing.

Skills Review

1. **Interviewing** To do a report, you want to interview an expert on solar energy. You call the expert, ask for an interview, and make an appointment. Write down at least three questions you might ask the expert.

2. **Reading a Newspaper** Use the information on pages 519–520 to answer these questions.
   a. Where would you find a story about a school that uses solar energy to provide heat?
   b. What questions would you expect the story to answer?
   c. Where would you find the editor's opinion on whether the decision to use solar energy is a good one?

EXPLORING
YOUR STATE'S HISTORY

In the twentieth century, Americans have been involved in four wars. They have lived through the country's worst depression and have traveled in outer space. These events may have changed your state and your hometown a great deal.

Perhaps the Western states have been changed the most by the events of this century. Sleepy little towns like Los Angeles and Phoenix have grown into large cities. Forgotten lands in Nevada, Utah, and Wyoming have become important because of their mineral wealth. All our states have been brought closer together by radio, television, and air travel.

The following activities may help you learn how your state has changed in this century.

Learning About People

1. Women have made great progress toward gaining equality in our society. One hundred years ago women did not even have the right to vote. Today women are judges, business leaders, police officers, construction workers, and athletes. Write a short report on a woman from your state whom you admire for her achievements.

2. The Great Depression, beginning in 1929, affected life in every state. It is hard to know what the depression was like if you did not live then. One way to learn more about it is to talk to someone who lived through it. Find a member of your family or community who lived in your state during the depression. Interview that person and give a talk to your class on what you learn.

Learning About Geography

3. Teddy Roosevelt and others had the wisdom to preserve beautiful areas as national parks. Find out if there are national parks in your state. Write to one of the parks for more information. Write a short report about the animals, plants, and natural features of the park. Draw pictures to go with your report.

4. Are there places in your state named after any of the people you studied in this unit? If so, make a list of some of them. Tell where they are.

Learning About Economics

5. Find out more about how technology has changed your state in the twentieth century. Are there industries in your state that have developed because of automobiles, airplanes, movies, television, computers, or space travel? On a map of your state, show where some of the new-technology industries are located.

6. Are there hydroelectric dams in your state? If so, where are they? How have they helped the economy of your state?

UNIT
10
Canada and Mexico

- **1519**
Hernando Cortés conquers the Aztecs

- **1600s**
French first settle in Canada

- **1754-1763**
French and Indian War

- **1763**
France loses its territory in North America

- **1810**
Miguel Hidalgo leads a revolution in Mexico

*O*ur country has particularly strong ties to our two closest neighbors, Canada and Mexico. Both Canada and Mexico share long borders with the United States.

On this page are pictures of the flags of Canada and Mexico and scenes from both countries. In this unit you will learn about the people, the land, and the history of both Canada and Mexico.

Think Beyond Why do you think it is important to study the history and people of Canada and Mexico?

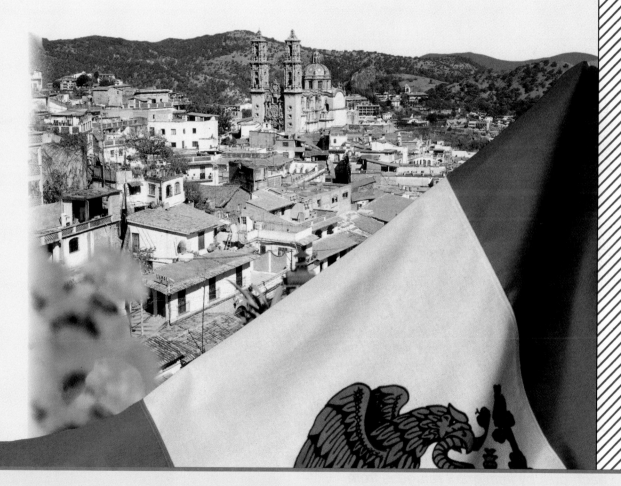

- **1821**
Mexico wins its independence from Spain

- **1910–1917**
Mexican revolution for land and liberty

- **1931**
Statute of Westminster gives more independence to Canada

- **1959**
St. Lawrence Seaway completed

- **1982**
Canada gets control over its Constitution

CHAPTER 22

Canada—
Neighbor to
the North

"As two proud and independent peoples, there is much that distinguishes us one from the other, but there is also much that we share: a vast continent, with its common hardships and uncommon duties; generations of mutual respect and support; and an abiding friendship that grows ever stronger. We are two nations, each built by immigrant refugees from tyranny and want, pioneers of a new land of liberty."

—President Ronald Reagan, 1987

Look for these important words:

Places
- Appalachian Highlands
- Halifax
- St. Lawrence River Lowlands
- Montreal
- Toronto
- Ottawa
- Canadian Shield
- Interior Plains
- Winnipeg
- Western Mountains
- Vancouver
- Arctic Islands
- Baffin Island
- Victoria Island

Look for answers to these questions:
1. How does Canada compare with the United States in size?
2. What is Canada's greatest natural resource?
3. What are the natural regions of Canada?
4. Where do most people in Canada live?

1 Canada's Geographical Regions

Canada, our neighbor to the north, is a huge country. It is the second-largest nation on Earth. Only the Soviet Union is larger. Canada is slightly bigger than China or the United States. Canada extends from close to the North Pole southward to the United States border. It stretches 3,223 miles (5,186 km) between the Pacific Ocean and the Atlantic Ocean.

The population of Canada, over 25 million people, is about one-ninth that of the United States. Most Canadians live in southeastern Canada within 200 miles (320 km) of the American border.

Canada is rich in natural resources. It has large areas of fertile soil, forests, oil and gas reserves, and mineral deposits. Canada's largest industries take advantage of this natural abundance. The leading industries include the production of vehicles, farming, wood products, fishing, and mining.

Canada's greatest natural resource is water. Almost one-half of all the world's fresh water lies in Canada. This country has more lakes than the rest of the countries in the world combined. No one has ever been able to count all the lakes in Canada.

There are six natural regions in Canada. They are the Appalachian Highlands, the St. Lawrence River Lowlands, the Canadian Shield, the Interior Plains, the Western Mountains, and the Arctic Islands. The geography of these regions determines much of Canadian life. In fact, a past leader of Canada called it "a nation of regions."

Appalachian Highlands

The **Appalachian Highlands** are a rugged area of low hills and dense woods. Summers are cool. Winters are

577

long with lots of snow. Most of the people in this region live near the coast. Off the coast lie the rich fishing areas of the Grand Banks. Near the coast the soil is more fertile than farther inland. Farmers grow hay and raise chickens, pigs, and dairy cows. Minks, foxes, and raccoons are raised for fur. The Appa-lachian forests are used to make wood pulp for newspapers and other products. Iron, coal, copper, asbestos, and zinc are mined.

There is no large city in this region. However, the port of **Halifax,** in Nova Scotia, is important because it remains free of ice all year.

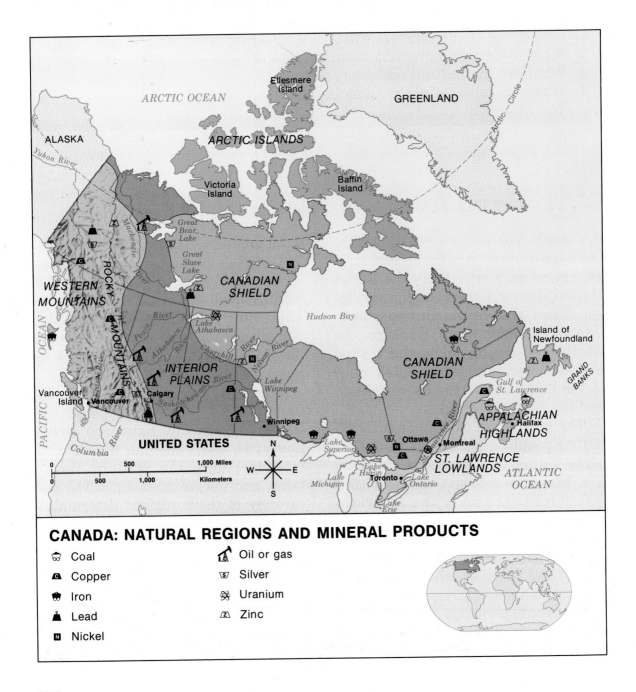

CANADA: NATURAL REGIONS AND MINERAL PRODUCTS

- Coal
- Copper
- Iron
- Lead
- Nickel
- Oil or gas
- Silver
- Uranium
- Zinc

St. Lawrence Lowlands

Canada's smallest natural region, the **St. Lawrence River Lowlands,** is also the most heavily populated. At least 40 Canadian cities have populations of over 50,000 people. Twenty-four of those cities are in the St. Lawrence River Lowlands. Among them are **Montreal** and **Toronto,** two of Canada's largest cities. Montreal has a population of 1,015,420. Just over 600,000 people live in Toronto, the third-largest city. **Ottawa,** the capital of Canada, is also in the St. Lawrence River Lowlands.

In 1959 Canada and the United States completed the St. Lawrence Seaway. This is a series of canals linking the river and the lakes between Montreal and Lake Erie. Using the Seaway, ships can travel from the Atlantic Ocean as far as Duluth, Minnesota, on Lake Superior.

Canadian Shield

The **Canadian Shield** is a vast, horseshoe-shaped region in the north of Canada. It makes up about one-half of Canada, an area larger than most countries. Fewer than 2 million people live in the Shield. The surface area is made of the oldest rock mass on the continent. The soil is thin.

During the Ice Age enormous glaciers covered the Shield. The movement of glaciers over the years created many small hollows. Water collected in these hollows, and they became lakes and swampy areas. The Shield is rich

This glacier, like a freeway of ice, cuts a wide path as it inches downhill. Melting ice forms a glacial lake at its foot.

in uranium, gold, copper, iron, and nickel. The numerous lakes and rivers of the Shield provide much of Canada's hydroelectric power. Great forests in the southern part supply wood for lumber and paper products.

Interior Plains

In the United States, the **Interior Plains** cover much of the central part of the country. The Interior Plains also extend north into Canada. In Canada this area of deep, fertile soil is one of the best areas in the world for growing wheat. Large deposits of oil, gas, and coal are also found in this region. Al-together, 3.5 million people live on the Interior Plains. **Winnipeg,** Canada's fourth-largest city, is on the plains.

Western Mountains

The Rocky Mountains and the Coast Ranges of the United States also extend into Canada. In Canada this mountainous region is called the **Western Mountains.** Thousands of tourists visit the Western Mountains. There they find natural beauty, clean air, lofty mountain peaks, and rushing rivers. Giant trees abound, including sweet-smelling cedars and stately Douglas firs.

Vast fields of wheat spread across Canada's fertile Interior Plains. Wheat is one of Canada's major exports.

The Western Mountains of Canada offer spectacular scenery of snow-peaked mountains, forests, and lakes.

The leading industries of the Western Mountains are logging, mining, farming, and the production of hydroelectric power. **Vancouver,** Canada's eighth-largest city, has a population of nearly half a million. It is located where the north arm of the Fraser River meets the Pacific Ocean.

The climate along Canada's southern Pacific coast is one of the country's wettest. More than 100 inches (254 cm) of rain fall yearly in some coastal areas. In winter, the climate is also warmer than other parts of Canada. Normal January temperatures in Vancouver range from 32 to 41°F (0 to 5°C).

Arctic Islands

Few people live in Canada's cold and rugged **Arctic Islands.** This chain of islands extends far to the north. The northern tip of Ellesmere Island is within 500 miles (805 km) of the North Pole. Some of the islands, like **Baffin** and **Victoria,** are very large. Baffin Island is larger than California.

The Canadian government thinks that there may be large oil deposits in the area. It will be very hard to recover this oil. The waters around the islands are frozen much of the time. Some people want to use submarines as freighters to move the oil.

 Reading Check

1. What are some of Canada's natural resources?
2. Where is Montreal located?
3. Where do most Canadians live?

Think Beyond How would you compare Canada's regions to America's?

Look for these important words:

Key Words
- Hudson's Bay Company
- French and Indian War
- Quebec Act
- British North America Act
- Statute of Westminster

- Commonwealth of Nations

People
- Count Frontenac
- Pierre Radisson
- Medard Groseilliers
- Louis Montcalm

- James Wolfe
- Alexander Mackenzie
- Simon Fraser
- David Thompson

Places
- New France
- Quebec

Look for answers to these questions:
1. Why does Canada have both a French and a British heritage?
2. What caused France to give up its claims in the new world?
3. Who were some important explorers of Canada?
4. When did Canada become completely independent of Britain?

2 Canada's History

Until 1763 the French controlled Canada. French missionaries, explorers, farmers, and fur traders helped settle the rugged northern land. They called it **New France.** The city of **Quebec,** on the St. Lawrence River, was the capital of New France. New France included the Mississippi River valley.

One of the great leaders of New France was **Count Frontenac.** He came to Quebec from France in 1672. He established a peaceful relationship between the settlers and nearby Indians. Frontenac made regular visits to Indian camps and participated in Indian activities. Sometimes he danced with the braves around the ceremonial fires, his face covered with paint. The Indians called him Great Father. His leadership helped the settlers protect their villages and their fur trade.

Count Frontenac, both dashing and clever, helped New France to prosper.

Traders traveled far into the North American interior in search of the wealth to be found in animal furs. The traders got along well with the Indians, who exchanged pelts for beads, knives, and iron products.

English Claims

England also had claims to northern Canadian lands. Most British colonists had settled in what was to become the United States. Some, however, had gone to Canada. Since the voyage of John Cabot in 1497, the English had fished off Newfoundland. Henry Hudson's discovery of Hudson Bay in 1610 established English claims to the Canadian north.

Surprisingly, England's strongest interest in Canada started with two Frenchmen. **Pierre Radisson** (ra•dee•SAWN) and **Medard Groseilliers** (may•DAR groh•ze•YAI) were fur traders. Most Canadian traders made the difficult journey to the north woods by land. There they would trap beaver and other animals. Radisson and his partner had a clever idea. They realized they could reach the fur country more easily by sailing into Hudson Bay.

Their first voyage yielded them a fortune in furs. They asked the French king to put up the money for more expeditions. He refused. Then he placed Groseilliers in jail for trading without a license.

In 1666 the two partners went to England. These rugged explorers became very popular with the English nobles. The nobles nicknamed them "Mr. Radishes and Mr. Gooseberry." King Charles of England agreed to help the young traders. In 1670 the king granted them permission to start a fur-trading business called the **Hudson's Bay Company.** The business proved to be very successful. As a result the English king became even more interested in Canadian lands.

The French and Indian War

Relations between France and Britain became increasingly difficult. Both claimed the Ohio River valley as well as the Hudson Bay area. The **French and Indian War** broke out in 1754. In the war many Indians fought on the side of the French.

The British sent large numbers of men, ships, and arms to Canada. They hoped to defeat the French easily. They had not counted, however, on the brilliant leadership of the French general **Louis Montcalm.** Time and again Montcalm's forces turned back the British.

In the summer of 1759, the British general **James Wolfe** decided on a new plan. With 8,000 men he traveled up the St. Lawrence River to the city of Quebec. His intention was to capture Quebec. From June until September, Wolfe tried, but failed, to take the city. The steep and rocky cliffs made it difficult for the British to attack. Winter was coming on. General Wolfe realized that the St. Lawrence River would soon freeze over. If that happened, they could not leave by ship. With time running out, Wolfe settled on a last, desperate attempt.

In darkness Wolfe and his men rowed upriver past Quebec. They scaled the difficult cliffs in the dead of night. They reached a flat plain behind the city. At sunrise the British attacked. The British won the fierce battle that followed, but both Wolfe and Montcalm were killed. The rest of Canada soon fell to the British.

In 1763 a peace treaty was signed. France gave its North American lands east of the Mississippi to Britain. Madame Pompadour, a friend of the French king, was not upset. "Canada," she announced, "was useful only to provide me with furs." French Canadians did not agree with her at all. Sixty thousand French settlers stayed on in Canada.

British Rule

In 1774 the British Parliament passed the **Quebec Act.** This law allowed French Canadians to keep their laws, to speak their own language, and to practice their own religion.

In 1776 the 13 American colonies rebelled against British rule. The British watched anxiously to see if Canada would also have a revolution. It never happened. Most Canadians were happy with British rule. The Quebec Act helped maintain French-Canadian loyalty.

Westward Movement

In the decades before and after 1800, explorers were pushing across the North American continent. In Canada three men stand out as brave explorers.

Alexander Mackenzie led the first expedition to cross Canada all the way to the Pacific. His epic journey was made in 1793. In 1808 **Simon Fraser** followed Canada's wildest river, now called the Fraser, to the Pacific Ocean.

David Thompson may have been Canada's greatest explorer. He was a master surveyor, astronomer, and mapmaker. The Indians respected him very much. They called him "Koo-koo-sint," the man who looks at the stars.

Thompson worked for the North West Company, a fur-trading business. In 1810 his employers gave him

David Thompson, an astronomer and expert surveyor, explored much of western Canada.

a difficult job. They knew the Americans were trying to reach the mouth of the Columbia River. Thompson was to get there before the Americans did. Thompson and his crew traveled by horse, on foot, and finally by canoe. Through the Canadian Rockies and down the mighty Columbia they struggled. The trip was long and hard. At last they saw the bright shoreline of the Pacific Ocean. There on the water's edge stood a rugged log fort—Fort Astoria. The Americans had arrived first!

Thompson continued to explore the West for 25 years. His huge map of western Canada was very accurate.

A canoe of the Hudson's Bay Company shoots the rapids. This picture was painted by Frances Ann Hopkins, who was married to a company agent. Can you see her in the canoe?

Becoming a Nation

The British Parliament passed the **British North America Act** in 1867. This law united all of Canada into one nation. It gave Canada a representative government. Under the law Britain held the final word in Canadian affairs. The British North America Act provided a framework for the new Canadian nation. Canada grew and prospered.

In 1931 Parliament passed the **Statute of Westminster.** This law gave Canada more independence. It could conduct its own foreign affairs. However, Canada still remained partly under British rule.

In 1982 Queen Elizabeth signed the papers giving Canada its constitution.

In 1965 Canada adopted its own flag, with the symbol of a maple leaf. The new flag showed Canada's growing independence from Britain.

Canada's constitution had been the British North America Act of 1867. This yellowing old document, tied up with a scarlet ribbon, rested in the House of Lords in Britain. The British Parliament, not the Canadian Parliament, made changes in the constitution.

In 1982 the British Parliament passed its last law dealing with Canada. At the request of Canada, the British voted to send the constitution to Canada. Canada also requested that a Charter of Rights and Freedoms be added to the constitution. This statement of rights is similar to our own Bill of Rights. In addition, it recognizes the equality of men and women under the law.

Now completely independent, Canada still holds to part of its British heritage. It remains a member of the **Commonwealth of Nations.** This is the name given to territories that give allegiance to the British crown. Many members of the Commonwealth are territories formerly ruled by Britain. Others remain under British control. Canadians are loyal to Elizabeth II, queen of Great Britain and head of the Commonwealth.

 Reading Check

1. Why did both France and England claim parts of Canada?
2. What happened in Quebec in 1759?
3. Name three Canadian explorers.

Think Beyond What advantages did Canada gain by becoming an independent nation?

People MAKE HISTORY

Frances Ann Hopkins
1838–1918

▶▶▶▶▶▶▶▶▶▶▶▶▶

More than a hundred years ago, fur traders, Indian guides, and agents for the Hudson's Bay Company canoed into remote areas of Canada. They paddled through dense fog on Lake Superior and struggled to control their canoes in the raging rapids of Canada's mighty rivers. Historians know of these adventures because they were painted by an artist named Frances Ann Hopkins.

Frances Ann Hopkins was born in London, England. Not much is known about her early training in art. However, she was probably influenced by members of her family. Her grandfather was a well-known portrait painter. Her father was a navy admiral and Arctic explorer who drew scenes of his travels.

In 1858 Hopkins moved to Canada to be with her husband, Edward Hopkins, who worked for the Hudson's Bay Company. At first, the family lived near Montreal, where she painted scenes of the city, the St. Lawrence River, and the Ottawa district. Later, she traveled throughout the Northwest in trading canoes with her husband. Along the way she sketched and painted scenes of what she saw. She often included herself in the canoe scenes.

In 1870 Hopkins may have been the only woman to travel with an expedition on the Red River. She later produced a large painting of this journey. The painting shows the beauty and adventure of this famous canoe trip.

Sometime during the 1870s, Hopkins returned to England to live. Her paintings and sketches were exhibited in several important museums and galleries there. However, her work was not as popular in Canada and did not sell well.

If Frances Ann Hopkins were alive today, she might be pleased to know that her art is now very much appreciated by Canadians. In 1988 Canada issued a commemorative stamp in her honor. In 1990 a major showing of her paintings was held in Thunder Bay, Ontario.

Think Beyond   Why do you think people in Canada did not at first appreciate Hopkins's paintings?

Majestic mountains like these greeted Hopkins on her journey through Canada.

587

SKILLS IN ACTION

READING A ROAD MAP

A road map shows you where places are. It also shows you how to get from place to place. This road map shows part of Washington state and Canada.

Road maps may be large or small. They may show a nation or just part of a city.

All road maps, however, use a grid of letters and numbers. They also have an index. The index gives the grid location for each listing. You can look up the name of a city in the map index. Then you can use grid numbers and letters to find the city on the map. For example, Bellingham is listed with the letter and number *B-4*. It is found in the square formed by the intersection of the "B" column and the "4" column.

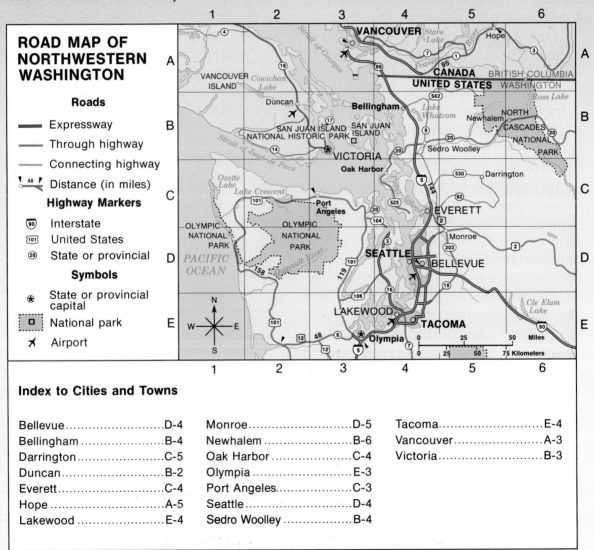

Index to Cities and Towns

588

Most road maps have a distance scale so you can measure distances between places. The scale on this map is in the lower right-hand corner. Most maps also show the actual number of miles between places. These places are marked by black wedges called distance markers. You can look at the legend to see what the distance markers look like. How far is it from Vancouver (A-3) to Bellevue (D-4)?

The map key also gives information about the kinds of roads shown on the map. It can help you plan the quickest route from one place to another. Look at the map key. It tells you that expressways are printed in blue. In some parts of the country expressways are also called freeways or turnpikes. Travel on expressways is usually quick because it is not interrupted by stoplights or crossroad traffic.

What color are through highways on the map? Through highways are main roads but, unlike expressways, they may have stoplights and crossroads.

A connecting highway is usually a two-lane road. What color does this map show for a connecting highway?

Symbols as well as colors are used to mark highways on road maps. Find the symbol for **interstate highways.** Interstate highways are expressways that cross several states. Find the symbol for United States highways. These highways also cross several states. They may be either broad expressways or two-lane roads. The symbols used for state or provincial highways identify roads that begin and end in one state or province. They often connect with roads in a bordering state or province.

The route numbers make it easy to talk about travel plans. For example, someone might say: "Here's how you get from Tacoma to North Cascades National Park. Take Interstate 5 north until you come to state highway 20. Take highway 20 east. Follow it to the park."

Try following this route on the map. Find Hope, British Columbia, in square A-5 of the map. With your finger, trace highway 1 west until it reaches Vancouver. Now find highway 99 and move your finger south until you come to the Canadian–United States border. What is the number of this expressway in the United States?

Usually road maps identify certain kinds of places with symbols. On this map the symbol of the airplane helps you locate airports. One airport shown on this map is near Seattle. In what squares are there other airports?

Another symbol on this map identifies a national park. According to the symbol, national parks are shown in a light green color. You will notice a small box within the national park symbol. This means that a small box will be used instead of a color if the park is very small. The symbol of the small box is used on this map to show San Juan Island National Historic Park.

CHECKING YOUR SKILLS

Use the map to answer these questions.

1. What state highways on the map pass into Darrington?

2. What is the shortest route from Bellingham to Monroe?

3. In what square is San Juan Island?

4. What national park is nearest Port Angeles?

5. Find Olympia. What two routes could you take to reach Port Angeles? Which is probably the fastest?

6. What is the distance between Port Angeles and Olympia?

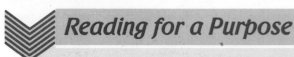
Look for these important words:

Key Words
- provinces
- House of Commons
- Senate
- prime minister
- ministers
- Separatists
- acid rain

Places
- Newfoundland
- Nova Scotia
- New Brunswick
- Prince Edward Island
- Quebec
- Ontario

- Manitoba
- Saskatchewan
- Alberta
- British Columbia
- Yukon Territory
- Northwest Territories
- Georges Bank

Look for answers to these questions:

1. How is the nation of Canada organized?
2. What is the structure of Canada's government? What is the head of government called?
3. What are some examples of cooperation between Canada and the United States?

3 Canada Today

Today Canada has one of the highest standards of living in the world. Canada has become a modern industrial power. It is a democratic nation respected around the globe.

Ottawa, Canada's capital, is Canada's twelfth-largest city. Ottawa is not the center of any important industry. Like Washington, D.C., Ottawa is important primarily because it is the center of Canada's national government. Canada's lawmaking body, or Parliament, is housed in three stone buildings that overlook the Ottawa River.

The Provinces

Canada today is a federation of ten **provinces** and two territories. A Canadian province is a political region like one of our states. The provinces are **Newfoundland, Nova Scotia,** **New Brunswick, Prince Edward Island, Quebec, Ontario, Manitoba, Saskatchewan** (suh•SKACH•uh•wuhn), **Alberta,** and **British Columbia.** The territories are the **Yukon** and the **Northwest Territories.** These are large areas in the far north with small populations.

Each province has its own government. Each provincial government makes laws about education, health, working conditions, and the use of natural resources. It also handles other matters within the province. Canadian provinces have a great deal of power and authority.

Canada's Parliament

The Canadian Parliament is made up of two houses—the **House of**

Commons and the **Senate.** The House of Commons is the more powerful and important of the two houses. This group has 295 members. Elections to choose members of the House of Commons are held at least every five years. New elections may be called at any time by the political party in power. The party in power has the most members in the House of Commons.

The leader of the majority party is the **prime minister.** The prime minister is the most important elected official in Canada. Like our President, the prime minister heads the executive branch of government. Unlike our President, the prime minister is not elected nationwide. The prime minister is first elected as a representative

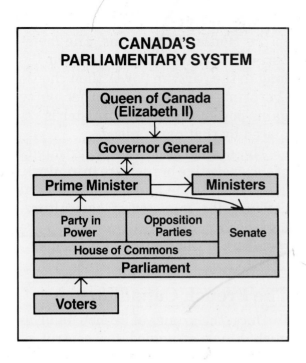

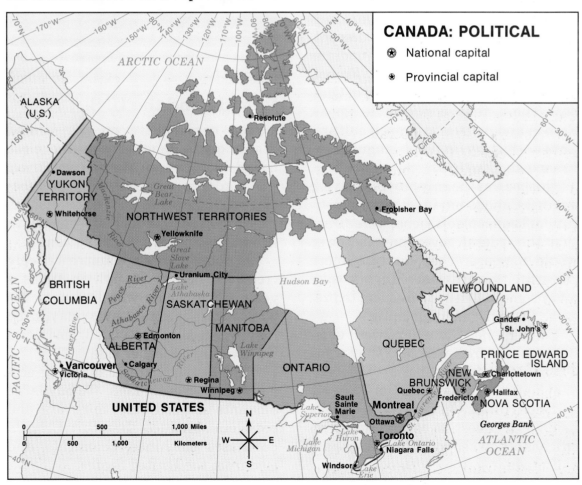

to the House of Commons. The members of the House of Commons who belong to the party in power then choose the prime minister. If another party gains power, the prime minister is replaced by that party's leader.

The people who head departments of the executive branch are **ministers.** They include the minister of national defense, the minister of agriculture, and the minister of transport. They are members of the House of Commons.

The French Canadians

Once, the armies of French and English kings struggled for control of Canada. Today, some of that conflict remains.

Almost one-half of Canada's 25 million people are of British descent. About one-third of all Canadians are of French descent. Most French Canadians live in the province of Quebec. There they continue to speak French and hold on to French culture. Canada has two official languages—French and English.

Quebec was the only province to vote against Canada having its own constitution. The people of Quebec were afraid that the federal government's power would increase. They feared a more powerful government might take away some of Quebec's freedom to preserve French Canadian culture.

Some French Canadians want Quebec to secede from Canada. They want Quebec to become a separate, independent nation. These people are known as **Separatists.** In 1980 a vote was held on the question of secession. The citizens of Quebec voted to remain part of Canada.

Canada prints signs in both English and French.

Canada and the U. S.

The border between the United States and Canada shows the close friendship between our two countries. The border is not protected in any special way. There are no fences. Visitors crossing the border are given a friendly welcome by each nation.

Citizens of both countries freely cross the border 70 million times a year. Some people who live near the border cross it almost every day. They may work, shop, or visit friends and relatives on the other side.

The United States has strong economic ties with Canada. We buy large amounts of wood pulp, minerals, and petroleum products. In return Canada purchases machines, chemicals, and food from the United States.

592

The United States and Canada worked together to build the St. Lawrence Seaway. This project is an example of the friendship and cooperation that exists between the nations.

The United States and Canada have also cooperated in space programs. With help from NASA, Canada launched its first satellite in 1962. Since then Canada has sent up other satellites.

More recently Canada and the United States have worked together on the space shuttle. One of the most important parts of the space shuttle is a mechanical arm. This arm can pick up and place objects in space. It was developed by Canadian scientists.

Although a lasting friendship exists between the United States and Canada, we have some disagreements.

Canadians are particularly upset about the air pollution caused by industries. Many of these are coal-burning power plants in the United States. When air pollutants combine with moisture in the atmosphere, **acid rain** results. Acid rain can cause fish to die in lakes and rivers. Acid rain may slow down growth of forests. Acid rain is affecting large parts of Canada and the United States. Both countries have been doing research on acid rain. In January 1986, a United States–Canada report agreed that acid rain is a serious problem. The United States and Canada have agreed to work to control air pollution.

Canada and the United States have also disagreed about fishing rights on the **Georges Bank.** This is a huge area off the coasts of Nova Scotia and

GEOGRAPHY CONNECTION

Billboards in Canada now urge people to "Join us against acid rain." Radio messages warn about acid rain's ill effects. Already there are 14,000 lakes in Canada that have no fish. The maple syrup and sugar industry in both Canada and the United States may also be in danger. However, Canada and the United States are not the only countries that are being affected.

Pollution from factories in Canada and the United States may end up in countries as far away as Great Britain and China. Pollution from those countries may also affect our lakes and rivers.

Passing laws against the amount of pollutants that may be released into the air can help stop acid rain. However, one

country cannot do the work alone. Countries all over the world need to join together to solve this problem.

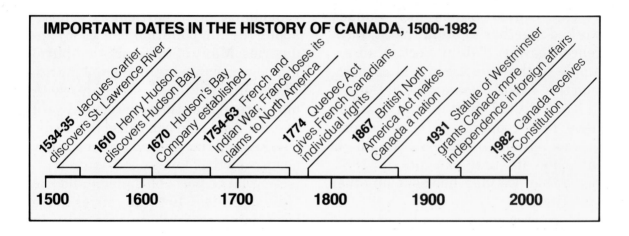

IMPORTANT DATES IN THE HISTORY OF CANADA, 1500-1982

1534-35 Jacques Cartier discovers St. Lawrence River

1610 Henry Hudson discovers Hudson Bay

1670 Hudson's Bay Company established

1754-63 French and Indian War; France loses its claims to North America

1774 Quebec Act gives French Canadians individual rights

1867 British North America Act makes Canada a nation

1931 Statute of Westminster grants Canada more independence in foreign affairs

1982 Canada receives its Constitution

1500 1600 1700 1800 1900 2000

Terry Fox runs in Quebec as part of his fund-raising marathon across Canada.

Maine. It is one of the world's richest fishing grounds. For many years, both Canada and the United States claimed Georges Bank.

This disagreement had to be settled by an international court. In 1984 the court awarded most of the northern portion of the Georges Bank to Canada. This area has the best fishing grounds for scallops. Fishers from the United States are upset by the court's decision.

There will always be challenges, both for nations and for individuals. The challenge met by one brave man, Terry Fox, inspired Canadians. Terry, who had lost his right leg to cancer, ran 3,339 miles (5,372 km) across Canada to raise funds for cancer research. Terry Fox died in 1981. Yet he remains a hero to all of Canada.

Reading Check

1. What is Canada's capital city?
2. What is the name of Canada's most important lawmaking body?
3. How is Canada's prime minister chosen?

Think Beyond How have the United States and Canada remained friendly?

THE MOUNTIES

Northwestern Canada in the 1800s was a wild frontier. Crime and violence were serious problems. So, the Canadian government sent a scout to this sparsely settled area in the 1870s to investigate. The scout reported that "the region is without law, order or security for life or property. Robbery and murder for years have gone unpunished. Indian massacres are unchecked." The scout recommended that a force on horseback be sent to keep the peace.

In 1873 the Canadian government took his advice. It organized a force called the North West Mounted Police. Later it would be called the Royal Canadian Mounted Police or the Mounties.

There were 300 men in the first group of Mounties. They rode fine horses and wore scarlet jackets and blue trousers with gold stripes.

The job of bringing peace to the Canadian west was huge. "No more wildly impossible undertaking was ever staged," said one of the early leaders. Yet the Mounties succeeded. Many people—traders, prospectors, and Indians—owed their lives to these mounted men.

The Mounties had help in their huge task. Indian leaders cooperated with them. One such leader was Crowfoot, chief of the Blackfeet. "The Mounted Police have protected us as the feathers of the bird protect it from the frosts of winter," he said.

The Mounties became famous for never giving up in their pursuit of a criminal. One man was very famous because he solved so many crimes. This man, Alick Pennycuick (pen•ee•kwɪk), became known as the Sherlock Holmes of the Mounted Police.

Today the Royal Canadian Mounted Police use horses only on parade. They carry out their work using cars, trucks, snowmobiles, airplanes, and boats. Women joined the Mounties for the first time in 1974.

The tradition of the Mounties is the same today as it has always been. Throughout Canada's vast spaces, the Mounties maintain the peace and see that justice is done.

Think Beyond   Why do you think Indian leaders were eager to cooperate with the Mounties?

Mounties on parade

595

Thinking Back

- Canada is rich in natural resources. Its most important resource is water.

- Canada has six natural regions. Most Canadians live in the St. Lawrence River Lowlands region.

- People from both England and France settled Canada. France was forced to give up its lands east of the Mississippi River after the French and Indian War.

- Thousands of French settlers remained in Canada. The Quebec Act allowed French Canadians to keep their culture. As a result, Canada has both a French and British heritage.

- Alexander Mackenzie, Simon Fraser, and David Thompson helped push the Canadian frontier westward across North America.

- The British North America Act of 1867 united all of Canada into one country. However, Canada did not achieve complete independence until 1982. Canada still remains a member of the Commonwealth of Nations.

- Canada today is a federation of ten provinces and two territories. The Parliament is made up of two houses. The head of government is the prime minister.

- Most French Canadians live in the province of Quebec. French and English are the official languages of Canada.

- The United States and Canada carry on extensive trade. Both are working to control the problem of acid rain.

Check for Understanding

Using Words

Number your paper from 1 to 10. Use the terms below to complete the sentences that follow.

Canadian Shield	**provinces**
House of Commons	**Quebec**
Ottawa	**Vancouver**
prime minister	**Winnipeg**
St. Lawrence Seaway	
St. Lawrence River Lowlands	

1. Most people in Canada live in the _____ .

2. Ocean-going ships can travel through the Great Lakes because in 1959 the United States and Canada built the _____ .

3. Most French Canadians live in the province of _____ .

4. _____ is the largest city in the Interior Plains region of Canada.

5. The capital of Canada is _____ .

6. The natural region that covers half of Canada is called the _____ .

7. _____ is a large city on the Pacific coast in British Columbia.

8. Canada's most important lawmaking body is the _____ .

9. Political regions in Canada that are similar to our states are called _____ .

10. The most important elected official in Canada is the _____ .

Reviewing Facts

1. What is Canada's greatest natural resource?
2. What was the basis of British claims to Canada?
3. Why did Canadians not join the rebellion against British rule during the American Revolution?
4. How did the French and Indian War affect Canada?
5. How did Canada gain full independence from Britain in 1982?

Thinking Critically

1. What qualities and skills must David Thompson have had?
2. How is the Canadian government similar to the government of the United States? What differences exist between the two?
3. Do you think Americans should be interested in Canadian events? Explain.

Writing About It

Review the information on Canada's geographical regions. Find the area that is most like the area in which you live. Then write two paragraphs comparing and contrasting the two areas.

Practicing Geography Skills

Reading a Road Map

Use the road map on page 588 to answer these questions.

1. In which square is Victoria?
2. How would you get from Newhalem to Tacoma?
3. How far is it from Hope to Vancouver?
4. What highway passes through Sedro Woolley?

On Your Own

Social Studies at Home

1. Trace the map of Canada on page 578. On your map, draw a red canoe on the river on which William Fraser traveled in 1808. Then draw a blue canoe on the river on which David Thompson traveled in 1810. Make up a map symbol for Fort Astoria and use it to locate the fort on your map. Finally, make a map key that explains the symbols on your map.
2. With your family's help, write a play about one part of Canada's history. You may choose to write about Count Frontenac, the French and Indian War, or how Canada became an independent nation. Choose classmates to perform in your play, and prepare to present it to the class.

Read More About It

The Journey of Shadow Bairns by Margaret Jean Anderson. Alfred A. Knopf. After unexpected adventures, orphaned Elspeth realizes her father's dream of settling on the Saskatchewan prairie.

Ten Moments in Canadian History by Marian Ogden Sketch. Campbell. These stories tell of the accomplishments of soldiers, adventurers, and ordinary people.

St. Lawrence by Trudy J. Hanmer. Franklin Watts. This book illustrates the history, culture, economy, and ecology of Canada's St. Lawrence River Lowlands region.

Very Last Time by Jan Andrews. Illustrated by Ian Wallace. Atheneum. This is the tale of an Inuit girl's expedition to dig for mussels in Canada's arctic north.

CHAPTER 23

Mexico—Neighbor to the South

❝As we rode along, we found that the scenery on the hilly parts was generally bleak and sterile, the grass dried up, and very little vegetation; but wherever we arrived at a valley sheltered from the sun's rays, there we found a little rivulet trickling through it, with water like liquid diamonds, bathing the trees and the flowers— the loveliest blossoming trees, mingled with bananas, oranges, and lemons, and interspersed with bright flowers, forming a natural garden and orchard. ❞

—Spanish lady residing in Mexico, 1840

Look for these important words:

Key Words
• Ring of Fire

Places
• Parícutin
• El Chichón
• Mexico City
• Gulf Coast

• Yucatán Peninsula
• Rio Grande
• Monterrey
• Veracruz
• Sierra Madre
• Durango
• Puebla
• Oaxaca

• Central Plateau
• Pacific Coast
• Mazatlán
• Puerto Vallarta
• Acapulco
• Baja California
• Ensenada
• Tijuana

Look for answers to these questions:
1. Why does Mexico have a wide variety of climates?
2. What kinds of natural regions are there in Mexico?
3. Where do most people in Mexico live?

1 *Mexico's Geography*

Americans like to vacation at Mexico's sunny beaches and other resort areas. For this reason some Americans think of Mexico as a warm and gentle place. Mexico actually is a land of great variety and contrast.

Mexico is about one-fourth as large as the United States. Its population is over 82 million.

Mexico is one of the most mountainous countries in the world. Only one-third of the country is level land. In the early sixteenth century, the Spanish conquistador Hernando Cortés was asked about Mexico's geography. He crumpled up a piece of paper and threw it down on a table. "That," he exclaimed, "is the map of Mexico!"

We know that climate changes as we move north or south away from the equator. Canada, for example, is generally colder than the United States because it is farther north. Climate also changes with elevation. Low-lying lands tend to be warmer than high, mountainous areas. Air in mountain regions does not hold heat as well as air at lower elevations.

Because of its many mountains, Mexico has a great variety of climates. They vary from the lowland rain forest climate to the cool air of the mountains.

Mexico also has great extremes of precipitation. In the northwest desert only a few drops of rain fall each year. In the eastern jungles 100 inches (254 cm) of rain may fall. One area, the Grijalva (gree•HAHL•vuh) River valley in the south, can receive 200 inches (508 cm) a year.

Ring of Fire

Perhaps the most awesome natural force in Mexico is the volcano. Mexico lies in a region called the **Ring of Fire.** This is a circular band of volcanoes located along the western coast of the

Americas and the eastern coast of Asia. The Ring of Fire contains active volcanoes and thousands of extinct ones.

In 1943 a farmer was working in his cornfield in western Mexico. He noticed a strange crack in his field. Out of the crack arose hot, smelly smoke. The next day the farmer returned to find a mound of volcanic lava.

For nine years lava poured from the center of the mound. Then, in only eight months, the lava piled up to a height of 2,000 feet (609.6 m) above the valley floor. It buried all villages and farms in the area. Now only the broken tower of a church sticks out through the lava. The name of this volcano is **Parícutin** (puh•REE•kuh•teen).

In 1982 an ancient volcano again erupted. This was **El Chichón** (chee•CHON) in the state of Chiapas in southern Mexico. There were two eruptions of El Chichón, each a week apart. The gases from the El Chichón eruptions produced the largest volcanic cloud in the Northern Hemisphere since 1912. Gas and ashes from the volcano shot 10 miles (16 km) into the sky. Rocks hailed on the surrounding countryside. Everywhere, roofs were crushed, trees turned to charcoal, and fields were covered with rock and ash. A fertile valley was turned into a wasteland, and thousands were killed.

Earthquakes and volcanoes often go together. Some of the world's worst earthquakes have occurred near the Ring of Fire. In September 1985, a terrible earthquake struck Mexico. In **Mexico City,** the nation's capital, as many as 10,000 people were killed. More than 2,000 buildings were destroyed or heavily damaged.

Five Natural Regions

Mexico has five natural regions. The natural features, climate, and products are different for each of these regions.

The **Gulf Coast** region, consisting of lowlands, is thinly populated.

A church steeple among hardened lava is all that remains of this Mexican village. It was destroyed in the 1940s by the erupting volcano Parícutin.

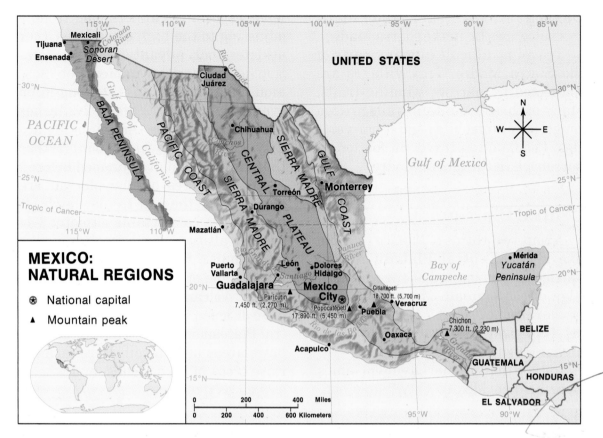

MEXICO:
NATURAL REGIONS

⊛ National capital

▲ Mountain peak

The region stretches from the jungles of the **Yucatán Peninsula** to the mouth of the **Rio Grande.** The Gulf Coast climate is quite warm. The northern part is a desert. The southern coast is a tropical rain forest. In this part of the Gulf Coast region farmers grow coffee, sugarcane, and bananas. Henequen, a plant used to make rope, is grown in the Yucatán.

Monterrey is this region's largest city. It is home to Mexico's large steel and automobile industries.

Much of the region's economic activity centers on the oil industry. Rich supplies of oil are found in the Gulf of Mexico.

The developing oil industry has led to the growth of the whole region, particularly the seaport of **Veracruz.** In earlier days Veracruz was surrounded by swamps and marshes. These areas harbored hordes of mosquitoes and other insects. The insects carried many deadly diseases. Veracruz was known as the City of Death.

Today Mexican people are clearing jungles and draining swamps along the Gulf Coast. This work has made Veracruz a safe place to live. It has also created more usable farmland in the region.

The Sierra Madre

Three mountain ranges combine to form the Y-shaped **Sierra Madre** (see•ER•uh MAHD•dray) region. These ranges are known as the Eastern, Southern, and Western Sierra Madre. This rugged region includes the cities of **Durango, Puebla,** and

Oaxaca (wuh·HAHK·uh). All of Mexico's volcanoes lie in the Sierra Madre.

Travel is difficult in many parts of the Sierra Madre. Tiny villages are connected by narrow, winding trails. Many of these mountain trails are too rough for automobiles and other vehicles. People often travel on foot or on horseback in the Sierra Madre.

Central Plateau

About two-thirds of Mexico's people live in the **Central Plateau** region. Mexico City is located at the southern edge of the plateau. Mexico City has an elevation of about 7,000 feet (2,134 m). No larger city in the world has a higher elevation.

In 1968 the Summer Olympic Games were held in Mexico City. Some athletes, especially runners, had trouble adjusting to the high elevation. Other athletes took advantage of the location. An American named Bob Beamon participated in the long-jump event. He jumped 29 feet, 2½ inches (8.9 m) through the thin air of Mexico City. This was two feet (0.6 m) farther than anyone had ever jumped before.

Temperatures on the plateau are much cooler than in the lowlands. It has a more comfortable climate. The average altitude of the whole region is more than a mile (1.6 km) above sea level. Some of Mexico's best farmland is here. Volcanoes in the Sierra Madre have dumped volcanic ash on the Central Plateau for years. This has created large areas of rich soil. Here farmers raise crops of corn, beans, and wheat, as well as livestock.

The white-topped mountain in the distance is the volcano Popocatépetl (poh·puh·KAT·uh·pehtl). Once it showered forth ash and lava. Now it is serenely quiet.

Sunny Acapulco on Mexico's Pacific Coast is a popular tourist resort.

Many types of cactus grow in the deserts of Baja California.

Pacific Coast

Tourists from around the world enjoy Mexico's **Pacific Coast.** Its weather is sunny, and it features many beautiful beaches. The cities of **Mazatlán, Puerto Vallarta** (PWER·toh vuh·YAHR·tuh), and **Acapulco** (ahk·uh·PUL·koh) are among the region's most popular resort communities. Farmers in this region grow corn, cotton, coffee, and cocoa.

The northern section of the Pacific Coast consists of the Sonoran Desert. The Morelos Dam on the Colorado River has changed part of this desert into good farmland.

Baja California

The peninsula of **Baja** (BAH·hah) **California** is 800 miles (1,287 km) long. *Baja* means "lower" in Spanish. The Pacific Coast Range forms the mountainous backbone of the Baja peninsula.

Baja California is a land of desert, rugged mountains, and wind-swept beaches. It attracts tourists and people who like to fish in the ocean. Nature lovers come to see the great gray whales in the shallow waters along the coast. The largest communities in this region are **Ensenada** and the border town of **Tijuana** (tee·uh·WAHN·uh).

Reading Check

1. Name Mexico's natural regions.
2. In what natural region is Mexico City located?
3. Why is there rich soil in the Central Plateau region?

Think Beyond How do you think the Ring of Fire got its name?

Look for these important words:

Key Words
- *encomiendas*
- *ejidos*
- mestizos
- liberals
- La Reforma
- peasants
- Cinco de Mayo

- estates
- Mexican Constitution of 1917

People
- Hernando Cortés
- Miguel Hidalgo
- Santa Anna
- Benito Juárez

- Porfirio Díaz
- Francisco Madero
- Pancho Villa
- Emiliano Zapata

Places
- Chihuahua

Look for answers to these questions:
1. Why did Mexican people rebel against Spain?
2. What troubles and successes did Mexico have after independence from Spain?
3. Why did Mexico go through a second revolution in the twentieth century?

2 Mexico's History

Hernando Cortés conquered the Aztec rulers of Mexico in 1519 and claimed their land for Spain. Cortés and other conquistadors were given large pieces of Mexican land by the Spanish king. These land grants were called **encomiendas** (en•ko•MYEN•dahs). The Spanish forced the Indians to work on these lands. At first the Indians were treated as slaves, but Spain outlawed Indian slavery in 1542. After that, the Indians had to work on the *encomiendas* only about 45 days every year. Some Indians were forced to work in the mines. Gold and silver from the mines made Spain rich.

The Indians were allowed to farm small communal plots on poor land. These plots, owned in common by a village rather than by individuals, were called **ejidos** (ay•HEE•dohs).

The Catholic Church became a powerful force in New Spain. It was because of Church leaders such as Bartolomé de las Casas that Indian slavery was ended. The Church also became very wealthy. During 300 years of Spanish rule, the Church acquired about half of all the Mexican lands. At one point the Church also held two-thirds of all the money in Mexico.

Independence Achieved

Life in New Spain was hard and cruel for Indians. Life was also harsh for **mestizos,** people of mixed Indian and Spanish ancestry. Neither Indians nor mestizos had much chance for education and prosperity. Most of the wealth and power belonged to people of pure Spanish ancestry.

In the early 1800s this situation began to change. Mestizo priests and lawyers started reading books about freedom and democracy. They had heard about the American and French revolutions. Many had read the American Declaration of Independence. Some of these priests and lawyers dreamed of liberty and equality for Mexico. They wanted to see mestizos have as much power as the Spaniards. Others dreamed of a new prosperity. Many of them dreamed of revolution.

Finally, many Mexican people could take no more of Spanish rule. In 1810 a revolution started. A mestizo priest, **Miguel Hidalgo,** rang a church bell to call for a people's revolt. Thousands of mestizos and Indians joined him. Hidalgo himself was captured and executed by the Spanish in 1811. The revolution continued, however, for ten more years. In 1821 Mexico finally won its freedom from Spain.

Juárez Brings Reforms

Independence failed to solve many of Mexico's problems. Mexico was poor, with the Church holding most of the money. Mexicans had no experience in ruling themselves. The Aztecs had obeyed one ruler. Then for 300 years a viceroy, the king's representative, had ruled. With independence came outbreaks of violence and civil war. Mexico was ruled off and on by one man, General Antonio Lopez de **Santa Anna.** More change was necessary if Mexico was to achieve peace and unity.

The person who did the most to create change in Mexico was **Benito Juárez** (HWAH·rays). In 1857 he became president of Mexico.

HISTORY CONNECTION

Mexico City was once the site of the proud Aztec city Tenochtitlán. The Great Temple in this city stood as the center of the Aztec Empire. In 1519 Spanish explorers conquered the Aztecs and destroyed the temple. As time passed, the temple was forgotten and became buried under the new Spanish buildings.

In 1978 workers digging a ditch in Mexico City rediscovered the Great Temple. When their shovels struck a huge stone, work was immediately stopped. Archaeologists were called in to investigate

the site. What they found were remains of the temple and elaborate carvings and statues that now connect us with the ancient Aztec civilization.

Juárez was a Zapotec Indian. He did not learn to speak Spanish until the age of 12. Juárez was a strong, honest leader, a man often compared to Abraham Lincoln. Juárez was supported by people calling themselves **liberals.** They believed in representative government and in laws based on a constitution. They also wanted private ownership of land.

The changes that Juárez and the liberals brought about were called **La Reforma**—"the reform." They established a new constitution. They took away the large landholdings of the Church. They broke up the *ejidos.* The land was divided among the Indian and mestizo **peasants.** Peasants are people who live and work on the land.

In 1862 the government of Benito Juárez ran out of money. Mexico owed a large amount of money to Britain, Spain, and France. Juárez told these nations that they would not be repaid for a few years. France then decided to invade Mexico. The French were supported by Mexican generals and others who did not like the reforms.

On May 5, 1862, a battle was fought at the city of Puebla. In this battle a small band of Mexicans defeated a large French army. The leader of the Mexican forces sent a telegram to Benito Juárez. It said, "The arms of the nation are covered with glory!" This battle is celebrated today as the Mexican national holiday **Cinco de Mayo.** *Cinco de Mayo* means "fifth of May." Cinco de Mayo is also celebrated by many Mexican Americans living in the United States.

Benito Juárez finally drove the French from Mexican soil in 1867. After the French left, Juárez returned to office as president. He was determined to make his country a better place to live. Under his leadership free public schools were established. New roads were built. Juárez served as president until his death in 1872.

At Puebla, on May 5, 1862, Mexicans defeated the rich and powerful French army. Although the victory gave Mexicans new hope, the French sent more troops. They governed Mexico for five years before the Mexicans at last drove them out.

The effort to achieve democracy and equality in Mexico came to an end in 1876. In that year **Porfirio Díaz** (DEE•ahz) led a revolt and took over as ruler of Mexico. Under Díaz the people stayed poor. They had little say in their government. Workers had to labor for low wages and could not form labor unions. Much of the land again ended up in the hands of large landholders. Large landholdings are called **estates.**

A Revolution Begins

In 1910 a Mexican writer named **Francisco Madero** ran for president against Díaz. During the election Díaz had Madero arrested and jailed. Many thousands of people voted for Madero anyway. Díaz announced, however, that Madero had received only 176 votes. Díaz declared that he himself had gathered over 1 million votes. The Mexican people were furious. They knew that Díaz had lied about the results of the voting. Within a few months a revolution had begun.

The first combat started in the rugged backcountry of **Chihuahua** (chee•WAH•wah). This area is in the northern part of the Western Sierra Madre. The leader there was named **Pancho Villa** (PAHN•cho VEE•yah). Villa was a cruel and violent man, but he was an excellent commander of soldiers. Before long, no train, estate, or government official was safe in the northern mountains.

Another leader of this Mexican revolution was fighting in the south of the country. His name was **Emiliano Zapata** (ay•mi•LYAH•noh sah•PAH•tah). Like Benito Juárez, Zapata was a man of high ideals and honesty. He wanted

Land for the peasants was a goal of Mexican revolutionary Emiliano Zapata.

nothing for himself. He wanted only that the land be owned by the people who worked on it. The slogan of his revolt was "Land and Liberty!"

Zapata had another favorite saying. He said, "It is better to die on your feet than to live on your knees." He was not afraid to die fighting for what he believed in.

Zapata and his men swarmed out of the mountains. They drove many rich landowners off their land, dividing up the great estates among the people. Zapata and his men often helped people farm land on the estates they had conquered.

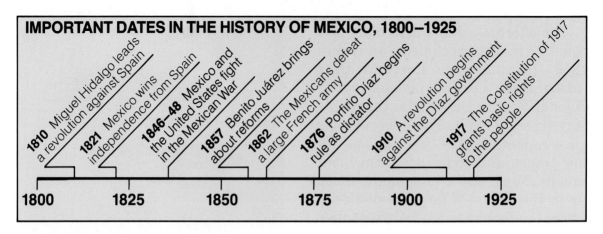

IMPORTANT DATES IN THE HISTORY OF MEXICO, 1800–1925

1810 Miguel Hidalgo leads a revolution against Spain

1821 Mexico wins independence from Spain

1846–48 Mexico and the United States fight in the Mexican War

1857 Benito Juárez brings about reforms

1862 The Mexicans defeat a large French army

1876 Porfirio Díaz begins rule as dictator

1910 A revolution begins against the Díaz government

1917 The Constitution of 1917 grants basic rights to the people

1800　1825　1850　1875　1900　1925

Zapata's colorful band of peasants marched across the country to Mexico City. There they met up with Pancho Villa and his men. Two ragtag armies of peasants, all Indians and mestizos,

The green, white, and red flag of Mexico is sold to people celebrating Constitution Day, an important national holiday.

had brought the Mexican government to its knees.

Terrified, Díaz resigned as president and fled to Europe. Zapata was eventually killed in an ambush, but the revolution went on. In 1917 Mexico's new political leaders called for a constitutional convention. They wanted to turn the ideals of Zapata and the other revolutionaries into law.

The Constitution of 1917

The **Mexican Constitution of 1917** gave workers the right to form labor unions. It gave the government control over education, farmland, and the oil industry. It limited the time a president could serve to just one term. This constitution is the heart and soul of Mexico's revolution.

Reading Check

1. Describe the influence of the Catholic Church in New Spain.
2. Why did Father Hidalgo call for a people's revolt?
3. What was *La Reforma*?

Think Beyond Why do you think Benito Juárez is compared to Abraham Lincoln?

608

People MAKE HISTORY

Father Hidalgo
1753–1812

►►►►►►►►►►►►►►►►►

In 1810 a Mexican priest rang a church bell and changed history. That priest was Father Miguel Hidalgo. Today Hidalgo is known as the Father of Mexican Independence.

Father Hidalgo was the priest for the small village of Dolores. Most of the people who lived in Dolores were poor Indians and mestizos. Father Hidalgo had helped them improve the economy by planting mulberry bushes, olive trees, and grapevines. With mulberry bushes, silkworms could be raised for spinning silk thread. Olive trees could produce olive oil. Grapevines could produce wine. Father Hidalgo then brought in beehives so that honey could be gathered. Father Hidalgo hoped that the people of Dolores could prosper selling silk, olive oil, wine, and honey.

Father Hidalgo's plan was good, but the Spanish government ruling Mexico at the time had other ideas. The Spanish leaders wanted Indians and mestizos to remain poor. They were suspicious that Father Hidalgo might have ideas other than economic ones—ideas of democracy and independence. Indeed, Father Hidalgo belonged to a secret society that planned a revolution against Spain. The Spanish authorities learned this and arrested one of the society's leaders.

When he discovered what had happened, Father Hidalgo acted. He rang the bell of his church to call the people of Dolores together. He told them that they would have to fight to win their freedom. "Down with bad government!" he cried out to them. "Long live Mexico!"

Father Hidalgo was a peaceful man and a deeply religious one. Suddenly, however, he found himself leading a great army that swept through Mexico. Thousands joined Hidalgo's forces.

Father Hidalgo was captured and executed in 1811. The Spaniards hoped this would end the fighting, but they were wrong. For ten more years, the Mexican people fought. Finally, in 1821, the last of the Spanish army fled the country. Mexico had won its independence!

Think Beyond   Do you think this revolution was anything like the American Revolution? Why or why not?

609

Reading for a Purpose

Look for these important words:

Key Words
- PRI

People
- Carlos Salinas de Gortari

Look for answers to these questions:
1. What is the structure of Mexico's government?
2. What is Mexico's most important political party?
3. What problems face Mexico today?
4. What are relations like between Mexico and the United States?

3 The Nation of Mexico Today

With a population of about 10 million people, Mexico City is one of the largest cities in the world. Like the country itself, Mexico City is a place of great contrasts. Modern skyscrapers cast shadows on lovely old colonial churches. Under the churches may lie the ruins of ancient Aztec structures. Horses and burros share the streets with automobiles. There are neighborhoods of beautiful homes, and there are tenements overcrowded with poor people.

Mexico City stands on the same site as did Tenochtitlán, the capital of the Aztecs. Tenochtitlán was built in the fourteenth century. This makes Mexico City the oldest city in the Western Hemisphere. As in Aztec times, the power and population of Mexico is centered in the capital.

Mexico's Government

In many ways Mexico's government is like that of the United States. Mexico is a democratic federation of 31 states. Like our country, Mexico has three branches of government. They are the legislative, judicial, and executive branches. The president, who serves as chief executive, is particularly powerful.

Mexico's National Palace is located on Constitution Plaza in Mexico City.

610

Mexico's government is also different from ours. In the United States the two leading political parties are the Democrats and the Republicans. During the last 50 years we have had five Democratic Presidents and six Republican Presidents.

In Mexico, at present, there is one political party that is stronger than the others. This party is the **PRI**, the Institutional Revolutionary party. The PRI has not lost an election since 1929. Another political party is the National Action party (PAN).

In the United States 13 colonies came together to form a federation of states. These states preserved many powers for themselves. In Mexico the federal government divided the country into 31 states. These states have very little power. Much of the country's political power is in the hands of its president.

Mexico and the World

Mexico's plans for the future have depended on oil. Vast new fields of

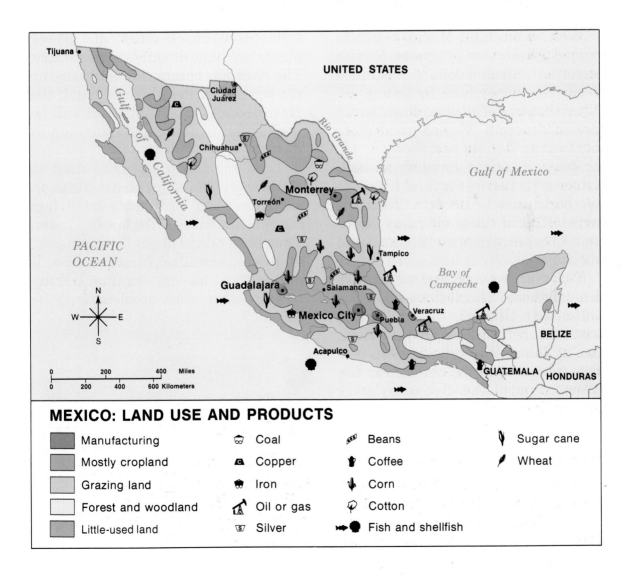

MEXICO: LAND USE AND PRODUCTS

Manufacturing	Coal	Beans	Sugar cane
Mostly cropland	Copper	Coffee	Wheat
Grazing land	Iron	Corn	
Forest and woodland	Oil or gas	Cotton	
Little-used land	Silver	Fish and shellfish	

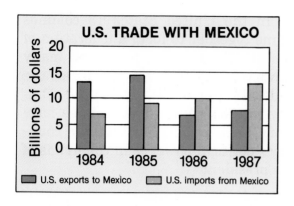

U.S. TRADE WITH MEXICO

Billions of dollars

1984 1985 1986 1987

■ U.S. exports to Mexico ■ U.S. imports from Mexico

Mexican oil were found in 1976. Mexico is now the fifth-leading producer of oil in the world. Some experts believe that Mexico will be the largest producer in the world by 1999.

With so much oil Mexico began to expand government programs. Mexico borrowed billions of dollars. It planned to pay the money back by selling oil. When the price of oil went down, so did Mexico's income. Mexico owed more money than it could pay.

Mexico is now tightening its belt, reducing its borrowing, and trying to pay back some of its debt. This is a period of hard times for many Mexicans. There is high unemployment and inflation. Poverty is increasing.

The man who is leading Mexico through these difficult times is **Carlos Salinas de Gortari.** He was elected president in 1988 for a six-year term. Two of Salinas's priorities are to promote advances in the democratic life of Mexico and to lead the country's war on poverty.

Mexico and the U. S.

The United States wants Mexico to be prosperous. To help Mexico develop its industries, American banks have loaned money to Mexico. If Mexico cannot repay its loans, the American economy will suffer.

Mexico is an important trading partner of the United States. Only Canada and Japan carry on more trade with the United States. We purchase Mexican cotton, sugar, coffee, shrimp, beef, minerals, and oil. Mexico buys machinery, automobiles, and chemicals from our country. Prosperity in Mexico will lead to even more trade.

We still have disagreements with Mexico, just as we do with Canada. Mexico has complained that American farmers are taking too much water from the Colorado River. American farmers, ranchers, cities, and power plants use huge amounts of this water. The river has become low and salty by the time it reaches Mexican soil. If the river becomes much saltier, it will be useless for drinking and irrigation in Mexico.

Leaders of both countries want to settle their shared problems. Mexican and American Presidents have had many conferences in the last few years. They have talked about fishing rights, oil prices, and illegal immigration. If our political leaders continue talking to each other, such problems may be solved.

Reading Check

1. In what ways is Mexico City a city of contrasts?
2. What is the name of Mexico's leading political party?
3. Give two examples of how the economies of Mexico and the United States are connected.

Think Beyond Why is the price of oil important to Mexico?

IN FOCUS

THE BALLET FOLKLÓRICO

At Mexican festivals, you can count on one thing: there will be plenty of dancing. Mexico has a tradition of dancing that goes back more than 1,000 years. Each of Mexico's many Indian tribes has its own dances, complete with unique costumes and special music. When the Spanish came to Mexico in the 1500s, they brought dances of their own. The Mexican people have combined these two traditions to create many different styles of dance.

The best way to see all the different types of Mexican dance is to watch the *Ballet Folklórico de Bellas Artes*, the Fine Arts Folk Ballet. The Ballet Folklórico was started in 1952 by Amalia Hernandez. She noticed that some of the dances were being forgotten as people moved to the cities from the small towns. She feared that these traditions would be lost forever.

A performance by the Ballet Folklórico is a journey through the history of Mexican dance. It starts with the solemn plume dance, an ancient Indian ritual. From there the performers seem to move through time and space, dancing as people did in different parts of Mexico during each era of Mexican history. They dance the Yaqui (YAHK•ee) Deer Dance, an Indian hunting ritual. They also perform dances from the Mexican Revolution period, complete with the drum-and-harp music of the era.

The Ballet Folklórico performs all over the world, but its home is the Palace of Fine Arts in Mexico City. The Palace is made of white marble, and its inside walls are painted with folk scenes by Mexico's finest artists. The stage curtain at the Palace is made of pieces of colored glass that form a picture of the great valley of south central Mexico, with its two tall volcanoes.

Thanks to the Ballet Folklórico, visitors need not travel all over Mexico to see its many traditional dances. They can enjoy the spectacle without journeying any farther than their seats at the Ballet Folklórico in Mexico City.

Think Beyond Why do you think it is important for the Mexican folk dances to be preserved?

Mexican folk dancers

SKILLS IN ACTION

UNDERSTANDING CLIMATE

Latitude and Climate

The Earth is divided into three major climate zones, depending on latitude. Separating these zones are parallels, or lines of latitude, with special names. You should remember that the equator is the parallel that divides the world into its northern and southern hemispheres. North of the equator are the Tropic of Cancer and the Arctic Circle. South of the equator are the Tropic of Capricorn and the Antarctic Circle.

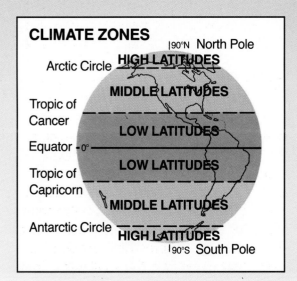

CLIMATE ZONES

The Tropics

The area between the Tropic of Cancer and the Tropic of Capricorn is the tropics. Remember that in the tropics the sun is almost directly overhead at noon all year long. The sun's rays produce high temperatures on the ground. For that reason the tropics are generally the warmest part of Earth.

Areas between the Tropic of Cancer and the Tropic of Capricorn are sometimes called **low latitude** areas. The latitude of

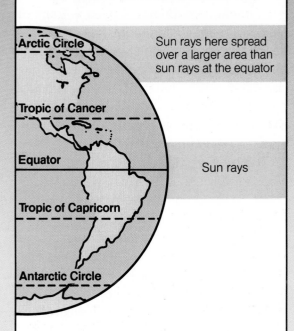

HOW THE SUN'S RAYS AFFECT THE EARTH'S CLIMATE ZONES

Sun rays here spread over a larger area than sun rays at the equator

Sun rays

Sun rays carry energy in the form of light and heat. The two bands of sun rays shown in the diagram have the same width and the same amount of energy. The tropics are the warmest climate zone because sun rays are more concentrated near the equator. Because of the way the Earth curves, sun rays that strike farther away from the equator cover a larger area of the Earth's surface. Therefore, regions farther from the equator are generally cooler because they receive less of the sun's heat and light.

the equator is 0°. Latitudes closest to the equator have low latitude numbers.

Southern Mexico and the state of Hawaii are in the tropics. The latitude of Honolulu, Hawaii, is about 21°N.

The Middle Latitudes

The **middle latitudes** are the second major climate area. There are two areas of middle latitudes. One is between the Tropic of Cancer and the Arctic Circle. The other is between the Tropic of Capricorn and the Antarctic Circle. The middle latitudes are also called the temperate zone.

In general, regions in the middle latitudes have warm summers and cold winters. This is because the angle of the sun's rays varies during the year. In summer the sun's rays are more direct and therefore are warming. In winter the sun's rays are slanted and do not heat the ground much.

The mainland United States lies totally within the middle latitudes of the Northern Hemisphere.

The Polar Regions

The **polar regions,** or **high latitudes,** form the third major climate area on Earth. The high latitudes are the latitudes closest to the North Pole and the South Pole. The region to the north of the Arctic Circle is called the **Arctic.** The region to the south of the Antarctic Circle is the **Antarctic.** These regions have the coldest climates on Earth.

The Arctic and Antarctic are so cold because the sun's rays are the most slanted there. Even in summer the sun does not appear far from the horizon. In winter near the poles the sun does not appear at all.

Parts of Alaska and northern Canada are within the Arctic region.

Precipitation

Latitude has a general effect on precipitation. Warm air can hold more moisture than cold air. The warmer the air, the more moisture it picks up from the ocean. Much moisture then falls as rain. The tropics have more precipitation than other areas because they are warmer. Mount Waialeale (wy•ahl•ay•AHL•ay) in the Hawaiian Islands has the most rainfall in the world. The average annual rainfall there is 460 inches (1,168 cm). The Arctic and Antarctic have little precipitation—fewer than 5 inches (12.7 cm) a year.

Winds

Latitude also has an effect on winds. Winds are caused by the uneven heating of the air. Warm air tends to rise. Cold air then moves to take its place. This action usually takes place in great circular movements. The winds near the equator generally blow from east to west. In the middle latitudes the winds generally blow from west to east.

Winds that generally blow in one direction are called **prevailing winds.** Prevailing winds can affect climate. Consider what happens on the west coast of North America. Winds blowing from the west bring much moisture from the Pacific Ocean. Average yearly rainfall in the coastal parts of northern California, Oregon, Washington, and western Canada ranges from 60 to 80 inches (152 to 203 cm).

In winter the prevailing winds on the east coast of North America are from the northwest. Therefore, they often bring cold, arctic air. In summer the prevailing winds on the east coast come from the southwest. They bring warm, moisture-filled air.

Look at the map on page 616. Notice that the interior of North America is drier than either the west or the east coast. If prevailing winds from the west carry moisture, why does much of the west have low precipitation? One reason is that winds usually drop moisture when they run into mountains. Therefore, with winds from the west, most moisture falls on the western sides of the mountains.

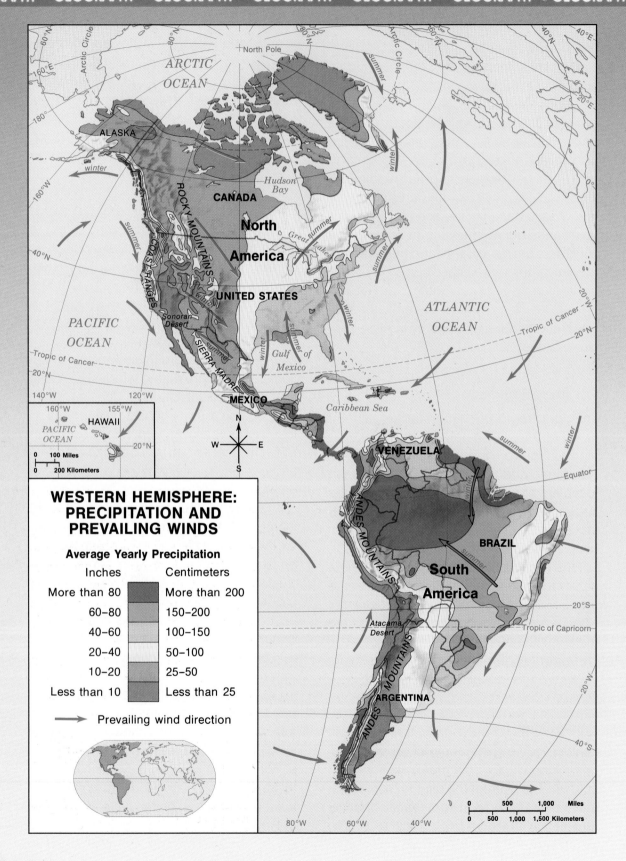

WESTERN HEMISPHERE: PRECIPITATION AND PREVAILING WINDS

Average Yearly Precipitation

Inches		Centimeters
More than 80		More than 200
60–80		150–200
40–60		100–150
20–40		50–100
10–20		25–50
Less than 10		Less than 25

→ Prevailing wind direction

ARCTIC OCEAN

ALASKA

CANADA

North America

Hudson Bay

ROCKY MOUNTAINS

COAST RANGES

UNITED STATES

PACIFIC OCEAN

Sonoran Desert

SIERRA MADRE

Great Lakes

ATLANTIC OCEAN

Tropic of Cancer

MEXICO

Gulf of Mexico

Caribbean Sea

PACIFIC OCEAN

HAWAII

0 100 Miles
0 200 Kilometers

160°W   155°W

VENEZUELA

Equator

ANDES MOUNTAINS

South America

BRAZIL

Atacama Desert

Tropic of Capricorn

ANDES MOUNTAINS

ARGENTINA

0   500   1,000   Miles
0   500 1,000 1,500 Kilometers

80°W   60°W   40°W

616

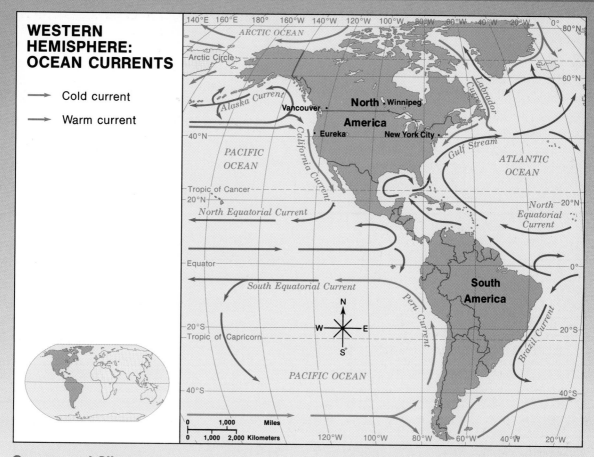

Oceans and Climate

Oceans can affect climate in two ways. Like the air, oceans have great circular currents. In the Northern Hemisphere these currents generally go in a clockwise direction. In the Southern Hemisphere they go in a counterclockwise direction. The **Gulf Stream** is the name of the current along the east coast of North America. It sweeps from south to north. Because it comes from tropical areas, the Gulf Stream is a warm current.

The current that sweeps down the west coast of North America comes from the north. It is a cold current. When warm air hits the cold water, fog is produced. Fog results in cooler temperatures. The average July temperature of Eureka, California, is 56°F (13.3°C). New York City, also on the ocean and at the same latitude, is warmer. It has an average July temperature of 77°F (25°C).

Water heats and cools more slowly than land does. For this reason, great bodies of water affect climate. In summer, oceans do not get as warm as the land. In winter they do not get as cool. Land near an ocean is warmer in winter and cooler in summer than land far from an ocean. Temperatures of places near an ocean do not vary as much as temperatures of places inland. The Canadian cities of Vancouver, British Columbia, and Winnipeg, Manitoba, are located on about the same latitude. Vancouver is on the ocean. Winnipeg is inland. The chart below shows the difference.

AVERAGE TEMPERATURES		
	January	July
Winnipeg	−4°F (−18°C)	68°F (20°C)
Vancouver	35.6°F (2°C)	62.6°F (17°C)

Elevation

The elevation of a place can affect its climate. Generally, the higher the elevation, the cooler the climate. In very hot climates, areas of high elevation are usually the most comfortable places to live.

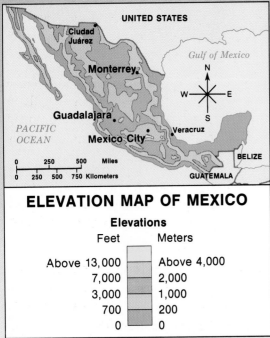

ELEVATION MAP OF MEXICO

Elevations

Feet	Meters
Above 13,000	Above 4,000
7,000	2,000
3,000	1,000
700	200
0	0

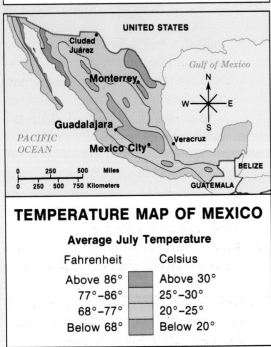

TEMPERATURE MAP OF MEXICO

Average July Temperature

Fahrenheit	Celsius
Above 86°	Above 30°
77°–86°	25°–30°
68°–77°	20°–25°
Below 68°	Below 20°

Look at the map of Mexico showing July temperatures. What is the average July temperature of Mexico City? of Veracruz?

Now look at the elevation map of Mexico. What is the elevation of Mexico City? What is the elevation of Veracruz? Why would Mexico City have cooler temperatures than Veracruz?

CHECKING YOUR SKILLS

Use what you have learned to answer these questions.

1. Which of the three major climate zones best fits each of these descriptions?

   a. The sun is low in the sky in summer. There is very little precipitation.

   b. The sun is overhead at noon. It is likely to be warm and rainy.

   c. It is warm in summer and cold in winter. Precipitation and temperature vary greatly.

2. What kind of winter climate is a city in the interior of Canada likely to have?

3. What kind of climate are you likely to find along a tropical coast? How would it compare to a place at the same latitude but at a higher elevation?

4. Find Nevada and California on the Atlas map in the back of your book. Then look at the map of prevailing winds on page 616. Why does Nevada have less precipitation than most of California?

5. If a town is at 50°N latitude, what is its climate likely to be?

6. What is the name of the warm ocean current off the east coast of North America?

7. How does the ocean temperature make coastal areas warmer in winter than places far from the ocean?

Thinking Back

- Mexico is a land of contrasts in both climate and precipitation. Mexico also has many volcanoes and has experienced some of the world's worst earthquakes.

- Mexico has five natural regions. Most of Mexico's people live in the Central Plateau region.

- Most of the wealth and power in New Spain belonged to people of pure Spanish ancestry. Life was difficult for the Indians and for *mestizos*. Miguel Hidalgo led a revolution against Spanish rule, and in 1821 independence was won.

- Independence failed to solve many of Mexico's problems. However, the government under Benito Juárez established a constitution and brought about changes to help the poor.

- These reforms were short-lived. The effort to achieve democracy and equality ended after Juárez's death.

- Another revolution and a new constitution finally brought about greater justice for all Mexicans.

- Mexico today is a democratic federation of 31 states. Its government has three branches, but the president holds most of the real power. There is only one strong political party.

- Mexico is a leading oil-producing nation. However, it faces many problems today, such as debt, unemployment, inflation, and poverty.

- Mexico is an important trading partner of the United States. Leaders work together to solve the disagreements between the two nations.

Check for Understanding

Using Words

Number your paper from 1 to 5. For each word below select the correct definition from the list that follows.

1. *ejidos*
2. *encomiendas*
3. *estates*
4. *mestizos*
5. *peasants*
   a. land owned in common by Mexican Indians or peasants
   b. poor people who live and work on the land
   c. large land holdings
   d. large grants of land given to the conquistadors
   e. people who have both Indian and Spanish ancestors

Reviewing Facts

1. Why is Mexico described as a land of great variety and contrast?
2. What kinds of farming and manufacturing take place in the Gulf Coast region of Mexico?
3. How is the Pacific Coast region different from the Central Plateau region? from the Sierra Madre region?

4. How was the Catholic Church a powerful force in New Spain?

5. How was life in New Spain difficult for mestizos and Indians?

6. What reforms did Benito Juárez bring to Mexico?

7. How did Emiliano Zapata bring about the downfall of dictator Porfirio Díaz?

8. How is Mexico's government similar to that of the United States?

9. Why does Mexico now face a period of hard times?

10. What disagreements do Mexico and the United States need to work out?

Thinking Critically

1. How did the colonial influence of Spain shape Mexico's history?

2. What did Miguel Hidalgo, Benito Juárez, and Emiliano Zapata each fight for? What similarities existed among the three men? What differences?

3. Do you think Americans should be interested in Mexico? Explain.

Writing About It

Write a travel brochure that tells about Mexico. In your brochure, describe Mexico's landscape and its climate. Explain why Mexico would be a good place for a vacation.

Practicing Geography Skills

Understanding Climate

Use pages 614 to 618 to answer the following questions.

1. What are the three major climate zones on Earth?

2. In which climate zone is the mainland United States?

3. Why do the tropics have more rain than other areas?

4. Name two ways in which the ocean affects climate.

5. How does elevation affect climate?

On Your Own

Social Studies at Home

1. The volcano Popocatépetl is shown on page 602. Ask your family to help you build a clay model of this volcano. You may want to streak your volcano with red paint so that the volcano appears to be erupting. Or, you may want to top it with sugar to make the mountain appear to be covered with snow. Take your model to class to share with your class.

2. Make a timeline that shows events from the time that Juárez became president in 1857 until he died in 1872. Illustrate your timeline and compare it with those of your classmates.

Read More About It

Aztecs by Barbara Beck. Franklin Watts. This reference book details the geography and history of Mexico and the life styles of its people.

In This Proud Land, the Story of a Mexican American Family by Bernard Wolf. J. B. Lippincott. This book describes an immigrant family's struggle against prejudice.

Mexico, Giant of the South by Eileen Latell Smith. Dillon Press. This book outlines Mexico's past and also contains a fact sheet about Mexico today.

Tame the Wild Stallion by Jeanne Williams. TCU Press. This tale describes life along the Mexican border after the conflict in 1846.

Hispanic Americans

The word *Hispanic* relates to the people, the culture, and the language of Spain and *Latin America*. Latin America is a huge region in the Western Hemisphere that includes all of South America and the southern part of North America. While most Hispanic, or Spanish-speaking, Americans were born in the United States, their ancestors came from many different countries. These countries include Mexico, Puerto Rico, Cuba, and other nations in Central and South America.

The number of Hispanic Americans is growing fast. In 1970 there were 9 million Hispanics in the United States. By 1980 that number had grown to almost 15 million. It is estimated that there will be 47 million Hispanic Americans living in the United States by the year 2020. This makes Hispanic Americans the fastest-growing minority in our country.

Six out of every ten Hispanic Americans live in the states of Arizona, California, New Mexico, and Texas. In towns and cities near the border of Mexico, Mexican Americans are often the majority. San Antonio, Texas, for example, has a population that is over one-half Mexican American.

Mexican Americans are the largest group among Hispanic Americans. Mexican Americans and other Hispanic groups have affected life in the United States in several ways. For example, many homes and buildings in our country are built in a style called

The Heard Museum of Anthropology and Primitive Arts, located in Phoenix, Arizona, is an example of Spanish Colonial architecture.

Spanish Colonial. Such buildings are often built of adobe and have red-tiled roofs. Many have an open area called a patio. This building style was brought from Spain and then Mexico.

Parts of our country were first explored and settled by the ancestors

of Mexican Americans. Spanish-speaking people brought the first cattle to the Western Hemisphere and started the first ranches. These early ranchers developed the gear, clothing, and language used by modern cowhands.

Spanish-speaking people also shared their laws with the people of the Southwest. The laws dealing with the right to use the water in streams in Southwestern states are based on Spanish and Mexican laws.

Mexican Americans have shared their food, clothing, and celebrations as well. When Americans go to a rodeo or eat barbeque, they are sharing in the Hispanic culture. Spicy foods such as tacos, chili, and enchiladas are popular throughout the country.

Mexican Americans observe a number of holidays which are also celebrated in Mexico. *Cinco de Mayo,* the Fifth of May, is special to Mexican Americans everywhere. Another important Mexican holiday celebrated in the United States is *Diez y Seis de Septiembre* (DEE·ays ee SAHYS day sep·tee·EM·bray), the Sixteenth of September. This holiday recalls the date in 1810 when Father Hidalgo

◀ The Fiesta Parade in San Antonio, Texas, is an example of Mexican-American influence on our culture.

began the fight which led to Mexico's freedom from Spain. Mexicans also share some American holidays. Mexicans and Texans hold a joint celebration of George Washington's birthday each February 22 in Laredo, Texas.

Mexican Americans are leaders in art, education, business, and government. One of the first Mexican Americans to gain high political office was Henry B. Gonzales (gohn·ZAH·lez) of San Antonio, Texas. He was elected to the United States House of Representatives in 1961. Henry Cisneros (sees·NAY·rohs) was elected mayor of San Antonio in 1981. He was the first Hispanic to be elected mayor of a major American city. In 1983 the citizens of New Mexico elected Toney Anaya (ah·NYE·uh) governor. Anaya was the first Hispanic to serve as governor of the state. The Hispanic culture of these Mexican Americans has contributed much to the United States.

Unit Review

Words to Remember

Number your paper from 1 to 5. Use the words below to replace the underlined words in the sentences that follow.

encomiendas   **provinces**
mestizos   **Separatists**
ministers

1. Canada is a federation of ten <u>political divisions similar to states</u>.

2. In Canada <u>people who are in charge of executive departments</u> are usually members of the House of Commons.

3. A number of Canadians with French ancestors and customs are <u>people who wish Quebec to be independent</u>.

4. Life in New Spain was hard for Indians and <u>people of mixed Indian and Spanish blood</u>.

5. The conquistadors were given <u>large grants of land</u>.

Focus on Main Ideas

1. What are the major natural resources of Canada? of Mexico?

2. Compare the climates of Mexico and Canada.

3. Who were the first Europeans to claim land in Canada? in Mexico?

4. How did Canada gain independence from Britain?

5. How did Mexico gain independence from Spain?

6. What is the Commonwealth of Nations?

7. How is America's economy tied to that of Mexico? of Canada?

8. Why is it significant that the United States' borders with Canada and Mexico are undefended?

9. How are the governments of Mexico and Canada alike? How do they differ?

10. How have history and geography made Canada and Mexico different?

Think/Write

The United States, Canada, and Mexico are the three largest nations in North America. Because they are neighbors, they share many common landforms and natural features. What other things do they share? What responsibilities do you think the people of the United States, Canada, and Mexico have to one another?

Activities

1. **Map Reading/Writing** Find a road map of Mexico or Canada. Plan a trip across the country. What highways will you travel? What sights will you see? Write down the plan of your trip.

2. **Research/Art** Make a poster or mural of Mexico or Canada. Include the flag, people, important resources, products, national holidays or festivals.

3. **Making a Table** Make a large table comparing Mexico and Canada. Compare the national flags, languages spoken, holidays, resources, and products.

4. Making a Timeline   Put these events in the correct order on a timeline.
- Mexico wins independence from Spain
- Mexican Constitution of 1917
- Jacques Cartier arrives in Canada.
- Britain gains control of Canada.
- Canada achieves independence from British Parliament.
- English land at Jamestown.
- Cortés conquers Mexico.

Skills Review

1. Reading a Road Map   Use the map to answer the questions that follow.

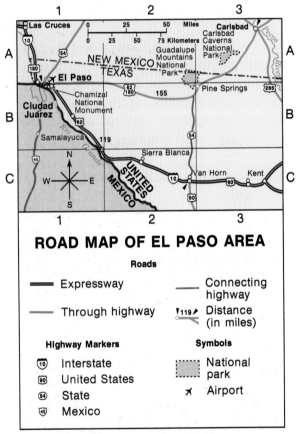

ROAD MAP OF EL PASO AREA

a. What town can be found in square C-3?

b. What kind of road connects Pine Springs (B-3) to El Paso (A-1)?

c. What route would you follow to go from Las Cruces, New Mexico (A-1), to Samalayuca (B-1) in Mexico?

d. What would be the best route to follow to travel from Sierra Blanca, Texas (C-2), to Guadalupe Mountains National Park?

2. Understanding Climate   Number your paper from 1 to 10. Choose the best word or phrase from the list below to complete the sentences that follow. You will use each term once.

Antarctic	**middle latitudes**
cooler	**prevailing winds**
equator	**Tropic of Cancer**
Gulf Stream	**tropics**
latitude	**warmer**

a. The __(1)__ is the parallel that divides the Earth into its northern and southern hemispheres.

b. Winds that usually blow in one direction are __(2)__.

c. The __(3)__ is a warm ocean current along the east coast of the United States.

d. Regions in the __(4)__, such as the United States, have warm summers and cold winters.

e. The __(5)__ is located in the polar region and has one of the coldest climates on the Earth.

f. The warmest part of the Earth is in the low latitudes, or __(6)__.

g. Land that is near an ocean is __(7)__ in summer and __(8)__ in winter than places inland.

h. The Earth is divided into three major climate zones based on __(9)__.

i. The __(10)__ is one of the parallels that divides the low latitudes from the middle latitudes.

Fourteen American states border on Canada. Four states border on Mexico. Every day thousands of people cross the borders to work, shop, or visit. Mexican Americans and Canadian Americans live in all parts of the United States.

The following activities will help you learn about connections between your state and our neighbors, Canada and Mexico.

Learning About Geography

1. How far is your town from the Mexican border? the Canadian border? Which border is closer?

2. Longitude is a measure of the distance east or west of a point in Greenwich, England. Find a map or an atlas with lines of longitude. Look for a Canadian town that is nearly the same longitude as your hometown. Use an atlas to write a short report about the town you choose. What is the population of the town? What is its elevation? What is its climate like?

3. Using a map or an atlas, find a Mexican town that is at the same longitude as your hometown. If there is none, select any Mexican town or city. Write a short report on that town.

4. Use a road atlas to plan the route you would follow to reach either Canada or Mexico from your hometown. About how many miles would you have to travel?

Learning About Economics

5. World trade is important. Are there products you use in your community or state that come from Canada or Mexico? What are they? Does your state export products to Canada or Mexico?

Learning About People

6. The picture below shows a dancer performing a traditional dance of Mexico. Mexican folk dances are often performed in the United States where there are large numbers of Mexican Americans. These citizens influence the culture of the state in which they live. Is there a Mexican American influence in your state? If so, explain what form it takes.

FOR YOUR REFERENCE

The National Anthem

The National Anthem

(1)

Oh! say, can you see, by the dawn's early light,
What so proudly we hailed at the twilight's last gleaming?
Whose broad stripes and bright stars, thro' the perilous fight,
O'er the ramparts we watched were so gallantly streaming?
And the rockets' red glare, the bombs bursting in air,
Gave proof thro' the night that our flag was still there.
Oh! say, does that star-spangled banner yet wave
O'er the land of the free and the home of the brave?

(2)

On the shore, dimly seen thro' the mist of the deep,
Where the foe's haughty host in dread silence reposes,
What is that which the breeze, o'er the towering steep,
As it fitfully blows, half conceals, half discloses?
Now it catches the gleam of the morning's first beam,
In full glory reflected, now shines on the stream.
'Tis the star-spangled banner. Oh! long may it wave
O'er the land of the free and the home of the brave!

(3)

And where is that band who so vauntingly swore
That the havoc of war and the battle's confusion
A home and a country should leave us no more?
Their blood has washed out their foul footstep's pollution.
No refuge could save the hireling and slave
From the terror of flight or the gloom of the grave,
And the star-spangled banner in triumph doth wave
O'er the land of the free and the home of the brave.

(4)

Oh! thus be it ever when freemen shall stand
Between their loved home and the war's desolation,
Blest with vict'ry and peace, may the Heav'n-rescued land
Praise the Pow'r that hath made and preserved us a nation.
Then conquer we must, when our cause it is just,
And this be our motto, "In God is our trust."
And the star-spangled banner in triumph shall wave
O'er the land of the free and the home of the brave.

"The Star-Spangled Banner" was written by Francis Scott Key and adopted as the national anthem in March of 1931. The Army and Navy had recognized it as such long before Congress approved it.

During the War of 1812, Francis Scott Key spent a night aboard a British warship in the Chesapeake Bay while trying to arrange for the release of an American prisoner. The battle raged throughout the night while the Americans were held on the ship. The next morning, when the smoke from the cannons finally cleared, Francis Scott Key was thrilled to see the American flag still waving proudly above Fort McHenry. It symbolized the victory of the Americans.

There are four verses to the National Anthem. In these four verses, Key wrote about how he felt when he saw the flag still waving over Fort McHenry. He wrote that the flag was a symbol of the freedom for which the people had fought so hard. Key also told about the pride he had in his country and the great hopes he had for the future of the United States.

The Pledge of Allegiance

The Pledge of Allegiance

I pledge allegiance to the flag
of the United States of America.
And to the republic
for which it stands,
One nation under God, indivisible,
with liberty and justice for all.

The flag is a symbol of the United States of America. The Pledge of Allegiance says that the people of the United States promise to stand up for their flag, their country, and the basic beliefs of freedom and fairness upon which the country was established.

IN CONGRESS, JULY 4, 1776.

The unanimous Declaration of the thirteen united States of America.

When in the Course of human events it becomes necessary for one people to dissolve the political bands which have connected them with another, and to assume among the powers of the earth, the separate and equal station to which the Laws of Nature and of Nature's God entitle them, a decent respect to the opinions of mankind requires that they should declare the causes which impel them to the separation.

We hold these truths to be self-evident, that all men are created equal, that they are endowed by their Creator with certain unalienable Rights, that among these are Life, Liberty and the pursuit of Happiness.—That to secure these rights, Governments are instituted among Men, deriving their just powers from the consent of the governed,—That whenever any Form of Government becomes destructive of these ends, it is the Right of the People to alter or to abolish it, and to institute new Government, laying its foundation on such principles and organizing its powers in such form, as to them shall seem most likely to effect their Safety and Happiness.

[Remainder of document text in period cursive script; signatures below include John Hancock and others.]

The Declaration of Independence

The Declaration of Independence
In Congress, July 4, 1776
The unanimous Declaration of the thirteen united States of America

When, in the Course of human events, it becomes necessary for one people to dissolve the political bands which have connected them with another, and to assume, among the powers of the earth, the separate and equal station to which the Laws of Nature and of Nature's God entitle them, a decent respect to the opinions of mankind requires that they should declare the causes which impel them to the separation.—

PREAMBLE *(tells why the Declaration was written)*
The members of the Continental Congress believed that they must be free from those who controlled them. They felt that they had the right to be a separate but equal nation. The Declaration was the explanation of why the people wanted to be a free nation.

We hold these truths to be self-evident, That all men are created equal, that they are endowed by their Creator with certain unalienable Rights, that among these are Life, Liberty, and the pursuit of Happiness.

That, to secure these rights, governments are instituted among Men, deriving their just powers from the consent of the governed,

That, whenever any Form of Government becomes destructive of these ends, it is the Right of the People to alter or to abolish it, and to institute new Government, laying its foundation on such principles, and organizing its powers in such form, as to them shall seem most likely to effect their Safety and Happiness. Prudence, indeed, will dictate that Governments long established should not be changed for light and transient causes; and, accordingly, all experience hath shown that mankind are more disposed to suffer, while evils are sufferable, than to right themselves by abolishing the forms to which they are accustomed. But when a long train of abuses and usurpations, pursuing invariably the same Object, evinces a design to reduce them under absolute Despotism, it is their right, it is their duty, to throw off such Government, and to provide new guards for their future security.—

STATEMENT OF RIGHTS *(tells what rights all people should have)*
The Continental Congress listed the following beliefs that were important to them: all people are equal, and have the right to life, to liberty, and to happiness. These rights cannot be taken away. When the government tries to take these rights away from the people, then the people have the right to change the government or do away with it. The people should form a new government that gives them these rights.

Such has been the patient sufferance of these Colonies; and such is now the necessity which constrains them to alter their former Systems of Government. The history of the present King of Great Britain is a history of repeated injuries and usurpations, all having in direct object the establishment of an absolute Tyranny over these States. To prove this, Let facts be submitted to a candid world.—

He has refused his Assent to Laws the most wholesome and necessary for the Public good.—

He has forbidden his Governors to pass Laws of immediate and pressing importance, unless suspended in their operation till his Assent should be obtained; and, when so suspended, he has utterly neglected to attend to them.—

He has refused to pass other Laws for the accommodation of large districts of people, unless those people would relinquish the right of Representation in the Legislature—a right inestimable to them, and formidable to tyrants only.—

He has called together legislative bodies at places unusual, uncomfortable, and distant from the depository of their public Records, for the sole purpose of fatiguing them into compliance with his measures.—

He has dissolved Representative Houses repeatedly, for opposing, with manly firmness his invasions on the rights of the people.—

He has refused for a long time after such dissolutions, to cause others to be elected; whereby the Legislative powers, incapable of Annihilation, have returned to the People at large for their exercise; the State remaining in the meantime exposed to all dangers of invasion from without, and convulsions within.—

He has endeavored to prevent the population of these States; for that purpose obstructing the Laws for Naturalization of Foreigners; refusing to pass others to encourage their migration hither, and raising the conditions of new Appropriations of Lands.—

He has obstructed the Administration of Justice, by refusing his Assent to Laws for establishing Judiciary powers.

He has made Judges dependent on his Will alone for the tenure of their offices, and the amount and payment of their salaries.—

A BILL OF INDICTMENT *(abuses of human rights by the king)*

The Declaration lists over twenty-five charges against the king. The colonists accused the king of mistreating them in order to gain total power over the colonies. To prove that they had the right to change their government, the colonists publicly listed the following wrongs:

King George III rejected many of the laws passed by colonial legislatures.

The king's governors could not approve any colonial law until the king approved the law. This often took many years.

People who settled in new areas were not fairly represented in the legislatures because the king's government did not redraw the boundaries of the legislative districts.

Members of the colonial assemblies often had to meet at inconvenient places.

The king's governors often dissolved colonial assemblies for disobeying their orders.

It often took a long time for new colonial assemblies to be elected.

In order for immigrants to settle in the undeveloped lands in the west, the laws made it easy to buy land and become a citizen. In 1763, King George III claimed the undeveloped lands in the west. The king also rejected most new laws about becoming a citizen.

The North Carolina legislature passed a law to establish a court system, but Britain objected. Therefore North Carolina did not have courts for several years.

In Britain, judges served as long as the king was satisfied with them. The king paid them. The colonies

He has erected a multitude of New Offices, and sent hither swarms of officers to harass our people and eat out their substance.—

He has kept among us, in times of peace, Standing Armies, without the Consent of our legislatures.—

He has affected to render the Military independent of, and superior to, the Civil power.

He has combined with others to subject us to a jurisdiction foreign to our constitution, and unacknowledged by our laws; giving his Assent to their Acts of pretended Legislation:—

For quartering large bodies of armed troops among us:—

For protecting them, by a mock Trial, from punishment for any Murders which they should commit on the Inhabitants of these States:—

For cutting off our Trade with all parts of the world:—

For imposing Taxes on us without our Consent:—

For depriving us in many cases, of the benefits of Trial by Jury;—

For transporting us beyond Seas to be tried for pretended offenses:—

For abolishing the free System of English Laws in a neighboring Province, establishing there an Arbitrary government, and enlarging its Boundaries, so as to render it at once an example and fit instrument for introducing the same absolute rule into these colonies:—

For taking away our Charters, abolishing our most valuable Laws, and altering fundamentally the Forms of our Governments:—

For suspending our own Legislatures, and declaring themselves invested with power to legislate for us in all cases whatsoever.—

He has abdicated Government here, by declaring us out of his Protection, and waging War against us.—

He has plundered our seas, ravaged our coasts, burnt our towns, and destroyed the Lives of our people.—

He is at this time transporting large Armies of foreign Mercenaries to complete the works of death, desolation, and tyranny, already begun with circumstances of Cruelty & perfidy scarcely paralleled in the most barbarous ages, and totally unworthy the Head of a civilized nation.—

He has constrained our fellow Citizens taken Captive on the high Seas, to bear Arms against their Country, to become the executioners of their friends and Brethren, or to fall themselves by their Hands.—

He has excited domestic insurrection amongst us, and has endeavored to bring on the inhabitants of our frontiers, the merciless Indian Savages, whose known rule of warfare, is an undistinguished destruction of all ages, sexes, and conditions.

In every stage of these Oppressions We have Petitioned for Redress, in the most humble terms: Our repeated Petitions have been answered only by repeated injury. A prince whose character is thus marked by every act which may define a Tyrant is unfit to be the ruler of a free people.—

Nor have We been wanting in our attentions to our British brethren. We have warned them from time to time of attempts by their legislature to extend an unwarrantable jurisdiction over us. We have reminded them of the circumstances of our emigration and settlement here. We have appealed to their native justice and magnanimity, and we have conjured them by the ties of our common kindred to disavow these usurpations, which would inevitably interrupt our connections and correspondence. They too have been deaf to the voice of justice and of consanguinity. We must, therefore, acquiesce in the necessity, which denounces our Separation, and hold them, as we hold the rest of mankind, Enemies in War, in Peace Friends.—

We, therefore, the Representatives of the united states of america, in General Congress, Assembled, appealing to the Supreme Judge of the world for the rectitude of our intentions, do, in the Name, and by authority of the good People of these Colonies, solemnly publish and declare, That these United Colonies are, and of Right ought to be Free and Independent States; that they are Absolved from all Allegiance to the

General Gage was told to use force if necessary to make the colonists obey the laws of Parliament.

The British seized colonial ships by force and destroyed many towns and the people living there.

The king hired and sent German troops to fight the colonists.

Americans who were captured when their ships were seized were forced to join the British navy.

The king's Governor in Virginia promised freedom to all black slaves who joined the British forces. The British also planned to use Indians to fight the colonists.

A STATEMENT OF INDEPENDENCE (explains colonial efforts to avoid separation)

King George III continued to take away all of the rights of the people of America. They asked that he be stopped, but the problems grew worse. The colonists said that the king was unfair and not fit to rule free people.

The people of America also asked the British people for help. They described all of the things that the king had done, but the British people did not listen. Therefore the American people declared their separation and referred to the British as their enemies in war and friends in peace.

The cries for help went unanswered, so the representatives of the people of the United States declared their independence. They broke all ties with Great Britain. As free states they declared that they had the right to make war and peace, trade, and do all the things free countries could do.

British Crown, and that all political connection between them and the State of Great Britain, is and ought to be totally dissolved; and that, as Free and Independent States, they have full Power to levy War, conclude Peace, contract Alliances, establish Commerce, and to do all other Acts and Things which Independent States may of right do.

And for the support of this Declaration, with a firm reliance on the protection of divine Providence, we mutually pledge to each other our Lives, our Fortunes, and our sacred Honor.—

To support the Declaration of Independence, the American people promised their lives, their fortunes, and their honor to each other.

The foregoing Declaration was, by order of Congress, engrossed and signed by the following members:—

New Hampshire
Josiah Bartlett
William Whipple
Matthew Thornton

Massachusetts Bay
Samuel Adams
John Adams
Robert Treat Paine
Elbridge Gerry

Rhode Island
Stephen Hopkins
William Ellery

Connecticut
Roger Sherman
Samuel Huntington
William Williams
Oliver Wolcott

New York
William Floyd
Philip Livingston
Francis Lewis
Lewis Morris

New Jersey
Richard Stockton
John Witherspoon
Francis Hopkinson
John Hart
Abraham Clark

Pennsylvania
Robert Morris
Benjamin Rush
Benjamin
 Franklin
John Morton
George Clymer
James Smith
George Taylor
James Wilson
George Ross

Delaware
Caesar Rodney
George Read
Thomas M'Kean

Maryland
Samuel Chase
William Paca
Thomas Stone
Charles Carroll
 of Carrollton

Virginia
George Wythe
Richard Henry Lee
Thomas Jefferson
Benjamin
 Harrison
Thomas Nelson, Jr.
Francis
 Lightfoot Lee
Carter Braxton

North Carolina
William Hooper
Joseph Hewes
John Penn

South Carolina
Edward Rutledge
Thomas
 Heyward, Jr.
Thomas Lynch, Jr.
Arthur Middleton

Georgia
Button Gwinnett
Lyman Hall
George Walton

Resolved, That copies of the Declaration be sent to the several assemblies, conventions, and committees, or councils of safety, and to the several commanding officers of the continental troops; that it be proclaimed in each of the United States, at the head of the army.

Members of the Continental Congress declared that copies of the Declaration be sent to all committees and commanders of the troops, and that it be announced in every state.

We the People of the United States, in Order to form a more perfect Union, establish Justice, insure domestic Tranquility, provide for the common defence, promote the general Welfare, and secure the Blessings of Liberty to ourselves and our Posterity, do ordain and establish this Constitution for the United States of America.

Article. I.

Section. 1. All legislative Powers herein granted shall be vested in a Congress of the United States, which shall consist of a Senate and House of Representatives.

Section. 2. The House of Representatives shall be composed of Members chosen every second Year by the People of the several States, and the Electors in each State shall have the Qualifications requisite for Electors of the most numerous Branch of the State Legislature.

No Person shall be a Representative who shall not have attained to the Age of twenty five Years, and been seven Years a Citizen of the United States, and who shall not, when elected, be an Inhabitant of that State in which he shall be chosen.

Representatives and direct Taxes shall be apportioned among the several States which may be included within this Union, according to their respective Numbers, which shall be determined by adding to the whole Number of free Persons, including those bound to Service for a Term of Years, and excluding Indians not taxed, three fifths of all other Persons. The actual Enumeration shall be made within three Years after the first Meeting of the Congress of the United States, and within every subsequent Term of ten Years, in such Manner as they shall by Law direct. The Number of Representatives shall not exceed one for every thirty Thousand, but each State shall have at Least one Representative; and until such enumeration shall be made, the State of New Hampshire shall be entitled to chuse three, Massachusetts eight, Rhode Island and Providence Plantations one, Connecticut five, New York six, New Jersey four, Pennsylvania eight, Delaware one, Maryland six, Virginia ten, North Carolina five, South Carolina five, and Georgia three.

When vacancies happen in the Representation from any State, the Executive Authority thereof shall issue Writs of Election to fill such Vacancies.

The House of Representatives shall chuse their Speaker and other Officers; and shall have the sole Power of Impeachment.

Section. 3. The Senate of the United States shall be composed of two Senators from each State, chosen by the Legislature thereof, for six Years; and each Senator shall have one Vote.

Immediately after they shall be assembled in Consequence of the first Election, they shall be divided as equally as may be into three Classes. The Seats of the Senators of the first Class shall be vacated at the Expiration of the second Year, of the second Class at the Expiration of the fourth Year, and of the third Class at the Expiration of the sixth Year, so that one third may be chosen every second Year; and if Vacancies happen by Resignation, or otherwise, during the Recess of the Legislature of any State, the Executive thereof may make temporary Appointments until the next Meeting of the Legislature, which shall then fill such Vacancies.

No Person shall be a Senator who shall not have attained to the Age of thirty Years, and been nine Years a Citizen of the United States, and who shall not, when elected, be an Inhabitant of that State for which he shall be chosen.

The Vice President of the United States shall be President of the Senate, but shall have no Vote, unless they be equally divided.

The Senate shall chuse their other Officers, and also a President pro tempore, in the Absence of the Vice President, or when he shall exercise the Office of President of the United States.

The Senate shall have the sole Power to try all Impeachments. When sitting for that Purpose, they shall be on Oath or Affirmation. When the President of the United States is tried, the Chief Justice shall preside: And no Person shall be convicted without the Concurrence of two thirds of the Members present.

Judgment in Cases of Impeachment shall not extend further than to removal from Office, and disqualification to hold and enjoy any Office of honor, Trust or Profit under the United States: but the Party convicted shall nevertheless be liable and subject to Indictment, Trial, Judgment and Punishment, according to Law.

Section. 4. The Times, Places and Manner of holding Elections for Senators and Representatives, shall be prescribed in each State by the Legislature thereof; but the Congress may at any time by Law make or alter such Regulations, except as to the Places of chusing Senators.

The Congress shall assemble at least once in every Year, and such Meeting shall be on the first Monday in December, unless they shall by Law appoint a different Day.

Section. 5. Each House shall be the Judge of the Elections, Returns and Qualifications of its own Members, and a Majority of each shall constitute a Quorum to do Business; but a smaller Number may adjourn from day to day, and may be authorized to compel the Attendance of absent Members, in such Manner, and under such Penalties as each House may provide.

Each House may determine the Rules of its Proceedings, punish its Members for disorderly Behaviour, and, with the Concurrence of two thirds, expel a Member.

Each House shall keep a Journal of its Proceedings, and from time to time publish the same, excepting such Parts as may in their Judgment require Secrecy; and the Yeas and Nays of the Members of either House on any question shall, at the Desire of one fifth of those Present, be entered on the Journal.

Neither House, during the Session of Congress, shall, without the Consent of the other, adjourn for more than three days, nor to any other Place than that in which the two Houses shall be sitting.

Section. 6. The Senators and Representatives shall receive a Compensation for their Services, to be ascertained by Law, and paid out of the Treasury of the United States. They shall in all Cases, except Treason, Felony and Breach of the Peace, be privileged from Arrest during their Attendance at the Session of their respective Houses, and in going to and returning from the same; and for any Speech or Debate in either House, they shall not be questioned in any other Place.

No Senator or Representative shall, during the Time for which he was elected, be appointed to any civil Office under the Authority of the United States, which shall have been created, or the Emoluments whereof shall have been encreased during such time; and no Person holding any Office under the United States, shall be a Member of either House during his Continuance in Office.

Section. 7. All Bills for raising Revenue shall originate in the House of Representatives; but the Senate may propose or concur with Amendments as on other Bills.

Every Bill which shall have passed the House of Representatives and the Senate, ...

The Constitution of the United States

The Constitution of the United States
PREAMBLE

We the people of the United States, in order to form a more perfect union, establish justice, insure domestic tranquility, provide for the common defense, promote the general welfare, and secure the blessings of liberty to ourselves and our posterity, do ordain and establish this CONSTITUTION for the United States of America.

PREAMBLE

The Preamble is the introduction to the Constitution. In the opening phrase, the authors make it clear that the United States government is established by its people and for its people. The Preamble also states the purposes for writing the Constitution, which are: a) to set up a better form of government, b) to develop a fair system of laws, c) to keep peace throughout the nation, d) to defend the people from foreign nations, e) to make a better way of life for the people, and f) to maintain freedom for the people and for future generations.

Three articles, or sets of guidelines, follow the Preamble. These articles are designed to divide government duties into three parts: the legislative branch (Article 1), the executive branch (Article 2), and the judicial branch (Article 3).

ARTICLE 1
Legislative Branch

SECTION 1. Congress

All legislative powers herein granted shall be vested in a Congress of the United States, which shall consist of a Senate and a House of Representatives.

SECTION 2. House of Representatives

1. Election and Term of Members. The House of Representatives shall be composed of members chosen every second year by the people of the several states, and the electors in each state shall have the qualifications requisite for electors of the most numerous branch of the state legislature.

2. Qualifications. No person shall be a Representative who shall not have attained to the age of twenty-five years, and been seven years a citizen of the United States, and who shall not, when elected, be an inhabitant of that state in which he shall be chosen.

ARTICLE 1
Legislative Branch

SECTION 1. Congress

Congress has the power to make laws. Congress is made up of two groups of representatives: the Senate and the House of Representatives.

SECTION 2. House of Representatives

1. Election and Term of Members. Members of the House of Representatives will be chosen every two years by the qualified voters in their states. Each member of the House of Representatives will meet the necessary requirements.

2. Qualifications. Members of the House of Representatives must be at least 25 years old, citizens of the United States for at least seven years, and live in the state which they will represent.

3. Determining Representation and Direct Taxes. Representatives and direct taxes shall be apportioned among the several states which may be included within this Union, according to their respective numbers, which shall be determined by adding to the whole number of free persons, including those bound to service for a term of years, and excluding Indians not taxed, three fifths of all other persons.* The actual enumeration shall be made within three years after the first meeting of the Congress of the United States, and within every subsequent term of ten years, in such manner as they shall by law direct. The number of Representatives shall not exceed 1 for every 30,000, but each state shall have at least one representative; and until such enumeration shall be made, the state of New Hampshire shall be entitled to choose three; Massachusetts, eight; Rhode Island and Providence Plantations, one; Connecticut, five; New York, six; New Jersey, four; Pennsylvania, eight; Delaware, one; Maryland, six; Virginia, ten; North Carolina, five; South Carolina, five; and Georgia, three.

*The Constitution is printed in black. Parts that are no longer in force and that have been changed by amendment are crossed out in color.

4. Filling Vacancies. When vacancies happen in the representation from any state, the executive authority thereof shall issue writs of election to fill such vacancies.

5. Officers, Impeachment. The House of Representatives shall choose their Speaker and other officers; and shall have the sole power of impeachment.

SECTION 3. Senate

1. Number, Term, and Selection of Members. The Senate of the United States shall be composed of two senators from each state, chosen by the legislature thereof, for six years; and each senator shall have one vote.

2. Alternating Terms, Filling Vacancies. Immediately after they shall be assembled in consequence of the first election, they shall be divided as equally as may be into three classes. The seats of the senators of the first class shall be vacated at the expiration of the second year, of the second class

---

3. Determining Representation and Direct Taxes. Taxes and the number of representatives depend on the number of people living in each state. Every ten years, the government must take a census, or count, of its population.

Originally, each state was given one representative for each 30,000 people; but since 1929, Congress has limited the number of representatives to 435.

Southern representatives wanted slaves to be included when deciding on the number of representatives, but not on the amount of tax to be paid. Northern representatives wanted the reverse. The three-fifths compromise settled this disagreement by stating that three-fifths of a state's slave population would be counted, both for deciding the number of representatives and the amount of taxes. Indians would not be included in the count at all.

Amendments 13 and 14 overruled the three-fifths compromise for blacks, but Indians were not included in the census until 1940.

4. Filling Vacancies. If there is a vacancy in the House of Representatives, the governor of the state involved must call a special election to fill it.

5. Officers, Impeachment. The House of Representatives chooses a Speaker, as its presiding officer, and its other officers. The House is the only government branch that may impeach, or charge, an official in the executive branch or a judge in the federal courts for a crime. Impeachment cases are tried in the Senate.

SECTION 3. Senate

1. Number, Term, and Selection of Members. In the Senate, each state will be represented by two senators. Until Amendment 17 was passed, state legislatures chose the senators for their states. Each senator serves six-year terms, and has one vote in Congress.

2. Alternating Terms, Filling Vacancies. One third of the senators are elected every two years for a six-year term. Senators are divided into three groups so that their terms end at different times. This allows at least two thirds

at the expiration of the fourth year, and of the third class at the expiration of the sixth year, so that one third may be chosen every second year; and if vacancies happen by resignation, or otherwise, during the recess of the legislature of any state, the executive thereof may make temporary appointments until the next meeting of the legislature, which shall then fill such vacancies.

3. Qualifications. No person shall be a senator who shall not have attained to the age of thirty years, and been nine years a citizen of the United States, and who shall not, when elected, be an inhabitant of that state for which he shall be chosen.

4. President of the Senate. The Vice President of the United States shall be President of the Senate, but shall have no vote, unless they be equally divided.

5. Other Officers. The Senate shall choose their other officers, and also a President *pro tempore,* in the absence of the Vice President, or when he shall exercise the office of President of the United States.

6. Impeachment Trials. The Senate shall have the sole power to try all impeachments. When sitting for that purpose, they shall be on oath or affirmation. When the President of the United States is tried, the Chief Justice shall preside; and no other person shall be convicted without the concurrence of two thirds of the members present.

7. Penalty for Conviction. Judgment in cases of impeachment shall not extend further than to removal from office, and disqualification to hold and enjoy any office of honor, trust, or profit under the United States; but the party convicted shall nevertheless be liable and subject to indictment, trial, judgment, and punishment, according to law.

SECTION 4. Elections and Meetings

1. Holding Elections. The times, places, and manner of holding elections for senators and representatives shall be prescribed in each state by the legislature thereof; but the Congress may at any time by law make or alter such regulations, except as to the places of choosing senators.

of the experienced senators to remain in the Senate after each election.

Amendment 17 permits state governors to appoint a senator in the event of an opening until the next election is held.

3. Qualifications. Senators must be at least 30 years old, citizens of the United States for at least nine years, and live in the state which they will represent.

4. President of the Senate. The Vice President is the presiding officer of the Senate, but does not have the power to vote unless there is a tie.

5. Other Officers. The Senate chooses its other officers and a president *pro tempore,* who serves if the Vice President is not present or becomes President.
Pro tempore is a Latin term meaning "for the time being."

6. Impeachment Trials. Only the Senate has the power of impeachment. If the President of the United States is tried for impeachment, the Chief Justice presides over the trial. In all other cases, the Vice President presides. A two-thirds vote is necessary before a conviction may be made.

7. Penalty for Conviction. The punishment for conviction in impeachment cases can only be removal from office and disqualification from ever holding office in the United States government again. The convicted person may also be tried in a normal court of law for the same charges.

SECTION 4. Elections and Meetings

1. Holding Elections. Each state may make its own rules about electing senators and representatives. However, Congress may change these rules at any time, except the rule stating the places where senators are chosen.

In 1872, Congress passed a law setting congressional elections to be held on the first Tuesday after the first Monday in November of even-numbered years.

2. Meetings. The Congress shall assemble at least once in every year, and such meeting shall be on the first Monday in December, unless they shall by law appoint a different day.

SECTION 5. Rules of Procedure

1. Organization. Each house shall be the judge of the elections, returns, and qualifications of its own members, and a majority of each shall constitute a quorum to do business; but a smaller number may adjourn from day to day, and may be authorized to compel the attendance of absent members, in such manner, and under such penalties, as each house may provide.

2. Rules. Each house may determine the rules of its proceedings, punish its members for disorderly behavior, and, with the concurrence of two thirds, expel a member.

3. Journal. Each house shall keep a journal of its proceedings, and from time to time publish the same, excepting such parts as may in their judgment require secrecy; and the yeas and nays of the members of either house on any question shall, at the desire of one fifth of those present, be entered on the journal.

4. Adjournment. Neither house, during the session of Congress, shall, without the consent of the other, adjourn for more than three days, nor to any other place than that in which the two houses shall be sitting.

SECTION 6. Privileges and Restrictions

1. Pay and Privileges. The senators and representatives shall receive a compensation for their services, to be ascertained by law, and paid out of the treasury of the United States. They shall in all cases, except treason, felony, and breach of the peace, be privileged from arrest during their attendance at the session of their respective houses, and in going to and returning from the same; and for any speech or debate in either house they shall not be questioned in any other place.

2. Restrictions. No senator or representative shall, during the time for which he was elected, be appointed to any civil office under the authority of the United States, which shall have been created, or the emoluments whereof shall have been increased, during such time; and no person holding any office under the United States shall be a member of either house during his continuance in office.

2. Meetings. Congress must meet once a year on the first Monday in December, unless Congress sets a different day. Amendment 20 changed this date to January 3.

SECTION 5. Rules of Procedure

1. Organization. Each house of Congress may decide if its members have been elected fairly and are able to hold office. Each house may do business only when a quorum, or a majority of its members, is present. Each house may punish members for not attending sessions.

2. Rules. Each house may decide on its own rules for doing business, punish its members, and remove a member from office if two thirds of the members agree.

3. Journal. Each house must keep records of its activities and publish these records from time to time. The *House Journal* and the *Senate Journal* are published at the end of each session. Votes must be recorded if one fifth of the members make this request.

4. Adjournment. When Congress is in session, neither house may take a recess for more than three days or move to another place unless the other house agrees.

SECTION 6. Privileges and Restrictions

1. Pay and Privileges. Members of Congress set their own salaries, which are to be paid by the federal government. Members of Congress cannot be arrested or sued for anything they say when Congress is in session.

This privilege is called **congressional immunity.**

Members of Congress may be arrested if they commit a crime.

2. Restrictions. Members of Congress may not hold any other government office while serving in Congress. A member of Congress may not resign from office and then take a position created during that member's term of office.

SECTION 7. Method of Passing Laws

1. Revenue Bills. All bills for raising revenue shall originate in the House of Representatives; but the Senate may propose or concur with amendments as on other bills.

2. How a Bill Becomes a Law. Every bill which shall have passed the House of Representatives and the Senate shall, before it becomes a law, be presented to the President of the United States; if he approve he shall sign it, but if not he shall return it, with his objections, to that house in which it shall have originated, who shall enter the objections at large on their journal, and proceed to reconsider it. If after such reconsideration two thirds of that house shall agree to pass the bill, it shall be sent, together with the objections, to the other house, by which it shall likewise be reconsidered, and if approved by two thirds of that house, it shall become a law. But in all such cases the votes of both houses shall be determined by yeas and nays, and the names of the persons voting for and against the bill shall be entered on the journal of each house respectively. If any bill shall not be returned by the President within ten days (Sundays excepted) after it shall have been presented to him, the same shall be a law, in like manner as if he had signed it, unless the Congress by their adjournment prevent its return, in which case it shall not be a law.

3. Presidential Approval or Veto. Every order, resolution, or vote to which the concurrence of the Senate and House of Representatives may be necessary (except on a question of adjournment) shall be presented to the President of the United States; and, before the same shall take effect, shall be approved by him, or, being disapproved by him, shall be repassed by two thirds of the Senate and House of Representatives, according to the rules and limitations prescribed in the case of a bill.

SECTION 8. Powers Granted to Congress
The Congress shall have power

1. Taxation. To lay and collect taxes, duties, imposts, and excises, to pay the debts and provide for the common defense and general welfare of the United States; but all duties, imposts, and excises shall be uniform throughout the United States;

SECTION 7. Method of Passing Laws

1. Revenue Bills. A **bill** is a proposal for a law. All **revenue,** or money-raising, bills must be introduced in the House of Representatives, but the Senate may suggest changes.

2. How a Bill Becomes a Law. After a bill is passed by the House of Representatives and the Senate, it must be sent to the President. If the President approves the bill, it becomes a law. If the President **vetoes,** or rejects, the bill, it is returned to the group that presented it, along with a list of objections. The bill is again presented for discussion. If two thirds of the House agree to pass the bill, they send it to the Senate for their vote. If two thirds of the Senate agree to pass the bill, it becomes a law. These votes must be recorded. If the President does not return a bill within ten days, two things may happen. If Congress is still in session during this time, the bill becomes a law. Or, if Congress ends its session within that same ten-day period, the bill does not become a law.

When a bill does not become a law because the Congress session has ended, it is called a **pocket veto.**

3. Presidential Approval or Veto. Congress takes votes, and passes orders and resolutions, some of which have the effect of law. Congress may decide on its own when to end the session. Other actions which have the effect of law must be signed or vetoed by the President. If the President approves the action, then it will take effect. If the President vetoes the action, it may again be presented to the House and the Senate for a two-thirds vote. If it is passed, the action will take effect.

SECTION 8. Powers Granted to Congress

1. Taxation. Congress may raise money to pay debts, defend the United States, and provide services for its people by collecting taxes. These may include taxes on goods coming into the country and taxes on goods that are made or sold within the country. The rate of tax must be the same in every state.

2. Borrowing Money. To borrow money on the credit of the United States;

3. Commerce. To regulate commerce with foreign nations, and among the several states, and with the Indian tribes;

4. Naturalization, Bankruptcy. To establish a uniform rule of naturalization, and uniform laws on the subject of bankruptcies throughout the United States;

5. Coinage, Weights, and Measures. To coin money, regulate the value thereof, and of foreign coin, and fix the standard of weights and measures;

6. Counterfeiting. To provide for the punishment of counterfeiting the securities and current coin of the United States;

7. Postal Service. To establish post offices and post roads;

8. Copyrights, Patents. To promote the progress of science and useful arts, by securing for limited times to authors and inventors the exclusive right to their respective writings and discoveries;

9. Federal Courts. To constitute tribunals inferior to the Supreme Court;

10. Crimes At Sea. To define and punish piracies and felonies committed on the high seas, and offenses against the law of nations;

11. Declarations of War. To declare war, grant letters of marque and reprisal, and make rules concerning captures on land and water;

---

2. Borrowing Money. Congress may borrow money for national use. This is usually done by selling government bonds.

3. Commerce. Congress may pass laws about trading with other countries, within the United States, and with Indians.

4. Naturalization, Bankruptcy. Congress may pass laws about **naturalization,** the process by which immigrants become United States citizens, and laws to protect people who declare **bankruptcy,** or cannot pay their debts. These laws must be the same in every state.

5. Coinage, Weights, and Measures. Congress may make money and decide its value. Congress also decides on the system of weights and measures to be used throughout the nation.

6. Counterfeiting. Congress may pass laws to punish people who make **counterfeit,** or fake, money, bonds, or stamps.

7. Postal Service. Congress can make rules about the postal system and roads used for mail delivery.

8. Copyrights, Patents. Congress can issue patents and copyrights to inventors and authors to protect the ownership of their works for a limited time.

9. Federal Courts. Congress can establish a system of federal courts under the Supreme Court.

10. Crimes At Sea. Congress can pass laws to punish people for crimes committed at sea against the United States or its people. Congress may also punish United States citizens for breaking international law.

11. Declarations of War. Only Congress may declare war.

However, some Presidents have taken military action without declaring war. In 1856, the United States agreed to an international law preventing **letters of marque and reprisal,** or licenses that allowed private ships to attack enemy ships during wartime.

12. The Army. To raise and support armies, but no appropriation money to that use shall be for a longer term than two years;

13. The Navy. To provide and maintain a navy;

14. Military Regulations. To make rules for the government and regulation of the land and naval forces;

15. The Militia. To provide for calling forth the militia to execute the laws of the Union, suppress insurrections, and repel invasions;

16. Control of the Militia. To provide for organizing, arming, and disciplining the militia, and for governing such part of them as may be employed in the service of the United States, reserving to the states respectively, the appointment of the officers, and the authority of training the militia according to the discipline prescribed by Congress.

17. National Capital and Other Property. To exercise exclusive legislation, in all cases whatsoever, over such district (not exceeding ten miles square) as may, by cession of particular states, and the acceptance of Congress, become the seat of the government of the United States; and to exercise like authority over all places purchased by the consent of the legislature of the state in which the same shall be, for the erection of forts, magazines, arsenals, dock-yards, and other needful buildings; and

18. Other Necessary Laws. To make all laws which shall be necessary and proper for carrying into execution the foregoing powers, and all other powers vested by this Constitution in the government of the United States, or in any department or officer thereof.

12. The Army. Congress can establish an army, but it cannot vote enough money to support it for more than two years.

This was designed to keep the army under nonmilitary control.

13. The Navy. Congress can establish a navy and vote enough money to support it for as long as necessary. No time limit was set because people thought the navy was less of a threat to people's liberty than the army.

14. Military Regulations. Congress may pass laws to rule the armed forces.

15. The Militia. Each state has its own volunteer military, now called the **National Guard.** Congress has now given the President the right to call the National Guard into service when it becomes necessary to enforce laws, to stop uprisings against the government, or to protect the United States.

16. Control of the Militia. Congress helps each state support the National Guard. Each state may appoint its own officers and train its own guard according to rules set by Congress.

17. National Capital and Other Property. Congress may pass laws to govern the nation's capital (Washington, D.C.) and any land on which government buildings are set.

18. Other Necessary Laws. Congress may pass other laws that are necessary to enforce all powers listed in this article and any other powers granted by the Constitution in governing the United States.

This is sometimes called the **elastic clause,** because it allows Congress to stretch its powers if new situations arise.

SECTION 9. Powers Denied to Congress

1. The Slave Trade. The migration or importation of such persons as any of the states now existing shall think proper to admit, shall not be prohibited by the Congress prior to the year one thousand eight hundred and eight, but a tax or duty may be imposed on such importation, not exceeding ten dollars for each person.

2. Writ of Habeas Corpus. The privilege of the writ of *habeas corpus* shall not be suspended, unless when in cases of rebellion or invasion the public safety may require it.

3. Bills of Attainder, Ex Post Facto Laws. No bill of attainder or *ex post facto* law shall be passed.

4. Direct Taxes. No capitation or other direct tax shall be laid, unless in proportion to the census or enumeration herein before directed to be taken.

5. Export Taxes. No tax or duty shall be laid on articles exported from any state.

6. Ports and Port Duties. No preference shall be given by any regulation of commerce or revenue to the ports of one state over those of another; nor shall vessels bound to, or from, one state, be obliged to enter, clear, or pay duties in another.

7. Public Money. No money shall be drawn from the treasury, but in consequence of appropriations made by law; and a regular statement and account of the receipts and expenditures of all public money shall be published from time to time.

SECTION 9. Powers Denied to Congress

1. The Slave Trade. Certain powers are not given to Congress.

Congress could not prevent slave trade until 1808, but it could put a tax of ten dollars on each slave brought into the United States. In 1808, a law was passed to stop slaves from being **imported,** or brought into, the United States.

2. Writ of *Habeas Corpus*. Every person held in jail is entitled to a hearing before a judge. The judge must then decide if there is enough evidence to charge that person with the crime. If not, the person must be released. The writ of *habeas corpus* is to be enforced except during a national emergency, such as an invasion or a rebellion. The right to *habeas corpus* is one of our most important guarantees of personal liberty.

3. Bills of Attainder, Ex Post Facto Laws. Congress cannot pass **bills of attainder,** or laws that convict and punish a person without a trial. Nor can Congress pass *ex post facto* laws, or laws that punish a person for an action that was legal when it was done. Congress also cannot pass laws to increase the punishment for a crime after it has been committed.

4. Direct Taxes. Congress cannot set a **capitation,** or direct tax on people, unless it is in proportion to the total population. This restriction was designed to stop Congress from trying to end slavery by taxing the slaves as free people.

5. Export Taxes. Congress cannot tax goods sent from one state to another or from a state to another country.

6. Ports and Port Duties. Congress cannot pass laws about trade that would favor one state over another. Congress cannot require ships from one state to pay a duty to enter another state.

7. Public Money. Congress cannot spend money from the United States treasury unless they **appropriate,** or pass a law giving permission. Congress may limit the amount of money the President may spend and can require a written record of all money spent by the government.

8. Titles of Nobility, Gifts. No title of nobility shall be granted by the United States; and no person holding any office of profit or trust under them shall, without the consent of the Congress, accept of any present, emolument, office, or title, of any kind whatever, from any king, prince, or foreign state.

SECTION 10. Powers Denied to the States

1. Absolute Restrictions. No state shall enter into any treaty, alliance, or confederation; grant letters of marque and reprisal; coin money; emit bills of credit; make anything but gold and silver coin a tender in payment of debts; pass any bill of attainder, *ex post facto* law, or law impairing the obligation of contracts; or grant any title of nobility.

2. Conditional Restrictions. No state shall, without the consent of the Congress, lay any imposts or duties on imports or exports, except what may be absolutely necessary for executing its inspection laws; and the net produce of all duties and imposts, laid by any state on imports or exports, shall be for the use of the treasury of the United States; and all such laws shall be subject to the revision and control of the Congress.

3. Other Conditional Restrictions. No state shall, without the consent of Congress, lay any duty of tonnage, keep troops or ships of war in time of peace, enter into any agreement or compact with another state, or with a foreign power, or engage in war, unless actually invaded, or in such imminent danger as will not admit of delay.

8. Titles of Nobility, Gifts. The United States government cannot grant titles of nobility. Government officials cannot accept gifts from other countries without the permission of Congress.

This clause was intended to prevent United States government officials from being bribed by other nations.

SECTION 10. Powers Denied to the States

1. Absolute Restrictions. Certain powers denied to the states are powers granted only to the federal government. No state government may make a treaty or form an agreement with any other nation. No state may permit its ships to attack enemy ships during wartime. No state may make its own money, grant credit, or accept anything other than gold or silver in payment of debt. No state may pass laws preventing the right to a hearing by a judge or punish a person for an act that was legal when it was done. Nor may a state pass laws that interfere with fulfilling contracts or that grant titles of nobility.

2. Conditional Restrictions. Some powers are granted to state governments with the approval of Congress. No state government may tax goods coming into its state unless Congress approves. States may charge a fee to inspect these goods, but profits must be given to the United States treasury.

This law may be changed by Congress. This restriction was designed to prevent individual states from trying to lessen government control of trade within the states and with other nations.

3. Other Conditional Restrictions. No state government may tax ships entering their ports unless Congress approves. No state may keep an army or navy other than the National Guard during times of peace. No state may make agreements with other states or nations, or go to war unless it is are actually invaded.

ARTICLE 2
Executive Branch

SECTION 1. President and Vice President

1. Term of Office. The executive power shall be vested in a President of the United States of America. He shall hold his office during the term of four years, and, together with the Vice President, chosen for the same term, be elected as follows:

2. The Electoral College. Each state shall appoint, in such manner as the legislature thereof may direct, a number of electors, equal to the whole number of senators and representatives to which the state may be entitled in the Congress; but no senator or representative, or person holding an office of trust or profit under the United States, shall be appointed an elector.

3. Original Electoral College Procedure. The electors shall meet in their respective states, and vote by ballot for two persons, of whom one at least shall not be an inhabitant of the same state with themselves. And they shall make a list of all the persons voted for, and of the number of votes for each; which list they shall sign and certify, and transmit sealed to the seat of the government of the United States, directed to the President of the Senate. The President of the Senate shall, in the presence of the Senate and House of Representatives, open all the certificates, and the votes shall then be counted. The person having the greatest number of votes shall be the President, if such number be a majority of the whole number of electors appointed; and if there be more than one who have such majority, and have an equal number of votes, then the House of Representatives shall immediately choose by ballot one of them for President; and if no person have a majority, then from the five highest on the list the said house shall in like manner choose the President. But in choosing the President, the votes shall be taken by states, the representation from each state having one vote; a quorum for this purpose shall consist of a member or members from two thirds of the states, and a majority of all the states shall be necessary to a choice. In every case, after the choice of the President, the person having the greatest number of votes of the electors shall be the Vice President. But if there should remain two or more who have equal votes, the Senate shall choose from them by ballot the Vice President.

4. Time of Elections. The Congress may determine the time of choosing the electors, and the day on which they shall give their votes; which day shall be the same throughout the United States.

ARTICLE 2
Executive Branch

SECTION 1. President and Vice President

1. Term of Office. The President of the United States **executes**, or carries out, our nation's laws. The term of office for both the President and the Vice President is four years.

2. The Electoral College. The Electoral College was established as a group of people chosen by the voters of each state to elect the President and Vice President. The number of electors in each state is equal to the number of that state's senators and representatives in Congress.

3. Original Electoral College Procedure. Originally, the President and Vice President were chosen by a group of electors. The president of the Senate opened all the votes of the electors and counted them. The President of the United States would be the person with the greatest number of votes if that number was a majority of the total number of appointed electors. If more than one person had a majority vote or if no one had the majority vote, then the House of Representatives chose the President.

Amendment 12 changed the procedure for electing the President and Vice President in 1804.

4. Time of Elections. Congress decides the day the electors are to be elected and the day when they are to vote for President and Vice President.

Today Presidential elections are held on the Tuesday after the first Monday in November.

5. Qualifications for the President. No person except a natural-born citizen, or a citizen of the United States at the time of the adoption of this Constitution, shall be eligible to the office of President; neither shall any person be eligible to that office who shall not have attained to the age of thirty-five years, and been fourteen years a resident within the United States.

6. Vacancies. In case of the removal of the President from office, or of his death, resignation, or inability to discharge the powers and duties of the said office, the same shall devolve on the Vice President, and the Congress may by law provide for the case of removal, death, resignation, or inability, both of the President and Vice President, declaring what officer shall then act as President, and such officer shall act accordingly, until the disability be removed, or a President shall be elected.

7. Salary. The President shall, at stated times, receive for his services a compensation, which shall neither be increased nor diminished during the period for which he shall have been elected, and he shall not receive within that period any other emolument from the United States, or any of them.

8. Oath of Office. Before he enter on the execution of his office, he shall take the following oath or affirmation:—"I do solemnly swear (or affirm) that I will faithfully execute the office of President of the United States, and will, to the best of my ability, preserve, protect, and defend the Constitution of the United States."

SECTION 2. Powers of the President

1. Military Powers. The President shall be Commander in Chief of the army and navy of the United States, and of the militia of the several states, when called into the actual service of the United States; he may require the opinion, in writing, of the principal officer in each of the executive departments, upon any subject relating to the duties of their respective offices, and he shall have power to grant reprieves and pardons for offenses against the United States, except in cases of impeachment.

5. Qualifications for the President. The President must be thirty-five years old, a citizen of the United States by birth, and must have been living in the United States for fourteen years or more.

6. Vacancies. If the President dies or is removed from office, the Vice President takes over the office.

In 1947, a law was passed that states that the following officials are in line for the Presidency if both the President and the Vice President are unable to serve: the Speaker of the House of Representatives, the President *pro tempore* of the Senate, and the Cabinet members in the order in which their offices were created.

7. Salary. The President receives a salary which can neither be raised nor lowered during a term of office. The President may not be paid any additional salary from the government.

Today the President's salary is $200,000 a year, plus expenses such as travel and entertainment.

8. Oath of Office. Before entering office, the President must make a promise to perform the duties faithfully and to protect the country's form of government.

Usually, the Chief Justice of the United States administers the oath of office, though that has not always been the case.

SECTION 2. Powers of the President

1. Military Powers. The President is commander in chief of the armed forces and the National Guard when it is called into service. The President may order information from the heads of all executive departments. The President may grant pardons or reprieves for federal crimes, except in cases of impeachment.

2. Treaties and Appointments. He shall have power, by and with the advice and consent of the Senate, to make treaties, provided two thirds of the senators present concur; and he shall nominate, and by and with the advice and consent of the Senate, shall appoint ambassadors, other public ministers and consuls, judges of the Supreme Court, and all other officers of the United States, whose appointments are not herein otherwise provided for, and which shall be established by law; but the Congress may by law vest the appointment of such inferior officers, as they think proper, in the President alone, in the courts of law, or in the heads of departments.

3. Filling Vacancies. The President shall have the power to fill up all vacancies that may happen during the recess of the Senate, by granting commissions which shall expire at the end of their next session.

SECTION 3. Duties of the President

He shall from time to time give to the Congress information of the state of the Union, and recommend to their consideration such measures as he shall judge necessary and expedient; he may, on extraordinary occasions, convene both houses, or either of them, and in case of disagreement between them, with respect to the time of adjournment, he may adjourn them to such time as he shall think proper; he shall receive ambassadors and other public ministers; he shall take care that the laws be faithfully executed, and shall commission all the officers of the United States.

SECTION 4. Impeachment

The President, Vice President, and all civil officers of the United States, shall be removed from office on impeachment for, and conviction of, treason, bribery, or other high crimes and misdemeanors.

2. Treaties and Appointments. The President has the power to make treaties, but they must be approved by a two-thirds vote of the Senate. The President may appoint government officials with Senate approval, but Congress may pass laws allowing the President, the courts, or executives to appoint officials without the Senate's approval.

3. Filling Vacancies. If a government official's position becomes available when Congress is not in session, the President can make a temporary appointment. When Congress is back in session, this appointment must be brought before the Senate for approval.

SECTION 3. Duties of the President

The President must report to Congress on the condition of the country.

Up to 1913, this report was made in writing. This information is now presented in the State of the Union Message, given at the opening session of Congress. In this speech, the President reports on problems facing the nation and suggests laws for Congress to pass.

The President may call special sessions of either house or call for the end of a session when the two houses cannot agree.

The President also receives, or refuses to receive, representatives of foreign governments, makes sure that the nation's laws are enforced, and appoints officials to the armed forces.

SECTION 4. Impeachment

The President, the Vice President, or any government official will be removed from office if impeached, or charged with, and found guilty of disloyalty, bribery, or other crimes.

Andrew Johnson was the only President to be impeached (1868); however, he was one vote short of being convicted. In 1974, Richard M. Nixon resigned from the Presidency after the House agreed to begin impeachment proceedings.

ARTICLE 3
Judicial Branch

SECTION 1. Federal Courts

The Supreme Court and Lower Federal Courts. The judicial power of the United States shall be vested in one Supreme Court, and in such inferior courts as the Congress may from time to time ordain and establish. The judges, both of the Supreme and inferior courts, shall hold their offices during good behavior, and shall, at stated times, receive for their services a compensation, which shall not be diminished during their continuance in office.

SECTION 2. Jurisdiction of the Federal Courts

1. General Jurisdiction. The judicial power shall extend to all cases, in law and equity, arising under this Constitution, the laws of the United States, and treaties made, or which shall be made, under their authority; to all cases affecting ambassadors, other public ministers and consuls; to all cases of admiralty and maritime jurisdiction; to controversies to which the United States shall be a party; to controversies between two or more states; between a state and citizens of another state; between citizens of different states; between citizens of the same state claiming lands under grants of different states; and between a state or the citizens thereof, and foreign states, citizens, or subjects.

2. The Supreme Court. In all cases affecting ambassadors, other public ministers and consuls, and those in which a state shall be party; the Supreme Court shall have original jurisdiction. In all the other cases before mentioned, the Supreme Court shall have appellate jurisdiction, both as to law and fact, with such exceptions, and under such regulations as the Congress shall make.

3. Trial by Jury. The trial of all crimes, except in cases of impeachment, shall be by jury; and such trial shall be held in the state where the said crimes shall have been committed; but when not committed within any state, the trial shall be at such place or places as the Congress may by law have directed.

ARTICLE 3
Judicial Branch

SECTION 1. Federal Courts

The power to decide legal cases is granted to the Supreme Court and to a system of lower courts established by Congress. The Supreme Court is the highest court.

The Constitution does not name the number of justices that should serve on the Supreme Court, but Congress establishes that number by law. There were originally six Supreme Court justices, but today there are nine.

SECTION 2. Jurisdiction of the Federal Courts

1. General Jurisdiction. Federal courts have the right to decide legal cases involving the interpretation of: a) the Constitution, b) federal laws, c) treaties, d) laws about ships at sea, and e) the federal government. Federal courts also have the right to decide cases involving disagreements between f) foreign officials, g) two or more state governments, h) citizens of different states, i) citizens of the same state claiming lands under grants of different states, and j) citizens of a state and a foreign nation or its citizens.

Amendment 11 changed this section so that a citizen of one state cannot sue a citizen of another state in a federal court.

2. The Supreme Court. The Supreme Court has two kinds of power: 1) original jurisdiction, which grants the right to decide cases being tried for the first time; 2) appellate jurisdiction, which grants the right to review cases that have already been tried in a lower court, in which the decision has been appealed, or questioned, by one side.

3. Trial by Jury. Every person charged with a crime is guaranteed a jury trial. The trial is to be held in the state where the crime was committed. If a crime is committed at sea or in a United States possession, Congress decides where the trial will take place.

Amendments 5, 6, and 7 extend and clarify people's rights to a trial by jury.

SECTION 3. Treason

1. Definition. Treason against the United States shall consist only in levying war against them, or in adhering to their enemies, giving them aid and comfort. No person shall be convicted of treason unless on the testimony of two witnesses to the same overt act, or on confession in open court.

2. Punishment. The Congress shall have power to declare the punishment of treason, but no attainder of treason shall work corruption of blood, or forfeiture, except during the life of the person attainted.

ARTICLE 4
Relations Among the States

SECTION 1. Official Records

Full faith and credit shall be given in each state to the public acts, records, and judicial proceedings of every other state. And the Congress may by general laws prescribe the manner in which such acts, records, and proceedings shall be proved, and the effect thereof.

SECTION 2. Privileges of Citizens

1. Privileges. The citizens of each state shall be entitled to all privileges and immunities of citizens in the several states.

2. Extradition. A person charged in any state with treason, felony, or other crime, who shall flee from justice, and be found in another state, shall, on demand of the executive authority of the state from which he fled, be delivered up, to be removed to the state having jurisdiction of the crime.

3. Fugitive Slaves. No person held to service or labor in one state, under the laws thereof, escaping into another, shall in consequence of any law or regulation therein, be discharged from such service or labor, but shall be delivered up on claim of the party to whom such service or labor may be due.

SECTION 3. Treason

1. Definition. Acts that may be considered treason are making war against the United States or helping its enemies. A person cannot be convicted of treason, or an attempt to overthrow the government, unless there are two witnesses to the act, or the person confesses to treason in court.

2. Punishment. Congress has the power to decide the punishment for treason. This punishment cannot extend to other members of the guilty person's family.

Congress set the punishment for treason at death or a prison term of at least five years and a $10,000 fine.

ARTICLE 4
Relations Among the States

SECTION 1. Official Records

Each state must honor the laws, official records and legal decisions of other states. Congress may pass laws to enforce this article.

SECTION 2. Privileges of Citizens

1. Privileges. Citizens going from one state to another have all rights of the state they are in.

Some rights, such as voting, may require people to live in their new state for a certain amount of time before they may vote as citizens of the new state.

2. Extradition. At the governor's request, a person charged with a crime who tries to escape justice by crossing into another state may be **extradited,** or returned, to the state in which the crime was committed.

If another governor feels that extradition may result in injustice to the accused person, extradition may be refused.

3. Fugitive Slaves. States are required to return runaway slaves to their owners.

Amendment 13 abolished slavery.

SECTION 3. New States and Territories

1. Admission of New States. New states may be admitted by the Congress into this Union; but no new state shall be formed or erected within the jurisdiction of any other state; nor any state be formed by the junction of two or more states, or parts of states, without the consent of the legislatures of the states concerned, as well as of the Congress.

2. Territories and Other Federal Property. The Congress shall have power to dispose of and make all needful rules and regulations respecting the territory or other property belonging to the United States; and nothing in this Constitution shall be so construed as to prejudice any claims of the United States, or of any particular state.

SECTION 4. Guarantees to the States

The United States shall guarantee to every state in this Union a republican form of government, and shall protect each of them against invasion; and on application of the legislature, or of the Executive (when the legislature cannot be convened), against domestic violence.

ARTICLE 5
Amending the Constitution

The Congress, whenever two thirds of both houses shall deem it necessary, shall propose amendments to this Constitution, or, on the application of the legislatures of two thirds of the several states, shall call a convention for proposing amendments, which, in either case, shall be valid to all intents and purposes, as part of this Constitution, when ratified by the legislatures of three fourths of the several states, or by conventions in three fourths thereof, as the one or the other mode of ratification may be proposed by the Congress; provided that no amendment which may be made prior to the year one thousand eight hundred and eight shall in any manner affect the first and fourth clauses in the ninth section of the first article; and that no state, without its consent, shall be deprived of its equal suffrage in the Senate.

ARTICLE 6
General Provisions

1. Public Debt. All debts contracted and engagements entered into, before the adoption of this Constitution, shall be valid against the United States under this Constitution, as under the Confederation.

SECTION 3. New States and Territories

1. Admission of New States. Congress has the power to admit new states to the Union. No new state can be made within the boundaries of another state. New states cannot be formed by combining two or more states without the approval of Congress and each state involved.

2. Territories and Other Federal Property. Congress has the power to make or change laws governing federal property, including territories and federally owned land within states, such as national parks.

SECTION 4. Guarantees to the States

Every state has the right to elect its own representatives to govern the state. The federal government must protect the states against invasion by other nations. If a state requests help, the federal government must call upon the National Guard to help that state.

ARTICLE 5
Amending the Constitution

Amendments, or changes, to the Constitution may be requested by a two-thirds vote of both the House and the Senate, or by a national convention called by Congress at the request of two thirds of the states. To pass an amendment, the legislatures of three quarters of the states must **ratify,** or approve, the request. No state may be denied equal representation in the Senate without the approval of that state.

ARTICLE 6
General Provisions

1. Public Debt. The Constitution promised that any debt owed by the United States before the Constitution went into effect would be honored.

2. Federal Supremacy. This Constitution, and the laws of the United States which shall be made in pursuance thereof, and all treaties made, or which shall be made, under the authority of the United States, shall be the supreme law of the land; and the judges in every state shall be bound thereby, anything in the constitution or laws of any state to the contrary notwithstanding.

3. Oaths of Office. The Senators and Representatives before mentioned, and the members of the several state legislatures, and all executive and judicial officers, both of the United States and of the several states, shall be bound by oath or affirmation to support the Constitution; but no religious test shall ever be required as a qualification to any office or public trust under the United States.

2. Federal Supremacy. This clause is known as the **supremacy clause,** which declares that the Constitution is the supreme, or highest, law in the nation. Laws made by the Constitution have more power than laws made by a state. If a state law does not agree with a federal law, the federal law is to be obeyed.

3. Oaths of Office. All federal and state officials must take an oath promising to follow and enforce the laws of the Constitution. There may be no religious requirements for holding a government office.

ARTICLE 7
Ratification

The ratification of the conventions of nine states shall be sufficient for the establishment of this Constitution between the states so ratifying the same.

ARTICLE 7
Ratification

In order for the Constitution to become law, nine states had to ratify the Constitution. Special conventions were held for this purpose, and the process took nine months to complete.

Amendments to the Constitution

Amendments to the Constitution

Many people felt it unfair that the Constitution did not provide a list of people's personal freedoms. Therefore, in its first session, Congress proposed twelve amendments to the Constitution. Ten of these amendments were ratified by the states in 1791, and are known as the Bill of Rights.

AMENDMENT 1
Freedom of Religion, Speech, Press, Assembly, and Petition (1791)

Congress shall make no law respecting an establishment of religion, or prohibiting the free exercise thereof; or abridging the freedom of speech, or of the press; or the right of the people peaceably to assemble, and to petition the government for a redress of grievances.

AMENDMENT 1
Freedom of Religion, Speech,
Press, Assembly, and Petition (1791)

Amendment 1 guarantees our five basic civil rights. It provides for a) freedom of religion, b) freedom of speech, c) freedom of the press, d) the right to assemble peacefully, and e) the right to protest government policies.

AMENDMENT 2
Right to Keep Arms (1791)

A well regulated militia being necessary to the security of a free state, the right of the people to keep and bear arms shall not be infringed.

AMENDMENT 3
Quartering Soldiers (1791)

No soldier shall, in time of peace, be quartered in any house, without the consent of the owner, nor in time of war, but in a manner to be prescribed by law.

AMENDMENT 4
Searches and Seizures (1791)

The right of the people to be secure in their persons, houses, papers, and effects, against unreasonable searches and seizures, shall not be violated, and no warrants shall issue but upon probable cause, supported by oath or affirmation, and particularly describing the place to be searched, and the persons or things to be seized.

AMENDMENT 5
Rights of Accused Persons (1791)

No person shall be held to answer for a capital, or otherwise infamous crime, unless on a presentment or indictment of a grand jury, except in cases arising in the land or naval forces, or in the militia, when in actual service in time of war or public danger; nor shall any person be subject for the same offense to be twice put in jeopardy of life or limb; nor shall be compelled in any criminal case to be a witness against himself, nor be deprived of life, liberty, or property, without due process of law; nor shall private property be taken for public use without just compensation.

AMENDMENT 2
Right to Keep Arms (1791)

This amendment means that the states may have an armed military, such as the National Guard. However, the federal government may pass laws about ownership and possession of weapons by private citizens.

AMENDMENT 3
Quartering Soldiers (1791)

Before the American Revolution, the colonists were forced to house British troops in their homes. Amendment 3 guarantees people the right to privacy and safety in their own homes. During times of peace, the federal government cannot force people to house soldiers in their homes. However, Congress may pass laws to this effect during wartime.

AMENDMENT 4
Searches and Seizures (1791)

Amendment 4 further guarantees the right to personal privacy and safety. In order for a law officer to search a person's house and belongings, a judge must issue a search warrant. There must be good reason for the search, and the warrant must describe the place to be searched and the people or things to be seized, or taken.

There are some exceptions to this amendment; for example, if police have witnessed a crime, they do not need a warrant. The Supreme Court ruled that any evidence obtained without a warrant cannot be used in a court of law.

AMENDMENT 5
Rights of Accused Persons (1791)

If a person is accused of a serious crime that is punishable by death, the evidence for the trial must be presented before a grand jury to decide if there is enough evidence to hold a trial. People cannot be tried twice for the same crime, nor be forced to give evidence against themselves. No person shall be fined, jailed, or executed by the federal government unless a fair trial has been given and one of these punishments has been ordered. The government cannot take a person's property for public use unless fair payment is made.

AMENDMENT 6
Jury Trial in Criminal Cases (1791)

In all criminal prosecutions, the accused shall enjoy the right to a speedy and public trial, by an impartial jury of the state and district wherein the crime shall have been committed, which district shall have been previously ascertained by law, and to be informed of the nature and cause of the accusation; to be confronted with the witnesses against him; to have compulsory process for obtaining witnesses in his favor, and to have the assistance of counsel for his defense.

AMENDMENT 7
Jury Trial in Civil Cases (1791)

In suits at common law, where the value in controversy shall exceed twenty dollars, the right of trial by jury shall be preserved, and no fact tried by a jury shall be otherwise reexamined in any court of the United States, than according to the rules of the common law.

AMENDMENT 8
Excessive Bail or Punishment (1791)

Excessive bail shall not be required, nor excessive fines imposed, nor cruel and unusual punishments inflicted.

AMENDMENT 9
Other Rights of the People (1791)

The enumeration in the Constitution of certain rights shall not be construed to deny or disparage others retained by the people.

AMENDMENT 6
Jury Trial in Criminal Cases (1791)

A person accused of a crime has a right to a public trial within a reasonable amount of time. The members of the jury should be residents of the state and district in which the crime was committed. The accused person must be informed of all charges and have the right to see, hear, and question any witnesses. If there are other witnesses that might help the accused, these witnesses may be ordered to testify in court. The accused person has a right to be defended by a lawyer.

Since 1942, the federal government must provide a lawyer free of charge to any accused person unable to pay for legal services.

AMENDMENT 7
Jury Trial in Civil Cases (1791)

In any federal civil case involving more than twenty dollars, a jury trial is guaranteed.

Civil cases are those involving two or more people over money, property, personal injury, or legal rights. Usually civil cases are not tried in federal courts unless much larger sums of money are involved.

AMENDMENT 8
Excessive Bail or Punishment (1791)

A person accused of a crime may be released from jail before the trial if bail is posted, or paid. **Bail** is an amount of money decided by the courts to be paid by the accused person. It serves as a guarantee that the accused person will appear for trial. If the accused person appears at the trial, bail is returned. A person convicted of a crime cannot be given unreasonable punishment, nor can "cruel or unusual" punishment be ordered. The Supreme Court has ruled that capital punishment, or punishment by death, is not cruel and unusual.

AMENDMENT 9
Other Rights of the People (1791)

The Constitution does not list every right guaranteed to the people of the United States. However, the federal government must respect all basic human rights.

AMENDMENT 10
Powers of the States and the People (1791)

The powers not delegated to the United States by the Constitution, nor prohibited by it to the states, are reserved to the states respectively, or to the people.

AMENDMENT 11
Suits Against States (1798)

The judicial power of the United States shall not be construed to extend to any suit in law or equity, commenced or prosecuted against one of the United States or citizens of another state, or by citizens or subjects of any foreign state.

AMENDMENT 12
Election of President and Vice President (1804)

The electors shall meet in their respective states, and vote by ballot for President and Vice President, one of whom, at least, shall not be an inhabitant of the same state with themselves; they shall name in their ballots the person voted for as President, and in distinct ballots the person voted for as Vice President; and they shall make distinct lists of all persons voted for as President, and of all persons voted for as Vice President, and of the number of votes for each, which lists they shall sign and certify, and transmit sealed to the seat of the government of the United States, directed to the President of the Senate;—the President of the Senate shall, in the presence of the Senate and House of Representatives, open all the certificates, and the votes shall then be counted;—the person having the greatest number of votes for President shall be the President, if such a number be a majority of the whole number of electors appointed; and if no person have such majority; then from the persons having the highest numbers not exceeding three on the list of those voted for as President, the House of Representatives shall choose immediately, by ballot, the President. But in choosing the President, the votes shall be taken by states, the representation from each state having one vote; a quorum for this purpose shall consist of a member or members from two thirds of the states, and a majority of all the states shall be necessary to a choice. And if the House of Representatives shall not choose a President whenever the right of choice shall devolve upon them, before the fourth day of March next following, then the Vice President shall act as President, as in the case of the death or other constitutional disability of the President. The person having the greatest number of votes as Vice President

AMENDMENT 10
Powers of the States
and the People (1791)

Amendment 10 is called the **reserved powers amendment.** The Constitution gives certain powers to the federal government in Article 1, Section 9, and others are given to the individual states in Article 1, Section 10. Any remaining powers belong to the states or to the people.

AMENDMENT 11
Suits Against States (1798)

A state government may be sued only in its own courts.

AMENDMENT 12
Election of President
and Vice President (1804)

Amendment 12 replaces the part of Article 2, Section 1 in which electors voted for the President and the Vice President on one ballot.
In 1800, Thomas Jefferson and Aaron Burr had the same number of electoral votes. Jefferson was finally elected President by the House of Representatives, but it took so long that people were afraid a President would not be named before Inauguration Day. This amendment was designed to prevent this from happening again.

Members of the Electoral College vote for one person as President and one person as Vice President. If no presidential candidate receives the majority of electoral votes, the House of Representatives chooses the President from the top three candidates. Each state casts only one vote. If the House fails to choose a President by the beginning of the new term, then the person who was elected Vice President acts as President.

Amendment 20 changed the date by which the House must make its Presidential selection. If no candidate for the Vice Presidency receives a majority, the Senate chooses from the top two candidates. A Vice President must meet the same qualifications as the President.

shall be the Vice President, if such number be a majority of the whole number of electors appointed, and if no person have a majority, then from the two highest numbers on the list the Senate shall choose the Vice President; a quorum for the purpose shall consist of two thirds of the whole number of senators, and a majority of the whole number shall be necessary to a choice. But no person constitutionally ineligible to the office of President shall be eligible to that of Vice President of the United States.

AMENDMENT 13
Abolition of Slavery (1865)

SECTION 1. Abolition of Slavery. Neither slavery nor involuntary servitude, except as a punishment for crime whereof the party shall have been duly convicted, shall exist within the United States, or any place subject to their jurisdiction.

SECTION 2. Enforcement. Congress shall have power to enforce this article by appropriate legislation.

AMENDMENT 14
Rights of Citizens (1868)

SECTION 1. Definition of Citizenship. All persons born or naturalized in the United States, and subject to the jurisdiction thereof, are citizens of the United States and of the state wherein they reside. No state shall make or enforce any law which shall abridge the privileges or immunities of citizens of the United States; nor shall any state deprive any person of life, liberty, or property, without due process of law; nor deny to any person within its jurisdiction the equal protection of the laws.

SECTION 2. Number of Representatives. Representatives shall be apportioned among the several states according to their respective numbers, counting the whole number of persons in each state, excluding Indians not taxed. But when the right to vote at any election for the choice of electors for President and Vice President of the United States, representatives in Congress, the executive and judicial officers of a state, or the

AMENDMENT 13
Abolition of Slavery (1865)

SECTION 1. Abolition of Slavery. People cannot be forced to work against their will unless they have been tried and convicted of a crime for which this means of punishment is ordered.

This amendment was a direct result of the Civil War and abolished, or ended, slavery in the United States and its territories.

SECTION 2. Enforcement. Congress may pass laws to enforce this article.

AMENDMENT 14
Rights of Citizens (1868)

SECTION 1. Definition of Citizenship. All persons born or naturalized in the United States are citizens of the United States and of the state in which they live. State governments may not deny any citizen the full rights of citizenship. Individual states may not set their own citizenship laws that would prevent any group of people from voting. States may not execute, fine, or imprison any citizen unless such action is ordered as punishment after a fair trial.

Also, Amendment 14 extends the due process clause of Amendment 5 to the states. According to due process of law, no state may take away the rights of a citizen, and all citizens must be protected equally under law.

SECTION 2. Number of Representatives. The number of representatives to Congress is determined by the number of people living in the state, except Indians. (Indians have been counted only since 1940.) The number of members in the House of Representatives will be reduced in any state that refuses to allow any 21-year-old male the right to vote.

members of the legislature thereof, is denied to any of the male inhabitants of such state, being twenty-one years of age and citizens of the United States, or in any way abridged, except for participation in rebellion or other crime, the basis of representation therein shall be reduced in the proportion which the number of such male citizens shall bear to the whole number of male citizens twenty-one years of age in such state.

SECTION 3. Penalty for Rebellion. No person shall be a senator or representative in Congress, or elector of President and Vice President, or hold any office, civil or military, under the United States, or under any state, who, having previously taken an oath, as a member of Congress, or as an officer of the United States, or as a member of any state legislature, or as an executive or judicial officer of any state, to support the Constitution of the United States, shall have engaged in insurrection or rebellion against the same, or given aid or comfort to the enemies thereof. But Congress may, by a vote of two thirds of each house, remove such disability.

SECTION 4. Public Debt. The validity of the public debt of the United States, authorized by law, including debts incurred for payment of pensions and bounties for services in suppressing insurrection or rebellion, shall not be questioned. But neither the United States nor any state shall assume or pay any debt or obligation incurred in aid of insurrection or rebellion against the United States, or any claim for the loss or emancipation of any slave; but all such debts, obligations, and claims shall be held illegal and void.

SECTION 5. Enforcement. The Congress shall have power to enforce, by appropriate legislation, the provisions of this article.

SECTION 3. Penalty for Rebellion. No person may hold or continue to hold office if that person has rebelled against the United States, or given aid or comfort to an enemy of the United States.

This section was originally added to punish the leaders of the Confederacy for failing to support the Constitution of the United States. If a government official rebelled against the government by joining the Confederacy, for example, that person could no longer vote or hold public office.

SECTION 4. Public Debt. The government is responsible for all public debts. It is not responsible for debts that are a result of any rebellion against the United States.

The government was ordered to pay back the debts resulting from the Civil War. However, money borrowed by the Confederacy was not to be repaid by the national government or any state governments. Nor would there be payment to slave owners who set their slaves free.

SECTION 5. Enforcement. Congress may pass laws to enforce this article.

AMENDMENT 15
Voting Rights (1870)

SECTION 1. Right to Vote. The right of citizens of the United States to vote shall not be denied or abridged by the United States or by any state on account of race, color, or previous condition of servitude.

SECTION 2. Enforcement. The Congress shall have power to enforce this article by appropriate legislation.

AMENDMENT 15
Voting Rights (1870)

SECTION 1. Right to Vote. No state may prevent any qualified citizens from voting simply because of race or color.

This amendment was designed to extend voting rights to blacks.

SECTION 2. Enforcement. Congress may pass laws to enforce this article.

AMENDMENT 16
Income Tax (1913)

The Congress shall have power to lay and collect taxes on incomes, from whatever source derived, without apportionment among the several states, and without regard to any census or enumeration.

AMENDMENT 16
Income Tax (1913)

Congress has the power to collect taxes based on incomes, not on the number of people living in the state.

Congress passed an income tax law in 1894. The Supreme Court later declared this law illegal according to Article 1, Section 2, Clause 3 and Article 1, Section 9, Clause 4 of the Constitution, which did not permit direct taxation unless it was based on the number of people in the state. Amendment 16 was a response to this unpopular Supreme Court decision. The amount of tax that citizens have to pay to the federal government does not have to be in proportion to the number of people living in the state, but can be based on personal income. Today income taxes are the federal government's main source of income.

AMENDMENT 17
Direct Election of Senators (1913)

SECTION 1. Method of Election. The Senate of the United States shall be composed of two senators from each state, elected by the people thereof, for six years; and each senator shall have one vote. The electors in each state shall have the qualifications requisite for electors of the most numerous branch of the state legislatures.

AMENDMENT 17
Direct Election of Senators (1913)

SECTION 1. Method of Election. Each state shall elect two senators for a term of six years.

The section changes Article 1, Section 3, Clause 1 of the Constitution, which granted state governments the right to elect their own state senators. Many people were dissatisfied because voters had such little control over the Senate. Amendment 17 allows the people of each state to elect their own senators. This helps to make the senators more responsible to the people they represent, which may give voters more voice in the government.

SECTION 2. Vacancies. When vacancies happen in the representation of any state in the Senate, the executive authority of such state shall issue writs of election to fill such vacancies: *Provided,* that the legislature of any state may empower the executive thereof to make temporary appointments until the people fill the vacancies by election as the legislature may direct.

SECTION 2. Vacancies. If a position in the state Senate becomes open, the state governor may call a special election. The state government may permit the governor to appoint a senator to serve until the next election is held.

SECTION 3. Exception. This amendment shall not be so construed as to affect the election or term of any senator chosen before it becomes valid as part of the Constitution.

SECTION 3. Exception. Senators already in office were not to be affected by this amendment.

AMENDMENT 18
National Prohibition (1919)

SECTION 1. Prohibition. After one year from the ratification of this article the manufacture, sale, or transportation of intoxicating liquors within, the importation thereof into, or the exportation thereof from the United States and all territory subject to the jurisdiction thereof for beverage purposes is hereby prohibited.

SECTION 2. Enforcement. The Congress and the several states shall have concurrent power to enforce this article by appropriate legislation.

SECTION 3. Time Limit for Ratification. This article shall be inoperative unless it shall have been ratified as an amendment to the Constitution by the legislatures of the several states, as provided in the Constitution, within seven years from the date of the submission hereof to the states by the Congress.

AMENDMENT 19
Women's Voting Rights (1920)

SECTION 1. Right to Vote. The right of citizens of the United States to vote shall not be denied or abridged by the United States or by any state on account of sex.

SECTION 2. Enforcement. Congress shall have power to enforce this article by appropriate legislation.

AMENDMENT 20
Terms of Office (1933)

SECTION 1. Beginning of Terms. The terms of the President and Vice President shall end at noon on the 20th day of January, and the terms of senators and representatives at noon on the 3d day of January, of the years in which such terms would have ended if this article had not been ratified; and the terms of their successors shall then begin.

AMENDMENT 18
National Prohibition (1919)

SECTION 1. Prohibition. This amendment, called **prohibition,** made it illegal to make, sell, or transport liquor within the United States, or transport it out of the United States or its territories.

SECTION 2. Enforcement. Both Congress and the states may pass laws to enforce this article.

SECTION 3. Time Limit for Ratification. Within seven years, a certain number of states had to ratify, or confirm, this amendment.

Amendment 18 was the first to include a time limit for approval. If not ratified within seven years, it would be repealed, or canceled.

AMENDMENT 19
Women's Voting Rights (1920)

SECTION 1. Right to Vote. All citizens have the right to vote, regardless of sex.

For many years, women had struggled to win **suffrage,** or the right to vote. Amendment 19 granted women the right to vote.

SECTION 2. Enforcement. Congress may pass laws to enforce this article.

AMENDMENT 20
Terms of Office (1933)

SECTION 1. Beginning of Terms. The President and Vice President take office on January 20; members of Congress take office on January 3.

The amount of time between the November election and the date the newly elected President, Vice President, and members of Congress took office was shortened by this amendment. Originally, newly-elected members did not begin their terms until March 4, and those who had been defeated remained in office for four months. Since these members had already been defeated by the voters, they were known as **lame ducks,** suggesting that the voters had clipped their "political wings." Amendment 20 is often called the **Lame Duck Amendment.**

SECTION 2. Beginning of Congressional Sessions. The Congress shall assemble at least once in every year, and such meeting shall begin at noon on the 3d day of January, unless they shall by law appoint a different day.

SECTION 3. Presidential Succession. If, at the time fixed for the beginning of the term of the President, the President-elect shall have died, the Vice President-elect shall become President. If a President shall not have been chosen before the time fixed for the beginning of his term, or if the President-elect shall have failed to qualify, then the Vice President-elect shall act as President until a President shall have qualified; and the Congress may by law provide for the case wherein neither a President-elect nor a Vice President-elect shall have qualified, declaring who shall then act as President, or the manner in which one who is to act shall be selected, and such person shall act accordingly until a President or Vice President shall have qualified.

SECTION 4. Elections Decided by Congress. The Congress may by law provide for the case of the death of any of the persons from whom the House of Representatives may choose a President whenever the right of choice shall have devolved upon them, and for the case of the death of any of the persons from whom the Senate may choose a Vice President whenever the right of choice shall have devolved upon them.

SECTION 5. Effective Date. Sections 1 and 2 shall take effect on the 15th day of October following the ratification of this article.

SECTION 6. Time Limit for Ratification. This article shall be inoperative unless it shall have been ratified as an amendment to the Constitution by the legislatures of three fourths of the several states within seven years from the date of its submission.

AMENDMENT 21
Repeal of National Prohibition (1933)

SECTION 1. Amendment 18 Repealed. The eighteenth article of amendment to the Constitution of the United States is hereby repealed.

SECTION 2. Prohibition by States Permitted. The transportation or importation into any state, territory, or possession of the United States for delivery or use therein of intoxicating liquors, in violation of the laws thereof, is hereby prohibited.

SECTION 3. Time Limit for Ratification. This article shall be inoperative unless it shall have been ratified as an amendment to the Constitution by conventions in the several states, as provided in the Constitution, within seven years from the date of the submission hereof to the states by Congress.

AMENDMENT 21
Repeal of National Prohibition (1933)

SECTION 1. Amendment 18 Repealed. Amendment 21 repealed Amendment 18.

This was the only amendment to be ratified by state conventions instead of state legislatures. Congress felt that this would give the people's opinions on prohibition a better chance to be heard.

SECTION 2. Prohibition by States Permitted. Bringing liquor into a state or territory that rules against it is illegal.

SECTION 3. Time Limit for Ratification. Amendment 21 would be repealed if it was not ratified within seven years of its proposal.

AMENDMENT 22
Two-Term Limit for Presidents (1951)

SECTION 1. Two-Term Limit. No person shall be elected to the office of President more than twice, and no person who has held the office of President, or acted as President, for more than two years of a term to which some other person was elected President shall be elected to the office of the President more than once. But this article shall not apply to any person holding the office of President when this article was proposed by the Congress, and shall not prevent any person who may be holding the office of President, or acting as President, during the term within which this article becomes operative from holding the office of President, or acting as President, during the remainder of such term.

SECTION 2. Time Limit for Ratification. This article shall be inoperative unless it shall have been ratified as an amendment to the Constitution by the legislatures of three fourths of the several states within seven years from the date of its submission to the states by the Congress.

AMENDMENT 22
Two-Term Limit for Presidents (1951)

SECTION 1. Two-Term Limit. A President may serve only two full terms in office. Any President who takes over for another President for less than two years may be elected for two more terms. This does not apply to the President in office at the time of this Amendment's proposal.

SECTION 2. Time Limit for Ratification. This Amendment would be repealed if it was not ratified within seven years of its proposal.

AMENDMENT 23
Presidential Electors for District of Columbia (1961)

SECTION 1. Number of Electors. The district constituting the seat of Government of the United States shall appoint in such manner as Congress may direct: A number of electors of President and Vice President equal to the whole number of senators and representatives in Congress to which the district would be entitled if it were a state, but in no event more than the least populous state; they shall be in addition to those appointed by the states, but they shall be considered, for the purposes of the election of President and Vice President, to be electors appointed by a state; and they shall meet in the district and perform such duties as provided by the twelfth article of amendment.

SECTION 2. Enforcement. The Congress shall have power to enforce this article by appropriate legislation.

AMENDMENT 24
Ban on Poll Tax in Federal Elections (1964)

SECTION 1. Poll Tax Illegal. The right of citizens of the United States to vote in any primary or other election for President or Vice President, for electors for President or Vice President, or for senator or representative in Congress, shall not be denied or abridged by the United States or any state by reason of failure to pay any poll tax or other tax.

SECTION 2. Enforcement. The Congress shall have power to enforce this article by appropriate legislation.

AMENDMENT 25
Presidential Disability and Succession (1967)

SECTION 1. Presidential Vacancy. In case of the removal of the President from office by his death or resignation, the Vice President shall become President.

SECTION 2. Vice Presidential Vacancy. Whenever there is a vacancy in the office of the Vice President, the President shall nominate a Vice President who shall take office upon confirmation by a majority vote of both houses of Congress.

AMENDMENT 23
Presidential Electors
for District of Columbia (1961)

SECTION 1. Number of Electors. People living in Washington, D.C., may vote for President. This amendment grants three electoral votes to the capital city.

SECTION 2. Enforcement. Congress may pass laws to enforce this article.

AMENDMENT 24
Ban on Poll Tax
in Federal Elections (1964)

SECTION 1. Poll Tax Illegal. No United States citizen may be prevented from voting in a presidential election because of failing to pay a **poll tax,** or a tax people paid before being allowed to vote, or any other tax.

The poll tax was one way to prevent blacks from voting. In 1966 the Supreme Court made poll taxes illegal.

SECTION 2. Enforcement. Congress may pass laws to enforce this article.

AMENDMENT 25
Presidential Disability
and Succession (1967)

SECTION 1. Presidential Vacancy. If the President resigns from or dies in office, the Vice President becomes President.

SECTION 2. Vice Presidential Vacancy. If the office of the Vice President becomes open, the President shall name someone to take office as long as both houses approve by a majority vote.

SECTION 3. Presidential Disability. Whenever the President transmits to the President *pro tempore* of the Senate and the Speaker of the House of Representatives his written declaration that he is unable to discharge the powers and duties of his office, and until he transmits to them a written declaration to the contrary, such powers and duties shall be discharged by the Vice President as Acting President.

SECTION 4. Determining Presidential Disability. Whenever the Vice President and a majority of either the principal officers of the executive departments, or of such other body as Congress may by law provide, transmit to the President *pro tempore* of the Senate and the Speaker of the House of Representatives their written declaration that the President is unable to discharge the powers and duties of his office, the Vice President shall immediately assume the powers and duties of the office as Acting President.

Thereafter, when the President transmits to the President *pro tempore* of the Senate and the Speaker of the House of Representatives his written declaration that no inability exists, he shall resume the powers and duties of his office, unless the Vice President and a majority of either the principal officers of the executive department or of such other body as Congress may by law provide transmit within four days to the President *pro tempore* of the Senate and the Speaker of the House of Representatives their written declaration that the President is unable to discharge the powers and duties of his office. Thereupon Congress shall decide the issue, assembling within 48 hours for that purpose if not in session. If the Congress, within 21 days after receipt of the latter written declaration, or, if Congress is not in session, within 21 days after Congress is required to assemble, determines by two-thirds vote of both houses that the President is unable to discharge the powers and duties of his office, the Vice President shall continue to discharge the same as Acting President; otherwise, the President shall assume the powers and duties of his office.

AMENDMENT 26
Voting Age (1971)

SECTION 1. Right to Vote. The right of citizens of the United States, who are 18 years of age or older, to vote shall not be denied or abridged by the United States or any state on account of age.

SECTION 2. Enforcement. The Congress shall have the power to enforce this article by appropriate legislation.

SECTION 3. Presidential Disability. If the President becomes unable to continue in office because of sickness or any other reason, the President must inform the Speaker of the House in writing. The Vice President will take over as Acting President until the Speaker is informed in writing that the President is able to resume office.

SECTION 4. Determining Presidential Disability. If the Vice President and a majority of the Cabinet inform the Speaker of the House that the President is unable to carry out the duties and powers of the office of the Presidency, the Vice President shall then serve as Acting President. When the President informs the Speaker of the House in writing that he is again able to serve, he shall take over the office. But, if the Vice President and a majority of executives inform the Speaker of the House that the President is still unable to serve, then Congress decides the issue.

AMENDMENT 26
Voting Age (1971)

SECTION 1. Right to Vote. All citizens 18 years or older have the right to vote.

SECTION 2. Enforcement. Congress may pass laws to enforce this article.

FACTS ABOUT THE STATES

State	Year of Statehood	Population*	Area (sq. mi.)	Capital	Origin of State Name
Alabama	1819	4,127,000	51,609	Montgomery	Choctaw, *alba ayamule*, "one who clears land and gathers food from it"
Alaska	1959	513,000	586,412	Juneau	Eskimo, *alayeska*, "great land"
Arizona	1912	3,466,000	113,909	Phoenix	Papago, *arizonac*, "place of the small spring"
Arkansas	1836	2,422,000	53,104	Little Rock	Quapaw, "the downstream people"
California	1850	28,168,000	158,693	Sacramento	Spanish, "an early paradise"
Colorado	1876	3,290,000	104,247	Denver	Spanish, "red land; red earth"
Connecticut	1788	3,241,000	5,009	Hartford	Mohican, *quinnitukqut*, "at the long tidal river"
Delaware	1787	660,000	2,057	Dover	Named for Lord de la Warr
Florida	1845	12,377,000	58,560	Tallahassee	Spanish, "land of flowers"
Georgia	1788	6,401,000	58,876	Atlanta	Named for King George II of England
Hawaii	1959	1,093,000	6,450	Honolulu	Polynesian, *Hawaiki* or *Owykee*, "homeland"
Idaho	1890	999,000	83,557	Boise	Shoshone, "light on the mountains"
Illinois	1818	11,544,000	56,400	Springfield	Algonquian, *iliniwek*, "men" or "warriors"
Indiana	1816	5,575,000	36,291	Indianapolis	Indian + a = "land of the Indians"
Iowa	1846	2,834,000	56,290	Des Moines	Dakota, *ayuba*, "beautiful land"
Kansas	1861	2,487,000	82,264	Topeka	Sioux, "land of the south wind people"
Kentucky	1792	3,721,000	40,395	Frankfort	Iroquois, *Kentake*, "meadowland"
Louisiana	1812	4,420,000	48,523	Baton Rouge	Named for King Louis XIV of France
Maine	1820	1,206,000	33,215	Augusta	Named after a French province
Maryland	1788	4,644,000	10,577	Annapolis	Named for Henrietta Maria, Queen Consort of Charles I of England
Massachusetts	1788	5,871,000	8,257	Boston	Algonquian, "at the big hill; place of the big hill"
Michigan	1837	9,300,000	58,216	Lansing	Chippewa, *mica gama*, "big water"
Minnesota	1858	4,306,000	84,068	St. Paul	Dakota Sioux, "sky-blue water"
Mississippi	1817	2,627,000	47,716	Jackson	Chippewa, *mici sibi*, "big river"
Missouri	1821	5,139,000	69,686	Jefferson City	Algonquian, "muddy water" or "people of the big canoes"
Montana	1889	804,000	147,138	Helena	Spanish, "mountainous"

*These population figures represent the most recent available estimates.

State	Year of Statehood	Population*	Area (sq. mi.)	Capital	Origin of State Name
Nebraska	1867	1,601,000	77,227	Lincoln	Omaha, *ni-bthaska*, "river in the flatness "
Nevada	1864	1,060,000	110,540	Carson City	Spanish, "snowy; snowed upon"
New Hampshire	1788	1,097,000	9,304	Concord	Named for Hampshire County, England
New Jersey	1787	7,720,000	7,836	Trenton	Named for the Isle of Jersey
New Mexico	1912	1,510,000	121,666	Santa Fe	Named by Spanish explorers from Mexico
New York	1788	17,898,000	49,576	Albany	Named after the Duke of York
North Carolina	1789	6,526,000	52,586	Raleigh	Named after King Charles II of England
North Dakota	1889	663,000	70,665	Bismarck	Sioux, *dakota*, "friend; ally"
Ohio	1803	10,872,000	41,222	Columbus	Iroquois, *oheo*, "beautiful, beautiful water"
Oklahoma	1907	3,263,000	69,919	Oklahoma City	Choctaw, "red people"
Oregon	1859	2,741,000	96,981	Salem	Algonquian, *wauregan*, "beautiful water"
Pennsylvania	1787	12,027,000	45,333	Harrisburg	Penn + *sylvania*, meaning "Penn's woods"
Rhode Island	1790	995,000	1,214	Providence	Dutch, "red-clay island"
South Carolina	1788	3,493,000	31,055	Columbia	Named after King Charles II of England
South Dakota	1889	715,000	77,047	Pierre	Sioux, *dakota*, "friend; ally"
Tennessee	1796	4,919,000	42,244	Nashville	Name of a Cherokee village
Texas	1845	16,780,000	267,338	Austin	Indian, *texia*, "friend; ally"
Utah	1896	1,691,000	84,916	Salt Lake City	"Land of the Ute" (an Indian tribe)
Vermont	1791	556,000	9,609	Montpelier	French, *vert*, "green" and *mont*, "mountain"
Virginia	1788	5,996,000	40,817	Richmond	Named after Elizabeth I of England
Washington	1889	4,619,000	68,192	Olympia	Named for George Washington
West Virginia	1863	1,884,000	24,181	Charleston	From the English-named state of Virginia
Wisconsin	1848	4,858,000	56,154	Madison	Possibly Algonquian, meaning "grassy place" or "place of the beaver"
Wyoming	1890	471,000	97,914	Cheyenne	Algonquian, *mache-weaming*, "at the big flats"
District of Columbia		620,000	67		Named after Christopher Columbus

*These population figures represent the most recent available estimates.

PRESIDENTS OF THE UNITED STATES

WASHINGTON

J. Q. ADAMS

CLEVELAND

T. ROOSEVELT

WILSON

CARTER

FILLMORE

LINCOLN

EISENHOWER

BUSH

NAME	YEARS IN OFFICE	HOME STATE
George Washington (1732–1799)	1789–1797	VA
John Adams (1735–1826)	1797–1801	MA
Thomas Jefferson (1743–1826)	1801–1809	VA
James Madison (1751–1836)	1809–1817	VA
James Monroe (1758–1831)	1817–1825	VA
John Quincy Adams (1767–1848)	1825–1829	MA
Andrew Jackson (1767–1845)	1829–1837	TN
Martin Van Buren (1782–1862)	1837–1841	NY
William Henry Harrison (1773–1841)	1841	OH
John Tyler (1790–1862)	1841–1845	VA
James K. Polk (1795–1849)	1845–1849	TN
Zachary Taylor (1784–1850)	1849–1850	LA
Millard Fillmore (1800–1874)	1850–1853	NY
Franklin Pierce (1804–1869)	1853–1857	NH
James Buchanan (1791–1868)	1857–1861	PA
Abraham Lincoln (1809–1865)	1861–1865	IL
Andrew Johnson (1808–1875)	1865–1869	TN
Ulysses S. Grant (1822–1885)	1869–1877	IL
Rutherford B. Hayes (1822–1893)	1877–1881	OH
James A. Garfield (1831–1881)	1881	OH
Chester A. Arthur (1830–1886)	1881–1885	NY
Grover Cleveland (1837–1908)	1885–1889	NY
Benjamin Harrison (1833–1901)	1889–1893	IN
Grover Cleveland (1837–1908)	1893–1897	NY
William McKinley (1843–1901)	1897–1901	OH
Theodore Roosevelt (1858–1919)	1901–1909	NY
William Howard Taft (1857–1930)	1909–1913	OH
Woodrow Wilson (1856–1924)	1913–1921	NJ
Warren G. Harding (1865–1923)	1921–1923	OH
Calvin Coolidge (1872–1933)	1923–1929	MA
Herbert Hoover (1874–1964)	1929–1933	CA
Franklin D. Roosevelt (1882–1945)	1933–1945	NY
Harry S. Truman (1884–1972)	1945–1953	MO
Dwight D. Eisenhower (1890–1969)	1953–1961	KA
John F. Kennedy (1917–1963)	1961–1963	MA
Lyndon B. Johnson (1908–1973)	1963–1969	TX
Richard M. Nixon (1913–)	1969–1974	CA
Gerald R. Ford (1913–)	1974–1977	MI
Jimmy Carter (1924–)	1977–1981	GA
Ronald Reagan (1911–)	1981–1989	CA
George Bush (1924–)	1989–	TX

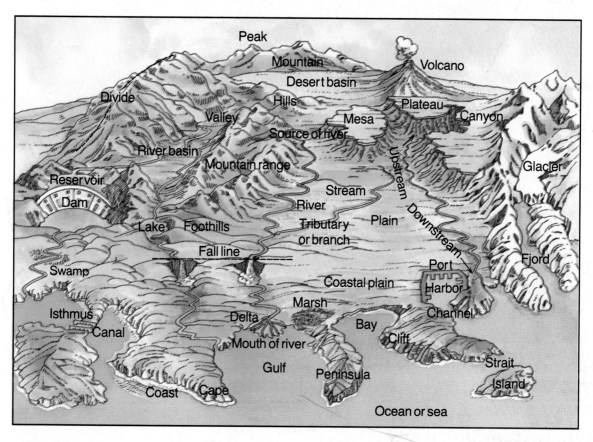

basin a land area mostly surrounded by higher land

bay a small area of ocean partly surrounded by land

canal a waterway dug across land for transportation or irrigation

canyon a narrow valley with high, steep sides

cape a point of land that extends into a body of water

channel a narrow waterway connecting two bodies of water; the deepest part of a waterway

cliff a high, steep wall of rock

continent one of the Earth's seven main landmasses

delta a piece of land formed by silt built up at a river's mouth

divide a high ridge of land between areas with different river basins

fall line the point where a river forms a waterfall as it drops to lower land

fjord a narrow inlet of the sea between high, steep banks

foothill a low hill at the base of a mountain

glacier a large mass of slow-moving ice spread over a land surface

gulf a large area of ocean partly surrounded by land

harbor a sheltered area along a seacoast where ships can anchor

highland a region of hills, mountains, or plateaus

hill a small, raised part of the land, lower than a mountain

isthmus a narrow strip of land connecting two larger land areas

lowland a low, mostly level land area

marsh an area of low, wet land

mesa a flat-topped hill with steep sides, common in dry areas

mountain range a group or chain of mountains

mouth (of river) the place where a river or stream empties into a larger body of water

peak the pointed top of a mountain

peninsula land surrounded by water on three sides

plain a large area of flat or gently rolling land

plateau an area of high, flat land

port a city or place where ships arrive and depart

prairie a broad, grassy plains region

rain forest a woodland with rain much of the year and marked by a dense growth of trees and plants

reservoir a lake where a large water supply is stored

source (of river) the place where a stream or river begins

strait a narrow water passage between two larger bodies of water

stream a small body of flowing water

swamp low, wet land

tributary a river or stream that flows into another river

tundra a broad, treeless plain in a polar region

valley low land between mountains or hills

volcano a hill or mountain formed when melted rock is forced through the Earth's surface

UNITED STATES OF AMERICA: POLITICAL

CANADA

Legend:
— National boundary
— State boundary
⊛ National capital
✴ State capital
• Other cities

0   100   200   300 Miles
0 100 200 300 400 Kilometers

R43

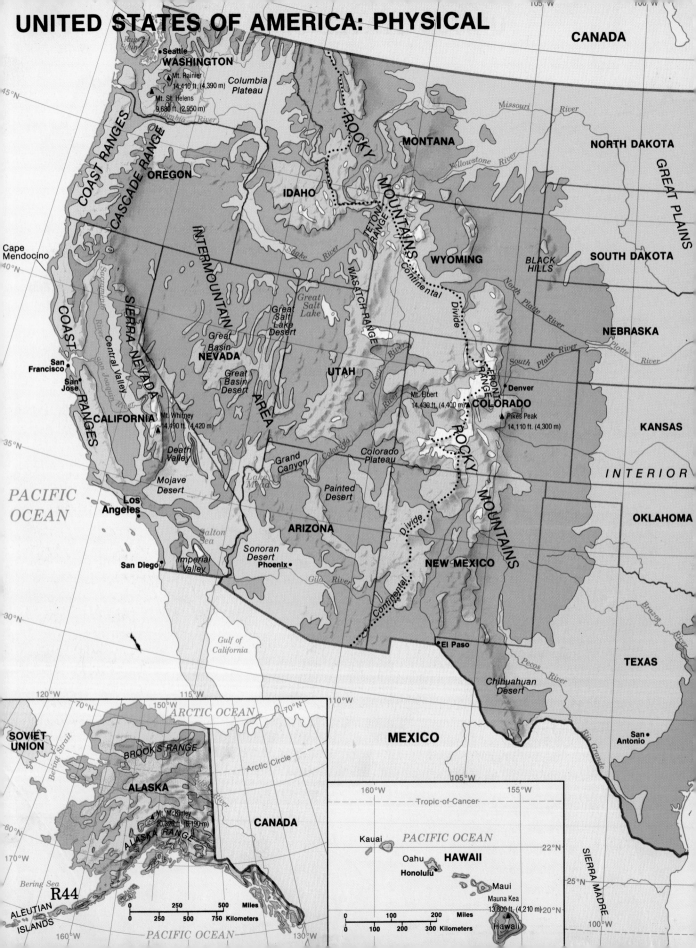

UNITED STATES OF AMERICA: PHYSICAL

CANADA

WASHINGTON
• Seattle
▲ Mt. Rainier
14,410 ft. (4,390 m)
▲ Mt. St. Helens
9,680 ft. (2,950 m)

Columbia Plateau

OREGON

COAST RANGES

CASCADE RANGE

Cape Mendocino

COAST RANGES

SIERRA NEVADA

INTERMOUNTAIN AREA

Columbia River

Snake River

ROCKY MOUNTAINS

MONTANA

NORTH DAKOTA

GREAT PLAINS

Missouri River

Yellowstone River

IDAHO

TETON RANGE

WASATCH RANGE

WYOMING

Continental Divide

SOUTH DAKOTA

BLACK HILLS

North Platte River

South Platte River

NEBRASKA

Platte River

San Francisco •
San Jose •

Sacramento River

Central Valley

San Joaquin River

Great Salt Lake

Great Salt Lake Desert

NEVADA

Great Basin

Great Basin Desert

UTAH

Green River

Colorado River

Mt. Elbert
14,430 ft. (4,400 m)

FRONT RANGE

• Denver
COLORADO

▲ Pikes Peak
14,110 ft. (4,300 m)

ROCKY MOUNTAINS

KANSAS

CALIFORNIA

▲ Mt. Whitney
14,490 ft. (4,420 m)

Death Valley

Mojave Desert

Lake Mead

Grand Canyon

Colorado Plateau

Painted Desert

INTERIOR

OKLAHOMA

PACIFIC OCEAN

Los Angeles •

Salton Sea

Imperial Valley

San Diego •

ARIZONA

Sonoran Desert

Phoenix •

Gila River

Continental Divide

NEW MEXICO

ROCKY MOUNTAINS

Gulf of California

• El Paso

Pecos River

Chihuahuan Desert

TEXAS

Rio Grande

San Antonio •

MEXICO

SIERRA MADRE

Inset: Alaska

SOVIET UNION

ARCTIC OCEAN

BROOKS RANGE

Arctic Circle

ALASKA

▲ Mt. McKinley
20,320 ft. (6,190 m)

ALASKA RANGE

CANADA

Bering Strait

Bering Sea

R44

ALEUTIAN ISLANDS

PACIFIC OCEAN

0   250   500 Miles
0   250   500   750 Kilometers

Inset: Hawaii

Tropic of Cancer

Kauai

PACIFIC OCEAN

Oahu
Honolulu

HAWAII

Maui

Mauna Kea
13,800 ft. (4,210 m)

Hawaii

0   100   200 Miles
0   100   200   300 Kilometers

THE WORLD: POLITICAL

—— National boundary

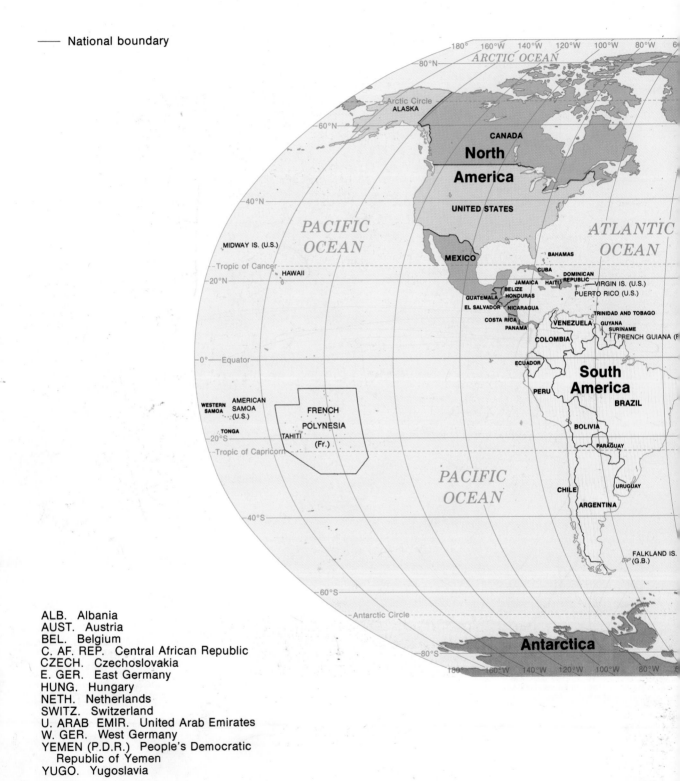

ALB. Albania
AUST. Austria
BEL. Belgium
C. AF. REP. Central African Republic
CZECH. Czechoslovakia
E. GER. East Germany
HUNG. Hungary
NETH. Netherlands
SWITZ. Switzerland
U. ARAB EMIR. United Arab Emirates
W. GER. West Germany
YEMEN (P.D.R.) People's Democratic
   Republic of Yemen
YUGO. Yugoslavia

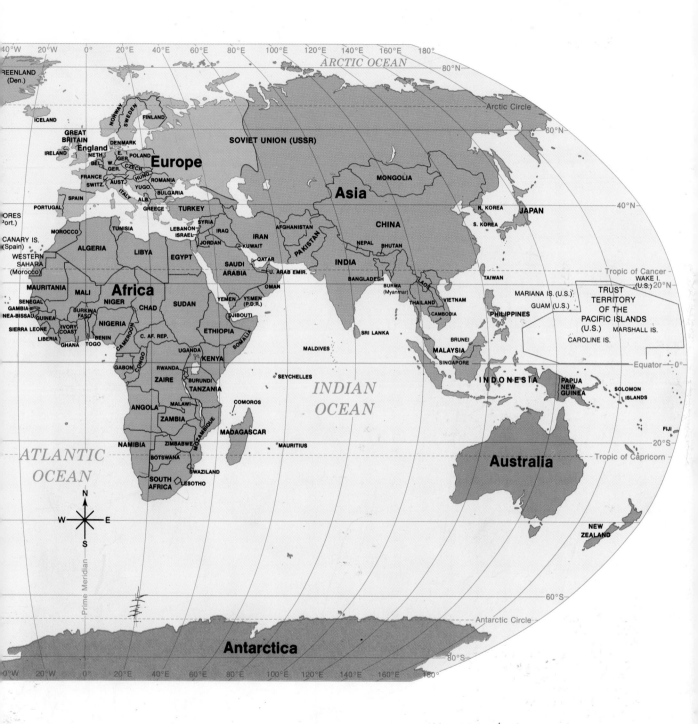

ARCTIC OCEAN

80°N

Arctic Circle

60°N

40°N

GREENLAND
(Den.)

ICELAND

GREAT
BRITAIN
England

IRELAND

NORWAY

SWEDEN

FINLAND

DENMARK

NETH.
BEL.

E.
GER.
W.
GER.

POLAND

CZECH

Europe

SOVIET UNION (USSR)

FRANCE

SWITZ.

AUST.

HUNG.

ROMANIA

ITALY

YUGO.

BULGARIA

ALB.

SPAIN

GREECE

TURKEY

PORTUGAL

Asia

MONGOLIA

N. KOREA

JAPAN

S. KOREA

CHINA

ORES
Port.)

CANARY IS.
(Spain)

MOROCCO

TUNISIA

LEBANON
ISRAEL

SYRIA

IRAQ

IRAN

AFGHANISTAN

PAKISTAN

NEPAL

BHUTAN

WESTERN
SAHARA
(Morocco)

ALGERIA

LIBYA

EGYPT

JORDAN

KUWAIT

QATAR

SAUDI
ARABIA

U. ARAB EMIR.

INDIA

Tropic of Cancer

TAIWAN

WAKE I.
(U.S.)

20°N

MAURITANIA

Africa

NIGER

CHAD

SUDAN

OMAN

YEMEN

YEMEN
(P.D.R.)

BANGLADESH

BURMA
(Myanmar)

LAOS

TRUST
TERRITORY
OF THE
PACIFIC ISLANDS
(U.S.)

MARIANA IS. (U.S.)

GUAM (U.S.)

MARSHALL IS.

MALI

DJIBOUTI

THAILAND

VIETNAM

CAMBODIA

PHILIPPINES

CAROLINE IS.

SENEGAL

GAMBIA

NEA-BISSAU

GUINEA

BURKINA
FASO

NIGERIA

ETHIOPIA

SRI LANKA

BRUNEI

SIERRA LEONE

IVORY
COAST

BENIN

CAMEROON

C. AF. REP.

SOMALIA

MALDIVES

MALAYSIA

LIBERIA

GHANA

TOGO

UGANDA

KENYA

SINGAPORE

Equator 0°

GABON

CONGO

RWANDA

BURUNDI

TANZANIA

SEYCHELLES

INDIAN
OCEAN

INDONESIA

PAPUA
NEW
GUINEA

SOLOMON
ISLANDS

ZAIRE

ANGOLA

MALAWI

COMOROS

ZAMBIA

MOZAMBIQUE

MADAGASCAR

FIJI

ATLANTIC
OCEAN

NAMIBIA

ZIMBABWE

MAURITIUS

20°S

BOTSWANA

Tropic of Capricorn

SWAZILAND

Australia

SOUTH
AFRICA

LESOTHO

N

W   E

S

NEW
ZEALAND

60°S

Antarctic Circle

Antarctica

80°S

40°W   20°W   0°   20°E   40°E   60°E   80°E   100°E   120°E   140°E   160°E   180°

Prime Meridian

0   500   1,000 1,500 2,000 Miles

0   1,000   2,000   Kilometers

R47

NORTH AMERICA: PHYSICAL

Europe

Asia

ARCTIC OCEAN

Bering Strait

Bering Sea

Greenland Sea

Greenland

Beaufort Sea

Baffin Bay

Yukon

Mt. McKinley
20,320 ft.
(6,194 m)

Gulf of Alaska

Mt. Logan
19,850 ft.
(6,050 m)

COAST MOUNTAINS

ROCKY

Great Bear Lake

Great Slave Lake

Mackenzie River

Hudson Strait

Labrador Sea

Great

Hudson Bay

Canadian   Shield

MOUNTAINS

Lake Winnipeg

Gulf of St. Lawrence

Columbia River

Lake Superior

St. Lawrence R.

Bay of Fundy

40°N

Plains

Missouri

Lake Huron

Lake Michigan

Lake Ontario

ATLANTIC

Great Salt Lake

Great Basin

Mt. Whitney
14,494 ft.
(4,418 m)

Death Valley
−282 ft.
(−86 m)

Colorado River

Pikes Peak
14,110 ft.
(4,301 m)

Missouri River

Ozark Plateau

Ohio River

Lake Erie

Tennessee R.

APPALACHIAN MTNS.

Plain

OCEAN

Mississippi River

Coastal

Tropic of Cancer

Gulf of California

SIERRA MADRE OCCIDENTAL

SIERRA MADRE ORIENTAL

Rio Grande

Citlaltépetl
18,700 ft. (5,700 m.)

Bay of Campeche

Yucatán Peninsula

Gulf of Mexico

Hispaniola

Sea

Caribbean

PACIFIC

Balsas de

OCEAN

Lake Nicaragua

Panama Canal

South

America

International boundary

▲ Mountain peak

N
W   E
S

0   300   600   Miles
0   300   600   900 Kilometers

R48

Equator

SOUTH AMERICA: PHYSICAL

Caribbean Sea

ATLANTIC

OCEAN

Lake Maracaibo

Orinoco River

Guiana

Angel Falls

Highlands

Equator

Amazon

Amazon River

Basin

PACIFIC

▲ Mt. Huascarán
22,205 ft. (6,768 m)

ANDES MOUNTAINS

Lake Titicaca

Mato Grosso

Brazilian Highlands

São Francisco River

Plateau

OCEAN

Atacama Desert

Chaco

Gran

Salado R.

Paraguay River

Uruguay River

Tropic of Capricorn

ATLANTIC

P a m p a s

OCEAN

ANDES

▲ Mt. Aconcagua
22,840 ft. (6,960 m)
(highest point in S. America)

Valdés Peninsula
(lowest point in S. America)

〰〰〰 International boundary

▲ Mountain peak

N
W · E
S

| 0 | | 250 | | 500 | Miles |
| 0 | 250 | 500 | 750 | | Kilometers |

R49

Cape Horn

Drake Passage

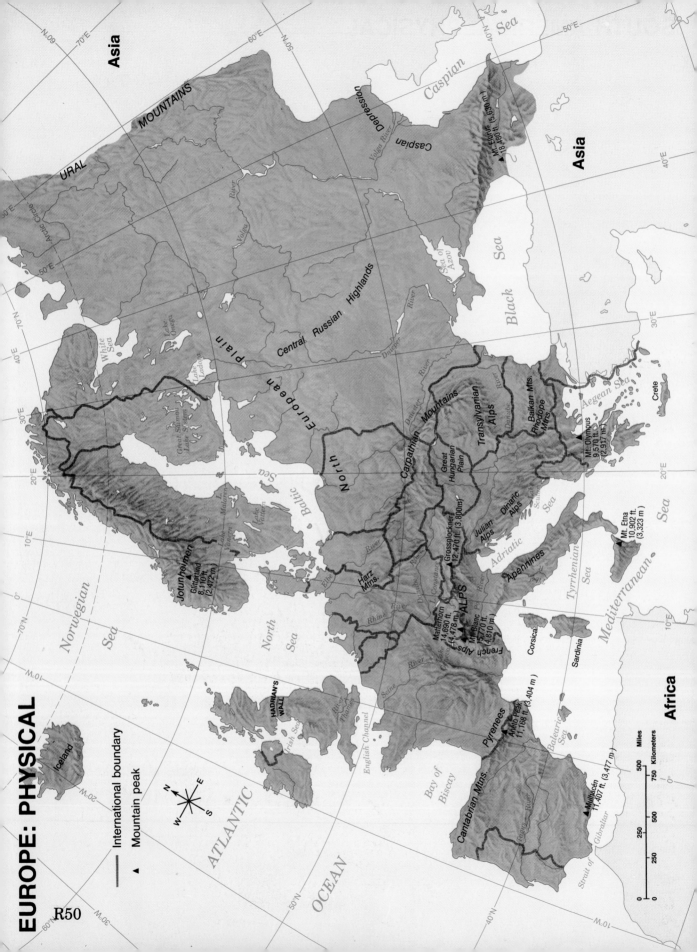

EUROPE: PHYSICAL

R50

Iceland

—— International boundary

▲ Mountain peak

N
W E
S

ATLANTIC

OCEAN

Norwegian Sea

HADRIAN'S WALL

Irish Sea

English Channel

River Thames

Bay of Biscay

North Sea

Seine River

Rhine River

Cantabrian Mtns.

Pyrenees
Aneto Peak
11,168 ft. (3,404 m) ▲

Mulhacén
11,407 ft. (3,477 m) ▲

Strait of Gibraltar

Tagus River

Balearic Sea

Africa

0   250   500   Miles
0 250 500 750 Kilometers

Jotunheimen
Glittertind ▲
8,110 ft.
(2,472 m)

L. Mjøsa

L. Vänern
L. Vättern

Baltic Sea

Arctic Circle

White Sea

Lake Ladoga

Lake Onega

Great Salina

Lake Segosero

URAL MOUNTAINS

Asia

European Plain

North

Central Russian Highlands

Volga

Volga River

Dnieper River

Don River

Caspian Depression

Caspian Sea

Sea of Azov

Black Sea

Mt. Elbrus (5,630 m) ▲
18,480 ft.

Asia

Harz Mtns.

Elbe River

Danube River

Dniester River

Carpathian Mountains

Great Hungarian Plain

Transylvanian Alps

Balkan Mts.
Rhodope Mts.

Grossglockner
12,470 ft. (3,800 m) ▲

ALPS

Matterhorn
14,690 ft.
(4,478 m) ▲

Mt. Blanc
15,770 ft.
(4,810 m) ▲

French Alps

Po River

Julian Alps

Dinaric Alps

Apennines

Adriatic Sea

Corsica

Sardinia

Tyrrhenian Sea

Mt. Etna
10,902 ft.
(3,323 m) ▲

Mediterranean Sea

Aegean Sea

Crete

Mt. Olympus
9,570 ft.
(2,917 m) ▲

ASIA: PHYSICAL

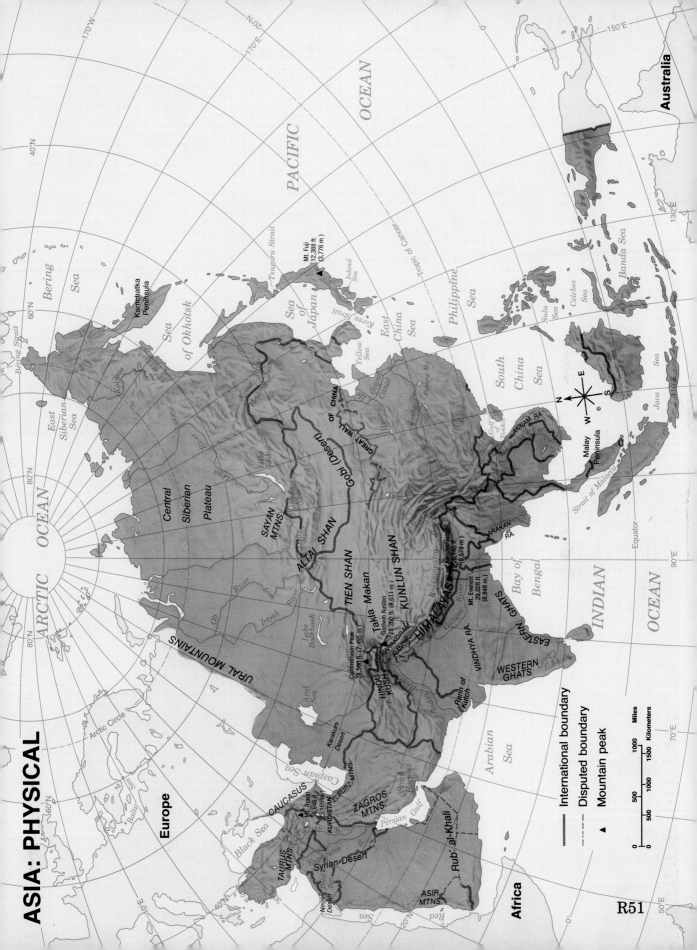

ARCTIC OCEAN

PACIFIC OCEAN

Europe

Africa

Australia

Bering Sea

East Siberian Sea

Sea of Okhotsk

Kamchatka Peninsula

Central Siberian Plateau

Lake Baikal

URAL MOUNTAINS

SAYAN MTNS.

ALTAI SHAN

TIEN SHAN

Gobi (Desert)

GREAT WALL OF CHINA

Takla Makan

KUNLUN SHAN

Lake Balkhash

Caspian Sea

Aral Sea

Karakum Desert

Ob River

Irtysh River

Amu Darya

CAUCASUS

Mt. Araxat
16,946 ft.
(5,165 m)

KURDISTAN

TAURUS MTNS.

ELBURZ MTNS.

ZAGROS MTNS.

Syrian Desert

Negev Desert

Black Sea

Baltic Sea

Euphrates R.

Tigris R.

Persian Gulf

Strait of Hormuz

Rub' al-Khali

ASIR MTNS.

Red Sea

Arabian Sea

HINDU KUSH

Communism Peak
24,590 ft. (7,495 m)

KARAKORAM RANGE

Godwin Austen
28,250 ft. (8,611 m)

HIMALAYAS

Mt. Everest
29,028 ft.
(8,848 m)

Kanchenjunga
28,146 ft.
(8,579 m)

Rann of Kutch

Ganges River

Brahmaputra R.

Indus R.

VINDHYA RA.

WESTERN GHATS

EASTERN GHATS

Bay of Bengal

INDIAN OCEAN

ARAKAN RA.

ANNAM RA.

Malay Peninsula

Strait of Malacca

Equator

South China Sea

Java Sea

Sulu Sea

Celebes Sea

Banda Sea

Philippine Sea

East China Sea

Yellow Sea

Gulf of Tonkin

Xi River

Chang Jiang

Grand Canal

Huang He

Amur River

Yellow River

Kolyma R.

Sea of Japan

Tsugaru Strait

Korea Strait

Mt. Fuji
12,388 ft.
(3,776 m)

Inland Sea

Tropic of Cancer

Gulf of Siam

Bering Strait

Arctic Circle

N
E
S
W

International boundary

Disputed boundary

▲ Mountain peak

Miles
Kilometers

0   500   1000

0   500   1000   1500

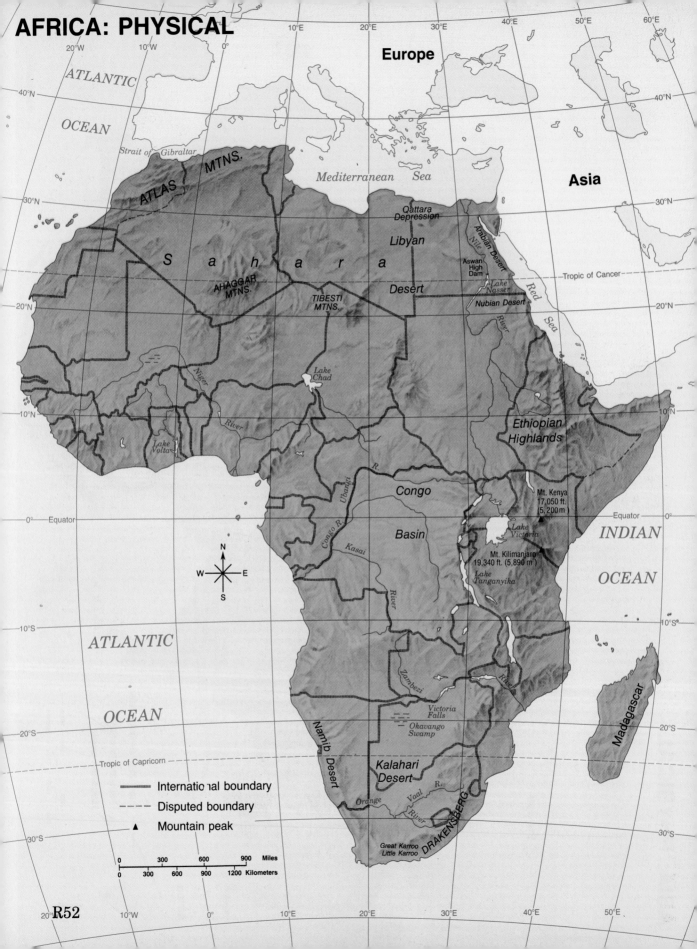

AFRICA: PHYSICAL

Europe

Asia

ATLANTIC

OCEAN

Mediterranean Sea

Strait of Gibraltar

ATLAS MTNS.

Qattara
Depression

Libyan

S a h a r a

AHAGGAR
MTNS.

TIBESTI
MTNS.

Desert

Arabian Desert

Aswan
High
Dam

Lake
Nasser

Nubian Desert

Nile River

Red Sea

Tropic of Cancer

Niger River

Lake
Chad

Lake
Volta

River

Ethiopian
Highlands

Congo

Ubangi R.

Congo R.

Kasai

Basin

Mt. Kenya
17,050 ft.
(5,200 m)

Lake
Victoria

Mt. Kilimanjaro
19,340 ft. (5,890 m)

Lake
Tanganyika

INDIAN

OCEAN

Equator

N
W E
S

River

Zambezi

Victoria
Falls

Okavango
Swamp

River

Madagascar

ATLANTIC

OCEAN

Namib Desert

Tropic of Capricorn

Kalahari
Desert

Orange

Vaal River

R.

DRAKENSBERG

Great Karroo
Little Karroo

International boundary

Disputed boundary

▲ Mountain peak

| 0 | 300 | 600 | 900 | Miles |
| 0 | 300 | 600 | 900 | 1200 | Kilometers |

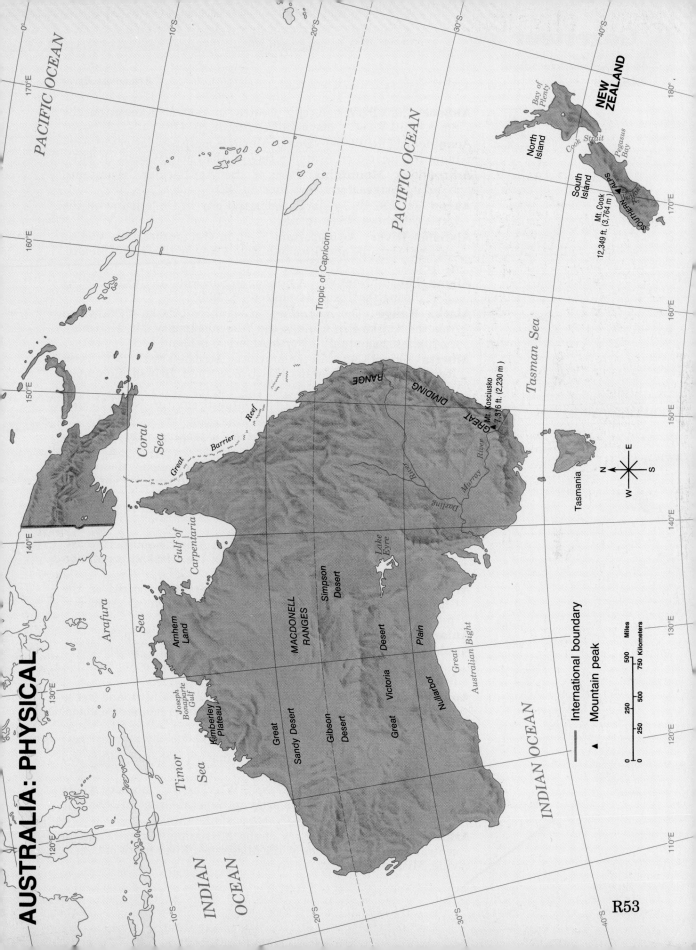

AUSTRALIA: PHYSICAL

PACIFIC OCEAN

INDIAN OCEAN

Timor Sea

Arafura Sea

Joseph Bonaparte Gulf

Kimberley Plateau

Arnhem Land

Gulf of Carpentaria

Coral Sea

Great Barrier Reef

Great Sandy Desert

Gibson Desert

MACDONELL RANGES

Simpson Desert

Lake Eyre

Great Victoria Desert

Nullarbor Plain

Great Australian Bight

INDIAN OCEAN

GREAT DIVIDING RANGE

Mt. Kosciusko
▲ 7,316 ft. (2,230 m)

Murray River

Darling River

Tasman Sea

Tasmania

PACIFIC OCEAN

NEW ZEALAND

Bay of Plenty

North Island

Cook Strait

Pegasus Bay

South Island

SOUTHERN ALPS

Mt. Cook
▲ 12,349 ft. (3,764 m)

Tropic of Capricorn

N
W — E
S

	Miles	
0	250	500
0	250	500	750 Kilometers

——— International boundary

▲ Mountain peak

R53

Abilene (39°N/97°W) A city located in central Kansas on the Smoky Hill River; a major railroad town. (p. 478)

Acapulco (17°N/100°W) One of Mexico's most popular resort communities; located on Acapulco Bay, on the Pacific Ocean. (p. 601)

Adirondack Mountains Part of the Appalachian Mountains; found in northeastern New York. (p. 42)

Akron (41°N/82°W) A large industrial city in Ohio; found on the Little Cuyahoga River. (p. 56)

Alabama River An important river in the southeastern U.S.A.; starts in Alabama and flows into Mobile Bay on the Gulf of Mexico. (p. 51)

Alamo, The (30°N/99°W) A mission in San Antonio, Texas, used as a fort during the Texas Revolution. (p. 394)

Alaska Range The mountains in southern Alaska that extend from the Alaska Peninsula to the Yukon boundary; Mt. McKinley, the highest mountain in North America, is found here. (p. 14)

Alberta One of Canada's ten provinces; bordered by the Northwest Territories, Saskatchewan, the U.S.A., and British Columbia. (p. 591)

Albuquerque (35°N/107°W) The largest city in New Mexico; located on the Rio Grande. (p. 62)

Aleutian Islands A chain of islands extending west from the Alaska Peninsula. (p. 508)

Allegheny Mountains A part of the Appalachian Mountains; parallel to the Blue Ridge Mountains; extend through Pennsylvania, Maryland, Virginia, and West Virginia. (p. 42)

Altamaha River A river that begins in southeastern Georgia and flows into the Atlantic Ocean. (p. 22)

Anchorage (61°N/150°W) A large city on Alaska's southern coast; main seaport of the state; almost half of the Alaskan population lives here. (p. 70)

Annapolis (39°N/77°W) The capital of Maryland; located on the Chesapeake Bay; home of the United States Naval Academy. (p. 257)

Antarctic Circle A line of latitude; located at 66½°S. (p. 30)

Apalachicola River An important river in the southeastern U.S.A.; starts in northwestern Florida and flows into Apalachicola Bay on the Gulf of Mexico. (p. 22)

Appalachian Highlands A rugged area of low hills and dense woods in eastern Canada; one of the six natural regions of Canada. (p. 578)

Appalachian Mountains A large chain of mountains that extends, in the United States, from Maine to northern Georgia and Alabama. (p. 14)

Appomattox Court House (37°N/79°W) The Virginia city where General Lee surrendered his army to General Grant in 1865; the Civil War ended here. (p. 437)

Arkansas River A tributary of the Mississippi River; begins in central Colorado and ends at the Mississippi River north of Greenville, Mississippi. (p. 22)

Badlands   *Cascade Range*

Badlands   A stretch of wild, rugged, dry land in South Dakota and North Dakota. (p. 56)

Baja Peninsula   A peninsula in Mexico; located between the Pacific Ocean and the Gulf of California; made up of desert, rugged mountains, and windswept beaches. (p. 601)

Baltimore (39°N/77°W)   A major seaport in Maryland; located on the Patapsco River at Chesapeake Bay. (p. 237)

Bering Strait   A narrow water passage that separates Asia from North America. (p. 86)

Berkshire Hills   The highlands located in western Massachusetts. (p. 198)

Billings (46°N/108°W)   A city in central Montana; located on the Yellowstone River. (p. 70)

Birmingham (34°N/87°W)   A large city in Alabama; located near iron and coal deposits. (p. 459)

Black Hills   A group of mountains in South Dakota; its highest peak, over 7,000 feet (2,133.6 m), is the highest place in the Plains states. (p. 56)

Boston (42°N/71°W)   The capital and largest city of Massachusetts; settled by Puritans in 1630. (p. 198)

British Columbia   One of Canada's ten provinces; located on the west coast of Canada and bordered by the Yukon Territory, the Northwest Territories, Alberta, the U.S.A., and the Pacific Ocean. (p. 591)

Brooks Range   The mountains in northern Alaska; a part of the Rocky Mountains. (p. 14)

Buffalo (43°N/79°W)   A city in western New York; located on the Niagara River at Lake Erie. (p. 42)

Cambridge (42°N/71°W)   A city in northeastern Massachusetts; located near Boston. (p. 198)

Canada   The country located to the north of the U.S.A.; these two countries share the longest undefended border in the world. (p. 578)

Canadian Shield   A large, horseshoe-shaped natural region in northern Canada; makes up about half of Canada. (p. 578)

Cape Canaveral (28°N/81°W)   A cape located on the east coast of Florida; Kennedy Space Center is found here. (p. 51)

Cape Cod   A cape in southeastern Massachusetts; located between Cape Cod Bay and the Atlantic Ocean; Pilgrims sailing on the *Mayflower* landed here. (p. 42)

Cape Horn   The southern tip of South America; a longer but easier way to travel from the Atlantic to the Pacific coast of the U.S.A. (p. 147)

Cape of Good Hope (34°N/19°E)   A cape on the southwestern coast of South Africa; first discovered by Bartholomeu Dias in 1487. (p. 147)

Caribbean Sea   A part of the Atlantic Ocean; found southeast of Florida. (p. 153)

Cascade Range   A mountain range in the western U.S.; extends north from California through Oregon and Washington; Mt. Rainier is the highest peak. (p. 14)

Charles River   A river located in eastern Massachusetts; separates Boston from Cambridge; flows into Boston Bay. (p. 279)

Charleston (33°N/80°W)   A city in South Carolina; a major port on the Atlantic Ocean; many French settled here in 1680. (p. 51)

Charlotte (35°N/81°W)   The largest city in North Carolina. (p. 51)

Chattahoochee River   An important river in the Southeast; forms part of the Georgia-Alabama border; begins in Georgia and flows into the Apalachicola River. (p. 51)

Chattanooga (35°N/85°W)   An industrial city on the Tennessee River in southeastern Tennessee. (p. 437)

Chesapeake Bay   A bay of the Atlantic Ocean; surrounded by Virginia and Maryland. (p. 42)

Chicago (42°N/88°W)   A city located in Illinois; third-largest city in the U.S.A. (p. 56)

Chihuahuan Desert   A part of the North American Desert; located in New Mexico and Texas. (p. 62)

Cleveland (41°N/82°W)   The largest city in Ohio; located at the mouth of the Cuyahoga River on Lake Erie. (p. 56)

Coast Ranges   The north-south chains of mountains found along the Pacific coast; receive heavy rainfall each year. (p. 14)

Coastal Plain   One of two major plains in the U.S.A.; found along the coasts of the Atlantic Ocean and the Gulf of Mexico. (p. 14)

Colorado Plateau   A major plateau in the southwestern U.S.A.; covers most of New Mexico and Arizona; the Colorado River cuts across it. (p. 14)

Colorado River   A major river of the southwestern U.S.A.; its basin extends from the Rocky Mountains to the Sierra Nevada, ending in the Gulf of California; carved out the Grand Canyon. (p. 22)

Columbia River   A river that begins in the Rocky Mountains in Canada; forms the Washington-Oregon border; supplies much of the area's water power. (p. 22)

Concord (42°N/71°W)   A town in Massachusetts near Boston; famous battle of the American Revolution took place here. (p. 289)

Connecticut River   The longest river in New England; begins in New Hampshire, flows south through Massachusetts and Connecticut, and ends in Long Island Sound. (p. 22)

Continental Divide   An imaginary line along the crest of the Rocky Mountains; separates rivers that flow west from those that flow east. (p. 22)

Cumberland Gap   A pass through the Appalachian Mountains; located in Tennessee; Daniel Boone traveled through this gap into Kentucky. (p. 341)

Dallas (33°N/97°W)   An industrial city in northeastern Texas; located on the Trinity River. (p. 62)

Death Valley   The lowest point in the Western Hemisphere; part of the Mojave Desert in California. (p. 70)

Delaware Bay   A part of the Atlantic Ocean; located between New Jersey and Delaware. (p. 42)

Delaware River   A river that begins in southern New York State and flows into the Atlantic Ocean at Delaware Bay; important transportation route in the northeastern U.S.A. (p. 42)

Detroit (42°N/83°W)   The largest city in Michigan; located on the Detroit River; center of automobile industry. (p. 56)

District of Columbia (39°N/77°W)   A special district, not part of any state, that contains only the city of Washington; the capital of the U.S.A.; located between Maryland and Virginia on the Potomac River. (p. 34)

Dodge City (38°N/100°W)   A city in southern Kansas; located on the Arkansas River; was a major railroad center on the Santa Fe Trail. (p. 478)

Durango (25°N/105°W)   A city located in the Sierra Madre region of Mexico. (p. 601)

El Paso (32°N/106°W)   A city at the western tip of Texas; located on the Rio Grande. (p. 62)

Ellesmere Island   The most northern of Canada's Arctic Islands. (p. 578)

Ensenada (32°N/116°W)   A city in northern Baja California, Mexico; located on the Pacific Ocean. (p. 601)

Erie Canal   The longest canal in the world; connects Troy (on the Hudson River) with Buffalo (on Lake Erie). (p. 364)

Everglades   A large area of wetlands located in southern Florida. (p. 51)

Fall Line   The point where the Piedmont meets the Coastal Plain in the eastern U.S.A.; rivers here form waterfalls. (p. 22)

Fort Sumter (33°N/80°W)   A fort on an island in the harbor of Charleston, South Carolina; the Civil War began here. (p. 437)

Frankfort (38°N/85°W)   The capital of Kentucky; located on the Kentucky River. (p. 51)

Fraser River   A river that begins in the Rocky Mountains in Canada and empties into the Pacific Ocean near Vancouver, British Columbia; Canada's wildest river. (p. 578)

Gary (42°N/87°W)   A city in Indiana; located on Lake Michigan; center of iron and steel manufacturing. (p. 56)

Georges Bank   A huge area off the coasts of Nova Scotia and Maine; one of the richest fishing grounds in the world; claimed by both Canada and the U.S.A. (p. 591)

Gettysburg (40°N/77°W)   A town in Pennsylvania; the greatest battle of the Civil War was fought here in 1863. (p. 437)

Gila River   A river that begins in New Mexico, flows through Arizona, and empties into the Colorado River near Yuma, Arizona. (p. 62)

Gonzales (30°N/98°W)   A city in central Texas; scene of the first battle in the Texas Revolution. (p. 394)

Grand Banks   A rich fishing area off the coast of Newfoundland; the southern edge of these banks is known as the Georges Bank. (p. 166)

Grand Canyon (36°N/113°W)   A famous canyon in Arizona, formed by the Colorado River; one of the world's natural wonders. (p. 22)

Great Basin   One of the driest parts of the country; located in Nevada, Utah, California, Idaho, Wyoming, and Oregon; includes the Great Salt Lake Desert, the Mojave Desert, and Death Valley. (p. 14)

Great Lakes   The largest group of freshwater lakes in the world; located in central North America; Canada-U.S. border passes through four of these five lakes. (p. 22)

Great Plains   The western part of the Interior Plains; receives less than 20 inches of rainfall each year. (p. 14)

Great Salt Lake (41°N/112°W)   The largest lake in the Great Basin; located in Utah. (p. 22)

Great Smoky Mountains   A part of the Appalachian Mountains; extend along the North Carolina-Tennessee border. (p. 51)

Green Mountains   A part of the Appalachian Mountains; extend from Canada through Vermont and into Massachusetts. (p. 42)

Grijalva River   A river in southeastern Mexico; flows into the Bay of Campeche. (p. 601)

Groton (41°N/72°W)   A town in southeastern Connecticut; located on Long Island Sound at the mouth of the Thames River; Fort Griswold is found here. (p. 198)

Guadalupe Mountains   A mountain range located in Texas and New Mexico; national park located in these mountains. (p. 62)

Guam   U.S. territory in the Pacific Ocean; largest of the Mariana Islands. (p. 540)

Gulf Coast   A region of Mexico located along the Gulf of Mexico. (p. 601)

Gulf of California   A part of the Pacific Ocean; located between Baja California, Mexico, and Sonora and Sinaloa, Mexico. (p. 601)

Gulf of Mexico   A body of water located on the southeast coast of North America; surrounded by the U.S.A., Cuba, and Mexico. (p. 14)

Halifax (45°N/64°W)   The capital of the province of Nova Scotia in Canada; a major port on the Atlantic Ocean; remains free of ice all year. (p. 578)

Havana (23°N/82°W)   The capital of Cuba; largest city in the West Indies; the American battleship *Maine* exploded here in 1898. (p. 506)

Hawaii   The largest of the Hawaiian Islands. (p. 9)

Hiroshima (34°N/132°E)   An industrial city in Japan; a single atomic bomb was dropped here on August 6, 1945. (p. 540)

Hispaniola   An island in the West Indies made up of Haiti and the Dominican Republic; located in the Caribbean Sea between Cuba and Puerto Rico. (p. 147)

Hollywood (34°N/118°W)   A part of the city of Los Angeles, California; center of the U.S. movie and television industries. (p. 70)

Hoover Dam   A dam built on the Colorado River at the Nevada-Arizona border; forms Lake Mead, one of the world's largest reservoirs. (p. 62)

Houston (30°N/95°W)   The largest city in Texas; third-largest port in the U.S.; leading industrial center in Texas. (p. 62)

Houston Ship Channel   A deep, narrow waterway that connects Houston, Texas, with the Gulf of Mexico. (p. 62)

Hudson Bay   A bay in Canada surrounded by the Northwest Territories, Manitoba, Ontario, and Quebec; connects with the Atlantic Ocean through the Hudson Strait. (p. 591)

Hudson River   Henry Hudson named this river for himself; located in New York State, it flows into the Atlantic Ocean; the New York State Barge Canal connects it with Lake Erie. (p. 42)

Illinois Waterway   A system of rivers and canals that connects Lake Michigan (at Chicago, Illinois) with the Illinois River and then with the Mississippi. (p. 22)

Imperial Valley   A valley in southern California; irrigation changed this desert into the largest lettuce-producing area in the U.S.A. (p. 70)

Independence (39°N/94°W)   A city in western Missouri; starting point of the Oregon Trail; Mormons lived here before they moved to Salt Lake City. (p. 383)

Indian Ocean   A body of water located between Africa, Asia, Australia, and Antarctica. (p. 61)

Indies   The islands of Southeast Asia. (p. 143)

Interior Plains   A landform located between the Appalachian Mountains and the Rocky Mountains; divided into the Central and Great plains. (p. 14)

Intermountain Region   A high, dry area of land that extends from west of the Rocky Mountains to east of the Sierra Nevada in California, and from Canada to Mexico. (p. 14)

Isthmus of Panama   A narrow strip of land that links North America and South America; separates the Atlantic and Pacific oceans. (p. 510)

Jackson (32°N/90°W)   Mississippi's capital and largest city; located on the Pearl River. (p. 51)

Jacksonville (30°N/82°W)   A city in northeastern Florida; located near the mouth of the St. Johns River. (p. 51)

James River   A river located in central Virginia; begins where the Jackson and Cowpasture rivers join; flows into Chesapeake Bay. (p. 22)

Jamestown (37°N/101°W)   The first permanent English settlement in America; located on the shore of the James River. (p. 51)

Kahoolawe (21°N/157°W)   One of the eight main islands of Hawaii; located west of Maui. (p. 9)

Kansas City (39°N/95°W)   The largest city in Missouri; located on the Missouri River on the Kansas-Missouri state line. (p. 56)

Kauai   The fourth-largest of the eight main Hawaiian Islands. (p. 9)

Kitty Hawk (36°N/76°W)   A small village in eastern North Carolina; the Wright brothers flew the first U.S. aircraft here on December 17, 1903. (p. 51)

Klondike (64°N/140°W)   An area in the Yukon Territory, Canada; gold was discovered here in 1896. (p. 508)

Lake Erie   The fourth-largest of the five Great Lakes; borders New York, Pennsylvania, and Ohio. (p. 22)

Lake Huron   The second-largest of the five Great Lakes; borders Michigan. (p. 22)

Lake Mead   A reservoir on the Colorado River; formed by the Hoover Dam; one of the world's largest reservoirs. (p. 70)

Lake Michigan   The third-largest of the five Great Lakes; borders Michigan, Indiana, Illinois, and Wisconsin. (p. 22)

Lake Okeechobee   The largest lake in the southern U.S.A.; located in central Florida along the northern edge of the Everglades. (p. 51)

Lake Ontario   The smallest of the five Great Lakes; borders New York. (p. 22)

Lake Superior   The largest of the five Great Lakes; borders Michigan, Wisconsin, and Minnesota. (p. 22)

Lanai   An island in central Hawaii; major pineapple-producing area. (p. 9)

Lexington (43°N/71°W)   A town near Boston, Massachusetts; first battle of the American Revolution took place here. (p. 289)

Lima (12°S/77°W)   The capital of Peru; located on the Rimac River; founded by Pizarro in 1535. (p. 153)

Lisbon (38°N/9°W)   The capital of Portugal; leading seaport of the country. (p. 143)

Little Bighorn River   A river in Wyoming; begins in northern Wyoming; flows into the Bighorn River; General Custer and all his men were killed here. (p. 70)

Long Island   An island located east of New York City and south of Connecticut; lies between Long Island Sound and the Atlantic Ocean. (p. 14)

Los Angeles (34°N/118°W)   The largest city in California; second-largest city in the U.S.A. (p. 70)

Louisville (38°N/86°W)   The largest city in Kentucky; located on the Ohio River. (p. 51)

Manhattan (42°N/74°W)   An island at the north end of New York Bay; surrounded by the Spuyten Duyvil Creek, the Harlem River, the East River, New York Bay, and the Hudson River. (p. 42)

Manitoba   A province in central Canada; bordered by Hudson Bay, Ontario, Minnesota, North Dakota, and Saskatchewan; located on the Interior Plains of Canada. (p. 591)

Massachusetts Bay   An inlet of the Atlantic Ocean on the east coast of Massachusetts; extends from Cape Ann to Cape Cod. (p. 42)

Maui   The second-largest island in Hawaii. (p. 9)

Mazatlán (23$\frac{1}{2}$°N/105°W)   The largest Mexican seaport on the Pacific coast; one of the region's most popular resort communities. (p. 601)

Memphis (35°N/90°W)   A city in the southwestern corner of Tennessee; located on the Mississippi River. (p. 51)

Mesabi Range   A range of mountains in northeastern Minnesota. (p. 56)

Mexico   The country to the south of the U.S.A. in North America; one of the most mountainous countries in the world. (p. 601)

Mexico City (19°N/99°W)   The capital of Mexico; located on the southern edge of the Central Plateau; has an elevation of about 7,000 feet. (p. 601)

Miami (26°N/80°W)   A city in southeastern Florida; located on Biscayne Bay; major Atlantic Ocean resort. (p. 51)

Milwaukee (43°N/88°W)   The largest city in Wisconsin; located on Lake Michigan. (p. 56)

Minneapolis (45°N/93°W)   The largest city in Minnesota; located on the Mississippi River; twin city with St. Paul. (p. 56)

Mississippi River   The largest river in the U.S.A.; source is Lake Itasca, Minnesota; flows into the Gulf of Mexico. (p. 22)

Missouri River   A tributary of the Mississippi; starts in southern Montana and joins the Mississippi near St. Louis, Missouri; forms parts of these borders: South Dakota-Nebraska, Nebraska-Iowa, Nebraska-Missouri, and Kansas-Missouri (p. 22)

Mobile (31°N/88°W)   A seaport in Alabama; located at the mouth of the Mobile River. (p. 51)

Mohawk River   A tributary of the Hudson River; parallels the New York State Barge Canal. (p. 48)

Mojave Desert   A desert in southern California. (p. 70)

Molokai   An island in Hawaii. (p. 9)

Monterrey (26°N/100°W)   A city in northeastern Mexico; largest city in the Gulf Coast region. (p. 601)

Montreal (45°N/73°W)   The largest city in Canada; located in the province of Quebec on the St. Lawrence Lowlands. (p. 591)

Mt. McKinley (64°N/150°W)   The highest mountain in North America; located in central Alaska. (p. 70)

Mt. Rainier (47°N/122°W)   The highest mountain in Washington state; highest point in the Cascade Range. (p. 70)

Mt. St. Helens (46°N/122°W)   A volcano in southern Washington state; last major eruption was in 1980. (p. 70)

Mt. Waialeale (22°N/160°W)   A mountain on Kauai Island in Hawaii; the wettest spot in the world. (p. 9)

Nagasaki (33°N/130°E)   A seaport city in southern Japan; an atomic bomb was dropped here on August 9, 1945. (p. 540)

New Brunswick   One of Canada's ten provinces; bordered by Quebec, the Gulf of St. Lawrence, Northumberland Strait, the Bay of Fundy, Maine, and Nova Scotia. (p. 591)

New England   An area along the Atlantic coast north of the Hudson River; includes Connecticut, Rhode Island, Massachusetts, New Hampshire, Vermont, and Maine. (p. 40)

New Orleans (30°N/90°W)   The largest city in Louisiana; major port located between the Mississippi River and Lake Pontchartrain. (p. 51)

New York City   *Pecos River*

New York City (41°N/74°W) The largest city in the U.S.A.; located in southeastern New York state at the mouth of the Hudson River. (p. 42)

New York State Barge Canal A system of four canals by which ships can travel across New York from Albany to Lake Erie. (p. 22)

Newfoundland An island in the Atlantic Ocean off the east coast of Canada; one of Canada's ten provinces. (p. 591)

Newport (74°N/71°W) A city on the southern end of Rhode Island; located at the mouth of Narragansett Bay (p. 198)

Norfolk (37°N/76°W) A city in southeastern Virginia; located on the Elizabeth River. (p. 51)

Northwest Territories One of Canada's two territories; located in the Far North; population is small. (p. 591)

Nova Scotia One of Canada's ten provinces; located on a peninsula. (p. 591)

Nueces River A river located in southern Texas; flows into Nueces Bay at the head of Corpus Christi Bay. (p. 478)

Oahu The third-largest of the eight main islands of Hawaii; Honolulu is located here. (p. 9)

Oaxaca (17°N/97°W) A city in southeastern Mexico; located in the Sierra Madre region. (p. 601)

Ohio River A major tributary of the Mississippi; starts in Pittsburgh, Pennsylvania, and ends in Cairo, Illinois, where it joins the Mississippi. (p. 22)

Okefenokee Swamp A swamp extending from southeastern Georgia to northeastern Florida. (p. 51)

Olympia (47°N/123°W) The capital of Washington; located on Puget Sound. (p. 70)

Omaha (41°N/96°W) The largest city in Nebraska; located on the Missouri River. (p. 56)

Ontario One of Canada's ten provinces; located between Quebec and Manitoba. (p. 591)

Ottawa (45°N/76°W) The capital of Canada; located in Ontario on the St. Lawrence Lowlands. (p. 591)

Ozark Highlands Plateau in southern U.S., extending from southwestern Missouri across Arkansas and into eastern Oklahoma. (p. 14)

Pacific Coast One of Mexico's five natural regions; includes the resort communities of Acapulco and Mazatlán. (p. 601)

Painted Desert An area of eroded land in central Arizona; the sand has been worn away and many-colored rocks show through. (p. 62)

Panama Canal A canal across the Isthmus of Panama; extends from the Caribbean Sea to the Bay of Panama. (p. 510)

Pearl Harbor (21°N/158°W) An inlet on the southern coast of Oahu, Hawaii; the Japanese attacked an American naval base here on December 7, 1941. (p. 540)

Pecos River A river in eastern New Mexico and western Texas; empties into the Rio Grande. (p. 62)

Pee Dee River   A river in North Carolina and South Carolina; formed where the Yadkin and Uharie rivers meet; empties into Winyah Bay. (p. 237)

Philadelphia (40°N/75°W)   A city in southeastern Pennsylvania; located where the Delaware and Schuylkill rivers meet; major U.S. port. (p. 42)

Pittsburgh (40°N/80°W)   The second-largest city in Pennsylvania; the Allegheny and Monongahela rivers meet here to form the Ohio River. (p. 42)

Platte River   A river in southern Iowa and northwestern Missouri; flows into the Missouri River. (p. 22)

Plymouth (41°N/71°W)   A town on Plymouth Bay in Massachusetts; site of the first settlement built by Pilgrims who sailed on the *Mayflower*. (p. 198)

Portsmouth (41½°N/71°W)   A town in southeastern Rhode Island; located on the Sakonnet River. (p. 198)

Potomac River   An important river on the Coastal Plain of the U.S.A.; begins in West Virginia and flows into Chesapeake Bay; Washington, D.C., is located on this river. (p. 51)

Prince Edward Island   One of Canada's ten provinces; located in the Gulf of St. Lawrence. (p. 591)

Puebla (19°N/98°W)   A city in southern Mexico; located in the rugged Sierra Madre region. (p. 601)

Puerto Rico   A commonwealth of the U.S.A.; an island located about 1,000 miles (1,600 km) southeast of Florida. (p. 510)

Puget Sound   An arm of the Pacific Ocean; extending 100 miles (160 km) into the state of Washington; Seattle is located on it. (p. 70)

Quebec (46°N/71°W)   The capital of the province of Quebec in Canada; located on the north side of the St. Lawrence River; first successful French settlement in the new world; established in 1608. (p. 591)

Red River   A tributary of the Mississippi River; rises in eastern New Mexico, flows across Louisiana and into the Mississippi River; forms the Texas-Oklahoma border. (p. 22)

Richmond (38°N/77°W)   The capital of Virginia; located on the fall line of the James River. (p. 51)

Rio Grande   A river that forms the Texas-Mexico border; begins in the Rocky Mountains in Colorado and empties into the Gulf of Mexico. (p. 22)

Rocky Mountains   A range of mountains covering much of the western U.S.A. and Canada; extend from Alaska to New Mexico; these mountains divide rivers that flow east from those that flow west. (p. 14)

St. Augustine (30°N/81°W)   A city in Florida on the Atlantic Ocean; oldest city founded by Europeans in the U.S.A. (p. 51)

St. Lawrence Lowlands   Canada's smallest and most populated natural region. (p. 578)

St. Lawrence River   A river that flows from the Great Lakes to the Atlantic Ocean. (p. 22)

St. Lawrence Seaway   A series of canals built between Montreal and Lake Erie to allow ships to travel from the Atlantic Ocean through Lake Superior. (p. 22)

St. Louis (39°N/90°W)   The largest city in Missouri; major Mississippi River port; known as the Gateway to the West. (p. 56)

Salt Lake City (41°N/112°W)   Utah's capital and largest city; located on the Jordan River. (p. 70)

Salt River   A river in eastern Arizona; flows into the Gila River near Phoenix; used for irrigation and water power. (p. 62)

San Antonio (29°N/98°W)   A city in central Texas; located on the San Antonio River; the Alamo is found here. (p. 62)

San Diego (35°N/117°W)   A large city on the coast of southern California. (p. 8)

San Francisco (38°N/122°W)   The largest city in northern California; located on San Francisco Bay. (p. 70)

San Joaquin River   One of two major rivers in California; flows into the Sacramento River near San Francisco Bay. (p. 70)

San Jose (37°N/122°W)   A large city in western California; one of the twenty largest cities in the U.S.A. (p. 8)

San Salvador   One of the islands in the Bahamas; located in the Atlantic Ocean; Columbus landed here in 1492. (p. 147)

Saratoga (43°N/74°W)   A village on the west bank of the Hudson River in eastern New York State; site of Revolutionary War battle; now called Schuylerville. (p. 289)

Saskatchewan   One of Canada's ten provinces; located between Alberta and Manitoba. (p. 591)

Savannah (32°N/81°W)   The oldest city in Georgia; located at the mouth of the Savannah River. (p. 51)

Savannah River   A river that forms the border between Georgia and South Carolina; flows into the Atlantic Ocean at Savannah, Georgia. (p. 22)

Seattle (48°N/122°W)   The largest city in Washington State; located on Puget Sound. (p. 70)

Sierra Madre   A Y-shaped region of Mexico made up of three mountain ranges: the Eastern, Southern, and Western Sierra Madre. (p. 601)

Sierra Nevada   The mountain range in eastern California that runs parallel to the Coast Ranges. (p. 14)

Snake River   A river that begins in the Rocky Mountains and flows west into the Pacific Ocean; was part of the Oregon Trail. (p. 345)

Sonoran Desert   One of the four areas of the North American Desert; one of the world's most beautiful deserts. (p. 601)

South Pass   A pass in southwestern Wyoming; crosses the Continental Divide; part of the Oregon Trail. (p. 383)

Springfield (40°N/90°W)   The capital of Illinois; home and burial place of Abraham Lincoln. (p. 56)

Strait of Magellan   A waterway from the Atlantic Ocean to the Pacific Ocean near the tip of South America. (p. 147)

Susquehanna River   A river in central New York, Pennsylvania, and Maryland; rises in Otsego Lake, New York, and empties into northern Chesapeake Bay. (p. 22)

Tampa (28°N/82°W)   A city in western Florida; located on the northeastern end of Tampa Bay. (p. 51)

Tampa Bay   An inlet of the Gulf of Mexico in western Florida; Hernando de Soto landed here to begin his search for gold. (p. 51)

Tennessee River   A tributary of the Mississippi River; begins in eastern Tennessee and flows into the Ohio River. (p. 51)

Teton Range   A part of the Rocky Mountains; begins in northwestern Wyoming and extends north into Yellowstone National Park. (p. 70)

Tijuana (32°N/117°W)   A large community on the Mexico-California border; popular resort town. (p. 601)

Tombigbee River   A river in Alabama; starts in Mississippi and joins with the Alabama River before flowing into Mobile Bay on the Gulf of Mexico. (p. 22)

Toronto (44°N/79°W)   The capital of the province of Ontario in Canada; located near the northwestern end of Lake Ontario; third-largest city in Canada. (p. 591)

Tucson (32°N/111°W)   A city in southeastern Arizona; located on the Santa Cruz River. (p. 62)

Tulsa (36°N/96°W)   A city in Oklahoma; located on the Arkansas River. (p. 62)

Valley Forge (40°N/75°W)   George Washington's winter camp near Philadelphia; the American army spent a cold winter here in 1777. (p. 289)

Vancouver (49°N/123°W)   Canada's eighth-largest city; located where the north arm of the Fraser River meets the Pacific Ocean. (p. 591)

Vancouver Island   An island off the southwest coast of British Columbia, Canada. (p. 578)

Veracruz (19°N/96°W)   A seaport in eastern Mexico; located on the Gulf of Mexico. (p. 601)

Vicksburg (32°N/91°W)   A city in western Mississippi; located on the Mississippi River. (p. 437)

Victoria Island   The third-largest of Canada's northern Arctic Islands. (p. 578)

Washington, D.C. (39°N/77°W)   The capital of the U.S.A.; located on the Potomac River in a special district that is not part of any state. (p. 8)

Western Mountains   A region in western Canada; name given to the Rocky Mountains and Coast Ranges in Canada. (p. 578)

White Mountains   Part of the Appalachian Mountains; located in New Hampshire. (p. 42)

Willamette Valley   A valley near Portland, Oregon; the Oregon Trail ended here. (p. 383)

Williamsburg (37°N/77°W)   A city in southeastern Virginia; located on a peninsula between the James and York rivers. (p. 51)

Wilmington (40°N/76°W)   A city in northern Delaware; located where the Delaware and Christina rivers meet Brandywine Creek. (p. 42)

Winnipeg (50°N/97°W)   The capital of the province of Manitoba in Canada; located on the Red River; fourth-largest city in Canada. (p. 591)

Yorktown (37°N/77°W)   A small town in Virginia; located on Chesapeake Bay; last major battle of the Revolutionary War was fought here in 1781. (p. 289)

Youngstown (41°N/81°W)   A city in northeastern Ohio; located on the Mahoning River. (p. 56)

Yucatán Peninsula   A peninsula in southeastern Mexico and northern Central America; separates the Gulf of Mexico from the Caribbean Sea. (p. 601)

Yukon River   A river that begins in southwestern Yukon Territory, Canada; flows through Alaska and into the Bering Sea. (p. 578)

Yukon Territory   One of Canada's two territories; bordered by the Arctic Ocean, the Northwest Territories, British Columbia, and Alaska. (p. 591)

abolish   *boycott*

This glossary contains important social studies words and their definitions. Each word is respelled as it would be in a dictionary. When you see this mark ′ after a syllable, pronounce that syllable with more force than the other syllables. The page number at the end of the definition tells where to find the word in your book.

add, āce, câre, pälm; end, ēqual; it, īce; odd, ōpen, ôrder; tŏŏk, pōōl; up, bûrn; yōō as u in *fuse;* oil; pout; ə as a in *above,* e in *sicken,* i in *possible;* o in *melon,* u in *circus;* **ch**eck; ri**ng**; **th**in; **th**is; zh as in *vision*

abolish (ə·bol′ish)   To put an end to. (p. 402)

abolitionist (ab·ə·lish′ə·nist)   A person who wished to end slavery. (p. 402)

acid rain (as′id rān)   Rain that contains acids formed when air pollutants combine with moisture in the atmosphere. (p. 593)

active volcano (ak′tiv vol·kā′nō)   A volcano that is erupting or is likely to erupt. (p. 16)

agriculture (ag′rə·kul·chər)   Farming. (p. 89)

ally (al′ī)   A friend in war. (p. 267)

almanac (ôl′mə·nak)   A yearly calendar that gives information about natural events. (p. 249)

amendment (ə·mend′mənt)   A change to the Constitution. (p. 328)

apprentice (ə·pren′tis)   Someone who works for a person skilled in a craft in order to learn that craft. (p. 227)

archaeologist (är·kē·ol′ə·jist)   A scientist who studies remains and artifacts to learn about the past. (p. 97)

archaeology (är·kē·ol′ə·jē)   The scientific study of artifacts and remains. (p. 97)

armistice (är′mə·stis)   An agreement to stop fighting. (p. 506)

artifact (är′tə·fakt)   An object used by people in the past. (p. 97)

assassination (ə·sas·ə·nā′shən)   Murder for a political reason. (p. 439)

assembly (ə·sem′blē)   A lawmaking body. (p. 119)

assembly line (ə·sem′blē līn)   A system of work in which the product to be assembled moves on a conveyor belt from one work station to another, while each worker stays in one place. (p. 515)

astronaut (as′trə·nôt)   An explorer of the moon and outer space. (p. 563)

authority (ə·thôr′ə·tē)   Control. (p. 198)

barter (bär′tər)   A system of exchanging goods and services without using money. (p. 203)

bauxite (bôk′sīt)   The ore from which aluminum is made. (p. 25)

Bill of Rights (bil uv rīts)   The first ten amendments to the Constitution. (p. 330)

blockade (blo·kād′)   The use of warships to prevent other ships from entering or leaving a harbor. (p. 423)

boycott (boi′kot)   To refuse to buy something in order to show disapproval. (p. 271)

broker (brō′kər)   A person who gets paid to buy and sell for someone else. (p. 239)

budget (buj′it)   A plan for controlling spending. (p. 560)

budget deficit (buj′it def′ə·sit)   The amount of money borrowed to pay for expenses. (p. 560)

bureaucracy (byŏŏ·rok′rə·sē)   A body of government officials and employees. (p. 533)

canyon (kan′yən)   A deep, narrow valley with steep sides. (p. 24)

cape (kāp)   A point of land that extends into a body of water. (p. 40)

capital (kap′ə·təl)   The money used to start a business; the equipment needed to run a business. (p. 495)

cardinal directions (kär′də·nəl di·rek′shənz)   The main directions—north, south, east, and west. (p. 7)

carpetbagger (kär′pit·bag·ər)   A Northerner who moved to the South to make profits after the Civil War. (p. 455)

carriers (kar′ē·ərz)   Large ships that serve as bases for fighter planes. (p. 540)

cartographer (kär·tog′rə·fər)   A person who draws maps. (p. 29)

cash crop (kash krop)   A crop grown to sell to make a profit. (p. 235)

casualty (kazh′ŏŏ·əl·tē)   A person killed or wounded in a war. (p. 429)

cavalry (kav′əl·rē)   An army unit that rides horses. (p. 424)

century (sen′chə·rē)   A period of 100 years. (p. 100)

chart (chärt)   A map. (p. 143)

checks and balances (cheks and bal′ən·səz)   A system in which each branch of the government has controls on the power of the other branches. (p. 326)

civil rights (siv′əl rīts)   The rights of citizens to equal treatment, both in law and in practice. (p. 552)

civilian (sə·vil′yən)   A person who is not a soldier. (p. 539)

civilization (siv·ə·lə·zā′shən)   A way of life that has large cities, complex government, and highly developed arts and sciences. (p. 89)

coke (kōk)   A fuel made from coal and used to make steel. (p. 458)

colonist (kol′ə·nist)   A person who comes from a mother country to live in a colony. (p. 156)

colony (kol′ə·nē)   A settlement ruled by a faraway country. (p. 156)

common (kom′ən)   A parklike pasture shared by the residents of a New England village. Also called a village green. (p. 198)

communism (kom′yə·niz·əm)   A social and economic system in which all land and industries are owned by the government. (p. 547)

compact (kom′pakt)   An agreement. (p. 177)

compass (kum′pəs)   An instrument used for finding directions. (p. 143)

compass rose (kum′pəs rōz)   The guide to directions on a map. (p. 7)

competition (kom·pə·tish′ən)   The effort of two or more companies to gain the business of the same customers. (p. 496)

compromise   *dwelling*

compromise (kom′prə·mīz) To give up some of what one wants in order to reach an agreement. (p. 324)

conquistador (kon·kis′tə·dôr) A Spanish conqueror. (p. 149)

conservation (kon·sər·vā′shən) Using a natural resource in a way that keeps it from being wasted or destroyed. (p. 28)

Constitution (kon·stə·too′shən) The fundamental law of the United States that provides a framework for our government. (p. 321)

constitutional (kon·stə·too′shən·əl) Lawful according to the United States Constitution. (p. 326)

consumer (kən·soo′mər) A person who uses goods or services; a buyer. (p. 494)

continent (kon′tə·nənt) One of the Earth's main landmasses. (p. 5)

cooperation (kō·op·ə·rā′shən) Working together for a common purpose. (p. 95)

corporation (kôr·pə·rā′shən) A company owned by stockholders who have each invested money in the company. (p. 495)

creditor (kred′i·tər) A person to whom money is owed. (p. 322)

crest (krest) High point. (p. 21)

cultivate (kul′tə·vāt) To prepare and use land to raise crops. (p. 57)

culture (kul′chər) The way of life shared by a group of people. (p. 90)

D day (dē dā) The greatest seaborne invasion in history, when the Allied forces landed in France during World War II. (p. 540)

debate (di·bāt′) A formal argument. (p. 409)

debtor (det′ər) A person who owes money. (p. 322)

decade (dek′ād) A period of ten years. (p. 99)

deciduous (di·sij′oo·əs) Shedding leaves in the fall. (p. 197)

declaration (dek·lə·rā′shən) A formal statement. (p. 287)

Declaration of Independence (dek·lə·rā′shən uv in·di·pen′dəns) The formal document that proclaimed the freedom of the American colonies from Britain, adopted on July 4, 1776. (p. 291)

degree (di·grē′) A unit of measure used to describe lines of latitude and lines of longitude. (p. 18)

delegate (del′ə·git or del′ə·gāt) A person elected by people to represent them. (p. 218)

delta (del′tə) Land formed at a river's mouth by silt. (p. 23)

demand (di·mand′) The wants and needs of consumers that result in the goods and services for which they are willing to pay. (p. 494)

democracy (di·mok′rə·sē) Rule by the people. (p. 1)

depression (di·presh′ən) A period of time during which there is little money and no economic growth. (p. 531)

descendant (di·sen′dənt) The offspring of an ancestor. (p. 95)

dictator (dik′tā·tər) A ruler who has no respect for individual rights. (p. 537)

drainage basin (drā′nij bā′sən) The area drained by a river system. (p. 21)

drought (drout) A long period of little or no rain. (p. 94)

dwelling (dwel′ing) A home. (p. 93)

earthworks (ûrth′wûrks) Walls of dirt. (p. 288)

Eastern Hemisphere (ēs′tərn hem′ə·sfir) The half of the Earth east of an imaginary line. (p. 5)

economic resources (ek·ə·nom′ik rē′sôr·sez) Resources used to produce goods and services. (p. 27)

economy (i·kon′ə·mē) The way people use resources to produce and sell goods and services. (p. 27)

editorial (ed·i·tôr′ē·əl) An article that gives the opinion of the editor. (p. 519)

ejidos (ā·hē′dōs) Communal plots that the Indians of Mexico were allowed to farm. (p. 604)

employee (im·ploi′ē) A person who is hired to work. (p. 496)

encomiendas (en·kō·me·en′däz) Large pieces of Mexican land given to the conquistadors by the Spanish king. (p. 604)

engineer (en·jə·nir′) A person who is responsible for designing something and seeing that it is built. (p. 363)

equator (i·kwā′tər) The imaginary line that circles the Earth halfway between the North Pole and the South Pole. (p. 4)

estate (ə·stāt′) A large landholding. (p. 607)

event (i·vent′) Something that happens or occurs. (p. 1)

executive (ig·zek′yə·tiv) The management branch of the government. (p. 326)

expedition (ek·spə·dish′ən) A journey or voyage taken for a special reason. (p. 144)

export (eks′pôrt) A product sent from one country to another. (p. 209)

extension of slavery (ik·sten′shən uv slā′vər·ē) The movement of slavery into new territories of the West. (p. 405)

extinct (ik·stingkt′) No longer in existence. (p. 110)

fact (fakt) A statement that can be proved to be true. (p. 244)

fair market price (fâr mär′kit prīs) The price at which businesses can make a profit and at which consumers will still buy a product. Also known as the market clearing price. (p. 495)

fall line (fôl līn) The point at which a river drops from the foothills to the plains, forming a waterfall. (p. 23)

federal (fed′ər·əl) A form of government in which states are united under a national government. (p. 324)

federation (fed·ə·rā′shən) An organization formed of many related groups; for example, skilled workers in different trades. (p. 466)

flatboat (flat′bōt) A large boat with a flat bottom. (p. 365)

flint (flint) A stone used for tools during the Stone Age. (p. 86)

foothills (fŏŏt′hilz) Low hills at the base of a mountain. (p. 14)

forty-niner (fôr·tē·nī′nər) A pioneer who went to California in the 1849 gold rush. (p. 382)

free enterprise (frē en′tər·prīz) An economic system in which businesses have the freedom to sell many kinds of goods and services, and people have the freedom to buy almost anything they need or want. (p. 493)

free states (frē stāts) States that did not allow slavery. (p. 401)

Freedmen's Bureau *indentured servant*

Freedmen's Bureau (frēd′mənz byŏŏr′ō) An agency that was set up to help former slaves. (p. 453)

frontier (frun·tir′) An area where settled land meets wilderness. (p. 207)

fugitives (fyŏŏ′jə·tivz) People who were seeking to escape from slavery. (p 402)

geography (jē·og′rə·fē) The study of the surface of the Earth and of how people use the Earth. (p. 1)

glacier (glā′shər) A large, moving ice mass. (p. 41)

glasnost (gläs′nōst) A Russian word that means "openness." (p. 559)

glider (glī′dər) An aircraft that has no engine. (p. 514)

globe (glōb) A model of the Earth. (p. 4)

government (guv′ərn·mənt) A group of people who make and carry out the rules by which a country's citizens live. (p. 1)

graph (graf) A visual way of comparing amounts. (p. 213)

grid (grid) A pattern of crossing lines or squares. (p. 9)

guarantee (gar·ən·tē′) A written promise that something will work. (p. 460)

hemisphere (hem′ə·sfir) Half a sphere. (p. 5)

heritage (her′ə·tij) Customs and beliefs handed down from the past. (p. 1)

historian (his·tôr′ē·ən) A person who studies the past. (p. 1)

history (his′tə·rē) The study of past events. (p. 1)

hogan (hō′gən) A round or six-sided dwelling made of logs and dried mud. (p. 120)

homesteader (hōm′sted·ər) A person who was given 160 acres of land by the government after living on it for five years. (p. 478)

hostages (hos′tij·əz) People held by enemies until certain demands are met. (p. 558)

human rights (hyŏŏ′mən rīts) The basic rights and freedoms of all people. (p. 547)

hydroelectric dam (hī·drō·i·lek′trik dam) A dam that produces electricity. (p. 534)

ideal (ī·dē′əl) A worthwhile goal. (p. 549)

igloo (ig′lŏŏ) A house made of snow blocks. (p. 122)

immigrant (im′ə·grənt) A person who comes from one country to live in another country. (p. 224)

import (im′pôrt) A product brought into a country from another country. (p. 209)

impressment (im·pres′mənt) The act of forcing American sailors to work on British ships. (p. 347)

inauguration (in·ô·gyə·rā′shən) The ceremony at which the President takes the oath of office. (p. 413)

indentured servant (in·den′chərd sûr′vənt) A person who agreed to work in the colonies in exchange for ocean passage. (p. 174)

independence (in·di·pen′dəns) Freedom from control by others. (p. 290)

Independence Day (in·di·pen′dəns dā) The day the Continental Congress voted to adopt the Declaration of Independence. We celebrate this day every year on July 4. (p. 291)

indigo (in′də·gō) A plant that produces a blue dye. (p. 235)

industrial (in·dus′trē·əl) Having many factories. (p. 458)

industry (in′dəs·trē) Manufacturing or business activity. (p. 26)

inflation (in·flā′shən) A situation that occurs when prices rise faster than wages. (p. 550)

influence (in′floo·əns) The power of people or things to act on others. (p. 220)

installment (in·stôl′mənt) One of several payments made on a debt at specific times until the whole debt is paid. (p. 515)

installment buying (in·stôl′mənt bī′ing) An arrangement in which a buyer at first pays only a small part of the selling price of an item and then continues to make regular payments until the debt is paid. (p. 515)

integration (in·tə·grā′shən) Full equality of all races in the use of public facilities. (p. 553)

interchangeable part (in·tər·chān′jə·bəl pärt) A part that can be taken out of one machine or object and put into another similar one. (p. 372)

interdependence (in·tər·di·pen′dəns) Depending on one another for the things we want and need. (p. 40)

interior drainage (in·tir′ē·ər drā′nij) An area where rivers do not flow into an ocean or gulf. (p. 24)

intermediate directions (in·tər·mē′dē·it di·rek′shənz) The directions northeast, northwest, southeast, and southwest. (p. 7)

invest (in·vest′) Using money in hopes of making a profit. (p. 460)

irrigation (ir·ə·gā′shən) The process of bringing water to farmland. (p. 26)

isthmus (is′məs) A neck, or narrow strip, of land connecting two larger land areas. (p. 510)

jazz (jaz) A kind of popular music that grew out of the heritage of African Americans. (p. 528)

journal (jûr′nəl) A daily record. (p. 145)

judicial (joo·dish′ əl) The branch of government that is the court system. (p. 326)

kayak (kī′ak) An Eskimo canoe made of a frame covered by animal skins. (p. 122)

labor (lā′bər) Work. (p. 496)

labor union (lā′bər yoon′yən) An organization of workers formed to protect their interests. (p. 466)

land bridge (land brij) A piece of land connecting Asia and North America during the Ice Age. (p. 85)

landforms (land′fôrmz) The shapes of the Earth's surface. (p. 6)

league (lēg)   A union of people joined for a common purpose. (p. 112)

legend (lej′ənd)   A story that may or may not be true. (p. 149)

legislative (lej′is·lā·tiv)   The lawmaking branch of government. (p. 326)

legislature (lej′is·lā·chər)   A state lawmaking body. (p. 454)

liberals (lib′ər·əlz)   People in Mexico who supported Juárez and wanted a representative government. (p. 606)

liberty (lib′ər·tē)   Freedom. (p. 270)

lines of latitude (līnz uv lat′ə·tōōd)   The imaginary lines on the Earth that run in an east-west direction. They are used to locate points on the Earth. Also known as parallels. (p. 18)

lines of longitude (līnz uv lon′jə·tōōd)   The imaginary lines on the earth that run in a north-south direction. They are used to locate points on the Earth. Also known as meridians. (p. 18)

locks (loks)   A system that allows boats to go higher and lower within a canal. (p. 364)

lodge (loj)   A circular house built over a shallow pit. (p. 115)

longhouse (long′hous)   A long dwelling made of poles and covered with elm bark. (p. 111)

majority (mə·jôr′ə·tē)   The greater number of people. (p. 328)

mammoth (mam′əth)   A huge, hairy, elephantlike animal that lived during the Ice Age. (p. 85)

manganese (mang′gə·nēz)   An element used to make steel. (p. 25)

map (map)   A drawing of all or part of the Earth. (p. 5)

map scale (map skāl)   A scale on a map that compares distance on the map to distance in the real world. (p. 8)

market clearing price (mär′kit klir′ing prīs)   The price at which businesses can make a profit and at which consumers will still buy a product. Also known as the fair market price. (p. 495)

marketing (mär′kit·ing)   In business, the job of finding and keeping customers. (p. 497)

mass production (mas prə·duk′shən)   A way of manufacturing that produces a huge amount of goods. (p. 372)

massacre (mas′ə·kər)   The killing of a group of people who cannot defend themselves. (p. 273)

meetinghouse (mē′ting·hous)   A church building that was also used for other public gatherings. (p. 198)

megalopolis (meg·ə·lop′ə·lis)   A widespread, highly populated area, usually made up of several cities and their suburbs. (p. 43)

mercenary (mûr′sə·ner·ē)   A hired soldier. (p. 290)

mesas (mā′səz)   Plateaus that rise sharply on all sides and have a level top. (p. 7)

mica (mī′kə)   A clear rock that comes apart in thin sheets. (p. 90)

migration (mī·grā′shən)   A movement from one country or region to another. (p. 85)

military draft (mil′ə·ter·ē draft)   A way of bringing people into the army. (p. 537)

militia (mə·lish′ə)   A military unit made up of volunteers. (p. 201)

minister (min′is·tər)   The head of a department of the executive branch within the Canadian system of government. (p. 592)

mission (mish′ən) A missionary settlement that included a church and buildings necessary for farming and ranching. (p. 158)

missionary (mish′ən·er·ē) A priest who hoped to convert Indians to the Christian faith. (p. 158)

module (moj′ool) A small, self-contained landing unit of a space-craft. (p. 563)

monopoly (mə·nop′ə·lē) Complete control over a product or service. (p. 274)

natural environment (nach′ər·əl in·vī′rən·mənt) The natural world around a person, including the land, water, climate, plants, and animals. (p. 105)

natural regions (nach′ər·əl rē′jənz) Large areas that have something natural in common, such as the same kinds of landforms or other natural features. (p. 13)

natural resources (nach′ər·əl rē′sôr·səz) Things found in nature that people use. (p. 25)

natural vegetation (nach′ər·əl vej·ə·tā′shən) Plants growing wild in an area. (p. 33)

naval stores (nā′vəl stôrz) The planks, masts, pitch, tar, and turpentine used in shipbuilding. (p. 197)

navigable (nav′ə·gə·bəl) Rivers that are wide, deep, and gentle enough for cargo-carrying boats. (p. 197)

navigation (nav·ə·gā′shən) The science of figuring out a ship's direction and location and the distance it travels. (p. 143)

navigator (nav′ə·gā·tər) A person who is able to find his or her way on the seas. (p. 139)

neutral (noo′trəl) Not taking sides in a war. (p. 347)

nomad (nō′mad) A person who has no fixed dwelling but generally moves and lives within a defined territory. (p. 116)

no-man's-land (nō′manz·land) The land separating opposing armies in trench warfare. (p. 522)

nonrenewable resources (non·ri·noo′ə·bəl rē′sôr·səz) Resources of which neither humans nor nature can make more. (p. 28)

norther (nôr′thər) A bitterly cold winter wind. (p. 33)

Northern Hemisphere (nôr′thern hem′ə·sfir) The half of the Earth that lies north of the equator. (p. 5)

northwest passage (nôrth·west′ pas′ij) A hoped-for waterway leading to Asia through North America. (p. 165)

obsidian (əb·sid′ē·ən) A glassy, black volcanic rock. (p. 90)

office (ôf′is) A job held to achieve the good of the community. (p. 200)

official (ə·fish′əl) A person either elected or appointed to do a community or government job. (p. 200)

opinion (ə·pin′yən) A statement that cannot be proved to be true. (p. 245)

overhead (ō′vər·hed) The amount of money it takes to run a business. (p. 495)

overseer (ō′vər·sē·ər) The person on a plantation who was directly responsible for field slaves. (p. 246) *palisade*   *rationing*

palisade (pal·ə·sād′) A wall or fence made of sharpened tree trunks. (p. 109)

peasants (pez′ənts) People who lived and worked on the land in Mexico. (p. 606)

pesticide (pes′tə·sīd) A chemical used to kill bugs. (p. 556)

petition (pə·tish′ən) A written request, for example, to Parliament. (p. 269)

petrochemical (pet·rō·kem′i·kəl) A chemical produced from oil. (p. 53)

petroleum (pə·trō′lē·əm) Crude oil. (p. 461)

phosphate (fos′fāt) A chemical compound used to make fertilizer and glass. (p. 53)

piecework (pēs′wûrk) Work done and paid for by the piece. (p. 464)

piedmont (pēd′mont) Gently rolling hills at the base of mountains. (p. 14)

pioneer (pī·ə·nir′) One of the first people to settle or enter a new territory. (p. 339)

plantation (plan·tā′shən) A large Southern farm. (p. 239)

planter (plan′tər) A person who owned a plantation. (p. 239)

poll tax (pōl taks) A tax paid in order to vote. (p. 456)

population density (pop·yə·lā′shən den′sə·tē) The number of people living in an area. (p. 410)

potash (pot′ash) A mineral used in fertilizers. (p. 64)

potlatch (pot′lach) A feast during which the host gave presents to guests, sometimes giving away all of his wealth. (p. 121)

prejudice (prej′o͞o·dis) Negative opinion about a group of people because of their race or religion. (p. 468)

presidio (pri·sid′ē·ō) A fort. (p. 158)

primary source (prī′mer·ē sôrs) Firsthand information from people who actually observed an event. (p. 427)

prime minister (prīm min′is·tər) The chief official of the government and leader of the majority party in Canada. (p. 591)

profit (prof′it) The money left over after expenses have been paid. (p. 172)

proprietor (prə·prī′ə·tər) A person who owned and ruled a colony. (p. 218)

province (prov′ins) A political region in Canada, like a state in the United States. (p. 590)

public service (pub′lik sûr′vis) Work that helps the community. (p. 241)

pueblo (pweb′lō) A village. (p. 152)

quartered (kwôr′tərd) Housed. (p. 275)

queue (kyo͞o) One braid of hair that hangs from the back of the head. (p. 467)

radiocarbon dating (rā·dē·ō·kär′bən dā′ting) A technique that determines approximately how old an object is by measuring the amount of radiocarbon it contains. (p. 97)

ratify (rat′ə·fī) To approve by voting. (p. 455)

rationing (rash′ə·ning) Limiting what people can buy. (p. 538)

raw materials   *shaman*

raw materials (rô mə·tir′ē·əlz) Natural resources that can be made into useful products. (p. 27)

reaper (rē′pər) A machine used to harvest grain. (p. 460)

refinery (ri·fī′nər·ē) A factory that changes oil into fuels. (p. 53)

reform (ri·fôrm′) A change for the better. (p. 487)

reformer (ri·fôr′mər) A person who works to bring about a change for the better. (p. 465)

refuge (ref′yōōj) A place of safety. (p. 223)

regiment (reg′ə·mənt) An organized group of soldiers. (p. 419)

regulate (reg′yə·lāt) To set rules for something. (p. 512)

relocation camp (rē·lō·kā′shən kamp) A prison-like camp to which Japanese Americans were forced to move during World War II. (p. 539)

renewable resources (ri·nōō′ə·bəl rē′sôr·səz) Resources that can be reused or remade by humans or nature. (p. 28)

repeal (ri·pēl′) To withdraw or cancel. (p. 270)

republic (ri·pub′lik) A form of government in which people elect representatives. (p. 321)

reservation (rez·ər·vā′shən) A piece of land on which Indians live. (p. 129)

reservoir (rez′ər·vwär) A lake that stores water held back by a dam. (p. 26)

resist (ri·zist′) To act against. (p. 275)

revolution (rev·ə·lōō′shən) A large, sudden change in government and people's lives. (p. 265)

river system (riv′ər sis′təm) A river and its tributaries. (p. 21)

runoff (run′ôf) Rain and snow that does not sink into the ground, but forms streams. (p. 21)

saga (sä′gə) A story about the deeds of the Vikings. (p. 140)

satellite (sat′ə·līt) A natural or artificial body that revolves around a planet. (p. 562)

scalawag (skal′ə·wag) A white Southerner who worked with the Northerners in the Reconstruction government. (p. 455)

scandal (skan′dəl) Any action that brings disgrace. (p. 558)

sea dog (sē dôg) A commander of an English warship. (p. 167)

secede (si·sēd′) To withdraw from the Union. (p. 413)

secession (si·sesh′ən) A state's withdrawal from the Union. (p. 408)

secondary source (sek′ən·der·ē sôrs) A description of an event not directly observed. (p. 428)

second-class citizen (sek′ənd·klas sit′ə·zən) A person who does not have the full rights of citizenship. (p. 454)

secret ballot (sē′krit bal′ət) A way to vote without anyone knowing how one has voted. (p. 455)

segregation (seg·rə·gā′shən) Separation of people due to the color of their skin. (p. 552)

senate (sen′it) One of the two houses of Congress. (p. 326)

shaman (shä′mən) An Indian priest and healer. (p. 105)

sharecropper (shâr′krop·ər)   A person who farms a rented piece of land and pays the landowner with a share of the crops. (p. 454)

silt (silt)   Fine bits of rock and soil carried by water. (p. 6)

slag (slag)   A waste product left over from making steel. (p. 458)

smelt (smelt)   To melt ore to separate out the metal. (p. 458)

society (sə·sī′ə·tē)   A broad grouping of people who are bound by common laws, traditions, and activities. (p. 241)

sod (sod)   The top layer of earth that includes both grass and grass roots. (p. 115)

Southern Hemisphere (suth′ərn hem′ə·sfir)   The half of the Earth that lies south of the equator. (p. 5)

space shuttle (spās shut′əl)   A spacecraft that can travel from Earth into space and back again. (p. 563)

specialize (spesh′əl·īz)   To spend most of one's time doing one kind of job. (p. 89)

sphere (sfir)   Anything shaped like a ball. (p. 4)

spiritual (spir′i·chōō·əl)   A religious folk song that originated among the blacks of the Southern United States. (p. 528)

spring (spring)   A place where underground water breaks through the earth's surface. (p. 120)

stampede (stam·pēd′)   To run away out of control. (p. 478)

staple food (stā′pəl fōōd)   The food that people depend on most for nourishment. (p. 119)

stations (stā′shənz)   Safe places to stay on the Underground Railroad. (p. 402)

steam engine (stēm en′jin)   An engine that works by heating water to make steam. (p. 366)

stock (stok)   Shares of ownership in a company. (p. 172)

stock market (stok mär′kit)   A place where people can buy and sell stocks. (p. 529)

stockholder (stok′hōl·dər)   A person who has invested money in a company and shares whatever profit the company makes. (p. 495)

stockyards (stok′yärdz)   Large pens built near railroads to hold cattle while they are waiting to be shipped. (p. 477)

stoop (stōōp)   A wide, high doorstep. (p. 221)

storm troopers (stôrm trōō′pərz)   A private army set up by the Nazis. (p. 536)

strait (strāt)   A narrow passageway between two bodies of water. (p. 85)

strategy (strat′ə·jē)   A long-range plan. (p. 423)

suburbs (sub′ûrbz)   Communities near a city. (p. 515)

suffrage (suf′rij)   The right to vote. (p. 516)

supply (sə·plī′)   The goods and services offered by businesses. (p. 494)

surplus (sûr′plus)   An amount more than is needed. (p. 89)

survey (sər·vā′)   To measure the land. (p. 322)

sweatshop (swet′shop)   A small factory that has poor working conditions. (p. 465)

symbol (sim′bəl)   Something that stands for something else. (p. 7)

tableland (tā′bəl·land) A plateau that rises sharply on all sides and has a level top. (p. 7)

tariff (tar′if) A tax on imported goods. (p. 399)

technology (tek·nol′ə·jē) The use of tools and knowledge to achieve practical aims. (p. 370)

telegraph (tel′ə·graf) A device for sending and receiving messages. (p. 459)

tenant farmer (ten′ənt fär′mər) A person who farms a rented piece of land, owns animals and tools, and pays the landowner with either crops or money. (p. 454)

tenement (ten′ə·mənt) A crowded, run-down apartment house. (p. 464)

tepee (tē′pē) A dwelling made by lashing poles together in the shape of a cone and covering the poles with animal skins. (p. 116)

territory (ter′ə·tôr·ē) An area of land belonging to a government. (p. 322)

terrorism (ter′ə·riz·əm) The use of violence to achieve publicity for a cause. (p. 558)

textile (teks′tīl) Cloth. (p. 52)

tidewater (tīd′wô·tər) A low coastal plain full of waterways. (p. 235)

totem (tō′tem) A spirit being. (p. 121)

town meeting (toun mē′ting) A meeting at which the town's needs and problems were discussed. (p. 200)

township (toun′ship) A square of land measuring 6 miles (10 km) on each side. (p. 322)

transcontinental railroad (trans·kon·tə·nen′təl rāl′rōd) The railroad that linked the East with the Pacific Coast. (p. 475)

travois (trə·voi′) A baggage carrier made by fastening two poles to an animal's harness. (p. 116)

treaty (trē′tē) A formal agreement to maintain peace. (p. 305)

trial by jury (trī′əl bī jŏŏr′ē) A trial in which a person accused of breaking the law is judged by a group of fellow citizens. (p. 268)

triangle trade route (trī′ang·gəl trād rōōt) An Atlantic trade route on which rum, molasses, and slaves were traded. (p. 210)

tributary (trib′yə·ter·ē) A stream or river that flows into another river. (p. 21)

tuberculosis (tōō·bûr·kyə·lō′sis) A contagious lung disease. (p. 512)

tundra (tun′drə) A broad, treeless plain in an arctic region. (p. 122)

tyranny (tir′ə·nē) Harsh and unjust rule. (p. 275)

unemployment (un·im·ploi′mənt) The condition of being without a job. (p. 533)

uranium (yŏŏ·rā′nē·əm) An ore used in producing nuclear energy. (p. 64)

vegetation (vej·ə·tā′shən) Plant life. (p. 30)

veto (vē′tō) To refuse to sign a proposed law. (p. 326)

viceroy (vīs′roi) A ruler appointed as a representative of a king. (p. 152)

volcano   *wood pulp*

volcano (vol·kā′nō)   A hill or mountain formed when melted rock is forced up through the Earth's surface. (p. 16)

wampum (wom′pəm)   Beads made from porcupine quills or sea-shells, used to help remember important events and also as money. (p. 111)

Western Hemisphere (wes′tərn hem′ə·sfir)   The half of the Earth west of an imaginary line. (p. 5)

wetlands (wet′landz)   Land areas, such as swamps and marshes, that contain large amounts of water. (p. 14)

wigwam (wig′wom)   A round, bark- or hide- covered shelter. (p. 111)

wood pulp (wŏŏd pulp)   A forest product used to make paper. (p. 25)

Page references for illustrations are set in boldface italic.

Key: (t) top, (b) bottom, (l) left, (r) right, (c) center.

Photographs

F. Cover(t), Carr Clifton/AllStock; F. Cover(b), Four By Five; Back Cover, Four By Five; iv(l), Grant Heilman/Grant Heilman Photography; iv(r), Larry Lefever/Grant Heilman Photography; v(l), Larry Lefever/Grant Heilman Photography; v(r), Helga Teiwes/Arizona State Museum, University of Arizona; vii(t), The Granger Collection; vi(b), The Granger Collection; vi(t), Art Resource; vii(b), Jamestown Yorktown Foundation; viii(r), Albany Institute of History and Art; ix(l), Albany Institute of History and Art; ix(r), reproduced from "A Window on Williamsburg," published by Colonial Williamsburg Foundation; x(t), The Granger Collection; x(b), The Granger Collection; xi(b), painting by C. C. A. Christensen, Museum of Church History and Art, The Church of Jesus Christ of Latter-Day Saints, used by permission; xii(l), The Granger Collection; xii(r), courtesy of Illinois Secretary of State, Jim Edgar; xiii(l), courtesy of Illinois Secretary of State, Jim Edgar; xiii(r), California Historical Society; xiv(l), The Granger Collection; xiv(r), The Bettmann Archive; xv(l), U. S. Postal Service; xvi, Wide World Photos; xvi, Historical Picture Service; xvii, Runk/Schoenberger/Grant Heilman Photography; 3(t), HBJ Photo; 3(b), NASA; 10-11, Warren Jacobi/Berg & Assoc.

CHAPTER 1: 12, M. Schneider/H. Armstrong Roberts; 15, Phil Degginger; 16, James Mason/Black Star; 17(t), The Bettmann Archive; 17(b), Culver Pictures; 23, Peter Beck/TSW/After-Image; 24, Tom Bean/The Stock Market; 27, Maxwell McKenzie/TSW/After-Image; 28, William Hubbel/Woodfin Camp & Assoc.; 29, Tom Tracy/TSW/After-Image; 32(t), E. R. Degginger; 32(b), Thomas Kitchin/Tom Stack & Assoc.; 33, C. T. Seymour/The Picture Cube.

CHAPTER 2: 38, Dave Millert/Tom Stack & Assoc.; 41(t), Catherine Ursillo/Photo Researchers; 41(b), Ruth Dixon; 43, J. Buchar/The Stockhouse; 44(t), John Elk III/Bruce Coleman, Inc.; 44(b), Wendell Metzens/Southern Stock Photos; 45, Larry Lefever/Grant Heilman Photography; 50(t), Tony Leonard/Shostal Assoc.; 50(bl), Cary Wolinsky/Stock, Boston; 50(br), Stacy Pick/Stock, Boston; 52(t), Milt and Joan Mann/Cameramann International; 52(b), Marting Rogers/TSW/After-Image; 54, Lowell Georgia/Photo Researchers; 58(t), Grant Heilman/Grant Heilman Photography; 58(b), Roger Malloch/Magnum Photos; 59, Dick Durrance II/Woodfin Camp & Assoc.; 60, Milt and Joan Mann/Cameramann International; 63(t), Billy E. Barner/Stock, Boston; 63(b), Allen Russell/Profiles West; 64(t), Mark Antman/The Image Works; 64(b), Scott Berner/The Stockhouse; 65(t), Craig Aurness/Woodfin Camp & Assoc.; 65(b), Shelly Katz/Black Star; 66, Alan Pitcairn/Grant Heilman Photography; 67(t), Brad Bower/Picture Group; 67(b), Thomas Sennett/Magnum Photos; 69, Joseph Tomala, Jr./Bruce Coleman, Inc.; 71, Mike and Carol Werner/Stock, Boston; 72, Michael Collier/Stock, Boston; 73, Lawrence Migdale/Photo Researchers.

CHAPTER 3: 87, Helga Teiwes/Arizona State Museum, University of Arizona; 88, Kent and Donna Dannen/Photo Researchers; 91, Tony Linck; 92, Gerald P. Smith, photographer/Chucalissa Museum; 94, David Muench; 95, Helga Teiwes/Arizona State Museum, University of Arizona; 98(t), AP/Wide World Photos; 98(b), AP/Wide World Photos.

CHAPTER 4: 104, The Granger Collection; 107, Milwaukee Public Museum; 110, American Museum of Natural History; 111, American Museum of Natural History; 112, Museum of the American Indian, Heye Foundation; 113, The Granger Collection; 114(b), The Granger Collection; 115, Historical Picture Service; 116, Thomas Gilcrease Institute of American History and Art; 117, National Museum of American Art, Smithsonian Institution, gift of Mrs. Joseph Harrison, Jr.; 119, Edward Curtis; 120, Craig Aurness/Woodfin Camp & Assoc.; 123(l), Matt Bradley/Tom Stack & Assoc.; 123(r), John Running/Stock, Boston; 130, David O. Bron/courtesy of Farm Journal; 132(t), Weiglen Photo; 135, Jerry Jacka; 136-137, The Granger Collection.

CHAPTER 5: 138, The Bettmann Archive; 140, Historical Picture Service; 144, The Granger Collection; 145, The Granger Collection; 146, Art Resource; 148, The Granger Collection; 151, The Granger Collection; 154, National Park Service, painting by Robert Giese; 155(b), Eric Carle/Stock, Boston; 156, The Bettmann Archive.

CHAPTER 6: 164, The Granger Collection; 168, The Granger Collection; 170, The Granger Collection; 171, Gary Millburn/Tom Stack & Assoc.; 173, Jamestown Yorktown Foundation; 174, Colonial Williamsburg Foundation; 175, The Granger Collection; 176, The Granger Collection; 177, The Granger Collection; 179, courtesy American Antiquarian Society; 180, Musuem of the City of New York; 181, The Bettmann Archive; 182(b), Library of Congress; 193, Plymouth Plantation; 194-195, New York Historical Assoc., Cooperstown.

CHAPTER 7: 196, The Granger Collection; 202, The Granger Collection; 203, Robert Arnold/Old Sturbridge Village; 204(t), The Bettmann Archive; 204(b), Sampler, NYC-TE-64, Index of American Design, National Gallery of Art, Washington; 205(t), Culver Pictures; 205(b), The Granger Collection; 207, The Granger Collection; 209, Old Dartmouth Historical Society; 211, Schomberg Collection; 212, The Mystic Seaport Museum.

CHAPTER 8: 216, Historical Picture Service; 220, Albany Institute of History and Art; 221, courtesy of Title Guarantee, New York; 222(t), The Granger Collection; 222(b), The Granger Collection; 224, Metropolitan Museum of Art, Rogers Fund, 1923; 225, Maryland Historical Society, Baltimore; 226, Shelburn Museum; 228, Hercules Incorporated, Wilmington, DE; 229(l), Collection-CIGNA Corporation, Philadelphia, PA; 229(r), The Granger Collection.

CHAPTER 9: 234, Historical Picture Service; 236, Enoch Pratt Free Library of Baltimore; 238, The Granger Collection; 242(t), Colonial Williamsburg Photograph; 242(b), reproduced from "A Window on Williamsburg," published by the Colonial Williamsburg Foundation and distributed by Holt, Rhinehart and Winston; 243, The Bettmann Archive; 247, courtesy American Antiquarian Society; 248, Library of Congress; 249, Maryland Historical Society, Baltimore; 250(tl), The Granger Collection; 250(tr), The Granger Collection; 250(bl), The Granger Collection; 250(bc), Moorland-Spingarn Research Center, Howard University; 250(br), The Granger Collection; 251, Colonial Williamsburg Foundation; 252, Historical Picture Service; 256, Colonial Williamsburg Foundation; 257(t), Colonial Williamsburg Foundation; 257(c), Colonial Williamsburg Foundation; 257(b), Colonial Williamsburg Foundation; 258(l), Colonial Williamsburg Foundation; 258(r), Colonial Williamsburg Foundation; 262-263, The Granger Collection.

CHAPTER 10: 264, The Granger Collection; 270, Brown Brothers; 271(t), The Granger Collection; 271(b), New York Public Library; 273, Library of Congress; 274, The Bettmann Archive; 276, Historical Society of Pennsylvania; 277, The Granger Collection; 280, Historical Picture Service; 281(t), The Granger Collection; 281(b), The Granger Collection.

CHAPTER 11: 286, The Granger Collection; 290, The Bettmann Archive; 291, Yale University Art Gallery; 292, William S. Weems/Woodfin Camp & Assoc.; 296, detail from "The Nationmakers" by Howard Pyle, photograph courtesy of the Brandywine River Museum; 297, Historical Picture Service; 298, The Metropolitan Museum of Art, gift of John Stewart Kennedy, 1897; 299, The Granger Collection; 300, The Granger Collection; 302(t), The Granger Collection; 302(b), Brown University Library, Anne S. K. Brown Military Collection, "Marion Crossing the Peedee River"; 303, Cliche Musees Nationaux, Paris; 306, Ahrens/H. Armstrong Roberts; 318-319, The Granger Collection.

CHAPTER 12: 320, The Granger Collection; 324, Architect of the United States Capitol, Washington, DC; 325, Keeper of the Seal; 328(t), The Granger Collection; 328(b), The Granger Collection; 329, Everett C. Johnson/TSW/After-Image; 332, The White House Historical Assoc., photo by The National Geographic Society; 333(t), The Granger Collection; 333(b), The Granger Collection; 335, HBJ Photo/Alec Duncan.

CHAPTER 13: 338, The Granger Collection; 340, The Granger Collection; 341, The Granger Collection; 342, The Granger Collection; 346, courtesy of Colorado Historical Society; 347, Historical Picture Service; 349, The Smithsonian Institution; 350, The Granger Collection; 351, The Granger Collection; 352(t), The Granger Collection; 352(b), The Granger Collection; 354, The Granger Collection; 355, The Granger Collection; 356, Jerome Tiger Art Co.; 357(t), Library of Congress; 357(b), courtesy of the New York Historical Society; 358(l), Library of Congress; 358(r), reprinted courtesy of *The Boston Globe*; 359(l), Newspaper Enterprise Association, Inc.; 359(r), copyright 1938, *Los Angeles Times*, reprinted by permission; 361, Dana Sumers/*Orlando Sentinel* ©1989, Washington Post Writers Group, reprinted with permission.

CHAPTER 14: 362, The Granger Collection; 365, Picture Collection, The Branch Libraries, The New York Public Library; 367, The Bettmann Archive; 368, Culver Pictures; 370, Yale University Art Gallery, Barfoot for Darton, "Progress of Cotton #9 Reeding or Drawing In," The Mabel Brandy Graven Collection; 371, The Granger Collection; 374, Library of Congress; 375, Library of Congress; 376, San Jacinto Museum of History Assoc., Houston, TX; 377(t), courtesy Archives Division, Texas State Library; 379, painting by C. C. A. Christensen, Museum of Church History and Art, The Church of Jesus Christ of Latter-Day Saints, used by permission; 381, New York Historical Society; 396-397, The Seventh Regiment Fund, Inc.

CHAPTER 15: 398, The Bettmann Archive; 401, The Granger Collection; 403, The Cincinatti Art Museum, Subscription Fund Purchase; 404(t), The Bettmann Archive; 404(b), The Bettmann Archive; 407, The Granger Collection; 408, Brown University Library, Anne S. K. Brown Military Collection, "Battle of Hickory Point"; 409, courtesy of Illinois Secretary of State, Jim Edgar; 414, The Granger Collection; 415, Brown Brothers.

CHAPTER 16: 418, Culver Pictures; 420, owned by Robert M. Hicklin, Jr.; 421, The Granger Collection; 422(t), The Bettmann Archive; 422(b), Culver Pictures; 424, Virginia Historical Society; 425, *The Innocent Victim*, from the collection of Dr. Josephine A. Dolan, Ph.D., from "Nursing in Society, a Historical Perspective," W. B. Saunders Company (14th ed., 1978); 426, *The Innocent Victim*, from the collection of Dr. Josephine A. Dolan, Ph.D., from "Nursing in Society, a Historical Perspective," W. B. Saunders Company (14th ed., 1978); 428, National Portrait Gallery, Washington, DC, lent by Serena Williams Miles Van Rensselaer; 430, Library of Congress; 432, The Granger Collection; 433, Library of Congress; 434, The Granger Collection; 435, National Archives; 436, The Bettmann Archive; 438, courtesy of The West Point Museum Collections, United States Military Academy, West Point, NY; 442, The Granger Collection; 445, The Mariner's Museum, Newport News, VA; 449, Official U. S. Signal Corps Photo; 450-451, The Granger Collection.

CHAPTER 17: 452, The Bettmann Archive; 454, The Granger Collection; 456, The Granger Collection; 458, The Granger Collection; 462, Library of Congress; 463, Steven J. Sherman; 464, Brown Brothers; 465, The Bettmann Archive; 466, California Historical Society; 467, The Granger Collection; 468, Visual Communications Photo Archive, Los Angeles, CA; 469(t), Florida State Archives; 469(b), Florida State Archives.

CHAPTER 18: 474, The Granger Collection; 476, The Granger Collection; 477, Thomas Gilcrease Institute of American History and Art, Tulsa, OK; 479, Nebraska State Historical Society, Solomon D. Butcher Collection; 483, Thomas Gilcrease Institute of American History and Art, Tulsa, OK; 484, The Bettmann Archive; 485, George D. Lepp/Comstock; 487, D. Kinsey Collection, Whatcom Museum Archive; 488, The Bettmann Archive; 490(t), The Granger Collection; 490(b), The Bettmann Archive; 493, Robert Frerck/Odyssey Productions; 494, Stuart Cohen/The Stock Market; 495, HBJ Photo; 496, HBJ Photo/Alec Duncan; 497(t), HBJ Photo/Alec Duncan; 497(b), The Murray Ohio Manufacturing Company; 502-503, NASA.

CHAPTER 19: 504, The Bettmann Archive; 506, Remington Art Museum; 508, The Bettmann Archive; 509, Smithsonian Institution; 511, The Bettmann Archive; 512, Woodfin Camp & Assoc.; 513(t), Culver Pictures; 513(b), Library of Congress; 513(inset), Biophoto Assoc./Photo Researchers; 515, Brown Brothers; 517, The Bettmann Archive; 518, Brown Brothers; 520, Wide World Photos; 523, National Archives.

CHAPTER 20: 526, The Bettmann Archive; 527, The Granger Collection; 528(l), Wide World Photos; 528(r), The Bettmann Archive; 529, Wide World Photos; 530, The Bettmann Archive; 531, Wide World Photos; 532, Wide World Photos; 533, The Bettmann Archive; 535(l), Florida State Archives; 535(b), Florida State Archives; 537, Wide World Photos; 538, Brian Parker/Tom Stack & Assoc.; 539, The Bettmann Archive; 542, Wide World Photos.

CHAPTER 21: 546, NASA; 548, AP/Wide World Photos; 549, UPI/Bettman Newsphotos; 550, Gerry Cranham/Photo Researchers; 551, UPI/Bettman Newsphotos; 553, Fred Ward/Black Star; 554, UPI/Bettman Newsphotos; 555, Tom Zimberoff/Sygma; 556(t), Erich Hartmann/Magnum Photos; 556(b), AP/Wide World Photos; 558, O. Franken/Sygma; 559, UPI/Bettman Newsphotos; 560, Dirck Halstead/Gamma-Liaison; 563, NASA; 564, Gabe Palmer/TSW/After-Image; 574-575(t), Robert Kraitz/TSW/After-Image; 574-575(r), Steve Vidler/TSW/After-Image; 574-575(b), HBJ Photo.

CHAPTER 22: 576, Dallas & John Heaton/TSW/After-Image; 579, John Running/Stock, Boston; 580, George Hunter/Shostal Assoc.; 581, Tom Devisser/Black Star; 582, Historical Picture Service; 583, The Granger Collection; 585(t), "David Thompson Taking an Observation," C. W. Jeffreys, Picture Division, Public Archives of Canada, Ottawa; 585(b), "Shooting the Rapids" by Frances Ann Hopkins (1838-1918) #C-2774, courtesy Picture Division, Public Archives of Canada, Ottawa; 586, Jonathan Wenk/Black Star; 587(t), Notman Photographic Archives, McCord Museum of Canadian History; 587(b), Galen Rowell/TSW/After-Image; 593, David M. Dennis/Tom Stack & Assoc.; 594, Wide World Photos; 595, Francis Lepine/Valen Photos.

CHAPTER 23: 598, Bryon Augustin/Tom Stack & Assoc.; 600, University of Texas at Austin; 602, John Running/Stock, Boston; 603(l), David C. Oshner/TSW/After-Image; 603(b), Jack Swenson/Tom Stack & Assoc.; 605, David Hisner/Photographers-Aspen; 606, The Granger Collection; 607, Brown Brothers; 609(t), The Institute of Texan Cultures; 609(b), The Institute of Texan Cultures; 610, Karl Kummels/Shostal Assoc.; 613, Randa Bishop/TSW/After-Image; 621, Ralph Krubner/H. Armstrong Roberts; 622, Alan Carey/The Image Bank.

FOR YOUR REFERENCE: 626-R1, Jon Feingersh/The Stock Market; R40(tl), The Granger Collection; R40(tcl), The Granger Collection; R40(tcr), The Granger Collection; R40(tr), The Granger Collection; R40(ctl), The Granger Collection; R40(ctr), The Granger Collection; R40(cbl), The Granger Collection; R40(cbr), AP/Wide World Photos; R40(bl), AP/Wide World Photos; R40(br), Maiman/Sygma.

Illustrations Karen Bauman: x. Walter Brooks: 93, 117(b), 129(t), 130(t), 132(bl), 200, 267, 325, 348. Larry Hughston: 160, 427, 422, 423, 445, 446. Intergraphics: 2, 46, 99, 100, 101, 124, 125, 128, 129, 134, 159–161, 184, 201, 213, 218, 230, 231, 237, 282, 283, 285, 327, 331, 364, 372, 376, 384, 470, 498, 561, 522, 591(t), 594, 608, 612, 614, 617(b). Eric Joyner: 309–314. Stephanie Pershing: 157, 199, 240. José Reyes: 114(t), 155(t), 182(t). John Rice: 82–83, 84, 377(b). Kazuhiko Sano: 92, 288. Carla Simmons: 96. Arvis Stewart: 387–392. Michael Sullivan: 183. Bill Walker: 304, 366.

Maps R. R. Donnelly Cartographic Services: 3–6, 8, 9, 14, 18, 19, 20, 22, 26, 34, 35, 40, 42, 46, 47, 48, 51, 56, 62, 70, 86, 90, 85, 106, 108 (Adapted with permission from *Indians of North America* ©1961, 1969, by the University of Chicago. All rights reserved.), 141, 198, 208, 210, 218(l), 237, 266, 269, 289, 323, 341(b), 380, 383, 394, 400, 406, 411, 437, 459, 471, 478, 480, 481, 500, 506(t), 508(t), 510, 540–441, 578, 588, 591(b), 601, 611, 616, 617(t), 618, 624, R42–R53.